CHANGZHOU STATISTICAL YEARBOOK

常州统计年鉴 2016

（总第26期 No.26）

常 州 市 统 计 局
国家统计局常州调查队 编

Compiled by Changzhou Municipal Statistics Bureau and
Changzhou Investigation Team of the national Bureau of Statistics

中国统计出版社
China Statistics Press

地区生产总值

Gross Domestic Product

单位：亿元(100 million yuan)

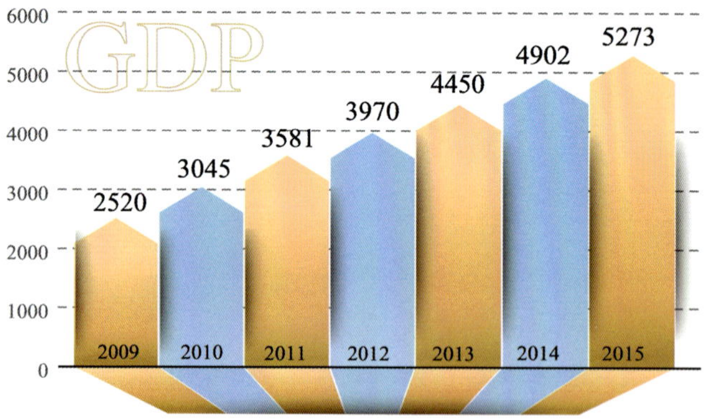

国民经济三次产业结构

Proportions in Gross Domestic Product

单位：%

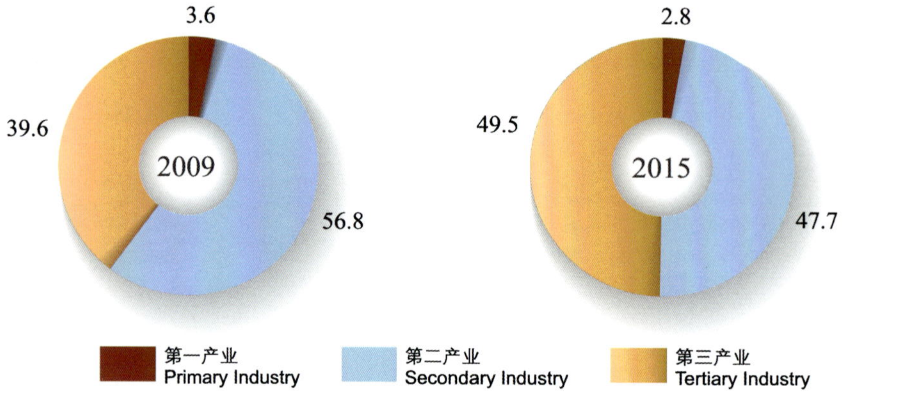

人均地区生产总值

Per Capita of Gross Domestic Product

单位：元(yuan)

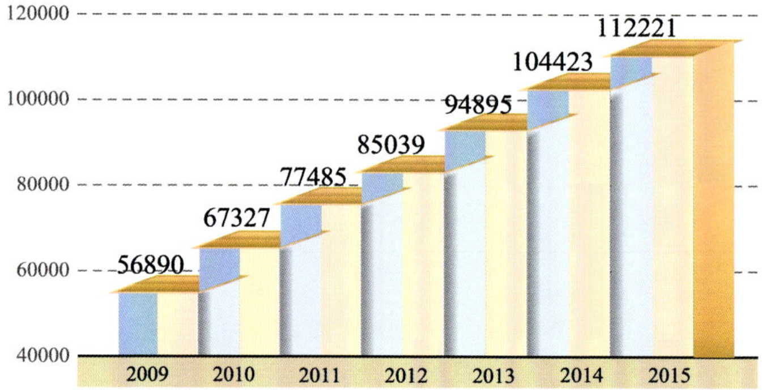

综合实力

固定资产投资完成额
Realized Investment in Fixed Assets

单位：亿元(100 million yuan)

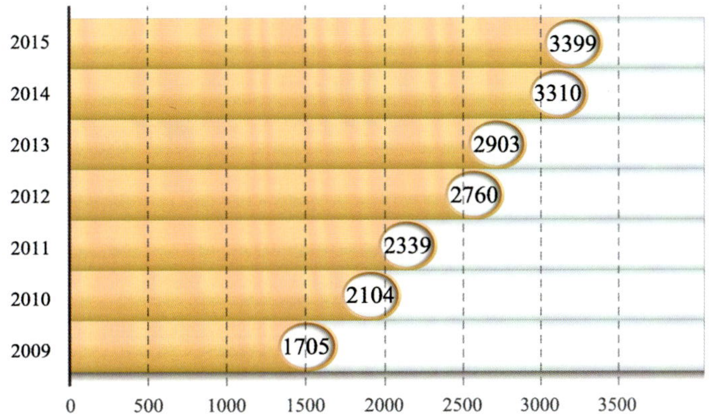

固定资产投资构成
Structure of Fixed Assets Investment

单位：%

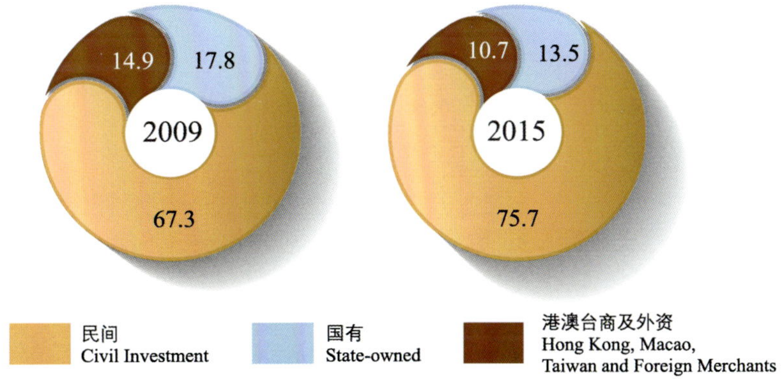

社会消费品零售总额
Total Retail Sales of Consumer Goods

单位：亿元(100 million yuan)

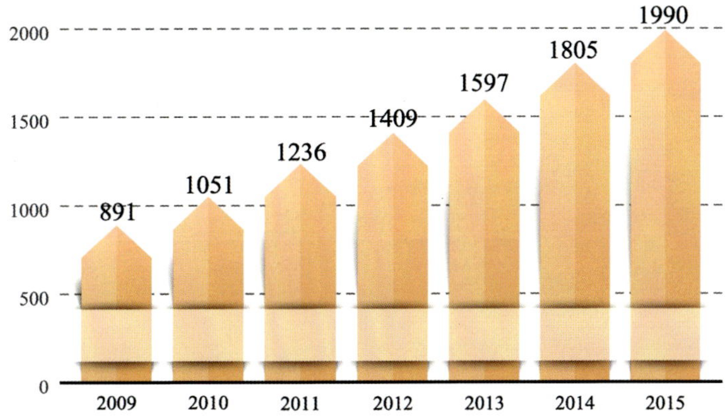

农林牧渔业总产值(现价)

Gross Output Value of Farming, Forestry, Animal Husbandry and Fishery (Current)

单位：亿元(100 million yuan)

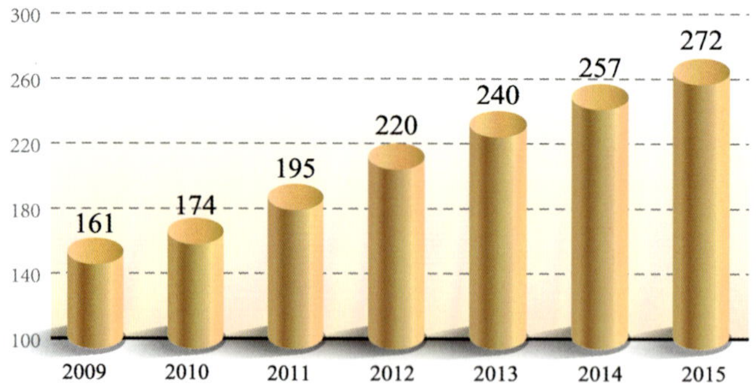

农村三次产业从业人员比重

Proportion of Employment in Tertiary Industry in Rural Area

单位：%

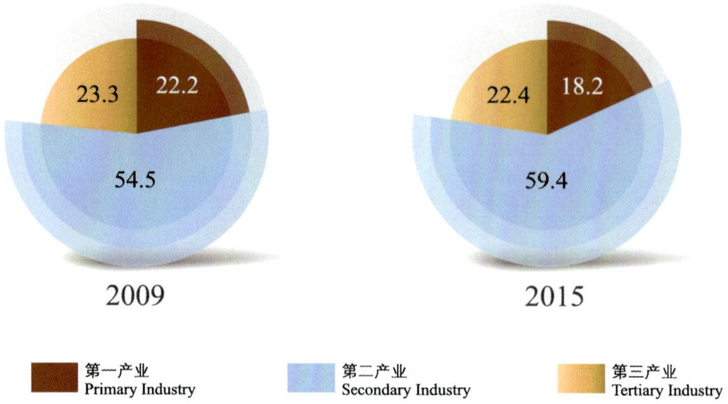

水稻单产

Per Hectare of Paddy Rice

单位：公斤/公顷(kg/hectare)

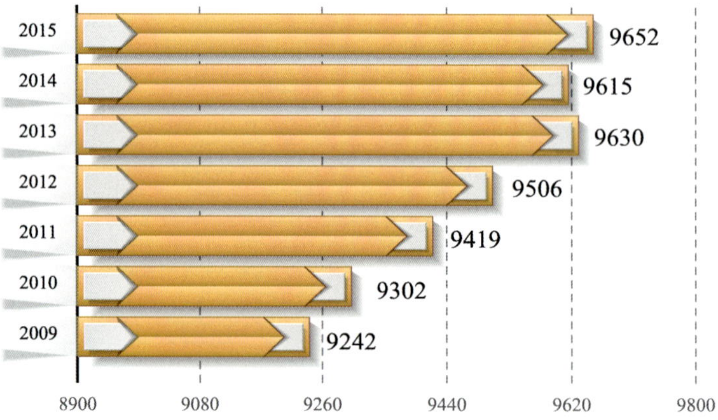

工业生产发展指数（以2000年为100）

Indices of Gross Industrial Output

(Calculated by Comparable Price:2000=100)

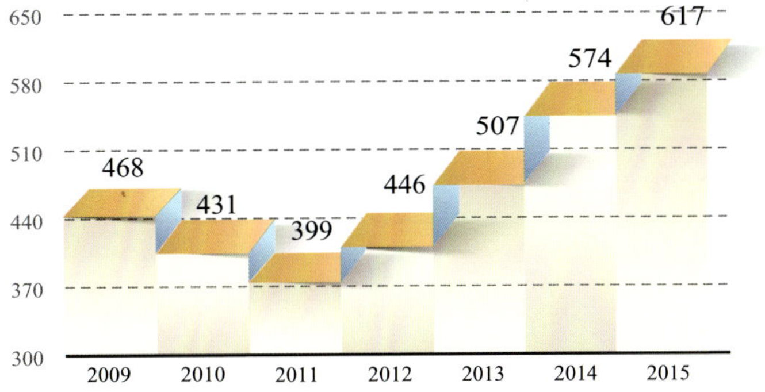

规模以上工业实现利润

Profit of Industries above Dseignated Size

单位：亿元(100 million yuan)

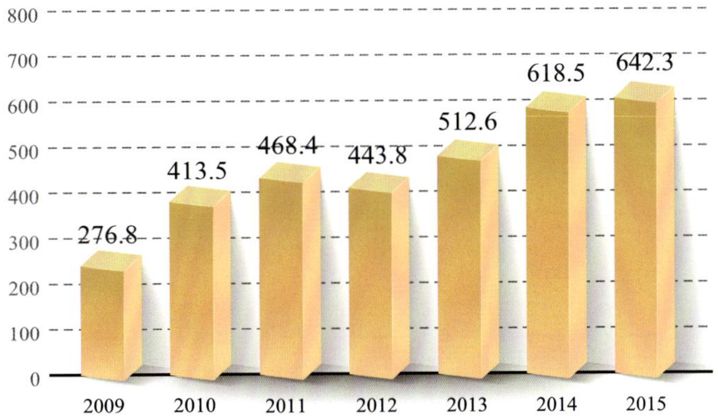

工业主要行业构成

Main Industry Structure

单位：%

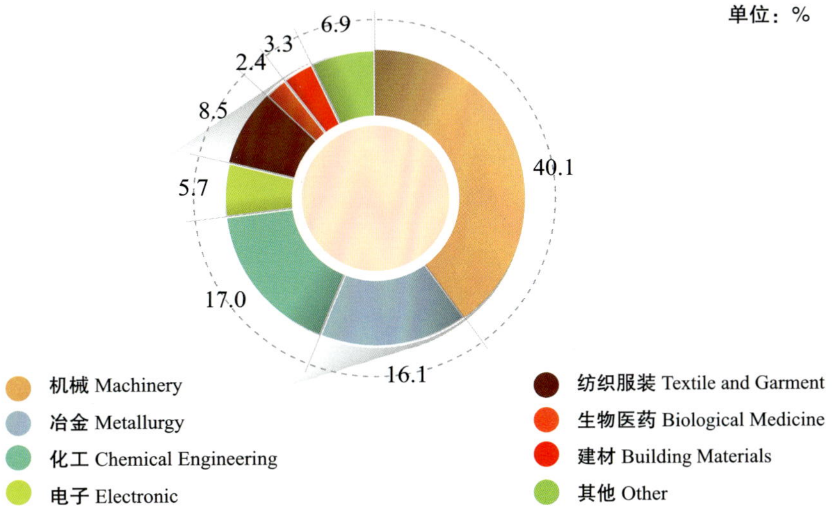

私营企业注册资本

Registered Capital of Private Enterprises

单位：亿元(100 million yuan)

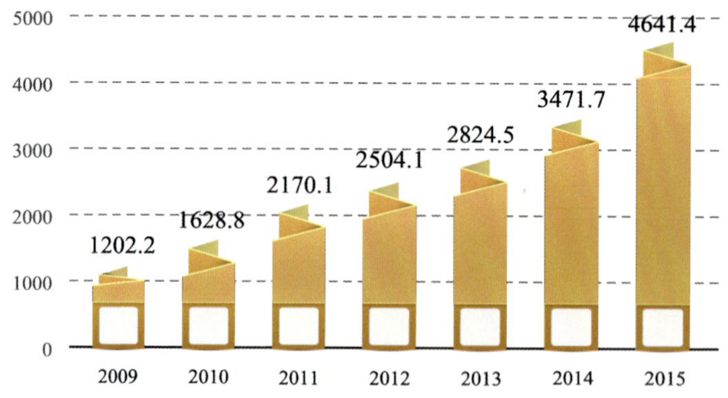

个私企业从业人数

Number of Employees in Individual and Private Enterprises at Year-end

单位：万人(10000 persons)

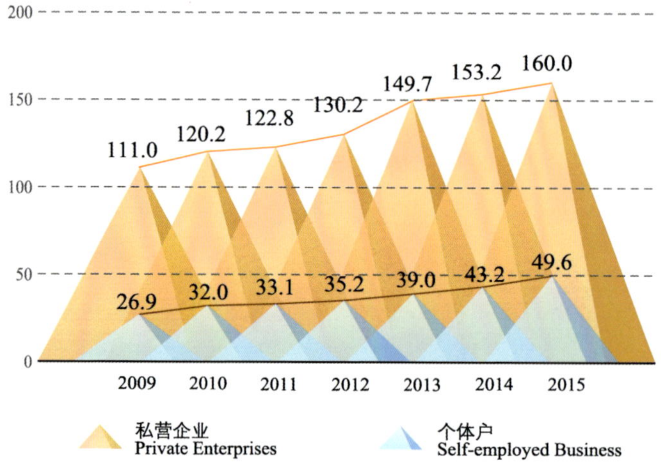

个私企业户数

Number of Individual and Private Economy at Year-end

单位：户(unit)

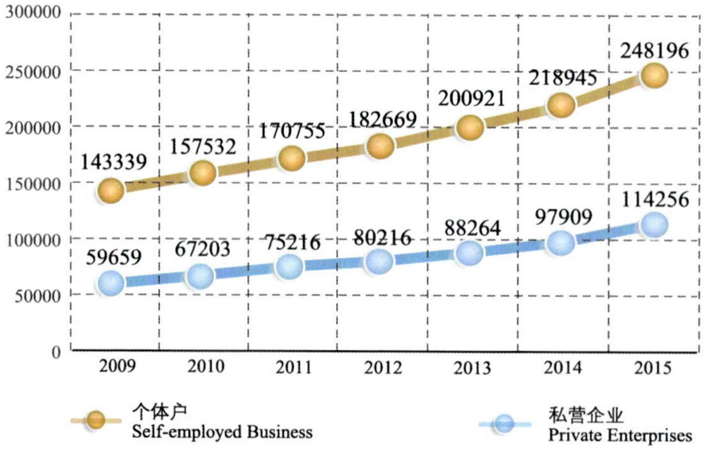

进出口总额

Total Imports and Exports

单位：亿美元(USD 100 million)

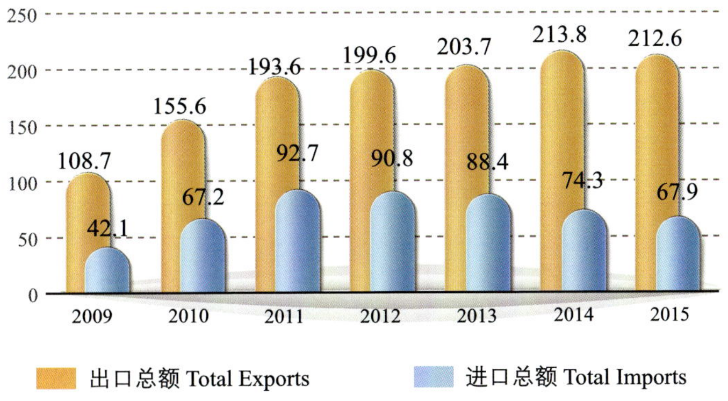

实际利用外资金额

Total Amount of Foreign Investment Actually Utilized

单位：亿美元(USD 100 million)

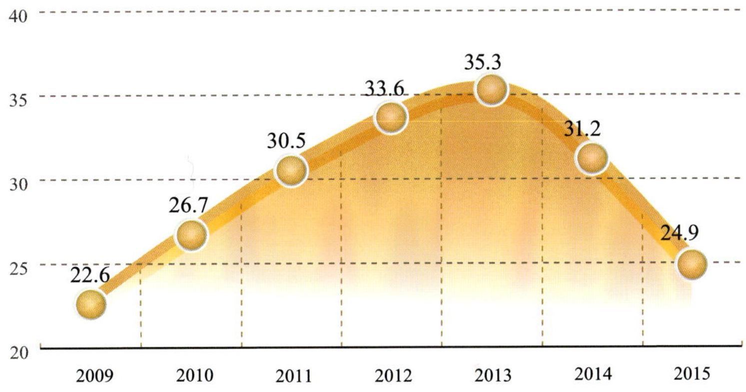

规模以上港澳台及外商投资企业工业总产值

Total Industrial Output of Hong Kong, Macao, Taiwan and Foreign Invested Companies Above the Designated Size

单位：亿元(100 million yuan)

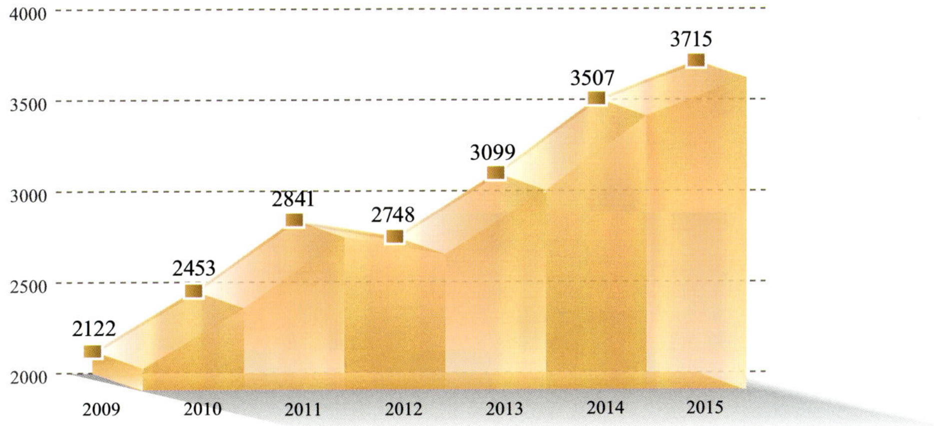

一般公共预算收入和支出

General Public Budgetary Revenue & Expenditure

单位：亿元（100 million yuan）

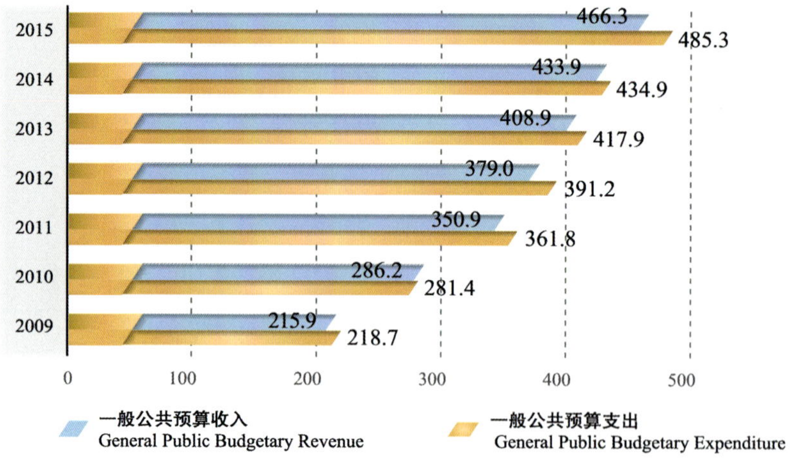

一般公共预算收入占GDP比重

Proportion of General Public Budgetary Revenue to GDP

单位：%

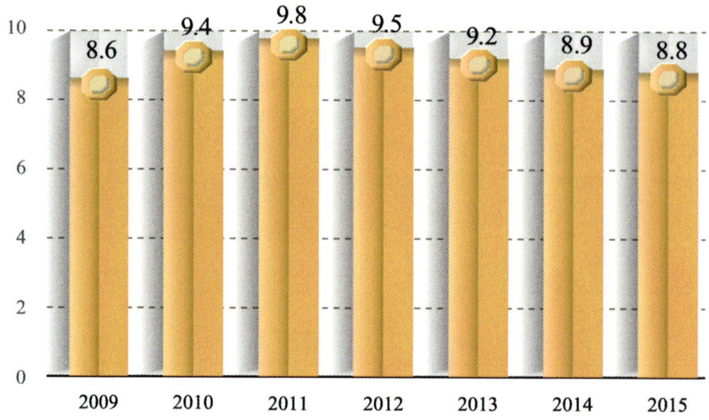

金融机构存贷款余额

Deposit and Loan Balance of National Banking Institutions

单位：亿元（100 million yuan）

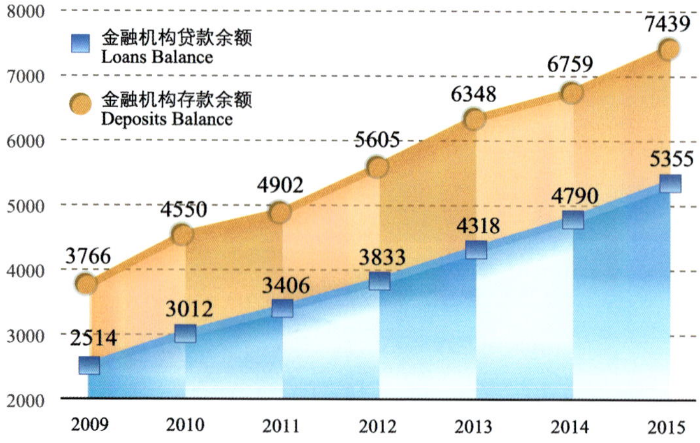

城镇常住居民人均可支配收入
Per Capita Disposable Income of Urban Residents

单位：元（yuan）

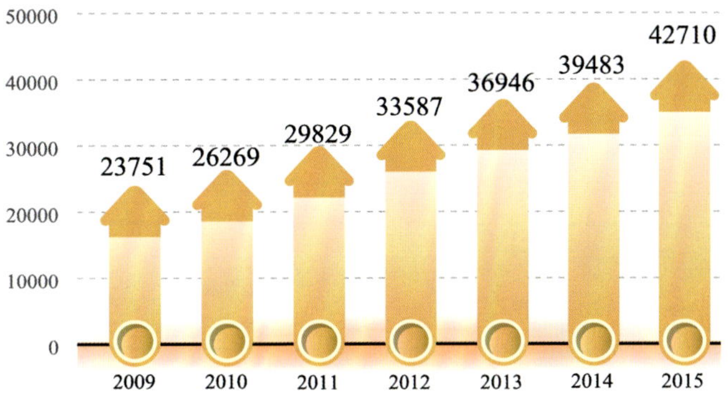

农村常住居民人均可支配收入
Per Capita Disposable Income of Rural Residents

单位：元(yuan)

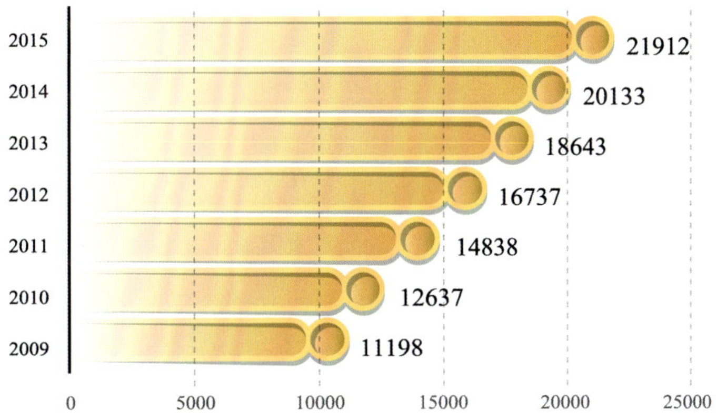

市区居民消费价格总指数（以上年价格为100）
Consumer Price Index of Urban Residents （Preceding Year=100）

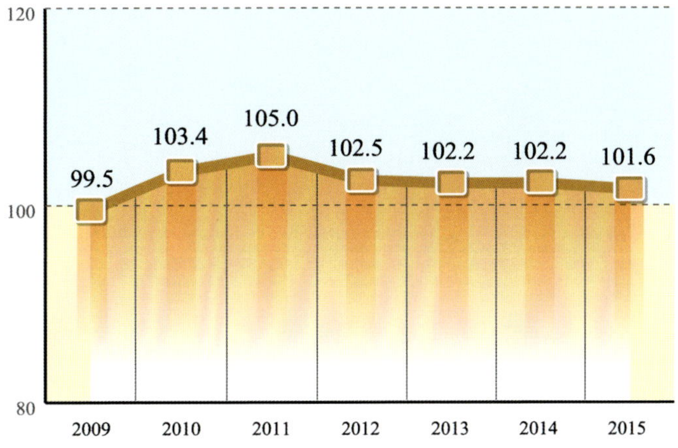

普通高等院校在校学生数

Students Enrollmed of Institutions of Higher Education

单位：人（person）

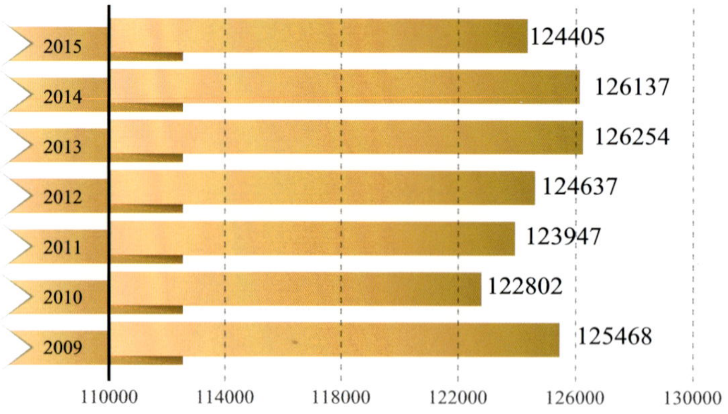

专利申请量、专利授权量

Number of Patent Authorizations Examined and Granted

单位：项（unit）

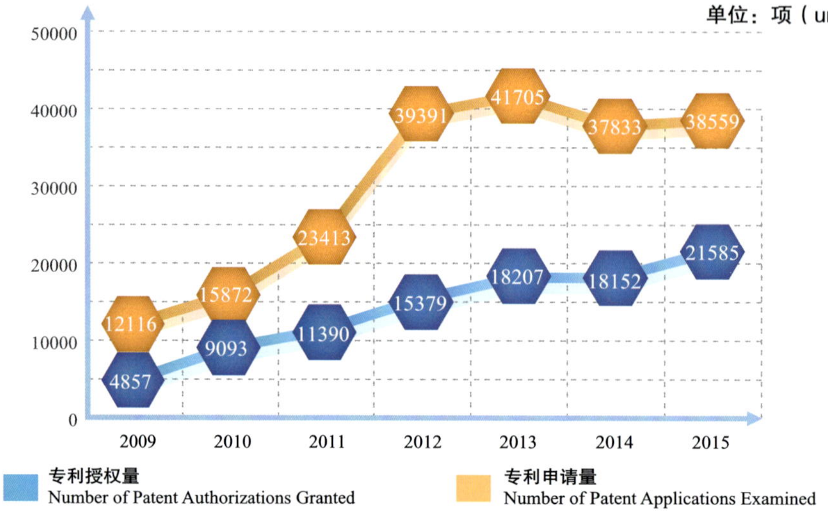

全社会卫生机构床位数

Beds of Health Care Institutions

单位：张（bed）

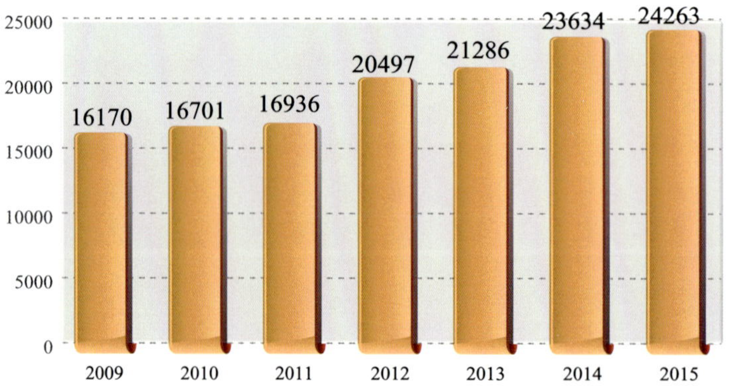

人均拥有道路面积

Per Capita Area of Roads

单位：平方米（sq.m）

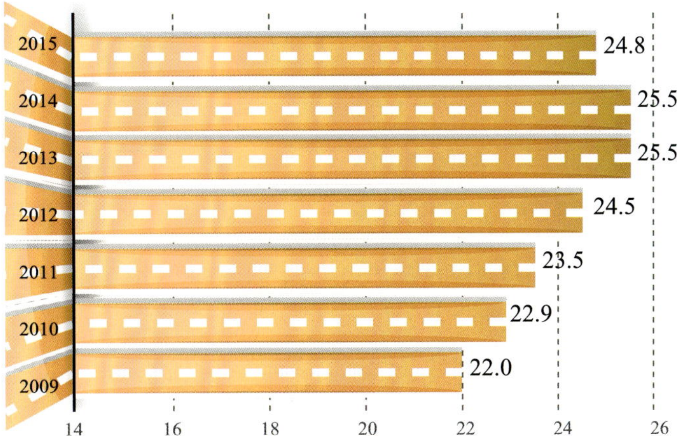

人均公园绿地面积

Per Capita Green Area of Parks

单位：平方米（sq.m）

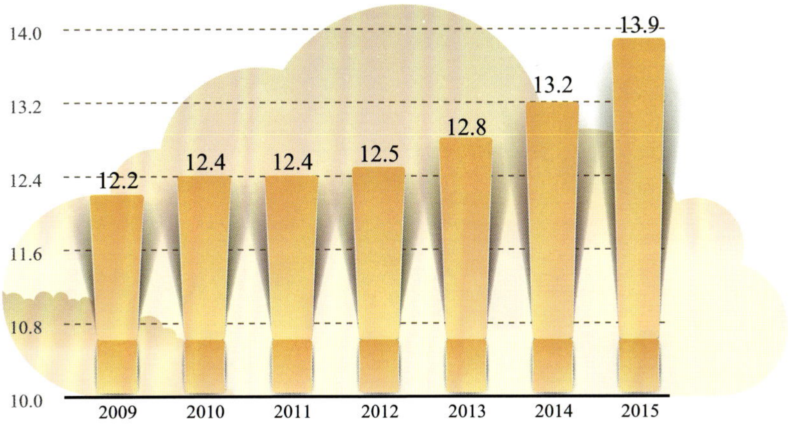

建成区面积

Area of Constructed Regions

单位：平方公里（sq.km）

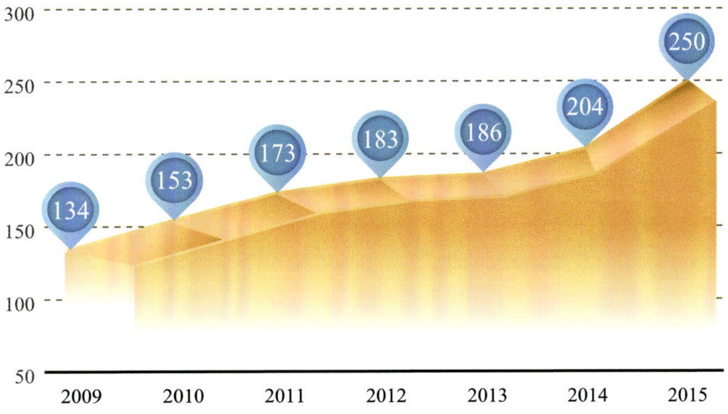

常州统计年鉴

2016 STATISTICAL YEARBOOK

编 者 说 明

一、《常州统计年鉴— 2016》是一本信息高度密集的资料和工具书。它以翔实的统计数据反映了 2015 年常州经济、科技、社会各方面的发展变革情况，以及历史年份和改革开放以来大量的统计数据。

二、全书内容分为22部分，即：1. 概述；2. 排名榜；3. 行政区划、自然概况；4. 综合；5. 人口；6. 从业人员、工资总额；7. 物价指数；8. 人民生活；9. 固定资产投资；10. 农业；11. 工业；12. 建筑业；13. 交通运输、邮电通信；14. 批发零售、住宿餐饮；15. 个体、私营经济；16. 对外经济、旅游；17. 能源消费；18. 财政、金融、保险；19. 城市建设、环境保护；20. 科技、教育、文化；21. 卫生、体育；22. 民政、司法、其他。书末附有主要统计指标解释等附录资料。

三、2015 年常州市部分行政区划调整：撤销金坛市，设立金坛区；撤销原武进区和戚墅堰区，设立新武进区；原武进区的奔牛镇划归新北区；原武进区的郑陆镇划归天宁区；原武进区的邹区镇划归钟楼区。本年鉴表中 2015 年全市数据包括金坛区、武进区、新北区、天宁区、钟楼区、溧阳市，市区中包含金坛区数据 (物价指数、居民家庭相关调查数据除外)，历史数据未作调整。

四、本书中所使用的度量衡单位采用国际统一标准计量单位，价值量指标凡未表明何种价格的，均为以现行价格计算。

五、本书中的简称和符号使用说明：“…”表示数据不足本表最小单位数；“空格”表示数据不详或无该项数据；“#”表示其中数。

《常州统计年鉴》公开出版以来，受到社会各界关心和支持，并提出了许多宝贵意见，对此，我们深表谢意。热忱欢迎读者继续对年鉴的不足之处批评指正，帮助我们进一步提高编辑水平。

Preface

I. Changzhou Statistical Yearbook-2015 is a reference book, which reflects the economic, scientific and technological, social development in Changzhou city in 2014 by means of full and accurate statistical data. It also provides abundant statistical data about past years and the years since reform and opening-up.

II. This book contains the following twenty-three parts: 1.General Description; 2.List of Top Strengths; 3. Division of Administration Areas and Natural Resources; 4.General Survey; 5.Population; 6.Employment and Total Wages; 7.Price Indices; 8.People’s Livelihood; 9.Investment in Fixed Assets; 10.Agriculture; 11.Industry; 12.Construction; 13.Transportation, Post and Telecommunications; 14. Wholesale and Retail, Accommodation and Catering; 15.Individual and Private Economy; 16.Foreign Economy and Tourism; 17.Energy Consumption; 18. Public Finance, Banking and Insurance; 19.Urban Construction and Environmental Protection; 20.Science Technology, Education and Culture; 21.Health and Sports; 22.Givil Administration Judicature and Others. In addition, Explanatory Notes on Main Statistical Indicators are provided at the end of each part.

III. Changzhou underwent an administrative-district readjustment in 2015. Jintan County-city was turned into Jintan District; Wujin District and Qi Shuyan District were merged into the new Wujin District; Zhenglu Town and Zouqu Town previously administrated by Wujin District were transferred to Tianning District and Zhonglou District respectively. All relevant 2015 data of Changzhou include Jintan District, Wujin District, Xinbei District, Tianning District, Zhonglou District and Liyang County-city. And all relevant 2015 data of Changzhou’s urban area (except CPI and urban-household-related data) include Jintan District. Historical data are not adjusted in accordance with the district readjustment.

IV. The units of measurement used in this book are internationally standard measurement units. Those undefined price indices should be calculated in accordance with current prices.

V. Abbreviations and Notations used in this book:

Aabove are referred to the statistical coverage of industrial enterprises “above designated size” for short. “…” indicates that the figure is not big enough to be measured with the smallest unit in the table, “(blank)” indicates that the data are not available, “#” indicates the items of the total.

Here we’d like to express our sincere thanks to the readers who have offered us so many invaluable suggestions on content selection and compilation of the yearbook. Our thanks also go to those friends in all circles of society who have shown their support and care to the publication of the yearbook. We welcome any suggestions and comments from readers so as to help us to further improve our work of compilation.

目 录

CONTENTS

第一篇 概 述

CHAPTER 1 GENERAL DESCRIPTION

第二篇 排名榜

CHAPTER 2 LIST OF TOP STRENGTHS

第三篇 行政区划 自然概况

CHAPTER 3 ADMINISTRATIVE DIVISION AND NATURAL RESOURCES

第四篇 综 合

CHAPTER 4 GENERAL SURVEY

第五篇 人 口

CHAPTER 5 POPULATION

第六篇 从业人员 工资总额

CHAPTER 6 EMPLOYMENT AND TOTAL WAGES

第七篇 物价指数

CHAPTER 7 PRICE INDEX

第八篇 人民生活

CHAPTER 8 PEOPLE'S LIVELIHOOD

第九篇 固定资产投资

CHAPTER 9 INVESTMENT IN FIXED ASSETS

第十篇 农 业

CHAPTER 10 AGRICULTURE

第十一篇 工 业

CHAPTER 11 INDUSTRY

第十二篇 建筑业

CHAPTER 12 CONSTRUCTION

第十三篇 交通运输 邮电通信

CHAPTER 13 TRANSPORTATION, POST AND TELECOMMUNICATIONS

第十四篇 贸易 住宿餐饮业

CHAPTER 14 TRADE, ACCOMMODATION AND CATERING TRADE

第十五篇　个体 私营经济

CHAPTER 15 INDIVIDUAL AND PRIVATE ECONOMY

第十六篇 对外经济 旅游

CHAPTER 16 FOREIGN ECONOMY AND TOUEISM

第十七篇 能源消费

CHAPTER 17 CONSUMPTION OF ENERGY

第十八篇 财政 金融 保险

CHAPTER 18 PUBLIC FINANCE, BANKING AND INSURANCE

第十九篇　城市建设 环境保护
CHAPTER 19 URBAN CONSTRUCTION AND ENVIRONMENTAL PROTECTION

第二十篇　科技 教育 文化
CHAPTER 20 SCIENCE, TECHNOLOGY, EDUCATION AND CULTURE

第二十一篇 卫生 体育

CHAPTER 21 HEALTH AND SPORTS

第二十二篇 民政 司法 其他

CHAPTER 22 CIVIL ADMINISTRATION, JUDICATURE AND OTHERS

附 录

APPENDIX

1

CHAPTER 1

概 述

GENERAL DESCRIPTION

常州统计年鉴

常州市
2015年国民经济和社会发展统计公报

2015年，面对错综复杂的宏观经济环境和艰巨繁重的改革发展任务，全市上下在市委、市政府的正确领导下，积极适应经济发展新常态，坚持开拓创新，加快转型发展，扎实做好稳增长、调结构、促改革、惠民生、防风险等各项工作，经济社会运行呈现总体平稳、稳中有优的态势。

一、综合经济

经济运行保持平稳。经初步核算，全年实现地区生产总值5273.2亿元，按可比价格计算增长9.2%，其中第一产业增加值146.6亿元，增长3.1%；第二产业增加值2516.0亿元，增长8.5%；第三产业增加值2610.6亿元，增长10.6%。全年服务业增加值占GDP比重达到49.5%，较上年提高1.5个百分点，服务业占比首次超过第二产业，经济结构实现由“二三一”向“三二一”的新格局转变。全市按常住人口计算的人均生产总值达112221元，按平均汇率折算达18018美元。

财政收入平稳增长。全年实现一般公共预算收入466.3亿元，增长7.5%，其中税收收入373.7亿元，增长7.3%，税收占比达到80.1%。主要税种中，增值税（含营改增）完成70.8亿元，增长6.4%；营业税完成113.8亿元，增长19.1%；企业所得税完成42.6亿元，增长1.4%。全年一般公共预算支出485.3亿元，增长11.6%。一般公共预算支出中教育支出79.2亿元，增长16.1%；科学技术支出22.7亿元，增长4.8%;社会保障和就业支出55.3亿元，增长12.4%；医疗卫生与计划生育支出38.5亿元，增长20.1%。

民营经济增幅放缓。2015年末，全市拥有私营企业和个体工商户36.3万户，注册资本4814.7亿元。全年民营经济完成增加值3541.4亿元，按可比价计算增长9.0%，增幅较上年回落1.1个百分点，占地区生产总值的比重为67.2%，较上年降低0.3个百分点。

二、农业与农村经济

农业生产保持稳定。2015年，全市完成农林牧渔业现价总产值271.8亿元，增长5.8%。其中，农业产值147.2亿元，增长6.1%；林业产值1.9亿元，增长4.8%；牧业产值38.8亿元，增长3.5%；渔业产值68.3亿元，增长5.5%；农林牧渔服务业产值15.6亿元，增长10.7%。全年粮食播种面积214.2万亩，粮食总产量108.3万吨，与上年相比分别下降3.2%、3.4%。水稻单产643.5公斤/亩、小麦单产356.3公斤/亩，水稻单产连续13年保持全省第一。

现代农业加快发展。农业物质技术装备水平不断提升。全市新建高标准农田6.26万亩，累计建成134.97万亩；新发展设施农业面积2.7万亩，累计建成46.5万亩；新发展高效设施渔业面积1.63万亩，累计建成19.71万亩，占全市水产养殖面积的比重达到33.58%；2015年全市农业综合机械化水平达到87%，农业信息化覆盖率达到60%，分别较上年提高1个、3个百分点。农业产业化经营稳步推进，全市91家市级以上农业产业化龙头企业实现销售618亿元，增长9.6%。

三、工业和建筑业

工业生产增幅趋缓。2015年，全市规模以上工业企业累计完成总产值11101.6亿元，规模以上工业增加值增长8.5%。全市规模以上重工业完成产值8326.4亿元，轻工业完成产值2775.2亿元。七大行业中，化工、机械、纺织服装、生物医药行业分别完成工业总产值1952.8亿元、4602.7亿元、976亿元、278.8亿元，分别增长14.9%、9.3%、7.2%、7%；电子、建材行业分别完成产值656.1亿元、376.4亿元，增长4.8%、0.3%；冶金行业完成产值

1849.8 亿元，下降 9.5%。

十大产业链贡献提升。2015 年，全市十大产业链规模以上工业企业累计完成产值 3816.8 亿元，增长 8.9%，增速高出全市规模以上工业平均增速 3.6 个百分点，对全市规模以上工业产值的贡献份额达到 52.6%。十大产业链中，太阳能光伏、汽车及零部件、轨道交通三大产业分别完成产值 633.6 亿元、656.2 亿元、411.5 亿元，分别增长 25.6%、15.8% 和 13.1%。

建筑行业发展平缓。建筑企业全年完成施工产值 1288.5 亿元，比上年增长 0.3%；施工面积 10051.0 万平方米，下降 6.4 %；竣工面积 3448.6 万平方米，下降 9.5%。建筑业按施工产值计算的全员劳动生产率为 27.9 万元 / 人，比上年下降 0.8%。

四、固定资产投资

投资结构不断优化。2015 年全市完成固定资产投资 3399 亿元，增长 6.7%，其中工业投资 1756.1 亿元，增长 6.5%，服务业投资 1636.7 亿元，增长 7.1%。投资结构不断优化，全市高新技术产业投资 794.6 亿元，增长 13.9%，增幅高于全市固定资产投资增幅 7.2 个百分点；工业投资中技改投入 1160.2 亿元，占工业投资比重 66.1%，较上年提高 6.2 个百分点。房地产投资持续下滑，2015 年全市完成房地产开发投资 508 亿元，同比下降 25.5%。全年商品房开发面积 3948.2 万平方米，比上年下降 11.5%，其中新开工面积 637.8 万平方米，比上年下降 30.4%。

五、国内贸易

消费市场保持稳定。2015 年全市实现社会消费品零售总额 1990.5 亿元，增长 10.3%，增幅与全省平均增幅持平，与上年相比下降 2.8 个百分点。按消费形态分，批发业实现零售额 240.1 亿元，增长 9.4%；零售业实现零售额 1585.7 亿元，增长 10.1%；餐饮业实现零售额 149.9 亿元，增长 14.2%；住宿业实现零售额 14.8 亿元，增长 4%。按单位经营所在地分，城镇消费品零售额 1861.1 亿元，增长 10.6%，农村消费品零售额 129.4 亿元，增长 5.7%。

六、开放型经济

对外贸易难中求进。2015 年，全市完成外贸出口 1319.2 亿元，比上年增长 0.5%。全年对“一带一路”国家和地区出口良好，其中对印度、东盟、中东出口分别增长 27.6%、12.3%、5%。全年完成高新技术产品出口 217.4 亿元，增长 9.7%；机电产品出口占全市出口总额的比重达 54.1%，较上年提高 1.6 个百分点。全年完成服务贸易进出口额 80 亿元，增长 5.1%;一般贸易出口 979 亿元，增长 0.5%。

外资项目有所突破。全年全市实际到账注册外资 24.9 亿美元，新增协议注册外资 3000 万美元以上项目 16 个，其中总投资超 10 亿美元的瑞声射频模组项目成功签约，波士顿锂电池、联合光伏、顺风光电科技等 3 个项目总投资超 5 亿美元。全年新增世界 500 强投资项目 5 个、增资项目 2 个，数量创近年新高。

对外合作不断加强。全年新备案境外投资项目 67 个，中方协议投资额 7.55 亿美元，同比增长 61.7%，其中涉及“一带一路”国家和地区项目 12 个，中方协议投资额 3.6 亿美元，占比达到 47.8%。全年完成服务外包合同额 3.8 亿美元，增长 21.5%；服务外包执行额 3.2 亿美元，增长 17.7%。

开发区建设提档升级。全市开发区实现一般公共预算收入 299.7 亿元，完成工业投入 1323.8 亿元，基础设施建设投入 297.4 亿元，全年实际到账外资 22.5 亿美元，新批协议注册外资 23.6 亿美元。西太湖科技产业园获批筹建省级高新区，常州高新区成功创建国家生态示范园区，武进高新区、武进经开区已通过了环保部、商务部、科技部对国家级生态工业示范园区的联合现场验收;中以、中德等国际合作园区加快建设。

对外交流不断深化。全年接待外宾 197 批、1025 人次，接待外国驻华使领馆官员 28 批、161 人次，外国友好城市团组 38 批、215 人次，外国来访记者 4 批、8 人次。2015 年新缔结友城两个，分别是智利拉塞雷纳市和巴西库里蒂巴市。

七、交通运输、邮政电信业和旅游业

交通运输业平稳发展。年末全市公路总里程9010公里，其中高速公路306公里。全年营业性客运量7673万人，比上年下降9.3%，货运量1.3亿吨，比上年增长0.9%。公路客运量5856万人，比上年下降13.5%，公路旅客周转量40.2亿人公里，下降4.1%；公路货运量1.1亿吨，下降0.5%，公路货物周转量117.3亿吨公里，增长5.5%。全年铁路客运量1369.2万人，增长11%。全年民用航空旅客吞吐量181.1万人次，货物邮吞吐量1.8万吨。全年港口货物吞吐量8984万吨，其中常州长江港货物吞吐量3619万吨。年末全市民用汽车拥有量96.8万辆，其中私人汽车82.1万辆，分别比上年增长10.9%和13.1%。

邮政通信业较快发展。全年邮政业务总量29.3亿元，比上年增长34.3%，全年邮政业务总收入26.0亿元，比上年增长31.6%。邮政业全年发送特快专递1.2亿件，增长46.9%。全市规模以上快递企业主营业务收入17.4亿元，增长40%。全年通信业务收入52.7亿元，比上年下降2.2%。年末全市固定电话用户133.0万户，移动电话用户514.4万户，其中3G用户132.2万户，4G用户260.4万户。年末互联网用户达199.8万户，增长25.3%，其中宽带网用户190.4万户，增长27.8%。

旅游业稳步发展。2015年全市实现旅游总收入731亿元，比上年增长11.7%，其中国内旅游收入718.4亿元，比上年增长12.3%，旅游外汇收入1.21亿美元，增长18.8%；旅游接待总人数5455.7万人次，比上年增长9.1%，其中接待国内游客5443.0万人次，增长9.1%，入境过夜旅游者12.7万人次，比上年增长5.4%。截至年底，全市共有省级以上旅游度假区4家，其中国家级旅游度假区1家；国家A级景区33家，其中5A级旅游区2家，4A级旅游区9家；全国工农业旅游示范点17家，江苏省四星级乡村旅游点25家，江苏省工业旅游点3家，江苏省自驾游基地6家；旅行社140家，1家旅行社进入全省旅行社20强；星级酒店56家，其中五星级酒店7家，四星级酒店21家。旅游产品不断丰富和升级，天目湖旅游度假区成功创建为首批国家级旅游度假区，金坛长荡湖成功创建为省级旅游度假区，春秋淹城国家5A级景区景观质量通过国家级评审，华夏宝盛园、江南环球港等新景区建成开放。2015年，常州成为大陆游客赴台湾自由行城市，常州机场新开通日本、台湾等多条境外航线。

八、金融业

金融信贷平稳运行。截至年末，全市金融机构人民币存款余额7438.7亿元，比年初新增512.3亿元，增长7.4%，其中住户存款3193.8亿元，增长4.7%。全市金融机构人民币贷款余额5354.6亿元，比年初新增564.8亿元，增长11.8%，住户贷款余额1233.8亿元，增长15.2%。金融改革创新取得积极进展，成功组建运营江南金融租赁有限公司。

保险业稳步发展。截至年末，全市保险公司共67家，其中产险公司28家，寿险公司39家。全年保费总收入156.6亿元，比上年增长15.6%，其中寿险104.9亿元，增长17.0%，财产险51.7亿元，增长13.2%。全年保险赔（结）款支出55.1亿元，比上年增长12.5%，其中寿险21.7亿元，下降6.5%，财产险33.4亿元，增长29.5%。

证券市场趋于活跃。截至年底，全市证券营业部总数达40个，资金账户总数96万户，持有A股市值1246.5亿元。证券市场全年各类证券交易总额32172.3亿元，比上年增长229%。其中，A股交易额28946.8亿元，增长275.9%；B股交易额35亿元，增长408.4%；基金成交额749.4亿元，增长132.0%；债券成交额2441.1亿元，增长39.6%。截至年末，全市共有上市公司38家，其中境内24家、境外14家，累计募集资金409亿元。年内新增上市企业两家，分别是常州强力电子新材料股份有限公司、常州腾龙汽车零部件股份有限公司，共募集资金7.1亿元。

九、科技创新

创新能力不断提高。全年完成专利申请38559件，其中发明专利13211件；专利授权21585件，其中发明专利授权2664件；

万人发明专利拥有量 18.78 件。全年新增高新技术企业 140 家，累计 1126 家；规模以上高新技术产业产值 4975.6 亿元，占规模以上工业总产值的比重达 43.4%。全年争取省级以上科技项目 530 项，争取经费超过 5.3 亿元。全年新增产学研合作项目 1116 项。2015 年全社会研究与发展（R&D）活动经费占地区生产总值比重为 2.67%。

创新平台加快建设。全年新增省级以上企业研发机构 73 家，累计建成“两站三中心”1159 个，其中省级以上 602 家。新增孵化器、加速器 16 家，累计 108 家；新增孵化、加速面积超 100 万平方米，累计达 800 多万平方米。积极推进江苏省智能装备产业技术创新中心及 4 家省产业研究院预备研究所建设，其中 2 家正式挂牌；完成 20 家市级重大公共研发机构的建设和提升。

推进苏南国家自主创新示范区建设。“一核两区多园”的常州苏南国家自主创新示范区建设框架基本形成。“中国以色列常州创新园”建设步伐加快；“常州国家科技领军人才创新驱动中心”成效明显；科教城省科技服务示范区特色鲜明；武进高新区及江南石墨烯研究院被列为科技部科技服务业区域和行业试点。

十、教育、文化、卫生和体育

教育现代化稳步推进。截至年末，全市拥有各级各类学校 691 所，在校学生 79.32 万人，教职工 5.7 万人。大力推进现代化学校建设，全市实施学校建设项目 108 个，完成投资 16 亿元。2015 年全市教育现代化建设综合得分为 88.06。教育教学质量不断提高，全市本二以上达线率达 77.46%，职业学校对口单招本科录取率连续 16 年位居全省第一。在 2015 年全国职业院校技能大赛中获得一等奖 8 个，二等奖 3 个；在全省职业学校技能大赛中获一等奖 51 个、二等奖 120 个，获奖数量、层次均居全省前列；五大学科竞赛获省一等奖共 335 个，二等奖共 547 个，在全省保持高位。办学品质不断提升，16 所高中的 17 个项目建成省级课程基地，建成职业教育集团 10 个、义务教育阶段教育集团 37 个，热点高中统招名额分配比例保持在 70%，流动就业人员随迁子女公办学校吸纳比例达 90.2%。职业教育全国领航，高标准完成“国家中等职业教育改革发展示范学校”建设工程，全市江苏省品牌和特色专业增至 45 个，建成并投入使用 5 个省级高水平示范性实训基地。

文化事业繁荣发展。年末全市共有艺术表演团体 11 个，群众艺术馆、文化馆 8 个，博物馆 26 个；公共图书馆 4 个，全年总流通 217.2 万人次；自办广播节目 7 套，电视台节目 7 套，有线电视、数字电视用户分别达 117.9 万户、116.6 万户。不断加强历史文化保护与传承，青果巷历史文化街区保护利用工程顺利推进，恽代英纪念馆建成开放。2015 年，国务院正式批复常州成为国家历史文化名城。文化精品生产再获丰收，原创大型锡剧《夕照青果巷》成功亮相第二届江苏省艺术展演月，获“省文华优秀剧目奖”，被列为全省重点剧目明年晋京演出，《龙城谍恋》、《幸福的红萝卜》、《千古词帝》、《帝国的最后一夜》等作品成绩突出。文化惠民活动扎实有效开展，组织全市 10 多家民办博物馆、100 多个社会文化团体、近 2000 名艺术家和文艺工作者全心参与，惠及市民再超百万。文化产业加快发展，“中华龙城（常州）创意产业基地一期”项目入选文化部 2015 年文化金融合作项目，常州创意产业基地荣获“国家电子商务示范区”称号。环太湖艺术城、东方盐湖城、华夏宝盛园等重点文化产业项目加快推进。2015 年全市文化产业增加值占地区生产总值的比重达 5.8%。

卫生事业健康发展。年末全市共有各级各类医疗卫生机构 1196 个，拥有总床位 24263 张，卫生技术人员 2.96 万人，其中执业（助理）医师 12009 人、注册护士 12531 人，全市每千人拥有执业（助理）医师 2.55 人。深入推进综合医改，11 家城市公立医院和 7 家县级公立医院同步实施医药价格综合改革，取消以药补医机制；构建分级诊疗制度，8 所二级以上医院与基层医疗机构共建 380 张床位的 21 个特色专科；大力发展社会资本办医，全年新增非公立医疗机构 72 家，床位 1200 张。稳步夯实基层基础，新农合参合率继续保持 100%，人均筹资标准达到 603 元，住院实际补偿比达 56.03%；实施基层医疗机构提档升级工程，新建和改扩建基层医疗机构 11 家。规范开展公共卫生服务，全市基本公共卫生服务人均补助标准达 50 元，服务内容扩大到 12 类 45 项；传染病发病率低于全省平均水平，数字化预防接种门诊建成率达

72.2%，全市居民电子健康档案建档率 80.7%。大力提升优质医疗，推进市妇保院、市一院钟楼院区、市三院公卫临床中心等重点建设项目，配合行政区划调整，增设 3 个急救分站。不断创优计生服务，实施单独两孩政策，受理城镇单独夫妇再生育申请 2114 对。

体育事业蓬勃发展。全市拥有体育场地 12340 个，其中体育场 26 个，体育馆 35 个。公共体育服务体系建设取得阶段性成果，常州市和辖市区全部创建成为“第一批江苏省公共体育服务体系示范区”。有序推进各级各类体育健身设施建设，年内开工建设 1 个区级全民健身中心，完成 4 个乡镇全民健身活动中心建设，建成 32 个全民健身示范工程，为自然村（居民小区）新建和更新 637 个健身路径，免费开展国民体质测试超 3 万人次。实施“提升农民体育工程”，乡镇农村“10 分钟体育健身圈”建设逐步推进。全年共成功举办中国羽毛球大师赛、西太湖国际半程马拉松赛、环太湖国际公路自行车赛（武进赛段）、第七届 U21 青年女曲亚洲杯赛、中塞国际男篮对抗赛等 5 项次国际性比赛，以及 26 项次全国比赛（含体育协会赛事）、14 项次省级比赛。2015 年，常州市共有 13 名运动员获得国际性比赛前三名，63 名运动员获得全国性比赛前三名；其中，2015 年 8 月俄罗斯喀山游泳世锦赛上，常州籍运动员史婧琳、沈铎和队友夺得女子 4×100 米混合泳接力赛金牌，全市世界冠军总人数达到 20 人。全年共组织中小学生田径、游泳、篮球、排球、足球、乒乓球、羽毛球、网球、棋类、射击、举重等 20 项 47 次中小学生体育比赛。

十一、人口、民生与社会保障

人口规模逐步扩大。截至年末，全市常住人口 470.1 万人，比上年末增长 0.1%，其中城镇人口 329.1 万人，城镇化率达到 70.0%。全市户籍总人口 370.9 万人，增长 0.6%。其中，男性 183.6 万人，增长 0.4%；女性 187.3 万人，增长 0.8%。户籍人口出生率 9.6‰，人口死亡率 7‰，人口自然增长率为 2.7‰。

就业工作积极推进。全市城镇新增就业 13.3 万人，扶持创业 12979 人，援助困难群体就业 11362 人，期末城镇登记失业率继续控制 4% 以内。成功组织“第二届常州市大学生创业大赛”，征集创业项目 330 个。在全省首推以“招工即招生、入企即入校、企校双师联合培养”为主要内容的企业新型学徒制。大力促进残疾人从业创业，全年新增残疾人就业 853 人。全年新增高技能人才 3.85 万人，每万名劳动者中高技能人才 824 人。

居民收入稳定增长。2015 年全市居民人均可支配收入 35379 元，增长 8.3%，其中城镇居民人均可支配收入 42710 元，增长 8.2%，农村居民人均可支配收入 21912 元，增长 8.8%，城乡收入比为 1.95：1。全市居民人均消费支出 22234 元，增长 7.9%，其中城镇居民人均消费支出 25358 元，增长 7.5%，农村居民人均消费支出 14764 元，增长 9.1%。2015 年，城镇居民恩格尔系数 28%，农村居民恩格尔系数 31.7%，分别较上年下降 0.3 个、0.1 个百分点。

居民消费价格温和上涨。全年居民消费价格总指数为 101.6，八大类消费品价格中交通和通讯类价格下降 4.4%，食品、衣着、家庭设备用品及维修服务、医疗保健和个人用品、居住、烟酒用品、娱乐教育文化用品及服务七大类消费价格指数分别为 104.0、103.1、102.4、101.4、101.2、101.1、100.9。

住房保障工作有序推进。保障性安居工程建设稳步推进，全年新开工保障房 19065 套，基本建成 15847 套。全年新增公共租赁住房家庭 953 户，其中实物配租家庭 710 户，租金补贴家庭 243 户。2015 年全市城镇住房保障体系健全率 93.41%。

社会保障提质增效。截至年末，全市企业职工养老保险参保人数 133.8 万人，比上年增长 2.5%；城镇职工基本医疗保险参保人数 188.1 万人，增长 5.5%；城镇失业保险参保人数 108.7 万人，增长 3.3%。养老、医疗、失业三大保险综合覆盖率达 98%。连续第 11 年调整企业退休人员基本养老金，人均增幅超过 10%。

社会福利事业不断提升。全市城乡低保标准实现大幅提高，天宁区、钟楼区、新北区城乡低保标准为 670 元 / 月，金坛区、溧阳市城乡低保标准均为 590 元 / 月，武进区城乡低保标准为 620 元 / 月。2015 年全市 23351 户、39734 人纳入低保范围，其中城镇低保对象 7906 户、13123 人，农村低保对象 15445 户，26611 人，累计发放保障金 1.77 亿元。全年医疗直接救助 152977 人次、医疗直接救助金额 5907.5 万元。年末全市拥有各类养老机构 108 个，养老机构床位数 21968 张，收养人数 12274 人。全年发行福利彩票 11.02 亿元。2015 年，全市各级慈善会募集到账资金 1.18 亿元，发放（支出）各类救助金 8646 万元，惠及困难对象 16 万人次。

十二、城乡建设和公用事业

路网建设持续推进。常溧高速、延政西路西延、金武路快速化改造建成通车，地铁 1 号线等在建工程进展顺利。劳动西路（五星路～龙江路）、三堡街（长江路～五星路）、福阳路（青洋路～北塘河西路）和飞龙西路等新建和大修工程建成通车，永宁北路（新一路～横塘河西路）、新堂北路（新一路～龙汇路）、新一路和龙汇路（竹林北路～新堂北路）等新建工程基本具备通车条件。

公共交通服务不断完善。截至年底，全市公交线路 306 条，公交营运车辆 3055 辆，营运出租汽车 3680 辆。城市居民公共交通出行分担率 28.9%，镇村公交开通率 100%。

公共服务能力提升。全年全社会用电量 408 亿千瓦时，比上年增长 3.3%，其中城乡居民生活用电 34.4 亿千瓦时，增长 6%。城区全年实现公共供水 2.5 亿立方米，供气 7.8 亿立方米，污水处理总量 2.27 亿立方米，新增道路照明灯 10316 盏。城市公用基础设施不断完善，建成 30 万立方米 / 日德胜河应急取水工程，自来水深度处理工艺改造工程西石桥水厂项目、魏村水厂项目顺利开工建设，市区老小区雨污分流改造和污水提升工程基本完成。

十三、生态建设和环境保护

生态绿城建设不断深化。年末建成区绿地面积 9782.1 公顷，其中公园绿地面积 2479.5 公顷。市区人均公园绿地 13.9 平方米，建成区绿化覆盖率达到 43.1%。建成环高架及延伸段、丽华路、光华路、大明路生态绿道、横塘河湿地公园和白荡河绿地。扎实推进村庄规划建设示范工作，完成 7 个美丽乡村示范村检查验收，推进 8 个美丽乡村示范村建设，农村人居环境持续提升。2015 年常州市获得中国人居环境奖。

环境质量持续改善。全市生态文明建设工程综合考核连续 4 年名列全省第二。2015 年，全市完成大气污染防治项目 1270 项，水环境整治项目 356 项。全年空气质量优良天数 258 天，比上年增加 22 天，优良率 70.7%。化学需氧量、氨氮、二氧化硫、氮氧化物排放量比上年分别削减 3.44%、3.61%、2.51%、2.74%，超额完成“十二五”总削减任务。

注：公报中各项统计数据除注明按可比价格计算外，均按现行价格计算。

STATISTICAL COMMUNIQUE OF CHANGZHOU ON THE 2015 LOCAL ECONOMIC AND SOCIAL DEVELOPMENT

Despite the complicated macro economic environment and the heavy tasks to maintain reform and development in 2015, under the strong leadership of the Changzhou Municipal Committee of Communist Party of China and the Changzhou Municipal People's Government, Changzhou actively adapted itself to the economic "new normal", adhered to innovation, accelerated transformation, and properly managed multiple tasks of stabilizing growth, restructuring industries, promoting reforms, improving people's living standards, and guarding against risks. As a result, the city maintained a steady economic and social development and made new achievements in 2015.

I. Overview of the Local Economy

The local economy maintained a steady growth. Preliminary accounting shows that Changzhou's gross domestic product (GDP) of 2015 hit 527.32 billion RMB, up by 9.2% (calculated at constant prices) in comparison to 2014. Of this total, the value added of the primary industry grew by 3.1% to 14.66 billion RMB, that of the secondary industry grew by 8.5% to 251.60 billion RMB, and that of the tertiary industry grew by 10.6% to 261.06 billion RMB. The value added of the tertiary industry accounted for 49.5% of the GDP, up by 1.5% over 2014. And this makes the tertiary industry take over the secondary industry to be the No.1 contributor to the GDP for the first time. As a result, the local economy was restructured from the previous structure in which the secondary industry was the lead contributor to GDP, the tertiary industry was the No.2 contributor, and the primary industry was the No.3 contributor to the new structure with the tertiary industry being the top contributor, the secondary industry being the No.2 contributor, and the primary industry being the No.3 contributor. The per capita GDP (by resident population) reached 112,221 RMB, equal to 18,018 US dollars (converted at the average exchange rate).

Fiscal revenues grew steadily. In 2015, the general public budgetary revenues grew by 7.5% to 46.63 billion RMB, among which tax revenues grew by 7.3% to 37.37 billion RMB, accounting for 80.1% of the total. And among all tax revenues, value added tax (VAT) revenues (including those transformed from the business tax) grew by 6.4% to 7.08 billion RMB, business tax revenues grew by 19.1% to 11.38 billion RMB, and corporate income tax revenues grew by 1.4% to 4.26 billion RMB. The general public spending in 2015 grew by 11.6% to 48.53 billion RMB, among which spending on education grew by 16.1% to 7.92 billion RMB, that on science and technology grew by 4.8% to 2.27 billion RMB, that on social security and employment grew by 12.4% to 5.53 billion RMB, and that on health care and family planning grew by 20.1% to 3.85 billion RMB.

The local private sector slowed down. By end of 2015, there were 363,000 private enterprises and individual businesses with a total registered capital of 481.47 billion RMB. The value added of the private sector grew by 9.0% (calculated at constant prices) to 354.14 billion RMB, down by 1.1% in comparison to the growth rate of 2014. And the private sector accounted for 67.2% of the GDP, down by 0.3% over the previous year.

II. Agriculture and Rural Economy

Agricultural production remained stable. In 2015, the total output value of agriculture, forestry, animal husbandry and fishing combined grew by 5.8% to 27.18 billion RMB (calculated at current prices), among which agriculture grew by 6.1% to 14.72 billion RMB, forestry grew by 4.8% to 190 million RMB, animal husbandry grew by 3.5% to 3.88 billion RMB, and fishing grew by 5.5% to 6.83 billion RMB. Furthermore, the output value of the agriculture-related service sectors reached 1.56 billion RMB, up by 10.7% over 2014. The sown area of grain was 2.142 million mu (1 mu = 0.0667 hectares) and the aggregate grain output reached 1.083 million tons, down by 3.2% and 3.4% respectively in comparison to 2014. The rice yield per unit reached 643.5 kg/mu, ranking the highest in Jiangsu for 13 years in a row, and the wheat yield per unit was 356.3 kg/mu.

Modern agriculture speeded up. Agricultural technology and equipment continued to develop. 62,600 mu of high-standard farming land, 27,000 mu of protected agricultural land and 16,300 mu of facility fishery area were created in 2015, making the city's total to 1.35 million mu, 465,000 mu and 197,100 mu (taking 33.58% of the city's total fishery area) respectively. Besides, the agricultural mechanization rate and the agricultural informationization coverage hit 87% and 60%, up by 1% and 3% respectively. Moreover, agricultural industrialization advanced steadily. 91 leading agricultural enterprises in Changzhou registered a sales volume of 61.8 billion RMB, up by 9.6% over 2014.

III. Industry and Construction

Industrial production slowed down. In 2015, the total output value of industrial enterprises above the designated size in Changzhou reached 1110.16 billion. And the value added of these enterprises grew by 8.5%. Of all the industrial output value, the output value of heavy-industry enterprises and light-industry enterprises above the designated size stood at 832.64 billion and 277.52 billion RMB. In terms of the industrial output value of seven industry sectors, the chemistry, machinery, textile&garments, bio-medicine, electronics and construction material sectors grew by 14.9%, 9.3%, 7.2%, 7%, 4.8% and 0.3% to 195.28 billion, 460.27 billion, 97.6 billion, 27.88 billion, 65.61billion and 37.64 billion RMB respectively. In contrast, the metallurgy sector fell by 9.5% to 184.98 billion RMB.

The ten major industrial chains made more contributions to the GDP. In 2015, the aggregate output value of industrial enterprises above the designated size in the ten major industrial chains grew by 8.9% to 381.68 billion RMB, 3.6% higher than the average growth rate of industrial enterprises above the designated size in all sectors. And the ten major industrial chains contributed to 52.6% of the city's total industrial output value of all industrial enterprises above the designated size. Among the ten major industrial chains, the solar pv, automobile&parts, and rail transportation sectors registered the output values of 63.36 billion, 65.62 billion and 41.15 billion RMB, up by 25.6%, 15.8% and 13.1% respectively.

The construction sector remained stable. In 2015, the construction output value of local construction enterprises was128.85 billion RMB, up by 0.3% over 2014. The floor space under construction fell by 6.4% to 100.510 million m2 and the floor space completed fell by 9.5% to 34.486 million m2. The per capita productivity of the construction sector fell by 0.8% to 279,000 RMB (calculated by the total construction output value).

IV. Fixed Asset Investment

The investment structure continued to improve. In 2015, fixed asset investments in Changzhou grew by 6.7% to 339.9 billion RMB, among which investments on the heavy and light industry grew by 6.5% to 175.61 billion RMB and investments on the tertiary industry grew by 7.1% to 163.67 billion RMB. Furthermore, the city's investment structure was optimized. Investments on hi-tech enterprises increased by 13.9% to 79.46 billion RMB, 7.2% higher than the general fixed-asset-investment growth rate. Of all investments on the heavy and light industry, those on technical innovation and upgrading grew by 6.2% to 116.02 billion RMB, accounting for 66.1% of the total industrial investments. In contrast, real estate investments continued to decline. In 2015, 50.8 billion RMB was invested in the property market, down by 25.5% in comparison to 2014. 39.482 million m2 of residential floor space was developed and 6.378 million m2 of residential floor space was newly started, down by 11.5% and 30.4% respectively.

V. Domestic Trade

The local consumption remained stable. In 2015, the total retail sales of consumer goods grew to 199.05 billion RMB at the provincial average rate, 10.3%, down by 2.8% over 2014. Grouped by consumption patterns, retail sales for the wholesale, retail, catering and hotel businesses reached 24.01 billion, 158.57 billion, 14.99 billion and 1.48 billion RMB respectively, up by 9.4%, 10.1%, 14.2% and 4% respectively. Areawise, retail sales in urban areas grew by 10.6% to 186.11 billion RMB and those in rural areas increased by 5.7% to 12.94 billion RMB.

VI. Open Economy

Foreign trade rose despite all the difficulties. Changzhou's exports in 2015 stood at 131.92 billion RMB, up by 0.5% over 2014. Exports to countries and regions alongside the Silk Road Economic Belt and Maritime Silk Road maintained a good momentum. For instance, exports to India, ASEAN and Middle East up by 27.6%, 12.3% and 5% respectively. And hi-tech exports grew by 9.7% to 21.74 billion RMB. Machinery and electronics exports took up 54.1% of the city's total export value, up by 1.6%. The total value of imports and exports of services in 2015 stood at 8 billion RMB, up by 5.1% over 2014. Exports of general trade increased by 0.5% to 97.9 billion RMB.

Breakthroughs were made in foreign investment. In 2015, 2.49 billion US dollars of foreign investment was actually utilized and 16 projects were signed, each with an agreed investment of above 30 million US dollars. Among these 16 projects, the AAC Technologies project was worth over 1 billion US dollars, and the Boston Lithium Battery project, the United PV project and the Shunfeng PV project had an investment of over 500 million US dollars each. Besides, 5 new projects and 2 capital-increase projects were invested by Global Fortune 500 companies throughout the year, making a record high in recent years.

International cooperation was strengthened. In 2015, 67 new outbound investment projects were recorded with a total agreed investment of 755 million US dollars from local enterprises, up by 61.7% over 2014. Among these projects, 12 were connected to the " One Belt and One Road" initiative with an agreed investment of 360 million US dollars, accounting for 47.8% of the total. Service outsource contracts worth of 380 million US dollars were signed and those worth of 320 million US dollars were executed, up by 21.5% and 17.7% respectively.

Local development zones were upgraded. In 2015, development zones across Changzhou registered a general public budgetary revenue of 29.97 billion RMB and made an industrial investment of 132.38 billion RMB as well as an infrastructure investment of 29.74 billion RMB. Besides, these development zones utilized a total foreign capital of 2.25 billion US dollars and secured an agreed registered foreign capital of 2.36 billion RMB. Moreover, the Changzhou West Taihu Lake Science and Technology Industrial Zone was given a go-ahead to build itself into a provincial hi-tech zone. The Changzhou National Hi-tech District was designated as a national eco-friendly demonstration zone. Besides, the Wujin National Hi-tech Industrial Zone and the Wujin Economic Zone also applied for the status of the national eco-friendly industrial demonstration zone, and passed the on-site inspection jointly conducted by the Ministry of Environmental Protection, Ministry of Commerce, and Ministry of Science and Technology. In addition, international cooperation parks like China-Israel (Changzhou) Innovation Park and Sino-German Innovation Park maintained a rapid growth.

International exchanges were deepened. Changzhou received 197 foreign delegations of 1025 foreign guests throughout 2015. Among them were 28 groups of 161 embassy and consulate officials, 38 delegations of 215 persons from the city's international sister cities, and 4 groups of 8 foreign journalists. Two more cities were added to Changzhou's international sister city list in 2015, namely, La Serena of Chile and Curitiba of Brazil.

VII. Transportation, Post, Telecommunications and Tourism

The local transportation developed smoothly. By end of 2015, the total length of highways in Changzhou reached 9,010 km with 306 km of expressways. In 2015, the total passenger traffic stood at 76.73 million persons, down by 9.3% over 2014. The total freight traffic reached 130 million tons, up by 0.9% over 2014. The Passenger traffic handled by highways fell by 13.5% to 58.56 million persons and the passenger flows were 4.02 billion person-kilometers, down by 4.1% over 2014. The freight traffic handled by highways down by 0.5% to 110 million tons and the freight flows were 11.73 billion ton-kilometers, up by 5.5% over 2014. The passenger traffic handled by railways increased by 11% to 13.692 million persons. Passengers and freight&mails handled by civil aviation reached 1.811 million persons and 18,000 tons respectively. Besides, the volume of freight handled by ports stood at 89.84 million tons, among which the volume handled by the Changzhou Yangtze River Port hit 36.19 million tons. By end of 2015, the total number of motor vehicles for civilian use grew by 10.9% to 968,000 in the city, among which privately- owned motor vehicles grew by 13.1% to 821,000.

Post and telecommunications services grew relatively fast. The total turnover and revenue of post services reached 2.93 billion and 2.6 billion RMB, up by 34.3% and 31.6% respectively. The express mail delivery stood at 120 million units, up by 46.9%. Moreover, express companies above the designated size made 1.74 billion RMB from their primary business, with an year-on-year increase of 40%. The telecommunications services registered a total revenue of 5.27 billion RMB, down by 2.2% over 2014. By end of 2015, there were 1.33 million fixed-line phone subscribers and 5.144 million mobile phone subscribers. Of the total mobile phone subscribers, 1.322 million were 3G-service subscribers and 2.604 million were 4G-service subscribers. In addition, internet users grew by 25.3% to 1.998 million, among which 1.904 million were broadband users, up by 27.8% over 2014.

Tourism enjoyed a steady growth. In 2015, the local tourism sector generated a total revenue of 73.1 billion RMB, with a year-on year growth of 11.7%. Of the total, the revenue from domestic tourism grew by 12.3% to 71.84 billion RMB and the revenue generated by international visits topped 121 million US dollars, up by 18.8% over the previous year. The city received 54.557 million throughout the year, up by 9.1% over 2014. Of the total, 54.43 million were domestic tourists, up by 9.1% and 127,000 were inbound overnight visitors, up by 5.4%. By end of 2015, Changzhou boasted 3 provincial and 1 national holiday resorts, and 33 national Class-A tourist attractions, among which were 2 5A attractions and 9 4A attractions. The city also had 17 national industrial and agricultural tourist demonstration sites, 25 4-star provincial countryside tourist sites, 3 provincial industrial tourist sites, and 6 provincial tourist bases for self-drive travels. There were also 140 local travel agencies and one of them made it to the top 20 in Jiangsu. Besides, there were 56 star hotels, among which were 7 5-star hotels and 21 4-star hotels. Tourist attractions were also enriched and upgraded in 2015. For example, the Tian Muhu Lake Resort was selected as one of the first national holiday resorts and the Changdang Lake Resort was designated as a provincial holiday resort. In addition, the 5A Yan-city tourist site passed the national review and the Baosheng Park and the South Jiangsu Gloabl Harbor Shopping Mall were newly opened up. Moreover, Changzhou became a Taiwan- free-travel source city in 2015. And new international air routes were opened to Japan, Taiwan, etc..

VIII. The Financial Sector

The local credit market remained stable. By end of 2015, RMB deposits of financial institutions across the city grew by 51.23 billion RMB to 743.87 billion RMB, up by 7.4% over 2014. Of the total, household savings grew by 4.7% to 319.38 billion RMB. Loans of all the financial institutions in the city increased by 56.48 billion RMB to 535.46 billion RMB, up by 11.8%. Of the total, household loans hit 123.38 billion RMB, up by 15.2%. Besides, progress was made in financial reforms and innovation. For instance, the Jiangnan Financial Leasing Co., Ltd. was successfully established and became operational.

The local insurance sector maintained a steady growth. By end of 2015, insurance companies across the city totaled 67, among which were 28 property insurance companies and 39 life insurance companies. Insurance premium throughout the year grew by 15.6% to 15.66 billion RMB, among which life insurance premium grew by 17.0% to 10.49 billion RMB while property insurance premium grew by 13.2% to 5.17 billion RMB. Insurance companies paid an indemnity of 5.51 billion RMB in 2015, up by 12.5% in comparison to 2014. Of the total, life indemnity stood at 2.17 billion RMB, down by 6.5% whereas property indemnity surged by 29.5% to 3.34 billion RMB.

The local stock market was active. By end of 2015, there were 40 securities business offices across the city, managing over 960,000 securities accounts with 124.65 billion RMB worth of A shares. The total securities transaction volume in 2015 surged by 229% to 3217.23 billion RMB, among which A-share transactions surged by 275.9% to 2894.68 billion RMB, B-share transactions surged by 408.4% to 3.5 billion RMB, fund transactions grew by 132.0% to 74.94 billion RMB, and bond transactions increased by 39.6% to 244.11 billion. By end of 2015, there were 38 publicly traded local companies with an aggregate financing of 40.9 billion RMB, among which 24 were domestically traded companies and 14 were internationally traded ones. Two companies had their Initial Public Offerings (IPO) in 2015, i.e. Changzhou Tronly New Electronic Material Co., Ltd and Changzhou Tenglong Auto Parts Co., Ltd, raising a total fund of 710 million RMB.

IX. Science and Technology Innovation

Local innovation continued to rise. In 2015, 38,559 patent applications were made, among which were 13,211 invention patent applications. 21,585 patents were granted, among which were 2,664 invention patents. Patents per 10,000 persons reached 18.78. Besides, 140 hi-tech companies were established in 2015, bringing the city's total to 1,126. The output value of hi-tech companies above the designated size hit 497.56 billion RMB, taking up 43.4% of the total output value of industrial enterprises above the designated size. Furthermore, 530 national and provincial science and technology programs were approved with a total national and provincial funding of 530 million RMB. In addition, 1,116 industry-academy-research integration projects were newly created in 2015. Research and development (R&D) expenditures in 2015 accounted for 2.67% of the GDP.

Innovation platforms were accelerated. In 2015, 73 new provincial and national corporate R&D institutions were created, bringing the city's total "Two Stations and Three Centers" R&D entities to 1,159. Of the total, 602 were national and provincial R&D entities. In addition, 16 incubators and accelerators were established with a floor space of over 1 million m2. By end of 2015, Changzhou boasted a total number of 108 incubators and accelerators with an aggregate floor space of over 8 million m2.

Construction work on the Jiangsu Smart Manufacturing Innovation Center and four provincial industrial research institutes was advanced, and two out of the four institutes were officially inaugurated. Moreover, 20 key municipal public R&D institutes were either completed or upgraded in 2015.

South Jiangsu Innovation Demonstration Zone was advanced. The main framework of the South Jiangsu Innovation Demonstration Zone (Changzhou section) was basically established with the Changzhou Science and Education Town as its core, Changzhou National Hi-tech District and Wujin National Hi-tech Industrial Zone as its key parts and multiple industrial parks as its main components. The China-Israel (Changzhou) Innovation Park was accelerated and the city's key-talent- innovation-driven strategy generated noticeable benefits. In addition, the provincial Science and Technology Service Demonstration Zone in the Science and Education Town was regarded as a featured demonstration zone. The Wujin National High-tech Industrial Zone and the Jiangnan Graphene Research Institute were designated as regional science & technology service pilot zone and industrial science & technology service pilot institute respectively by the Ministry of Science and Technology.

X. Education, Culture, Public Health and Sports

Educational modernization was steadily advanced. By end of 2015, the city had a total number of 691 schools with 793,200 registered students and 57,000 faculties. Modernization of schools was vigorously advanced. For instance, 108 school construction projects were implemented with a total investment of 1.6 billion RMB. In 2015, Changzhou scored 88.06 points in terms of educational modernization. Education quality continued to improve. For instance, 77.46% of national college entrance exam takers in the city reached the second-tier college admission line in 2015. The higher technical education admission rate of the city's vocational school graduates remained the highest in Jiangsu for 16 years in a row. In addition, the city's vocational schools won 8 first prizes and 3 second prizes in the 2015 National Vocational School Skill Competition and 51 first prizes and 120 second prizes in the 2015 Jiangsu Provincial Vocational School Skill Competition, achieving a high position in Jiangsu. Moreover, students from Changzhou won 335 provincial first prizes and 547 provincial second prizes in five major national competitions (mathematics, physics, chemistry, biology, and information technology). Local schools also made great progress in 2015. For example, 16 senior high schools established 17 provincial curriculum programs. 10 vocational education school groups and 37 compulsory education school groups were set up. And 70% of popular senior high school's annual student recruitment numbers were allocated through the unified municipal senior high school entrance exam. Plus, 90.2% of migrant worker's children were admitted to local public schools. Changhzou also took a leading position in vocational education in China. The year 2015 witnessed the city's successful completion of the "Model School of National Secondary Vocational Education Reform and Development" project. By end of 2015, the city had 45 provincial brand and featured disciplines, and 5 provincial high-level model training bases were completed and became operational.

The local cultural service prospered. By end of 2015, there were 11 arts performance associations, 8 arts&cultural galleries and 26 museums. There were also 4 public libraries, which received 2.172 million persons in 2015. The city also had 7 local radio programs and 7 local TV programs, with subscribers to cable TV programs and digital TV programs hitting 1.179 million and 1.166 million respectively. Furthermore, preservation and inheritance work on history and culture was enhanced in 2015. For example, the preservation and utilization work on the Qingquo Alley Historical and Cultural Block progressed smoothly. And the memorial hall of the famous martyr of Communist Party of China, Yun Daiying, was established and opened to the public. In 2015, the State Council officially designated Changzhou as a famous national historic and cultural city. In addition, several exquisite art works were produced throughout the year. For instance, the original Xi opera drama the Sunset of Qingguo Alley was successfully staged in the second Jiangsu Art Show Month and received the Jiangsu Wenhua Outstanding Drama Award. It was also selected as a key provincial drama to be performed in Beijing next year. Besides, dramas like Love in the Dragon City, Happy Carrot, Great Poetry Emperor and Last Night of Empire also won great recognition. Cultural campaigns to entertain the public were also carried out, with over 10 private museums, over 100 cultural societies and almost 2000 artists and cultural workers participating in them. As a result, millions of citizens enjoyed tangible benefits. Moreover, the cultural industry sustained a rapid growth in 2015. The first-phase Dragon City Creativity Industry Base was selected as a cultural-financial cooperation project by the Culture Ministry. The base also received the title of National E-commerce Demonstration Zone. Meanwhile, the Taihu Lake Art Town, the Oriental Salt Lake Resort and the Baosheng Park were all constructed at a faster pace. In 2015, the value added of the local cultural industry accounted for 5.8% of the GDP.

The local public health service enjoyed a healthy development. By end of 2015, there were 1,196 medical institutions and 24,263 hospital beds across the city. The city's medical staff totaled 29,600, among which were 12,009 licensed/assistant doctors and 12,531 registered nurses. On average, every one thousand citizens had 2.55 licensed/assistant doctors. Comprehensive medical reforms were also deepened. For example, 11 municipal public hospitals and 7 county-level ones took a coordinated step to implement the comprehensive drug price reforms and abolish the traditional drug-profit-based hospital funding practice. The categorized diagnosis and treatment system was established. And 8 first and second class hospitals teamed up with grass-root level medical institutions to set up 380 hospital beds and 21 featured medical departments. In addition, private capital was attracted to the public health undertakings. For instance, 72 private medical institutions were newly established with 1,200 beds in 2015. Furthermore, the fundamentals of the health care system were consolidated. The participation rate of the new rural cooperative medical system (NCMS) continued to be at 100% with the per capita premium reaching 603 RMB. Meanwhile, the actual reimbursement rate for inpatient treatments climbed to 56.03%. Throughout the year, grass-root level medical institutions were upgraded, 11 of which were newly built, renovated or expanded. In addition, public health services were delivered in a standard manner. The per capita subsidy for basic public health services reached 50 RMB and service types were expanded to 12 categories of 45 items. The city's infectious disease morbidity rate was also below the provincial average. By end of 2015, 72.2% of the city's vaccination outpatient services were digitalized and 80.7% of citizens had e-medical records. Premium medical services were improved as well. Key medical facility projects - the new headquarters of the Changzhou Maternal and Child Care Hospital, the Zhonglou District compound of the Changhzhou First People's Hospital, and the clinical center of the Changzhou Third People's Hospital, etc. - were advanced. With the readjustment of the city's administrative districts, 3 new first-aid substations were set up in 2015. Moreover, family-planning services were continuously improved. With the full implementation of the two-child policy, 2,114 local couples filed applications for a second child throughout 2015.

The local sports service boomed. By end of 2015, Changzhou boasted 12,340 playgrounds, among which were 26 stadiums and 35 gymnasiums. New achievements were made in the public sports service system. Both the city and all its districts &county-level cities were selected among the first batch of Jiangsu Municipal Public Sports Service Demonstration Zones. Construction work of sports facilities was advanced in an orderly manner. In 2015, the construction work of one district-level sports center started and 4 township-level sports centers and 32 sports demonstration projects were completed. 637 community fitness lanes were built or upgraded. Besides, free physical fitness tests were provided to 30,000 persons. Efforts were made to improve sports facilities and ensure the availability of fitness facilities within 10-minute walk in townships and rural areas. 5 international sports games were held throughout 2015 (China Badminton Masters, West Taihu Lake International Half-marathon Race, Tour de Taihu Lake International Road Cycling Race (Wujin section), 7th U21 Female Hockey Asian Championship, 2015 China-Serbia Men's International Basketball

Challenge). And 26 national sports games (including tournaments of national sports associations) and 14 provincial sports games were also hosted in Changzhou in 2015. Also in 2015, 13 athletes from the city made it to the top 3 in international sports games and 63 made it to the top 3 in national sports games. For instance, in the 2015 World Swimming Championships in Russia, athletes Shi Qianlin and Shen Duo from Changzhou won the gold medal for the women's 4*100 medley relay together with their teammates. And this made the total number of Changzhou gold medalists to 20. Plus, 47 elementary and high school sports competitions in 20 categories (track and field, swimming, basketball, volleyball, football, table tennis, badminton, tennis, chess games, shooting, weight lifting, etc.) were organized in 2015.

XI. Population, People's Livelihood and Social Security

The local population was on a steady rise. By end of 2015, there were 4.701 million permanent residents with a year-on-year growth of 0.1%, among which 3.291 million were urban residents. And the urbanization rate reached 70.0%. The total number of registered residents grew by 0.6% to 3.709 million, among which 1.836 million were males, up by 0.4% and 1.873 million were females, up by 0.8%. The birth rate and death rate of the registered residents stood at 9.6‰ and 7‰ respectively, with a natural population growth rate of 2.7‰.

Efforts were made to promote employment. In 2015, 133,000 persons were newly employed, 12,979 persons started their own business with government support, and 11,362 disadvantaged persons became employed with government aids. And the registered urban unemployment rate remained below 4%. Besides, the second Changzhou College Student Entrepreneurship Competition was successfully organized and 330 business proposals were collected subsequently. The new enterprise-school apprenticeship system was initiated, which brought companies and schools together to produce workers in a targeted manner. Moreover, employment and entrepreneurship for the handicapped were actively promoted with 853 disabled persons being newly employed in 2015. The year 2015 also witnessed an increase of 38,500 highly-skilled talents and the number of highly-skilled talents per 10,000 workers reached 824.

People's incomes were on a steady rise. In 2015, the per capita disposable income of the city's residents increased by 8.3% to 35,379 RMB, among which the per capita disposable income of urban residents grew by 8.2% to 42,710 RMB while that of rural residents increased by 8.8% to 21,912 RMB. The ratio of the urban residents' income to the rural residents' income stood at 1.95:1. The per capita spending in 2015 grew by 7.9% to 22,234 RMB, among which the per capita spending of urban residents grew by 7.5% to 25,358 RMB and that of rural residents increased by 9.1% to 14,764. The Engel Coefficient of urban residents and rural residents stood at 28% and 31.7%, down by 0.3% and 0.1% respectively over 2014.

CPI grew at a mild pace. The city's general Consumer Price Index (CPI) stood at 101.6 in 2015. Among the eight major categories of consumer goods, the prices of transportation and telecommunications fell by 4.4%. CPI for food, garments, home appliances&maintenance, health care&individual goods, housing, cigarettes&wine, and entertaining&educational&cultural goods and services stood at 104.0, 103.1, 102.4, 101.4, 101.2, 101.1, and 100.9 respectively.

Security housing was advanced in an orderly manner. Construction work on security housing units was well underway. In 2015, 19,065 new security housing units were started and 15,847 security housing units were basically completed. 953 new households enjoyed public rental housing, among which 710 households were given rental housing units directly and 243 households received rental subsidies. In 2015, 93.41% of the city's urban security housing system was completed.

Social security was improved. By end of 2015, 1.338 million residents joined the enterprise employee's endowment insurance system, up by 2.5% over the previous year. 1.881 million residents joined the urban worker's basic medical insurance system, up by 5.5% over 2014. 1.087 million residents joint the urban unemployment insurance system, up by 3.3%. The three major insurance systems (endowment insurance, medical insurance, and unemployment insurance) covered 98% of the total population. Besides, pensions to retirees grew for 11 years in a row, with a per capita growth rate of above 10%.

Social welfare continued to improve. The year 2015 saw a substantial increase of Changzhou's basic living allowances. The basic living allowance for residents in Tianning District, Zhonglou District and Xinbei District stood at 670 RMB per month, that in Jintan District and Liyang County-city stood at 590 RMB, and that in Wujin District stood at 620 RMB. In 2015, 23,351 households and 39,734 persons were covered by the basic living allowance system, among which were 7,906 urban households of 13,123 residents and 15,445 rural households of 26,611 residents. A total sum of 177 million RMB worth of basic living allowances was handed out. In 2015, 152,997 residents received direct medical aids of 59.075 million RMB. By end of 2015, there were 108 aged care institutions with 21,968 beds, accommodating 12,274 persons. In addition, the sales volume of lottery tickets throughout the year was 1.102 billion RMB. In 2015, local charity organizations collected a total donation of 118 million RMB and handed out a total relief fund of 86.46 million RMB, covering 160,000 persons in need.

XII. City Construction and Public Utilities

The local road network continued to develop. In 2015, Changzhou-Liyang Expressway, the west extension line of West Yanzheng Rd. and the fast-track upgrading project of Jintan-Wujin Highway were completed and became fully operational. And Changzhou Metro Line 1 was being built smoothly throughout the year. West Laodong Rd. (from Wuxing Rd. to Longjiang Rd), Sanbao Street (from Changjiang Rd. to Wuxing Rd.), Fuyang Rd. (from Qingyang Rd. to West Bei Tanghe Rd.) and West Feilong Rd. were either renovated or newly built and became fully operational. The newly built roads like North Yongning Rd. (from Xinyi Rd. to West Heng Tanghe Rd.), North Xintang Rd. (from Xinyi Rd. to Longhui Rd.), Xinyi Rd. and Longhui Rd. (from North Zulin Rd. to North Xintang Rd.) were almost ready for operation.

Public transportation services continued to improve. By end of 2015, there were 306 bus lines, 3,055 buses and 3,680 taxis. 28.9% of residents' local travel and commuting was made via public transportation. Besides, bus lines were extended to all local towns, townships and villages.

Public utility services improved. In 2015, the total local power consumption grew by 3.3% to 40.8 billion kWh, among which the household power consumption of urban and rural residents grew by 6% to 3.44 billion kWh. Besides, the city's annual water and gas supplies hit 250 million and 780 million cubic meters respectively. 227 million cubic meters of sewage was treated and 9,338 lamps were installed throughout the year. In addition, public utility infrastructure continued to improve. For instance, the Ri Desheng River Emergency Water Intake project with a capacity of 300,000 cubic meteres was completed. Upgrading projects of tap water deep processing techniques like the the Xishi Bridge Water Plant and Weicun Village Water Plant were also started. Besides, infrastructure upgrading projects on rainwater-sewage diversion and sewage treatment in old neighborhoods were largely completed.

XIII. Ecology and Environmental Protection

The eco-city campaign deepened. By end of 2015, there were 9,782.1 hectares of green land, among which were 2,479.5 hectares of green park land. The per capita green park space hit 13.9 m2 and the city's green coverage rate reached 43.1%. Besides, green lanes were built alongside the city's elevated highways, their extension lines, Lihua Rd., Guanghua Rd., and Da Guangming Rd in 2015. And the Hengtang River Wetland Park and Baidang River Green Land were also completed. Efforts to plan and build model villages were also underway. For instance, 7 local villages were approved to be Beautiful Countryside Model Villages and 8 other villages were on their way to become such model villages. Plus, living conditions in rural areas continued to improve. Changzhou received the National Award for Best Living Environment in 2015.

The local environment continued to improve. The year 2015 saw continued environmental improvements and marked the 4th consecutive year in which Changzhou ranked the 2nd place in terms of environmental achievements among all cities in Jiangsu. Throughout 2015, 1270 air-pollution prevention & treatment programs and 356 water quality treatment programs were implemented. As a result, there were 258 days with good air quality throughout the year, up by 22 days in comparison to 2014. That is to say, 70.7% of all the days throughout 2015 had good air quality. In addition, 2015 also witnessed the reduction of COD,ammonia nitrogen, sulfur dioxide, and oxynitride emissions by 3.44%, 3.61%, 2.51% and 2.74% respectively, thus making the city overfulfill its total emission cut goal for the 12th Five Year Plan period.

Note:otherwise said to be calculated at comparable prices, all figures in the communique were calculated at current prices.

2

CHAPTER 2

排 名 榜

LIST OF TOP STRENGTHS

2-1 工业企业主营业务收入前 100 名单位（2015 年）
TOP 100 INDUSTRIAL ENTERPRISES BY MAIN BUSINESS INCOME（2015）

序号 No.	企业名称 Name of Enterprises	序号 No.	企业名称 Name of Enterprises
1	中天钢铁集团有限公司	26	常州亿晶光电科技有限公司
2	亚邦投资控股集团有限公司	27	溧阳市光明金属有限责任公司
3	江苏申特钢铁有限公司	28	常州神力电机股份有限公司
4	东方润安集团有限公司	29	常州同泰高导铜线有限公司
5	常州天合光能有限公司	30	江苏金昇实业股份有限公司
6	新阳科技集团有限公司	31	常州安凯特电缆有限公司
7	常州南海铜业有限公司	32	百兴集团有限公司
8	常州金源铜业有限公司	33	常州华利达服装集团有限公司
9	江苏上上电缆集团有限公司	34	江苏国强镀锌实业有限公司
10	国茂减速机集团有限公司	35	江苏华鹏变压器有限公司
11	江苏江南实业集团有限公司	36	江苏中再生投资开发有限公司
12	常州亚邦化学有限公司	37	江苏亿禾新材料有限公司
13	常州东昊化工有限公司	38	南车戚墅堰机车有限公司
14	新誉集团有限公司	39	常州旷达织物整理有限公司
15	华润包装材料有限公司	40	常州华盛恒能光电有限公司
16	江苏今创投资经营有限公司	41	常州市英中电气有限公司
17	江苏科茵格特种沥青有限公司	42	常州格力博有限公司
18	江苏诚达石化工业有限公司	43	常州常松金属复合材料有限公司
19	莱尼电气线缆（中国）有限公司	44	现代（江苏）工程机械有限公司
20	瑞声声学科技（常州）有限公司	45	常州东风农机集团有限公司
21	新华昌集团有限公司	46	盘固水泥集团有限公司
22	江苏旷达汽车织物集团股份有限公司	47	江苏雷利电机股份有限公司
23	江苏振达钢铁有限公司	48	森萨塔科技（常州）有限公司
24	光宝科技（常州）有限公司	49	常州东芝变压器有限公司
25	天合光能（常州）科技有限公司	50	江苏易成电力器材有限公司

2-1　续表　continued

序号 No.	企业名称 Name of Enterprises	序号 No.	企业名称 Name of Enterprises
51	常州西电变压器有限责任公司	76	江苏常发农业装备股份有限公司
52	江苏丰润电器集团有限公司	77	金坛市海林稀土有限公司
53	常州明谛树脂有限公司	78	江苏中东化肥股份有限公司
54	江苏正昌集团有限公司	79	常州科研试制中心有限公司
55	常州海杰冶金机械制造有限公司	80	瑞声光电科技（常州）有限公司
56	常州武矿电气设备有限公司	81	中盐常州化工股份有限公司
57	南车戚墅堰机车车辆工艺研究所有限公司	82	常州老三集团有限公司
58	溧阳市宏峰水泥有限公司	83	常州昌瑞汽车部品制造有限公司
59	江苏金峰水泥集团有限公司	84	常州东奥服装有限公司
60	江苏金坛汽车工业有限公司	85	常州市名杰建材设备制造有限公司
61	常州岩松金属制品有限公司	86	常州祥明电机有限公司
62	亚邦医药股份有限公司	87	溧阳市新金峰水泥有限公司
63	常柴股份有限公司	88	江苏新鸿联集团有限公司
64	江苏顺风光电科技有限公司	89	常州润源电力建设有限公司
65	常州久日化学有限公司	90	常州市环银物资有限公司
66	中盐金坛盐化有限责任公司	91	常州昊邦汽车零部件有限公司
67	常州协鑫光伏科技有限公司	92	常州常益建设工程构件有限公司
68	常州兆阳能源科技有限公司	93	常州市新东方电缆有限公司
69	常州星宇车灯股份有限公司	94	江苏华电戚墅堰发电有限公司
70	江苏常隆化工有限公司	95	江苏富民新材料有限公司
71	常州首创服饰有限公司	96	常州市同和纺织机械制造有限公司
72	国电常州发电有限公司	97	江苏洛克集团电气有限公司
73	常州市正和电磁线有限公司	98	溧阳市万兴特种建材有限公司
74	今创集团股份有限公司	99	江苏长海复合材料股份有限公司
75	正信光伏有限公司	100	常州四药制药有限公司

2-2 工业企业实现利税前 100 名单位（2015 年）
TOP 100 INDUSTRIAL ENTERPRISES BY PROFITS AND TAXES（2015）

序号 No.	企业名称 Name of Enterprises	序号 No.	企业名称 Name of Enterprises
1	江苏申特钢铁有限公司	26	新华昌集团有限公司
2	常州天合光能有限公司	27	江苏上上电缆集团有限公司
3	亚邦投资控股集团有限公司	28	常州同泰高导铜线有限公司
4	新誉集团有限公司	29	中盐金坛盐化有限责任公司
5	东方润安集团有限公司	30	溧阳市新金峰水泥有限公司
6	常州南海铜业有限公司	31	常州旷达织物整理有限公司
7	瑞声声学科技（常州）有限公司	32	溧阳市光明金属有限责任公司
8	国茂减速机集团有限公司	33	常州首创服饰有限公司
9	江苏今创投资经营有限公司	34	常州华盛恒能光电有限公司
10	江苏江南实业集团有限公司	35	江苏旷达汽车织物集团股份有限公司
11	中天钢铁集团有限公司	36	常州润源电力建设有限公司
12	国电常州发电有限公司	37	常州市环银物资有限公司
13	江苏金峰水泥集团有限公司	38	森萨塔科技（常州）有限公司
14	天合光能（常州）科技有限公司	39	盘固水泥集团有限公司
15	莱尼电气线缆（中国）有限公司	40	江苏科茵格特种沥青有限公司
16	今创集团股份有限公司	41	常州神力电机股份有限公司
17	江苏亿禾新材料有限公司	42	江苏国强镀锌实业有限公司
18	江苏诚达石化工业有限公司	43	常州久日化学有限公司
19	江苏华电戚墅堰发电有限公司	44	百兴集团有限公司
20	常州四药制药有限公司	45	江苏常发农业装备股份有限公司
21	江苏振达钢铁有限公司	46	常州星宇车灯股份有限公司
22	常州安凯特电缆有限公司	47	江苏金昇实业股份有限公司
23	溧阳市宏峰水泥有限公司	48	常州市嘉业铸造有限公司
24	江苏易成电力器材有限公司	49	江苏长海复合材料股份有限公司
25	江苏华鹏变压器有限公司	50	常州千红生化制药股份有限公司

2-2　续表　continued

序号 No.	企业名称 Name of Enterprises	序号 No.	企业名称 Name of Enterprises
51	江苏雷利电机股份有限公司	76	江苏常宝钢管股份有限公司
52	江苏中再生投资开发有限公司	77	江苏新鸿联集团有限公司
53	常州太平通讯科技有限公司	78	常州小糸今创交通设备有限公司
54	常州亿晶光电科技有限公司	79	江苏斯达工业科技有限公司
55	常州市英中电气有限公司	80	常州市正和电磁线有限公司
56	常州协鑫光伏科技有限公司	81	常州常益建设工程构件有限公司
57	梅特勒-托利多（常州）测量技术有限公司	82	正信光伏有限公司
58	常州华利达服装集团有限公司	83	溧阳市四方不锈钢制品有限公司
59	常州海杰冶金机械制造有限公司	84	江苏武进不锈股份有限公司
60	常州市临江化工有限公司	85	江苏弘博新材料有限公司
61	常州市新东方电缆有限公司	86	常州祥明电机有限公司
62	江苏丰润电器集团有限公司	87	常州昊邦汽车零部件有限公司
63	江苏顺风光电科技有限公司	88	常州明谛树脂有限公司
64	江苏正昌集团有限公司	89	常州博瑞电力自动化设备有限公司
65	常州港华燃气有限公司	90	江苏瑞昕金属制品科技有限公司
66	常州科研试制中心有限公司	91	江苏鸿瑞昌泰纺织有限公司
67	常州金源铜业有限公司	92	常州兆阳能源科技有限公司
68	常州市名杰建材设备制造有限公司	93	常州格力博有限公司
69	安费诺（常州）高端连接器有限公司	94	常州龙宇江庆新材料科技有限公司
70	卡尔迈耶（中国）有限公司	95	江苏富民新材料有限公司
71	常州市同和纺织机械制造有限公司	96	常州龙宇颜料化学有限公司
72	常州西电变压器有限责任公司	97	溧阳市万兴特种建材有限公司
73	常州新奥燃气发展有限公司	98	常州合力电器有限公司
74	常州市天盛工程机械有限公司	99	常州市滔邦精密机械有限公司
75	常州东芝变压器有限公司	100	柳工常州挖掘机有限公司

2-3 工业企业实现利润前 100 名单位（2015 年）
TOP 100 INDUSTRIAL ENTERPRISES BY PROFITS（2015）

序号 No.	企业名称 Name of Enterprises	序号 No.	企业名称 Name of Enterprises
1	新誉集团有限公司	26	常州华盛恒能光电有限公司
2	亚邦投资控股集团有限公司	27	盘固水泥集团有限公司
3	常州南海铜业有限公司	28	江苏诚达石化工业有限公司
4	江苏申特钢铁有限公司	29	江苏国强镀锌实业有限公司
5	国茂减速机集团有限公司	30	常州旷达织物整理有限公司
6	瑞声声学科技（常州）有限公司	31	江苏科茵格特种沥青有限公司
7	常州天合光能有限公司	32	溧阳市新金峰水泥有限公司
8	江苏金峰水泥集团有限公司	33	常州同泰高导铜线有限公司
9	江苏亿禾新材料有限公司	34	江苏旷达汽车织物集团股份有限公司
10	国电常州发电有限公司	35	江苏常发农业装备股份有限公司
11	江苏今创投资经营有限公司	36	常州首创服饰有限公司
12	莱尼电气线缆（中国）有限公司	37	常州星宇车灯股份有限公司
13	今创集团股份有限公司	38	常州千红生化制药股份有限公司
14	常州安凯特电缆有限公司	39	中盐金坛盐化有限责任公司
15	东方润安集团有限公司	40	常州四药制药有限公司
16	江苏江南实业集团有限公司	41	常州华利达服装集团有限公司
17	江苏华电戚墅堰发电有限公司	42	江苏长海复合材料股份有限公司
18	森萨塔科技（常州）有限公司	43	梅特勒-托利多（常州）测量技术有限公司
19	常州久日化学有限公司	44	溧阳市光明金属有限责任公司
20	江苏华鹏变压器有限公司	45	江苏中再生投资开发有限公司
21	江苏易成电力器材有限公司	46	常州市环银物资有限公司
22	常州润源电力建设有限公司	47	天合光能（常州）科技有限公司
23	中天钢铁集团有限公司	48	安费诺（常州）高端连接器有限公司
24	溧阳市宏峰水泥有限公司	49	江苏金昇实业股份有限公司
25	江苏上上电缆集团有限公司	50	常州市新东方电缆有限公司

2-3 续表 continued

序号 No.	企业名称 Name of Enterprises	序号 No.	企业名称 Name of Enterprises
51	江苏雷利电机股份有限公司	76	常州博瑞电力自动化设备有限公司
52	常州市临江化工有限公司	77	常州市天盛工程机械有限公司
53	常州神力电机股份有限公司	78	柳工常州挖掘机有限公司
54	常州亿晶光电科技有限公司	79	瑞声光电科技（常州）有限公司
55	常州太平通讯科技有限公司	80	江苏弘博新材料有限公司
56	常州港华燃气有限公司	81	常州东风农机集团有限公司
57	常州市嘉业铸造有限公司	82	江苏武进不锈股份有限公司
58	江苏振达钢铁有限公司	83	常州市万顺纺织集团有限公司
59	常州新奥燃气发展有限公司	84	江苏鸿瑞昌泰纺织有限公司
60	常州市同和纺织机械制造有限公司	85	麦格纳动力总成（常州）有限公司
61	卡尔迈耶（中国）有限公司	86	江苏瑞昕金属制品科技有限公司
62	常州协鑫光伏科技有限公司	87	常州艾贝服饰有限公司
63	常州市名杰建材设备制造有限公司	88	江苏丰润电器集团有限公司
64	常州小糸今创交通设备有限公司	89	常州市正和电磁线有限公司
65	常州海杰冶金机械制造有限公司	90	江苏顺风光电科技有限公司
66	百兴集团有限公司	91	雅柯斯电力科技（中国）有限公司
67	常州市英中电气有限公司	92	新华昌集团有限公司
68	常州科研试制中心有限公司	93	江苏正昌集团有限公司
69	江苏常宝钢管股份有限公司	94	常州昊邦汽车零部件有限公司
70	常州金源铜业有限公司	95	江苏钢锐精密机械有限公司
71	江苏省激素研究所股份有限公司	96	常州永安公共自行车系统股份有限公司
72	常州西电变压器有限责任公司	97	南车戚墅堰机车车辆工艺研究所有限公司
73	特雷克斯（常州）机械有限公司	98	常州龙宇江庆新材料科技有限公司
74	常州龙宇颜料化学有限公司	99	东嘉麻棉（常州）有限公司
75	常州东芝变压器有限公司	100	常州明谛树脂有限公司

2-4 批发贸易业企业商品销售总额前 10 名单位（2015 年）
TOP TEN WHOLESALE TRADE ENTERPRISES BY COMMODITIES SALES VOLUME（2015）

序号 No.	单位名称 Name of Units	序号 No.	单位名称 Name of Units
1	华润化工新材料有限公司	6	江苏金坛众泰汽车销售有限公司
2	中石化销售有限公司江苏常州石油分公司	7	常州大华进出口（集团）有限公司
3	常州市化工轻工材料总公司	8	常州怡锋达物资有限公司
4	江苏省烟草公司常州市公司	9	江苏亚邦进出口有限公司
5	常州海江国际贸易有限公司	10	常州对外贸易有限公司

2-5 批发贸易业企业利税总额前 10 名单位（2015 年）
TOP TEN WHOLESALE TRADE ENTERPRISES BY PROFITS AND TAXES（2015）

序号 No.	单位名称 Name of Units	序号 No.	单位名称 Name of Units
1	江苏省烟草公司常州市公司	6	常州海江国际贸易有限公司
2	中石化销售有限公司江苏常州石油分公司	7	江苏亚邦医药营销有限公司
3	五矿西电（常州）钢材加工有限公司	8	常州特耐炉料有限公司
4	梅特勒-托利多（常州）称重系统设备有限公司	9	金坛市汇隆祥棉业有限公司
5	常州市中油石油销售有限公司	10	常州市四季禽业有限公司

2-6 零售贸易业企业商品销售总额前 10 名单位（2015 年）
TOP TEN RETAIL TRADE ENTERPRISES BY COMMODITIES SALES VOLUME（2015）

序号 No.	单位名称 Name of Unitss	序号 No.	单位名称 Name of Units
1	江苏明都汽车集团有限公司	6	中国石油天然气股份有限公司江苏常州销售分公司
2	国药控股常州有限公司	7	常州百货大楼股份有限公司
3	上药集团常州药业股份有限公司	8	常州之星汽车有限公司
4	月星集团有限公司	9	常州苏宁云商商贸有限公司
5	江苏万帮明都汽车有限公司	10	常州宝尊汽车销售服务有限公司

2-7　零售贸易业企业利税总额前 10 名单位（2015 年）
TOP TEN RETAIL TRADE ENTERPRISES BY PROFITS AND TAXEX（2015）

序号 No.	单位名称 Name of Units	序号 No.	单位名称 Name of Units
1	常州百货大楼股份有限公司	6	溧阳八佰伴商贸中心有限公司
2	月星集团有限公司	7	常州泰富百货集团有限责任公司
3	上药集团常州药业股份有限公司	8	常州金店有限公司
4	常州新世纪商城有限公司	9	常州中天汽车有限公司
5	国药控股常州有限公司	10	金坛大统华购物中心有限公司

2-8　批发零售贸易业企业利润总额前 10 名单位（2015 年）
TOP TEN WHOLESALE AND RETAIL TRADE ENTERPRISES IN PROFITS （2015）

序号 No.	单位名称 Name of Units	序号 No.	单位名称 Name of Units
1	江苏省烟草公司常州市公司	6	常州海江国际贸易有限公司
2	常州百货大楼股份有限公司	7	上药集团常州药业股份有限公司
3	五矿西电（常州）钢材加工有限公司	8	常州特耐炉料有限公司
4	常州市中油石油销售有限公司	9	常州新世纪商城有限公司
5	月星集团有限公司	10	梅特勒-托利多（常州）称重系统设备有限公司

2-9　餐饮业企业营业收入前 10 名单位（2015 年）
TOP TEN CATERING TRADE ENTERPRISES IN BUSINESS INCOME（2015）

序号 No.	单位名称 Name of Unitss	序号 No.	单位名称 Name of Units
1	大娘水饺餐饮集团股份有限公司	6	常州富都青枫苑宾馆有限公司
2	常州丽华快餐集团有限公司	7	常州听松楼花园酒店有限公司
3	常州扬子餐饮管理有限公司	8	常州奥体明都国际饭店有限公司
4	常州福记餐饮投资管理有限公司	9	常州市怡佳逸高酒店管理有限公司
5	江苏大城小爱餐饮管理有限公司	10	常州锦湖酒店管理有限公司

2-10 餐饮业企业利税总额前 10 名单位（2015 年）
TOP TEN CATERING TRADE ENTERPRISES BY PROFITS AND TAXEX（2015）

序号 No.	单位名称 Name of Units	序号 No.	单位名称 Name of Units
1	大娘水饺餐饮集团股份有限公司	6	常州富都青枫苑宾馆有限公司
2	溧阳泰丰餐饮有限公司	7	常州市百德江南餐饮管理有限公司
3	常州市竺山湖小镇酒店管理有限公司	8	常州奥体明都国际饭店有限公司
4	常州扬子餐饮管理有限公司	9	江苏大城小爱餐饮管理有限公司
5	常州福记餐饮投资管理有限公司	10	常州金色南都国际大酒店有限公司

2-11 住宿业企业营业收入前 10 名单位（2015 年）
TOP TEN HOTELS BY BUSINESS INCOME（2015）

序号 No.	单位名称 Name of Units	序号 No.	单位名称 Name of Units
1	溧阳亚东实业发展有限公司	6	溧阳宾馆有限公司
2	常州九洲花园大酒店有限公司	7	常州富都溪湖国际大饭店有限公司
3	常州波尔曼旅游投资发展有限公司	8	溧阳市金峰国际饭店管理有限公司
4	常州富都大酒店有限公司	9	常州锦江国际大酒店有限公司
5	江苏天目湖宾馆有限公司	10	常州大酒店有限公司

2-12 住宿业企业利税总额前 10 名单位（2015 年）
TOP TEN HOTELS BY PROFITS AND TAXEX（2015）

序号 No.	单位名称 Name of Unitss	序号 No.	单位名称 Name of Units
1	溧阳亚东实业发展有限公司	6	常州市明都大饭店管理有限公司
2	溧阳宾馆有限公司	7	常州常瑞宾馆
3	江苏天目湖宾馆有限公司	8	常州市中天凤凰大酒店有限公司
4	常州市和平假日大饭店有限公司	9	金坛颐丰大酒店有限公司
5	溧阳市金峰国际饭店管理有限公司	10	常州富都大酒店有限公司

2-13 住宿餐饮企业利润总额前 10 名单位（2015 年）
TOP TEN ACCOMMODATION AND CATERING TRADE ENTERPRISES BY PROFITS（2015）

序号 No.	单位名称 Name of Units	序号 No.	单位名称 Name of Units
1	溧阳亚东实业发展有限公司	6	溧阳宾馆有限公司
2	大娘水饺餐饮集团股份有限公司	7	常州常瑞宾馆
3	常州市和平假日大饭店有限公司	8	常州如家快捷酒店有限公司
4	常州市竺山湖小镇酒店管理有限公司	9	常州市百德江南餐饮管理有限公司
5	溧阳泰丰餐饮有限公司	10	常州市明都大饭店管理有限公司

2-14 成交额超亿元市场前 10 名单位（2015 年）
TOP TEN MARKETS WITH TANSACTION VOLUME ABOVE RMB100 MILLION （2015）

序号 No.	单位名称 Name of Units	序号 No.	单位名称 Name of Units
1	江苏凌家塘市场发展有限公司	6	江苏长江塑料化工交易市场有限公司
2	江苏湖塘纺织城投资发展有限公司	7	常州钢材现货交易市场有限公司
3	常州淮都金属城有限公司	8	江苏苏浙皖边界市场发展有限公司
4	常州市武进汽车城投资发展有限公司	9	常州市武进邹区灯具城
5	常州市武进夏溪花木市场发展有限公司	10	江苏万商商贸城有限责任公司

2-15 出口额前 10 名单位（2015 年）
TOP TEN ENTERPRISES IN EXPORT VALUE（2015）

序号 No.	单位名称 Name of Unitss	序号 No.	单位名称 Name of Units
1	常州天合光能有限公司	6	常州格力博有限公司
2	常州大华进出口（集团）有限公司	7	常州对外贸易有限公司
3	华润包装材料有限公司	8	天合光能（常州）科技有限公司
4	常州华利达服装集团有限公司	9	常州机械设备进出口有限公司
5	森萨塔科技（常州）有限公司	10	常州大亚进出口有限公司

2-16 驰名商标和著名商标一览
RENOWNED AND DISTINGUISHED BRANDS

企业名称 Name of Enterprises	商标名称 Brand Name	主要产品 Mostly Product	颁布时间 Time of Release	所在地区 Region
驰名商标 Renowned Brand				
常柴股份有限公司	CHANGCHAI及图; 常柴CC及图	柴油机	1995年	钟楼区
常州东风农机集团有限公司	东风及图；DF及图	拖拉机	1999年	钟楼区
新科电子集团有限公司	新科Shinco	影碟机	1999年	武进区
江苏正昌集团有限公司	正　昌	饲料机械	2000年	溧阳市
常州常发动力机械有限公司	常　发	柴油机	2002年	武进区
黑牡丹（集团）股份有限公司	黑牡丹HEIMUDAN及图	牛仔布、色织布	2005年	天宁区
江苏华鹏变压器有限公司	华鹏HUA PENG	变压器	2005年	溧阳市
江苏庄臣同大有限公司	全无敌	杀虫剂、蚊香	2006年	新北区
江苏上上电缆集团有限公司	上上及图	电线、电缆	2006年	溧阳市
江苏新鸿联集团有限公司	红联及图	灯　具	2006年	武进区
亚邦投资控股集团有限公司	亚邦及图	染料、涂料	2007年	武进区
江苏兰陵化工集团有限公司	兰陵及图	防腐涂料、防火涂料	2008年	武进区
顶呱呱彩棉服饰有限公司	顶呱呱	内衣等	2008年	武进区
江苏天容集团股份有限公司	溧化LIHUA及图	农　药	2008年	溧阳市
亚邦投资控股集团有限公司	光辉GUANGHUI及图	油漆、耐酸漆	2009年	武进区
江苏庄臣同大有限公司	爱家及图	空气清新剂、杀害虫剂等	2009年	新北区
常州市武进五洋纺织机械有限公司	五洋WYFJ及图	针织机械、编织机	2010年	武进区
江苏迪邦三星轴承有限公司	三鑫SANXIN及图	圆柱滚子轴承、四列圆锥滚子轴承	2010年	武进区
江苏旷达汽车织物集团股份有限公司	旷　达	装饰布	2010年	武进区
江海环保股份有限公司	江海及图	水质稳定剂	2010年	武进区
国茂减速机集团有限公司	国茂GUOMAO及图	减速机	2010年	武进区
江苏洛基木业有限公司	洛基LODGI及图	地板、铺地木材、非金属地板等	2010年	武进区
江苏开利地毯股份有限公司	天目湖及图	地　毯	2010年	溧阳市
江苏天容集团股份有限公司	天容及图	杀害虫剂、除草剂、消灭有害植物剂	2010年	溧阳市
常州光洋轴承股份有限公司	NRB	轴承（机器零件）、传动轴承	2011年	新北区
常州银河电器有限公司	BILIN	晶体管（电子）、半导体器件、晶片（锗片）	2011年	新北区
常州市常欣电子衡器有限公司	常欣CHANGXIN及图	超载限制器	2011年	新北区
灵通投资集团有限公司	LING TONG及图	金属陈列架	2011年	武进区
常州迪邦纺织有限公司	迪邦DiBang	纱、线、棉线和棉纱	2011年	武进区
江苏太阳宝新能源有限公司	太阳宝	太阳能热水器	2011年	武进区
江苏亚示照明集团有限公司	YASHIPS	灯、照明器	2011年	武进区
江苏裕成电子有限公司	裕成YUCHENG及图	自行车发动机	2011年	武进区

注：驰名商标和著名商标按当年行政区划口径统计。
Note: Nation-wide famous brands and famous brands are counted in accordance with the city’s administrative districts of the year.

2-16 续表 1　continued 1

企业名称 Name of Enterprises	商标名称 Brand Name	主要产品 Mostly Product	颁布时间 Time of Release	所在地区 Region
常州玉宇电光器件有限公司	玉　宇	灯泡、电灯	2011年	武进区
常州市武进五洋纺织机械有限公司	柳绿LLPJ及图	纺织织物、布、编织织物	2011年	武进区
今创集团股份有限公司	KTK及图	车辆行李架、车辆座位、车辆内装饰品	2011年	武进区
新城控股集团有限公司	新城及图	建筑、砖石建筑、商业摊位及商店的建筑	2011年	武进区
江苏省激素研究所股份有限公司	金珠及图	农　药	2012年	金坛市
冶建新材料股份有限公司	天虎及图	涂　料	2012年	溧阳市
江苏瑞阳化工股份有限公司	瑞阳RUI YANG及图	季戊四醇、盐类	2012年	溧阳市
常州市国宇环保科技有限公司	玉宇及图	硝酸银、催化剂	2012年	武进区
江苏晨光涂料有限公司	晨光CHENGUANG及图	氯磺化聚乙烯工业涂料	2012年	武进区
常州华通焊业股份有限公司	華通HUATONG及图	金属焊丝	2012年	武进区
常州市润源经编机械有限公司	润源及图	纺织工业用机器	2012年	武进区
常州市钱璟康复器材有限公司	钱璟及图	按摩器械等	2012年	武进区
江苏众恒染整有限公司	众恒ZHONGHENG及图	针织牛仔布	2012年	武进区
江苏天香集团有限公司	香雪及图	味　精	2012年	武进区
江苏金鼎电动工具集团有限公司	金鼎及图	电动手工具等	2012年	武进区
江苏长海复合材料股份有限公司	常海CHANGHAI及图	热敷胶粘纤维布等	2012年	武进区
江苏南洋木业有限公司	第1330307号图形	成品木材等	2012年	武进区
亚邦化工集团有限公司	金囤及图	农　药	2012年	武进区
常州远东连杆集团有限公司	滆湖GH及图	连杆总成	2012年	武进区
江苏华光粉末有限公司	剑亮及图	粉末涂料	2012年	武进区
常州方圆制药有限公司	创成及图	化学药物制剂	2012年	新北区
江苏华冠电器集团有限公司	华程HUACHENG HC	配电柜等	2012年	新北区
常州市康辉医疗器械有限公司	康辉及图	外科器械	2012年	新北区
江苏久信医用净化工程有限公司	久信JIU XIN及图	空气净化等	2012年	新北区
常州市瑞悦车业有限公司	富满及图	车辆内装饰品等	2012年	新北区
常州星宇车灯股份有限公司	星宇及图	照明防护装置等	2012年	新北区
江苏三恒科技集团有限公司	三　恒	报警器等	2012年	新北区
江苏华达化工集团有限公司	常恒CHANGHENG及图	胶粘剂等	2012年	新北区
常州市常蒸蒸发器有限公司	常蒸及图	蒸发器	2012年	新北区
吟飞科技（江苏）有限公司	吟飞Ringway	乐　器	2012年	新北区
大娘水饺餐饮集团股份有限公司	吴大娘WU DA NIANG 及图	餐厅等	2012年	天宁区
常州亚玛顿股份有限公司	亞瑪頓	光学玻璃等	2012年	天宁区
常州东风农机集团有限公司	DFAM及图	拖拉机等	2012年	钟楼区

2-16 续表 2 continued 2

企业名称 Name of Enterprises	商标名称 Brand Name	主要产品 Mostly Product	颁布时间 Time of Release	所在地区 Region
常州祥兴电机有限公司	第965963号图形	马达及其部件	2012年	戚墅堰区
江苏南方卫材医药股份有限公司	妙手及图形	外科敷料，医用橡皮膏，医用胶布等	2013年	武进区
江苏南方通信科技有限公司	精科及图形	电缆、电线、电源材料等	2013年	武进区
常州市棱光化工材料有限公司	棱光及图形	铝鞋眼	2013年	武进区
常州市武进广宇花辊机械有限公司	广宇及图	轧花机、织机（机器）等	2013年	武进区
江苏华鑫合金有限公司	热工及图形	热电耦丝、补偿导线	2013年	武进区
百兴集团有限公司	百兴及图	密封物	2013年	武进区
常州玉宇电光器件有限公司	Yuyu	照明器；灯泡；灯等	2013年	武进区
常州南苑塑料有限公司	南苑NANYUAN及图	容器用非金属盖；封口用非金属盖；非金属瓶盖	2013年	武进区
江苏上能变压器有限公司	上能Sunel	变压器、高压防爆配电设备、电器联接器等	2013年	天宁区
江苏天目湖宾馆有限公司	天目湖及图	鱼制食品	2013年	溧阳市
江苏保龙机电制造有限公司	保龙及图	刨削机；刨花机；原木传送机；木材加工机等	2013年	溧阳市
江苏竹箦阀业有限公司	竹机ZJ	闸 阀	2013年	溧阳市
江苏波仕曼制衣有限公司	波仕曼及图形	服装、袜、游泳衣等	2013年	金坛市
江苏贝德莱特太阳能科技有限公司	BadeLite	太阳能热水器、太阳能集热器、空气调节设备等	2013年	新北区
常州千红生化制药股份有限公司	怡 开	人用药、原料药、生化药品等	2013年	新北区
常茂生物化学工程股份有限公司	图 形	酸、酒石酸等	2013年	新北区
常州长江玻璃有限公司	长江CHANGJIANG及图	车窗玻璃、钢化玻璃	2013年	新北区
常州一步干燥设备有限公司	一步YIBU及图	食品工业用机械及部件、制药工业用机械及部件、林产化学设备等	2014年	武进区
常州市华立液压润滑设备有限公司	华润HUARUN及图形	液压润滑设备、液压元件、油箱等	2014年	武进区
中韩科技有限公司	中 韩	冰柜；冰箱；饮水机等	2014年	武进区
中天钢铁集团有限公司	ZENITH及图	未加工或半加工普通金属、铸钢等	2014年	武进区
江苏科利达装饰材料有限公司	科利达KLD	木材、地板、非金属建筑材料等	2014年	武进区
夏溪花木市场控股有限公司	夏溪花木市场及图	市场研究，推销（替他人），组织商业或广告交易会	2014年	武进区
常州华日升反光材料股份有限公司	通明及图	反光膜	2015年	钟楼区
常州市锦纶厂有限公司	威美Weimei及图	丙纶丝、锦纶丝	2015年	钟楼区
常州环球地毯制造有限公司	环球HUANQIU	地毯	2015年	钟楼区
江苏亚飞电线电缆有限公司	豪格HAOGE及图	聚氯乙烯绝缘电线橡套电缆	2015年	武进区
常州奥兰通标识有限公司	奥兰通及图	金属标志牌、金属数字牌	2015年	武进区
常州市武起汽车电机有限公司	常乐changle及图	起动机、电机	2015年	武进区
溧阳市天目湖玉莲珍稀茶果场	玉莲及图	茶	2015年	溧阳市
江苏卓云豆宝食品有限公司	康力KANGLI及图	葡萄糖酸内酯	2015年	新北区
常州市南港港口机械有限公司	NGPMC及图	起重机、装卸设备	2015年	新北区
常州市宏发纵横新材料科技有限公司	PGTEX	纺织织物	2015年	新北区

2-16 续表 3　continued 3

企业名称 Name of Enterprises	商标名称 Brand Name	主要产品 Mostly Product	颁布时间 Time of Release	所在地区 Region
著名商标 Distinguished Brand				
金坛正信光伏电子有限公司	ZNSHINE	半导体单晶硅、多晶硅、传感器、灯光调节器	2013年	金坛市
江苏蓝色星球环保科技股份有限公司	蓝色星球及图	制冷剂；三氟乙醇；三氟乙烯等	2013年	金坛市
江苏南顺食品有限公司	满天星及图形	挂面；面粉；大米	2013年	金坛市
金坛市金旺包装科技有限公司	图　形	包装机；装填机；瓶子盖塞机等	2013年	金坛市
江苏高高制衣有限公司	GAOGAO及图形	服装，衬衫，西服等	2013年	金坛市
常州港华丝绢工艺制品有限公司	佩贝雅及图	钱包、学生用书包、背包、小皮夹、购物袋、海滨浴场用手提袋、帆布背包、购物网袋、手提包	2013年	金坛市
江苏五香居食品有限公司	五香居	卤制肉类食品，卤制禽类食品，卤制水产类食品	2013年	金坛市
常州华钛化学股份有限公司	图　形	工业用化学品、紫外线吸收剂、光引发剂	2013年	金坛市
金坛柴油机有限公司	天鹅及图形	柴油机、发电机组	2013年	金坛市
江苏旺达喷灌机有限公司	大网及图形	排水机、农业用排灌机、泵等	2013年	金坛市
常州而今太阳能设备制造有限公司	而今ERJIN	太阳能收集器、太阳能热水器、太阳能淋浴器	2013年	金坛市
常州朗博汽车零部件有限公司	JMP及图形	橡皮圈、密封用橡皮圈、橡皮减震器等	2013年	金坛市
盘固水泥集团有限公司	盘固及图形	水　泥	2013年	金坛市
金坛市博天鞋业有限公司	博天BOTIAN	鞋（脚上的穿着物）	2013年	金坛市
江苏茅山青锋茶叶有限公司	金鹿及图形	茶　叶	2013年	金坛市
金坛市方麓茶场有限公司	百园春及图形	茶　叶	2013年	金坛市
江苏鑫品茶业有限公司	鑫品及图形	茶、茶叶代用品	2013年	金坛市
金坛市御庭春茶业有限公司	天壶及图形	茶、茶叶代用品	2013年	金坛市
江苏申特钢铁有限公司	G及图	生铁或半锻造铁；铁条；未加工或半加工铸铁等	2013年	溧阳市
江苏鹏程钢结构有限公司	蒙杰及图	金属棚；金属建筑物；建筑用金属架等	2013年	溧阳市
溧阳市天目湖茶叶研究所	伍员山伍员飞翠及拼音	茶	2013年	溧阳市
常州市富月砝码有限公司	富月及图	衡器；衡量器具；砝码等	2013年	溧阳市
常州乔尔塑料有限公司	乔尔塑料及英文	未加工塑料；有机硅树脂；未加工合成树脂等	2013年	溧阳市
冶建新材料股份有限公司	J及图	涂　料	2013年	溧阳市
溧阳市天目春雨茶业有限公司	天目春雨及图	茶叶；茶叶代用品	2013年	溧阳市
江苏扬子水泥有限公司	长荡湖及图	水　泥	2013年	溧阳市
江苏保龙机电制造有限公司	保龙及图	刨削机；刨花机；原木传送机；木材加工机等	2013年	溧阳市
江苏华能建设工程集团有限公司	苏华及图	锅炉清垢与修理；炉子维修；供暖设备的安装与修理等	2013年	溧阳市
重庆啤酒集团常州天目湖啤酒有限公司	天目湖及图	啤酒等	2013年	溧阳市
溧阳市重型机械厂有限公司	麦重及图	破碎机；喂料机等	2013年	溧阳市
溧阳市天目湖玉莲珍稀茶果场	玉莲及图	茶；茶叶代用品	2013年	溧阳市

2-16 续表 4 continued 4

企业名称 Name of Enterprises	商标名称 Brand Name	主要产品 Mostly Product	颁布时间 Time of Release	所在地区 Region
江苏天目湖宾馆有限公司	天目湖及图	鱼制食品	2013年	溧阳市
江苏省社渚轴承有限公司	球星牌及图	轴　承	2013年	溧阳市
江苏金峰水泥集团有限公司	金峰牌及拼音	水　泥	2013年	溧阳市
江苏省前峰茶厂	前峰及图	茶　叶	2013年	溧阳市
江苏竹箦阀业有限公司	竹机 ZJ	闸　阀	2013年	溧阳市
江苏力乐汽车部件股份有限公司	力乐及图	汽车配件（汽车座椅调角器滑槽）	2013年	溧阳市
常州市格林照明灯具制造有限公司	GREEN	灯；照明防护装置；照明器械及装置等	2013年	戚墅堰区
常州兰锦橡塑有限公司	兰陵及图	衬垫；机器上密封垫（减震）；隔音材料等	2013年	戚墅堰区
江苏华旺科技有限公司	联旺 LIANWANG	电源材料（电线、电缆）；绝缘铜线；合金线（保险丝）等	2013年	戚墅堰区
常州欧尔特机械进出口有限公司	欧亚特及图	农业机械；收割机；柴油机等	2013年	戚墅堰区
常州市向利防静电装饰材料有限公司	向利拼音及图	金属地板、水泥用金属加固材料、金属铺路块料	2013年	戚墅堰区
常州市同和纺织机械制造有限公司	TONGHE	纺织工业用机器、纺织机、精纺机等	2013年	戚墅堰区
江苏凯隆电器有限公司	KRAO 及图形	断路器、高低压开关板、工业操作遥控电器设备等	2013年	戚墅堰区
常州亚联灯具有限公司	FANOYA	路灯、探照灯、安全灯等	2013年	戚墅堰区
常州三毛纺织集团有限公司	三猫及图形	呢　绒	2013年	天宁区
常州市恒丰铜材有限公司	恒丰及拼音	电源材料（电线、电缆）；绝缘铜线；镀银丝等	2013年	天宁区
常州兰陵制药有限公司	兰陵 LANLING	西　药	2013年	天宁区
常州市兰翔电器有限公司	兰翔及图	高低压开关板，配电箱（电），配电盘等	2013年	天宁区
常州强声纺织有限公司	强声纺织及拼音	棉织品；凸纹条格细平布；粗斜纹布等	2013年	天宁区
常州金源铜业有限公司	金线加图形	金属杆、金属板条	2013年	天宁区
常州新华陵汽车电器有限公司	超灵 CL	汽车配件	2013年	天宁区
常州丽华快餐集团有限公司	丽华快餐	餐厅、快餐馆、流动饮食供应等	2013年	天宁区
月星集团有限公司	图　形	家具、非纺织品壁饰（家具），陈列架等	2013年	天宁区
常州制药厂有限公司	常药图及拼音	西药、原料药	2013年	天宁区
常州联发凯迪机械有限公司	LF 图形	拖拉机、电动车辆、机动三轮车	2013年	武进区
江苏武进不锈股份有限公司	WUJIN	钢管、金属管道、金属管	2013年	武进区
常州市新亚不锈钢管有限公司	双牛及图	金属管	2013年	武进区
常州百川新型护栏有限公司	百川及图	栏杆、非金属建筑材料、建筑用塑料板等	2013年	武进区
江苏南方轴承股份有限公司	NF 图形	轴承（机器零件）、滚动轴承（滚柱）、传动轴轴承	2013年	武进区
江苏恒立高压油缸股份有限公司	HENGLI 及图	液压元件	2013年	武进区
常州市泽源化工有限公司	常源及图	未加工环养树脂，未加工合成树脂，未加工人造树脂	2013年	武进区

2-16 续表 5　continued 5

企业名称 Name of Enterprises	商标名称 Brand Name	主要产品 Mostly Product	颁布时间 Time of Release	所在地区 Region
常州金鼎电器有限公司	鼎克及图	绝缘铜线、电容器、变压器	2013年	武进区
江苏亚飞电线电缆有限公司	豪格HAOGE及图	聚氯乙稀绝缘电线橡套电缆	2013年	武进区
常州气弹簧有限公司	常　弹	气弹簧	2013年	武进区
常州市新盛电器有限公司	新盛鹰及图	光通讯设备，内部通讯装置，分线盒（电）	2013年	武进区
常州苏特轴承制造有限公司	WJS	轴承（机器零件）、传动轴承、滚动轴承（滚柱）	2013年	武进区
常州华通新立地板有限公司	华通及图形	金属地板	2013年	武进区
江苏德哲木业有限公司	德哲dez及图	地板，非金属地板，非金属建筑材料	2013年	武进区
常州乐士雷利电机有限公司	雷利及图	马达和引擎起动器，机器、引擎或发动机用控制装置，步进电机	2013年	武进区
江苏华阳电器有限公司	华　阳	马达和引擎起动器、发电机、冰箱电机	2013年	武进区
常州市武进五洋纺织机械有限公司	艾诗丽及图	服装、袜、手套（服装）	2013年	武进区
江苏新洛凯机电有限公司	洛　凯	变压器（电）；电开关；断路器等	2013年	武进区
常州煜明电子有限公司	煜明电子及图	家用遥控器	2013年	武进区
江苏金牛线缆集团有限公司	金　牛	电缆电线	2013年	武进区
江苏联凯农业装备集团有限公司	常联发	柴油机、收割机、农业机械	2013年	武进区
江苏玉兰木业有限公司	图　形	金属地板，建筑用金属框架	2013年	武进区
常州市欧太装饰材料有限公司	欧运及图	非金属地板，拼花地板，非金属建筑材料	2013年	武进区
常州东吴链传动制造有限公司	东传及图	非陆地车辆传动链	2013年	武进区
南京化工学院常州市武进水质稳定剂厂	颂歌及图	水质稳定剂	2013年	武进区
江苏双菱链传动有限公司	双菱及图	滚子链条	2013年	武进区
夏溪花木市场控股有限公司	夏溪花木市场及图	市场研究，推销（替他人），组织商业或广告交易会	2013年	武进区
江苏猴王涂料有限公司	猴王及图	涂　料	2013年	武进区
江苏智思机械集团有限公司	zs及图	工业用卷烟机，烟草加工机	2013年	武进区
常州市武进五菱柴油机有限公司	五菱牌及图	柴油机	2013年	武进区
常州市永安电机有限公司	M及图	电　机	2013年	武进区
江苏常发农业装备股份有限公司	常　发	拖车（车辆），拖拉机，陆地车辆动力装置	2013年	武进区
常州欧凯电器有限公司	OUCK	马达和引擎发动机、发电机、非陆地车辆传动马达	2013年	武进区
常州市凯凯照明电器有限公司	KK及图	照明灯（照明灯笼），汽车防眩装置（灯具），弧光灯	2013年	武进区
江苏常发农业装备股份有限公司	常　发	泵、发电机	2013年	武进区
创生医疗器械（中国）有限公司	创生及图	骨科手术器械	2013年	武进区
江苏立华牧业有限公司	雪山及图	活家禽	2013年	武进区

2-16 续表 6 continued 6

企业名称 Name of Enterprises	商标名称 Brand Name	主要产品 Mostly Product	颁布时间 Time of Release	所在地区 Region
金隆科技集团有限公司	华隆及图	染 料	2013年	武进区
普罗斯电器（中国）有限公司	PLUSRITE	灯 泡	2013年	武进区
常州神龙饲料有限公司	水神及图	饲料（包括非医用饲料添加剂及催化剂）	2013年	武进区
江苏省范群干燥设备厂有限公司	范群FANQUN及图	食品加工机（电动），制药加工工业用机器，化学工业用电力机械	2013年	武进区
江苏康进医疗器材有限公司	康进及图	医疗器械和仪器、医用注射器、医用针	2013年	武进区
常州市翟家果品专业合作社	常溪及图	鲜水果	2013年	武进区
江苏润德医用材料有限公司	润德及图	橡皮塞子，密封橡皮圈，接头用密封物	2013年	武进区
常州华日升反光材料股份有限公司	通明及图	反光膜	2013年	武进区
常州钢筘有限公司	蓝箭及图	梳理机用齿条，钢筘	2013年	武进区
江苏尼高科技有限公司	尼高科技及图形	建筑灰浆、石膏、非金属建筑材料	2013年	武进区
常州市范群干燥设备有限公司	范干及图形	热风循环节能烘箱，节能气流干燥机，真空低温干燥器等	2013年	新北区
常州天合光能有限公司	天合光能	太阳能电池	2013年	新北区
华润包装材料有限公司	华蕾及英文	树 脂	2013年	新北区
新阳科技集团有限公司	图形及拼音	苯二甲酸酐、苯乙烯、合成树脂	2013年	新北区
常州清红化工有限公司	清红及拼音	硫酸；硫酸二甲酯；苯二甲酸酐	2013年	新北区
常州新区怡泰食品有限公司	怡 泰	即溶麦片、饮料	2013年	新北区
江苏英伦美家家居有限公司	英伦美家	装饰织品；布；床单等	2013年	新北区
常州依丽雅斯纺织品有限公司	ELISE	织物、床上用覆盖物、纺织品或塑料帘	2013年	新北区
常州市正阳焊接材料有限公司	金阳英文及图形	金属焊丝、金属焊条、金焊料等	2013年	新北区
常州普莱克红梅色母料有限公司	速彩达拼音及图	塑料色母料	2013年	新北区
江苏考普乐新材料股份有限公司	考普乐KFCC	铝涂料；银涂料；涂层（油漆）等	2013年	新北区
常州卡米文化传播有限公司	炮炮兵	广告、媒体展示商品、广告设计	2013年	新北区
常州市武滚轴承有限公司	W图形	滚针轴承	2013年	新北区
常州佳讯光电产业发展有限公司	不凡BUFAN及图	半导体器件，电器接插件，晶体管（电子)等	2013年	新北区
江苏凯特汽车部件有限公司	大亚DAYA	车轮毂；车辆减震器；轮辐夹钳等	2013年	新北区
常州市佳乐车辆配件制造有限公司	佳乐大通及图形	车辆保险杠；车辆内装饰品；后视镜等	2013年	新北区
常州千红生化制药股份有限公司	怡 开	人用药、原料药、生化药品等	2013年	新北区
常州亨达车业部件有限公司	一帆顺YIFANSHUN	汽车照明设备、车灯、车辆反光镜等	2013年	新北区
江苏贝德莱特太阳能科技有限公司	BadeLite	太阳能热水器、太阳能集热器、空气调节设备等	2013年	新北区
江苏华生塑业有限公司	华生及图形	塑料管、管子接头、非金属软管	2013年	新北区

2-16 续表 7　continued 7

企业名称 Name of Enterprises	商标名称 Brand Name	主要产品 Mostly Product	颁布时间 Time of Release	所在地区 Region
常州丰盛光电科技股份有限公司	Julite	半加工塑料物质、有机玻璃、塑料板等	2013年	新北区
常州市宏发纵横新材料科技股份有限公司	PGTEX	纺织织物、航空气球用不透气织物、纺织用玻璃纤维织物等	2013年	新北区
常州能源设备总厂有限公司	CEEF及图形	载热体加热炉	2013年	新北区
常林股份有限公司	CHANGLIN	装载机；压路机；平地机等	2013年	新北区
常州市曙光车业有限公司	知音及图形	车辆油箱盖（气）、车辆内装饰品、车辆转向信号灯等	2013年	新北区
常泰建筑装璜工程有限公司	常　泰	供暖设备的安装与修理、建筑、室内装潢等	2013年	钟楼区
常州市明景电子有限公司	MINKING	摄像机；录像机；电子防盗装置等	2013年	钟楼区
江苏裕兴薄膜科技股份有限公司	裕兴及图形	聚酯薄膜、绝缘材料、非包装用塑料聚酯薄膜等	2013年	钟楼区
常州市万象化工机械有限公司	万　象	石油开采、石油精炼工业用机器设备，石油化工设备等	2013年	钟楼区
常州科研试制中心有限公司	KS及图形	地质勘探、采矿选矿用设备等	2013年	钟楼区
常州瑞和泰食品有限公司	瑞和泰	推销（替他人）；商业管理咨询；商业信息	2013年	钟楼区
常州红梅乳业有限公司	红梅及图形	牛奶、牛奶饮料（以牛奶为主的）、牛奶制品等	2013年	钟楼区
常州月兔调味食品有限公司	月兔牌及图形	味　精	2013年	钟楼区
凡登（常州）新型金属材料技术有限公司	fundant	钢丝；普通金属合金丝；金属绳等	2014年	金坛市
江苏康友医用器械有限公司	康　友	注射器；输血器；输液器	2014年	金坛市
江苏瑞东农药有限公司	瑞东及图	消灭有害动物制剂；消灭有害植物制剂；除草剂等	2014年	金坛市
盛利维尔（中国）新材料技术有限公司	sunnywell	钢丝；普通金属合金丝（除保险丝外）；金属绳等	2014年	金坛市
晨风（金坛）服饰有限公司	晨风及拼音	服装；童装；游泳衣等	2014年	金坛市
金坛鑫田柴油机有限公司	鑫田英文及图	农业机械；柴油机；汽油机等	2014年	金坛市
江苏鑫田电子科技有限公司	鑫　田	灯；日光灯管；照明用发光管等	2014年	金坛市
常州亿晶光电科技有限公司	EGNG及图	太阳能电池；太阳能电池组（件）；太阳能电池片等	2014年	金坛市
江苏龙泉太阳能科技有限公司	龙全及拼音	太阳能热水器；浴用加热器；太阳能集热器等	2014年	金坛市
常州金土木工程仪器有限公司	金土木	测力计；测压仪器；观测仪器等	2014年	金坛市
金坛市明日春花盆有限公司	树春及图	花盆；花和植物用盆（花展用）；非纸制花盆套	2014年	金坛市
江苏华兴电子有限公司	fy及图	扼流圈（阻抗）；磁芯材料和器件；变压器等	2014年	金坛市
江苏鸿瑞昌泰纺织有限公司	HRCT及图	毛毯；床上用毯；纺织品毛巾等	2014年	金坛市
江苏丰登作物保护股份有限公司	丰登拼音及图	农　药	2014年	金坛市
金坛丰登酒业有限公司	丰登及图	酒	2014年	金坛市
江苏波仕曼制衣有限公司	波仕曼拼音及图	服装；领带；围巾等	2014年	金坛市
中盐金坛盐化有限责任公司	金赛盐业英文及图	岩盐；原盐；工业用盐	2014年	金坛市

2-16 续表 8　continued 8

企业名称 Name of Enterprises	商标名称 Brand Name	主要产品 Mostly Product	颁布时间 Time of Release	所在地区 Region
溧阳市天目湖白埂茶场	碧波拼音及图	茶；茶叶代用品	2014年	溧阳市
江苏上齿集团有限公司	上溧及图	陆地车辆传动齿轮；陆地车辆减速齿轮	2014年	溧阳市
溧阳市周城汤山茶厂	九龙及图	茶　叶	2014年	溧阳市
溧阳市天目云露茶业有限公司	天目云露及图	茶；茶饮料；茶叶代用品	2014年	溧阳市
江苏维多股份有限公司	Vitasweet及图	人造增填剂（化学制剂）；工业用淀粉；工业用葡萄糖等	2014年	溧阳市
江苏华鹏变压器有限公司	JSHP	变压器	2014年	溧阳市
溧阳市天目湖田家山茶果场	田家山TJS及图	茶；茶叶代用品	2014年	溧阳市
江苏天目湖生态农业有限公司	富子fz	茶　叶	2014年	溧阳市
江苏天目湖旅游股份有限公司	天目湖英文及图	观光旅游；安排游览；旅行预定等	2014年	溧阳市
江苏竹溪活性炭有限公司	竹溪拼音及图	活性炭	2014年	溧阳市
溧阳市幽香苏茶有限公司	幽香苏及图	咖啡；茶；糖等	2014年	溧阳市
江苏金源锻造股份有限公司	金石及拼音	金属锻造；金属冶炼；研磨加工等	2014年	溧阳市
溧阳市天目湖玉枝特种茶果园艺场	玉枝及图	茶；茶叶代用品	2014年	溧阳市
常州市惠信纸业有限公司	惠信及图	纸或塑料杯；纸盘；引用器皿等	2014年	戚墅堰区
常州新区金利达电子有限公司	金利达拼音及图	非医用x光产生器械和设备；非医用x光防护设备	2014年	戚墅堰区
常州市申达涂料有限公司	申达拼音及图	涂层（油漆）；底漆；防水粉（涂料）等	2014年	戚墅堰区
蓝豹股份有限公司	蓝豹LANBAO	服　装	2014年	戚墅堰区
常州市新东方电缆有限公司	神鸡及图	电线；电缆	2014年	戚墅堰区
江苏常宝钢管股份有限公司	环球及图	钢管；钢带；钢胚	2014年	戚墅堰区
常州市宏达机床数控设备有限公司	宏瑞达	机械台架；切削工具（包括机械刀片）；刀座	2014年	戚墅堰区
江苏江南农村商业银行股份有限公司	图　形	资本投资；金融服务；担保等	2014年	天宁区
常州曼淇威电气产品有限公司	曼淇威及图	发电机；马达和引擎起动器等	2014年	天宁区
常州华利达服装集团有限公司	王子甲PRINCE ARMOR	服　装	2014年	天宁区
常州艾贝服饰有限公司	ABLE JEANS	服装；披肩；领带等	2014年	天宁区
常州月夜灯芯绒有限公司	图　形	布；粗斜纹布；松劲布等	2014年	天宁区
常州航月纺织机件有限公司	航月英文及图	纺织机；纺织工业用机；钢令等	2014年	天宁区
大娘水饺餐饮集团股份有限公司	WU DA NIANG及图	饺子；盒饭；面条等	2014年	天宁区
常州四药制药有限公司	奥　克	西　药	2014年	天宁区
常州克劳诺斯特种轴承制造有限公司	NBI	轴承（机器零件）；装卸设备；精加工机器等	2014年	武进区
侨裕控股集团有限公司	侨裕QIAOYU及图	椅子；沙滩椅；床等	2014年	武进区

2-16 续表 9　continued 9

企业名称 Name of Enterprises	商标名称 Brand Name	主要产品 Mostly Product	颁布时间 Time of Release	所在地区 Region
江苏佳得顺热能设备有限公司	GardenSun及图	炉子（取暖器具）；燃气炉；烤肉炉等	2014年	武进区
江苏永阳涂料有限公司	永阳拼音及图	油漆；涂料	2014年	武进区
常州市龙鑫化工机械有限公司	化宝拼音及图	化学工业用电动机械；油漆加工用机器；制牙膏设备等	2014年	武进区
常州强力电子新材料股份有限公司	强　力	照相用感光剂；显影剂；光引发剂	2014年	武进区
常州市赛欧地板有限公司	大欧DAOU及图	地板；非金属地板；非金属建筑材料等	2014年	武进区
新誉集团有限公司	图　形	铁路车辆；牵引机；机车等	2014年	武进区
常州查家湾生态林果专业合作社	查家湾及图	鲜水果；鲜葡萄；梨等	2014年	武进区
江苏超凡标牌股份有限公司	超凡及图	金属标志牌；金属纪念牌；金属识别牌等	2014年	武进区
津通集团有限公司	津　通	金融信息；不动产出租；不动产代理等	2014年	武进区
江苏朝晖化工有限公司	朝晖及图	油漆；防火漆；稀料等	2014年	武进区
江苏佳华新材料科技有限公司	斯普佳及图	表面活性化学剂；乳化剂；防水浆消泡剂等	2014年	武进区
常州灵特尔轻便展示系统有限公司	LINTEL及图	陈列架；支架（家具）；金属家具等	2014年	武进区
江苏新瑞重工科技有限公司	SHINRI	金属加工机械；铸造机械；模压加工机器等	2014年	武进区
常州武进长城工具有限公司	CHANGCHENG及图	非手工操作手工具；电动螺丝刀；电动板手等	2014年	武进区
常州科威天使环保科技有限公司	春江拼音及图	水净化化学品；工业用洗净剂；工业用化学品等	2014年	武进区
江苏华艺装饰工程有限公司	建雅拼音及图	金属百叶窗；金属门设置；建筑幕墙等	2014年	武进区
江苏新科电器有限公司	shinco	空气调节装置	2014年	武进区
常州市永明机械制造有限公司	常明拼音及图	合成纤维设备；塑料挤出腹膜机；织机（机器）等	2014年	武进区
江苏恒力电机集团股份有限公司	WUDIAN及图	直流起动机	2014年	武进区
常州市传动输送机械有限公司	霸宇及图	电动滚筒；机器、马达和引擎调速器；非陆地车辆用减速齿轮等	2014年	武进区
江苏容天乐机械股份有限公司	WJT	滚珠轴承；轴承（机器零件）；轴承滚珠圈等	2014年	武进区
江苏昌盛电缆集团有限公司	昌盛拼音及图	防火线缆；电线；电缆	2014年	武进区
常州市云涛洁具有限公司	云涛拼音及图	玛瑙浴缸；脸盆；抽水马桶等	2014年	武进区
江苏海鸥冷却塔股份有限公司	图　形	水冷却装置；冷却设备和装置	2014年	武进区
江苏南方卫材医药股份有限公司	妙手拼音及图	绷带；外科敷料；医用橡皮膏等	2014年	武进区
江苏博大木业有限公司	博瑞得及图	地板；树脂复合板；贴面板等	2014年	武进区
江苏玉兰木业有限公司	帕伦克拼音及图	地板；贴面板；树脂复合板凳	2014年	武进区
江苏吉祥贺盛食品有限公司	贺盛及图	味精；调味品	2014年	武进区
常州市源恩合成材料有限公司	源恩拼音及图	工业用粘合剂；有机硅树脂；鞋粘合剂等	2014年	武进区
常州市锦纶厂有限公司	威美拼音及图	丙纶丝；锦纶丝	2014年	武进区

2-16 续表 10 continued 10

企业名称 Name of Enterprises	商标名称 Brand Name	主要产品 Mostly Product	颁布时间 Time of Release	所在地区 Region
常州市华立液压润滑设备有限公司	华润拼音及图	液压润滑设备；液压元件	2014年	武进区
常州市洁丽木业有限公司	洁丽拼音及图	地板；护墙板；已加工木材等	2014年	武进区
江苏华鑫合金有限公司	热工拼音及图	热点耦丝；补偿导线	2014年	武进区
江海环保股份有限公司	江海及图	水质稳定及	2014年	武进区
常州市钱璟康复器材有限公司	钱璟及图	按摩器材；健美按摩设备；医用体育活动器材（康复运动器材）等	2014年	武进区
常州市牛塘化工厂有限公司	牛塘拼音及图	氰尿酸聚丁脂；癸二酸二酰肼；三羟二基尿酸脂等	2014年	武进区
江苏武东机械有限公司	武东WD及图	机器、马达和引擎调速器；联轴器；传动装置（机器）等	2014年	武进区
常州市铭锦弹簧有限公司	铭锦拼音及图	车辆减震弹簧；车辆悬挂弹簧；陆地车辆动力装置等	2014年	武进区
英特曼电工（常州）有限公司	Etman及图	插头、插座及其他接触器（电）；电开关、电器接插件；电器联接器等	2014年	武进区
江苏宏事达电气制造有限公司	宏事达	衡器；量具；一般测量仪表	2014年	武进区
江苏武进液压启闭机有限公司	五叶WY及图	液压启闭机	2014年	武进区
常州市运河焊材有限公司	大运河YH及图	焊　丝	2014年	武进区
江苏贝尔装饰材料有限公司	贝尔BEIER	木材；铺地木材；制家用器具用木材等	2014年	武进区
江苏恒耐炉料集团有限公司	恒耐HN及图	耐火材料	2014年	武进区
常州市宇锋车业有限公司	宇锋及图	三轮运货车；机动自行车；小型机动车等	2014年	武进区
江苏南方通信科技有限公司	精科拼音及图	电缆；电线；电源材料（电线、电缆）	2014年	武进区
江苏友奥电器有限公司	YOAU	空气调节设备；干燥设备；灯等	2014年	武进区
常州精科实业有限公司	CONTIN	钟表及其零部件；计时器（时钟）；记时计	2014年	武进区
江苏聚荣制药集团有限公司	聚荣拼音及图	人用药	2014年	武进区
江苏环球龙圣环境科技发展有限公司	宇球拼音及图	水冷却装置；冷却设备和装置等	2014年	武进区
江苏新洛凯机电有限公司	洛凯ROCOI	非陆地车辆传动马达；定子（机器零件）；马达和引擎用风扇等	2014年	武进区
常州市武起汽车电机有限公司	常乐拼音及图	起动机；电机	2014年	武进区
江苏赛鑫树脂有限公司	方鑫拼音及图	未加工环氧树脂；未加工合成树脂；未加工人造树脂等	2014年	武进区
常州市安江车辆部件厂	禾　安	车辆保险杆；后视镜；车辆内装饰品等	2014年	新北区
常州市怡江汽车部件有限公司	TYJ	车辆灯；车辆前灯；车辆用反射镜等	2014年	新北区
江苏莱赛光电技术有限公司	LAISAI	测距设备；水平仪；测量仪器（勘测仪器)等	2014年	新北区
常州恐龙园股份有限公司	中华恐龙园英文及图	游乐园	2014年	新北区
常州宝隆冶金设备制造有限公司	宝　隆	轧钢机滚筒；轧钢机；滚筒（机器零件）等	2014年	新北区
常州赛尔克瑞特电气有限公司	ESEC常赛电气	配电箱（电）；配电控制台（电）；高低压开关板等	2014年	新北区
常州西玛特电器有限公司	XMT及图	感应器（电）；热调节装置；自动定时开关等	2014年	新北区

2-16 续表 11　continued 11

企业名称 Name of Enterprises	商标名称 Brand Name	主要产品 Mostly Product	颁布时间 Time of Release	所在地区 Region
常州市后肖宇虹铝幕墙制造有限公司	图　形	金属板条；金属片和金属板；金属建筑材料等	2014年	新北区
江苏宏微科技股份有限公司	MACMIC及图	半导体；太阳能电池；整流用电力装置等	2014年	新北区
江苏米多装饰有限公司	米多MIDO及图	室内装潢修理；室内装潢；粉饰等	2014年	新北区
汉得利（常州）电子股份有限公司	波　束	传感器；防盗报警器；蜂音器等	2014年	新北区
常州西夏墅工具协会	西夏墅工具拼音及图	刀具（机器零件）；切削工具（包括机械刀片）；金属加工机械等	2014年	新北区
常州光阳摩托车有限公司	光　阳	摩托车；摩托车零组件	2014年	新北区
常州华科聚合物股份有限公司	新　盛	未加工合成树脂；未加工人造树脂；未加工的人造合成树脂等	2014年	新北区
常州市西夏墅工具研究所有限公司	合力LH	刀具（机器零件）；切削工具（包括机械刀片）	2014年	新北区
常州耀春格瑞纺织品有限公司	春格儿及英文	床罩；被子；丝毯等	2014年	新北区
常州市第八纺织机械有限公司	华发拼音及图	纺织机械及另件；针织机械及另件	2014年	新北区
常州市南港港口机械有限公司	NGPMC及图	起重机；装卸设备	2014年	新北区
吟飞科技（江苏）有限公司	吟飞英文及图	乐器；电子乐器；打击乐器等	2014年	新北区
江苏中江焊丝有限公司	鲀鱼TY及图	金属焊丝；金属焊条；铜焊及焊接用金属棒等	2014年	新北区
常州市永光车业有限公司	永兆拼音及图	汽车灯；车辆灯	2014年	新北区
常州天山重工机械有限公司	TSHI及图	机器传动装置；非陆地车辆变速箱；非陆地车辆齿轮传动装置等	2014年	新北区
常州太平通讯科技有限公司	太平通信拼音及图	光通信设备；分线盒（电）；电源材料（电线、电缆）等	2014年	新北区
常州太平洋电力设备（集团）有限公司	常太及图	配电箱（电）；配电控制台（电）；高低压开关板等	2014年	新北区
常州市墅乐厨具有限公司	墅乐SHULE	家用压面机	2014年	新北区
常州天马集团有限公司	天马及图形	纺织用玻璃纤维织物	2014年	新北区
常州市建筑科学研究院股份有限公司	常建科TC及图	质量检测；质量评估；材料测试等	2014年	钟楼区
江苏国光信息产业股份有限公司	国　光	通信设备；程控交换设备；计算机外部设备等	2014年	钟楼区
常州远东塑料机械有限公司	远东拼音及图	塑料打包带	2014年	钟楼区
常州格力博有限公司	greenworks及图	电瓶；电池充电器；电池等	2014年	钟楼区
江苏双桂坊餐饮管理有限公司	双桂坊	自助餐饮；餐厅；饭店等	2014年	钟楼区
江苏丽岛新材料股份有限公司	丽岛LIDAO	建筑用金属包层；金属地板；金属建筑材料等	2014年	钟楼区
江苏洛克电气有限公司	洛克LK及图	电　机	2014年	钟楼区
常州东风农机集团有限公司	常拖拼音及图	农业机械；犁；收割脱粒机等	2014年	钟楼区

2-16 续表 12 continued 12

企业名称 Name of Enterprises	商标名称 Brand Name	主要产品 Mostly Product	颁布时间 Time of Release	所在地区 Region
常州博瑞油泵油嘴有限公司	BOST及图	发动机喷油嘴；密封接头（发动机部件）；气动元件等	2015年	金坛区
江苏斯威克新材料有限公司	斯威克英文及图	合成树脂（半成品）；非包装用塑料膜；未加工或半加工树胶等	2015年	金坛区
江苏鑫隆复合工程材料有限公司	双　鑫	汽车用垫毯；乙烯地板覆盖物；塑料或橡胶地板革等	2015年	金坛区
金坛市茅麓茶厂	巨鹿及图	茶　叶	2015年	金坛区
江苏力合粘合剂有限公司	力合及图	粘合剂	2015年	金坛区
江苏省健尔康医用敷料有限公司	JIANERKANG及图	卫生绷带；外科用纱布；医用棉等	2015年	金坛区
江苏峨嵋动力机械有限公司	金田拼音及图	柴油机；汽油机；发动机喷油嘴等	2015年	金坛区
江苏金动动力机械有限公司	金动拼音及图	柴油机；汽油机	2015年	金坛区
常州瑞华电力电子器件有限公司	申社及图	半导体器件；控制板（电）；整流用电力装置等	2015年	金坛区
江苏凯灵汽车电器有限公司	凯灵LK及图	汽车综合开关；汽车地板	2015年	金坛区
江苏飞洋鱼制衣有限公司	飞洋鱼	衣物；衬衫；套服等	2015年	金坛区
金坛市江南制粉有限公司	沁雪及图	谷类制品；米；生糯粉等	2015年	金坛区
金坛市江南春米业有限公司	蘇及图	米；面粉；谷类制品等	2015年	金坛区
江苏金唐农业科技有限公司	绿坛英文及图	鲜水果；新鲜蔬菜；水芹（新鲜蔬菜）等	2015年	金坛区
江苏联盟化学有限公司	联福拼音及图	三盐基性硫酸铅；二盐基亚磷酸铅等	2015年	溧阳市
常州市宏豪制钢有限公司	宏豪及图	钢条；铁板；金属板条等	2015年	溧阳市
申芝电梯有限公司	申　芝	电梯（滑雪运送机除外）；电梯（升降机）；带式输送机等	2015年	溧阳市
江苏盛德电子仪表有限公司	晟德及图	计量仪表；电度表	2015年	溧阳市
江苏安靠智能输电工程科技股份有限公司	安　靠	电力电缆连接件等	2015年	溧阳市
溧阳市康达化工有限公司	南大及图	合成胶	2015年	溧阳市
溧阳市利达有机硅科技有限公司	科达及图	工业用粘合剂和胶	2015年	溧阳市
常州嘉仁禾化学有限公司	嘉仁禾英文及图	盐类（化学制剂）；硬脂酸盐类；稳定剂等	2015年	溧阳市
冶建新材料股份有限公司	天虎TH及图	涂　料	2015年	溧阳市
溧阳市四方不锈钢制品有限公司	利洋四方LYSF及图	金属管道弯头；金属管道接头；金属阀门等	2015年	溧阳市
江苏国强镀锌实业有限公司	图　形	镀锌铁塔；公路防碰撞用金属栅栏；金属护栏等	2015年	溧阳市
江苏山湖电缆有限公司	山湖牌及图	电缆；电线；接线盒	2015年	溧阳市
常州宝丽丝纤维有限公司	博　洋	纱；丝纱；麻纱线等	2015年	溧阳市
江苏科信燃气设备有限公司	科信及图	调压阀；阀（机器零件）；压力阀（机器部件）等	2015年	天宁区
常州船用电缆有限责任公司	海豹拼音及图	电线；电缆	2015年	天宁区
常州东方伊思达染织有限公司	伊思达	纱；精纺棉；细线和细纱等	2015年	天宁区
常州灵泰面料科技有限公司	LINGTEX	布；织物；装饰织品等	2015年	天宁区

2-16 续表 13 continued 13

企业名称 Name of Enterprises	商标名称 Brand Name	主要产品 Mostly Product	颁布时间 Time of Release	所在地区 Region
常州腾跃不锈钢管有限公司	三李及图	金属管道配件；金属管；金属套筒（金属制品）等	2015年	天宁区
江苏吉春医用器材有限公司	吉春及图	一次性使用注射器；输液器；输血器	2015年	天宁区
江苏骠马智能装备股份有限公司	骠马涂装	涂漆机；喷漆枪；油漆喷枪等	2015年	天宁区
常州特种变压器有限公司	稳福拼音及图	变压器（电）；配电箱（电）	2015年	天宁区
江苏上能新特变压器有限公司	上能Sunel	变压器；高压防爆配电装置；电器联接器等	2015年	天宁区
常州旭荣针织印染有限公司	NEW WIDE及图	布；织物；无纺布等	2015年	天宁区
常嘉建设集团有限公司	图　形	建筑；商业摊位及商店的建筑；室内装潢等	2015年	天宁区
江苏佳尔科药业集团有限公司	佳尔科拼音及图	医用激素；医用营养品；原料药等	2015年	天宁区
常州一步干燥设备有限公司	一步YIBU及图	食品工业用机械及部件；制药工业用机械及部件；林产化学设备等	2015年	天宁区
江苏先锋干燥工程有限公司	先锋拼音及图	化学工业用电动机械；制药加工工业用机器；焦化设备等	2015年	天宁区
常州市久虹医疗器械有限公司	JIUHONG	医用导管；镊子（医用钳）；外科用移植物（人造材料）等	2015年	武进区
西太湖环境建设集团有限公司	西太湖XITAIHU	庭院风景布置；风景设计；园艺等	2015年	武进区
江苏竹展吉泰克科技有限公司	SZZ及图	铁路车辆；车辆座位等	2015年	武进区
常州科普动力机械有限公司	koop	泵（机器、发动机或马达部件）；混凝土振动器；柴油机（陆地车辆用的除外）等	2015年	武进区
常州晶雪冷冻设备有限公司	晶雪及图	保温用非导热材料；防热散发合成物；防潮建筑材料等	2015年	武进区
常州金信诺凤市通信设备有限公司	FIRNIC	电器接插件；光通信设备；电器联接器等	2015年	武进区
江苏格林保尔光伏有限公司	Gppv	电池极板；电池；太阳能电池等	2015年	武进区
江苏二传机械有限公司	图　形	万向节；机器轴；机器传动装置等	2015年	武进区
江苏恒泰泳池设备有限公司	图　形	水净化装置；水净化设备和机器；游泳池用氯化装置等	2015年	武进区
常州嬉戏谷有限公司	嬉戏谷英文及图	观光旅游；旅行陪伴；安排游览等	2015年	武进区
常州市联谊特种不锈钢管有限公司	常润及图	金属管道配件；钢管；金属管等	2015年	武进区
常州腾龙汽车零部件股份有限公司	CZTL及图	压缩空气管用金属配件；金属管；通风和空气调节设备用金属管等	2015年	武进区
常州市武进协昌机械有限公司	协昌拼音及图	橡胶塑料工业设备	2015年	武进区
常州市武进广宇花辊机械有限公司	广宇CY	轧花机；织机（机器）；纺织工业用机器等	2015年	武进区
江苏常武起动电机有限公司	常威拼音及图	汽车发电机；汽车起动机	2015年	武进区
常州市长润石油有限公司	江	各种机油；工业脂；高温脂	2015年	武进区
江苏圣乐机械有限公司	圣盛拼音及图	钢模板；金属建筑材料；金属铸模等	2015年	武进区
常州凯达轧辊集团有限公司	凯达及图	铸铁轧辊	2015年	武进区
江苏恒鑫富奥汽车零部件有限公司	恒鑫拼音及图	汽车零部件（不包括轮胎）；摩托车零部件（不包括轮胎）	2015年	武进区
江苏龙城精锻有限公司	图　形	陆地车辆传动齿轮；陆地车辆传动马达；陆地车辆传动轴等	2015年	武进区
常州快克锡焊股份有限公司	QUICK	电焊设备；电测量仪器等	2015年	武进区

2-16 续表 14 continued 14

企业名称 Name of Enterprises	商标名称 Brand Name	主要产品 Mostly Product	颁布时间 Time of Release	所在地区 Region
江苏河马井股份有限公司	河马拼音及图	塑料管；管子接头；非金属软管	2015年	武进区
江苏丰顺新材料科技有限公司	FENGSHUN及图	金属建筑材料；建筑用金属板；铝塑板（以铝为主）等	2015年	武进区
江苏苏宏医疗器械有限公司	苏　宏	秤、衡器	2015年	武进区
江苏安普特防爆科技有限公司	安普特防爆英文及图	电脑计量加油机；加油站发油泵；加油站汽油泵等	2015年	武进区
常州市翰琪电机有限公司	前程及图	电子工业设备；机器、马达和发动机连杆	2015年	武进区
常州佳辰地板集团有限公司	佳辰拼音及图	地　板	2015年	武进区
大澳电器（江苏）有限公司	新澳玛拼音及图	陆地车辆传动马达；陆地车辆电力发动机；陆地车辆动力装置等	2015年	武进区
常州神力电机股份有限公司	常神拼音及图	电机；发电机及其部件	2015年	武进区
常州威克医疗器械有限公司	图　形	泌尿科器械及器具；止血缝合器械；缝合材料等	2015年	武进区
江苏安格特新材料科技有限公司	安格特AGT	未加工塑料；聚丙烯；聚氯乙烯树脂等	2015年	武进区
中韩科技有限公司	中　韩	冰柜；冰箱；饮水机等	2015年	武进区
江苏红日防静电地板有限公司	红日及图	地板；建筑用木材；铺地木材	2015年	武进区
江苏双奇地板有限公司	双　奇	木地板；非金属地板等	2015年	武进区
江苏凯莱木业有限公司	凯莱KAILAI	地板；非金属建筑材料；非金属地板等	2015年	武进区
常州新鸿联家具有限公司	鸿联拼音及图	家具；金属家具；办公用家具等	2015年	武进区
常州市腾田液压机械有限公司	腾田TENT及图	液压机；活塞（机器或发动机部件等	2015年	武进区
常州市薛巷电讯元件有限公司	桑乐拼音及图	电线；电线接插件；电连接器等	2015年	武进区
江苏日盈电子股份有限公司	图　形	电器接插件；电线；电线连接物等	2015年	武进区
常州市赛力木业有限公司	圣力及图	地板；镶花地板等	2015年	武进区
常州永盛包装有限公司	永盛及图	包装机械；胶带分配机	2015年	武进区
常州市科沛达超声工程设备有限公司	科沛达及拼音	电焊机；清洗设备；工业用振荡器（机器）等	2015年	武进区
常州华日新材有限公司	图　形	合成树脂塑料；未加工塑料；丙烯酸树脂（未加工）等	2015年	新北区
江苏常胜电器有限公司	图　形	温度控制器；保险丝；熔断器等	2015年	新北区
远电控股（集团）有限公司	FE及图	断路器；高低压开关板；配电箱（电）等	2015年	新北区
常州市伟泰电子科技有限公司	伟　泰	铁路道岔遥控电动设备；工业操作遥控电力装置；工业操作遥控电器设备等	2015年	新北区
常州新区常工电子计算机有限公司	雲楊UPCLOUD	测量器械和仪器；计算机程序（可下载软件）；计量仪器等	2015年	新北区
常州英泊索尔新能源有限公司	英泊索尔及图	电热水器；太阳能集热器；太阳能热水器等	2015年	新北区
常州市东海橡胶厂有限公司	CZDH及图	非金属软管；橡胶圈；密封物等	2015年	新北区
江苏普立泳池设备有限公司	普立及图	游泳池（非金属结构）；非金属地砖；防水卷材等	2015年	新北区
常州天目湖南山竹海食品有限公司	南山天目湖竹海	香肠；干食用菌等	2015年	新北区
常州市阳光药业有限公司	图　形	人用药；药用胶囊；医药制剂等	2015年	新北区

2-16 续表 15 continued 15

企业名称 Name of Enterprises	商标名称 Brand Name	主要产品 Mostly Product	颁布时间 Time of Release	所在地区 Region
常州大江饲料有限公司	常大拼音及图	饲料；动物催肥剂；动物食品等	2015年	新北区
江苏卓云豆宝食品有限公司	康力拼音及图	防水浆消泡剂；葡萄糖酸盐；葡萄糖酸内酯等	2015年	新北区
常茂生物化学工程股份有限公司	图 形	酸；酒石酸；人造增甜剂等	2015年	新北区
江苏常隆化工有限公司	天宁及图	农 药	2015年	新北区
常州方圆制药有限公司	创成及图	医药制剂；化学药物制剂	2015年	新北区
常州市长力冲压机床有限公司	万	内燃机配件；机器飞轮；机器联动机件等	2015年	新北区
常州东风轴承有限公司	DFB	传动轴轴承；滚珠轴承（滚柱）；机器用耐磨轴承等	2015年	新北区
常州海弘电子有限公司	长江及图	F	2015年	新北区
江苏华冠电器集团有限公司	华程拼音及图	配电柜（电）；配电控制台（电）；控制板（电）等	2015年	新北区
常州联力自动化科技有限公司	联力拼音及图	用于计算机操作仪器的机械装置；工业操作遥控电力装置；工业操作遥控电器设备	2015年	新北区
江苏德春电力科技有限公司	德春电器及图	电开关；接线盒（电）；高低压开关板等	2015年	新北区
特瑞斯能源装备股份有限公司	TRUBILITY	煤气管道用调节和安全附件；煤气设备用的调节和安全附件；蒸发器等	2015年	新北区
常州九鼎车业有限公司	JUDNG	车辆灯；灯等	2015年	新北区
常州市飞拓模塑有限公司	飞拓拼音及图	后视镜；车辆内装饰；车辆保险杆等	2015年	新北区
常州市盛扬电动自行车有限公司	盛扬拼音及图	电动车辆；机动自行车；三轮运货车等	2015年	新北区
常州恐龙园股份有限公司	恐龙宝贝	游戏机；玩具；扑克牌等	2015年	新北区
江苏久信医疗科技股份有限公司	久信拼音及图	空气净化；空气除臭；空气清新等	2015年	新北区
中海油常州环保涂料有限公司	阿沃德	油漆；涂料	2015年	钟楼区
江苏大使同丰涂料有限公司	同丰及图	涂层（油漆）；金属用保护制剂等	2015年	钟楼区
江苏腾奇电力设备科技有限公司	图 形	变压器用片式散热器	2015年	钟楼区
常州兆阳能源科技有限公司	SRSUNRISE	电池；单晶硅；多晶硅等	2015年	钟楼区
常州市英中电气有限公司	YZ及图	绝缘材料；电线绝缘物；绝缘体等	2015年	钟楼区
江苏瞬通交通设施有限公司	瞬通及图	栏杆；非金属建筑材料；公路防撞非金属栏等	2015年	钟楼区
常州盛德无缝钢管有限公司	图形	钢管；金属管；金属管道等	2015年	钟楼区
常州华联保健敷料有限公司	华联及图	医用敷料；医用胶布；止血栓等	2015年	钟楼区
常州常松金属复合材料有限公司	常松及图	金属片和金属板；钢板；金属建筑材料等	2015年	钟楼区
常州机械设备进出口有限公司	AMEG亚美柯及图	柴油机；汽油机；发电机等	2015年	钟楼区
常州昊邦汽车零部件有限公司	HAOB	车辆座位；车辆减震器；车辆底盘等	2015年	钟楼区
常州金店有限公司	JY皆是缘及拼音	宝石（珠宝）；黄金首饰；铂金首饰等	2015年	钟楼区
常州环球地毯制造有限公司	环球拼音及图	地 毯	2015年	钟楼区
常州马复兴餐饮管理有限公司	馬複興	饭店；快餐馆；茶馆等	2015年	钟楼区

2-17 名牌产品一览
GENERAL VIEW OF FAMOUS BRAND PRODUCTS

企业名称 Name of Enterprises	产品名称 Product Name	颁布时间 Time of Release
中国名牌产品　China Top Brand Products		
江苏上上电缆集团	上上牌交联聚乙烯电力电缆	2004年
黑牡丹（集团）股份有限公司	黑牡丹牌牛仔布	2005年
常州月夜灯芯绒有限公司	月夜牌灯芯绒	2005年
常柴股份有限公司	常柴牌单缸柴油机	2005年
江苏常发集团常州常发动力机械有限公司	常发牌单缸柴油机	2005年
江苏华鹏变压器有限公司	华鹏牌干式电力变压器	2005年
江苏华鹏变压器有限公司	华鹏牌110KV及以下油浸式电力变压器	2005年
常州华电变压器集团公司常州变压器厂	常州牌110KV及以下油浸式电力变压器	2005年
常州天马集团有限公司	天马牌无碱玻璃纤维短切原丝毡	2005年
江苏多棱数控机床股份有限公司	SDL牌重型数控镗铣床	2006年
常州东风农机集团有限公司	东风牌手扶拖拉机	2006年
江苏常发集团常州常发动力机械有限公司	常发牌手扶拖拉机	2006年
新科电子集团有限公司	新科、Shinco牌激光视盘机	2006年
江苏康泰氟化工有限公司	蓝色星球牌HFC-134A制冷剂	2006年
江苏常隆化工有限公司	天宁牌吡虫啉杀虫剂	2006年
江苏同大股份有限公司	全无敌牌气雾杀虫剂	2006年
月星集团有限公司	月星牌实木家具	2006年
江苏鸿联集团有限公司	红联牌室内灯具	2006年
常州天马集团有限公司	天马牌玻璃纤维土工格栅	2006年
江苏金鼎电动工具集团有限公司	金鼎牌电动工具	2007年
常州市永明机械制造有限公司	常明牌PP编织物机	2007年
常州市武进不锈钢管厂有限公司	阳湖牌锅炉用不锈钢无缝钢管	2007年
江苏常隆化工有限公司	天宁牌乙草胺	2007年
常林股份有限公司	常林牌装载机	2007年
新科电子集团有限公司	新科、Shinco牌家用分体空调	2007年

2-17 续表 1　continued 1

企业名称 Name of Enterprises	产品名称 Product Name	颁布时间 Time of Release
江苏名牌产品　Jiangsu Famous Brand Products		
常州天合光能有限公司	天合光能牌地面用晶体硅光伏组件	2013年
江苏裕成电子有限公司	裕成牌微型动圈式受话器、扬声器	2013年
常州星海电子有限公司	灵杰牌硅半导体塑封二极管	2013年
江苏波仕曼制衣有限公司	波仕曼牌羽绒服	2013年
江苏旷达汽车织物集团股份有限公司	旷达牌汽车内饰面料	2013年
顶呱呱彩棉服饰有限公司	顶呱呱牌棉针织内衣	2013年
江苏中东化肥股份有限公司	中东牌复混肥料（复合肥料）	2013年
常州亚邦化学有限公司	亚邦牌顺丁烯二酸酐	2013年
江苏丰登作物保护股份有限公司	丰登牌三唑类杀菌剂	2013年
江苏省激素研究所股份有限公司	金珠牌除草剂、杀虫剂、植物生长调节剂	2013年
常州市国宇环保科技有限公司	玉宇牌化学试剂硝酸银	2013年
金坛市农用水泵厂	国农牌自吸泵	2013年
常州亚美柯机械设备有限公司	亚美柯牌单缸柴油机	2013年
常州市永安电机有限公司	永安牌房间空调器用电动机	2013年
常州乐士雷利电机有限公司	雷利牌步进电机	2013年
大澳电器（江苏）有限公司	新澳玛牌永磁直流电机	2013年
常州市武起汽车电机有限公司	常乐牌QDJ系列起动机	2013年
常州市润源经编机械有限公司	润源牌经编机	2013年
卡尔迈耶（中国）有限公司	KARL MAYER牌经编机	2013年
常柴股份有限公司	常柴牌内燃机	2013年
常州常发动力机械有限公司	常发牌单缸柴油机、系列旋耕机、手扶拖拉机	2013年
江苏金鼎电动工具集团有限公司	金鼎牌电动工具	2013年
常州能源设备总厂有限公司	CEEF（图形）、先锋牌有机热载体炉	2013年
江苏武进不锈股份有限公司	WujIN牌不锈钢管、钢制管件	2013年
江苏保龙机电制造有限公司	保龙（图形）牌木材加工机械	2013年
江苏维尔利环保科技股份有限公司	维尔利牌管式超滤垃圾渗滤液处理装置	2013年
国茂减速机集团有限公司	国茂牌减速机	2013年
常州科研试制中心有限公司	KS牌矿用防爆无轨车	2013年

2-17 续表 2 continued 2

企业名称 Name of Enterprises	产品名称 Product Name	颁布时间 Time of Release
常州联发凯迪机械有限公司	联发凯迪牌轮式拖拉机	2013年
常州市瑞悦车业有限公司	富满牌汽车内饰	2013年
常州太平洋电力设备（集团）有限公司	常太牌高低压成套开关设备、高压真空断路器	2013年
江苏安靠智能输电工程科技股份有限公司	安靠牌高压及超高压交联聚乙烯绝缘电力电缆附件系列产品	2013年
江苏恒立高压油缸股份有限公司	恒立hengli牌液压油缸	2013年
江苏鑫和泰机械集团有限公司	常动牌单缸柴油机机体	2013年
常州市永明机械制造有限公司	常明牌PP编织物机	2013年
常州纺兴精密机械有限公司	飞霞牌喷丝板	2013年
江苏南方轴承股份有限公司	南方牌滚针轴承	2013年
江苏长海复合材料股份有限公司	常海牌薄型玻璃纤维短切毡	2013年
盘固水泥集团有限公司	盘固牌通用硅酸盐水泥	2013年
江苏扬子水泥有限公司	长荡湖牌通用硅酸盐水泥	2013年
江苏尼高科技有限公司	尼高科技牌建筑外墙保温材料	2013年
江苏太阳宝新能源有限公司	太阳宝牌太阳能热水器	2013年
常州而今太阳能设备制造有限公司	而今牌家用太阳能热水系统	2013年
吟飞科技（江苏）有限公司	吟飞牌电子乐器	2013年
常州侨裕旅游用品有限公司	侨裕牌便携式折叠椅	2013年
江苏洛基木业有限公司	洛基牌浸渍纸层压木质地板	2013年
常州市赛力木业有限公司	圣力牌浸渍纸层压木质地板	2013年
常州森鸿装饰材料有限公司	博鸿牌浸渍纸层压木质地板	2013年
江苏科利达装饰材料有限公司	科利达牌浸渍纸层压木地板	2013年
常州市佳安装饰材料有限公司	好佳好牌浸渍纸层压木质地板	2013年
常州市森尼装饰材料有限公司	森尼牌浸渍纸层压木质地板	2013年
常州市赛欧地板有限公司	大欧牌浸渍纸层压木质地板	2013年
常州市欧太装饰材料有限公司	欧运牌浸渍纸层压木质地板	2013年
溧阳军荣旅游用品有限公司	JUNRONG牌旅行箱包	2013年
常州精科实业有限公司	CONTIN牌指针式石英钟	2013年
常州世纪鸟电动车制造有限公司	世纪鸟牌电动自行车	2013年
灵通展览系统股份有限公司	灵通（LINGTONG）牌展览展示器材	2013年

2-17 续表 3　continued 3

企业名称 Name of Enterprises	产品名称 Product Name	颁布时间 Time of Release
江苏易成电力器材有限公司	易成牌氯化聚氯乙烯及硬聚氯乙烯塑料电缆导管	2013年
常州常松金属复合材料有限公司	常松牌金属复合板	2013年
江苏江南冷轧薄板有限公司	江南龙牌镀锌卷	2013年
江苏江南铁合金有限公司	江南龙牌低碳低硅钛铁	2013年
常州凯达重工科技有限公司	凯达牌铸铁、铸钢轧辊	2013年
常州四药制药有限公司	奥克牌奥克系列产品	2013年
常州四药制药有限公司	缬克牌缬克系列产品	2013年
常州四药制药有限公司	兰苏牌兰苏系列产品	2013年
常州制药厂有限公司	常药牌卡托普利系列	2013年
常州制药厂有限公司	盐酸多西环素	2013年
常州制药厂有限公司	复方利血平片	2013年
常州制药厂有限公司	瑞舒伐他汀	2013年
常州华森医疗器械有限公司	常胜牌肋骨接骨板	2013年
江苏康进医疗器材有限公司	康进牌一次性使用输液器带针	2013年
江苏康友医用器械有限公司	一次性使用注射器带针	2013年
江苏康友医用器械有限公司	康友牌一次性使用无菌注射器	2013年
江苏吉祥贺盛食品有限公司	贺盛牌鸡精调味料	2013年
江苏南顺食品有限公司	满天星牌小麦粉	2013年
金坛市江南制粉有限公司	沁雪牌水磨糯米粉	2013年
江苏常州城北国家粮食储备库	诚百牌大米	2013年
常州长江水产有限公司冷冻加工厂	江南牌冻银鱼	2013年
江苏三德利牧业发展有限公司	金茅鸡牌金茅草鸡	2013年
常州市康乐农牧有限公司	中东牌商品猪	2013年
金坛市方麓茶场有限公司	百园春牌金坛雀舌茶	2013年
江苏省前峰茶厂	前峰牌绿茶	2013年
常州公路运输集团有限公司	交通运输服务	2013年
常州中房物业有限公司	物业管理服务	2013年
常州中华恐龙园有限公司	景区游乐服务	2013年
江苏奥新电梯有限公司	电梯服务	2013年

2-17 续表 4 continued 4

企业名称 Name of Enterprises	产品名称 Product Name	颁布时间 Time of Release
常州大华进出口（集团）有限公司	外贸流通服务	2013年
月星集团有限公司	家具流通服务	2013年
江苏正平技术服务事务所有限公司	检验检测、技术服务	2013年
常州市维益专利事务所	专利服务	2013年
常州产权交易所	产权交易服务	2013年
常州银河世纪微电子有限公司	G 牌硅塑封微型贴片半导体分立器件	2014年
江苏众恒染整有限公司	众恒牌针织牛仔布	2014年
江苏华达化工集团有限公司	常恒牌 1-萘胺、 1-萘酚系列产品	2014年
常茂生物化学工程股份有限公司	图形牌 L（+）-酒石酸、 L-苹	2014年
冶建新材料股份有限公司	天虎牌 TH -2型硅酸锌车间底漆	2014年
江海环保股份有限公司	江海牌 JH -水处理剂系列产品	2014年
常州科威天使环保科技有限公司	天使牌水处理剂聚丙烯酰胺	2014年
江苏南方通信科技有限公司	精科牌铜芯聚烯烃绝缘铝塑综合护套市内通信电缆、层绞式通信用室外光缆	2014年
江苏海鸥冷却塔股份有限公司	海鸥牌玻璃纤维增强塑料冷却塔	2014年
江苏友奥电器有限公司	友奥（YOAU）牌移动式空调器	2014年
江苏友奥电器有限公司	友奥（YOAU）牌除湿机	2014年
江苏峨嵋动力机械有限公司	金田牌单缸基本型柴油机	2014年
金坛柴油机有限公司	天鹅牌柴油机	2014年
江苏天元工程机械有限公司	TEEYER牌蒸压加气混凝土切割机	2014年
江苏上能新特变压器有限公司	SUNEL牌10KV系列干式变压器	2014年
凡登（常州）新型金属材料技术有限公司	fundant牌切割钢丝	2014年
常州市第八纺织机械有限公司	华发牌高精度分段整经机	2014年
江苏恒耐炉料集团有限公司	恒耐牌水泥窑用高强度莫来石浇注料	2014年
常州亚玛顿股份有限公司	亚玛顿牌多功能高效减反增透光伏玻璃	2014年
常州协鑫光伏科技有限公司	GCL牌太阳能级多晶硅片	2014年
中韩科技有限公司	中韩牌家用冷藏冷冻箱	2014年
常州华通新立地板有限公司	华通牌防静电活动地板	2014年
江苏南洋木业有限公司	南洋（图案）牌实木地板	2014年
常州市东家装饰材料有限公司	东家牌浸渍纸层压木质地板	2014年

2-17 续表 5　continued 5

企业名称 Name of Enterprises	产品名称 Product Name	颁布时间 Time of Release
常州华日升反光材料股份有限公司	通明牌反光膜	2014年
江苏红日防静电地板有限公司	红日牌防静电活动地板	2014年
江苏金源锻造股份有限公司	金石牌MW级风力发电机齿轮箱配套锻件	2014年
江苏国强镀锌实业有限公司	国强牌低压流体输送用焊接镀锌钢管、普通流体输送管道用埋弧焊钢管、石油天然气工业管线输送用钢管、波形梁护栏	2014年
常州市常蒸蒸发器有限公司	常蒸及图牌常蒸牌蒸发器、冷凝器（高效节能换热器）	2014年
江苏中友精密制管有限公司	中友牌直缝焊接钢管	2014年
江苏江南创佳型材有限公司	创佳牌铝合金型材	2014年
常州华通焊业股份有限公司	华通牌碳钢焊丝	2014年
常州市恒丰铜材有限公司	镀银丝牌镀银丝及绞线	2014年
江苏康华医疗器材有限公司	常宝牌一次性使用无菌注射器、输液器	2014年
常州华联保健敷料有限公司	华联牌创可贴	2014年
常州市钱璟康复器材有限公司	钱璟牌康复训练器械	2014年
江苏久信医疗科技股份有限公司	久JIUXIN信及图牌整体数字化洁净手术室	2014年
金坛市后渎特种水产养殖场有限公司	苏标牌长荡湖中华绒螯蟹	2014年
常州市常洛果品专业合作社	苏常鲜牌绿色食品葡萄	2014年
江苏新城房产股份有限公司	房地产相关服务	2014年
江苏凌家塘市场发展有限公司	江苏服务业名牌	2014年
江苏光辉灯具市场有限公司	江苏服务业名牌	2014年
常州电梯工程有限公司	电梯服务	2014年
常州恐龙谷温泉有限公司	景区游乐服务	2014年
常州市春秋乐园旅游发展有限公司	景区游乐服务	2014年
常嘉建设集团有限公司	建筑相关服务	2014年
常州市保利大剧院管理有限公司	江苏服务业名牌	2014年
常州市新北区西夏墅镇人民政府	西夏墅硬质合金刀具	2014年
常州市武进区郑陆镇人民政府	郑陆不锈钢管	2014年
常州市武进区横林镇人民政府	横林强化木地板	2014年

2-17 续表 6 continued 6

企业名称 Name of Enterprises	产品名称 Product Name	颁布时间 Time of Release
江苏立华牧业有限公司	雪山鸡	2015年
常州阳湖新月茶业有限公司	阳湖新月茶	2015年
常州市常洛果品专业合作社	猕猴桃	2015年
金坛丰登酒业有限公司	黄酒（封缸酒）	2015年
金坛市金土地有机稻米专业合作社	“黄金村”牌有机软米	2015年
江苏鑫品茶业有限公司	金坛雀舌茶	2015年
江苏茅山青锋茶叶有限公司	茅山青锋	2015年
中天钢铁集团有限公司	钢筋混凝土用热轧光圆钢筋	2015年
江苏双奇地板有限公司	浸渍纸层压木质地板	2015年
江苏亚邦染料股份有限公司	分散染料	2015年
南京化工学院常州市武进水质稳定剂厂	水处理剂 2-膦酸基-1，2，4-三羧基丁烷；羟基亚乙基二膦酸等	2015年
常州洪都电动车有限公司	电动自行车	2015年
江苏玉兰木业有限公司	浸渍纸层压木质地板	2015年
江苏博大木业有限公司	热固性树脂浸渍纸高压装饰层积板	2015年
江苏兰陵化工集团有限公司	涂料	2015年
江苏晨光涂料有限公司	内外墙涂料	2015年
常州常发制冷科技有限公司	冰箱、空调用蒸发器、冷凝器	2015年
江苏南方卫材医药股份有限公司	一次性伤口敷料	2015年
江苏凯莱木业有限公司	浸渍纸层压木质地板	2015年
江苏常发农业装备股份有限公司	轮式拖拉机	2015年
江苏贝尔装饰材料有限公司	浸渍纸层压木质地板	2015年
江苏洛凯机电股份有限公司	智能电网断路操作机构	2015年
江苏龙城精锻有限公司	汽车发电机转子用精锻爪极	2015年
常州晶雪冷冻设备有限公司	组合冷库用隔热夹芯板	2015年
常州市云涛洁具有限公司	玻璃纤维增强塑料浴缸	2015年
常州市武进中天机房设备有限公司	新型环保防静电活动地板	2015年
江苏丰顺新材料科技有限公司	建筑幕墙用铝塑复合板	2015年
江苏新瑞重工科技有限公司	V系列立式加工中心	2015年
新誉集团有限公司	CRH5A、成都地铁1号线空调系统	2015年

2-17 续表 7　continued 7

企业名称 Name of Enterprises	产品名称 Product Name	颁布时间 Time of Release
今创集团股份有限公司	轨道交通站台屏蔽门	2015年
今创集团股份有限公司	一等车客室座椅	2015年
卡尔迈耶（中国）有限公司	整经机	2015年
江苏悦达卡特新能源有限公司	生物柴油	2015年
普罗斯电器（中国）有限公司	高强度气体放电灯	2015年
江苏上上电缆集团有限公司	上上牌电线电缆	2015年
江苏华鹏变压器有限公司	华鹏牌电力变压器	2015年
江苏正昌集团有限公司	正昌牌制粒机	2015年
江苏正昌集团有限公司	正昌牌粉碎机	2015年
江苏正昌集团有限公司	正昌牌成套工程设备	2015年
江苏开利地毯股份有限公司	天目湖牌地毯	2015年
江苏开磷瑞阳化工股份有限公司	瑞阳牌工业用季戊四醇	2015年
江苏金峰水泥集团有限公司	通用硅酸盐水泥	2015年
布勒（常州）机械有限公司	布勒牌饲料机械	2015年
溧阳市重型机械厂有限公司	麦重牌破碎机	2015年
江苏上齿集团有限公司	汽车、工程车螺旋锥齿轮	2015年
江苏竹溪活性炭有限公司	竹溪牌活性炭	2015年
江苏竹箦阀业有限公司	ZJ牌阀门	2015年
常州乔尔塑料有限公司	JOEL乔尔塑料牌UFC氨基模塑颗粒料	2015年
江苏保龙设备制造有限公司	保龙牌风力发电塔架	2015年
常州光洋轴承股份有限公司	滚针轴承系列、滚子轴承系列、离合器分离轴承系列、汽车轮毂轴承系列、推力轴承系列	2015年
常州市宏发纵横新材料科技股份有限公司	连续树脂基预浸料用多轴向经编增强复合材料	2015年
华润包装材料有限公司	瓶用聚对苯二甲酸乙二醇酯（PET）树脂	2015年
常州千红生化制药股份有限公司	肝素钠	2015年
常州千红生化制药股份有限公司	胰激肽原酶	2015年
常州天马集团有限公司（原建材二五三厂）	不饱和聚酯树脂、玻璃纤维制品	2015年
常州星宇车灯股份有限公司	星宇牌汽车车灯	2015年
梅特勒-托利多（常州）测量技术有限公司	电子衡器	2015年
特瑞斯能源装备股份有限公司	燃气调压箱	2015年

2-17 续表 8 continued 8

企业名称 Name of Enterprises	产品名称 Product Name	颁布时间 Time of Release
江苏省健尔康医用敷料有限公司	脱脂纱布	2015年
江苏鸿瑞昌泰纺织有限公司	毛毯	2015年
常州市龙泉太阳能设备厂	太阳能热水器	2015年
中盐金坛盐化有限责任公司	盐	2015年
常州市新东方电缆有限公司	电线电缆	2015年
常州神力电机股份有限公司	电机	2015年
江苏常宝钢管股份有限公司	无缝钢管	2015年
常州格力博有限公司	格力博牌新型节能环保园林机械	2015年
常州东风农机集团有限公司	拖拉机	2015年
常州华威电子有限公司	铝电解电容器	2015年
常州船用电缆有限责任公司	船用电线电缆	2015年
常州四药制药有限公司	卡前列素氨丁三醇注射液	2015年
常州四药制药有限公司	注射用兰索拉唑	2015年
江苏骠马智能装备股份有限公司	乘用车清洁涂装自动化生产线	2015年
常州市武进广宇花辊机械有限公司	非织造布热轧机	2015年
常州光辉化工有限公司	油漆、涂料	2015年
黑牡丹（集团）股份有限公司	色织牛仔布	2015年
常州华利达服装集团有限公司	服装	2015年
津通集团有限公司	津通国际工业园服务	2015年
溧阳申菱电梯工程有限公司	电梯安装、改造、维保服务	2015年
常州三晶世界科技产业发展有限公司	科技企业孵化服务	2015年
江苏米多装饰有限公司	设计施工服务	2015年
常州市建筑科学研究院股份有限公司	建设工程质量检测服务	2015年
江苏汇菱电梯有限公司	电梯销售、安装、维修保养服务	2015年
常州港华燃气有限公司	城市天然气供应服务	2015年
常州丽华快餐集团有限公司	集体用餐配送膳食	2015年

2-17 续表 9　continued 9

企业名称 Name of Enterprises	产品名称 Product Name	颁布时间 Time of Release
常州名牌产品　Changzhou Famous Brand Products		
溧阳市天目湖白埂茶场	绿　茶	2013年
溧阳市横涧竹下茶场	绿　茶	2013年
溧阳市玉莲生态农业开发有限公司	天目湖白茶	2013年
江苏省前峰茶厂	绿　茶	2013年
溧阳市上兴茶厂	绿　茶	2013年
溧阳市白露山生态农业发展有限公司	挂面、花式挂面	2013年
溧阳市缪氏大闸蟹专业合作社	大闸蟹	2013年
江苏全福农牧实业有限公司	分割鸡	2013年
溧阳市天目湖春芽茶场	绿　茶	2013年
溧阳市天目湖伍员山食品有限公司	野山笋	2013年
溧阳市海斌粮食作物专业合作社	大　米	2013年
溧阳市天目一奇食品有限公司	真空包装鱼头	2013年
溧阳市梅坞生态园艺有限公司	茶　叶	2013年
江苏曹山紫竹林生态农业发展有限公司	绿　茶	2013年
溧阳市天目云露茶业有限公司	绿　茶	2013年
金坛市上清茅山农产品开发有限公司	大　米	2013年
江苏省薛埠粮食储备直属库	大　米	2013年
金坛市茅麓锡峰茶场	绿　茶	2013年
常州市圣王果蔬有限公司	无花果茶	2013年
金坛市茅麓茶厂	绿　茶	2013年
金坛市麓雨茶场	绿　茶	2013年
江苏金唐农业科技有限公司	无节水芹	2013年
金坛市社头水平牛肉食品有限公司	酱卤牛肉	2013年
金坛市二呆子牛肉有限公司	酱卤牛肉	2013年
金坛市昌玉红香芋专业合作社	红香芋	2013年
常州市翟家果品专业合作社	翠冠梨	2013年
常州市常洛果品专业合作社	葡　萄	2013年
常州神力电机股份有限公司	风力发电机定子铁芯	2013年
常州制药厂有限公司	马来酸依那普利片	2013年
江苏省社渚轴承有限公司	圆锥滚子轴承	2013年

2-17 续表 10 continued 10

企业名称 Name of Enterprises	产品名称 Product Name	颁布时间 Time of Release
常州制药厂有限公司	复方利血平片	2013年
常州市第八纺织机械有限公司	华发牌整经机	2013年
常州依丽雅斯纺织品有限公司	窗帘布	2013年
金坛市德博密封技术有限公司	低压变、高强度汽车用HNBR橡胶密封圈	2013年
常州市世兴医疗器械公司	医用电动铣磨钻	2013年
常州华德机械有限公司	高速列车转向架轴箱	2013年
常州山由帝衫防护材料制造有限公司	高效节能隔热遮阳窗膜	2013年
江苏润利锅炉有限公司	锅　炉	2013年
常州市震华干燥设备有限公司	EYH型二维运动混合机	2013年
常州奥琳斯邦热能设备有限公司	蒸压釜	2013年
常州华通新立地板有限公司	防静电活动地板	2013年
常州市久虹医疗器械有限公司	JHY 型一次性使用活体取样钳	2013年
常州市金致机械制造有限公司	JHY系列行星齿轮减速器	2013年
常州市美隆机房设备有限公司	防静电活动地板	2013年
常州市欧普莱斯装饰材料有限公司	浸渍纸层压木质地板	2013年
江苏武进不锈股份有限公司	不锈钢管及钢制管件	2013年
常州市耀邦摩擦材料厂	摩擦材料原料	2013年
常州市君豪纺织品有限公司	服装面料	2013年
常州市佳平装饰材料有限公司	浸渍纸层压木质地板	2013年
常州市正航装饰材料有限公司	热固性树脂浸渍纸高压层积板	2013年
常州帝豪装饰材料有限公司	浸渍纸层压木质地板	2013年
常州市玉燕冷藏设备厂	组合冷库用隔热夹芯板	2013年
江苏科力农业资源科技有限公司	有机-无机复混肥料	2013年
江苏龙城洪力液压设备有限公司	液压冷拔机	2013年
江苏恒源园艺用品有限公司	园艺用支柱	2013年
常州世纪鸟电动车制造有限公司	电动自行车	2013年
常州虹波涂料有限公司	漆包绕组线绝缘漆	2013年
常州中南化工有限公司	制盐阻垢剂	2013年
常州中南化工有限公司	灰水阻垢分散剂	2013年
常州市华鼎机械制造有限公司	数控龙门铣床	2013年
江苏开利地毯股份有限公司	地　毯	2013年

2-17 续表 11　continued 11

企业名称 Name of Enterprises	产品名称 Product Name	颁布时间 Time of Release
常州市双爱家私有限公司	电脑桌	2013年
大澳电器（江苏）有限公司	永磁直流电机	2013年
常州市钱璟康复器材有限公司	康复训练器械	2013年
江苏恒立高压油缸股份有限公司	液压油缸	2013年
常州辰盛绝缘新材料有限公司	二芳基乙烷绝缘油	2013年
常州华森医疗器械有限公司	骨科植入物、吻（缝）合器	2013年
常州市国宇环保科技有限公司	硝酸银	2013年
常州市武进第二齿轮有限公司	小功率柴油机齿轮	2013年
江苏南方卫材医药股份有限公司	医用胶布（医用橡皮膏）	2013年
常州市东家装饰材料有限公司	浸渍纸层压木质地板	2013年
江苏龙城精锻有限公司	汽车发电机精锻爪极	2013年
常州市赛欧地板有限公司	浸渍纸层压木质地板	2013年
万桦（常州）新材料科技有限公司	PU合成革新材料	2013年
常州南苑塑料有限公司	铝箔封口塑料盖	2013年
常州盛来太阳能科技有限公司	太阳能热水器	2013年
常州市武进晨光金属涂料有限公司	汽车涂料	2013年
常州市泰尔木业有限公司	浸渍纸层压木质地板	2013年
江苏朝晖化工有限公司	工业防腐涂料	2013年
常州苏特轴承制造有限公司	摩托车连杆支承用滚针和保持架组件	2013年
常州市亚达轧辊有限公司	轧　辊	2013年
常州市润源经编机械有限公司	经编机	2013年
常州强力电子新材料股份有限公司	六芳基二咪唑光刻胶引发剂	2013年
常州康普药业有限公司	复方地芬诺酯片	2013年
常州康普药业有限公司	盐酸苯海索片	2013年
常州顺安水泥有限公司	普通硅酸盐水泥	2013年
常州紫寅电子电路有限公司	印制电路板	2013年
江苏飞翔木业有限公司	浸渍纸层压木质地板	2013年
常州市江南诚信制冷设备厂	组合冷库用隔热夹芯板	2013年
常州和圆钢管有限公司	无缝钢管	2013年
常州市江洋不锈钢有限公司	不锈钢管	2013年
溧阳市华鹏电机配件有限公司	电动机铸件	2013年

2-17 续表 12 continued 12

企业名称 Name of Enterprises	产品名称 Product Name	颁布时间 Time of Release
常州市恒成塑料机械有限公司	塑料成套编织机械	2013年
常州市月仙冷藏设备有限公司	组合冷库用隔热夹芯板	2013年
常州山鹰纸业纸品有限公司	瓦楞纸板、纸箱	2013年
常州瑞华电力电子器件有限公司	电力半导体模块	2013年
金坛市晨光轻工机械有限公司	直列式灌装机	2013年
常州远东塑料机械有限公司	包装用聚酯捆扎带	2013年
江苏瞬通交通设施有限公司	护　栏	2013年
江苏弘州金福车业有限公司	摩托车	2013年
常州市宇峰电源有限公司	3V锂锰扣式电池	2013年
常州市鼎亨机电设备有限公司	潜水搅拌机	2013年
常州市万象化工机械有限公司	蒸压釜	2013年
常州西电变压器有限责任公司	电力变压器	2013年
常州宣纳尔新能源科技有限公司	太阳能热水器	2013年
常州赛迪电气制造有限公司	电动工具	2013年
常州星亚服装有限公司	单、夹服装	2013年
常州市宏大电气有限公司	织物含潮率在线监测及控制系统	2013年
常州市兰翔电器有限公司	高低压配电柜	2013年
纳图（常州）电气有限公司	低压开关柜	2013年
常州特种变压器有限公司	电力变压器、箱式变压器、组合式美变	2013年
常州船用电缆有限责任公司	船用/矿用电线电缆	2013年
常州佳卓特种车辆有限公司	拖挂式运马车	2013年
江苏集盛星泰新能源科技有限公司	双电层超级电容器	2013年
常州明杰模具有限公司	核电、汽车、锻造及制管等工模具	2013年
常州曼淇威电气产品有限公司	单相电容运转异步电动机系列	2013年
常州市伯山机械有限公司	造纸机械 复卷机	2013年
常州美高塑件有限公司	汽车配件	2013年
常州永杰蒸发器有限公司	蒸发器	2013年
江苏港益重工股份有限公司	起重机	2013年
常州华日新材有限公司	不饱和聚酯树脂	2013年
江苏三恒科技股份有限公司	矿用无线通信系统	2013年
江苏东方印务有限公司	纸制品包装	2013年

2-17 续表 13　continued 13

企业名称 Name of Enterprises	产品名称 Product Name	颁布时间 Time of Release
常州明远宏图幕墙有限公司	氟碳铝幕墙板	2013年
东嘉麻棉（常州）有限公司	亚麻纱	2013年
常州新区金康精工机械有限公司	双头立式绕线机	2013年
常州钢构建设工程有限公司	网架、钢结构	2013年
汉得利（常州）电子有限公司	宽频式闪光灯信号器	2013年
常州海弘电子有限公司	印制板	2013年
常州澳弘电子有限公司	印制板	2013年
江苏先昌电能部件有限公司	软化护栏、公交座椅	2013年
常州华科树脂有限公司	不饱和聚酯树脂	2013年
常州市厦科动力机械有限公司	柴油水泵机组	2013年
常州市金牛研磨有限公司	砂　布	2013年
常州市豪来邦机电有限公司	闸　阀	2013年
常州光洋轴承股份有限公司	滚动轴承	2013年
常州宝隆冶金设备制造有限公司	锻钢轧辊	2013年
江苏考普乐新材料股份有限公司	环保型功能性氟碳涂料	2013年
常州鸿尔达车业有限公司	电动自行车	2013年
常州常瑞天力动力机械有限公司	单缸柴油机	2013年
常州市瑞悦车业有限公司	汽车前组合灯	2013年
常州天山重工机械有限公司	高精度高速重载硬齿面齿轮（轴）	2013年
常州市康迪医用吻合器有限公司	吻（缝）合器	2013年
常州市厦科动力机械有限公司	SH风冷型柴油机及柴油机组	2013年
常州市安江车辆部件厂	保险杠、仪表台	2013年
江苏康力生物科技发展有限公司	食品添加剂（复配豆制品消泡剂、单双硬脂酸甘油酯、葡萄糖酸内酯）	2013年
常州市恒力机械有限公司	PP编织物机	2013年
溧阳市特种变压器电器设备有限公司	高、低压成套开关设备	2013年
江苏国强镀锌实业有限公司	低压流体输送用焊接镀锌钢管	2013年
溧阳市嘉雄不锈钢设备有限公司	不锈钢卫生管道及阀门流体配件	2013年
溧阳市万兴特种建材有限公司	预应力混凝土用钢绞线	2013年
常州乔尔塑料有限公司	高档复合UFC颗粒料	2013年
江苏上齿集团有限公司	汽车及工程车螺旋锥齿轮	2013年
江苏金源锻造股份有限公司	风电增速箱零部件	2013年

2-17 续表 14 continued 14

企业名称 Name of Enterprises	产品名称 Product Name	颁布时间 Time of Release
常州博尼特种钢管有限公司	高精密不锈钢无缝毛细管	2013年
江苏常净环保科技有限公司	模块式布袋除尘器	2013年
江苏保龙设备制造有限公司	风力发电塔架	2013年
溧阳圣泰重型机械有限公司	风电设备	2013年
溧阳市华鹏电力仪表有限公司	DDZY83单相费控智能电能表	2013年
常州市瑞腾塑胶有限公司	聚碳酸酯（PC）中空板	2013年
江苏立达电梯有限公司	电　梯	2013年
江苏安靠智能输电工程科技股份有限公司	交联聚乙烯绝缘电力电缆连接件	2013年
立诚包装有限公司	宽幅柔版预印彩色瓦楞纸板	2013年
常州吉恩化工有限公司	氨基酸保护剂	2013年
常州吉恩化工有限公司	碱金属盐	2013年
江苏富深协通数码技术有限公司	富深协通住房公积金管理信息系统软件服务	2013年
江苏富深协通数码技术有限公司	富深协通财政一体化业务管理系统软件服务	2013年
常州市维邦网络软件有限公司	维邦统计数据处理平台系统软件服务	2013年
江苏启航开创软件有限公司	启航医院信息管理系统软件服务	2013年
江苏金马扬名信息技术有限公司	服务家庭社区的心脏三维远程信息诊断系统软件服务	2013年
常州外事旅游汽车集团有限公司	汽车销售服务	2013年
天宁区兰陵卢记聚德园饭店	餐饮服务	2013年
常州银河湾电脑数码城有限公司	电脑、数码及IT产品零售与服务	2013年
常州德嘉美吉特科技五金城有限公司	运营管理服务	2013年
常州恒生科技园有限公司	科技孵化及招商运营服务	2013年
常州公路运输集团有限公司	道路运输服务	2013年
常州大酒店有限公司	酒店管理服务	2013年
江苏双桂坊餐饮管理有限公司	餐饮销售服务	2013年
常州电梯工程有限公司	电梯维修保养	2013年
常州瑞和泰食品有限公司	副食品销售	2013年
常州糖烟酒股份有限公司	糖烟酒销售	2013年
常州市天华新能源科技有限公司	光伏技术服务	2013年
江苏安邦物流有限公司	仓储型物流服务	2013年
江苏后肖幕墙装饰有限公司	幕墙装饰	2013年
常州市圣王果蔬有限公司	金　瓜	2014年

2-17 续表 15　continued 15

企业名称 Name of Enterprises	产品名称 Product Name	颁布时间 Time of Release
常州市双丰水产养殖专业合作社	中华绒螯蟹	2014年
常州礼新果品专业合作社	鲜食葡萄	2014年
常州市祝庄园艺有限公司	红掌花卉	2014年
常州市西湖山庄水产科技有限公司	青　虾	2014年
常州希望粮食购销有限公司	大　米	2014年
江苏天目湖生态农业有限公司	天目湖白茶	2014年
溧阳市凌峰生态农业开发有限公司	茶　叶	2014年
溧阳市水西茶场	绿　茶	2014年
溧阳市天目湖溪水园生态农业发展有限公司	白　茶	2014年
金坛市福地春茶叶有限公司	绿　茶	2014年
江苏佳泽粮油有限公司	大　米	2014年
金坛市金鑫茶场	金坛雀舌茶	2014年
金坛市德润轩茶业开发有限公司	红　茶	2014年
金坛市万方光头牛肉有限公司	真空包装牛肉	2014年
常州市常丰食品有限公司	肉制品	2014年
金坛市荣华制粉厂	水磨糯米粉	2014年
溧阳市天目湖玉枝特种茶果园艺场	天目湖白茶	2014年
溧阳市周城汤山茶厂	绿　茶	2014年
溧阳市天目湖燕山茶园有限公司	绿　茶	2014年
溧阳市天目佳生态农业有限公司	绿　茶	2014年
溧阳市天目湖茶叶研究所	绿　茶	2014年
常州市雅浦酿酒有限公司	雅浦黄酒	2014年
常州市西湖山庄水产科技有限公司	中华绒螯蟹	2014年
常州市杨程禹渔业专业合作社	青　鱼	2014年
江苏佳尔科药业集团有限公司	菌宝牌灵芝孢子粉胶囊	2014年
西玛（常州）通用设备有限公司	搅拌机、过滤机、混合机、容器	2014年
常州领航电子有限公司	全自动（智能型）饮料机	2014年
江苏远传智能科技有限公司	远传水表	2014年
江苏裕兴薄膜科技股份有限公司	功能聚酯薄膜	2014年
常州奥立思特电子有限公司	电　机	2014年
常州合天电力设备有限公司	太阳能交直流发电系统	2014年

2-17 续表 16 continued 16

企业名称 Name of Enterprises	产品名称 Product Name	颁布时间 Time of Release
常州贝斯塔德机械股份有限公司	切割/帘线钢丝湿拉机	2014年
江苏宏源中孚防水材料有限公司	弹性体改性沥青防水卷材	2014年
江苏欧美电子科技有限公司	音视频连接线	2014年
江苏银晶光电科技发展有限公司	LED平板灯	2014年
常州市日新树脂有限公司	不饱和聚酯树脂	2014年
常州市华荣友佳纺织染整有限公司	色织牛仔布	2014年
常州市中迈源纺织机械有限公司	全闭环双针床电子贾卡经编机	2014年
常州市武进金宁纺织有限公司	牛仔布面料	2014年
常州市兰贵人纺织品有限公司	牛仔布面料	2014年
常州市佳友线盘有限公司	塑料线盘	2014年
常州科普动力机械有限公司	柴油发电机组	2014年
常州百佳薄膜科技有限公司	PVC-B面膜	2014年
常州市蓝托金属制品有限公司	飞机用坐具类零件	2014年
常州市常武欣摄石化配件有限公司	法　兰	2014年
江苏中友精密制管有限公司	冷拔精密焊接钢管	2014年
江苏宏亿钢管有限公司	精密无缝钢管	2014年
常州宏鹄焊接材料有限公司	碳钢药芯焊丝	2014年
常州优尼克包装有限公司	集装袋	2014年
常州市伟宇精密机械有限公司	塑料挤出平膜扁丝机组	2014年
常州科威天使环保科技有限公司	絮凝剂	2014年
常州强力先端电子材料有限公司	肟酯类高感度光引发剂	2014年
江海环保股份有限公司	水处理剂	2014年
常州盛德无缝钢管有限公司	高压锅炉用无缝钢管	2014年
冶建新材料股份有限公司	环保型无溶剂超长效防腐涂料	2014年
中安（常州）电气有限公司	油浸式非晶合金配电变压器	2014年
溧阳市裕达机械有限公司	饲料机械	2014年
江苏冠宇机械设备制造有限公司	带升降设备的立体车库	2014年
江苏东方印务有限公司	印刷品	2014年
江苏良友农牧机械有限公司	饲料机械	2014年
立诚包装有限公司	环保瓦楞纸板	2014年
江苏通达机械设备制造有限公司	双气垫带式输送机	2014年

2-17 续表 17 continued 17

企业名称 Name of Enterprises	产品名称 Product Name	颁布时间 Time of Release
江苏六和新能源设备科技有限公司	小型垂直轴风力发电设备	2014年
江苏鑫林钢铁有限公司	热轧带肋钢筋	2014年
溧阳市中兴环保机械有限公司	脉冲袋式除尘器	2014年
江苏恒祥石化工程有限公司	铸铁板式空气预热器	2014年
常州华利达服装集团有限公司	服　装	2014年
常州盛天传动件有限公司	链轮、链条等传动件	2014年
常州市拓源电气制造有限公司	低压成套开关设备和控制设备	2014年
常州源普液压设备有限公司	润滑站	2014年
常州老三集团有限公司	老三服饰	2014年
常州旭荣针织印染有限公司	针织面料	2014年
江苏默顿电气有限公司	电容补偿投切开关	2014年
常州亚玛顿股份有限公司	多功能高效减反增透光伏玻璃	2014年
常州亚美柯机械设备有限公司	单杠柴油机	2014年
冶建新材料股份有限公司	TH-2型硅酸锌车间底漆	2014年
江苏竹溪活性炭有限公司	活性炭	2014年
常州亚泰焊材有限公司	气体保护电弧焊用碳钢焊丝	2014年
江苏维多股份有限公司	阿斯巴甜	2014年
江苏联盟化学有限公司	PVC复合稳定剂	2014年
江苏山湖电缆有限公司	物理发泡同轴射频电缆	2014年
江苏苏阳电工机械有限公司	高速笼绞机	2014年
江苏通洋船舶有限公司	船、艇	2014年
常州市赛尔交通器材有限公司	轨道交通用前组合灯系列	2014年
江苏恒亮离心机制造有限公司	卧式螺旋卸料沉降离心机	2014年
江苏省巨变变压器有限公司	35KV及以下电力变压器	2014年
金坛市明日春花盆有限公司	实木复合花盆	2014年
江苏源力汽车内饰件有限公司	汽车内饰件	2014年
常州市华辉油泵油嘴厂	油泵、油嘴	2014年
常州金马炉业设备有限公司	锅炉链条炉排	2014年
常州液压成套设备厂有限公司	液压启闭机及接力器	2014年
江苏河马井股份有限公司（常州市河马塑胶有限公司）	塑料检查井	2014年
常州博万达汽车安全设备有限公司	BWD型汽车安全带	2014年

2-17 续表 18 continued 18

企业名称 Name of Enterprises	产品名称 Product Name	颁布时间 Time of Release
江苏福昌环保科技集团有限公司	免助燃有机化工废渣焚烧炉	2014年
江苏亚示照明集团有限公司	照明灯具	2014年
常州牛顿力称重系统有限公司	电子台秤	2014年
常州市武进电力管件有限公司	压力管件元件	2014年
常州市科能电器有限公司	SF6气体泄漏监控报警系统	2014年
常州腾龙汽车零部件股份有限公司	汽车空调用软管及软管组合件	2014年
普罗斯电器（中国）有限公司	高强度气体放电灯	2014年
常州信发汽车配件有限公司	电磁开关	2014年
常州康普药业有限公司	盐酸氯丙嗪片	2014年
常州市运河焊材有限公司	气体保护焊丝	2014年
中韩科技有限公司（原江苏德莱仕电器有限公司）	家用冷藏冷冻箱	2014年
常州乐士雷利电机有限公司	排水电机	2014年
江苏宇通干燥工程有限公司	干燥设备	2014年
常州腾跃不锈钢管有限公司	无缝不锈钢管	2014年
常州姚氏同德化工有限公司	水处理剂 有机膦酸盐	2014年
常州市金陵干燥设备有限公司	干燥设备	2014年
常州市武进洛阳新型保温材料厂	硬质聚氨酯泡沫	2014年
常州市武进红光无线电有限公司	电源适配器	2014年
常州佳辰地板集团有限公司	架空活动地板	2014年
常州市鼎鸿木业有限公司	浸渍纸层压木质地板	2014年
常州市武进骏宇汽配涂料有限公司	制动气室系列	2014年
常州市武进永达机械轴承有限公司	铆钉式长圆柱滚针轴承	2014年
江苏夏博士节能工程股份有限公司	太阳能热水器（平板型太阳能集热器）	2014年
常州绿地缘木业有限公司	浸渍纸层压木质地板	2014年
常州克迈特数控科技有限公司	数控加工中心	2014年
常州欧密格光电科技有限公司	LED发光二级管	2014年
新誉集团有限公司	轨道车辆用空调系统	2014年
江苏新瑞重工科技有限公司	V系列立式加工中心	2014年
江苏顺风光电科技有限公司	太阳能电池片	2014年
常州力安液压设备有限公司	大型液压油缸	2014年
常州市国宇环保科技有限公司	羧甲基纤维素钠	2014年

2-17 续表 19 continued 19

企业名称 Name of Enterprises	产品名称 Product Name	颁布时间 Time of Release
常州光辉生物科技有限公司	阿斯巴甜	2014年
常州通宝光电制造有限公司	车用LED模组及灯具	2014年
常州市思可达塑业有限公司	改性聚丙烯粒料	2014年
常州光洋轴承股份有限公司	汽车变速箱用同步器中间环	2014年
常州海克莱化学有限公司	（甲基）丙烯酸特种酯	2014年
常州协鑫光伏科技有限公司	太阳能电池用多晶硅片	2014年
常州市后肖宇虹铝幕墙制造有限公司	铝单板（氟碳）	2014年
江苏鸿响光学玻璃有限公司	非球面透镜	2014年
常州市联顺车辆配件厂	汽车内外饰塑料装饰件	2014年
常州大利节能新材料有限公司	玻璃微纤维深冷绝热材料	2014年
常州市东晨车辆部件有限公司	汽车安全带	2014年
常州天盛重工机械股份有限公司	挖掘机斗杆	2014年
常州市利凯车辆配件厂	带有可调节尾箱固定机构的电动自行车车架	2014年
常州环能涡轮动力股份有限公司	涡　轮	2014年
江苏华生塑业有限公司	PVC管材管件	2014年
常州捷佳创精密机械有限公司	多晶链式制绒设备	2014年
常州市天龙光电设备有限公司	铸造（锭）机	2014年
常州市欣欣制冷设备有限公司	家用电冰箱蒸发器	2014年
江苏大和新材料有限公司	包装材料	2014年
常州市赛嘉机械有限公司	智能控制整经机	2014年
常州五王电机有限公司	单相罩极电动机	2014年
常州雷利电机科技有限公司	排水泵用电动机	2014年
江苏天元工程机械有限公司	蒸压加气混凝土切割机	2014年
江苏德春电力科技有限公司	交流高压六氟化硫负荷开关	2014年
常州亨达车业部件有限公司	汽车后视镜（含广角后视镜）、汽车补盲外后视镜	2014年
常州市佳乐车辆配件制造有限公司	汽车空调系统壳体及金属支架	2014年
常州市明宇交通器材有限公司	汽车灯具	2014年
常州市飞拓模塑有限公司	汽车车灯	2014年
常州市厦科动力机械有限公司	高压清洗机	2014年
常州市丰宇五金工艺有限公司	丰宇牌网蓝	2014年
常州协发机械制造有限公司	高铁动力机壳	2014年

2-17 续表 20 continued 20

企业名称 Name of Enterprises	产品名称 Product Name	颁布时间 Time of Release
江苏恒鑫富奥汽车零部件有限公司	制动气室	2014年
常州生物医药孵化器有限公司	生物医药专业科技创业服务	2014年
常州迪诺恐龙谷温泉有限公司	景区温泉服务	2014年
常州航天信息有限公司	防伪税控系统及增值产品的销售和服务	2014年
武进区湖塘欧帝皇家副食品商行	红葡萄酒销售服务	2014年
常州德邦货运代理有限公司	物流零担货物运输	2014年
溧阳市天目湖蓓茗休闲山庄	休闲观光服务	2014年
江苏景尚旅业集团股份有限公司	旅游项目管理与服务	2014年
常州贝尔电梯工程有限公司	电梯安装维保服务	2014年
常州蓝城信息科技有限公司	智能视频分析系统	2014年
常州市汇菱电梯有限公司	电梯安装维保服务	2014年
常州市新怡华超市连锁有限公司	超市经营商贸服务	2014年
常州岳洋通商贸有限公司	钢铁贸易服务	2014年
常州钢材现货交易市场有限公司	钢材市场服务	2014年
常嘉建设集团有限公司	建筑相关服务	2014年
中国华电常州变压器工程技术中心有限公司	变压器技术培训服务	2014年
常州市天宁高新技术创业服务中心	科技创业孵化服务	2014年
常州市陈娟南方鱼府	餐饮服务	2014年
月星集团有限公司	家具销售服务	2014年
常州交服出租车有限公司	出租车服务	2014年
江苏省邮政公司常州分公司	邮政服务	2014年
常州政成物流有限公司	物流服务	2014年
常州产权交易所	产权交易、招投标服务	2014年
常州港华燃气有限公司	天然气供应与服务	2014年
常州丽华快餐集团有限公司	中式快餐（套餐）销售和服务	2014年

2-17 续表 21　continued 21

企业名称 Name of Enterprises	产品名称 Product Name	颁布时间 Time of Release
常州市传动输送机械有限公司	电动滚筒	2015年
智思控股集团有限公司	烟草加工机械	2015年
常州常矿起重机械有限公司	起重机	2015年
常州倍安特动力机械有限公司	风冷柴油机	2015年
常州市威德达耐火板有限公司	热固型树脂浸渍纸高压装饰层积板	2015年
常州市双进电子有限公司	印刷线路板	2015年
常州阿斯盾木业有限公司	浸渍纸层压木质地板	2015年
常州市武进中天机房设备有限公司	防静电活动地板	2015年
江苏金球链传动有限公司	链条	2015年
常州市福兴电器有限公司	节能灯、卤素灯、LED灯、JDD和玻璃罩	2015年
常州市科协减速机制造有限公司	摆线针轮减速机	2015年
江苏丰顺包装容器有限公司	铁桶	2015年
江苏聚荣制药集团有限公司	安神补脑液	2015年
常州市新星原制冷设备有限公司	组合冷库用隔热夹芯板	2015年
常州市新盛电器有限公司	射频同轴集束连接器	2015年
常州市武进恒通金属钢丝有限公司	铝包钢、铜包钢、钢丝系列、铝包钢丝护栏	2015年
常州金海防静电地板有限公司	PVC防静电地板	2015年
江苏安普特防爆科技有限公司	阻隔防爆撬装式汽车加油（气）装置	2015年
常州神龙管业有限公司	不锈钢焊管、钛焊管、钛合金焊管	2015年
常州市双马医疗器材有限公司	一次性实用输液器带针	2015年
常州普江不锈钢管有限公司	无缝不锈钢管	2015年
常州远东连杆集团有限公司	内燃机连杆	2015年
江苏武进液压启闭机有限公司	液压启闭机	2015年
常州市博聪儿童用品股份有限公司	机动车儿童成员用约束系统	2015年
常州液压成套设备厂有限公司	液压启闭机及接力器	2015年
上海振华重工（集团）常州油漆有限公司	氟碳面漆	2015年
常州市凯迪电器有限公司	升降电机	2015年
常州市晨晟木业有限公司	浸渍纸层压木质地板	2015年
常州埃姆基冷冻设备有限公司	钢制制冷阀门	2015年
江苏百博木业有限公司	浸渍纸层压木质地板	2015年
常州市腾田液压机械有限公司	精密液压冷拔机组	2015年

2-17 续表 22 continued 22

企业名称 Name of Enterprises	产品名称 Product Name	颁布时间 Time of Release
常州市武进洋泽织造有限公司	色织牛仔布	2015年
常州市润达照明电器有限公司	艺术庭院灯	2015年
常州市盈能电气有限公司	排水型电柜除湿机	2015年
常州胜威塑料有限公司	塑料包装容器	2015年
碳元科技股份有限公司	石墨烯导热膜	2015年
常州市新月成套冷藏设备有限公司	组合冷库用隔热夹芯板	2015年
常州煜明电子有限公司	高光、镜面、平板液晶、LED电视面框	2015年
常州南方盛达不锈钢制品有限公司	无缝不锈钢管	2015年
常州福伦特无铅焊料有限公司	高耐磨颗粒增强锡基巴氏合金焊丝	2015年
常州华岳电子有限公司	无极荧光灯	2015年
江苏海定工程机械有限公司	桥梁支座	2015年
江苏中宇电力器材有限公司	电力金具	2015年
金坛市金盛喷灌设备有限公司	涂塑软管	2015年
江苏蓝色星球环保科技股份有限公司	HFC-134a	2015年
江苏亚邦强生药业有限公司	头孢类口服固体制剂	2015年
江苏晨洋电缆有限公司	电线电缆	2015年
金坛市鸿图橡塑制品有限公司	O型橡胶密封圈	2015年
凡登（常州）新型金属材料技术有限公司	切割钢线	2015年
江苏力合粘合剂有限公司	聚氨酯粘合剂	2015年
江苏柚山建材有限公司	水泥	2015年
常州市利来密封件有限公司	旋转轴唇形密封圈	2015年
江苏金洋造船有限公司	内河钢质船舶	2015年
江苏立华生物肥料有限公司	有机肥料	2015年
金坛市金旺包装科技有限公司	全自动水平式袋装机	2015年
金坛市新华门窗装璜有限公司	建筑外窗	2015年
金坛市大地复合肥制造有限公司	复合肥	2015年
常州大利节能新材料有限公司	陶瓷纤维材料	2015年
常州常京化学有限公司	增粘树脂、补强树脂、粘合树脂	2015年
常州依梯凯动力机械有限公司	单缸风冷柴油机	2015年
常州市宏发纵横新材料科技股份有限公司	连续树脂基预浸料用多轴向经编增强复合材料	2015年
江苏沃尔夫机械有限公司	砂浆成套设备及配件	2015年

2-17 续表 23　continued 23

企业名称 Name of Enterprises	产品名称 Product Name	颁布时间 Time of Release
常州亚邦化学有限公司	顺酐、富马酸	2015年
常州华碧宝特种新材料有限公司	玻璃纤维壁布	2015年
常州世博乐克机械制造有限公司	玉米收割机用链轮	2015年
常州市正阳焊接材料有限公司	气体保护药芯焊丝	2015年
常州市第八纺织机械有限公司	经编机	2015年
常州八益电缆股份有限公司	核电站用1E级高性能电缆	2015年
常州九鼎车业有限公司	汽车灯具	2015年
常州市伟达科技有限公司	电动车车架	2015年
常州市正阳焊接材料有限公司	气体保护焊丝	2015年
常州普莱克红梅色母料有限公司	塑料色母料系列产品	2015年
常州联力自动化科技有限公司	矿用隔爆兼本质安全型真空组合开关	2015年
常州千红生化制药股份有限公司	胰激肽原酶	2015年
常州千红生化制药股份有限公司	肝素钠原料药及其制剂	2015年
常州有则科技有限公司	太阳能级硅片	2015年
特瑞斯能源装备股份有限公司	燃气调压装置	2015年
常州福兰德电器有限公司	温度控制器	2015年
常州汉森机械有限公司	拖拉机前置装载机	2015年
吟飞科技（江苏）有限公司	电子乐器	2015年
常州君合科技股份有限公司	太阳能硅片清洗剂	2015年
江苏华达化工集团有限公司	1-萘胺、1-萘酚系列产品	2015年
常茂生物化学工程股份有限公司	酒石酸、阿斯巴甜	2015年
常州市宏光机械有限公司	钣金件	2015年
江苏久信医疗科技股份有限公司	整体洁净数字化手术室系统	2015年
常州太平洋电力设备（集团）有限公司	高低压成套开关设备、高压真空断路器、电力变压器、箱式变电站	2015年
江苏维尔利环保科技股份有限公司	膜生化反应器加纳滤组合系统装备	2015年
常州东风轴承有限公司	自动变速箱用轴承	2015年
常州华生制药有限公司	奥氮平片	2015年
常州市申宏电力设备有限公司	高低压成套设备	2015年
常州常捷科技有限公司	金属化薄膜电容器	2015年
常州声泰龙电子音响有限公司	扬仕苹果时尚音响	2015年
江苏华冠电器集团有限公司	高低压开关设备	2015年

2-17 续表 24 continued 24

企业名称 Name of Enterprises	产品名称 Product Name	颁布时间 Time of Release
常州市永光车业有限公司	摩托车灯具	2015年
江苏浩峰汽车附件有限公司	汽车空调电机PWM控制模块	2015年
常州市五一灯具有限公司	汽车前组合灯	2015年
溧阳市凯瑞地毯制造有限公司	机织地毯	2015年
江苏国强镀锌实业有限公司	低压流体输送用焊接镀锌钢管	2015年
江苏司能润滑科技有限公司	润滑油	2015年
江苏富昌机械设备有限公司	埋刮板输送机	2015年
江苏富昌机械设备有限公司	皮带输送机	2015年
江苏富昌机械设备有限公司	斗式提升机	2015年
江苏中兴西田数控科技有限公司	伺服压力机	2015年
常州海大生物饲料有限公司	配合饲料	2015年
溧阳市精卫新型材料有限公司	液体水泥助磨剂	2015年
溧阳市新力机械铸造有限公司	高精度液压铸件	2015年
江苏通达机械设备制造有限公司	斗式提升机	2015年
江苏通达机械设备制造有限公司	埋刮板输送机	2015年
江苏国强镀锌实业有限公司	波形梁护栏	2015年
江苏国强镀锌实业有限公司	低压流体输送管道用螺旋缝埋弧钢管	2015年
江苏保龙机电制造有限公司	木材加工机械	2015年
溧阳康达威实业有限公司	硅橡胶	2015年
江苏威司顿印刷科技有限公司	预涂感光版	2015年
溧阳市虹翔机械制造有限公司	铸件产品	2015年
常州亚泰焊割科技有限公司	数控切割机	2015年
溧阳市濑江防火门有限公司	防火门	2015年
溧阳市天目助剂有限公司	工业甲醛溶液	2015年
溧阳市东晨服饰制伞有限公司	雨　具	2015年
常州宝丽丝纤维有限公司	纱　线	2015年
常州爱斯特空调设备有限公司	屋顶式空气调节机组	2015年
常州纺兴精密机械有限公司	喷丝板	2015年
江苏科信燃气设备有限公司	城镇燃气调压器	2015年
常州灵泰面料科技有限公司	弹力面料	2015年
常州众杰复合材料有限公司	玻璃纤维织物	2015年

2-17 续表 25　continued 25

企业名称 Name of Enterprises	产品名称 Product Name	颁布时间 Time of Release
常州市隆龙升经编机械有限公司	经编机、织机（机器）、纺织工业用机器、纺织机、织布机、电动织毯机、合成纤维设备等	2015年
常州制药厂有限公司	卡托普利系列、沙利度胺片、复方硫酸双肼屈嗪片	2015年
常州市同和纺织机械制造有限公司	集聚纺自动落纱细纱机系列	2015年
江苏凯隆电器有限公司	智能型万能式断路器	2015年
常州市新东方电缆有限公司	电线电缆	2015年
常州精研科技有限公司	笔记本金属扇叶 /BACH	2015年
常州华阳汽车附件有限公司	铝滑轨	2015年
江苏坚力电子科技股份有限公司	电源滤波器	2015年
常州鼎唐电机有限公司	电　机	2015年
常州明景智能科技有限公司	红外一体化智能高速云台摄像机	2015年
常州常松金属复合材料有限公司	金属复合板	2015年
常州格力博有限公司	新型节能环保园林机械	2015年
常州海川卓越密封材料有限公司	旋转轴唇形密封圈	2015年
江苏徕兹光电科技股份有限公司	手持式激光测距仪	2015年
江苏丽岛新材料股份有限公司	彩色功能型铝材	2015年
常州第二电子仪器有限公司	激光测距仪	2015年
常州正大面粉有限公司	小麦粉	2015年
江苏艺林园花木有限公司	樟树苗木	2015年
常州市科丰葡萄专业合作社	鲜食葡萄	2015年
常州市康惠保健品有限公司	肉制品	2015年
常州市祝庄园艺有限公司	凤梨花卉	2015年
常州市黄天荡螃蟹专业合作社	中华绒螯蟹	2015年
常州金英王生态农业有限公司	瓜果蔬菜	2015年
金坛市生态良种茶场	绿　茶	2015年
金坛市鑫园粉茶有限公司	超微绿茶粉	2015年
金坛市金土地有机稻米专业合作社	有机软米	2015年
常州市圣王果蔬有限公司	无花果	2015年
常州市高露达饮用水有限公司	纯净水、天然泉水、天然矿泉水	2015年
常州新区怡泰食品有限公司	固体饮料	2015年
江苏常州城北国家粮食储备库	大　米	2015年
溧阳市欣龙生态农业发展有限公司	白　茶	2015年

2-17 续表 26 continued 26

企业名称 Name of Enterprises	产品名称 Product Name	颁布时间 Time of Release
溧阳市天目湖羽韵茶场	白茶（绿茶）	2015年
溧阳市桂林茶场	绿茶（沙河桂茗）	2015年
溧阳市金山茶业有限公司	绿　茶	2015年
溧阳市天目湖满山跑绿壳蛋鸡散养场	绿壳鸡蛋	2015年
溧阳市太云白茶生态庄园	绿　茶	2015年
溧阳市天目湖环湖茶场	环湖翠柏	2015年
溧阳市天目湖小胖子腌制食品厂	腌腊肉制品	2015年
常州市鑫灿食品有限公司	糕　点	2015年
常州红谷粮食贸易有限公司	大　米	2015年
常州市阳光营养食品有限公司	阳光月饼	2015年
常州月兔调味食品有限公司	味精、鸡精、汤料	2015年
钟楼区永红蔡氏天香斋梨膏糖厂	梨膏糖	2015年
常州翔宇资源再生科技有限公司	电子废弃物的处理和再生利用（铜粉及铜米）	2015年
津通集团有限公司	津通国际工业园服务	2015年
常州市和平环卫服务有限公司	环卫服务	2015年
江苏海之客农业发展有限公司	农副产品销售	2015年
江苏盐道物流股份有限公司	物　流	2015年
常州黑牡丹置业有限公司	房地产	2015年
溧阳市天目湖南山竹海温泉度假有限公司	温泉服务	2015年
常州市青洋置业有限公司	新动力创业中心服务	2015年
常州通用自来水有限公司	自来水生产、供应及服务	2015年
常州龙澄污水处理厂	工业废水处理	2015年
江苏鑫洋装饰工程有限公司	建筑装饰装修服务	2015年
常州海誓山盟珠宝有限公司	纯银饰品销售	2015年
尤尼泰（常州）税务师事务所有限公司	涉税服务	2015年
江苏安迅电梯工程有限公司	电梯安装、维修保养	2015年

3

CHAPTER 3

行政区划 自然概况

ADMINISTRATIVE DIVISION AND NATURAL RESOURCES

常州统计年鉴

3 行政区划　自然概况
ADMINISTRATIVE DIVISION AND NATURAL RESOURCES

行政区划　自然概况

行政区划

常州市下辖溧阳市及金坛、武进、新北、天宁、钟楼五区。溧阳市下辖10镇、1个街道办事处、51个居民委员会（社区居委会）和175个村民委员会；金坛、武进、新北、天宁、钟楼区下辖24个街道办事处、26个镇，326个居民委员会（社区居委会）和473个村民委员会。

位　置

常州地处江苏省南部，沪宁线中段，属长江三角洲沿海经济开放区。位于北纬31° 09′至32° 04′，东经119° 08′至120° 12′之间，北倚长江天堑，南与安徽省交界，东濒太湖与无锡市相连，西与南京、镇江两市接壤。

常州水陆空交通便利。沪宁铁路、沪宁与宁杭高速公路、312国道、京杭大运河穿境而过。全市水网纵横交织，连江通海。长江常州港为一类口岸，常州民航站已开通至首尔、香港、北京、广州、大连、厦门、深圳、海口、西安等国内外20多个大中城市的航线。

地　势

常州地貌类型属高沙平原，山丘平圩兼有。南为天目山余脉，西为茅山山脉，北为宁镇山脉尾部，中部和东部为宽广的平原、圩区。境内地势西南略高，东北略低，高低相差1.5～2米左右。

面　积

常州市总面积4372平方公里，市区面积为2838平方公里。

河　流

常州境内河道纵横交织，湖塘星罗棋布。著名的有泊洮湖（长荡湖）、滆湖、太湖三大天然湖泊，并有沙河（天目湖）、大溪两大人工水库，贯通全境的京杭大运河更是支流密布，脉脉相连，形成江河相通，三湖相连的水系网络。

ADMINISTRATIVE DIVISION AND NATURAL RESOURCES

Administrative Division

Changzhou has under its jurisdiction Liyang County-city, Jintan District, 1 sub-districts,Wujin District, Xinbei District, Tianning District and Zhonglou District. Liyang County-city has under its jurisdiction 10 towns, 51 community committees and 175 village committees. Jintan District, Wujin District, Xinbei District, Tianning District and Zhonglou District have under their jurisdiction 24 sub-districts, 26 towns, 326 community committees and 473 village committees.

Location

Changzhou, located in the southeast of Jiangsu province and the central section of Shanghai-Nanjing railway, belongs to the coastal economic open zone. Between north latitude 31°09' to 32°04' and east longitude 119°08' to 120°12', bordering the great Yangtze River in the north, Anhui province in the south and facing Taihu Lake and Wuxi city in the east and neighboring Nanjing city, Zhenjiang city in the west.

Changzhou is easily accessed by water, land and air since it is traversed by railways and expressways, including Shanghai-Nanjing Railway, Shanghai-Nanjing expressway, Nanjing-Hangzhou Expressway, Yangtze Riverside Expressway, Wuxi-Yixing Expressway,Yangzhou-Liyang Expressway, National Highway 312 and Beijing-Hangzhou Grand Canal； Besides, it owns the crisscross network of waters, connecting Yangtze River and leading to the sea. Changzhou Port of the Yangtze River is listed as the state category-1 port; and Changzhou civil airport has scheduled flights to more than 20 large and medium size domestic and foreign cities, such as Seoul , Hongkong , Beijing, Guangzhou, Dalian, Xiamen, Shenzhen, Haikou and Xi’an, etc.

Topography

The relief type of Changzhou is combined with plain and hills and polders. It has Tianmu Mountain ranges in the south, Maoshan Mountain ranges in the west, Tailing edge of Ningzhen Mountain in the north, vast plain and polder in the central section and east. The terrain is relatively higher in southwest and relatively lower in the northeast with a difference of 1.5～2 meters.

Area

The total area of Changzhou is 4372sq.km,The urban area covers2838sq.km.

Rivers

The rivers cross the city in a crisscross pattern, and lakes spread all over the city like the stars in the sky and scattered like the pieces on a chessboard.There are three famous natural lakes, such as Taohu Lake （Changdang Lake）, Gehu Lake, Taihu Lake and two artificial reservoirs, namely, Shahe （Tianmu）, Daxi reservoirs. The Beijing-Hangzhou Grand Canal goes through the city properly with many branches interlinked with rivers, which forms the water system network of canal, rivers interlinked and three lakes connected.

3-1 行政区划（1983-2015 年）
ADMINISTRATIVE DIVISION（1983-2015）

单位：个（unit）

年 份 Year	街道办事处 Urban Subdistrict Office	居民委员会（社区居委会） Neighborhhood Committee（Community Committee）	镇人民政府 Town Governments	乡人民政府 Township Governments	村民委员会 Villagers Committee
1983	18	236	7	136	1868
1984	18	265	7	136	1886
1985	19	288	16	125	1914
1986	18	303	16	125	1922
1987	18	329	22	119	1918
1988	19	336	35	106	1922
1989	18	339	39	102	1969
1990	18	363	39	102	1920
1991	18	375	48	93	1919
1992	18	388	49	88	1913
1993	20	414	65	72	1913
1994	19	429	71	66	1915
1995	18	450	74	63	1908
1996	18	460	81	56	1907
1997	19	471	81	56	1903
1998	19	482	81	55	1902
1999	20	505	70	9	1900
2000	23	344	70	9	1888
2001	25	336	70	9	1104
2002	22	339	70	9	1103
2003	27	273	65		1085
2004	27	273	65		1092
2005	24	293	64		1092
2006	16	289	64		1092
2007	20	291	37		1078
2008	20	304	37		1073
2009	21	292	37		940
2010	21	323	37		807
2011	21	359	37		782
2012	21	354	37		777
2013	21	377	37		650
2014	21	377	37		650
2015	25	377	36		648

3-2　行政区划和土地面积（2015 年底）
ADMINISTRATIVE DIVISION AND LAND AREA（END OF 2015）

单位：个（unit）

地　区	Region	镇 Town	村民委员会 Villagers Committee	街　道 Subdistrict	居民委员会（社区居委会） Neighborhood Committee（Community Committee）	土地面积（平方公里） Area of Land（sq.km）
全　市	**Whole Municipality**	**36**	**648**	**25**	**377**	**4372.15**
市　区	**Urban Area**	**26**	**473**	**24**	**326**	**2837.63**
金坛区	Jintan District	6	98	3	22	975.68
武进区	Wujin District	11	197	5	119	1065.27
新北区	Xinbei District	7	60	3	65	508.91
天宁区	Tianning District	1	60	6	68	154.84
钟楼区	Zhonglou District	1	58	7	52	132.93
县级市	**Cities at Country Level**	**10**	**175**	**1**	**51**	**1534.52**
溧阳市	Liyang City	10	175	1	51	1534.52

3-3 分地区镇、街道数及名称（2015 年底）
NUMBER AND NAME OF SUBDISTRICT AND TOWN BY REGION（END OF 2015）

单位：个（unit）

指 标	Item	镇、街道数 Number of Subdistricts and Towns	镇、街道名称 Names of Subdistricts and Towns
总 计	**Total**	**61**	
街 道	**Subdistrict**	**25**	
按地区分	By Region		
市 区	Urban Area	24	
金坛区	Jintan Distric	3	尧塘、西城、东城
武进区	Wujin District	5	南夏墅、西湖、丁堰、戚墅堰、潞城
新北区	Xinbei Distric	3	河海、三井、龙虎塘
天宁区	Tianning District	6	天宁、兰陵、茶山、雕庄、红梅、青龙
钟楼区	Zhonglou District	7	南大街、荷花池、新闸、五星、永红、北港、西林
溧阳市	Liyang City	1	昆仑
镇	**Town**	**36**	
按地区分	By Region		
市 区	Urban Area	26	
金坛区	Jintan City	6	金城、薛埠、直溪、儒林、朱林、指前
武进区	Wujin District	11	湖塘、前黄、洛阳、遥观、横林、横山桥、牛塘、嘉泽、湟里、雪堰、礼嘉
新北区	Xinbei District	7	春江、新桥、孟河、西夏墅、薛家、罗溪、奔牛
天宁区	Tianning District	1	郑陆
钟楼区	Zhonglou District	1	邹区
溧阳市	Liyang City	10	溧城、社渚 、南渡、上兴、别桥、上黄、竹箦、戴埠、埭头、天目湖

4

CHAPTER 4

常州统计年鉴

综　合

GENERAL SURVEY

4 综　合
GENERAL SURVEY

从统计数字看 2015 年的常州
CHANGZHOU IN STATISTICS OF 2015

一、常州的人口

POPULATION OF CHANGZHOU

年末常住人口	Permanent Population at Year-end	470.14 万人	(10000 persons)
# 城镇人口	Urban Population	329.10 万人	(10000 persons)
人口密度	Density of population	1075 人 / 平方公里	(person/sq.km)

二、常州在全省的地位

POSITION OF CHANGZHOU IN JIANGSU PROVINCE

地区生产总值	Gross Domestic Product	居全省第 6 位	No.6 in Jiangsu
人均地区生产总值	Per Capita GDP	居全省第 4 位	No.4 in Jiangsu
一般公共预算收入	General Public Budgetary Revenue	居全省第 7 位	No.7 in Jiangsu
固定资产投资完成额	Realized Investment in Fixed Assets	居全省第 6 位	No.6 in Jiangsu
社会消费品零售总额	Total Retail Sales of Consumer Goods	居全省第 6 位	No.6 in Jiangsu
进出口总额	Total Imports and Exports	居全省第 5 位	No.5 in Jiangsu
# 出　口	Exports	居全省第 5 位	No.5 in Jiangsu
全体居民人均可支配收入	Per Capita Disposable Income of All Residents	居全省第 4 位	No.4 in Jiangsu

三、常州市区的市政建设和公用事业

URBAN CONSTRUCTION AND PUBLIC UTILITIES OF CHANGZHOU

年末建成区面积	Total Area of the Constructed Regions at Year-end	250.31 平方公里	(sq.km)
年末城市道路长度	Length of Roads at Year-end	2444 公里	(km)
年末城市道路面积	Area of Roads at Year-end	4432 万平方米	(10000 sq.m)
年末城市桥梁数	Number of Bridges in Urban Area at Year-end	1222 座	(unit)
公共汽车客运总数	Total Volume of Passengers Traffic by Public Buses	34054 万人次	(10000 person-times)
年末供水综合生产能力	Production Capacity of Water Supply at Year-end	172.0 万吨 / 日	(10000 tons/day)
生活用水量	Water for Livelihood	15009 万立方米	(10000 m3)
年末家庭燃气用户数	Number of Consumer of Gas and LPG at Year-end	63.21 万户	(10000 household)
燃气普及率	Percentage of Population with Access to Gas and LGP	100.0%	
年末城市园林绿地面积	Total Area of Parks,Gardens and Green Area in City at Year-end	10768 公顷	(hectare)
建城区绿化覆盖率	Coverage Rate of Green Area in the Constructed Area	43.1%	

四、常州的经济

ECONOMIC OF CHANGZHOU

	2015年实绩 Achievements in 2015	人均水平 Per Capita	日均水平 Per Dialy
地区生产总值 Gross Domestic Produc	5273.15亿元 （100 million yuan）	112221元 （yuan）	144470万元 （10000 yuan）
# 第三产业 Tertiary Industry	2610.56亿元 （100 million yuan）	55554元 （yuan）	71519万元 （10000 yuan）
农林牧渔业总产值 Total Output Value of Farming,forestry,Animal Husbandry and Fishing	271.76亿元 （100 million yuan）	5783元 （yuan）	7445万元 （10000 yuan）
# 农　业 Agriculture	147.24亿元 （100 million yuan）	3133元 （yuan）	4034万元 （10000 yuan）
规模以上工业总产值 Gross Output Value of Industrial Enterprises above Designated Size	11101.64亿元 （100 million yuan）	236260元 （yuan）	304155万元 （10000 yuan）
社会消费品零售总额 Total Retail Sales of Consumer Goods	1990.45亿元 （100 million yuan）	42360元 （yuan）	54533万元 （10000 yuan）
进出口总额 Total Imports and Exports	280.46亿美元 （USD 100 million）	5969美元 （USD）	7684万美元 （USD 10000）
# 出　口 Exports	212.58亿美元 （USD 100 million）	4524美元 （USD）	5824万美元 （USD 10000）
实际到帐注册外资 Foreign Capital Actually Utilized	24.87亿美元 （USD 100 million）	529美元 （USD）	681万美元 （USD 10000）
固定资产投资额 Realized Investment in Fixed Assets	3398.97亿元 （100 million yuan）	72335元 （yuan）	93122万元 （10000 yuan）
房地产开发企业竣工住宅建筑面积 Completed Housing Area by Real Estate Development Enterrpises	766.65万平方米 （10000 sq.m）	1.63平方米 （sq.m）	21004平方米 （sq.m）
财政收入 Financial Revenue	1367.54亿元 （100 million yuan）	2910元 （yuan）	37467万元 （10000 yuan）
#一般公共预算收入 General Public Budgetary Revenue	466.28亿元 （100 million yuan）	9923元 （yuan）	12775万元 （10000 yuan）
邮电业务收入 Revenue from Post & Telecommunication Services	78.66亿元 （100 million yuan）	1674元 （yuan）	2155万元 （10000 yuan）
全社会用电量 Total Electricity Consumed	408.04亿千瓦时 （100 million kw.h）	8684千瓦时 （kw.h）	11179万千瓦时 （10000 kw.h）
#工业用电量 Industrial Electricity Consumption	325.49亿千瓦时 （100 million kw.h）	6927千瓦时 （kw.h）	8918万千瓦时 （10000 kw.h）

注：本表人均指标按常住人口计算。
Note: The per capita indicators in this table are calculated by the resident population .

4-1 历年地区生产总值
GROSS DOMESTIC PRODUCT OVER THE YEARS

单位：万元（10000 yuan）

年 份 Year	地区生产总值 Gross Domestic Product	其中 of which 工 业 Industry	建筑业 Construction	按产业分 Grouped by Industries 第一产业 Primary Industry	第二产业 Secondary Industry	第三产业 Tertiary Industry
1949	24979	3129	64	17434	3193	4352
1950	28470	4339	124	18951	4463	5056
1951	31080	5114	196	19497	5310	6273
1952	34493	5980	640	21086	6620	6787
1953	38228	7865	466	21944	8331	7953
1954	37536	7978	504	20704	8482	8350
1955	37985	6959	580	21262	7539	9184
1956	42016	8849	864	21606	9713	10697
1957	41120	10565	845	20269	11410	9441
1958	50377	17632	1652	20110	19284	10983
1959	53880	22848	1730	16766	24578	12536
1960	62495	26005	1676	18720	27681	16094
1961	45580	16001	741	16215	16742	12623
1962	46409	14311	779	19128	15090	12191
1963	49362	14513	905	22345	15418	11599
1964	53181	16711	967	24631	17678	10872
1965	62909	20524	1025	29268	21549	12092
1966	68993	24176	1119	31178	25295	12520
1967	63602	19306	1099	30983	20405	12214
1968	62681	21798	1098	27946	22896	11839
1969	71965	28420	1220	29154	29640	13171
1970	81090	37189	1977	27892	39166	14032
1971	96559	45761	2401	33300	48162	15097
1972	108835	53487	3248	33843	56735	18257
1973	122521	63108	4483	35367	67591	19563
1974	125285	66170	4133	35160	70303	19822
1975	131084	74137	4177	30945	78314	21825
1976	144282	81957	4680	35323	86637	22322
1977	154405	94311	5273	30472	99584	24349
1978	175707	105407	7061	38525	112468	24714
1979	201753	112412	10069	49760	122481	29512
1980	227642	133235	9494	48897	142729	36016
1981	247378	147001	11128	51946	158129	37303
1982	260487	147281	13188	62795	160469	37223

4-1 续表 continued　　　　单位：万元（10000 yuan）

年 份 Year	地区生产总值 Gross Domestic Product	其中 of which		按产业分 Grouped by Industries		
		工 业 Industry	建筑业 Construction	第一产业 Primary Industry	第二产业 Secondary Industry	第三产业 Tertiary Industry
1983	298476	166110	14052	70682	180162	47632
1984	387700	203098	15810	97530	218908	71262
1985	495896	280504	24307	105195	304811	85890
1986	547374	297125	30914	117724	328039	101611
1987	664549	376766	35493	125279	412259	127011
1988	821138	461754	44232	153477	505986	161675
1989	872397	483264	38403	165070	521667	185660
1990	948687	540600	39010	176805	579610	192272
1991	1021751	610693	45427	160573	656120	205058
1992	1443961	859302	70666	190338	929968	323655
1993	2238962	1366806	114855	250531	1481661	506770
1994	3149332	1861541	147619	338176	2009160	801996
1995	3697000	2028562	177858	398160	2206420	1092420
1996	4311541	2236314	228743	455496	2465057	1390988
1997	4701069	2400789	257378	443684	2658167	1599218
1998	5045974	2526923	283356	444352	2810279	1791343
1999	5387217	2689386	305633	440113	2995019	1952085
2000	6006573	3019891	346956	451378	3366847	2188348
2001	6729008	3416841	390760	471137	3807601	2450270
2002	7606035	3877933	437108	488378	4315041	2802616
2003	9014200	4689100	513400	471800	5202500	3339900
2004	11021900	5929600	689000	541900	6618600	3861400
2005	13081800	7199500	791000	596200	7990500	4495100
2006	15851100	8750400	794100	660700	9544500	5645900
2007	19135000	10476100	875200	743200	11351300	7040500
2008	22663200	12094000	1076500	845000	13170500	8647700
2009	25199300	13016300	1281000	917500	14297300	9984500
2010	30448900	15308600	1528200	997800	16836800	12614300
2011	35809900	17689100	1819300	1117800	19508400	15183700
2012	39698700	19005500	2002100	1263700	21007600	17427400
2013	44500000	20529200	2206100	1303300	22734100	20462600
2014	49018700	21701900	2384800	1384600	24081100	23553000
2015	52731500	22699900	2467500	1465500	25160400	26105600

注：1、2000-2003年数据根据第一次经济普查结果进行了调整，2005-2007年数据根据第二次经济普查结果进行了调整，2013年数据根据第三次经济普查结果进行了调整。
2、2013年起，根据国家统计局有关规定：第三产业中增加农林牧渔服务业、开采铺助活动、金属制品、机械和设备修理业。

Note: 1、The data collected during 2000-2003 were adjusted according to the record of the first Economic Census; and the data collected during 2005-2007 were adjusted according to the record of the second Economic Census.
2、In accordance with relevant regulations of National Bureau of Statistics, service industry for farming, forestry, animal husbandary and fishery, auxiliary activity for mining as well as repairment for metal works, machinery and equipment shall be added to the tertiary industry from Year 2013.

4-2 地区生产总值指数（1978-2015 年，上年 =100）
GROSS DOMESTIC PRODUCT INDEX NUMBER （1978-2015，PRECEDING YEAR=100）

按可比价格计算　　Calculated by comparable price

年 份 Year	地区生产总值 Gross Domestic Product	其中 of which 工 业 Industry	按产业分 Grouped by Industries 第一产业 Primary Industry	第二产业 Secondary Industry	第三产业 Tertiary Industry	人均地区生产总值 Per Capita Gross Domestic Product
1978	100.0	100.0	100.0	100.0	100.0	100.0
1979	108.6	106.2	104.4	108.0	117.9	107.8
1980	112.2	118.1	97.4	116.4	115.2	111.3
1981	108.5	110.9	103.2	111.3	102.2	107.6
1982	104.1	101.8	113.5	102.9	98.9	103.1
1983	114.8	114.4	108.4	113.9	127.8	113.8
1984	126.6	121.4	131.0	120.7	146.0	125.7
1985	122.8	132.4	97.9	133.7	110.1	122.2
1986	105.9	103.8	103.2	105.4	110.5	105.2
1987	116.3	122.1	96.0	121.1	114.3	115.1
1988	110.6	113.6	99.7	113.9	104.1	109.3
1989	94.7	94.0	102.9	92.8	98.3	93.5
1990	107.9	111.6	98.8	110.8	101.3	106.5
1991	107.3	114.9	88.8	114.6	102.2	106.4
1992	134.8	136.4	107.9	136.5	150.6	134.0
1993	133.9	139.5	110.1	137.8	135.6	133.4
1994	116.6	112.7	114.2	112.3	130.2	116.1
1995	113.6	113.1	109.6	113.1	116.5	112.8
1996	110.8	108.8	105.6	109.6	116.0	109.8
1997	109.1	108.3	101.3	108.5	113.1	108.2
1998	110.8	111.4	100.0	111.3	112.8	110.3
1999	110.2	110.7	104.6	110.6	110.6	110.1
2000	111.0	111.3	104.3	111.3	112.1	110.9
2001	112.0	113.1	105.7	112.9	112.0	111.7
2002	112.4	113.5	105.2	113.4	112.3	112.1
2003	114.5	117.3	102.4	116.5	113.3	113.7
2004	115.5	118.1	102.7	117.6	114.1	114.6
2005	115.1	116.5	105.0	116.3	114.8	113.6
2006	115.2	117.6	105.0	115.8	115.5	112.0
2007	115.6	117.3	103.5	116.2	116.0	112.6
2008	112.4	112.6	103.8	112.1	113.7	110.4
2009	111.7	110.4	104.7	110.8	114.1	110.5
2010	113.1	113.3	104.3	113.2	113.6	110.7
2011	112.2	112.6	103.9	112.2	112.8	109.8
2012	111.5	111.7	104.7	111.7	111.6	110.4
2013	110.9	111.6	102.8	111.2	111.2	110.4
2014	110.1	109.8	103.0	109.5	111.5	110.0
2015	109.2	108.3	103.1	108.5	110.6	109.1

4-3　地区生产总值指数（1978-2015 年，1978 年 =100）
GROSS DOMESTIC PRODUCT INDEX NUMBER（1978-2015，1978=100）

按可比价格计算　　Calculated by comparable price

年　份 Year	地区生产总值 Gross Domestic Product	其中 of which 工　业 Industry	按产业分 Grouped by Industries 第一产业 Primary Industry	第二产业 Secondary Industry	第三产业 Tertiary Industry	人均地区生产总值 Per Capita Gross Domestic Product
1978	100.0	100.0	100.0	100.0	100.0	100.0
1979	108.6	106.2	104.4	108.0	117.9	107.8
1980	121.8	125.4	101.7	125.7	135.8	120.0
1981	132.1	139.1	105.0	139.9	138.8	129.1
1982	137.5	141.6	119.2	144.0	137.3	133.1
1983	157.8	162.0	129.2	164.0	175.5	151.5
1984	199.7	196.7	169.2	197.9	256.2	190.4
1985	245.2	260.4	165.6	264.6	282.1	232.7
1986	259.7	270.3	170.9	278.9	311.7	244.8
1987	302.0	330.0	164.1	337.8	356.2	281.7
1988	334.0	374.9	163.6	384.7	370.9	307.9
1989	316.3	352.4	168.3	357.0	364.5	287.9
1990	341.3	393.3	166.3	395.6	369.3	306.6
1991	366.2	451.9	147.7	453.4	377.4	326.2
1992	493.7	616.4	159.4	618.8	568.4	437.2
1993	661.0	859.9	175.5	852.8	770.8	583.2
1994	770.7	969.1	200.4	957.6	1003.5	677.1
1995	875.6	1096.0	219.6	1083.1	1169.1	763.7
1996	970.1	1192.5	231.9	1187.1	1356.2	838.6
1997	1058.4	1291.5	234.9	1288.0	1533.9	907.4
1998	1172.7	1438.7	234.9	1433.5	1730.2	1000.8
1999	1292.3	1592.6	245.7	1585.5	1913.6	1101.9
2000	1434.5	1772.6	256.3	1764.7	2145.1	1222.0
2001	1606.6	2004.8	270.9	1992.3	2402.5	1365.0
2002	1805.8	2275.4	285.0	2259.3	2698.0	1530.2
2003	2067.6	2669.0	291.8	2632.1	3056.8	1739.8
2004	2388.1	3152.1	299.7	3095.3	3487.8	1993.8
2005	2748.7	3672.2	314.7	3599.8	4004.0	2265.0
2006	3166.5	4318.5	330.4	4168.6	4624.6	2536.8
2007	3660.5	5065.6	342.0	4843.9	5364.5	2856.4
2008	4114.4	5703.9	355.0	5430.0	6099.4	3153.5
2009	4595.8	6297.1	371.7	6016.4	6959.5	3484.6
2010	5197.8	7134.6	387.7	6810.6	7905.9	3857.5
2011	5832.0	8033.5	402.8	7641.5	8917.9	4235.5
2012	6502.7	8973.5	421.7	8535.6	9952.4	4676.0
2013	7211.5	10014.4	433.5	9487.8	11067.0	5162.3
2014	7939.8	10995.8	446.5	10389.1	12339.8	5678.5
2015	8670.3	11908.4	460.4	11272.2	13647.8	6195.2

4-4 历年地区生产总值构成
PROPORTIONS IN GROSS DOMESTIC PRODUCT OVER THE YEARS

单位：%

年 份 Year	地区生产总值 Gross Domestic Product	其中 of which 工业 Industry	其中 of which 建筑业 Construction	按产业分 Grouped by Industries 第一产业 Primary Industry	按产业分 Grouped by Industries 第二产业 Secondary Industry	按产业分 Grouped by Industries 第三产业 Tertiary Industry
1949	100	12.5	0.3	69.8	12.8	17.4
1950	100	15.2	0.4	66.6	15.7	17.8
1951	100	16.5	0.6	62.7	17.1	20.2
1952	100	17.3	1.9	61.1	19.2	19.7
1953	100	20.6	1.2	57.4	21.8	20.8
1954	100	21.3	1.3	55.2	22.6	22.2
1955	100	18.3	1.5	56.0	19.8	24.2
1956	100	21.1	2.1	51.4	23.1	25.5
1957	100	25.7	2.1	49.3	27.7	23.0
1958	100	35.0	3.3	39.9	38.3	21.8
1959	100	42.4	3.2	31.1	45.6	23.3
1960	100	41.6	2.7	30.0	44.3	25.8
1961	100	35.1	1.6	35.6	36.7	27.7
1962	100	30.8	1.7	41.2	32.5	26.3
1963	100	29.4	1.8	45.3	31.2	23.5
1964	100	31.4	1.8	46.3	33.2	20.4
1965	100	32.6	1.6	46.5	34.3	19.2
1966	100	35.0	1.6	45.2	36.7	18.1
1967	100	30.4	1.7	48.7	32.1	19.2
1968	100	34.8	1.8	44.6	36.5	18.9
1969	100	39.5	1.7	40.5	41.2	18.3
1970	100	45.9	2.4	34.4	48.3	17.3
1971	100	47.4	2.5	34.5	49.9	15.6
1972	100	49.1	3.0	31.1	52.1	16.8
1973	100	51.5	3.7	28.9	55.2	16.0
1974	100	52.8	3.3	28.1	56.1	15.8
1975	100	56.6	3.2	23.6	59.7	16.6
1976	100	56.8	3.2	24.5	60.0	15.5
1977	100	61.1	3.4	19.7	64.5	15.8
1978	100	60.0	4.0	21.9	64.0	14.1
1979	100	55.7	5.0	24.7	60.7	14.6
1980	100	58.5	4.2	21.5	62.7	15.8
1981	100	59.4	4.5	21.0	63.9	15.1
1982	100	56.5	5.1	24.1	61.6	14.3

4-4 续表 continued　　　　单位：%

年 份 Year	地区生产总值 Gross Domestic Product	其 中 of which 工 业 Industry	建筑业 Construction	按产业分 Grouped by Industries 第一产业 Primary Industry	第二产业 Secondary Industry	第三产业 Tertiary Industry
1983	100	55.7	4.7	23.7	60.4	16.0
1984	100	52.4	4.1	25.2	56.5	18.4
1985	100	56.6	4.9	21.2	61.5	17.3
1986	100	54.3	5.6	21.5	59.9	18.6
1987	100	56.7	5.3	18.9	62.0	19.1
1988	100	56.2	5.4	18.7	61.6	19.7
1989	100	55.4	4.4	18.9	59.8	21.3
1990	100	57.0	4.1	18.6	61.1	20.3
1991	100	59.8	4.4	15.7	64.2	20.1
1992	100	59.5	4.9	13.2	64.4	22.4
1993	100	61.0	5.1	11.2	66.2	22.6
1994	100	59.1	4.7	10.7	63.8	25.5
1995	100	54.9	4.8	10.8	59.7	29.5
1996	100	51.9	5.3	10.6	57.2	32.3
1997	100	51.1	5.5	9.4	56.5	34.0
1998	100	50.1	5.6	8.8	55.7	35.5
1999	100	49.9	5.7	8.2	55.6	36.2
2000	100	50.3	5.8	7.5	56.1	36.4
2001	100	50.8	5.8	7.0	56.6	36.4
2002	100	51.0	5.8	6.4	56.8	36.8
2003	100	52.0	5.7	5.2	57.7	37.1
2004	100	53.8	6.3	4.9	60.1	35.0
2005	100	55.0	6.0	4.6	61.0	34.4
2006	100	55.2	5.0	4.2	60.2	35.6
2007	100	54.7	4.6	3.9	59.3	36.8
2008	100	53.4	4.7	3.7	58.1	38.2
2009	100	51.7	5.1	3.6	56.8	39.6
2010	100	50.3	5.0	3.3	55.3	41.4
2011	100	49.4	5.1	3.1	54.5	42.4
2012	100	47.9	5.0	3.2	52.9	43.9
2013	100	46.1	5.0	2.9	51.1	46.0
2014	100	44.3	4.9	2.8	49.2	48.0
2015	100	43.0	4.7	2.8	47.7	49.5

注：1、2000-2003年数据根据第一次经济普查结果进行了调整，2005-2007年数据根据第二次经济普查结果进行了调整，2013年数据根据第三次经济普查结果进行了调整。
2、2013年起，根据国家统计局有关规定：第三产业中增加农林牧渔服务业、开采辅助活动、金属制品、机械和设备修理业。

Note: 1、The data collected during 2000-2003 were adjusted according to the record of the first Economic Census; and the data collected during 2005-2007 were adjusted according to the record of the second Economic Census.
2、In accordance with relevant regulations of National Bureau of Statistics, service industry for farming, forestry, animal husbandary and fishery, auxiliary activity for mining as well as repairment for metal works, machinery and equipment shall be added to the tertiary industry from Year 2013.

4-5 历年分地区人均生产总值
PER CAPITA OF GROSS DOMESTIC PRODUCT BY REGION OVER THE YEARS

单位：元（yuan）

年份 Year	全市 Whole Municipality	市区 Urban Area	溧阳市 Liyang City	年份 Year	全市 Whole Municipality	市区 Urban Area	溧阳市 Liyang City
1949	144	183	73	1983	985	1276	518
1950	163	208	89	1984	1272	1615	748
1951	174	223	98	1985	1620	2101	901
1952	190	238	117	1986	1775	2271	1007
1953	206	262	114	1987	2134	2722	1231
1954	198	252	112	1988	2606	3225	1597
1955	196	249	115	1989	2732	3404	1618
1956	213	279	118	1990	2935	3709	1662
1957	205	264	119	1991	3136	4000	1740
1958	243	321	135	1992	4404	5568	2499
1959	253	342	128	1993	6806	8569	4075
1960	291	400	123	1994	9532	11714	6121
1961	211	289	80	1995	11117	13870	7912
1962	212	285	90	1996	12847	15369	9294
1963	219	283	120	1997	13892	16204	8174
1964	229	290	126	1998	14842	16962	8869
1965	264	343	139	1999	15834	18323	9431
1966	283	373	140	2000	17635	20744	10344
1967	256	323	143	2001	19704	23370	11563
1968	247	327	124	2002	22215	26744	13005
1969	279	375	133	2003	26149	31920	15415
1970	308	429	126	2004	31665	38601	18968
1971	358	485	198	2005	32116	34874	24456
1972	397	529	245	2006	37809	40574	29658
1973	441	583	264	2007	44452	46994	36039
1974	445	604	239	2008	51746	53788	43186
1975	462	645	221	2009	56890	60756	48488
1976	504	696	261	2010	67327	71812	56784
1977	535	739	273	2011	77485	81897	66934
1978	605	810	309	2012	85039	90107	73768
1979	689	914	334	2013	94895	99368	85538
1980	771	1000	405	2014	104423	110921	94224
1981	832	1088	432	2015	112221	115494	97055
1982	867	1120	454				

注： 1.2005年起人均地区生产总值按常住人口计算。
2.2000-2003年数据根据第一次经济普查结果进行了调整，2005-2007年数据根据第二次经济普查结果进行了调整，2013年数据根据第三次经济普查结果进行了调整。

Note: 1.Per capita regional GDP is calculated as per permanent population since 2005.
2.The data collected during 2000-2003 were adjusted according to the record of the first Economic Census; and the data collected during2005-2007 were adjusted according to the record of the second Economic Census.

4-6 分地区生产总值（2015年）
GROSS DOMESTIC PRODUCT BY REGION（2015）

单位：亿元（100 million yuan）

指 标	Item	全 市 Whole Municipality	其中 of which 市 区 Urban Area
地区生产总值	**Gross Domestic Product**	**5273.15**	**4548.57**
按产业分	**Grouped by Industries**		
第一产业	Primary Industry	146.55	100.22
第二产业	Secondary Industry	2516.04	2162.16
第三产业	Tertiary Industry	2610.56	2286.19
按国民经济行业分	**Grouped by Sector**		
农林牧渔业	Farming,Forestry,Animal Husbandry and Fishery	155.97	107.51
工 业	Industry	2269.99	1971.60
建筑业	Construction	246.75	191.26
交通运输、仓储业和邮政业	Transportation , Storage and Post	194.01	166.46
信息传输、软件和信息技术服务业	Information Transmission, Software and IT Services Industry	107.34	92.67
批发和零售业	Retail and Wholesale Industries	735.40	612.95
住宿和餐饮业	Accommodation and Catering Services	130.07	115.48
金融业	Financial	299.48	263.38
货币金融服务	Monetary and financial services	236.85	207.39
资本市场服务及其他金融业	Capital market services and other financial industries	49.22	43.09
保险业	Insurance	13.41	12.90
房地产业	Real Estate	269.11	237.51
房地产开发经营业	Real Estate Development Industry	145.38	136.30
物业管理、中介服务业和其他房地产	Property Management, Agency Service Industry and Other Real Estate	24.74	19.52
自有房地产经营活动	Business operation of self-owned assets	98.99	81.69
租赁和商务服务业	Leasehold and Business in Services	274.47	246.46
科学研究和技术服务业	Scientific Researches and Technical Services	66.64	62.27
水利、环境和公共设施管理业	Water Conservancy, Environment and Public Facility Management	81.26	75.93
居民服务、修理和其他服务业	Residential Services, Repairing and other Services Industry	99.32	88.22
教 育	Education	99.91	93.34
卫生和社会工作	Health, Social Work	47.67	44.53
文化、体育和娱乐业	Culture, Sports and Entertainment	84.41	74.96
公共管理、社会保障和社会组织	Public Administration， Social Security and Social Organizations	111.35	104.04

4-7 地区生产总值收入法构成项目（2015 年）
INCOM APPROACH COMPONENT OF GROSS REGIONAL PRODUCT（2015）

单位:亿元 （100 million yuan）

指 标	Item	全 市 Whole Municipality	其中 of which 市 区 Urban Area
地区生产总值	**Gross Domestic Product**	**5273.15**	**4548.57**
劳动者报酬	Compensation of Employees	1912.60	1645.66
生产税净额	Net Taxex on Production	905.28	787.27
固定资产折旧	Depreciation of Fixed Assets	837.91	731.09
营业盈余	Operating Surplus	1617.36	1384.55

4-8 按支出法计算的地区生产总值（2015）
GROSS DOMESTIC PRODUCT BY EXPENDITURE APPROACH（2015）

单位:亿元 （100 million yuan）

指 标	Item	全 市 Whole Municipality	其中 of which 市 区 Urban Area
地区生产总值	**Gross Domestic Product**	**5273.15**	**4548.57**
最终消费	**Final Consumption**	**2076.72**	**1788.28**
居民消费	Resident Consumption	1687.41	1446.29
农村居民	Village Residents	1330.47	1126.10
城镇居民	Urban Residents	356.94	320.19
政府消费	Government Consumption	389.31	341.99
资本形成总额	**Total Capital**	**2919.85**	**2567.80**
固定资本形成总额	Fixed Capital	2871.85	2526.78
存货增加	Goods in Stock	48.00	41.02
货物和服务净出口	**Net Export of Goods and Services**	**276.58**	**192.49**

4-9　分行业地区生产总值指数（2015 年）
GROSS DOMESTIC PRODUCT INDEX BY INDUSTRY AREAS (2015)

按可比价计算，上年 = 100　　　　Calculated by comparable price，Preceding year=100

指　标	Item	全　市 Whole Municipality	其中 of which 市　区 Urban Area
地区生产总值	**Gross Domestic Product**	**109.2**	**109.5**
按产业分	**Grouped by Industries**		
第一产业	Primary Industry	103.1	103.4
第二产业	Secondary Industry	108.5	109.4
第三产业	Tertiary Industry	110.6	109.9
按国民经济行业分	**Grouped by Sector**		
农林牧渔业	Farming,Forestry,Animal Husbandry and Fishery	103.1	103.4
工　业	Industry	108.3	109.4
建筑业	Construction	110.8	110.8
交通运输、仓储业和邮政业	Transportation , Storage and Post	110.4	108.4
信息传输、软件和信息技术服务业	Information Transmission, Software and IT Services Industry	122.1	118.1
批发和零售业	Retail and Wholesale Industries	108.1	106.5
住宿和餐饮业	Accommodation and Catering Services	109.8	103.9
金融业	Financial	110.8	110.9
货币金融服务	Monetary and financial services	101.1	101.0
资本市场服务及其他金融业	Capital market services and other financial industries	201.4	202.3
保险业	Insurance	114.9	131.3
房地产业	Real Estate	101.5	102.4
房地产开发经营业	Real Estate Development Industry	99.6	101.3
物业管理、中介服务业和其他房地产	Property Management, Agency Service Industry and Other Real Estate	101.8	101.1
自有房地产经营活动	Business operation of self-owned assets	105.0	105.0
租赁和商务服务业	Leasehold and Business in Services	120.1	116.5
科学研究和技术服务业	Scientific Researches and Technical Services	136.8	152.4
水利、环境和公共设施管理业	Water Conservancy, Environment and Public Facility Management	108.6	123.1
居民服务、修理和其他服务业	Residential Services, Repairing and other Services Industry	108.6	101.9
教　育	Education	110.9	108.1
卫生和社会工作	Health and Social Work	102.1	113.1
文化、体育和娱乐业	Culture, Sports and Entertainment	139.9	130.9
公共管理、社会保障和社会组织	Public Administration， Social Security and Social Organizations	102.6	109.2

4-10 主要年份社会经济主要指标
MAJOR SOCIAL AND ECONOMIC INDICATORS IN MAIN YEARS

指标	Item	1990	1995	2000	2005	2010	2015
人口与就业	**Population and Employment**						
人口	**Population**						
年末户籍人口（万人）	Year-end Household Population (10000 persons)	324.85	333.65	341.48	351.63	360.80	370.85
年末常住人口（万人）	Year-end Permanent population (10000 persons)				412.80	459.33	470.14
就业	**Employment**						
从业人员（万人）	Employment (10000 persons)	186.06	188.78	179.36	222.31	272.00	281.00
在岗职工人数（万人）	Number of Fully Employed Staff and Workers (10000 persons)	56.17	54.42	40.39	35.11	36.70	67.47
宏观经济	**Macroeconomy**						
国民经济核算	**National Accounting**						
地区生产总值（亿元）	Gross Domestic Products (100 million yuan)	94.87	369.70	600.66	1308.18	3044.89	5273.15
#工业	Industy	54.06	202.86	301.99	719.95	1530.86	2269.99
按产业分	Grouped by Industries						
第一产业	Primary Industry	17.68	39.82	45.14	59.62	99.78	146.55
第二产业	Secondary Industry	57.96	220.64	336.68	799.05	1683.68	2516.04
第三产业	Tertiary Industry	19.23	109.24	218.83	449.51	1261.43	2610.56
固定资产投资	**Investment in Fixed Assets**						
固定资产投资完成额（亿元）	Realized Investment in Fixed Assets (100 million yuan)	22.71	115.06	163.43	769.80	2103.55	3398.97
#房地产开发	Real Estate Investment	0.95	18.47	29.98	114.27	446.96	508.04
财政	**Government Finance**						
财政总收入（亿元）	Financial Revenue (100 million yuan)	13.10	28.50	60.23	220.45	841.67	1367.54
#一般公共预算收入	General Public Budgetary Revenue			32.25	94.99	286.18	466.28
一般公共预算支出（亿元）	General Public Budgetary Expenditure (100 million yuan)			31.83	97.85	281.44	485.33
#用于教育	Education Expenditure			6.12	13.47	40.61	79.21
吸收外资	**Forign Capital Inducement**						
协议外资项目（个）	Protocol foreign investment projects (unit)	40	292	167	509	327	255

注：固定资产投资完成额2015年以前主要年份数据为全社会口径。
Note:The statistical caliber of total investment in fixed assets before 2015 covered the whole society.

4-10　续表 1　continued 1

指　标	Item	1990	1995	2000	2005	2010	2015
协议（合同）外资金额（亿美元）	Amount of Foreign Capital in the Newly Signed Agreements（USD 100 million）	0.18	8.87	10.03	28.51	47.42	27.69
实际到帐注册外资（亿美元）	Foreign Capital Actually Utilized（USD 100 million）	0.07	3.29	7.00	7.31	26.70	24.87
产　业	**Industries**						
农　业	**Agriculture**						
耕地面积（千公顷）	Cultivated Areas（1000 hectares）	204.54	200.88	204.25	176.32	150.39	149.94
从业人员（万人）	Employment（10000 persons）	135.80	136.31	128.67	126.86	133.95	129.40
农林牧渔业总产值（亿元）	Gross Output Value of Agriculture（100 million yuan）	29.06	74.74	85.88	104.10	174.09	271.76
主要农副产品产量	**Output of Major Farm and Sideline Products**						
粮　食（万吨）	Grain（10000 tons）	164.50	159.57	136.22	98.06	115.16	108.31
油　料（吨）	Oil-Bearing Crop（ton）	63899	72786	91629	85960	40035	36006
水产品（吨）	Aquatic Products（ton）	53149	90571	111188	130198	147938	177892
蚕　茧（吨）	Silkworm Cocoons（ton）	8726	10055	4815	2843	671	187
水　果（吨）	Fruits（ton）	9670	22716	29639	67275	99565	128971
茶　叶（吨）	Tea（ton）	3730	2550	2680	2762	3464	2819
工　业	**Industry**						
规模以上工业企业主要经济指标	**Major Economy Indictors of Industrial Enterprises above Designated Size**						
工业总产值（亿元）	Gross Output Value of Industry（100 million yuan）	196.20	579.62	874.63	2504.19	7396.09	11101.64
主营业务收入（亿元）	Main Business Income（100 million yuan）	160.85	542.82	836.10	2459.56	7274.88	11500.68
利税总额（亿元）	Total Pre-tax Profits（100 million yuan）	13.21	34.65	59.64	161.84	620.18	1031.88
利润总额（亿元）	Total Profits（100 million yuan）	5.26	11.83	25.44	96.23	413.47	642.27
建筑业	**Construction**						
建筑业总产值（亿元）	Gross Output Value of Construction（100 million yuan）	8.64	30.93	123.18	283.48	735.61	1288.52
房屋竣工建筑面积（万平方米）	Floor Space of Buildings Completed（10000 sq.m）	193.97	194.70	630.28	1588.83	2659.14	3448.59
交通运输、邮电通信	**Transportation,Post and Telecommunications**						
货物运输量（万吨）	Freight Traffic（10000 tons）	4375	5804	4696	6032	13109	12954

4-10 续表 2 continued 2

指 标	Item	1990	1995	2000	2005	2010	2015
旅客发送量（万人次）	Number of Passenger Despatched （10000 person-times）	5048	7270	10196	15235	29361	7673
邮电业务收入（亿元）	Total Busines Volume of Post and Tele-communications（100 million yuan）	0.65	5.46	16.84	34.36	55.69	78.66
年末固定电话用户（万户）	Number of Fixed Telephone Subscribers at Year-end（10000 Subscribers）	15.57	19.79	75.88	202.08	159.58	132.99
年末移动电话用户（万户）	Number of Mobile Telephone Subscribers at Year-end （10000 Subscribers）		1.80	56.68	207.46	501.39	514.35
电话交换机容量（万门）	Capacity of Telephone Exchanges （10000 line）	5.16	29.79	118.30	160.33	284.41	319.01
国内商业	**Domestic Trade**						
社会消费品零售总额（亿元）	Total Retail Sales of Consumer Goods （100 million yuan）	38.19	131.78	202.31	444.94	1051.46	1990.45
对外经济贸易	**Foreign Trade**						
进出口总额（亿美元）	Total Exports and Imports （USD 100 million）	0.62	9.93	28.22	83.34	222.78	280.46
进 口	Imports	0.12	2.24	9.62	22.09	67.19	67.88
出 口	Exports	0.50	7.69	18.60	61.24	155.58	212.58
国际旅游	**International Tourism**						
来常旅游人数（万人次）	Number of Tourists from Abroad （10000 person-times）	0.70	1.95	3.31	18.20	35.91	12.70
旅游外汇收入（亿美元）	Foreign Exchange Earnings from Tourism （USD 100 million）		0.10	0.24	1.44	3.47	1.21
金融、保险	**Banking & Insurance**						
金融机构存款余额（亿元）	Deposit Balance of Financial Institutions （100 million yuan）	59.37	257.61	629.36	1649.61	4550.47	7438.68
金融机构贷款余额（亿元）	Loans Balance of Financial Institutions （100 million. yuan）	74.24	211.88	389.26	1113.25	3011.67	5354.58
保险费收入（亿元）	Income From Insurances （100 million yuan）	1.00	4.44	12.10	37.88	86.53	156.56
保险赔（结）款支出（亿元）	Expenditure for Insurance Claims （100 million yuan）	0.25	1.28	3.59	10.42	18.76	55.10
教育、科技	**Education,Science and Technology**						
教 育	**Education**						
专任教师数（万人）	Full-time Teachers （10000 persons）	2.52	2.74	2.82	3.16	3.46	3.79
#普通高等学校	Institutions of Higher Education	0.07	0.10	0.12	0.45	0.54	0.57
普通中学	Regular Secondary Schools	0.91	0.96	1.04	1.29	1.39	1.40
小 学	Primary Schools	1.31	1.36	1.30	1.14	1.19	1.37

注：2015年旅游外汇收入只统计入境过夜旅游者，与往年统计口径不同。
Note:The earning from the International Tourism only includes the part from the Inbound Overnight Touristsin1 in 2015,The statistical caliber is diffirent from former years.

4-10 续表 3 continued 3

指　标	Item	1990	1995	2000	2005	2010	2015
在校学生数（万人）	Students Enrollment（10000 persons）	46.10	50.19	57.10	64.88	60.39	62.46
#普通高等学校	Institutions of Higher Education	0.51	1.16	2.00	9.54	12.28	12.44
普通中学	Regular Secondary Schools	14.90	15.86	18.23	22.07	18.84	16.25
小 学	Primary Schools	27.70	27.16	30.01	24.46	22.15	27.37
科　技	**Science and Technology**						
专利申请量（项）	Number of Patent Applications Examined（unit）		547	837	2696	15872	38559
专利授权量（项）	Number of Patent Authorizations Granted（unit）		255	731	1240	9093	21585
家庭、生活、卫生	**Family, Livelihood and Health Care**						
家　庭	**Family**						
家庭总户数（万户）	Total Number of Household（10000 households）	106.91	114.00	117.89	121.97	127.11	130.24
平均每户家庭人口（人）	Average Number of Household Size（person）	3.04	2.93	2.90	2.88	2.84	2.85
婚　姻	**Marriages and Divorces**						
准予登记结婚（对）	Marriage Leagally Registered（couple）	24093	31889	23916	26536	33182	34105
准予登记离婚数（对）	Divorce Leagally Registered（couple）	604	1399	2203	5001	7795	10324
住　宅	**Housing**						
农村居民人均住房面积（平方米）	Per Capita Living Space Of Rural Residents（sq.m）	31.66	35.90	49.27	56.20	58.40	63.98
生　活	**People's Livelihood**						
农村居民人均纯收入（元）	Per Capita Net Income Of Rural Residents（yuan）	1401	3397	4430	7002	12637	21912
农村居民人均生活消费支出（元）	Per Capita Living Expenditure of Rural Residents（yuan）	1231	2952	3243	5712	9924	14764
工　资	**Wages**						
在岗职工工资总额（亿元）	Total Wages of Fully Employde Staff and Workers（100 million yuan）	12.90	38.68	48.97	78.57	161.50	475.70
卫　生	**Health Care**						
医　院（包括卫生院，个）	Hospitals（include Township Hospitals,unit）	163	161	117	113	91	109
医　生（人）	Doctors（person）	6144	7073	7779	8356	9962	12637
医院床位数（包括卫生院，张）	Number of Hospital Beds（include Township Hospitals,unit）	9495	10339	10730	11734	15263	22741

注：根据国家城乡一体化住户调查制度，从2014年起按新口径公布居民收支数据。2015年农民人均纯收入为农村常住居民人均可支配收入。
Note: According to the national urban and rural integration households survey system, the data of residents' income and expenditure shall be calculated based on new statistic calibers from Year 2014.In Year 2015 the indicator of per capita net income of rural residents is adjusted to per capita disposable income of permanent rural residents

4-11 主要年份市区社会经济主要指标
MAJOR SOCIAL AND ECONOMIC INDICATORS OF URBAN DISTRICTS IN MAIN YEARS

指　标	Item	1990	1995	2000	2005	2010	2015
人口与就业	**Population and Employment**						
人　口	**Population**						
年末户籍人口（万人）	Year-end Household Population（10000 persons）	195.24	202.20	208.18	220.76	227.75	291.25
年末常住人口（万人）	Year-end Permanent population（10000 persons）				286.73	329.13	394.05
就　业	**Employment**						
从业人员（万人）	Employment（10000 persons）	117.84	118.01	111.55	148.55	186.92	231.58
在岗职工人数（万人）	Number of Fully Employed Staff and Workers（10000 persons）	45.19	42.44	29.90	25.36	26.22	61.70
宏观经济	**Macroeconomy**						
国民经济核算	**National Accounting**						
地区生产总值（亿元）	Gross Domestic Products（100 million yuan）	72.06	279.19	430.89	981.45	2316.26	4548.57
#工　业	Industy	45.91	170.20	239.46	571.46	1229.12	1971.60
按产业分	Grouped by Industries						
第一产业	Primary Industry	9.07	20.95	22.75	27.03	47.64	100.22
第二产业	Secondary Industry	48.54	179.22	256.10	620.51	1316.20	2162.16
第三产业	Tertiary Industry	14.44	79.02	152.04	333.91	952.42	2286.19
固定资产投资	**Investment in Fixed Assets**						
固定资产投资完成额（亿元）	Realized Investment in Fixed Assets（100 million yuan）	17.09	85.23	126.90	609.75	1649.98	2956.57
#房地产开发	Real Estate Investment	0.78	14.62	25.46	97.76	401.22	467.74
财　政	**Government Finance**						
财政收入（亿元）	Financial Revenue（100 million yuan）	11.66	23.99	50.77	182.12	710.11	1158.93
#一般公共预算收入	General Public Budgetary Revenue			27.60	79.14	239.15	410.09
一般公共预算支出	General Public Budgetary Expenditure			25.41	79.80	225.81	423.95
#用于教育	Education Expenditure			4.05	9.55	28.40	67.97
价　格	**Price**						
居民消费价格指数（上年=100）	Consumer Price Index（preceding year=100）	104.2	114.9	99.5	102.8	103.4	101.6
商品零售价格指数（上年=100）	Retail Price Index（preceding year=100）	103.4	112.8	98.0	101.3	102.7	100.1
吸收外资	**Forign Capital Inducement**						
协议外资项目（个）	Protocol foreign Investment projects（unit）	39	243	132	355	208	241

注：本表资料除了1990、1995、2000年城市建设指标外均含武进区数据，2015年起市区包含金坛区数据。
Note: The data in this table（except the 1990, 1995 and 2000 city construction data）include Wujin District. In 2015, the city's urban area now includes Jintan District.

4-11　续表 1　continued 1

指　标	Item	1990	1995	2000	2005	2010	2015
协议（合同）外资金额（亿美元）	Amount of Foreign Capital in the Newly Signed Agreements（USD 100 million）	0.15	7.05	4.78	20.33	31.61	24.63
实际到帐注册外资（亿美元）	Foreign Capital Actually Utilized（USD 100 million）	0.07	3.29	7.00	7.31	26.70	23.81
产　业	**Industries**						
农　业	**Agriculture**						
耕地面积（千公顷）	Cultivated Areas（1000 hectares）	97.01	94.80	88.75	64.27	59.25	92.01
从业人员（万人）	Employment（10000 persons）	76.65	75.96	71.22	75.19	81.99	97.64
农林牧渔业总产值（亿元）	Gross Output Value of Agriculture（100 million yuan）	15.48	39.34	43.81	47.90	78.39	185.91
主要农副产品产量	**Output of Major Farm and Sideline Products**						
粮　食（万吨）	Grain（10000 tons）	89.07	81.30	66.11	39.28	34.22	54.41
油　料（吨）	Oil-Bearing Crop（ton）	11710	12068	17412	8489	3922	9737
水产品（吨）	Aquatic Products（ton）	16049	45321	35588	57173	52783	114027
水　果（吨）	Fruits（ton）	6038	18527	21811	49747	56204	105771
工　业	**Industry**						
规模以上工业企业主要经济指标	**Major Economy Indictors of Industrial Enterprises above Designated Size**						
工业总产值（亿元）	Gross Output Value of Industry（100 million yuan）	163.78	474.76	730.74	2032.39	5873.16	9888.90
主营业务收入（亿元）	Main Business Income（100 million yuan）	136.76	446.40	704.23	2016.20	5789.68	10277.66
利税总额（亿元）	Total Pre-tax Profits（100 million yuan）	11.67	28.13	50.94	119.96	442.32	909.36
利润总额（亿元）	Total Profits（100 million yuan）		4.45	12.85	73.99	297.35	569.03
建筑业	**Construction**						
建筑业总产值（亿元）	Gross Output Value of Construction（100 million yuan）			46.65	154.51	375.25	722.98
房屋竣工建筑面积（万平方米）	Floor Space of Buildings Completed（10000 sq.m）		80.50	320.17	830.89	1191.62	1926.80
交通运输、邮电通信	**Transportation,Post and Telecommunications**						
货物运输量（万吨）	Freight Traffic（10000 tons）	2349	4483	3100	3857	8933	10477
旅客发送量（万人次）	Number of Passenger Despatche（10000 person-times）	2849	4383	6924	10308	20625	6595
邮电业务收入（亿元）	Total Busines Volume of Post and Tele-communications（100 million yuan）	0.55	4.42	14.11	27.74	44.48	70.62
年末固定电话用户（万户）	Number of Fixed Telephone Subscribers at Year-end（10000 Subscribers）	2.46	11.68	53.43	145.97	112.63	112.14
年末移动电话用户（万户）	Number of Mobile Telephone Subscribers at Year-end（10000 Subscribers）		1.35	46.96	162.58	383.62	444.06
电话交换机容量（万门）	Capacity of Telephone Exchanges（10000 line）	4.23	21.53	82.45	114.35	202.74	307.90

4-11 续表 2 continued 2

	指 标 Item	1990	1995	2000	2005	2010	2015
国内商业	**Domestic Trade**						
社会消费品零售总额（亿元）	Total Retail Sales of Consumer Goods (100 million yuan)	26.21	84.99	133.88	329.21	788.45	1715.15
对外经济贸易	**Foreign Trade**						
进出口总额（亿美元）	Total Exports and Imports （USD 100 million）	0.61	9.43	25.15	76.03	199.49	272.11
进 口	Imports	0.11	2.22	8.81	21.11	63.43	66.91
出 口	Exports	0.50	7.21	16.34	54.92	136.06	205.12
国际旅游	**International Tourism**						
来常旅游人数（万人次）	Number of Tourists from Abroad (10000 person-times)	0.65	1.90	3.11	17.28	34.25	12.25
旅游外汇收入（亿美元）	Foreign Exchange Earnings from Tourism (USD 100 million)		0.09	0.23	1.38	3.31	1.16
金融保险	**Banking & Insurance**						
金融机构存款余额（亿元）	Deposit Balance of Financial Institutions (100 million yuan)	46.24	205.93	511.00	1375.25	3800.47	6572.31
金融机构贷款余额（亿元）	Loans Balance of Financial Institutions (100 million yuan)	58.52	170.12	324.19	966.84	2518.92	4655.86
保险费收入（亿元）	Income From Insurances (100 million yuan)	0.84	4.38	10.27	30.54	73.12	144.51
保险赔（结）款支出（亿元）	Expenditure for Insurance Claims (100 million yuan)	0.19	1.16	3.04	8.97	15.39	50.09
教育、科技	**Education,Science and Technology**						
教 育	**Education**						
专任教师数（万人）	Full-time Teachers (10000 persons)	1.59	1.76	1.82	2.15	2.42	3.22
#普通高等学校	Institutions of Higher Education	0.07	0.10	0.12	0.45	0.54	0.57
普通中学	Regular Secondary Schools	0.56	0.60	0.64	0.79	0.86	1.12
小 学	Primary Schools	0.75	0.78	0.75	0.71	0.76	1.13
在校学生数（万人）	Students Enrollment (10000 persons)	28.82	15.94	37.33	46.45	46.28	55.21
#普通高等学校	Institutions of Higher Education	0.51	1.16	2.00	9.54	12.22	12.39
普通中学	Regular Secondary Schools	9.17	9.84	11.11	13.52	12.37	13.58
小 学	Primary Schools	16.46	15.95	17.69	15.95	15.89	23.48
科 技	**Science and Technology**						
专利申请量（项）	Number of Patent Applications Examined (unit)				1976	12278	37460
专利授权量（项）	Number of Patent Authorizations Granted (unit)				1021	7559	20643

4-11　续表 3　continued 3

指　标	Item	1990	1995	2000	2005	2010	2015
家庭、生活、环境	**Family, Livelihood and Environment**						
家　庭	**Family**						
家庭总户数（万户）	Total Number of Household（10000 households）	63.65	67.67	70.77	74.36	79.54	103.99
平均每户家庭人口（人）	Average Number of Household Size（person）	3.07	2.98	2.94	2.97	2.86	2.8
婚　姻	**Marriages and Divorces**						
准予登记结婚（对）	Marriage Leagally Registered（couple）	11058	19048	14848	17002	19730	25271
准予登记离婚数（对）	Divorce Leagally Registered（couple）	496	1165	1280	3494	5084	8059
住　宅	**Housing**						
城市居民人均使用面积（平方米）	Per Capita Usable Floor Space of Urban Residents（sq.m）	13.22	15.04	15.19	21.04	24.91	33.08
生　活	**People's Livelihood**						
城镇居民人均可支配收入（元）	Per Capita Disposable Income Of Urban Residents（yuan）	1769	5632	8540	14589	26269	43642
城镇居民人均生活消费支出（元）	Per Capita Living Expenditure of Urban Residents（yuan）	1498	4426	6759	10718	17124	25922
工　资	**Wages**						
在岗职工工资总额（亿元）	Total Wages of Fully Employed Staff and Workers（100 million yuan）	10.82	31.91	38.59	60.26	124.85	447.79
卫　生	**Health Care**						
医　院（包括卫生院，个）	Hospitals（include Township Hospitals,unit）	90	91	64	61	47	82
医　生（人）	Doctors（person）	4636	5146	5616	4751	5771	10698
医院床位数（包括卫生院，张）	Number of Hospital Beds （include Township Hospitals,unit）	6506	7236	7774	8467	11151	19975
城市建设	**Urban construction**						
自来水供水量（万吨）	Annual Consumption of Tap Water（100 million tons）	25994	11257	16631	32384	21981	25048
城市排水管道长度（公里）	Length of Sewer Piplelines of Urban Districts（km）	231	698	929	2918	3627	5503
用电量（亿千瓦时）	Electric Power Consumption （100 milliom kwh）	14.72	22.44	32.74	143.21	215.17	339.93
城市煤气供应量（万立方米）	Goal Gas Supply of Urban Districts（10000 m^3）	1601	1783	4256	8030	48099	77578
年末出租车运营数（辆）	Number of Operating Taxi at Year-end（coach）	137	592	1443	1842	2542	3321
年末运营公交车辆数（辆）	Number of Public Transit Vehicles at Year-end（coach）	232	307	1572	2105	2518	2858
铺装道路长度（公里）	Length of Paved Roads（km）	336	483	697	3584	1753	2444
公园绿地面积（公顷）	Green Space of Park（hectare）	121	283	458	1568	1632	2479

注：根据国家城乡一体化住户调查制度，从2014年起按新口径公布居民收支数据，城镇居民人均可支配收入调整为城镇常住居民人均可支配收入。

Note: According to the national urban and rural integration households survey system, the data of residents' income and expenditure shall be calculated based on new statistic calibers from Year 2014, The indicator of per capita disposable income of urban residents is changed to that of per capita disposable income of permanent urban residents.

4-12 主要年份社会经济主要指标增长速度
GROWTH RATE OF MAJOR SOCIAL AND ECONOMIC INDICATORS IN MAIN YEARS

单位：%

指 标	Item	2015年比下列各年增长 Growth Rates of 2015 over Following Years				
		1978	1990	2000	2010	2014
人口与就业	**Population and Employment**					
年末总人口	Total Population at year-end	27.4	14.2	8.6	2.8	0.6
从业人员	Number of Employed Persons	88.1	51.0	56.7	3.3	0.0
宏观经济	**Macroeconomy**					
地区生产总值	Gross Domestic Product	85.7倍	24.4倍	5.0倍	66.8	9.2
#工　业	Industry	116.8倍	28.9倍	5.6倍	66.9	8.3
按产业分	Grouped by Industries					
第一产业	Primary Industry	3.6倍	1.8倍	80.3	18.8	3.1
第二产业	Secondary Industry	111.72倍	27.5倍	5.4倍	65.5	8.5
第三产业	Tertiary Industry	135.4倍	35.9倍	5.4倍	72.6	10.6
固定资产投资完成额	Realized Investment in Fixed Assets	3818.1倍	148.7倍	19.8倍	61.6	6.7
一般公共预算收入	General Public Budgetary Revenue			13.5倍	62.9	7.5
一般公共预算支出	General Public Budgetary Expenditure			14.2倍	72.4	11.6
协议外资项目	Protocol foreign Investment projects Signed		537.5	52.7	-22.0	-23.2
协议（合同）外资金额	Amount of Foreign Capital in the Newly Signed Agreements		152.8倍	176.0	-41.6	-19.7
实际到帐注册外资	Foreign Capital Actually Utilized		354.3倍	2.6倍	-6.9	-20.3
产　业	**Industries**					
农林牧渔业总产值	Gross Output Value of Agriculture	38.0倍	8.4倍	216.4	56.1	5.8
规模以上工业总产值	Total Output Value of Industry above Designated Size		55.6倍	11.7倍	50.1	5.3
建筑业总产值	Gross Output Value of Construction		148.1倍	9.5倍	75.2	0.3
邮电业务收入	Total Busines Volume of Post and Telecommunications		120.0倍	3.7倍	41.2	6.9
社会消费品零售总额	Total Retail Sales of Consumer Goods	412.0倍	51.1倍	8.8倍	88.8	10.3
进出口总额	Total Exports and Imports		451.4倍	8.9倍	25.9	-2.7

注：地区生产总值按可比价计算。
Note:GDP can be calculated by comparable price.

4-12 续表 continued　　　　单位：%

指　标	Item	2015年比下列各年增长 Growth Rates of 2015 over Following Years 1978	1990	2000	2010	2014
进　口	Imports		564.7倍	6.1倍	1.0	-8.9
出　口	Exports		424.2倍	10.4倍	36.6	-0.5
金融机构存款余额	Deposit Balance of Financial Institutions		124.3倍	10.8倍	63.5	7.4
金融机构贷款余额	Loans Balance of Financial Institutions	7435.9倍	71.1倍	12.8倍	77.8	11.8
保费收入	Income From Insurances		155.6倍	11.9倍	80.9	15.6
保险赔（结）款支出	Expenditure for Insurance Claims		219.4倍	14.3倍	1.9倍	12.4
教育、科技	**Education,Science and Technology**					
在校学生数	Students Enrollment	4.3	35.5	9.4	3.4	3.3
#普通高等学校	Institutions of Higher Education	310.0倍	23.4倍	5.2倍	1.3	-1.4
普通中学	Regular Secondary Schools	-24.6	9.1	-10.9	-13.8	0.0
小　学	Primary Schools	-27.9	-1.2	-8.8	23.5	8.1
专利申请量	Number of Patent Applications Examined			45.1倍	1.4倍	1.9
专利授权量	Number of Patent Authorizations Granted			28.5倍	1.4倍	18.9
家庭、生活、环境	**Family,Livelihood and Environment**					
城镇常住居民人均可支配收入	Per Capita Disposable Income of Permanent Urban Residents					8.2
城镇常住居民人均消费性支出	Per Capita Consuming Expenditures of Permanent Urban Residents					7.5
农村常住居民人均可支配收入	Per Capita Disposable Income of Permanent Rural Residents					8.8
农村常住居民人均生活消费支出	Per Capita Consuming Expenditures of Permanent Rural Residents					9.1
医　生	Doctors	318.3	105.7	62.5	26.9	5.0
医院、卫生院床位数	Number of Hospital Beds	225.7	139.5	111.9	49.0	2.6
自来水供水量	Annual Volume of Tap Water Supply	21.7	-3.6	50.6	14.0	17.7
城市排水管道长度	Length of Sewer Piplelines of Urban Districts	38.3倍	22.8倍	492.4	51.7	12.9
用电量	Electric Power Consumption		12.9倍	448.8	40.1	3.3
城市煤气供应量	Goal Gas Supply of Urban Districts		47.5倍	17.2倍	61.3	22.3

注：居民收支2014年起口径有调整，故2015年与2014年之前年份数据不可比，增幅栏数据空缺。
Note: The statistical caliber of resident income had been adjusted since Year 2014. So the data of Year 2015 is incomparable with that before Year 2014 with column of growth rate left blank.

4-13 主要时期社会经济主要指标平均增长率
AVERAGE GROWTH RATE OF MAJOR SOCIAL AND ECONOMIC INDICATORS OF MAIN PERIOD

单位：%

指 标	Item	"十五"时期 "Tenth Five-Year Plan" Period	十一五"时期 "Eleventh Five-Year Plan" Period	"十二五"时期 "Twelfth Five-Year Plan" Period	1979～2015
年末总人口	Year-end Population	0.6	0.5	0.6	0.7
从业人员	Number of Employed Persons	3.3	4.1	0.7	1.7
地区生产总值	Gross Domestic Product	13.9	13.6	10.8	12.8
第一产业	Primary Industry	4.2	4.3	3.5	4.2
第二产业	Secondary Industry	15.3	13.6	10.6	13.6
第三产业	Tertiary Industry	13.3	14.6	11.5	14.2
固定资产投资完成额	Realized Investment in Fixed Assets	36.3	22.3	15.7	25.0
一般公共预算收入	General Public Budgetary Revenue	24.1	24.7	10.3	
一般公共预算支出	General Public Budgetary Expenditure	25.2	23.5	9.1	
协议外资项目	Protocol foreign Investment projects	25.0	-8.5	-4.9	
协议（合同）外资金额	Amount of Foreign Capital in the Newly Signed Agreements	36.9	10.7	-10.2	
实际到帐注册外资	Foreign Capital Actually Utilized	5.5	29.6	-1.4	
农林牧渔业总产值	Total Output value of Farming,Forestry,Animal Husbandry and Fishing	3.9	10.8	9.3	
规模以上工业总产值	Total Output Value of Industry above Designated Size	23.4	24.2		
货物运输量	Freight Traffic	5.1	16.8		
旅客发送量	Number of Passenger Despatched	8.4	13.9		
邮电业务收入	Total Busines Volume of Post and Telecommunications	15.3	10.1	7.2	
社会消费品零售总额	Total Retail Sales of Consumer Goods	17.0	18.8	13.6	17.7
进出口总额	Total Exports and Imports	24.2	21.7	4.7	
进　口	Imports	18.1	24.9	0.2	
出　口	Exports	26.9	20.5	6.4	
城镇常住居民人均可支配收入	Per Capita Disposable Income of Permanent Urban Residents	11.3	12.5	10.6	
城镇常住居民人均消费性支出	Per Capita Consuming Expenditures of Permanent Urban Residents	9.7	9.8	9.1	
农村常住居民人均可支配收入	Per Capita Disposable Income of Permanent Rural Residents	9.6	12.5	12.2	
农村常住居民人均生活消费支出	Per Capita Consuming Expenditures of Permanent Rural Residents	12.0	11.7	10.3	
在岗职工年平均工资	Average Annual Wage of Fully Employed Staff and Workers	14.8	14.0	9.9	14.1
医　生	Doctors	1.4	3.6	4.9	3.9
在校学生数	Students Enrollment	2.6	-1.4	0.7	0.1
#高等学校	Institutions of Higher Education	36.7	5.2	0.3	16.8

注：1、固定资产投资"九五"、"十五"、"十一五"时期平均增长率为全社会固定资产投资平均增长率。
2、2014年起城乡居民收入是城乡住户调查一体化改革后的新口径数据。2014年以前，城镇居民人均可支配收入为市区数，农村居民可支配收入为全市农民人均纯收入。

Note：1、The average growth rate of fixed assets investment in the periods of Ninth Five-Year Plan, Tenth Five-Year Plan and Eleventh Five- year Plan is that of the total investment in fixed assets...
2、Disposable incomes of urban and rurual residents were calculated in line with standards set out after the integration of urban and rural surveys in 2014. Before 2014, the disposable income of urban residents was the disposable income of downtown residents, and the disposable income of rural residents was the net income of all rurual residents.

4-14　主要年份社会经济发展结构指标
STRUCTURAL INDICATORS ON ECONOMIC AND SOCIAL DEVELOPMENT IN MAIN YEARS

单位：%

指　标	Item	1990	1995	2000	2005	2010	2015
人　口	**Population**						
常住人口城乡结构	Urban and Rural Structure of Permanent population				100.0	100.0	100.0
城　镇	Urban				60.3	63.9	70.0
农　村	Rural				39.7	36.1	30.0
户籍人口性别结构	Sexual Structure of Household Population	100.0	100.0	100.0	100.0	100.0	100.0
男	Male	51.5	51.4	50.8	50.5	50.0	49.5
女	Female	48.5	48.6	49.2	49.5	50.0	50.5
就　业	**Employment**						
从业人员产业结构	Industrial Structure	100.0	100.0	100.0	100.0	100.0	100.0
第一产业	Primary Industry	35.9	29.4	28.9	13.5	8.7	10.9
第二产业	Secondary Industry	45.6	47.3	43.6	53.4	55.5	51.1
第三产业	Tertiary Industry	18.5	23.3	27.5	33.1	35.7	38.0
国民经济核算	**National Accounting**						
地区生产总值产业结构	Industrial Structure	100.0	100.0	100.0	100.0	100.0	100.0
第一产业	Primary Industry	18.6	10.8	7.5	4.3	3.3	2.8
第二产业	Secondary Industry	61.1	59.7	56.1	61.1	55.3	47.7
第三产业	Tertiary Industry	20.3	29.5	36.4	34.6	41.4	49.5
固定资产投资	**Investment in Fixed Assets**						
固定资产投资结构	Structure of fixed assets investment	100.0	100.0	100.0	100.0	100.0	100.0
#工业投资	Industrial investment	70.4	47.7	36.3	59.7	56.1	51.7
第三产业投资	Investment in Tertiary Industry	27.4	50.5	59.9	39.5	43.2	48.2
#房地产开发	Real Estate Development	4.1	16.1	18.3	14.8	21.2	14.9
财　政	**Government Finance**						
一般公共预算收入结构	Structure of General Public Budgetary Rerenue			100.0	100.0	100.0	100.0
#税收收入	Income from Taxes			92.1	84.1	83.1	80.1
吸收外资	**Utilization of Foreign Capital**						
实际吸收外资结构	Structure of Foreign Capital Actually Utilized		100.0	100.0	100.0	100.0	100.0
#合资企业	Joint-ventures		86.4	51.5	22.1	24.5	9.4
合作企业	Cooperative Enterprises		4.2	9.1	4.0	0.1	…
独资企业	Foreign Funded Enterprises		9.4	39.4	73.9	75.4	90.6

注：1、2015年全社会从业人员三次产业结构根据人口抽样调查数据计算。
　　2、固定资产投资结构2015年前主要年份为全社会投资口径。

Note：1.Employment structure of the three industries in 2015 was calculated on the basis of population survey data.
　　2.The statistical caliber of fixed assets investment structure before 2015 covered the whole society.

4-14 续表 1 continued 1

单位：%

指 标	Item	1990	1995	2000	2005	2010	2015
农 业	**Agriculture**						
农林牧渔业总产值结构	Structure of Gross Agricultural Output Value	100.0	100.0	100.0	100.0	100.0	100.0
农 业	Planting	61.9	59.7	59.8	48.2	54.6	54.2
林 业	Forestry	0.6	0.7	1.0	1.2	0.7	0.7
牧 业	Animal Husbandry	28.5	23.4	15.1	18.0	15.7	14.3
渔 业	Fishery	8.9	16.1	24.1	27.9	24.4	25.1
农林牧渔服务业	Service Industry for Planting, Forestry, Animal Husbandry and Fishery				4.7	4.6	5.7
工 业	**Industry**						
工业总产值结构	Structure of Gross Industrial Output Value	100.0	100.0	100.0	100.0	100.0	100.0
轻工业	Light Industry	49.5	40.0	41.4	34.9	21.6	25.0
重工业	Heavy Industry	50.5	60.0	58.6	65.1	78.4	75.0
建筑业	**Construction**						
建筑业企业总产值结构	Structure of Total Output Value of Construction Enterprises		100.0	100.0	100.0	100.0	100.0
#房屋土木工程建筑业	Building and Civil Engineering Construction		78.6	75.1	79.7	79.2	76.9
建筑安装业	Installation		11.7	13.8	11.2	12.4	15.3
建筑装饰业	Decoration		9.6	11.1	5.2	6.5	7.8
运输业	**Transportation**						
货运量结构	Structure of Freight Traffic	100.0	100.0	100.0	100.0	100.0	100.0
铁 路	Railways	2.9	3.2	4.7	4.9	1.7	0.8
公 路	Highways	67.3	61.2	71.0	82.1	88.5	82.4
水 运	Waterway	29.9	35.6	24.2	13.0	9.8	16.8
民用航空	Civil Aviation	…	…	…	…	…	…
国内商业	**Domestic Trade**						
社会消费品零售总额结构	Total Retail Sale of Consumer Goods		100.0	100.0	100.0	100.0	100.0
批发零售贸易业	Wholesale,Retail Sales		66.5	75.9	88.7	92.2	91.7
住宿餐饮业	Accommodation,Catering Trade		4.6	7.0	10.0	7.8	8.3
其 他	Others		28.8	17.1	1.3		
对外经济贸易	**Foreign Trade**						
进出口结构	Structure of Imports and Exports	100.0	100.0	100.0	100.0	100.0	100.0
出 口	Exports	80.8	77.5	65.9	73.5	69.8	75.8
进 口	Imports	19.2	22.5	34.1	26.5	30.2	24.2
金 融	**Banking**						
金融机构贷款结构	Structure Loans in Banking Institutions		100.0	100.0	100.0	100.0	100.0
#短期贷款	Short-term Loans		74.3	82.0	63.7	50.5	49.1
中长期贷款	Medium-term and Long-term Loans		11.8	8.5	26.0	46.7	44.6

注：2015年建筑业企业总产值结构中的建筑装饰业包含建筑装饰和其他建筑业。
Note: Decoration industry in the Structure of Total Output Value of Construction Enterprises of Year 2015 includes building decoration and other construction.

4-14 续表2 continued 2

单位：%

指 标	Item	1990	1995	2000	2005	2010	2015
教 育	**Education**						
在校学生结构	Structure of Student Enrollment	100.0	100.0	100.0	100.0	100.0	100.0
# 大学生	College and University Students	1.1	2.3	3.5	14.7	20.3	19.9
中学生	Secondary School Students	38.8	43.6	43.9	47.6	43.0	36.1
小学生	Primary School Students	60.1	54.1	52.6	37.7	36.7	43.8
专任教师结构	Full-time Teachers by Type	100.0	100.0	100.0	100.0	100.0	100.0
# 高等教育	Higher Education	2.8	3.5	4.4	14.3	15.6	15.0
普通中学	Regular Secondary Schools	35.9	35.2	36.7	40.8	40.2	36.9
小 学	Primary Schools	51.9	49.6	46.0	36.2	34.4	36.2
生 活	**Livelihood**						
城镇居民消费结构	Consumption Structure of Urban Residents	100.0	100.0	100.0	100.0	100.0	100.0
食品烟酒	Food, Tobacco and Liquor		54.9	40.1	35.9	32.7	28.0
衣 着	Clothing		10.4	7.9	9.7	9.5	7.4
生活用品及服务	Articles for Daily Use and Services	5.0	5.7	10.5	6.5	6.6	6.1
医疗保健	Medicine and Medical Services	1.5	1.4	6.1	7.6	6.5	6.5
交通通信	Transportation and Communication	3.0	4.7	5.9	12.2	17.1	15.2
教育文化娱乐	Education, Culture and Entertainment	6.7	9.7	12.2	13.8	15.0	13.4
居 住	Housing	7.5	8.6	11.0	9.9	8.2	20.9
其他商品和服务	Other Commodities and Services	3.6	4.6	6.3	4.3	4.3	2.6
农村居民消费结构	Consumption Structure of Rural Residents		100.0	100.0	100.0	100.0	100.0
食品烟酒	Food, Tobacco and Liquor		49.9	43.1	39.8	35.1	31.7
衣 着	Clothing		7.1	5.5	6.5	7.7	7.4
生活用品及服务	Articles for Daily Use and Services		8.5	5.1	6.1	5.6	6.1
医疗保健	Medicine and Medical Services		2.0	5.5	6.6	7.4	8.3
交通通信	Transportation and Communication		1.8	8.1	11.6	13.9	12.1
教育文化娱乐	Education, Culture and Entertainment		12.4	11.8	13.1	16.2	11.0
居 住	Housing		15.8	17.8	14.0	11.5	19.6
其他商品和服务	Other Commodities and Services		2.5	3.1	2.4	2.6	3.9
卫 生	**Public Health**						
卫生机构数结构	Number of Health Institutions	100.0	100.0	100.0	100.0	100.0	100.0
# 医院（包括卫生院）	Hospitals（include Township Hospitals）	18.3	18.8	15.0	8.9	8.4	9.1
门诊部、所	Clinics	77.1	76.0	79.2	36.9	30.6	33.9
卫生技术人员结构	Structure of Medical Technical Personnel	100.0	100.0	100.0	100.0	100.0	100.0
# 医 生	Doctors	47.5	47.3	46.5	46.8	45.4	42.7
护师、护士	Nurses	26.5	28.0	29.7	32.8	35.5	35.0

注：城镇居民消费结构2015年为全市口径，2015年以前年份为市区口径。
Note: The data of consumption structure of urban resudents in Year 2015 refers to whole municipality, while that of years before Year 2015 focuses on urban area.

4-15 主要年份社会经济发展相对指标
RELATIVE INDICATORS ON ECONOMIC AND SOCIAL DEVELOPMENT IN MAIN YEARS

指标	Item	1990	1995	2000	2005	2010	2015
人　口	**Population**						
出生率（‰）	Birth Rate（‰）	15.1	11.7	12.6	8.3	7.8	9.6
死亡率（‰）	Death Rate（‰）	6.4	6.4	6.8	6.2	8.5	7.0
自然增长率（‰）	Natural Growth Rate（‰）	8.7	5.3	5.8	2.1	-0.7	2.7
登记失业率（%）	Registered Unemployment Rate in Urban Areas（%）			3.0	3.6	2.6	1.9
国民经济核算	**National Accounting**						
经济增长贡献率（%）	Growth Rate of Economy（%）						
#工　　业	Industy	75.2	30.5	53.4	61.6	43.7	26.9
按产业分	Grouped by Industries						
第一产业	Primary Industry	15.4	11.0	1.8	2.6	1.5	2.2
第二产业	Secondary Industry	76.0	36.0	60.0	66.6	48.4	29.1
第三产业	Tertiary Industry	8.7	53.0	38.2	30.8	50.1	68.8
人均地区生产总值（元）	Per Capita Gross Domestic Product（yuan）	2935	11117	17635	32116	67327	112221
固定资产投资	**Investment in Fixed Assets**						
固定资产投资占地区生产总值比例（%）	Proportion of investment in fixed assets to regional GDP（%）	23.9	31.1	27.2	58.8	69.1	64.5
财　政	**Government Finance**						
全市财政收入占地区生产总值比例（%）	Proportion of Government Revenue to GDP（%）	13.8	7.7	10.0	16.9	27.6	25.9
一般公共预算收入占地区生产总值比例（%）	Proportion of General Public Budget Revenue to GDP（%）			5.4	7.3	9.4	8.8
吸收外资	**Utilization of Foreign Capital**						
实际利用外资额占签订利用外资比例（%）	Proportion of Foreign Capital Actually Utilized（%）	38.0	37.0	69.8	25.6	56.3	89.9
农　业	**Agriculture**						
平均每个农村人口占有耕地（平方米）	Cultivated Land per Rural Population（sq.m）	844	840	862	749	633	668
每公顷耕地农业机械总动力（千瓦）	Total Power of Agricultural Machinery per Hectare of Cultivated Land（kw）	5.72	6.83	8.21	9.19	9.99	9.53

4-15　续表 1　continued 1

指　标	Item	1990	1995	2000	2005	2010	2015
农民人均农产品产量（公斤）	Output of Farm Products per Agricultural Laborer（kg）						
粮　食	Grain	506.40	478.25	398.90	278.88	319.17	292.06
油　料	Oil-bearing Crops	19.67	21.82	26.83	24.45	11.10	9.71
茶　叶	Tea	1.15	0.76	0.79	0.79	0.96	0.76
水　果	Fruits	2.98	6.81	8.68	19.13	27.60	34.78
猪　肉	Pork	21.55	26.97	18.83	18.46	16.57	19.57
水产品	Aquatic Products	16.36	27.15	32.51	37.03	41.00	47.97
每公顷播种面积农产品产量（公斤）	Output of Farm Crops per Hectare of Sown Area（kg）						
粮　食	Grain	5720	6666	6982	6772	7131	7586
棉　花	Cotton	552	577	967	764	843	891
油　料	Oil-bearing Crops	1594	1644	1850	1952	2030	2417
工　业	**Industry**						
资产负债率（%）	Asstes-Liability Ratio（%）		64.82	61.70	65.61	59.89	57.52
成本费用利润率（%）	Ratio of Pre-tax Profits to Gross Output Value （%）		2.23	3.13	4.06	6.13	5.95
工业产品销售率（%）	Ratio of Industrial Products Sales（%）		96.13	97.12	97.77	98.45	99.17
全员劳动生产率（万元/人）	Overall Labor Productivity（10000 yuan/person）		2.36	4.41	9.83	18.30	30.88
建筑业	**Construction**						
全员劳动生产率（万元/人，按施工产值计算）	Overall Labor Productivity（yuan/person, In Terms of Construction Output Value）	1.13	3.98	7.75	16.31	22.06	27.37
交通、通信业	**Transportation and Telecommunication Services**						
每万人拥有公共车辆（标台）	Number of Public Transit Vehicles Owned per 10000 Persons（set）	4.30	4.80	15.60	9.02	13.10	20.50
移动电话普及率（部/百人）	Access to Mobile Telephone（set/100 persons）		0.54	16.64	45.50	138.97	139.11

注：每万人拥有公交车辆数从2013年起按交通部规定采用建成区人口计算。
Note: Since 2013, the number of buses per 10,000 people has been calculated according to the population of built-up area as required by the Ministry of Transport of the People’s Republic of China.

4-15 续表 2 continued 2

指 标	Item	1990	1995	2000	2005	2010	2015
国内商业	**Domestic Trade**						
人均社会消费品零售额（元）	Per Capita Consumption Retail Sale（yuan）	1182	3963	5940	12702	29264	42360
对外经济贸易	**Foreign Trade and Economic Cooperation**						
进出口总额占地区生产总值比例（%）	Ratio of Total Imports and Exports and Gross Domestic Product（%）	3.10	22.43	38.89	52.18	49.53	33.12
出口总额占地区生产总值比例（%）	Ratio of Total Exports and Gross Domestic Product（%）	2.51	17.38	25.64	38.35	34.59	25.10
教 育	**Education**						
学龄儿童入学率（%）	Rate of School-age Children Enrollment（%）	100.00	99.65	100.00	100.00	100.00	100.00
中学毕业生升学率（%）	Rate of Secondary School Graduates Entering Higher Level Schools（%）	49.02	72.53	90.28	96.51	99.90	99.90
平均每个教师负担学生数（人）	Number of Students Burdened Per Teacher（person）	18.28	18.32	20.22	20.51	17.45	16.52
高等学校	Institutions of Higher Education	7.30	12.17	16.23	21.13	22.75	21.88
普通中学	Regular Secondary School	16.46	16.45	17.61	17.12	13.54	11.63
小 学	Primary School	21.17	19.97	23.08	21.37	18.62	19.98
婚 姻	**Marriage**						
离婚率（‰）	Divorce Rate（‰）	0.19	0.42	0.65	1.43	2.16	2.78
生 活	**Livelihood**						
城市与农村居民收入比例	Proportion of Income of Urban Residents to Income of Rural Residents	1.26:1	1.66:1	1.93:1	2.08:1	2.08:1	1.95:1
卫 生	**Health Care**						
每万人拥有医院数（包括卫生院，个）	Number of Hospitals Per 10000 Persons（unit）	0.50	0.48	0.34	0.32	0.26	0.29
每万人拥有医生数（人）	Number of Doctors Per 10000 Persons（person）	18.91	21.20	22.78	23.76	27.61	34.08
每万人拥有医院床位数（包括卫生院，张）	Number of Hospital Beds Per 10000 Persons（bed）	29.23	30.99	31.42	33.37	42.30	61.32
城市建设	**Urban Construction**						
人均公园绿地面积（平方米）	Per Capita Green Area of Park（sq.m）	1.83	4.10	5.64	7.10	12.35	13.85
建成区绿化覆盖率（%）	Coverage Rate of Green Areas（%）	15.13	29.80	31.69	38.80	42.15	43.08
人均拥有道路面积（平方米）	Per Capita Area of Road（sq.m）	5.50	6.50	10.68	17.90	22.88	24.76

4-16 常州国民经济主要指标占全省的比重（2015 年）
PERCENTAGE OF CHANGZHOU'S MAJOR NATIONAL ECONOMIC INDICATORS IN THE PROVINCE（2015）

指 标	Item	常州市 Changzhou City	江苏省 Jiangsu Province	常州市占全省的比重（%）Percentage of Changzhou in Jiangsu
土地面积（平方公里）	Area of Land （sq.km）	4372	107200	4.1
常住人口（万人）	Permanent Populationn（10000 persons）	470.14	7976.30	5.9
全社会从业人员（万人）	Social Employment（10000 persons）	281.00	4758.50	5.9
地区生产总值（亿元）	Gross Domestic Product（100 million yuan）	5273.15	70116.38	7.5
第一产业	Primary Industry	146.55	3987.94	3.7
第二产业	Secondary Industry	2516.04	32043.63	7.9
第三产业	Tertiary Industry	2610.56	34084.81	7.7
固定资产投资完成额（亿元）	Investment in Fixed Assets（100 million yuan）	3398.97	45905.17	7.4
一般公共预算收入（亿元）	General Public Budgetary Revenue（100 million yuan）	466.28	8028.59	5.8
一般公共预算支出（亿元）	General Public Budgetary Expenditure（100 million yuan）	485.33	9681.47	5.0
全体居民人均可支配收入（元）	Per Capita Disposable Income of All Residents（yuan）	35379	29539	高出全省5840元
城镇常住居民人均可支配收入（元）	Per Capita Disposable Income of Permanent Urban Residents（yuan）	42710	37173	高出全省5537元
农村常住居民人均可支配收入（元）	Per Capita Net Income of Rural Residents（yuan）	21912	16257	高出全省5655元
金融机构贷款余额（亿元）	Deposit Balance of Financial Institutions（100 million yuan）	7438.68	107873.03	6.9
#住户存款	Household deposits	3193.77	40562.97	7.9
金融机构贷款余额（亿元）	Loans Balance of Financial Institutions（100 million yuan）	5354.58	78866.34	6.8
粮食产量（万吨）	Output of Grain（10000 tons）	108.31	3561.34	3.0
油料产量（万吨）	Output of Oil-bearing Crops（10000 tons）	3.60	143.11	2.5
社会消费品零售总额（亿元）	Total Retail Sales of Consumer Goods（100 million yuan）	1990.45	25876.77	7.7
进出口总额（亿美元）	Total Exports & Imports（USD 100 million）	280.46	5456.14	5.1
#出 口	Exports	212.58	3386.68	6.3
实际到帐注册外资（亿美元）	Foreign Capital Actually Utilized（USD 100 million）	17.21	242.75	7.1

注：实际到账注册外资为商务部认定数。
Note: The quantity of paid-up foreign capital was recorded in accordence with the amount recognized by the Ministry of Commerce of the People's Republic of China.

4-17 分地区社会经济主要指标（2015 年）
MAJOR SOCIAL AND ECONOMIC INDICATORS BY REGION （2015）

指 标	Item	金坛区 Jintan District	武进区 Wujin District	新北区 Xinbei District	天宁区 Tianning District	钟楼区 Zhonglou District	溧阳市 Liyang City
人口与就业	**Population and Employment**						
年末总户数（万户）	Total Number of Households at Year-end（10000 households）	20.28	32.87	17.83	17.23	15.78	26.25
年末户籍总人口（万人）	Total Population at Year-end （10000 persons）	54.93	93.03	54.89	46.18	42.22	79.60
年末常住人口（万人）	Permanent Population at Year-end（10000 persons）	55.90	143.62	68.88	63.92	61.73	76.09
#城镇人口	Non-agricultural Population	33.56	94.80	41.40	56.49	57.96	44.89
年末在岗职工人数（万人）	Number of Staff & Workers Employed at Year-end （10000 persons）	7.80	21.99	14.25	10.38	7.29	5.77
年末私营企业从业人员（万人）	Employees of Urban Private Enterprises at Year-end （10000 persons）	17.32	55.88	28.23	14.80	12.90	21.08
年末个体从业人员（万人）	Urban Self-employed Individuals at Year-end（10000 persons）	5.30	12.64	8.53	7.78	7.59	6.88
城镇登记失业人员（人）	Urban Registered Unemployed Persons at Year-end （person）	3162	12644	1662	6396	5212	4544
综合经济	**Aggregative Economy**						
地区生产总值（亿元）	Gross Domestic Product （100 million yuan）	525.49	1830.00	1050.12	632.19	595.96	738.15
#工 业	Industry	222.65	972.23	540.29	169.89	185.69	311.86
按产业分	Grouped by Industries						
第一产业	Primary Industry	32.32	38.76	17.45	8.71	2.97	46.32
第二产业	Secondary Industry	266.11	1018.98	564.89	187.91	211.38	367.07
第三产业	Tertiary Industry	227.06	772.26	467.78	435.57	381.61	324.76
地区生产总值指数（上年=100）	Gross Domestic Product Index Number（Preceding Year=100）	113.8	108.0	110.7	108.2	107.2	103.1
#工 业	Industry	114.0	106.9	110.1	104.1	105.7	99.3
按产业分	Grouped by Industries						
第一产业	Primary Industry	103.5	103.8	103.1	102.3	101.7	102.9
第二产业	Secondary Industry	114.1	106.7	109.9	104.6	105.9	99.8
第三产业	Tertiary Industry	114.9	110.9	112.5	110.4	108.4	108.3
固定资产投资	**Investment in Fixed Assets**						
固定资产投资完成额（亿元）	Realized Investment in Fixed Assets（100 million yuan）	336.23	971.53	783.34	360.60	369.77	442.40
#工业投资	Industrial investment	238.10	552.65	482.26	74.50	72.03	322.10
房地产投资	Investment in Real Estate	25.94	159.26	92.41	90.85	99.28	40.30

4-17 续表 1 continued 1

指 标	Item	金坛区 Jintan District	武进区 Wujin District	新北区 Xinbei District	天宁区 Tianning District	钟楼区 Zhonglou District	溧阳市 Liyang City
财 政							
财政收入（亿元）	Financial Revenue（100 million yuan）	123.13	378.00	205.32	77.57	61.83	208.61
#一般公共预算收入	General Public Budgetary Revenue	36.15	140.38	97.59	44.79	35.97	56.19
#各项税收	Taxes	31.19	115.42	78.50	38.04	30.06	46.08
财政支出（亿元）	Fiscal Expenditure（100 million yuan）	112.99	279.51	101.66	26.27	26.87	189.93
#一般公共预算支出	General Public Budgetary Expenditure	46.59	141.72	63.02	24.60	23.84	61.38
工 业	**Industry**						
规模以上工业企业主要经济指标	**Main Indicators of Enterprises Above Designated Size**						
企业单位数（个）	Number of Enterprises Above Designated Size（unit）	436	1678	991	413	334	392
内资企业	Domestic-funded Enterprises	340	1425	717	338	273	342
港、澳、台商投资企业	Enterprises with Investment from Hongkong,Macao and Taiwan	37	102	70	41	26	18
外商投资企业	Enterprises with Foreign Investment	59	151	204	34	35	32
工业总产值（亿元）	Gross Industrial Output Value（100 million yuan）	1025.53	4273.20	2623.68	1035.57	930.92	1212.73
内资企业	Domestic-funded Enterprises	757.77	3451.58	1054.17	633.31	659.01	830.78
港、澳、台商投资企业	Enterprises with Investment from Hongkong,Macao and Taiwan	148.46	492.22	330.78	163.44	132.27	317.40
外商投资企业	Enterprises with Foreign Investment	119.31	329.40	1238.73	238.82	139.64	64.55
#制造业	Manufacturing	1017.04	4218.06	2592.71	1010.30	930.92	1201.08
#重工业	Heavy Industry	716.68	2977.62	2301.77	493.74	747.09	1089.49
总资产（亿元）	Total Assets（100 million yuan）	894.70	3425.83	1987.64	553.48	592.93	953.36
负债合计（亿元）	Total Liabilities（100 million yuan）	596.95	1865.61	1103.89	278.09	319.27	672.15
主营业务收入（亿元）	Main Business Income（100 million yuan）	1047.28	4567.20	2629.79	1063.96	969.43	1223.03
利税总额（亿元）	Total Pre-tax Profits（100 million yuan）	112.47	368.01	216.74	107.41	86.72	122.52
利润总额（亿元）	Total Profits（100 million yuan）	78.51	241.03	126.04	68.11	55.34	73.24
贸易、外经	**Trade, Foreign Trade**						
社会消费品零售总额（亿元）	Total Retail Sales of Consumption Goods（100 million yuan）	222.61	479.86	263.95	429.65	319.08	275.30
进出口总额（亿美元）	Total Imports & Exports（USD 100 million）	15.56	94.26	106.53	31.56	24.06	8.35

注：五区财政总收入、总支出均不含社保基金。
Note: Social security fund is excluded in total financial revenue and financial expenditure of five districts.

4-17 续表 2 continued 2

指 标	Item	金坛区 Jintan District	武进区 Wujin District	新北区 Xinbei District	天宁区 Tianning District	钟楼区 Zhonglou District	溧阳市 Liyang City
#出 口	Exports	11.46	68.07	75.97	27.48	21.95	7.46
新签外资项目数（个）	The Number of new foreign inrestment projents Signed （unit）	26	108	72	14	21	14
协议合同外资金额（万美元）	Amount of Negotiated Investment from Abroad（USD 100 million）	8286	123685	27485	12314	14417	30522
实际到帐注册外资（万美元）	Foreign Capital Actually Utilized（USD 100 million）	6756	67265	37073	6166	10131	10620
教育、卫生	**Education and Public Health**						
普通中学学校数（个）	Number of Regular Secondary Schools（unit）	24	42	20	7	6	36
小学学校数（个）	Number of Primary Schools（unit）	30	61	27	21	24	38
普通中学在校学生数（人）	Number of Student Enrollment of Regular Secondary Schools（ person）	18736	49738	21797	6156	4332	26710
小学在校学生数（人）	Number of Student Enrollment of Primary Schools（ person）	25871	97250	43135	34060	34413	38898
普通中学专任教师数（人）	Number of Full-time Teachers of Regular Secondary Schools（person）	2171	3652	1754	502	299	2806
小学专任教师数（人）	Number of Full-time Teachers of Primary Schools（person）	1819	4170	1907	1809	1617	2366
幼儿园数（个）	Number of Kindergartens（unit）	45	70	42	35	39	62
入园儿童数（人）	Number of Newly Enrolled in Kindergartens（ persons）	13328	35695	21921	15012	17375	19855
卫生机构数（个）	Number of Health Institutions（unit）	183	326	147	182	119	239
#医院、卫生院	Hospitals and Health care centers	18	27	15	13	9	27
卫生机构床位数（张）	Number of Beds in Health Institutions（unit）	2472	4649	1393	11209	1723	2817
#医院、卫生院	Hospitals and Health care centers	2272	4319	1100	10811	1473	2766
卫生技术人员（人）	Number of Medical Personnel（person）	2789	5869	2319	12031	2556	4052
#执业（助理）医师	Practicing （Assistant） Doctors	1258	2529	1040	4361	1041	1780
人民生活	**People's Livelihood**						
全体常住居民人均可支配收入（元）	Per Capita Disposable Income of All Residents（yuan）	29852	35874	35009	41368	41209	28737
全体常住居民人均消费性支出（元）	Per Capita Consuming Expenditures of All Residents（yuan）	16813	21095	21868	24726	24762	17527
城镇常住居民人均可支配收入（元）	Per Capita Disposable Income of Urban Residents（yuan）	40002	44738	44767	42736	42350	38445
城镇常住居民人均生活消费支出（元）	Per Capita Consuming Expenditures of Permanent Urban Residents （yuan）	21270	25006	26472	25422	25346	20294
农村常住居民人均可支配收入（元）	Per Capita Disposable Income of Permanent Rural Residents（yuan）	20427	23531	22738	22042	22194	19880
农村居民人均生活消费支出（元）	Per Capita Consuming Expenditures of Permanent Rural Residents（yuan）	12674	15650	16079	14885	15045	15003

5

CHAPTER 5

人 口

POPULATION

5 人 口 POPULATION

2015 年主要统计指标
MAJOR STATISTICAL INDICATORS OF 2015

年底总户数	Total Households	130.24万户	(10000 households)
比上年增长	Over the Previous Year	0.6%	
年底总人口	Total Population	370.85万人	(10000 persons)
比上年增长	Over the Previous Year	0.6%	
年底市区人口	Urban Districts Population	291.25万人	(10000 persons)
比上年增长	Over the Previous Year	0.7%	
年底常住人口	Permanent population	470.14万人	(10000 persons)
比上年增长	Over the Previous Year	0.1%	

5-1 历年年末户籍户数、人口数
YEAR-END HOUSEHOLDS AND POPULATION OVER THE YEARS

年 份 Year	总户数（万户） Total Number of Households（10000 households）	总人口（万人） Total Population（10000 persons）	城镇人口（万人） Urban Population（10000 persons）	年平均人口（万人） Average Population Per Year（10000 persons）	平均每户人口（人） Average Person Per Household（person）
1949	40.88	173.89	33.77	173.89	4.25
1950	42.37	176.45	31.86	175.17	4.16
1951	43.52	179.87	30.44	178.16	4.13
1952	44.23	183.34	31.31	181.61	4.15
1953	45.76	187.99	32.46	185.67	4.11
1954	45.86	191.54	34.38	189.77	4.18
1955	46.96	196.35	36.82	193.95	4.18
1956	47.03	198.34	37.45	197.35	4.22
1957	47.94	203.70	38.79	201.02	4.25
1958	48.60	211.66	48.22	207.68	4.36
1959	50.31	214.43	49.18	213.05	4.26
1960	50.87	215.49	50.04	214.96	4.24
1961	52.86	215.57	45.10	215.53	4.08
1962	53.18	222.13	39.49	218.85	4.18
1963	54.67	229.31	39.15	225.72	4.19
1964	55.26	235.39	38.84	232.35	4.26
1965	55.78	240.79	39.48	238.09	4.32
1966	56.20	246.69	40.12	243.74	4.39
1967	57.60	250.36	41.10	248.53	4.35
1968	59.10	256.51	43.01	253.44	4.34
1969	60.47	260.19	36.82	258.35	4.30
1970	61.93	266.82	37.58	263.51	4.31
1971	63.33	272.22	38.61	269.52	4.30
1972	64.16	275.67	39.00	273.95	4.30
1973	65.71	279.95	41.97	277.81	4.26
1974	66.81	282.61	40.86	281.28	4.23
1975	68.01	284.69	40.74	283.65	4.19
1976	69.98	287.32	42.25	286.01	4.11
1977	71.63	289.64	42.75	288.48	4.04
1978	73.23	291.00	45.22	290.32	3.97
1979	74.41	294.42	51.79	292.71	3.96
1980	77.19	295.92	53.48	295.17	3.83
1981	79.93	298.75	55.17	297.34	3.74
1982	81.59	301.98	57.68	300.37	3.70

5-1 续表 continued

年 份 Year	总户数 （万户） Total Number of Households (10000 households)	总人口 （万人） Total Population (10000 persons)	城镇人口 （万人） Urban Population (10000 persons)	年平均人口 （万人） Average Population Per Year (10000 persons)	平均每户人口 （人） Average Person Per Household (person)
1983	83.73	304.26	59.47	303.12	3.63
1984	85.60	305.48	61.46	304.87	3.57
1985	88.21	306.87	64.20	306.18	3.48
1986	91.06	309.74	67.92	308.31	3.40
1987	93.67	313.22	69.21	311.48	3.34
1988	100.32	317.06	75.08	315.14	3.16
1989	104.80	321.65	79.32	319.36	3.07
1990	106.91	324.85	81.40	323.25	3.04
1991	108.61	326.87	82.80	325.86	3.01
1992	110.41	328.57	97.58	327.72	2.98
1993	111.63	329.33	115.11	328.95	2.95
1994	111.84	331.44	116.02	330.39	2.96
1995	114.00	333.65	120.48	332.55	2.93
1996	114.73	337.54	124.71	335.60	2.94
1997	115.69	339.23	128.47	338.39	2.93
1998	116.57	340.75	130.43	339.99	2.92
1999	117.44	339.71	139.43	340.23	2.89
2000	117.89	341.48	147.81	340.60	2.90
2001	118.65	341.52	152.40	341.50	2.88
2002	119.74	343.24	157.82	342.38	2.86
2003	121.04	346.22	201.01	344.73	2.86
2004	121.63	348.96	206.75	347.59	2.87
2005	121.97	351.63	212.56	350.30	2.88
2006	122.32	354.67	223.99	353.15	2.90
2007	122.21	357.38	264.84	356.03	2.92
2008	123.40	358.74	268.66	358.06	2.91
2009	125.47	359.82	272.27	359.28	2.87
2010	127.11	360.80	293.74	360.31	2.84
2011	128.10	362.86	303.16	361.83	2.83
2012	128.75	364.77	310.31	363.82	2.83
2013	128.81	365.91	316.48	365.34	2.84
2014	129.42	368.64	322.64	367.28	2.85
2015	130.24	370.85	329.10	369.75	2.85

注:2003年前城镇人口为非农业人口数据，2006年起城镇人口按常住人口计算。

Note： The data of urban population belong to the data of non-agricultural before the year of 2003，the urban population is calculated as permanent population since 2006.

5-2 历年人口自然变动情况
POPULATION NATURAL CHANGE OVER THE YEARS

年 份 Year	出生人数（人） Birth Population (person)	出生率（‰） Birth Rate (‰)	死亡人数（人） Death Population (person)	死亡率（‰） Death Rate (‰)	自然增长人数(人) Natural Growth Population (person)	自然增长率（‰） Natural Growth Rate (‰)
1949	68233	39.2	28572	16.4	39661	22.8
1950	69811	39.9	28921	16.5	40890	23.3
1951	73147	41.1	28458	16.0	44689	25.1
1952	76275	42.0	28956	15.9	47319	26.1
1953	79065	42.6	28832	15.2	50233	27.1
1954	74832	39.4	23251	12.3	51581	27.2
1955	70118	36.2	21094	10.9	49024	25.3
1956	70379	35.7	23938	12.1	46441	23.5
1957	73364	36.5	19413	9.7	53951	26.8
1958	64609	31.1	18203	8.8	46406	22.3
1959	44026	20.7	26971	12.7	17055	8.0
1960	44985	20.9	32791	15.3	12194	5.7
1961	46124	21.4	26508	12.3	19616	9.1
1962	80239	36.7	20515	9.4	59724	27.3
1963	89412	39.6	18889	8.4	70523	31.2
1964	83705	36.0	18644	8.0	65061	28.0
1965	77946	32.7	18188	7.6	59758	25.1
1966	73364	30.1	16995	7.0	56369	23.1
1967	73418	29.5	16405	6.6	57013	22.9
1968	75064	29.6	15607	6.2	59457	23.5
1969	71259	27.6	14611	5.7	56648	21.9
1970	70116	26.6	16094	6.1	54022	20.5
1971	66295	24.6	16815	6.2	49480	18.4
1972	56287	20.5	16850	6.2	39437	14.4
1973	46210	16.6	17319	6.2	28891	10.4
1974	43963	15.6	17964	6.3	25999	9.2
1975	42669	15.0	17906	6.3	24763	8.7
1976	40004	14.0	17748	6.2	22256	7.8
1977	42121	14.6	18985	6.6	23136	8.0
1978	41310	14.2	18293	6.3	23017	7.9
1979	37548	12.8	18392	6.3	19156	6.5
1980	35260	11.9	19086	6.5	16174	5.5
1981	46288	15.6	18865	6.3	27423	9.2
1982	46030	15.3	18086	6.0	27944	9.3

5-2 续表 continued

年 份 Year	出生人数（人） Birth Population (person)	出生率（‰） Birth Rate (‰)	死亡人数（人） Death Population (person)	死亡率（‰） Death Rate (‰)	自然增长人数(人) Natural Growth Population (person)	自然增长率（‰） Natural Growth Rate (‰)
1983	32485	10.7	19710	6.5	12775	4.2
1984	29331	9.6	19340	6.3	9991	3.3
1985	30971	10.1	19082	6.2	11889	3.9
1986	40329	13.1	19067	6.2	21262	6.9
1987	47636	15.3	19274	6.2	28362	9.1
1988	48901	15.5	20204	6.4	28697	9.1
1989	50730	15.9	19115	6.0	31615	9.9
1990	48772	15.1	20595	6.4	28177	8.7
1991	41384	12.7	20412	6.3	20972	6.4
1992	39676	12.1	20979	6.4	18697	5.7
1993	37130	11.3	20176	6.1	16954	5.2
1994	35638	10.8	20248	6.1	15390	4.7
1995	38830	11.7	21292	6.4	17538	5.3
1996	33464	10.0	22239	6.6	11225	3.3
1997	48469	14.3	20008	5.9	28461	8.4
1998	40230	11.8	22255	6.5	17975	5.3
1999	31975	9.4	20355	6.0	11620	3.4
2000	42845	12.6	22998	6.8	19847	5.8
2001	28713	8.4	18720	5.5	9993	2.9
2002	30949	9.0	19746	5.8	11203	3.2
2003	25490	7.4	19867	5.8	5623	1.6
2004	27992	8.1	24266	7.0	3726	1.1
2005	29049	8.3	21624	6.2	7425	2.1
2006	28166	8.0	21465	6.1	6701	1.9
2007	27236	7.7	23811	6.7	3425	1.0
2008	25273	7.1	24734	6.9	539	0.2
2009	26142	7.3	27577	7.7	-1435	-0.4
2010	27950	7.8	30510	8.5	-2560	-0.7
2011	29007	8.0	22144	6.1	6863	1.9
2012	34352	9.5	28625	7.9	5727	1.6
2013	33666	9.2	28502	7.8	5164	1.4
2014	37647	10.3	24962	6.8	12685	3.5
2015	35522	9.6	25699	7.0	9823	2.7

5-3 分地区户数和人口情况（2015年底）
NUMBER OF HOUSHOLD AND POPULATION BY REGION（END OF 2015）

地 区 Region		总户数（户）Total Number of Households（household）	户籍人口（人）Household register Population（person）	按性别分 By Sex		按年龄分 By Age		常住人口（万人）permanent population（10000 persons）	其中 of which
				男 Male	女 Female	#18岁以下 Age 18 and Under	#60岁以上 Age 60 and Over		#城镇人口 Urban Population
总 计	**Total**	**1302366**	**3708519**	**1835823**	**1872696**	**494418**	**821974**	**470.14**	**329.10**
市 区	Urban Area	1039852	2912540	1434347	1478193	390468	645818	394.05	284.21
金坛区	Jintan District	202836	549294	272510	276784	60662	125695	55.90	33.56
武进区	Wujin District	328692	930345	457570	472775	124792	216013	143.62	94.80
新北区	Xinbei District	178264	548870	270443	278427	83278	104336	68.88	41.40
天宁区	Tianning District	172278	461807	226434	235373	62763	104870	63.92	56.49
钟楼区	Zhonglou District	157782	422224	207390	214834	58973	94904	61.73	57.96
溧阳市	Liyang City	262514	795979	401476	394503	103950	176156	76.09	44.89

5-4 分地区暂住人口情况
TEMPORARY RESIDENT POPULATION BY REGION

单位：人（person）

指 标 Item		全 市 Whole Municipality	市 区 Urban Area	其中 of which					溧阳市 Liyang City
				金坛区 Jintan District	武进区 wujin District	新北区 Xinbei District	天宁区 Tianning District	钟楼区 Zhonglou District	
总 计	**Total**	**1718247**	**1625569**	**84045**	**807037**	**362586**	**179606**	**192295**	**92678**
按时间分	By Time								
半年以下	Less than Six Months	639196	614201	38656	335648	155346	41448	43103	24995
半年至五年	Six Months to Five Years	1061859	995190	45203	462930	206107	135534	145416	66669
五年以上	More than Five Years	17192	16178	186	8459	1133	2624	3776	1014
按活动类型分	By Active Type								
#务 工	Engaged into Industry or Project	456219	434735	26388	198009	133573	27730	49035	21484
务 农	Engaged into Agriculture	49909	49096	6397	37387	3682	1120	510	813
经 商	Business	45303	42751	1615	13007	10507	6797	10825	2552
服 务	Service	53980	50729	4598	8259	14199	15001	8672	3251

注：公安部门调整了暂住人口统计时间，本表是截止到2016年6月30日的暂住人口。
Note:The public security authority adjusted the statistical survey date of temporary resident population. This table of Temporary Resident Population by Region refers to the population as of June 30, 2016.

5-5 分地区人口自然增长和迁移情况（2015 年）
NATURAL GROWTH AND MIGRATION OF POPULATION BY REGION（2015）

地 区	Region	出生人数（人）Birth Population (person)	出生率（‰）Birth Rate (‰)	死亡人数（人）Death Population (person)	死亡率（‰）Death Rate (‰)
总 计	**Total**	**35522**	**9.6**	**25699**	**7.0**
市 区	Urban Area	26885	9.2	20778	7.1
金坛区	Jintan District	4710	8.5	4355	7.9
武进区	Wujin District	8452	9.1	6794	7.3
新北区	Xinbei District	6165	11.3	3675	6.8
天宁区	Tianning District	3867	8.4	3149	6.8
钟楼区	Zhonglou District	3691	8.8	2805	6.7
溧阳市	Liyang City	8637	10.9	4921	6.2

5-5 续表 continued

地 区	Region	自然增长人数（人）Natural Growth Population (person)	自然增长率（‰）Natural Growth Rate (‰)	迁入人数（人）Number of the Transferred From Outside (person)	迁出人数（人）Number of the Transferred to Outside (person)
总 计	**Total**	**9823**	**2.7**	**36140**	**15843**
市 区	Urban Area	6107	2.1	32659	13066
金坛区	Jintan District	355	0.6	2562	2325
武进区	Wujin District	1658	1.8	13010	4287
新北区	Xinbei District	2490	4.6	7243	2015
天宁区	Tianning District	718	1.6	4895	2013
钟楼区	Zhonglou District	886	2.1	4949	2426
溧阳市	Liyang City	3716	4.7	3481	2777

5-6　预期寿命
LIFE EXPECTANCY

单位：岁（age）

年　代	year	平均预期寿命 Average Life Expectancy	其　中 of which 男 性 Male	女 性 Female
全　市	**Whole Municipality**			
第三次人口普查（1982 年）	The Third Census （1982）	67.8	66.5	73.2
第四次人口普查（1990 年）	The Forth Census （1990）	72.2	70.1	74.3
第五次人口普查（2000 年）	The Fifth Census （2000）	75.5	73.3	77.8
第六次人口普查（2010 年）	The Sixth Census （2010）	77.6	75.8	79.7
市　区	**Urban Area**			
第一次人口普查（1953 年）	The First Census （1953）	63.3	62.9	66.6
第二次人口普查（1964 年）	The Second Census （1964）	57.1	54.3	60.7
第三次人口普查（1982 年）	The Third Census （1982）	71.6	69.1	74.4
第四次人口普查（1990 年）	The Forth Census （1990）	74.7	72.7	76.6
第五次人口普查（2000 年）	The Fifth Census （2000）	77.8	75.8	79.8
第六次人口普查（2010 年）	The Sixth Census （2010）	79.0	77.7	80.5

5-7　分地区计划生育情况（2015 年）
STATISTICS ON BIRTH CONTROL BY REGION（2015）

地 区	Region	计划生育率（%） Family Planning Rate （%）	育龄妇女人数（万人） Number of Woman of Child-bearing Age（10000 persons）	其 中 of which 已婚育龄妇女数 Number ofMarried Woman of Child-bearing Age	现家庭只有一个孩子的妇女人数（万人） Number of Woman Owns One-child in Family （10000 persons）
全 市	**Whole Municipality**	**99.4**	**119.93**	**85.36**	**63.99**
市 区	Urban Area	99.4	100.03	71.30	53.41
金坛区	Jintan District	99.3	14.51	11.04	8.84
武进区	Wujin District	99.1	34.75	22.73	16.48
新北区	Xinbei District	99.5	20.87	15.35	11.13
天宁区	Tianning District	99.8	14.56	10.82	8.45
钟楼区	Zhonglou District	99.5	15.34	11.35	8.52
溧阳市	Liyang City	99.3	19.90	14.06	10.58

6

CHAPTER 6

从业人员 工资总额

EMPLOYMENT AND TOTAL WAGES

常州统计年鉴

6 从业人员　工资总额 EMPLOYMENT AND TOTAL WAGES

2015 年主要统计指标 MAJOR STATISTICAL INDICATORS OF 2015

年底全社会从业人员	Number of Employment	281.00万人	(10000 persons)
城镇非私营单位年底从业人员	Number of Employed Persons of Urban Non-Private Entities by the End of Year	69.89万人	(10000 persons)
城镇非私营单位从业人员平均工资	Average wage of Employees of non-private units in urban areas	70144元	(yuan)
私营单位从业人员平均工资	Average Wage of Employees of Private Entities	43032元	(yuan)

6-1　历年年末从业人员及构成
NUMBER AND COMPOSITION OF EMPLOYED PERSONS OVER THE YEARS

年　份 Year	年末从业人员（万人） Number of Employed persons（10000 persons）	其　中　of　which 第一产业 Primary Industry	第二产业 Secondary Industry	第三产业 Tertiary Industry	构　成（%） Composition（%）	其　中　of　which 第一产业 Primary Industry	第二产业 Secondary Industry	第三产业 Tertiary Industry
1949	67.24	56.96	4.08	6.20	100	84.7	6.1	9.2
1950	70.06	58.53	5.46	6.07	100	83.5	7.8	8.7
1951	72.82	61.64	5.49	5.69	100	84.6	7.5	7.8
1952	78.04	65.81	6.44	5.79	100	84.3	8.3	7.4
1953	80.06	66.77	7.46	5.83	100	83.4	9.3	7.3
1954	82.70	69.68	7.38	5.64	100	84.3	8.9	6.8
1955	84.64	72.22	6.85	5.57	100	85.3	8.1	6.6
1956	84.81	71.67	7.13	6.01	100	84.5	8.4	7.1
1957	84.80	71.31	7.41	6.07	100	84.1	8.7	7.2
1958	87.44	62.17	18.78	6.49	100	71.1	21.5	7.4
1959	87.82	63.36	17.30	7.16	100	72.1	19.7	8.2
1960	89.23	67.06	14.61	7.61	100	75.2	16.4	8.5
1961	91.28	69.54	13.28	8.47	100	76.2	14.5	9.3
1962	98.92	80.91	8.98	9.03	100	81.8	9.1	9.1
1963	101.81	84.14	8.93	8.74	100	82.6	8.8	8.6
1964	100.72	82.34	10.05	8.33	100	81.8	10.0	8.3
1965	106.33	85.77	11.36	9.21	100	80.7	10.7	8.7
1966	106.80	85.30	12.60	8.90	100	79.9	11.8	8.3
1967	110.36	88.85	12.78	8.73	100	80.5	11.6	7.9
1968	115.08	92.74	13.39	8.95	100	80.6	11.6	7.8
1969	118.59	95.82	14.13	8.64	100	80.8	11.9	7.3
1970	127.24	100.81	16.10	10.33	100	79.2	12.7	8.1
1971	131.32	101.71	18.83	10.78	100	77.5	14.3	8.2
1972	134.45	101.22	21.40	11.83	100	75.3	15.9	8.8
1973	136.12	100.92	22.72	12.48	100	74.1	16.7	9.2
1974	138.01	100.05	24.71	13.25	100	72.5	17.9	9.6
1975	138.69	97.10	27.79	13.80	100	70.0	20.0	10.0
1976	140.81	97.19	30.58	13.04	100	69.0	21.7	9.3
1977	144.43	93.53	36.11	14.79	100	64.8	25.0	10.2
1978	149.35	90.36	40.20	18.79	100	60.5	26.9	12.6
1979	151.59	92.75	43.17	15.67	100	61.2	28.5	10.3
1980	155.45	90.25	49.18	16.02	100	58.1	31.6	10.3
1981	157.23	87.90	51.84	17.49	100	55.9	33.0	11.1
1982	160.65	84.48	55.32	20.85	100	52.6	34.4	13.0

6-1 续表 continued

年 份 Year	年末从业人员（万人）Number of Employed persons（10000 persons）	其 中 of which			构 成（%）Composition（%）	其 中 of which		
		第一产业 Primary Industry	第二产业 Secondary Industry	第三产业 Tertiary Industry		第一产业 Primary Industry	第二产业 Secondary Industry	第三产业 Tertiary Industry
1983	168.92	87.09	59.26	22.57	100	51.6	35.1	13.4
1984	173.73	78.25	67.98	27.50	100	45.0	39.1	15.8
1985	178.64	70.19	77.50	30.96	100	39.3	43.4	17.3
1986	181.69	67.84	80.62	33.23	100	37.3	44.4	18.3
1987	187.00	65.96	84.95	36.09	100	35.3	45.4	19.3
1988	185.59	65.24	86.90	33.44	100	35.2	46.8	18.0
1989	184.55	66.88	84.09	33.58	100	36.2	45.6	18.2
1990	186.06	66.82	84.83	34.42	100	35.9	45.6	18.5
1991	187.39	67.33	84.15	35.90	100	35.9	44.9	19.2
1992	187.00	65.03	84.80	37.17	100	34.7	45.3	19.9
1993	188.65	63.70	86.56	38.39	100	33.8	45.9	20.3
1994	187.19	61.42	85.75	40.02	100	32.8	45.8	21.5
1995	188.78	55.51	89.23	44.04	100	29.4	47.3	23.3
1996	188.75	53.68	88.02	47.05	100	28.4	46.6	24.9
1997	185.23	54.69	84.05	46.49	100	29.5	45.4	25.1
1998	183.96	55.04	80.17	48.75	100	29.9	43.6	26.5
1999	185.60	54.38	79.64	51.57	100	29.3	42.9	27.8
2000	179.36	51.82	78.13	49.41	100	28.9	43.6	27.5
2001	189.11	49.81	85.26	54.04	100	26.3	45.1	28.6
2002	192.14	46.22	88.47	57.45	100	24.1	46.0	29.9
2003	199.74	38.77	98.92	62.05	100	19.4	49.5	31.1
2004	217.42	34.57	114.52	68.32	100	15.9	52.7	31.4
2005	222.31	30.01	118.71	73.58	100	13.5	53.4	33.1
2006	225.81	27.32	123.52	74.97	100	12.1	54.7	33.2
2007	233.18	25.88	129.65	77.65	100	11.1	55.6	33.3
2008	242.71	24.76	136.16	81.79	100	10.2	56.1	33.7
2009	251.56	24.40	140.87	86.29	100	9.7	56.0	34.3
2010	272.00	23.66	151.23	97.10	100	8.7	55.6	35.7
2011	277.72	22.26	153.21	102.25	100	8.0	55.2	36.8
2012	280.99	21.76	155.59	103.66	100	7.7	55.4	36.9
2013	280.90	31.50	147.20	102.20	101	11.2	52.4	36.4
2014	281.00	30.80	145.80	104.40	100	11.0	51.9	37.1
2015	281.00	30.70	143.50	106.80	100	10.9	51.1	38.0

注：2013年起全社会从业人员及三次产业从业人员根据人口抽样调查数据推算。
Note:Starting from 2013,Employees of the whole society and that of the three industries are calculated on the basis of the population survey data.

6-2 主要年份城镇非私营单位在岗职工人数和工资情况
THE NUMBER AND THE WAGES OF FULLY EMPLOYED STAFF AND WORKERS OF URBAN NON-PRIVATE ENTITIES IN MAIN YEARS

年份 Year	年底在岗职工人数（万人） Number of Fully Employed Staff and Workers by the End of Year (10000 persons)	在岗职工工资总额（万元） Total Wages of Fully Employed Staff and Workers (10000 yuan)	在岗职工年平均工资（元） Average Annual Wage of Fully Employed Staff and Workers (yuan)	年份 Year	年底在岗职工人数（万人） Number of Fully Employed Staff and Workers by the End of Year (10000 persons)	在岗职工工资总额（万元） Total Wages of Fully Employed Staff and Workers (10000 yuan)	在岗职工年平均工资（元） Average Annual Wage of Fully Employed Staff and Workers (yuan)
1949	3.91	1472	376	1991	56.14	144208	2558
1952	6.44	3077	508	1992	56.15	178846	3147
1957	11.03	4854	573	1993	57.53	242714	4216
1962	16.51	7942	531	1994	55.52	325767	5887
1965	18.51	8266	572	1995	54.42	386820	7098
1970	13.45	9988	499	1996	53.70	430388	7984
1971	24.83	12021	512	1997	49.69	456656	8594
1972	26.03	12895	500	1998	46.67	455656	9570
1973	26.44	13423	507	1999	44.75	479067	10514
1974	27.21	13836	512	2000	40.39	489699	11542
1975	28.35	14341	517	2001	37.66	518441	13108
1976	30.26	14899	508	2002	35.90	552293	14907
1977	31.94	15343	493	2003	34.67	607812	17259
1978	36.63	19255	534	2004	34.84	698249	19985
1979	39.14	22002	580	2005	35.11	785656	22990
1980	40.99	27169	690	2006	35.47	928432	26553
1981	42.61	28835	697	2007	35.51	1076918	30413
1982	44.24	32000	737	2008	35.92	1253405	34834
1983	46.31	34859	764	2009	35.97	1410417	39220
1984	47.97	45634	973	2010	36.70	1615042	44214
1985	50.27	58411	1196	2011	48.31	2271309	49755
1986	51.89	71936	1417	2012	46.80	2590106	55764
1987	53.80	83035	1588	2013	69.58	3936560	61225
1988	55.44	102877	1902	2014	69.69	4450228	67396
1989	55.12	112962	2052	2015	67.47	4756976	70850
1990	56.17	128994	2333				

注：从2011年起，在岗职工人数中包含了劳务派遣人员，在岗职工工资中包括了用人单位使用的劳务派遣人员工资。

Note: Starting from 2011, the number of dispatched workers is included in the number of Fully Employed Staff and Workers; and the wages of dispatched workers are included in the salaries of Fully Employed Staff and Workers.

6-3 分地区城镇就业和失业变动情况（2015 年）
URBAN EMPLOMENT AND UNEMPLOYMENT CHANGE BY REGION（2015）

单位：人（person）

指 标	Item	全 市 Whole Municipality	其 中 of which 市 区 Urban Area	溧阳市 Liyang City
上年末结转失业人数	Number of Unemployed Persons Carried Forward at Previous Year-end	32044	27884	4160
本年新登记失业人数	Number of Newly Registered Unemployed Persons at This Year	84349	80368	3981
#女 性	Female	43010	41322	1688
#由就业转失业人数	Number of Employed Persons Changed to Unemployed	60696	57732	2964
本年失业人员就业数	Number of Employment of Former Unemployed Persons	80099	76502	3597
#女 性	Female	40174	38658	1516
年末实有登记失业人数	Actual Registered Unemployed Persons at Year-end	33620	29076	4544
#女 性	Female	14450	12487	1963
#由就业转失业人数	Long-term Unemployed Persons	17656	14167	3489
登记失业率（%）	Registered Unemployment Rate （%）	1.89	1.89	1.91

6-4 失业人员安置情况（2011-2015 年）
UNEMPLOYED PERSONS ALLOCATION （2011-2015）

单位：人（person）

指 标	Item	2011	2012	2013	2014	2015
当年登记失业人数	Number of Registered Unem ployed Persons at This Year	87152	82967	84797	84572	84349
当年已安置就业人数	Number of Arranged Empl oyed Persons at This Year	84142	78734	81810	82141	80099
年末实有登记失业人数	Actual Number of Registered Unemployed Persons at Year-end	32650	34013	32699	32044	33620
登记失业率（%）	Registered Unemployment Rate （%）	2.58	2.37	2.14	1.91	1.89

6-5　分地区城镇非私营单位从业人员（2015 年底）
NUMBER OF EMPLOYED PERSONS OF URBAN NON-PRIVATE ENTITIES BY REGION (END OF 2015)

指　标	Item	全　市 Whole Municipality	市　区 Urban Area
总　计	**Total**	**698933**	**639257**
#女　性	Female	297277	274314
按执行会计制度分	**Grouped by Accounting System Executed**		
#企　业	Enterprises	560480	521819
事　业	Institutions	101898	87494
机　关	Government Agencies	36292	29681
按登记注册类型分	**Grouped by Type of Registration**		
内　资	Domestic-funded	414999	368098
国　有	State-owned	159325	134472
集　体	Collective-owned	14606	13833
股份合作	Share-holding Cooperative	1562	1416
联　营	Joint Ownership	260	260
有限责任公司	Limited Liability Corporations	169059	161701
股份有限公司	Share-holding Corporations Ltd.	65190	51625
其　他	Others	4997	4791
港澳台商投资	Investment from Hongkong, Macao and Taiwan	144574	138306
外商投资	Foreign Investment	139360	132853
按国民经济行业分	**Grouped by Economic Sector**		
农林牧渔业	Farming,Forestry,Animal Husbandry and Fishery	578	231
制造业	Manufacturing	333549	316864
电力、热力、燃气及水的生产和供应业	Production and Supply of Electricity, Heat, Gas and Water Industry	7658	6905
建筑业	Construction	80932	69624
批发和零售业	Wholesale and Retail Trade	21461	19583
交通运输、仓储和邮政业	Transportation , Storage and Post	19860	18283
住宿和餐饮业	Accommodation and Catering Services	16698	15705
信息传输、软件和信息技术服务业	Information Transmission, Software and IT Services Industry	6523	6078
金融业	Banking	23337	22249
房地产业	Real Estate Industry	10100	9180
租赁和商务服务业	Rent and Business Services	20071	17702
科学研究和技术服务	Scientific Researches and Technical Services	12363	11841
水利、环境和公共设施管理业	Water Conservancy, Environment and Public Facilities Management	11776	9744
居民服务、修理和其他服务业	Residential Services, Repairing and other Services Industry	593	546
教　育	Education	54763	47504
卫生和社会工作	Health and Social Work	31380	27386
文化、体育和娱乐业	Culture, Sports and Entertainment	7255	6731
公共管理、社会保障和社会组织	Public Administration, Social Security and Social Organizations	40036	33101

注：从业人员中包含了劳务派遣人员。
Note:Dispatched workers are included in Employed Persons

单位：人（person）

金坛区 Jintan District	武进区 wujin District	其 中 of which #经开区 Economic Development Zone	新北区 Xinbei District	天宁区 Tianning District	钟楼区 Zhonglou District	溧阳市 Liyang City
80951	**226201**	**41346**	**144691**	**112035**	**75379**	**59676**
34774	97255	16118	56796	55194	30295	22963
62638	190103	35652	124200	84535	60343	38661
13642	26404	4300	10304	24423	12721	14404
4577	9624	1394	10187	2978	2315	6611
59226	119309	20672	56646	77562	55355	46901
19267	34327	4436	21923	33019	25936	24853
2542	4889	1839	2492	1984	1926	773
228	562	150	366	155	105	146
			3	246	11	
29261	71710	13272	21154	23653	15923	7358
5590	6318	975	10345	18130	11242	13565
2338	1503		363	375	212	206
9088	81894	17147	20585	17645	9094	6268
12637	24998	3527	67460	16828	10930	6507
157	70			4		347
34515	126165	32436	100602	26889	28693	16685
822	1942	1159	787	3354		753
14773	41343	1025	3172	7164	3172	11308
1815	4790	237	2259	5207	5512	1878
2044	388		1390	6287	8174	1577
335	1147	153	1186	12104	933	993
346	276		3935	1198	323	445
879	1903			15491	3976	1088
831	2547	179	1937	1654	2211	920
4535	2030	40	1722	4582	4833	2369
1446	4336	34	2632	1449	1978	522
1747	2449	313	2986	832	1730	2032
24	119	34	191	121	91	47
8770	17605	2733	5628	8203	7298	7259
3496	6634	1389	1884	13191	2181	3994
376	2048	75	2071	435	1801	524
4040	10409	1539	12309	3870	2473	6935

6-6 分地区城镇非私营单位在岗职工人数（2015 年底）
NUMBER OF ON-POST STAFF AND WORKERS OF URBAN NON-PRIVATE ENTITIES BY REGION （END OF 2015）

指　标	Item	全　市 Whole Municipality	市　区 Urban Area
总　计	**Total**	**674684**	**617014**
按执行会计制度分	**Grouped by Accounting System Executed**		
#企　业	Enterprises	542411	504632
事　业	Institutions	96517	83066
机　关	Government Agencies	35493	29053
按登记注册类型分	**Grouped by Type of Registration**		
内　资	Domestic-funded	398423	353518
国　有	State-owned	154598	131029
集　体	Collective-owned	12542	11788
股份合作	Share-holding Cooperative	1435	1289
联　营	Joint Ownership	257	257
有限责任公司	Limited Liability Corporations	165406	158283
股份有限公司	Share-holding Corporations Ltd.	59587	46480
其　他	Others	4598	4392
港澳台商投资	Investment from Hongkong, Macao and Taiwan	139409	133151
外商投资	Foreign Investment	136852	130345
按国民经济行业分	**Grouped by Economic Sector**		
农林牧渔业	Farming,Forestry,Animal Husbandry and Fishery	569	226
制造业	Manufacturing	327238	310578
电力、热力、燃气及水的生产和供应业	Production and Supply of Electricity, Heat, Gas and Water Industry	7627	6874
建筑业	Construction	79680	68513
批发和零售业	Wholesale and Retail Trade	20360	18754
交通运输、仓储和邮政业	Transportation , Storage and Post	19415	17968
住宿和餐饮业	Accommodation and Catering Services	14641	13778
信息传输、软件和信息技术服务业	Information Transmission, Software and IT Services Industry	6394	5952
金融业	Banking	18953	17871
房地产业	Real Estate Industry	9431	8632
租赁和商务服务业	Rent and Business Services	19684	17326
科学研究和技术服务	Scientific Researches and Technical Services	11404	10962
水利、环境和公共设施管理业	Water Conservancy, Environment and Public Facilities Management	10072	8240
居民服务、修理和其他服务业	Residential Services, Repairing and other Services Industry	541	494
教　育	Education	52588	45634
卫生和社会工作	Health and Social Work	30189	26553
文化、体育和娱乐业	Culture, Sports and Entertainment	6817	6325
公共管理、社会保障和社会组织	Public Administration, Social Security and Social Organizations	39081	32334

注：城镇非私营单位在岗职工人数中包含了劳务派遣人员。
"Note:The number of dispatched workers is included in the number of Fully Employed Staff and Workers of non-private companies in urban areas.

单位：人（person）

		其 中 of which					
	金坛区 Jintan District	武进区 wujin District	其 中 of which #经开区 Economic Development Zone	新北区 Xinbei District	天宁区 Tianning District	钟楼区 Zhonglou District	溧阳市 Liyang City
	77995	**219870**	**40847**	**142484**	**103790**	**72875**	**57670**
	60648	184722	35379	122392	77781	59089	37779
	12721	25608	4080	10062	23177	11498	13451
	4532	9470	1388	10030	2733	2288	6440
	56524	117068	20404	55559	71329	53038	44905
	18966	33609	4303	21475	32036	24943	23569
	1749	4674	1735	2443	1407	1515	754
	138	558	146	366	126	101	146
				3	246	8	
	28493	70565	13245	20666	23139	15420	7123
	5041	6285	975	10245	14062	10847	13107
	2137	1377		361	313	204	206
	9059	78122	16949	20459	16481	9030	6258
	12412	24680	3494	66466	15980	10807	6507
	157	65			4		343
	34058	122156	32175	99382	26648	28334	16660
	822	1940	1159	770	3342		753
	14044	41167	1024	3146	7071	3085	11167
	1629	4376	233	2226	5128	5395	1606
	2020	375		1378	6044	8151	1447
	335	1084	153	1184	10296	879	863
	221	275		3935	1198	323	442
	873	1893			11464	3641	1082
	619	2534	179	1735	1609	2135	799
	4392	1999	40	1662	4464	4809	2358
	1342	3706	34	2605	1375	1934	442
	1028	2401	313	2981	501	1329	1832
	24	110	25	153	117	90	47
	8677	17102	2558	5464	7741	6650	6954
	3401	6404	1346	1854	12807	2087	3636
	352	2028	75	1902	405	1638	492
	4001	10255	1533	12107	3576	2395	6747

6-7　全市城镇非私营单位从业人员及平均工资（2015 年）
EMPLOYEES OF CITY'S URBAN NON-PRIVATE UNIES, AVERAGE WAGES AND MEDIAN WAGES （2015）

指　标	Item	年底从业人员人数（人）Number of Persons Employed at Year-end (person)
总　计	**Total**	**698933**
按地区分	**Grouped by Region**	
市　区	Urban Area	639257
金坛区	Jintan District	80951
武进区	Wujin District	226201
新北区	Xinbei District	144691
天宁区	Tianning District	112035
钟楼区	Zhonglou District	75379
溧阳市	Liyang City	59676
按执行会计制度分	**Grouped by Accounting System Executed**	
#企　业	Enterprises	560480
事　业	Institutions	101898
机　关	Government Agencies	36292
按登记注册类型分	**Grouped by Type of Registration**	
内　资	Domestic-funded	414999
国　有	State-owned	159325
集　体	Collective-owned	14606
股份合作	Share-holding Cooperative	1562
联　营	Joint Ownership	260
有限责任公司	Limited Liability Corporations	169059
股份有限公司	Share-holding Corporations Ltd.	65190
其　他	Others	4997
港澳台商投资	Investment from Hongkong, Macao and Taiwan	144574
外商投资	Foreign Investment	139360
按国民经济行业分	**Grouped by Economic Sector**	
农林牧渔业	Farming,Forestry,Animal Husbandry and Fishery	578
制造业	Manufacturing	333549
电力、热力、燃气及水的生产和供应业	Production and Supply of Electricity, Heat, Gas and Water Industry	7658
建筑业	Construction	80932
批发和零售业	Wholesale and Retail Trade	21461
交通运输、仓储和邮政业	Transportation , Storage and Post	19860
住宿和餐饮业	Accommodation and Catering Services	16698
信息传输、软件和信息技术服务业	Information Transmission, Software and IT Services Industry	6523
金融业	Banking	23337
房地产业	Real Estate Industry	10100
租赁和商务服务业	Rent and Business Services	20071
科学研究和技术服务	Scientific Researches and Technical Services	12363
水利、环境和公共设施管理业	Water Conservancy, Environment and Public Facilities Management	11776
居民服务、修理和其他服务业	Residential Services, Repairing and other Services Industry	593
教　育	Education	54763
卫生和社会工作	Health and Social Work	31380
文化、体育和娱乐业	Culture, Sports and Entertainment	7255
公共管理、社会保障和社会组织	Public Administration, Social Security and Social Organizations	40036

注：从业人员工资中包含了劳务派遣人员工资。
Note: The wages of dispatched workers are included in the salaries of Employed Persons.

年底在岗职工人数（人）Number of Fully Employed Staff and Workers by the End of Year（person）	从业人员工资总额（万元）Total Wages ofPersons Employed（10000 yuan）	在岗职工 工资总额（万元）Total Wages of Fully Employed Staff （10000 yuan）	从业人员平均工资（元）Average Wage of Persons Employed（yuan）	在岗职工平均工资（元）Average Wag off and Workers（yuan）
674684	**4876845**	**4756976**	**70144**	**70850**
617014	4477935	4366703	70425	71120
77995	467722	455819	59088	59721
219870	1448298	1422869	64335	65047
142484	1129647	1103699	78141	77607
103790	885390	848334	78882	81069
72875	546878	535983	73154	74376
57670	398909	390273	67132	67965
542411	3674144	3578020	65900	66278
96517	863775	843512	85289	87978
35493	337389	333908	93214	94258
398423	2980056	2914803	72229	73544
154598	1372087	1352158	86404	87771
12542	99191	92560	68394	74339
1435	8826	8192	56506	57165
257	2152	2143	79981	80266
165406	950194	930948	56250	56413
59587	521866	504714	81969	86117
4598	25739	24088	52928	53553
139409	879339	868299	61276	62699
136852	1017450	973874	73106	71299
569	4184	4149	72384	72909
327238	2216559	2177721	66660	66776
7627	76123	75908	98592	98774
79680	338796	332154	42496	42357
20360	128023	122523	59463	60386
19415	129840	127743	65233	65583
14641	88710	71573	53553	49137
6394	64203	63562	91432	92119
18953	294505	282931	130053	150263
9431	95185	92884	91630	95520
19684	105229	101616	52842	52044
11404	103836	98101	84715	86677
10072	64457	59345	57112	61973
541	3650	3387	61659	63908
52588	467698	459982	85833	87860
30189	279830	273628	90186	91871
6817	53879	51841	75208	76949
39081	362139	357932	90673	91759

6-8　市区城镇非私营单位从业人员平均工资（2015 年）
AVERAGE WAGES OF EMPLOYEES OF NON-PRIVATE UNITS IN THE URBAN AREA （2015）

指　标	Item	从业人员平均工资（元）Average Wage of Persons Employed（yuan）	在岗职工平均工资（元）Average Wage of Staff and Workers（yuan）
总　计	**Total**	**70425**	**71120**
按执行会计制度分	**Grouped by Accounting System Executed**		
#企　业	Enterprises	66324	66704
事　业	Institutions	86680	89386
机　关	Government Agencies	94678	95733
按登记注册类型分	**Grouped by Type of Registration**		
内　资	Domestic-funded	72419	73740
国　有	State-owned	86888	88114
集　体	Collective-owned	67520	73696
股份合作	Share-holding Cooperative	56222	56926
联　营	Joint Ownership	79981	80266
有限责任公司	Limited Liability Corporations	55721	55842
股份有限公司	Share-holding Corporations Ltd.	90708	96404
其　他	Others	52920	53575
港澳台商投资	Investment from Hongkong, Macao and Taiwan	61664	63179
外商投资	Foreign Investment	73917	72036
按国民经济行业分	**Grouped by Economic Sector**		
农林牧渔业	Farming,Forestry,Animal Husbandry and Fishery	72281	72996
制造业	Manufacturing	66879	67007
电力、热力、燃气及水的生产和供应业	Production and Supply of Electricity, Heat, Gas and Water Industry	97876	98074
建筑业	Construction	40996	40812
批发和零售业	Wholesale and Retail Trade	60104	60921
交通运输、仓储和邮政业	Transportation , Storage and Post	65006	65351
住宿和餐饮业	Accommodation and Catering Services	54195	49405
信息传输、软件和信息技术服务业	Information Transmission, Software and IT Services Industry	91392	92098
金融业	Banking	129866	151254
房地产业	Real Estate Industry	95420	98844
租赁和商务服务业	Rent and Business Services	55538	54678
科学研究和技术服务	Scientific Researches and Technical Services	85621	87446
水利、环境和公共设施管理业	Water Conservancy, Environment and Public Facilities Management	57358	63000
居民服务、修理和其他服务业	Residential Services, Repairing and other Services Industry	60224	62507
教　育	Education	86593	88667
卫生和社会工作	Health and Social Work	91618	92979
文化、体育和娱乐业	Culture, Sports and Entertainment	76258	78031
公共管理、社会保障和社会组织	Public Administration, Social Security and Social Organizations	91698	92792

注：从业人员工资中包含了劳务派遣人员工资。
Note: The wages of dispatched workers are included in the salaries of Employed Persons.

7

CHAPTER 7

物价指数

PRICE INDEX

7 物价指数 PRICE INDEX

2015 年主要统计指标
MAJOR STATISTICAL INDICATORS OF 2015

市区居民消费价格指数（以上年价格为100）	Consumer Price Index of Urban Residents （Preceding Year=100）	101.6
#食　品	Food	104.0
市区商品零售价格指数（以上年价格为100）	Retail Price Index of Urban Commodities （Preceding Year=100）	100.1
#食　品	Food	103.9

7-1　市区居民消费价格指数（1984-2015 年，以上年价格为 100）
CONSUMER PRICE INDEX OF URBAN RESIDENTS（1984-2015, PRECEDING YEAR=100）

年 份 Year	居民消费价格指数 Consumer Price Index	其中 of which						衣着类 Clothing
		食品类 Food	其中 of which					
			粮 食 Grain	肉禽及其制品 Meat and Poultry	水产品 Aquatic Products	菜 类 Vegetables	其中 of which 鲜 菜 Fresh Vegetables	
1984	102.6	103.9	99.9	105.3	127.9		101.2	99.5
1985	112.9	119.0	100.7	118.1	148.5		160.7	100.1
1986	106.1	108.5	98.4	111.4	102.3		116.9	101.0
1987	116.2	112.9	104.1	115.5	118.1		128.2	108.0
1988	123.3	130.2	102.2	135.3	129.3		153.0	120.3
1989	116.1	112.9	101.2	115.5	119.9		98.3	125.6
1990	104.2	102.3	101.8	101.2	102.7		105.9	110.0
1991	108.4	111.3	155.9	97.9	107.4		139.8	105.6
1992	108.2	109.9	159.2	103.0	112.1		99.7	103.5
1993	121.7	123.0	153.1	112.6	142.0		138.8	111.6
1994	122.4	131.1	159.0	140.9	119.1	134.8	137.2	115.3
1995	114.9	117.9	129.1	122.9	115.6	121.0	122.8	118.0
1996	110.2	108.9	107.4	105.6	105.0	131.7	133.7	114.1
1997	101.9	98.7	83.6	105.3	97.1	94.6	93.1	102.1
1998	101.6	97.8	101.7	90.5	92.6	105.2	105.7	101.5
1999	98.3	94.0	97.7	84.9	90.6	95.3	94.8	97.8
2000	99.5	95.5	80.5	96.1	95.2	110.4	110.9	95.3
2001	100.1	97.4	91.4	97.4	95.3	93.3	92.0	94.4
2002	98.5	97.8	96.1	97.7	93.0	111.1	109.7	99.5
2003	100.7	102.8	102.8	104.6	98.9	110.5	111.4	97.4
2004	104.3	113.2	140.2	122.1	119.2	93.8	93.3	98.5
2005	102.8	104.7	99.7	106.2	101.3	107.7	108.5	97.1
2006	101.8	104.7	103.9	99.2	108.2	108.0	108.9	99.7
2007	103.3	110.4	104.2	125.1	111.8	116.4	117.1	100.4
2008	105.2	112.3	113.9	121.1	112.6	104.7	103.6	102.4
2009	99.5	101.3	106.9	91.0	102.0	115.8	116.9	102.6
2010	103.4	107.4	119.8	101.5	114.3	114.8	115.3	102.4
2011	105.0	111.7	116.0	121.6	113.9	107.6	106.6	101.6
2012	102.5	104.9	105.3	103.0	107.0	105.5	106.2	101.6
2013	102.2	103.5	103.5	103.3	104.4	106.6	107.1	101.6
2014	102.2	102.7	101.6	100.1	98.4	97.4	96.6	104.2
2015	101.6	104.0	102.1	103.9	100.6	108.0	108.4	103.1

of		which						
家庭设备及用品类 Household Appliances	医疗保健及个人用品 Health Care and Personal Articles	交通和通讯工具类 Means of Transportation and Commun -ication	娱乐教育文化用品类 Recreational, Educational and Cultural Goods	居住类 Housing	服务项目类 Service	其 中 of which 学杂保育费 Tuition and Children Care	修理及其他服务费 Repair and Other Services	医疗保健服务 Medical and Health Care Services
98.6	106.3		99.7		104.3	116.4	106.9	100.0
101.0	102.4		100.5		109.8	127.3	118.1	100.0
102.6	100.8		101.5		106.6	104.4	113.5	102.3
106.9	104.9		103.2		108.5	100.0	115.4	105.4
111.0	117.5		107.7		117.6	100.4	133.7	100.0
114.7	112.2		121.3		115.7	148.3	123.4	100.0
101.3	101.0		97.2		114.1	102.7	109.6	332.4
102.1	101.5		96.1		111.5	100.0	115.4	100.0
103.7	109.6		90.4		121.1	148.0	103.2	100.0
112.2	108.9		102.3		140.3	130.1	148.2	231.5
111.8	103.3	105.7	109.6	113.5	117.6	117.1	120.0	114.4
105.3	103.9	103.8	105.8	111.9	121.6	128.7	123.8	100.0
101.6	108.7	97.2	113.0	126.0	112.3	115.7	100.4	101.4
101.9	102.1	100.1	103.6	109.7	113.2	127.3	100.2	100.1
95.9	98.7	100.5	101.5	117.7	112.8	109.2	108.3	138.7
98.4	102.4	102.7	98.0	106.5	108.5	122.1	100.9	118.9
99.7	101.8	97.6	101.7	103.8	111.7	128.7	100.0	108.8
98.5	101.6	97.6	112.8	99.7	110.5	138.5		116.9
97.5	100.3	98.2	97.5	100.7	99.5	102.3		100.0
93.9	98.2	98.9	99.4	103.7	101.1	103.7		100.0
98.3	93.6	100.2	99.2	103.3	100.8	100.0		100.0
100.2	100.2	99.7	103.6	106.5	104.9	112.5		101.0
101.6	101.1	99.3	96.2	106.3	101.8	99.0		103.4
101.4	100.9	96.8	96.2	104.2	99.4	97.5		100.0
103.8	102.0	99.2	97.9	106.5	102.0	101.1		100.0
101.3	100.4	94.9	98.6	97.9	99.5	100.0		100.3
101.8	101.5	100.1	99.7	104.1	102.2	100.1		102.1
106.3	102.4	100.0	101.5	104.4	103.0	100.7		102.4
107.2	99.6	99.4	101.0	102.5	103.0	102.0		100.0
102.5	102.0	100.5	101.3	102.5	102.3	99.5		100
103.6	102.1	100.1	100.6	103.0	102.5	100.6		100.0
102.4	101.4	95.6	100.9	101.2	101.5	100.9		102.4

7-2　市区商品零售价格指数（1984-2015 年，以上年价格为 100）
RETAIL PRICE INDEX OF URBAN COMMODITIES（1984-2015, PRECEDING YEAR=100）

年 份 Year	商品零售价格指数 Retail Price Index of commodities	其 中							
		食品类 Food	其 中 of which				饮 料烟酒类 Beverages, Tobacco and Liquor	服 装鞋帽类 Clothing, Shoes and Hats	纺织品类 Textiles
			粮 食 Grain	肉禽及制品 Meat and Poultry	水产品 Aquatic Products	鲜 菜 Fresh Vegetables			
1984	102.5	103.9	99.9	105.3	127.9	101.2	99.3	99.6	99.2
1985	113.2	119.0	100.7	118.1	148.5	160.7	100.8	100.1	100.0
1986	106.1	108.5	98.4	114.4	102.3	116.9	101.9	100.8	101.3
1987	110.4	112.9	104.1	115.5	118.1	128.2	107.2	109.8	104.2
1988	123.8	130.2	102.2	135.3	129.3	153.0	124.1	120.9	118.9
1989	116.1	112.9	101.2	115.5	119.9	98.3	109.9	124.6	128.4
1990	103.4	102.3	101.8	101.2	102.7	105.9	97.6	109.8	110.5
1991	108.1	111.3	155.9	97.9	107.4	139.8	104.8	106.1	103.4
1992	107.0	109.9	159.2	103.0	112.1	99.7	111.3	104.3	101.3
1993	119.9	123.0	153.1	112.6	142.0	138.8	107.8	114.4	100.8
1994	118.9	134.9	154.7	135.6	121.2	137.6	108.2	118.3	111.6
1995	112.8	123.2	130.1	125.0	115.4	127.6	108.1	119.0	113.4
1996	107.8	109.4	111.8	105.7	105.4	132.2	107.8	117.8	112.4
1997	100.2	97.0	82.3	101.6	97.8	93.5	97.7	102.8	105.8
1998	98.8	98.4	101.6	93.4	93.1	106.3	99.1	102.7	100.7
1999	97.3	93.3	98.0	85.5	91.5	95.3	99.6	98.6	99.6
2000	98.0	94.0	80.6	94.3	95.7	110.4	95.9	97.2	94.1
2001	97.3	98.6	105.5	99.2	94.2	94.7	98.3	90.8	90.3
2002	99.0	99.3	97.2	99.0	94.2	105.6	94.2	100.8	106.0
2003	100.8	103.0	103.3	105.0	98.9	111.4	105.0	98.0	98.3
2004	103.7	114.0	139.2	123.9	119.5	92.8	101.6	97.3	100.0
2005	101.3	104.7	99.8	105.9	101.3	109.1	101.3	96.0	100.8
2006	100.6	104.4	102.9	98.6	108.2	108.9	97.3	97.0	99.9
2007	102.4	110.6	103.3	125.8	111.7	117.1	101.1	100.1	102.2
2008	104.7	112.6	113.9	121.8	111.8	103.6	103.9	102.7	103.7
2009	99.6	101.8	107.1	92.7	101.7	116.9	101.5	103.2	101.9
2010	102.7	107.8	120.0	100.8	114.1	115.3	100.5	102.5	109.5
2011	104.4	111.5	116.0	120.3	114.2	106.6	103.9	103.4	132.1
2012	101.7	105.1	105.3	103.3	107.8	106.2	103.3	105.6	131.5
2013	101.3	103.6	103.5	103.6	104.4	107.1	100.5	101.6	93.7
2014	101.4	102.7	101.6	100.3	98.5	96.6	99.3	104.1	103.3
2015	100.1	103.9	102.1	103.9	100.6	108.4	101.3	103.3	103.5

of which									
中西药品类 Traditional Chinese and Western Medicines	化妆品类 Cosmetics	书报杂志类 Newspapers and Magazines	文化体育用品类 Cultural and Sports Goods	日用品类 Articles for Daily Use	家用电器类 Household Appliances	首饰类 Jewelry	燃料类 Fuels	建筑装璜材料类 Building Decoration Materials	机电产品类 Mechanical and Electrical Products
106.3		100.0	99.5	100.5	98.4		100.0		
102.4		116.3	101.7	103.4	99.2		100.0		
100.8		125.4	106.9	102.1	101.3		100.0		
104.9		100.0	115.9	112.4	100.3		100.0		
117.5		116.2	108.2	115.7	107.7		100.0	127.8	
112.2		198.4	112.6	117.9	118.5		100.0	120.6	
101.0		110.9	109.5	107.4	96.2		161.9	101.7	
101.5		100.3	101.6	102.5	96.5		143.9	100.3	
109.6		108.1	100.7	105.8	91.4		141.8	100.8	
108.9		105.9	105.4	113.4	104.5		201.9	125.8	
103.7	133.0	135.2	107.4	114.0	105.9	114.2	124.5	103.5	
103.3	109.4	126.8	103.9	109.0	100.9	99.6	107.9	100.1	92.6
106.9	102.1	138.1	102.1	106.5	99.6	99.0	111.8	99.1	94.9
102.0	101.2	116.4	99.2	102.8	100.0	100.7	103.7	102.7	93.3
98.8	104.1	115.7	98.0	100.5	89.8	91.7	102.6	99.9	97.4
102.2	101.8	102.5	99.0	100.1	97.7	94.2	99.7	101.2	99.5
101.7	98.8	108.4	99.8	101.2	98.5	109.0	118.1	97.0	98.1
99.6	91.0	110.5	95.6	98.9	98.1	93.7	100.9	95.6	96.7
93.3	100.3	95.4	99.1	99.6	100.0	101.8	99.7	102.0	96.5
98.2	102.3	99.6	99.3	99.9	93.7	118.6	112.0	101.1	
92.2	100.7	100.2	100.2	100.6	94.8	114.2	107.6	104.6	
99.6	101.8	100.4	95.6	101.4	96.9	105.3	111.4	106.0	
98.3	100.1	96.6	98.4	101.4	94.0	119.1	110.9	111.4	
100.0	99.6	97.2	95.9	100.6	98.0	105.2	102.5	109.3	
102.1	99.7	105.0	93.7	105.0	98.0	110.6	109.7	107.8	
100.2	100.3	124.5	92.2	101.6	94.5	98.5	88.9	98.4	
97.7	101.6	101.6	101.2	101.8	93.7	108.0	111.0	108.0	
101.9	95.9	100.7	95.4	104.5	102.7	117.0	108.6	105.8	
98.3	102.9	101.0	102.1	103.6	97.9	99.6	102.0	97.4	
103.5	106.8	100.2	100.2	101.9	101.3	91.6	102.1	99.8	
103.6	103.7	103.6	100.9	100.9	101.1	92.3	101.6	100.1	
101.2	100.1	104.2	98.6	100.2	101.3	93.1	87.8	98.2	

7-3　市区居民消费价格指数（2015 年，以上年价格为 100）
CONSUMER PRICE INDEX OF URBAN RESIDENTS（2015, PRECEDING YEAR=100）

指　标	Item	2015
居民消费价格指数	**Residents Consumer Price Index**	**101.6**
服务项目价格指数	Price index of Service	101.5
消费品价格指数	Price index of Consumer Goods	101.6
食　品	Food	104.0
#粮　食	Grain	102.1
肉禽及其制品	Meat and Poultry	103.9
水产品	Aquatic Products	100.6
鲜　菜	Fresh Vegetables	108.4
烟酒及用品	Tobacco and Liquor and Articles	101.1
烟　草	Tobacco	101.7
酒	Liquor	99.3
衣　着	Clothing	103.1
服　装	Garments	102.3
衣着材料	Clothing Material	101.6
鞋袜帽	Shoes,Socks and Caps	105.7
衣着加工服务	Clothing Making Services	103.6
家庭设备用品及服务	Household Appliances and Services	102.4
耐用消费品	Durable Consumer Goods	103.1
室内装饰品	Interior Decorations	103.6
床上用品	Bed Articles	103.9
家庭日用杂品	Daily Use Household Articles	100.8
家庭服务及加工维修服务	Household Services,Processing and Repairing Services	102.3
医疗保健及个人用品	Health Care and Personal Articles	101.4
医疗保健	Medicine and Healthcare	102.4
个人用品及服务	Individual Articals and Services	99.6
交通和通讯	Transportation and Communication	95.6
交　通	Transportation	94.1
通　信	Communication	100.3
娱乐教育文化用品及服务	Recreational,Educational and Cultural Goods and Services	100.9
文娱用耐用消费品及服务	Durable Consumer Goods for Recreational Use and Services	99.9
教　育	Education	101.0
文化娱乐用品	Cultural and Recreational Articles	101.4
旅游及外出	Tour and External Business	100.8
居　住	Housing	101.2
建房及装修材料	Building Materials	99.6
租　房	Rent	100.3
自有住房	Housing	103.0
水、电、燃料	Water,Electricity and Fuels	99.2

7-4 市区商品零售价格指数（2015 年，以上年价格为 100）
RETAIL PRICE INDEX OF URBAN COMMODITIES（2015, PRECEDING YEAR=100）

指 标	Item	2015
商品零售价格指数	**Retail Price Index of commodities**	**100.1**
食 品	Food	103.9
#粮 食	Grain	102.1
淀粉及制品	Starches and Related Product	101.9
干豆类及豆制品	Bean and Its Products	101.7
油 脂	Oil or Fat	92.8
肉禽及其制品	Meat, Poultry and Related Product	103.9
蛋	Eggs	94.4
水产品	Aquatic Products	100.6
菜	Vegetables	108.0
#鲜 菜	Fresh Vegetables	108.4
调味品	Flavoring	105.0
糖	Carbohydrate	102.3
干鲜瓜果	Dried and Fresh Fruits and Melons	102.8
糕点饼干面包	Cake， Biscuit and Brad	105.0
奶及奶制品	Milk and Its Products	100.8
在外用膳食品	Out Ward Dinner	106.4
其它食品	Others Foods	100.2
饮料烟酒	Beverages,Tobacco and Liquor	101.3
服装鞋帽	Clothing,Shoes and Hats	103.3
纺织品	Textiles	103.5
家用电器及音像器材	Household Appliances and Acoutic and Visual Equipment	101.3
文化办公用品	Cultural Stationery	98.4
日用品	Articles for Daily Use	100.2
体育娱乐用品	Sports and Entertainment Articles	98.6
交通、通信用品	Tansportation and Telecommunication Facilities	98.9
家 具	Furniture	104.6
化妆品	Cosmetics	100.1
金银珠宝	Jewellery	93.1
中西药品及医疗保健用品	Chinese and Western Medicine and Medical care Articles	101.2
书报杂志及电子出版物	Newspaper, Magazine & Electronic Publication	104.2
燃 料	Fuels	87.8
建筑材料及五金电料	Construction Materials & Hardware Materials	98.2

7-5　市区分月主要农副产品价格（2015 年）
MAIN AGRICULTURAL AND SIDELINE PRODUCTS IN URBAN AREA BY MONTH（2015）

品　种	Name	规格等级	Specification and Grade	1 月 Jan.	2 月 Feb.
粳　米	Polished Rice	特　一	Special First Grade	5.6	5.6
植物油	Vegetable Oil	豆　油	Soybean Oil	8.1	8.2
猪　肉	Pork	去骨后腿肉	Thigh Meat without Bone	24.0	23.8
鸡	Chicken	活草鸡	Live Chicken	30.8	31.7
鲜　蛋	Fresh Eggs	新鲜完整	Fresh and Whole	10.5	10.1
鲢　鱼	Silver Carp	1.0千克以上	Above 1.0 Kilogram	13.9	14.0
鲫　鱼	Crucian	活200克左右	Live and Weight about 200 Gram	16.4	16.5
虾	Shrimps	活河虾	Live Shimps	137.9	141.5
大白菜	Chinese Cabbage	一　等	First Grade	2.3	2.6
油　菜	Rape	一　等	First Grade	4.4	4.9
芹　菜	Celery	一　等	First Grade	6.7	7.3
黄　瓜	Cucumber	一　等	First Grade	8.5	9.1
西红柿	Tomato	一　等	First Grade	7.8	9.4
萝　卜	Radish	一　等	First Grade	3.4	3.7
青　椒	Green Pepper	一　等	First Grade	10.4	12.5
生　姜	Ginger	一　等	First Grade	18.6	13.4
豆　芽	Bean Sprout	一　等	First Grade	4.8	5.6
苹　果	Apples	一　级	First Grade	14.4	15.2
梨	Pears	一　级	First Grade	7.0	7.1
香　蕉	Bananas	一　级	First Grade	7.6	8.8

单位：元/千克（yuan/kg）

3月 Mar.	4月 Apr.	5月 May	6月 June	7月 July	8月 Aug.	9月 Sept.	10月 Oct.	11月 Nov.	12月 Dec.
5.6	5.7	5.7	5.6	5.6	5.6	5.6	5.6	5.7	5.7
8.1	8.1	8.2	8.0	8.0	7.9	8.1	8.1	8.1	8.1
22.9	22.3	22.6	24.0	26.2	28.0	28.0	27.1	26.6	26.4
31.1	30.9	30.5	31.2	31.2	31.2	31.2	31.2	31.2	31.2
9.1	8.4	8.4	8.1	8.4	9.6	10.3	9.0	9.0	9.1
14.1	14.6	15.0	15.1	15.4	15.0	14.2	14.2	13.7	13.2
16.3	16.5	17.3	17.6	18.9	19.9	18.1	17.6	17.6	17.4
141.1	145.9	104.8	96.6	133.2	146.0	142.7	142.3	138.5	141.8
3.1	3.6	3.1	3.3	3.6	3.4	3.2	3.1	2.7	2.5
4.3	4.9	4.9	5.4	7.2	6.0	5.3	4.3	4.0	6.0
6.2	6.2	7.9	8.1	7.6	6.9	6.4	6.0	6.0	6.6
6.9	6.8	5.7	5.1	6.3	6.7	5.9	5.3	6.8	9.2
8.8	8.6	6.7	4.9	6.4	7.3	7.5	7.6	7.9	8.9
3.3	3.2	3.0	3.1	3.3	3.6	3.6	3.4	3.0	3.0
11.2	11.4	10.7	9.4	9.2	9.0	9.1	9.1	9.4	10.0
13.4	14.6	15.2	15.2	15.2	14.7	13.5	12.7	12.5	12.0
5.2	5.0	5.0	5.0	5.0	5.0	5.0	5.0	5.0	5.0
15.0	14.7	14.8	14.6	14.5	14.7	14.4	13.7	13.4	13.2
7.1	7.4	8.1	8.4	8.5	8.6	8.4	8.0	7.8	8.0
8.6	7.6	8.0	7.4	7.0	6.9	6.5	6.1	5.7	5.7

8

CHAPTER 8

人民生活

PEOPLE' S LIVELIHOOD

常州统计年鉴

8 人民生活
PEOPLE'S LIVELIHOOD

2015 年主要统计指标
MAJOR STATISTICAL INDICATORS OF 2015

全体居民人均可支配收入	Per Capita Disposable Income of All Residents	35379元	(yuan)
比上年增长	Over the Previous Year	8.3%	
全体居民人均消费支出	Per Capita Consuming Expenditures of All Residents	22234元	(yuan)
比上年增长	Over the Previous Year	7.9%	
城镇常住居民人均可支配收入	Per Capita Disposable Income of Permanent Urban Residents	42710元	(yuan)
比上年增长	Over the Previous Year	8.2%	
城镇常住居民人均消费支出	Per Capita Consuming Expenditures of Permanent Urban Residents	25358元	(yuan)
比上年增长	Over the Previous Year	7.5%	
农村常住居民人均可支配收入	Per Capita Disposable Income of Permanent Rural Residents	21912元	(yuan)
比上年增长	Over the Previous Year	8.8%	
农村常住居民人均消费支出	Per Capita Consuming Expenditures of Permanent Rural Residents	14764元	(yuan)
比上年增长	Over the Previous Year	9.1%	

8-1　城乡居民家庭人均收入和消费支出（1984-2015 年）
PER CAPITA ANNUAL INCOME AND LIVING EXPENDITURE OF URBAN HOUSEHOLDS （1984-2015）

单位:元（yuan）

年 份 Year	全体常住居民人均可支配收入 Per Capita Disposable Income of the Resident Population	全体常住居民人均消费支出 Per Capita Consumer Spending of the Resident Population	城镇常住居民人均可支配收入 Per Capita Disposable Income of the Urban Resident	城镇常住居民人均消费支出 Per Capita Consumer Spending of the Urban Residents	农村常住居民人均可支配收入 Per Capita Disposable Income of the Rural Residents	农村常住居民人均消费支出 Per Capita Consumer Spending of the Rural Residents
1984			701	595		
1985			889	746	618	563
1986			1089	918	777	697
1987			1236	1059	855	782
1988			1417	1359	1108	1161
1989			1559	1469	1301	1305
1990			1769	1498	1401	1231
1991			1996	1705	1318	1205
1992			2509	2000	1588	1442
1993			3195	2456	2041	1762
1994			4617	3503	2707	2259
1995			5632	4426	3397	2952
1996			6743	4946	4172	3598
1997			6853	5442	4216	3754
1998			7107	5282	4289	3045
1999			7874	6107	4313	3316
2000			8540	6759	4430	3243
2001			9406	7526	4719	3277
2002			9933	7973	5138	3698
2003			11303	8944	5550	3953
2004			12867	9878	6235	4793
2005			14589	10718	7002	5712
2006			16649	12503	8001	6518
2007			19089	13789	9033	7400
2008			21592	14967	10171	8128
2009			23751	15961	11198	8843
2010			26269	17124	12637	9924
2011			29829	18893	14838	11208
2012			33587	20519	16737	12027
2013			36946	23090	18643	13563
2014	32662	20608	39483	23590	20133	13529
2015	35379	22234	42710	25358	21912	14764

注：2014年起城乡居民收入是城乡住户调查一体化改革后的新口径数据。2013年以前，城镇居民人均可支配收入为市区数，农村居民人均可支配收入为全市农民人均纯收入。

Note: Disposable incomes of urban and rurual residents were calculated in line with standards set out after the integration of urban and rural surveys in 2014. Before 2014, the disposable income of urban residents was the disposable income of downtown esidents, and the disposable income of rural residents was the net income of all rurual residents.

8-2 全市居民家庭收支基本情况（2015 年）
BASIC CONDITION OF INCOME AND EXPENDITURE OF HOUSEHOLDS OF WHOLE MUNICIPALITY（2015）

指标	Item	全体居民 All Residents		城镇居民 Urban Residents		农村居民 Rural Residents	
		绝对数 Value	比上年增长(%) Over the Previous Year(%)	绝对数 Value	比上年增长(%) Over the Previous Year(%)	绝对数 Value	比上年增长(%) Over the Previous Year(%)
常住居民人均可支配收入（元）	**Per Capita Disposable Income of Permanent Residents（yuan）**	**35379**	**8.3**	**42710**	**8.2**	**21912**	**8.8**
按收入来源分	**Grouped by Source of Income**						
工资性收入	Income from Wages and Salaries	21780	8.1	26394	8.1	13236	8.4
经营净收入	Operating Net Income	5799	9.0	6124	8.3	5088	9.4
财产净收入	Net Property Income	2591	7.7	3784	7.7	409	11.2
转移净收入	Net Transfer Income	5210	8.9	6408	8.9	3180	9.5
按地区分	**Grouped by Region**						
市　区	Urban Area	37779	8.2	43642	8.1	23180	8.7
天宁区	Tianning District	41368	8.2	42736	8.2	22042	8.5
钟楼区	Zhonglou District	41209	8.3	42350	8.3	22194	8.3
新北区	Xinbei District	35009	8.3	44767	8.1	22738	8.9
武进区	Wujin District	35874	8.2	44738	8.0	23531	8.6
金坛区	Jintan District	29852	8.6	40002	8.4	20427	9.0
溧阳市	Liyang City	28737	8.5	38445	8.2	19880	9.1
常住居民人均消费支出（元）	**Per Capita Consuming Expenditure of Permanent Residents（yuan）**	**22234**	**7.9**	**25358**	**7.5**	**14764**	**9.1**
按支出项目分	**Grouped by Item**						
食品烟酒	Food, Tobacco and Liquor	6410	7.4	7101	6.4	4678	8.8
衣　着	Clothing	1688	8.3	1881	7.2	1088	9.8
居　住	Residence	4617	5.6	5292	4.5	2891	5.9
生活用品及服务	Articles for Daily Use and Services	1344	8.1	1537	8.6	903	8.4
交通通信	Transportation and Communications	3153	7.6	3848	10.0	1788	8.7
教育文化娱乐	Education, Culture and Entertainment	2875	12.5	3387	11.2	1623	16.6
医疗保健	Medicine and Medical Services	1506	8.6	1655	9.0	1219	9.8
其他商品及服务	Other Commodities and Services	640	7.3	657	5.0	573	8.6
按地区分	**Grouped by Region**						
市　区	Urban Area	23497	7.8	25922	7.5	15615	9.0
天宁区	Tianning District	24726	7.8	25422	7.7	14885	8.9
钟楼区	Zhonglou District	24762	8.2	25346	8.2	15045	9.0
新北区	Xinbei District	21868	7.6	26472	7.0	16079	9.0
武进区	Wujin District	21095	7.7	25006	7.1	15650	9.1
金坛区	Jintan District	16813	8.1	21270	7.5	12674	9.1
溧阳市	Liyang City	17527	8.3	20294	7.4	15003	9.5
恩格尔系数（%）	**Engel Coefficient（%）**	**28.8**	**-0.2个百分点**	**28.0**	**-0.3个百分点**	**31.7**	**-0.1个百分点**
人均住房建筑面积（平方米）	**Per Capita Construction Area of Housing（m^2）**	**50.1**	**3.1**	**44.1**	**0.9**	**63.98**	**7.2**

注：2015年市区不含金坛数据。
Note:The 2015 data of Changzhou's urban area do not include Jintan District.

8-3　全市居民家庭人口分组（2015 年）
GROUPING OF POPULATION OF HOUSEHOLDS OF WHOLE MUNICIPALITY （2015）

指　标	Item	总平均 Average
调查样本住户数	**Number of Sample Households Surveyed**	**951.75**
城镇住户	Urban Households	632.83
农村住户	Rural Households	318.92
期内住户常住成员数	**Permanent Members of Households within The Period**	**2.95**
劳动力人数	**Number of Labor Force**	**2.36**
按从业类型分	Grouped by Type of Employment	
从业人数	Number of Employed Persons	1.83
雇 主	Employers	0.05
公职人员	Public Employees	0.03
事业单位人员	Public Institution Personnel	0.12
国有企业雇员	State-owned Enterprise Employees	0.07
其他雇员	Other Employees	1.19
农业自营	Agricultural Self-employed	0.20
非农自营	Non-agricultural Self-employed	0.17
未从业人数	Unemployed	0.53
按是否离退休分	Grouped by Whether or Not Retired	
行政事业单位离退休	Retirement from Administrative Institutions	0.07
其他单位离退休	Retirement from Other Units	0.42
未退休	Not Retired	1.87
平均每一就业者负担人数	**Number of Persons Supported by Each Employee**	**1.61**

单位:人（person）

按收入水平分组 Grouped by Level of Income				
低收入户 Low Income Households	中低收入户 Lower Middle Income Households	中等收入户 Middle Income Households	中高收入户 Upper Middle Income Households	高收入户 High Income Households
190.50	**191.17**	**190.92**	**191.08**	**188.08**
70.50	102.17	129.92	154.08	176.17
120.00	89.00	61.00	37.00	11.92
3.17	**3.23**	**2.88**	**2.74**	**2.72**
2.32	**2.56**	**2.38**	**2.29**	**2.25**
1.79	2.05	1.86	1.71	1.72
0.03	0.05	0.04	0.04	0.09
0.01	0.01	0.01	0.07	0.09
0.02	0.04	0.10	0.19	0.27
0.04	0.04	0.05	0.09	0.12
1.15	1.51	1.32	1.07	0.89
0.37	0.25	0.19	0.14	0.03
0.18	0.16	0.16	0.12	0.23
0.53	0.51	0.52	0.58	0.53
0.01	0.02	0.05	0.08	0.21
0.23	0.42	0.46	0.58	0.40
2.09	2.13	1.86	1.62	1.64
1.78	**1.57**	**1.54**	**1.60**	**1.58**

8-4　全市居民家庭人均收入情况（2015 年）
PER CAPITA INCOME OF HOUSEHOLDS OF WHOLE MUNICIPALITY （2015）

指　标	Item	总平均 Average
全体居民人均可支配收入	**Per Capita Disposable Income**	**35378.90**
工资性收入	Income from Wages and Salaries	21779.50
工　资	Wages	20768.56
实物福利	Benefit in Kind	79.67
其 他	Others	931.27
经营净收入	Operating Net Income	5798.80
第一产业	Primay Industry	1230.50
第二产业	Secondary Industry	2177.15
第三产业	Tertiary Industry	2391.14
财产净收入	Net Property Income	2590.60
利息净收入	Net Interest Income	119.05
红利收入	Dividend	360.98
储蓄性保险净收益	Net Income from Depositing Insurance	3.64
转让承包土地经营权租金净收入	Net Rent Income by Transfer of Contracted Land Use Rights	70.78
出租房屋财产性收入	House Renting Income	438.51
出租机械、专利、版权等资产的收入	Income from Leasing Assets of Machinery, Patent and Copyright	0.32
其他财产净收入	Other Net Property Income	40.91
其　他	Others	1556.40
转移净收入	Net Transfer Income	5210.00
转移性收入	Transfer Income	7620.24
养老金或离退休金	Pension or Retirement Pay	5917.98
社会救济和补助	Social Relief and Subsidies	41.36
政策性生活补贴	Policy-guaranteed Living Allowances	26.93
报销医疗费	Reimbursement of Medical Expenses	284.68
家庭外出从业人员寄回带回收入	Income Sent or Brought Back by Household Members Working Outside	571.87
赡养收入	Alimony	405.59
其他经常转移收入	Other Regular Transfer Income	335.74
#失业保险金	Unemploment Insurance Benefits	7.86
从政府和组织得到的实物产品和服务折价	Physical Products and Discounted Service Obtained from Government and Organizations	8.99
现金政策性惠农补贴	Policy-guaranteed Agricultural Subsidies in Cash	27.12

单位:元（yuan）

按收入水平分组 Grouped by Level of Income				
低收入户 Low Income Households	中低收入户 Lower Middle Income Households	中等收入户 Middle Income Households	中高收入户 Upper Middle Income Households	高收入户 High Income Households
14181.51	**23080.59**	**30387.33**	**40524.07**	**75333.13**
9763.68	16018.02	19099.86	23606.71	43922.25
9497.65	15689.14	18333.54	22485.97	41058.88
26.27	56.25	73.26	113.51	143.25
239.76	272.63	693.07	1007.23	2720.11
2028.85	2500.21	3972.92	5858.08	16127.44
1267.01	951.12	1531.39	1799.53	619.36
203.78	330.41	376.80	1739.75	9113.86
558.06	1218.68	2064.73	2318.80	6394.21
814.97	1402.23	1985.68	2857.71	6496.32
-5.87	-4.19	-19.41	-34.51	720.91
80.56	178.87	160.30	55.21	1440.00
	3.85		8.64	6.49
137.08	81.15	58.90	62.74	0.96
106.09	263.39	405.65	560.31	952.89
1.47				
4.91	-22.84	-7.73	23.84	229.95
490.74	902.01	1387.97	2181.47	3145.13
1574.01	3160.12	5328.87	8201.57	8787.13
3015.45	4647.29	7291.16	11011.46	13526.35
1909.25	3604.06	6015.01	9442.77	9731.46
56.82	74.45	24.00	40.55	2.63
18.71	6.41	20.71	33.61	61.20
185.93	174.83	398.97	277.98	418.05
405.41	243.44	386.95	317.63	1623.16
339.82	201.65	257.11	504.75	787.05
64.22	297.59	151.48	359.87	875.32
	26.07	9.11	1.83	
9.65	6.14	7.29	12.83	9.56
25.65	38.72	29.66	21.47	17.91

8-4 续表 continued

指　标	Item	总平均 Average
转移性支出	Transfer Expenditure	2410.24
个人所得税	Personal Income tax	123.53
社会保障支出	Expenditure on Social Security	1502.02
个人缴纳的养老保险	Pension Fund Paid by Individual	1017.17
个人缴纳的医疗保险	Medical Treatment Fund Paid by Individual	426.67
个人缴纳的失业保险	Unemployment Fund Paid by Individual	45.81
其他社会保障支出	Other Expenditurte on Social Security	12.36
外来从业人员寄给家人的支出	Remittances made by migrant workers to their families	0.42
赡养支出	Expenditure on Support	133.04
其他转移性支出	Other Transfer Expenditure	651.24
非收入所得	**Non-income Earnings**	**1612.59**
出售资产所得	Earnings from Assets Sold	346.39
股票、基金、收藏品本金所得	Principal of Stock, Fund and Collection	10.92
股票、基金、收藏品所得（含亏损）	Earning （deficit） from Stock, Fund and Collection	67.61
生产性固定资产所得	Revenues generated by production-based fixed assets	2.07
拆迁征地补偿所得	Earning from Compensation for Housing Demolition and Land Acquisition	209.80
其他财物和收回其他投资本金所得	Earning of Other Property and Recovery of Other Investment Principals	55.99
非经常性转移所得	Earning from Occasional Transfer	795.60
博彩所得	Lottery	11.24
婚丧嫁娶礼金所得	Cash Gifts of Wedding and Funeral	281.80
遗产及一次性馈赠所得	Inheritance and One-time Presents	90.44
一次性赔偿所得	Lump-sum Compensation	5.79
提取住房公积金	Withdrawal of Public Accumulation Fund for Housing Construction	29.74
调查补贴	Investigation Subsidy	227.32
其他非经常性转移所得	Other Earnings from Occasional Transfer	149.26
其他非收入所得	Other Non-income Earnings	470.60
借贷性所得	**Debit and Credit Income**	**1396.74**
提取储蓄存款	Withdrawal of Savings Deposits	1223.09
借入款	Loan	96.86
收回借出款	Recovery of Loan	61.60
收回储蓄性保险本金	Recovery of Principal of Savings Insurance	1.40
住房贷款	Bank Loan for Housing Purchasing	2.78
汽车贷款	Car Loans	11.01

单位:元（yuan）

按收入水平分组 Grouped by Level of Income				
低收入户 Low Income Households	中低收入户 Lower Middle Income Households	中等收入户 Middle Income Households	中高收入户 Upper Middle Income Households	高收入户 High Income Households
1441.45	1487.17	1962.30	2809.90	4739.22
10.63	6.85	20.95	99.87	531.83
1181.55	1218.97	1316.00	1745.10	2172.65
816.15	889.70	866.44	1145.45	1438.73
340.04	298.00	396.95	533.63	606.60
14.23	25.45	35.57	56.68	107.52
11.13	5.82	17.04	9.34	19.79
1.94				
32.31	93.13	72.31	156.07	341.69
215.02	168.23	553.03	808.86	1693.05
2148.81	**1250.02**	**2244.63**	**797.47**	**1573.17**
71.09	365.36	549.16	30.60	754.29
	17.27			39.05
				370.72
	9.39			
70.97	316.14	530.10	13.10	103.19
0.11	22.56	19.06	17.49	241.33
412.18	861.97	1157.45	765.54	810.92
1.49	33.02	4.77	6.68	8.12
59.36	207.80	676.91	225.79	267.27
48.04	109.08	116.92	139.94	38.95
5.42	3.66	1.02	19.38	
		15.34	20.08	126.07
209.87	209.20	227.92	275.08	220.28
87.99	299.21	114.57	78.59	150.22
1665.55	22.69	538.02	1.34	7.96
695.62	**646.69**	**1833.15**	**1250.31**	**2811.24**
502.81	633.58	1424.93	1044.48	2751.07
43.32		327.67	106.45	19.52
148.82		32.77	85.85	39.05
			6.30	1.25
0.66	5.83		7.24	
	7.28	47.79		0.35

8-5 全市城镇居民家庭人均收入情况（2015 年）
PER CAPITA INCOME OF URBAN HOUSEHOLDS OF WHOLE MUNICIPALITY (2015)

指 标	Item	总平均 Average
城镇居民人均可支配收入	**Per Capita Disposable Income of Urban Residents**	**42710.30**
工资性收入	Income from Wages and Salaries	26394.40
工 资	Wages	25004.70
实物福利	Benefit in Kind	96.08
其 他	Others	1293.62
经营净收入	Operating Net Income	6124.10
第一产业	Primay Industry	96.06
第二产业	Secondary Industry	2851.91
第三产业	Tertiary Industry	3176.13
财产净收入	Net Property Income	3783.70
利息净收入	Net Interest Income	173.28
红利收入	Dividend	501.77
储蓄性保险净收益	Net Income from Depositing Insurance	5.10
转让承包土地经营权租金净收入	Net Rent Income by Transfer of Contracted Land Use Rights	5.80
出租房屋财产性收入	House Renting Income	594.47
出租机械、专利、版权等资产的收入	Income from Leasing Assets of Machinery, Patent and Copyright	
其他财产净收入	Other Net Property Income	58.46
其 他	Others	2444.82
转移净收入	Net Transfer Income	6408.10
转移性收入	Transfer Income	9411.04
养老金或离退休金	Pension or Retirement Pay	7588.36
社会救济和补助	Social Relief and Subsidies	40.37
政策性生活补贴	Policy-guaranteed Living Allowances	32.32
报销医疗费	Reimbursement of Medical Expenses	314.06
家庭外出从业人员寄回带回收入	Income Sent or Brought Back by Household Members Working Outside	493.21
赡养收入	Alimony	466.23
其他经常转移收入	Other Regular Transfer Income	466.05
#失业保险金	Unemploment Insurance Benefits	10.25
从政府和组织得到的实物产品和服务折价	Physical Products and Discounted Service Obtained from Government and Organizations	8.87
现金政策性惠农补贴	Policy-guaranteed Agricultural Subsidies in Cash	1.57

单位：元（yuan）

按收入水平分组 Grouped by Level of Income				
低收入户 Low Income Households	中低收入户 Lower Middle Income Households	中等收入户 Middle Income Households	中高收入户 Upper Middle Income Households	高收入户 High Income Households
18545.22	**28162.27**	**36913.83**	**47746.47**	**91998.05**
13166.80	17523.22	23425.75	29091.26	54304.78
12744.71	16875.45	22289.19	27591.98	50628.37
37.15	59.09	117.04	97.37	191.39
384.94	588.68	1019.51	1401.91	3485.02
1548.75	2625.48	3470.98	5733.69	19493.93
85.41	228.05	21.91	3.50	131.38
149.16	270.77	928.90	1977.92	12446.48
1314.17	2126.66	2520.17	3752.27	6916.06
1832.27	2491.07	3081.99	3590.62	8803.49
-33.20	-28.35	-10.26	-87.38	1159.32
88.90	223.71	91.90	121.01	2219.66
5.88			10.09	10.50
6.15	11.74	0.63	9.40	
223.24	486.47	518.30	531.06	1349.44
0.03	-42.20	-20.89	32.20	369.10
1541.28	1839.70	2502.32	2974.25	3695.46
1997.40	5522.49	6935.11	9330.90	9395.86
4050.23	7432.99	9733.65	12365.07	15114.80
3129.84	6414.38	8642.17	10308.15	10623.52
94.63	27.01	21.50	47.69	
22.51	16.73	29.38	14.93	85.43
216.42	242.35	314.46	452.79	375.92
130.08	31.20	152.21	370.04	2017.46
276.45	347.31	157.20	786.54	847.24
167.04	347.18	409.03	368.88	1157.07
	45.78	2.59		
9.71	4.90	6.64	15.26	8.16
3.57	1.93	1.04	0.79	

8-5 续表 continued

指　标	Item	总平均 Average
转移性支出	Transfer Expenditure	3002.94
个人所得税	Personal Income tax	175.32
社会保障支出	Expenditure on Social Security	1711.34
个人缴纳的养老保险	Pension Fund Paid by Individual	1138.93
个人缴纳的医疗保险	Medical Treatment Fund Paid by Individual	501.97
个人缴纳的失业保险	Unemployment Fund Paid by Individual	60.99
其他社会保障支出	Other Expenditurte on Social Security	9.44
外来从业人员寄给家人的支出	Remittances made by migrant workers to their families	0.62
赡养支出	Expenditure on Support	170.33
其他转移性支出	Other Transfer Expenditure	945.34
非收入所得	**Non-income Earnings**	**1289.02**
出售资产所得	Earnings from Assets Sold	460.04
股票、基金、收藏品本金所得	Principal of Stock, Fund and Collection	16.45
股票、基金、收藏品所得（含亏损）	Earning （deficit） from Stock, Fund and Collection	101.83
拆迁征地补偿所得	Earning from Compensation for Housing Demolition and Land Acquisition	268.73
其他财物和收回其他投资本金所得	Earning of Other Property and Recovery of Other Investment Principals	73.03
非经常性转移所得	Earning from Occasional Transfer	820.69
博彩所得	Lottery	4.98
婚丧嫁娶礼金所得	Cash Gifts of Wedding and Funeral	289.85
遗产及一次性馈赠所得	Inheritance and One-time Presents	97.40
一次性赔偿所得	Lump-sum Compensation	5.28
提取住房公积金	Withdrawal of Public Accumulation Fund for Housing Construction	44.79
调查补贴	Investigation Subsidy	234.85
其他非经常性转移所得	Other Earnings from Occasional Transfer	143.54
其他非收入所得	Other Non-income Earnings	8.30
借贷性所得	**Debit and Credit Income**	**1718.39**
提取储蓄存款	Withdrawal of Savings Deposits	1527.40
借入款	Loan	111.55
收回借出款	Recovery of Loan	72.40
收回储蓄性保险本金	Recovery of Principal of Savings Insurance	0.34
住房贷款	Bank Loan for Housing Purchasing	4.18
汽车贷款	Car Loans	2.51

单位：元（yuan）

按收入水平分组 Grouped by Level of Income				
低收入户 Low Income Households	中低收入户 Lower Middle Income Households	中等收入户 Middle Income Households	中高收入户 Upper Middle Income Households	高收入户 High Income Households
2052.83	1910.50	2798.54	3034.16	5718.94
12.73	8.34	118.51	92.68	734.20
1574.95	1253.74	1797.28	1556.69	2506.59
1063.55	854.33	1171.84	1042.97	1643.77
478.42	363.20	550.14	447.68	704.11
31.41	33.17	62.68	55.98	135.70
1.58	3.05	12.62	10.07	23.01
2.73				
66.71	110.12	101.18	271.69	342.21
395.71	538.29	781.57	1113.10	2135.94
637.39	**1321.86**	**2125.01**	**693.09**	**1802.85**
102.47	453.33	816.73	73.03	947.78
	26.88			60.54
			56.56	514.23
101.80	396.21	816.11	15.18	
0.68	30.23	0.62	1.28	373.00
516.90	860.72	1308.28	606.83	854.78
2.61	1.56	9.67	6.23	5.66
86.57	263.53	723.04	66.89	344.77
77.08	118.66	163.50	86.12	37.39
1.14		25.08	0.79	
	12.95	9.08	128.24	90.07
227.00	220.79	263.14	239.43	225.83
122.51	243.23	114.78	79.14	151.06
18.01	7.81		13.23	0.30
779.76	**1009.66**	**2384.79**	**927.13**	**3884.52**
493.50	1009.66	1874.98	785.72	3882.05
52.65		485.52	28.28	
213.45		13.81	113.13	
				1.93
9.49		10.48		
10.67				0.54

8-6 全市农村居民家庭人均收入情况（2015 年）
PER CAPITA INCOME OF RURAL HOUSEHOLDS OF WHOLE MUNICIPALITY （2015）

指　标	Item	总平均 Average
农村居民人均可支配收入	**Per Capita Disposable Income of Rural Residents**	**21912.33**
工资性收入	Income from Wages and Salaries	13235.90
工　资	Wages	12894.78
实物福利	Benefit in Kind	48.84
其 他	Others	292.27
经营净收入	Operating Net Income	5087.90
第一产业	Primay Industry	3058.68
第二产业	Secondary Industry	1001.80
第三产业	Tertiary Industry	1027.43
财产净收入	Net Property Income	409.00
利息净收入	Net Interest Income	19.65
红利收入	Dividend	93.46
储蓄性保险净收益	Net Income from Depositing Insurance	0.89
转让承包土地经营权租金净收入	Net Rent Income by Transfer of Contracted Land Use Rights	150.90
出租房屋财产性收入	House Renting Income	135.09
出租机械、专利、版权等资产的收入	Income from Leasing Assets of Machinery, Patent and Copyright	0.71
其他财产净收入	Other Net Property Income	8.29
其　他	Others	
转移净收入	Net Transfer Income	3179.50
转移性收入	Transfer Income	4555.22
养老金或离退休金	Pension or Retirement Pay	2838.80
社会救济和补助	Social Relief and Subsidies	51.49
政策性生活补贴	Policy-guaranteed Living Allowances	18.43
报销医疗费	Reimbursement of Medical Expenses	263.94
家庭外出从业人员寄回带回收入	Income Sent or Brought Back by Household Members Working Outside	874.12
赡养收入	Alimony	329.16
其他经常转移收入	Other Regular Transfer Income	72.37
#失业保险金	Unemploment Insurance Benefits	3.35
从政府和组织得到的实物产品和服务折价	Physical Products and Discounted Service Obtained from Government and Organizations	10.96
现金政策性惠农补贴	Policy-guaranteed Agricultural Subsidies in Cash	95.95

单位：元（yuan）

按收入水平分组 Grouped by Level of Income				
低收入户 Low Income Households	中低收入户 Lower Middle Income Households	中等收入户 Middle Income Households	中高收入户 Upper Middle Income Households	高收入户 High Income Households
9469.27	**15837.75**	**20429.01**	**25849.78**	**39437.13**
5644.80	9355.42	14667.89	18898.78	18140.19
5520.98	9167.38	14453.88	18387.73	17426.49
13.72	25.03	36.19	115.42	59.22
110.10	163.01	177.81	395.64	654.48
1782.95	3089.03	2758.32	2320.01	16274.22
1791.32	1685.17	2023.17	1564.20	8645.79
112.98	401.16	288.82	62.71	4379.20
-121.35	1002.70	446.33	693.10	3249.22
272.52	373.66	410.28	263.02	737.74
24.17	25.28	9.70	-16.11	56.26
45.48	76.11	115.28	70.10	161.81
				4.74
142.26	195.75	135.44	134.11	143.28
47.79	68.88	149.53	59.31	361.82
3.67				
9.16	7.64	0.33	15.59	9.83
1768.99	3019.64	2592.53	4367.98	4284.98
3269.91	3861.47	3997.43	5763.12	6088.88
1322.87	2502.45	2623.45	3621.07	4243.78
81.89	28.20	109.12		33.16
6.66	10.64		37.90	40.78
275.11	101.97	281.54	606.78	68.96
778.39	795.97	578.31	1161.98	1108.00
656.15	288.93	147.28	180.56	395.61
68.02	99.79	122.97	45.92	14.55
		15.64		
6.40	8.20	14.64	13.68	11.85
74.42	25.32	120.12	95.22	172.20

8-6 续表　continued

指　标	Item	总平均 Average
转移性支出	Transfer Expenditure	1375.72
个人所得税	Personal Income tax	17.01
社会保障支出	Expenditure on Social Security	1257.06
个人缴纳的养老保险	Pension Fund Paid by Individual	901.22
个人缴纳的医疗保险	Medical Treatment Fund Paid by Individual	317.52
个人缴纳的失业保险	Unemployment Fund Paid by Individual	16.37
其他社会保障支出	Other Expenditurte on Social Security	21.95
赡养支出	Expenditure on Support	64.52
其他转移性支出	Other Transfer Expenditure	37.12
非收入所得	**Non-income Earnings**	**2251.86**
出售资产所得	Earnings from Assets Sold	121.86
股票、基金、收藏品本金所得	Principal of Stock, Fund and Collection	
股票、基金、收藏品所得（含亏损）	Earning （deficit） from Stock, Fund and Collection	
生产性固定资产所得	Revenues generated by production-based fixed assets	6.15
拆迁征地补偿所得	Earning from Compensation for Housing Demolition and Land Acquisition	93.38
其他财物和收回其他投资本金所得	Earning of Other Property and Recovery of Other Investment Principals	22.33
非经常性转移所得	Earning from Occasional Transfer	746.03
博彩所得	Lottery	23.61
婚丧嫁娶礼金所得	Cash Gifts of Wedding and Funeral	265.91
遗产及一次性馈赠所得	Inheritance and One-time Presents	76.70
一次性赔偿所得	Lump-sum Compensation	6.80
提取住房公积金	Withdrawal of Public Accumulation Fund for Housing Construction	
调查补贴	Investigation Subsidy	212.46
其他非经常性转移所得	Other Earnings from Occasional Transfer	160.55
其他非收入所得	Other Non-income Earnings	1383.97
借贷性所得	**Debit and Credit Income**	**761.26**
提取储蓄存款	Withdrawal of Savings Deposits	621.87
借入款	Loan	67.81
收回借出款	Recovery of Loan	40.26
收回储蓄性保险本金	Recovery of Principal of Savings Insurance	3.50
住房贷款	Bank Loan for Housing Purchasing	
汽车贷款	Car Loans	27.81

单位：元（yuan）

按收入水平分组 Grouped by Level of Income				
低收入户 Low Income Households	中低收入户 Lower Middle Income Households	中等收入户 Middle Income Households	中高收入户 Upper Middle Income Households	高收入户 High Income Households
1500.93	841.83	1404.90	1395.14	1803.90
1.89	11.43	5.37	5.61	63.96
1437.22	710.67	1316.24	1295.70	1588.85
1149.14	442.99	1036.98	857.95	1057.74
263.36	230.50	258.03	381.25	476.33
8.77	5.03	16.24	27.16	26.40
15.95	32.16	4.98	29.33	28.38
53.17	72.99	29.90	63.15	107.54
8.65	46.73	53.39	30.68	43.55
4956.25	**1208.30**	**1360.97**	**2443.68**	**1470.27**
		272.55	2.61	337.24
		28.43		
		186.65		286.41
		57.46	2.61	50.83
454.97	314.23	1059.76	795.92	1133.04
			123.50	0.49
16.39	22.74	375.49	272.88	673.54
126.50	12.86	50.00	54.13	152.80
10.71	5.54	8.33	3.12	6.18
208.58	179.53	204.26	215.63	260.94
92.79	93.56	421.68	126.65	39.08
4501.28	894.07	28.66	1645.15	
562.84	**207.66**	**1403.58**	**767.73**	**853.28**
562.84	187.89	1403.58	639.78	254.99
	19.78		27.82	314.74
			100.14	114.45
				18.88
				150.21

8-7　全市居民家庭人均消费支出情况（2015 年）
PER CAPITA LIVING EXPENDITURES OF HOUSEHOLDS OF WHOLE MUNICIPALITY （2015）

指　标	Item	总平均 Average
全体居民人均消费支出	**Per Capita Consumption Expenditures**	**22234.10**
食品烟酒	**Food, Tobacco and Liquor**	**6410.20**
食　品	Food	4034.56
谷　物	Grain	366.99
薯　类	Tubers	22.83
豆　类	Beans	65.02
食用油	Oil and Fat	146.44
蔬菜和食用菌	Vegetables and Edible Fungi	643.27
肉　类	Meat	836.01
禽　类	Poultry	262.06
水产品	Aquantic Products	504.62
蛋　类	Eggs	105.22
奶　类	Milk	246.85
干鲜瓜果类	Dried and Fresh Melons and Fruits	484.36
糖果糕点类	Sweet and Cake	153.66
其他食品	Other Food	197.24
烟　酒	Tobacco and Liquor	900.43
烟　草	Tobacco	667.88
酒　类	Liquor	232.55
饮　料	Beverages	101.09
饮食服务	Catering service	1374.12
食堂用餐	Canteen Dining	52.15
其他在外饮食	Eating Outside	1311.56
食品加工服务费	Service Fee of Food Processing	10.41
衣　着	**Clothing**	**1687.80**
衣　类	Garments	1338.01
鞋　类	Footware	349.79

单位：元（yuan）

按收入水平分组 Grouped by Level of Income				
低收入户 Low Income Households	中低收入户 Lower Middle Income Households	中等收入户 Middle Income Households	中高收入户 Upper Middle Income Households	高收入户 High Income Households
12045.81	**15283.33**	**20424.41**	**25173.65**	**41582.26**
4018.91	**5124.20**	**6407.23**	**7349.35**	**9827.24**
2933.46	3443.18	4046.75	4725.39	5328.06
336.07	321.93	349.42	386.68	456.53
23.78	14.90	17.27	26.09	33.91
56.79	58.78	70.82	73.48	67.37
122.39	127.53	147.12	159.99	183.03
492.90	537.13	670.34	781.64	778.25
628.96	774.31	880.66	967.71	972.23
189.63	229.86	281.22	300.18	326.87
321.93	405.94	482.63	662.15	701.78
83.83	97.28	103.39	122.39	124.42
178.29	227.65	264.92	258.68	319.46
266.61	367.70	423.03	598.44	831.25
85.01	105.21	152.25	169.73	278.22
147.27	174.96	203.68	218.23	254.74
560.49	731.85	879.92	975.24	1450.63
421.16	554.62	661.03	724.32	1045.43
139.33	177.23	218.89	250.92	405.20
55.88	81.74	90.52	103.45	186.75
469.08	867.44	1390.04	1545.27	2861.80
17.50	39.96	65.40	83.84	61.15
441.41	821.42	1307.78	1450.85	2791.82
10.17	6.05	16.86	10.58	8.84
774.45	**1089.95**	**1492.26**	**1986.54**	**3391.50**
587.51	819.90	1195.69	1622.32	2710.91
186.93	270.06	296.57	364.22	680.59

8-7 续表 continued

指 标	Item	总平均 Average
居 住	**Residence**	**4617.40**
租赁房房租	Rent of Rental Housing	69.08
住房维修及管理	Housing Repairmen and Management	782.56
水电燃料及其他	Water, Electricity, fuel and Others	686.14
自有住房折算租金	Computed Rents of Owner-occupied Housing	3001.79
物业管理费	Property management fees	77.83
生活用品及服务	**Articles for Daily Use and Services**	**1343.70**
家具及室内装饰品	Furniture and Upholstery	276.27
. 家用器具	Home Appliances	306.47
家用纺织品	Home Textiles	110.31
家庭日用杂品	Household Articles for Daily Use	364.41
个人用品	Personal Articles	210.06
家庭服务	Household Services	76.19
交通通信	**Transportation and Communications**	**3152.80**
. 交 通	Transportation	2388.26
交通工具	Means of Transportation	1331.54
交通费	Transportation Fare	101.93
交通工具用燃料	Feul for Means of Transportation	559.23
交通工具使用及维修	Usage and Maintenance of Means of Transportation	395.56
#车辆保险支出	Expenditure on Vehicle Insurance	148.68
通 信	Post and Telecommunication	764.54
通信工具	Telecommunication Facilities	227.15
通信服务	Communication Service	537.39
教育文化娱乐	**Education, Culture and Entertainment**	**2875.40**
教 育	Education	1119.51
文化娱乐	Culture and Entertainment	1755.89
医疗保健	**Medicine and Medical Services**	**1506.40**
医疗器具及药品	Medical Appliance and Medicine	628.02
医疗服务	Medical Service	878.38
其他用品和服务	**Other Articles and Service**	**640.40**
其他用品	Other Articles	371.63
其他服务	Other Services	268.77

单位：元（yuan）

按收入水平分组 Grouped by Level of Income				
低收入户 Low Income Households	中低收入户 Lower Middle Income Households	中等收入户 Middle Income Households	中高收入户 Upper Middle Income Households	高收入户 High Income Households
2724.89	**3544.34**	**3880.19**	**5395.23**	**8141.23**
68.23	70.65	43.38	93.59	70.68
535.57	763.77	322.79	489.77	1889.66
525.44	569.76	717.90	791.10	874.81
1585.17	2078.69	2751.29	3928.62	5108.25
10.48	61.47	44.83	92.14	197.84
550.60	**727.87**	**1255.84**	**1635.60**	**2818.63**
32.66	68.56	316.54	193.91	855.59
143.04	213.13	304.00	409.96	508.80
43.03	64.09	88.77	176.73	200.62
249.17	266.21	321.47	433.84	593.92
49.82	83.13	182.31	299.25	490.90
32.88	32.75	42.76	121.90	168.80
993.21	**1804.08**	**3207.96**	**3482.84**	**6932.97**
524.67	1232.36	2456.53	2635.60	5656.87
100.18	655.01	1466.81	1469.70	3315.18
51.69	83.01	96.37	116.70	174.92
221.16	302.49	522.62	666.06	1198.08
151.63	191.85	370.72	383.14	968.68
64.47	61.29	167.79	174.95	306.16
468.54	571.72	751.43	847.24	1276.10
91.05	115.72	206.90	217.62	553.78
377.49	456.00	544.53	629.62	722.32
1476.61	**1653.79**	**2096.52**	**3278.30**	**6423.89**
998.09	981.92	870.56	1188.38	1625.39
478.52	671.87	1225.96	2089.92	4798.50
1221.53	**1054.65**	**1563.11**	**1521.87**	**2311.11**
429.86	408.38	512.15	778.48	1097.26
791.67	646.27	1050.96	743.38	1213.84
285.61	**284.45**	**521.29**	**523.93**	**1735.70**
130.79	143.54	274.57	293.28	1115.47
154.82	140.91	246.72	230.66	620.23

8-8　全市城镇居民家庭人均消费支出情况（2015 年）
PER CAPITA LIVING EXPENDITURES OF URBAN HOUSEHOLDS OF WHOLE MUNICIPALITY （2015）

指　标	Item	总平均 Average
城镇居民人均消费支出	**Per Capita Consumption Expenditures of Urban Residents**	**25358.10**
食品烟酒	**Food, Tobacco and Liquor**	**7100.60**
食　品	Food	4468.82
谷　物	Grain	386.44
薯　类	Tubers	22.78
豆　类	Beans	70.93
食用油	Oil and Fat	157.15
蔬菜和食用菌	Vegetables and Edible Fungi	724.15
肉　类	Meat	891.16
禽　类	Poultry	284.98
水产品	Aquantic Products	576.04
蛋　类	Eggs	112.71
奶　类	Milk	291.13
干鲜瓜果类	Dried and Fresh Melons and Fruits	571.32
糖果糕点类	Sweet and Cake	181.16
其他食品	Other Food	198.87
烟　酒	Tobacco and Liquor	923.75
烟　草	Tobacco	683.98
酒　类	Liquor	239.77
饮　料	Beverages	116.70
饮食服务	Catering service	1591.34
食堂用餐	Canteen Dining	51.36
其他在外饮食	Eating Outside	1529.95
食品加工服务费	Service Fee of Food Processing	10.03
衣 着	**Clothing**	**1880.80**
衣　类	Garments	1502.11
鞋　类	Footware	378.69

单位：元（yuan）

按收入水平分组	Grouped by Level of Income			
低收入户 Low Income Households	中低收入户 Lower Middle Income Households	中等收入户 Middle Income Households	中高收入户 Upper Middle Income Households	高收入户 High Income Households
14674.20	**18360.86**	**23033.43**	**28553.83**	**46530.16**
4827.39	**5977.48**	**6760.21**	**8191.48**	**10557.08**
3551.14	4146.81	4316.66	5148.56	5466.27
333.61	356.95	380.18	365.83	518.21
18.55	19.48	22.03	23.70	31.96
64.26	73.04	73.94	71.45	73.03
140.12	141.83	145.28	179.46	186.41
617.45	715.83	696.79	841.95	774.27
745.32	886.97	890.97	1026.55	937.63
236.86	275.29	274.30	337.39	313.65
431.49	507.62	550.28	725.39	711.12
99.01	105.45	109.81	121.33	132.90
255.05	313.69	255.27	299.63	340.32
354.10	432.09	545.27	715.92	889.63
112.84	136.09	165.30	218.81	299.62
142.48	182.48	207.25	221.14	257.51
559.21	690.37	829.40	936.46	1759.28
412.48	504.03	660.58	663.20	1294.64
146.72	186.34	168.82	273.25	464.65
83.24	79.12	101.13	146.69	189.50
633.80	1061.18	1513.02	1959.77	3142.03
14.34	44.90	79.51	58.49	67.88
611.99	1003.04	1421.07	1892.83	3065.65
7.47	13.24	12.44	8.46	8.49
824.26	**1299.94**	**1759.86**	**2195.26**	**3723.30**
612.81	1013.98	1433.80	1785.28	2995.52
211.45	285.96	326.07	409.97	727.78

8-8 续表 continued

指　标	Item	总平均 Average
居　住	**Residence**	**5291.60**
租赁房房租	Rent of Rental Housing	67.56
住房维修及管理	Housing Repairmen and Management	889.37
水电燃料及其他	Water, Electricity, fuel and Others	688.56
自有住房折算租金	Computed Rents of Owner-occupied Housing	3536.74
物业管理费	Property Management fees	109.37
生活用品及服务	**Articles for Daily Use and Services**	**1537.10**
家具及室内装饰品	Furniture and Upholstery	325.66
. 家用器具	Home Appliances	333.62
家用纺织品	Home Textiles	123.73
家庭日用杂品	Household Articles for Daily Use	393.48
个人用品	Personal Articles	269.36
家庭服务	Household Services	91.24
交通通信	**Transportation and Communications**	**3848.30**
. 交　通	Transportation	2916.05
交通工具	Means of Transportation	1552.16
交通费	Transportation Fare	127.37
交通工具用燃料	Feul for Means of Transportation	715.23
交通工具使用及维修	Usage and Maintenance of Means of Transportation	521.28
#车辆保险支出	Expenditure on Vehicle Insurance	203.69
通　信	Post and Telecommunication	932.25
通信工具	Telecommunication Facilities	305.31
通信服务	Communication Service	626.94
教育文化娱乐	**Education, Culture and Entertainment**	**3387.40**
教　育	Education	1214.49
文化娱乐	Culture and Entertainment	2172.91
医疗保健	**Medicine and Medical Services**	**1655.00**
医疗器具及药品	Medical Appliance and Medicine	726.58
医疗服务	Medical Service	928.42
其他用品和服务	**Other Articles and Service**	**657.30**
其他用品	Other Articles	382.60
其他服务	Other Services	274.70

单位：元（yuan）

按收入水平分组 Grouped by Level of Income				
低收入户 Low Income Households	中低收入户 Lower Middle Income Households	中等收入户 Middle Income Households	中高收入户 Upper Middle Income Households	高收入户 High Income Households
3727.29	**4061.90**	**4801.82**	**6053.29**	**8487.41**
72.19	105.49	23.16	82.96	48.28
861.14	524.54	367.00	753.24	2082.03
504.85	662.15	667.89	840.48	814.81
2249.26	2688.33	3644.20	4256.88	5310.89
39.85	81.39	99.56	119.72	231.40
584.74	**1024.52**	**1280.79**	**1862.43**	**3301.31**
38.81	236.97	113.72	180.81	1185.72
126.37	259.11	384.19	426.66	532.67
41.07	64.95	96.60	241.19	203.88
273.85	277.99	367.78	480.67	619.79
83.89	147.47	256.85	367.59	561.11
20.75	38.02	61.65	165.50	198.13
1254.04	**2605.57**	**3499.94**	**3587.94**	**9313.38**
671.92	1803.26	2661.54	2549.85	7788.50
133.33	960.66	1391.48	1062.81	4773.77
66.44	98.42	132.21	146.03	214.68
296.93	416.01	685.48	817.43	1531.92
175.21	328.17	452.37	523.58	1268.13
66.20	156.51	232.82	214.65	392.24
582.13	802.30	838.40	1038.08	1524.88
123.88	231.47	213.65	291.78	740.54
458.25	570.83	624.74	746.31	784.34
2004.72	**1805.04**	**2979.58**	**3683.60**	**7183.54**
1302.20	742.26	1209.53	1321.13	1561.24
702.52	1062.78	1770.06	2362.47	5622.30
1261.24	**1252.83**	**1452.75**	**2274.03**	**2199.92**
311.25	574.54	642.62	1162.16	1065.19
949.99	678.30	810.12	1111.87	1134.72
190.53	**333.58**	**498.49**	**705.80**	**1764.23**
71.62	156.80	275.93	392.20	1157.52
118.91	176.78	222.56	313.60	606.71

8-9　全市农村居民家庭人均消费支出情况（2015 年）
PER CAPITA LIVING EXPENDITURES OF RURAL HOUSEHOLDS OF WHOLE MUNICIPALITY （2015）

指　标	Item	总平均 Average
农村居民人均消费支出	**Per Capita Consumption Expenditures of Rural Residents**	**14763.60**
食品烟酒	**Food, Tobacco and Liquor**	**4677.90**
食　品	Food	2944.78
谷　物	Grain	306.03
薯　类	Tubers	21.45
豆　类	Beans	49.53
食用油	Oil and Fat	116.49
蔬菜和食用菌	Vegetables and Edible Fungi	447.35
肉　类	Meat	676.50
禽　类	Poultry	201.35
水产品	Aquantic Products	335.77
蛋　类	Eggs	84.08
奶　类	Milk	146.43
干鲜瓜果类	Dried and Fresh Melons and Fruits	287.23
糖果糕点类	Sweet and Cake	91.28
其他食品	Other Food	181.28
烟　酒	Tobacco and Liquor	797.33
烟　草	Tobacco	593.69
酒　类	Liquor	203.64
饮　料	Beverages	64.80
饮食服务	Catering service	870.99
食堂用餐	Canteen Dining	50.26
其他在外饮食	Eating Outside	810.29
食品加工服务费	Service Fee of Food Processing	10.44
衣　着	**Clothing**	**1087.90**
衣　类	Garments	838.32
鞋　类	Footware	249.58

单位：元（yuan）

按收入水平分组 Grouped by Level of Income				
低收入户 Low Income Households	中低收入户 Lower Middle Income Households	中等收入户 Middle Income Households	中高收入户 Upper Middle Income Households	高收入户 High Income Households
9928.34	**11083.72**	**13404.23**	**17764.48**	**22586.28**
3497.94	**3696.21**	**4090.49**	**5879.36**	**6499.63**
2555.64	2502.83	2836.87	3175.55	3752.36
336.07	296.85	294.00	281.29	324.69
34.09	17.47	8.73	9.97	39.46
57.53	41.13	43.31	58.50	48.91
104.11	115.99	99.34	142.39	123.43
441.30	372.23	403.43	437.59	601.96
572.08	585.59	648.46	750.81	847.35
171.24	171.28	190.20	221.31	260.16
269.25	254.54	319.79	336.63	517.19
84.88	65.53	85.57	84.37	102.67
96.03	114.70	182.83	193.23	145.32
198.69	226.80	309.40	322.28	387.96
55.33	67.37	79.15	140.79	119.83
135.04	173.36	172.65	196.40	233.43
541.55	590.68	623.17	1168.51	1125.88
401.51	436.04	452.76	890.50	836.60
140.04	154.64	170.41	278.01	289.28
61.66	44.07	51.51	80.02	91.94
339.09	558.63	578.94	1455.27	1529.45
10.40	25.67	39.28	118.83	62.77
316.58	524.66	529.07	1327.95	1453.71
12.12	8.31	10.59	8.48	12.98
523.88	**954.44**	**1101.19**	**1376.92**	**1520.21**
407.46	712.60	853.91	1051.96	1197.05
116.42	241.83	247.27	324.96	323.16

8-9 续表 continued

指　标	Item	总平均 Average
居 住	**Residence**	**2890.60**
租赁房房租	Rent of Rental Housing	68.75
住房维修及管理	Housing Repairmen and Management	506.30
水电燃料及其他	Water, Electricity, fuel and Others	644.40
自有住房折算租金	Computed Rents of Owner-occupied Housing	1666.77
物业管理费	Property Management fees	4.38
生活用品及服务	**Articles for Daily Use and Services**	**903.40**
家具及室内装饰品	Furniture and Upholstery	163.40
. 家用器具	Home Appliances	245.40
家用纺织品	Home Textiles	79.84
家庭日用杂品	Household Articles for Daily Use	299.23
个人用品	Personal Articles	73.80
家庭服务	Household Services	41.73
交通通信	**Transportation and Communications**	**1788.20**
. 交　通	Transportation	1353.15
交通工具	Means of Transportation	864.52
交通费	Transportation Fare	53.39
交通工具用燃料	Feul for Means of Transportation	268.39
交通工具使用及维修	Usage and Maintenance of Means of Transportation	166.85
#车辆保险支出	Expenditure on Vehicle Insurance	51.11
通　信	Post and Telecommunication	435.05
通信工具	Telecommunication Facilities	86.92
通信服务	Communication Service	348.13
教育文化娱乐	**Education, Culture and Entertainment**	**1623.10**
教　育	Education	878.85
文化娱乐	Culture and Entertainment	744.25
医疗保健	**Medicine and Medical Services**	**1219.40**
医疗器具及药品	Medical Appliance and Medicine	428.09
医疗服务	Medical Service	791.31
其他用品和服务	**Other Articles and Service**	**573.10**
其他用品	Other Articles	328.23
其他服务	Other Services	244.87

单位：元（yuan）

按收入水平分组 Grouped by Level of Income				
低收入户 Low Income Households	中低收入户 Lower Middle Income Households	中等收入户 Middle Income Households	中高收入户 Upper Middle Income Households	高收入户 High Income Households
2010.93	**2129.99**	**2622.40**	**3478.76**	**4400.21**
18.58	107.25	35.23	9.72	176.55
85.66	89.66	494.11	1018.08	916.82
555.30	591.05	603.00	667.99	823.50
1351.29	1339.62	1481.47	1777.64	2478.07
0.10	2.41	8.58	5.33	5.28
457.67	**649.54**	**813.96**	**1243.93**	**1418.13**
18.82	42.63	94.69	242.32	453.60
142.02	199.60	248.90	255.59	392.08
44.48	55.82	58.55	166.14	80.78
194.95	248.60	279.79	428.44	356.79
26.44	51.58	66.05	123.84	106.68
30.95	51.30	65.98	27.60	28.19
563.61	**824.33**	**1726.20**	**2300.89**	**3731.16**
259.06	439.69	1333.62	1780.11	3139.72
57.74	55.47	836.75	1149.12	2385.44
25.57	44.90	65.52	83.76	46.95
125.96	176.16	263.57	310.14	486.99
49.78	163.16	167.79	237.09	220.35
11.32	75.09	53.25	53.77	59.81
304.55	384.65	392.58	520.78	591.44
51.42	76.10	56.94	124.19	133.25
253.13	308.55	335.64	396.59	458.18
1105.83	**1353.60**	**1406.30**	**1196.45**	**3168.64**
809.46	843.04	977.23	660.91	1102.28
296.38	510.55	429.06	535.55	2066.37
1311.52	**977.72**	**1242.65**	**1605.06**	**978.81**
470.26	511.11	385.94	396.82	369.20
841.26	466.61	856.71	1208.24	609.61
456.95	**497.89**	**401.05**	**683.11**	**869.48**
256.36	234.87	210.36	396.40	579.06
200.60	263.02	190.69	286.71	290.42

8-10 分地区全体常住居民收支情况（2015 年）
THE INCOME AND EXPENDITURE OF ALL THE RESIDENTS IN THE REGION （2015）

指　标	Item	全　市 Whole Municipality
家庭成员情况	**Basic Situation of Households**	
调查户数（户）	Number of Households Surveyed （household）	951.75
平均每户家庭常住人口（人）	Average Household Size （person）	2.95
# 从业人员	Average Number of Employees per Household	1.83
平均每一从业者负担人数（包括从业者本人）	Number of Persons Supported by Each Employee（including the employee himself or herself）	1.61
家庭收支情况	**Family Income and Expenditure**	
人均可支配收入（元）	Per Capita Disposable Income （yuan ）	35379
工资性收入	Income from Wages and Salaries	21780
经营净收入	Operating Net Income	5799
财产净收入	Net Property Income	2591
转移净收入	Net Transfer Income	5210
人均消费支出（元）	Per Capita Annual Living Expenditure	22234
食品烟酒	Food, Tobacco and Liquor	6410
衣　着	Clothing	1688
居　住	Residence	4617
生活用品及服务	Articles for Daily Use and Services	1344
交通通信	Transportation and Communications	3153
教育文化娱乐	Education, Culture and Entertainment	2875
医疗保健	Medicine and Medical Services	1506
其他商品及服务	Other Commodities and Services	640

注：2015年市区不含金坛数据。
Note:The 2015 data of Changzhou's urban area do not include Jintan District.

市 区 Urban Area	其 中 of which					溧阳市 Liyang City
	金坛区 Jintan District	武进区 wujin District	新北区 Xinbei District	天宁区 Tianning District	钟楼区 Zhonglou District	
569.92	188.33	188.00	131.33	120.83	129.75	193.33
3.04	2.79	3.18	3.27	2.98	2.64	2.85
1.79	1.95	1.96	2.09	1.62	1.41	1.81
1.70	1.43	1.62	1.56	1.84	1.88	1.57
37779	29852	35874	35009	41368	41209	28737
23335	18953	22189	21815	25644	25717	16881
6025	5145	7234	5600	5975	5865	5460
2795	2219	2396	2320	3645	3471	2876
5625	3535	4055	5273	6105	6157	3520
23497	16813	21095	21868	24726	24762	17527
6740	5908	6802	6309	7035	7240	5935
1748	1437	1276	1644	1837	1896	1450
4874	2564	3905	4638	5145	5221	2855
1455	958	1103	1295	1603	1467	1081
3411	2290	3157	3085	3497	3536	2105
3034	2011	2480	2623	3344	3139	2075
1578	1188	1708	1570	1636	1581	1600
657	457	663	705	631	683	426

8-11 分地区城镇常住居民收支情况（2015 年）
THE INCOME AND EXPENDITURE OF URBAN RESIDENTS IN THE REGION （2015）

指　标	Item	全 市 Whole Municipality
家庭成员情况	**Basic Situation of Households**	
调查户数（户）	Number of Households Surveyed （household）	632.83
平均每户家庭常住人口（人）	Average Household Size （person）	2.95
# 从业人员	Average Number of Employees per Household	1.66
平均每一从业者负担人数（包括从业者本人）	Number of Persons Supported by Each Employee（including the employee himself or herself）	1.77
家庭收支情况	**Family Income and Expenditure**	
人均可支配收入（元）	Per Capita Disposable Income （yuan ）	42710
工资性收入	Income from Wages and Salaries	26394
经营净收入	Operating Net Income	6124
财产净收入	Net Property Income	3784
转移净收入	Net Transfer Income	6408
人均消费支出（元）	Per Capita Annual Living Expenditure	25358
食品烟酒	Food, Tobacco and Liquor	7101
衣　着	Clothing	1881
居　住	Residence	5292
生活用品及服务	Articles for Daily Use and Services	1537
交通通信	Transportation and Communications	3848
教育文化娱乐	Education, Culture and Entertainment	3387
医疗保健	Medicine and Medical Services	1655
其他商品及服务	Other Commodities and Services	657

市 区 Urban Area	其中 of which 金坛区 Jintan District	武进区 wujin District	新北区 Xinbei District	天宁区 Tianning District	钟楼区 Zhonglou District	溧阳市 Liyang City
427.00	100.33	131.08	84.33	101.83	108.75	106.33
2.95	2.88	3.13	3.16	2.94	2.63	2.95
1.66	1.58	1.81	1.97	1.55	1.37	1.58
1.78	1.82	1.73	1.60	1.89	1.91	1.86
43642	40002	44738	44767	42736	42350	38445
26925	25144	29565	27698	26277	26279	22800
6434	5653	6358	6471	6182	6059	6499
3726	4006	3560	3846	3827	3651	4495
6556	5199	5254	6753	6450	6362	4651
25922	21270	25006	26472	25422	25346	20294
7145	7338	8036	7324	7014	7244	6758
1908	1915	1574	2097	1853	1980	1760
5368	2612	4203	5749	5426	5312	3225
1619	1278	1269	1548	1699	1526	1290
4087	3284	4273	4088	3662	3650	2250
3418	2690	3087	3265	3470	3274	2570
1695	1653	1871	1644	1678	1705	1950
682	500	693	757	619	655	491

8-12 分地区农村常住居民收支情况（2015 年）
THE INCOME AND EXPENDITURE OF RURAL RESIDENTS IN THE REGION （2015）

指 标	Item	全 市 Whole Municipality
家庭成员情况	**Basic Situation of Households**	
调查户数（户）	Number of Households Surveyed （household）	318.92
平均每户家庭常住人口（人）	Average Household Size （person）	2.96
#从业人员	Average Number of Employees per Household	2.15
平均每一从业者负担人数（包括从业者本人）	Number of Persons Supported by Each Employee（including the employee himself or herself）	1.37
家庭收支情况	**Family Income and Expenditure**	
人均可支配收入（元）	Per Capita Disposable Income （yuan）	21912
工资性收入	Income from Wages and Salaries	13236
经营净收入	Operating Net Income	5088
财产净收入	Net Property Income	409
转移净收入	Net Transfer Income	3180
人均消费支出（元）	Per Capita Annual Living Expenditure	14764
食品烟酒	Food, Tobacco and Liquor	4678
衣 着	Clothing	1088
居 住	Residence	2891
生活用品及服务	Articles for Daily Use and Services	903
交通通信	Transportation and Communications	1788
教育文化娱乐	Education, Culture and Entertainment	1623
医疗保健	Medicine and Medical Services	1219
其他商品及服务	Other Commodities and Services	573

市 区 Urban Area	其 中 of which					溧阳市 Liyang City
	金坛区 Jintan District	武进区 wujin District	新北区 Xinbei District	天宁区 Tianning District	钟楼区 Zhonglou District	
143.92	88.00	56.92	47.00	19.00	21.00	87.00
3.26	2.69	3.30	3.46	3.21	2.74	2.74
2.16	2.20	2.32	2.30	2.00	1.57	2.09
1.51	1.22	1.43	1.50	1.61	1.74	1.31
23180	20427	23531	22738	22042	22194	19880
14395	13237	11919	14418	13654	13687	11445
5005	4681	8453	4506	2569	3629	4480
404	569	775	402	1224	1083	1372
3376	1940	2384	3413	4595	3795	2583
15615	12674	15650	16079	14885	15045	15003
4578	4588	5085	4567	4635	4884	5180
1174	996	860	1188	1170	828	1160
3306	2520	3490	3365	3272	2832	2510
942	662	873	978	1156	1092	890
2006	1372	1602	2049	1554	2259	1970
1729	1385	1635	1815	1609	1423	1630
1287	759	1482	1478	795	1197	1270
595	392	622	639	695	531	393

8-13　全市居民主要消费品人均消费量（2015 年）
PER CAPITA CONSUMPTION ON MAJOR CONSUMER GOODS OF RESIDENTS OF WHOLE MUNICIPALITY (2015)

指　标	Item	全体居民家庭 Whole Municipality	城镇居民家庭 Urban Households	农村居民家庭 Rural Households
大 米（千克）	Rice（kg）	42.88	43.96	40.74
食用植物油（千克）	Edible Vegetable Oil（kg）	11.40	12.23	9.74
鲜 菜（千克）	Fresh Vegetables（kg）	94.46	114.97	53.94
猪 肉（千克）	Pork（kg）	24.56	25.25	23.21
牛 肉（千克）	Beef（kg）	3.40	4.41	1.40
羊 肉（千克）	Mutton（kg）	0.92	0.96	0.82
鸡（千克）	Chieken（kg）	7.34	8.18	5.69
鸭（千克）	Duck（kg）	2.00	2.39	1.25
鱼（千克）	Aquantic Products（kg）	14.80	15.93	12.57
虾（千克）	Shrimp（kg）	4.02	4.98	2.12
鲜 蛋（千克）	Eggs（kg）	9.62	10.66	7.57
鲜乳品及酸奶（千克）	Fresh Milk and Yogurt（kg）	17.58	22.46	7.93
水 果（千克）	Fruits（kg）	41.69	47.74	29.74
糕 点（千克）	Cakes（kg）	6.13	7.58	3.25
茶 叶（千克）	Tea（kg）	0.27	0.29	0.24
啤 酒（千克）	Beer（kg）	4.22	3.68	5.28
白 酒（千克）	Liquor（kg）	3.53	3.02	4.54
果 酒（千克）	Wine（kg）	0.28	0.39	0.05
生活用水（立方米）	Household Water Consumption（cubic meters）	46.60	53.75	32.47
生活用电（千瓦时）	Household Power Consumption（kwh）	797.97	841.00	712.95
管道天然气（立方米）	Pipeline Gas（cubic meters）	37.55	52.58	7.87
液化石油气（千卡）	Liquified Petroleum Gas（kc）	17.11	11.99	27.22

8-14 每百户居民家庭年末耐用消费品拥有量（2015）
NUMBER OF DURABLE CONSUMER GOODS OWNED PER 100 HOUSEHOLDS AT YEAR-END （2015）

指　标	Item	全体居民家庭 Whole Municipality	城镇居民家庭 Urban Households	农村居民家庭 Rural Households
家用汽车（辆）	Family Car （unit）	40.85	48.34	26.00
摩托车（辆）	Motorcycle （unit）	25.22	16.12	43.27
助力车（辆）	Scooter （unit）	97.74	91.53	110.06
洗衣机（台）	Washing Machine （unit）	100.32	101.58	97.80
电冰箱（台）	Refrigerator （unit）	102.14	102.11	102.19
微波炉（台）	Microwave Oven （unit）	92.74	95.87	86.54
彩色电视机（台）	Color TV Set （unit）	185.24	194.68	166.50
空调（台）	Air Conditioner （unit）	196.20	222.07	144.86
热水器（台）	Shower Heater （unit）	101.89	103.46	98.77
消毒碗柜（台）	Disinfectant Cupboard （unit）	4.94	6.79	1.25
洗碗机（台）	Dishwasher （unit）	0.74	0.95	0.31
排油烟机（台）	Smoke Exhaust（unit）	82.47	90.53	66.47
固定电话（部）	Telephone （set）	82.24	80.71	85.29
移动电话（部）	Mobile Telephone （set）	228.09	237.18	210.06
计算机（台）	Family Computer （unit）	85.05	103.75	47.95
摄像机（架）	Pickup Camera （unit）	8.76	10.64	5.02
照相机（架）	Camera （unit）	37.68	47.83	17.56
中高档乐器（件）	Medium and High Class Music Instruments （unit）	5.03	6.77	1.57
健身器材（套）	Healthy Equipment （unit）	7.55	9.61	3.45
组合音响（套）	Hi-Fi Stereo Component System （unit）	16.41	17.88	13.48

9

CHAPTER 9

固定资产投资

INVESTMENT IN FIXED ASSETS

常州统计年鉴

9 固定资产投资
INVESTMENT IN FIXED ASSETS

2015 年主要统计指标
MAJOR STATISTICAL INDICATORS OF 2015

固定资产投资完成额	Realized Investment in Fixed Assets	3398.97 亿元	(100 million yuan)
比上年增长	Over the Previous Year	6.7%	
在建项目个数	Number of projects under Construction	4475 个	(unit)
比上年增长	Over the Previous Year	9.5%	
民间投资	Nongovernmental Investment	2573.76 亿元	(100 million yuan)
比上年增长	Over the Previous Year	4.3%	
公共基础设施投资	Public Infrastructure Investment	637.40 亿元	(100 million yuan)
比上年增长	Over the Previous Year	9.4%	
工业投资	Transformation and Renovation Investment	1756.13 亿元	(100 million yuan)
比上年增长	Over the Previous Year	6.5%	
第三产业投资	Investment in Tertiary Industry	1636.65 亿元	(100 million yuan)
比上年增长	Over the Previous Year	7.1%	
房地产开发投资	Real Estate Investment	508.04 亿元	(100 million yuan)
比上年增长	Over the Previous Year	-25.5%	

9-1　历年固定资产投资完成额
REALIZED INVESTMENT IN FIXED ASSETS OVER THE YEARS

单位：万元（10000 yuan）

年　份 Year	全　市 Whole Municipality	其 中 of which 市　区 Urban Area	年　份 Year	全　市 Whole Municipality	其 中 of which 市　区 Urban Area
1949	31	24	1983	31428	43426
1950	129	105	1984	60334	53083
1951	148	94	1985	104735	93054
1952	456	257	1986	161834	127213
1953	494	394	1987	201796	156071
1954	557	431	1988	259486	201601
1955	829	659	1989	212533	163734
1956	1323	1032	1990	227093	170921
1957	964	654	1991	309921	237860
1958	6490	5657	1992	443866	355392
1959	8246	7390	1993	879129	706406
1960	11184	10223	1994	964621	777442
1961	3189	2975	1995	1150612	852333
1962	1198	913	1996	1242072	922999
1963	1070	825	1997	1319585	1009095
1964	1714	1454	1998	1401110	1066040
1965	1279	1060	1999	1448908	1117208
1966	1537	1238	2000	1634262	1268963
1967	793	578	2001	1906854	1509623
1968	749	555	2002	2500118	1977105
1969	1397	1037	2003	4465944	3583446
1970	2398	1823	2004	5886129	4730966
1971	3411	3075	2005	7698021	6097516
1972	4944	4219	2006	9515629	7386948
1973	5900	4832	2007	12039417	9327048
1974	3994	3486	2008	14481662	11028826
1975	3490	3119	2009	17047690	13340391
1976	3528	3194	2010	21035519	16489817
1977	3093	2634	2011	23389418	18211797
1978	8852	7553	2012	27601436	21660862
1979	13203	11327	2013	29028402	22672613
1980	23699	26313	2014	33100503	26030559
1981	24198	30321	2015	33989667	29565715
1982	36336	46289			

注：2013年以前固定资产投资完成额为全社会口径。
Note：The statistical caliber of total investment in fixed assets before 2013 covered the whole society.

9-2 固定资产投资完成额（1985-2015 年）
REALIZED INVESTMENT IN FIXED ASSETS（1985-2015）

单位：万元（10000 yuan）

年 份 Year	固定资产投资完成额 Realized Investment in Fixed Assets	其 中 of which					
		第一产业 Primary Industry	第二产业 Secondary Industry	其中 of which 工业投资 Industrial Investment	第三产业投资 Investment in Tertiary Industry	公共基础设施投资 Public Infrastructure Investment	民间投资 Civil Investment
1985	104735	952	62475	61503	41308		
1986	161834	3732	98907	98383	59195		
1987	201796	1499	142569	135828	57728		
1988	259486	1244	190533	189871	67709		
1989	212533	2932	170954	170860	38647		
1990	227093	4642	160225	159955	62226	17820	95088
1991	309921	2789	256344	225608	50788	24629	94167
1992	443866	3176	332873	331741	107817	34729	76327
1993	879129	1309	528769	499487	349051	91302	199902
1994	964621	4889	509772	453869	449960	140547	262832
1995	1150612	9776	559360	548978	581476	153314	295241
1996	1242072	6088	604167	597020	631817	278333	375196
1997	1319585	19848	568241	559112	731496	308134	475233
1998	1401110	34000	536977	526974	830133	453150	479621
1999	1448908	55225	528263	520078	865420	547041	753172
2000	1634262	49771	604813	593913	979678	532296	888199
2001	1906854	53626	837711	830062	1015517	628214	1078742
2002	2500118	29619	1252088	1237465	1218411	699987	1445567
2003	4465944	20138	2591293	2508342	1854513	1262439	2666795
2004	5886129	5643	3451340	3425615	2429146	1597078	3533558
2005	7698021	11902	4648555	4597843	3037564	2042125	4798730
2006	9515629	20219	5653538	5629015	3841872	1857842	6307633
2007	12039417	6455	6870313	6808672	5162649	2284530	7987997
2008	14481662	29965	8391957	8315442	6059740	2428248	9626044
2009	17047690	39949	9788147	9710508	7219594	3555953	11469166
2010	21035519	73876	11865093	11804077	9096550	3403292	14816856
2011	23389418	100341	12958199	12934251	10330878	2958588	17051330
2012	27601436	58109	15339739	15259792	12203588	4020574	19730820
2013	29028402	54853	15450260	15411954	13523289	3895875	21235173
2014	33100503	42379	16842902	16802033	16215222	5828272	24678074
2015	33989667	23471	17599661	17561343	16366535	6373954	25737634

注：1、2013年以前固定资产投资完成额为全社会口径。
2、公共基础设施投资指电力、燃气、水的生产和供应业；交通运输、仓储和邮政业；电信、广播电视和卫星传输服务业；水利、环境和公共设施管理业；教育、卫生、社会保障和社会福利业；文化、体育、娱乐等行业的投资。

Note: 1.The statistical caliber of total investment in fixed assets before 2013 covered the whole society.
2.Public infrastructure investment refers to the investment in production and supply of electricity, gas and water; transportation, storage and postal industries; telecommunications, radio and television and satellite transmission services; water conservancy, environment and public facility management industries; education, health, social security and social welfare; and culture, sports, entertainment industries and so on.

9-3　分地区固定资产投资完成额（2015 年）
REALIZED INVESTMENT IN FIXED ASSETS BY REGION（2015）

指　标	Item	全　市 Whole Municipality	市　区 Urban Area
投资总额	**Total Investment**	**33989667**	**29565715**
按建设性质分	**Grouped by Type of Construction**		
新　建	New Construction	9970208	8500618
扩　建	Expansion	12858621	10384811
改　建	Reconstruction	1326589	1267309
其　它	Others	9834249	9412977
按构成分	**Grouped by Composition**		
建筑工程	Construction	18058036	15690433
安装工程	Installation	1898085	1355516
设备工器具购置	Purchase of Equipment and Investment	11193005	10186677
其他费用	Others	2840541	2333089
按经济类型分	**Grouped by Economic Types**		
国有及国有控股企业	State-owned and State Holding Enterprises	4603382	4333711
非国有投资	Non State-owned Investment	29386285	25232004
民间投资	Civil Investment	25737634	21791351
外商及港澳台商投资	Foreign Merchants & Hong Kong, Macao and Taiwan	3648651	3440653
按登记注册类型分	**Grouped by Registration Status**		
内　资	Domestically-Funded	30119569	25903615
国　有	State-owned	4387277	4120106
集　体	Collective-owned	1132969	1129929
股份合作	Share-holding Cooperative	26693	15161
集体联营	State-owned Joint Operation	2800	2800
国有独资公司	State-funded Corporations	216105	213605
其它有限责任公司	Other Limited Liability Corporations	3503713	3379991
股份有限公司	Share-holding Corporations Ltd.	686436	566611
私　营	Private	19888441	16219635
其　他	Others	275135	255777
港澳台商投资	Investment from Hong Kong, Macao and Taiwan	1896335	1797733
外商投资	Enterprises withForeign Investment	1752316	1642920
个体经营	Individual	221447	221447
个体户	Self-employed Individuals	204187	204187

单位：万元（10000 yuan）

	其 中 of which					
金坛区 Jintan District	武进区 wujin District	其中 of which # 经开区 Economic Development Zone	新北区 Xinbei District	天宁区 Tianning District	钟楼区 Zhonglou District	溧阳市 Liyang City
3362304	**9715279**	**2226047**	**7833394**	**3605968**	**3697744**	**4423952**
1546433	2445478	319020	2207829	51960	856897	1469590
1401862	3552785	1549642	1451178	2392455	1434775	2473810
97183	904894	28361	103702	76990	82258	59280
316826	2812122	329024	4070685	1084563	1323814	421272
1485558	5557134	1026041	2733172	2934821	2015065	2367603
222511	436342	116358	201246	157003	129439	542569
1478816	2845529	748680	4430872	391267	970618	1006328
175419	876274	334968	468104	122877	582622	507452
302081	1106358	100585	1134257	328401	278305	269671
3060223	8608921	2125462	6699137	3277567	3419439	4154281
2856509	7487808	2066197	5458833	2858119	3034639	3946283
203714	1121113	59265	1240304	419448	384800	207998
3146240	8580806	2163422	6566914	3101440	3228463	4215954
173406	1082060	100585	1134257	328401	258850	267171
59115	516641	204295	336623	148593	68957	3040
	7450	1150	7711			11532
					2800	
128675	24298				19455	2500
285089	1242782	251187	913442	431877	475577	123722
238534	169849	34494	36433	111714	10081	119825
2256621	5371425	1431534	4104129	2058712	2368029	3668806
4800	166301	140177	34319	22143	24714	19358
89718	513393	29685	441884	332077	362210	98602
113996	607720	29580	798420	87371	22590	109396
12350	13360	3360	26176	85080	84481	
12350	13360	3360	17576	76420	84481	

9-3 续表 continued

指 标	Item	全 市 Whole Municipality	市 区 Urban Area
按产业分	**Grouped by Industries**		
第一产业	Primary Industry	23471	10220
第二产业	Secondary Industry	17599661	14378674
#工 业	Industry	17561343	14340356
第三产业	Tertiary Industry	16366535	15176821
按国民经济行业分	**Grouped by Sector**		
农林牧渔业	Farming,Forestry,Animal Husbandry and Fishery	23471	10220
采矿业	Mining	13058	
制造业	Manufacturing	16962652	13910671
电力、热力、燃气及水的生产和供应业	Production and Supply of Electricity, Heat, Gas and Water Industry	585633	429685
建筑业	Construction	38318	38318
批发和零售业	Wholesale and Retail Trade	1319264	1207881
交通运输、仓储和邮政业	Transportation , Storage and Post	2281880	2236526
住宿和餐饮业	Accommodation and Catering Services	554639	519755
信息传输、软件和信息技术服务业	Information Transmission, Software and IT Services Industry	610615	553195
金融业	Banking	86102	86102
房地产业	Real Estate Industry	6545242	5916433
租赁和商务服务业	Rent and Business Services	900855	808246
科学研究和技术服务	Scientific Researches and Technical Services	473448	459142
水利、环境和公共设施管理业	Water Conservancy, Environment and Public Facilities Management	2045106	1988278
居民服务、修理和其他服务业	Residential Services, Repairing and other Services Industry	176258	172458
教 育	Education	534475	516376
卫生和社会工作	Health and Social Work	148958	145332
文化、体育和娱乐业	Culture, Sports and Entertainment	584917	463196
公共管理、社会保障和社会组织	Public Administration, Social Security and Social Organizations	104776	103901

单位：万元（10000 yuan）

其中 of which						
金坛区 Jintan District	武进区 wujin District	其中 of which # 经开区 Economic Development Zone	新北区 Xinbei District	天宁区 Tianning District	钟楼区 Zhonglou District	溧阳市 Liyang City
10220						13251
2381038	5526960	1346885	4822589	744967	758114	3220987
2381038	5526460	1346885	4822589	744967	720296	3220987
971046	4188319	879162	3010805	2861001	2939630	1189714
10220						13251
						13058
2364992	5328514	1184859	4753065	738837	720296	3051981
16046	197946	162026	69524	6130		155948
	500				37818	
59292	95084	50500	164142	277094	596274	111383
233662	369816	119437	529053	215774	290238	45354
22701	8860	860	62908	303364	112922	34884
	153708	94948	14610	96269	117546	57420
21000			4790	35972	24340	
345463	2065547	157151	1378052	996854	1107290	628809
92741	155902	63965	165819	148876	238431	92609
27505	126270	5443	22973	209645	68778	14306
44232	956946	337325	433903	275735	116157	56828
10182	7650	4650	15809	77890	59427	3800
	122098	1500	117073	98826	125279	18099
17416	53120	3123	22431	26669	25348	3626
87052	43508	12500	55042	87563	42065	121721
9800	29810	27760	24200	10470	15535	875

9-4　分地区工业各行业固定资产投资完成额（2015 年）
INVESTMENTS IN FIXED ASSETS OF INDUSTRIAL TRADES BY REGION（2015）

单位：万元（10000 yuan）

行　业	Sector	全　市 Whole Municipality	市　区 Urban Area	溧阳市 Liyang City
采矿业	Mining	13058		13058
农副食品加工业	Food Processing	107793	63358	44435
食品制造业	Food Production	144362	95082	49280
酒、饮料和精制茶制造业	Beverages and Refined Tea Manufacturing	39814	35744	4070
纺织业	Textile Industry	554569	471779	82790
纺织服装、服饰业	Textile and clothing Industry	191706	134827	56879
皮革、毛皮、羽毛及其制品和制鞋业	Leather, Fur, Feathers and Their Products, and Footwear Industry	54450	50270	4180
木材加工及木、竹、藤、棕、草制品业	Timber Processing, Bamboo, Cane, Palm Fiber and Straw Products	101364	84701	16663
家具制造业	Furniture Manufacturing	33971	24771	9200
造纸及纸制品业	Papermaking and Paper Products	141887	119910	21977
印刷和记录媒介复制业	Printing and Recorded Media Duplication Industry	127096	79626	47470
文教、工美、体育和娱乐用品制造业	Cultural & Educational, Arts & Crafts, Sports & Entertainment Articles Manufacturing	173322	95212	78110
石油加工、炼焦及核燃料加工业	Petroleum Processing, Coking and Nuclear Fuel Processing	50137	32677	17460
化学原料及化学制品制造业	Raw Chemical Materials and Chemica Products	1328179	968906	359273
医药制造业	Medical and Pharmaceutical Products	449293	415782	33511
化学纤维制造业	Chemical Fiber	231309	205139	26170
橡胶和塑料制品业	Rubber and Plastic Products Industry	564564	491004	73560
非金属矿物制品业	Nonmetal Mineral Products	798304	588259	210045
黑色金属冶炼及压延加工业	Smelting and Pressing of Ferrous Metals	412624	321391	91233
有色金属冶炼及压延加工业	Smelting and Pressing of Nonferrous Metals	291335	242645	48690
金属制品业	Metal Products	1126653	911471	215182
通用设备制造业	General Equipment Manufacturing	2636198	2071484	564714
专用设备制造业	For Special Purposes Equipment Manufacturing	1817741	1317799	499942
汽车制造业	Automotive Industry	1206209	1096382	109827
铁路、船舶、航空航天和其他运输设备制造	Railways, Shipping, Aerospace and other Transportation Equipment Manufacturing	563061	533244	29817
电气机械及器材制造业	Electric Equipment and Machinery	2224165	1973657	250508
计算机、通信和其他电子设备制造	Computer, Communications and other Electronic Equipment Manufacturing	946579	891219	55360
仪器仪表制造业	Instrumentation Manufacturing	458566	428791	29775
其他制造业	Other Manufacturings	158594	136984	21610
废弃资源综合利用业	Comprehensive Utilization of Waste Resources Industry	28807	28557	250
电力、热力生产和供应业	Production and Supply of Electricity & Heat Industry	474041	335636	138405
燃气生产和供应业	Production and Supply of Gas Industry	26394	25394	1000
水的生产和供应业	Production and Supply of water Industry	85198	68655	16543

9-5 分地区新增固定资产（2015 年）
NEWLY ADDED FIXED ASSETS BY REGION （2015）

单位：万元（10000 yuan）

指 标	Item	全 市 Whole Municipality	市 区 Urban Area	溧阳市 Liyang City
总 计	**Total**	**26114399**	**22138343**	**3976056**
按建设性质分	**Grouped by Type of Construction**			
新 建	New Construction	6056186	5139728	916458
扩 建	Expansion	10917010	8543302	2373708
改 建	Reconstruction	1049771	1009419	40352
其 它	Others	8091432	7445894	645538
按经济类型分	**Grouped by Economic Types**			
国有及国有控股企业	State-owned and State Holding Enterprises	2778102	2716382	61720
非国有投资	Non State-owned Investment	23336297	19421961	3914336
民间投资	Civil Investment	20665783	16945490	3720293
外商及港澳台商投资	Foreign Merchants & Hong Kong, Macao and aiwan	2670514	2476471	194043
按登记注册类型分	**Grouped by Registration Status**			
内 资	Domestically-Funded	23292429	19510416	3782013
国 有	State-owned	2738669	2676949	61720
集 体	Collective-owned	702704	699664	3040
股份合作	Share-holding Cooperative	23311	13448	9863
集体联营	Collective-owned Joint Operation	2800	2800	
国有独资公司	State-funded Corporations	39433	39433	
其它有限责任公司	Other Limited Liability Corporations	2926330	2745319	181011
股份有限公司	Share-holding Corporations Ltd.	451949	396882	55067
私 营	Private	16193552	12737003	3456549
其 他	Others	213681	198918	14763
港澳台商投资	Investment from Hong Kong, Macao and Taiwan	1372669	1253266	119403
外商投资	Enterprises with Foreign Investment	1297845	1223205	74640
个体经营	Individual	151456	151456	

9-5 续表　Continued　　　　单位：万元（10000 yuan）

指　标	Item	全　市 Whole Municipality	市　区 Urban Area	溧阳市 Liyang City
按产业分	**Grouped by Industries**			
第一产业	Primary Industry	19891	10220	9671
第二产业	Secondary Industry	14586762	11778107	2808655
#工　业	Industry	14562829	11754174	2808655
第三产业	Tertiary Industry	11507746	10350016	1157730
按国民经济行业分	**Grouped by Sector**			
农林牧渔业	Farming,Forestry,Animal Husbandry and Fishery	19891	10220	9671
采矿业	Mining	11179		11179
制造业	Manufacturing	14200378	11419153	2781225
电力、热力、燃气及水的生产和供应业	Production and Supply of Electricity, Heat, Gas and Water Industry	351272	335021	16251
建筑业	Construction	23933	23933	
批发和零售业	Wholesale and Retail Trade	1047133	938800	108333
交通运输、仓储和邮政业	Transportation , Storage and Post	1233662	1205071	28591
住宿和餐饮业	Accommodation and Catering Services	464302	449424	14878
信息传输、软件和信息技术服务业	Information Transmission, Software and IT Services Industry	431465	426045	5420
金融业	Banking	78152	78152	
房地产业	Real Estate Industry	4531552	3789523	742029
租赁和商务服务业	Rent and Business Services	815104	730196	84908
科学研究和技术服务	Scientific Researches and Technical Services	482077	471577	10500
水利、环境和公共设施管理业	Water Conservancy, Environment and Public Facilities Management	1486509	1441749	44760
居民服务、修理和其他服务业	Residential Services, Repairing and other Services Industry	143419	139619	3800
教　育	Education	329812	319912	9900
卫生和社会工作	Health and Social Work	87933	87912	21
文化、体育和娱乐业	Culture, Sports and Entertainment	302465	198750	103715
公共管理、社会保障和社会组织	Public Administration, Social Security and Social Organizations	74161	73286	875

9-6 分地区工业各行业新增固定资产（2015 年）
NEW FIXED ASSETS OF INDUSTRIAL SECTORS BY REGION （2015）

单位：万元（10000 yuan）

行业	Sector	全市 Whole Municipality	市区 Urban Area	溧阳市 Liyang City
采矿业	Mining	11179		11179
农副食品加工业	Food Processing	96036	54378	41658
食品制造业	Food Production	110427	66147	44280
酒、饮料和精制茶制造业	Beverages and Refined Tea Manufacturing	37656	33586	4070
纺织业	Textile Industry	466534	383744	82790
纺织服装、服饰业	Textile and clothing Industry	151661	100277	51384
皮革、毛皮、羽毛及其制品和制鞋业	Leather, Fur, Feathers and Their Products, and Footwear Industry	45662	41482	4180
木材加工及木、竹、藤、棕、草制品业	Timber Processing, Bamboo, Cane, Palm Fiber and Straw Products	79889	69362	10527
家具制造业	Furniture Manufacturing	29949	21249	8700
造纸及纸制品业	Papermaking and Paper Products	131275	109600	21675
印刷和记录媒介复制业	Printing and Recorded Media Duplication Industry	120973	74503	46470
文教、工美、体育和娱乐用品制造业	Cultural & Educational, Arts & Crafts, Sports & Entertainment Articles Manufacturing	156510	84600	71910
石油加工、炼焦及核燃料加工业	Petroleum Processing, Coking and Nuclear Fuel Processing	41363	23903	17460
化学原料及化学制品制造业	Raw Chemical Materials and Chemica Products	1130614	788375	342239
医药制造业	Medical and Pharmaceutical Products	363778	332747	31031
化学纤维制造业	Chemical Fiber	174225	148055	26170
橡胶和塑料制品业	Rubber and Plastic Products Industry	449876	392416	57460
非金属矿物制品业	Nonmetal Mineral Products	627394	442236	185158
黑色金属冶炼及压延加工业	Smelting and Pressing of Ferrous Metals	336231	247582	88649
有色金属冶炼及压延加工业	Smelting and Pressing of Nonferrous Metals	254913	206223	48690
金属制品业	Metal Products	967649	784312	183337
通用设备制造业	General Equipment Manufacturing	2279792	1747094	532698
专用设备制造业	For Special Purposes Equipment Manufacturing	1578175	1132203	445972
汽车制造业	Automotive Industry	940378	886235	54143
铁路、船舶、航空航天和其他运输设备制造	Railways, Shipping, Aerospace and other Transportation Equipment Manufacturing	431193	402621	28572
电气机械及器材制造业	Electric Equipment and Machinery	1980154	1722146	258008
计算机、通信和其他电子设备制造	Computer, Communications and other Electronic Equipment Manufacturing	724511	676552	47959
仪器仪表制造业	Instrumentation Manufacturing	366911	337136	29775
其他制造业	Other Manufacturings	102035	86025	16010
废弃资源综合利用业	Comprehensive Utilization of Waste Resources Industry	24614	24364	250
电力、热力生产和供应业	Production and Supply of Electricity & Heat Industry	311155	295154	16001
燃气生产和供应业	Production and Supply of Gas Industry	7600	7350	250
水的生产和供应业	Production and Supply of water Industry	32517	32517	

9-7　分地区固定资产投资效果（2015 年）
EFFECT OF FIXED ASSETS INVESTMENT BY REGION （2015）

指　标	Item	全　市 Whole Municipality	市　区 Urban Area	溧阳市 Liyang City
施工项目数（个）	Projects under Construction （unit）	4475	3667	808
#本年新开工	Beginning Projects in this Year	3902	3188	714
本年建成投产项目数（个）	Number of Projects Completed （unit）	4069	3342	727
项目建成投产率（%）	Rate of Projects Completed and Put into Use （%）	90.9	91.1	90.0
计划总投资（万元）	Plan of General Investment （10000 yuan）	83580179	73663713	9916466
本年完成投资（万元）	Completed Investment Value this year （10000 yuan）	33989667	29565715	4423952
建设周期（年）	Construction Cycle （year）	2.5	2.5	2.2
本年新增固定资产（万元）	Newly Increased Fixed Assets this year （10000 yuan）	26114399	22138343	3976056
固定资产交付使用率（%）	Rate of Fixed Assets Put into Use （%）	76.8	74.9	89.9
本年施工房屋面积（万平方米）	Floor Space of Buildings under Construction this year （10000 sq.km）	6589.15	5996.69	592.47
#住　宅	Residential Buildings	2894.89	2661.58	233.31
本年竣工房屋面积（万平方米）	Floor Space of Buildings Completed this year （10000 sq.km）	2678.07	2284.13	393.94
#住　宅	Residential Buildings	694.18	609.21	84.97
房屋竣工率（%）	Rate of Buildings Completed （%）	40.6	38.1	66.5

9-8 分地区固定资产投资资金来源（2015 年）
CAPITAL RESOURCE OF FIXED ASSET INVESTMENT BY REGION （2015）

单位：万元（10000 yuan）

指 标	Itemr	全 市 Whole Municipality	市 区 Urban Area	溧阳市 Liyang City
资金来源总计	**Total Capital Sources**	**37955447**	**33037025**	**4918422**
上年末结余资金	Balance of Last Year	2616653	2224548	392105
本年资金来源	Total Funds of This Year	35338794	30812477	4526317
国家预算内资金	State Budgetary Appropriation	614325	609825	4500
国内贷款	Domestic Loans	5638610	3926819	1711791
利用外资	Foreign Investment	518719	508519	10200
# 外商直接投资	Forcign Direct Investment	68749	58549	10200
自筹资金	Fundraising	23360601	20908384	2452217
其他资金来源	Other Fund Resources	5206539	4858930	347609
附：本年各项应付款	**Accounts Payable of This Year**	**4601789**	**4058217**	**543572**
# 工程款	Funds of Projects	2516370	2211799	304571

9-9 分地区房地产开发投资资金来源（2015 年）
FUNDING SOURCES FOR REAL ESTATE DEVELOPMENT & INVESTMENT BY REGION（2015）

单位：万元（10000 yuan）

指 标	Item	全 市 Whole Municipality	市 区 Urban Area	溧阳市 Liyang City
资金来源总计	**Total Capital Sources**	**9572723**	**8651489**	**921234**
上年末结余资金	Balance of Last Year	2265714	1873609	392105
本年资金来源	Total Funds of This Year	7307009	6777880	529129
国内贷款	Domestic Loans	1157529	1095329	62200
利用外资	Foreign Investment	7109	7109	
# 外商直接投资	Foreign Direct Investment	7109	7109	
自筹资金	Fundraising	1619376	1466934	152442
其他资金来源	Other Fund Resources	4522995	4208508	314487
附：本年各项应付款	**Accounts Payable of This Year**	**1754348**	**1617883**	**136465**
# 工程款	Funds of Projects	1189320	1117195	72125

9-10　房地产开发主要指标（1990-2015 年）
MAJOR INDICATORS OF REAL ESTATE DEVELOPMENT （1990-2015）

单位：万元、万平方米（10000 yuan、10000 sq.m）

年　份 Year	房地产开发投资额 Investment in Real Estate Development	商品房屋施工面积 Construction Area of Commodity Housing	其中 of which 住　宅 Residence	商品房屋竣工面积 Completion Area of Commodity Housing	其中 of which 住　宅 Residence	商品房屋销售面积 Sales Area of Commodity Housing	其中 of which 住　宅 Residence
1990	9384	34.15	30.86	19.38	16.78		
1991	18274	61.87	54.58	28.53	23.51	16.91	
1992	34620	125.50	107.98	40.27	34.59	24.32	
1993	106860	206.39	175.07	99.08	82.86	44.95	
1994	157903	316.28	175.64	144.78	113.07	61.19	
1995	184684	258.48	181.05	120.28	101.41	70.74	61.20
1996	153586	248.16	163.46	134.28	104.96	80.78	72.65
1997	187827	241.81	161.21	121.65	88.20	93.16	85.64
1998	223200	315.52	234.31	132.77	104.08	103.61	93.67
1999	255026	346.92	288.73	169.31	143.19	135.36	123.15
2000	299834	407.39	343.75	204.02	160.96	149.26	133.59
2001	321709	487.47	398.14	192.98	169.51	172.85	162.39
2002	410169	526.05	439.66	268.79	226.74	248.61	223.82
2003	527754	645.00	489.23	249.17	190.56	205.91	170.48
2004	978955	991.33	744.99	250.33	187.75	236.56	196.68
2005	1142730	1246.07	953.78	520.72	397.84	422.53	363.29
2006	1710416	1706.26	1350.55	397.78	297.58	479.12	407.89
2007	2250453	2190.26	1700.02	616.25	486.21	579.49	514.52
2008	3089162	2577.34	1844.19	685.14	541.65	504.49	425.53
2009	3062037	2748.89	1995.22	749.81	547.12	922.64	802.50
2010	4469606	3208.11	2192.84	732.50	486.98	915.75	775.14
2011	5659063	3926.82	2712.48	682.22	472.38	661.12	537.94
2012	5970105	4314.38	3047.37	927.33	642.50	756.81	664.99
2013	6988469	4732.18	3354.49	1155.54	889.72	875.98	769.45
2014	6815257	4459.64	3015.00	846.65	578.00	787.50	674.66
2015	5080400	3948.18	2691.96	766.65	547.31	784.25	672.86

9-11 分地区房地产开发企业经营情况（2015 年）
MANAGEMENT OF REAL ESTATE DEVELOPMENT ENTERPRISES BY REGION （2015）

行 业	Sector	全 市 Whole Municipality	市 区 Urban Area	溧阳市 Liyang City
开发企业个数（个）	**Number of Development Enterprises （unit）**	**451**	**402**	**49**
内 资	Domestically-Funded	370	329	41
国 有	State-owned	4	4	
国有独资公司	Share-Owned Companies	10	5	5
其他有限责任公司	Limited liability Corpora-tion	37	36	1
股份有限公司	Share-holding Corporations Ltd.	4	4	
私营有限责任公司	Private Limited Liability Corporation	310	277	33
私营股份有限公司	Private Share-holding Corporations Ltd.	5	3	2
港澳台商投资	Investment from Hong Kong, Macao and Taiwan	60	53	7
外商投资	Enterprises with Foreign Investment	21	20	1
平均从业人员（人）	**Average Number of Employed Persons （person）**	**12003**	**10635**	**1368**
土地开发及购置	**Land Area （sq.m）**			
待开发土地面积（平方米）	Land Space Needed to Development（sq.m）	1891487	1797332	94155
本年购置土地面积（平方米）	Land Space Purchases of This Year（sq.m）	393183	390394	2789
本年土地成交款（万元）	Total Value of Land Purchased（10000 yuan）	123976	123641	335
经营情况（万元）	**Management Condition （10000 yuan）**			
实收资本	Paid-up Capital	7615308	7342689	272619
资产总计	Total Assets	34218493	31668275	2550218
累计折旧	Accumulated Depreciation of Fixed Assets	251364	212195	39168
# 本年折旧	Depreciation of This Year	54404	45102	9303
负债总计	Total Liabilities	24500523	22322070	2178453
所有者权益	Owner's Equity	9717970	9346205	371766
主营业务收入	Operating Income	5923819	5503085	420733
土地转让收入	Income from Land Transferred	35252	35252	
商品房屋销售收入	Income from Commercial Houses Sold	5768696	5381904	386792
房屋出租收入	Housing Rental Income	47671	38253	9418
其他收入	Other Incomes	72201	47677	24524
主营业务成本	Operational Cost	4981698	4632175	349523
销售费用	Sales Expenses	156036	149140	6896
主营业务税金及附加	Business Tax and Extra Charges	457167	423555	33613
其他业务利润	Other Business Profits	10781	11776	-994
管理费用	Management Expenses finance Charge	244295	221839	22457
财务费用	finance Charge	127682	116592	11090
投资收益	Income from Investment	514881	514820	62
营业利润	Operating Surpius	449130	461884	-12754
营业外收入	Nonbusiness Income	33408	33002	407
营业外支出	Nonbusiness Expenditure	29053	28814	239
利润总额	Total Profits	484364	496950	-12586

9-12　分地区房地产开发投资完成额（2015 年）
TOTAL INVESTMENT IN REAL ESTATE DEVELOPMENT BY REGION （2015）

指　标	Item	全　市 Whole Municipality	市　区 Urban Area
投资完成额	**Total Investment**	**5080400**	**4677391**
按构成分	**Grouped by Composition**		
建筑工程	Construction	3953012	3679530
安装工程	Installation	477021	455620
设备工器具购置	Purchase of Equipment and Investment	56397	56097
其他费用	Others	593970	486144
按工程用途分	**Grouped by Use of funds**		
住　宅	Residential Buildings	3595833	3224373
#90 平方米及以下	under 90 square meters	1000559	940875
144 平方米以上	upon 144 square meters	792174	697859
办公楼	Office Buildings	172557	172487
商业营业用房	Buildings for Business Use	602271	575784
其　他	Others	709739	704747
按登记注册类型分	**Grouped by Registration Status**		
内　资	Domestically-Funded	3649164	3270031
国　有	State-owned	104550	104550
国有独资公司	State-funded Corporations	145712	48433
其它有限责任公司	Other Limited Liability Corporations	655184	655184
股份有限公司	Share-holding Corporations Ltd.	1463	1463
私营有限责任公司	Private Limited Liability Company	2719280	2447947
私营股份有限公司	Private Share-holding Corporations Ltd.	22975	12454
港澳台商投资	Investment from Hong Kong, Macao and Taiwan	1151419	1147299
外商投资	Enterprises with Foreign Investment	279817	260061

单位：万元（10000 yuan）

金坛区 Jintan District	武进区 wujin District	其中 of which #经开区 Economic Development Zone	新北区 Xinbei District	天宁区 Tianning District	钟楼区 Zhonglou District	溧阳市 Liyang City
259367	**1592594**	**81002**	**924106**	**908523**	**992801**	**403009**
204771	1269209	61693	698393	738103	769054	273482
14813	192232	18292	97353	96290	54932	21401
1567	13698	5	30927	9196	709	300
38216	117455	1012	97433	64934	168106	107826
174147	1150920	68487	694472	624404	580430	371460
43670	348060	9959	158477	210945	179723	59684
26015	212711	7493	185814	142336	130983	94315
3350	54792		24383	41177	48785	70
37369	161062	9447	107385	130680	139288	26487
44501	225820	3068	97866	112262	224298	4992
241084	1165142	59982	658719	575677	629409	379133
104550						
	24298			4680	19455	97279
11508	357799	5526	119401	85942	80534	
463	1000					
124563	782045	54456	539318	485055	516966	271333
					12454	10521
9091	297669	17600	201459	276870	362210	4120
9192	129783	3420	63928	55976	1182	19756

9-13　房地产开发企业房屋建设情况（2015 年）
CONSTRUCTION OF BUILDINGS DEVELOPED BY REAL ESTATE COMPANIES（2015）

指　标	Item	施工面积（万平方米）Floor Space under Construction（10000 sq.m）	其中 of which #本年新开工 Floor Space Started This Year	竣工面积（万平方米）Floor Space Completed（10000 sq.m）	竣工价值（万元）Value Completed（10000 yuan）
总　计	**Total**	**3948.18**	**637.77**	**766.65**	**2380312**
#溧阳市	Liyang City	274.14	59.19	107.95	392019
按经济成份分	**By Economic Sector**				
国　有	State-owned	81.39	78.14	3.25	9727
其　它	Others	3866.79	559.63	763.40	2370585
按用途分	**By Use**				
住　宅	Residential Buildings	2691.96	439.88	547.31	1740885
#90 平方米及以下	under 90 square meters	571.67	102.35	104.82	298209
144 平方米以上	upon 144 square meters	587.83	61.51	133.65	446488
# 别墅、高档公寓	Villas, Top Grade Apartments	230.03	6.40	73.91	259344
办公楼	Office Buildings	222.33	15.78	24.74	71492
商业营业用房	Buildings for Business Use	498.56	73.21	92.82	316149
其　他	Others	535.33	108.90	101.78	251786

9-14　市区房地产开发企业房屋建设情况（2015 年）
CONSTRUCTION OF BUILDINGS DEVELOPED BY REAL ESTATE COMPANIES IN URBAN AREA（2015）

指　标	Item	施工面积（万平方米）Floor Space under Construction（10000 sq.m）	其中 of which #本年新开工 Floor Space Started This Year	竣工面积（万平方米）Floor Space Completed（10000 sq.m）	竣工价值（万元）Value Completed（10000 yuan）
总　计	**Total**	**3674.04**	**578.57**	**658.71**	**1988293**
金坛区	Jintan District	295.87	162.98	13.58	47421
武进区	wujin District	1329.58	133.32	167.22	537592
#经开区	Economic Development Zone	138.14	13.19	32.20	90326
新北区	Xinbei District	856.25	118.04	180.42	576180
天宁区	Tianning District	717.19	78.22	224.43	672754
钟楼区	Zhonglou District	475.15	86.02	73.06	154346
按经济成份分	**By Economic Sector**				
国　有	State-owned	81.39	78.14	3.25	9727
其　它	Others	3592.66	500.44	655.46	1978566
按用途分	**By Use**				
住　宅	Residential Buildings	2469.23	396.09	462.34	1419831
#90 平方米及以下	under 90 square meters	550.84	97.11	98.71	270202
144 平方米以上	upon 144 square meters	550.04	54.34	114.60	386775
# 别墅、高档公寓	Villas, Top Grade Apartments	219.79	5.05	66.85	230648
办公楼	Office Buildings	222.28	15.78	24.69	71343
商业营业用房	Buildings for Business Use	458.72	64.29	78.34	283596
其　他	Others	523.81	102.42	93.33	213523

9-15 房地产开发企业商品房销售和出租情况（2015 年）
SOLD AND LEASEDCOMMODITY HOUSES OF REAL ESTATE DEVELOPMENT COMPANIES（2015）

指 标	Item	销售面积（万平方米）Actually Sales（10000sq.m）	其中 of which 现 房 Existing house	期 房 Future marketable housing	待售面积（万平方米）Needed to sales（10000sq.m）
总 计	**Total**	**784.25**	**223.35**	**560.90**	**632.77**
#溧阳市	Liyang City	62.74	37.75	24.99	65.38
按经济成份分	**By Economic Sector**				
国 有	State-owned	25.09	22.63	2.46	31.23
其 它	Others	759.16	200.72	558.44	601.54
按用途分	**By Use**				
住 宅	Residential Buildings	672.86	163.53	509.33	268.78
#90 平方米及以下	under 90 square meters	94.07	13.84	80.23	23.17
144 平方米以上	upon 144 square meters	126.39	43.56	82.83	117.99
# 别墅、高档公寓	Villas, Top Grade Apartments	29.09	12.32	16.77	49.86
办公楼	Office Buildings	15.29	8.68	6.61	47.66
商业营业用房	Buildings for Business Use	60.66	29.49	31.17	198.84
其 他	Others	35.44	21.66	13.78	117.48

9-15 续表 Continued

指 标	Item	销售额（万元）Total Actually（10000 yuan）	其中 of which 现 房 Existing house	期 房 Future marketable housing	出租面积（万平方米）Rent（10000sq.m）
总 计	**Total**	**4967728**	**1267395**	**3700333**	**9.05**
#溧阳市	Liyang City	376908	176643	200265	0.58
按经济成份分	**By Economic Sector**				
国 有	State-owned	91942	81481	10461	0.00
其 它	Others	4875786	1185914	3689872	9.05
按用途分	**By Use**				
住 宅	Residential Buildings	4198970	916401	3282569	0.00
#90 平方米及以下	under 90 square meters	547804	70658	477146	0.00
144 平方米以上	upon 144 square meters	1001990	342132	659858	0.00
# 别墅、高档公寓	Villas, Top Grade Apartments	293694	129477	164217	0.00
办公楼	Office Buildings	106832	62819	44013	4.80
商业营业用房	Buildings for Business Use	594066	249113	344953	1.86
其 他	Others	67860	39062	28798	2.38

9-16　市区房地产开发企业商品房销售和出租情况（2015 年）
COMMODITY HOUSES OF REAL ESTATE DEVELOPMENT COMPANIESSOLD AND LEASED IN URBAN AREA（2015）

指　标	Item	销售面积（万平方米）Actually Sales（10000sq.m）	其中 of which 现　房 Existing house	期　房 Future marketable housing	待售面积（万平方米）Needed to sales（10000sq.m）
总 计	**Total**	**721.51**	**185.60**	**535.91**	**567.40**
金坛区	Jintan District	93.74	34.58	59.16	81.58
武进区	wujin District	227.12	44.83	182.28	154.28
# 经开区	Economic Development Zone	29.23	7.57	21.66	12.32
新北区	Xinbei District	163.46	40.94	122.51	126.85
天宁区	Tianning District	135.30	47.45	87.84	155.69
钟楼区	Zhonglou District	101.90	17.80	84.11	49.00
按经济成份分	**By Economic Sector**				
国　有	State-owned	25.09	22.63	2.46	31.23
其　它	Others	696.42	162.97	533.45	536.17
按用途分	**By Use**				
住　宅	Residential Buildings	612.34	126.63	485.71	229.57
#90 平方米及以下	under 90 square meters	91.82	13.08	78.74	22.28
144 平方米以上	upon 144 square meters	118.37	41.37	77.00	105.16
# 别墅、高档公寓	Villas, Top Grade Apartments	28.36	11.81	16.55	44.33
办公楼	Office Buildings	15.29	8.68	6.61	46.95
商业营业用房	Buildings for Business Use	58.61	28.81	29.80	176.02
其　他	Others	35.27	21.49	13.78	114.86

9-16 续表　Continued

指　标	Item	销售额（万元）Total Actually（10000 yuan）	其中 of which 现　房 Existing house	期　房 Future marketable housing	出租面积（万平方米）Rent（10000sq.m）
总 计	**Total**	**4590820**	**1090752**	**3500068**	**8.47**
金坛区	Jintan District	544712	161287	383425	0.04
武进区	wujin District	1462427	289091	1173336	4.88
# 经开区	Economic Development Zone	157793	42800	114993	0.00
新北区	Xinbei District	992022	194513	797509	0.00
天宁区	Tianning District	896833	287666	609167	2.69
钟楼区	Zhonglou District	694826	158195	**536631**	0.87
按经济成份分	**By Economic Sector**				
国　有	State-owned	91942	81481	10461	0.00
其　它	Others	4498878	1009271	3489607	8.47
按用途分	**By Use**				
住　宅	Residential Buildings	3840701	745269	3095432	0.00
#90 平方米及以下	under 90 square meters	532828	66512	466316	0.00
144 平方米以上	upon 144 square meters	926846	319535	607311	0.00
# 别墅、高档公寓	Villas, Top Grade Apartments	285445	123950	161495	0.00
办公楼	Office Buildings	106832	62819	44013	4.80
商业营业用房	Buildings for Business Use	575647	243822	331825	1.29
其　他	Others	67640	38842	28798	2.38

10

CHAPTER 10

农 业

AGRICULTURE

常州统计年鉴

10 农 业 AGRICULTURE

2015 年主要统计指标 MAJOR STATISTICAL INDICATORS OF 2015

年底乡村实有从业人员	Number of Persons Employed In Rural Area at Year-end	129.40 万人	(10000 persons)
比上年增长	Over the Previous Year	-0.8%	
农林牧渔业总产值	Total Output value of Farming,Forestry,Animal Husbandry and Fishing	271.76 亿元	(100 million yuan)
比上年增长	Over the Previous Year	5.8%	
粮食总产量	Total Output of Grain	108.31 万吨	(10000 tons)
比上年增长	Over the Previous Year	-3.4%	
油料总产量	Total Output of Oil-Bearing	3.60 万吨	(10000 tons)
比上年增长	Over the Previous Year	-13.7%	

10-1　分地区农林牧渔业总产值（1978-2015 年）
GROSS OUTPUT VALUE OF FARMING, FORESTRY, ANIMAL HUSBANDARY AND FISHERY BY REGION（1978-2015）

按现价计算 At Current Prices　　　　单位：亿元（100 million yuan）

年　份 Year	全　市 Whole Municipality	其　中　of　which 市　区 Urban Area	 溧阳市 Liyang City
1978	6.96	3.75	1.96
1979	8.13	4.00	2.15
1980	8.12	3.89	2.54
1981	8.14	3.99	2.48
1982	9.66	4.75	2.85
1983	10.08	5.04	2.95
1984	13.71	6.97	4.08
1985	15.10	8.08	4.27
1986	17.42	9.63	4.39
1987	19.17	10.19	5.00
1988	25.01	13.07	6.79
1989	26.87	14.40	6.76
1990	29.06	15.48	7.52
1991	27.78	16.22	6.46
1992	35.22	19.59	8.03
1993	45.95	26.05	10.65
1994	63.64	34.30	16.43
1995	74.74	39.34	20.02
1996	87.28	44.98	24.13
1997	82.16	43.64	21.45
1998	84.01	43.96	22.15
1999	83.67	42.77	22.37
2000	85.88	43.81	22.06
2001	89.37	44.94	23.21
2002	92.67	45.89	24.53
2003	90.63	42.62	24.52
2004	99.42	46.03	27.16
2005	104.10	47.90	28.64
2006	101.99	46.65	27.74
2007	108.87	49.16	30.41
2008	149.77	69.60	45.11
2009	160.77	73.91	49.59
2010	174.08	78.39	54.57
2011	194.68	86.69	62.02
2012	219.58	97.99	69.75
2013	240.11	106.99	75.89
2014	256.81	112.99	81.67
2015	271.76	185.91	85.85

注:1、2006年至2008年数据依据第二次农业普查数据作相应调整。
　2、2015年行政区划调整，市区包含金坛区数据。

Note: 1、The data from year 2006 to year 2008 was adjusted in accordance with the data of the second agricultural census.
　2、With the administrative district adjustment in 2015, the city's urban area now includes Jintan District.

10-2 历年年末耕地面积
YEAR-END AREA UNDER CULTIVATION OVER THE YEARS

单位：千公顷（1000 hectares）

年 份 Year	全 市 Whole Municipality	其 中 of which 市 区 Urban Area	溧阳市 Liyang City
1949	232.64	109.48	73.15
1950	234.05	109.49	74.55
1951	234.91	109.51	75.40
1952	235.41	108.91	75.53
1953	234.47	108.63	75.22
1954	235.91	108.29	76.78
1955	235.93	107.93	76.84
1956	232.55	107.07	74.13
1957	231.33	106.19	75.24
1958	216.47	99.67	68.01
1959	217.58	103.18	68.15
1960	214.83	101.77	68.00
1961	213.75	101.10	68.15
1962	217.05	103.02	67.94
1963	217.53	103.28	68.05
1964	218.49	103.34	68.95
1965	218.25	103.29	68.86
1966	217.29	102.93	68.25
1967	215.02	102.22	67.53
1968	213.95	101.55	67.13
1969	212.49	100.87	66.46
1970	209.59	100.90	65.61
1971	211.12	101.96	65.81
1972	211.61	101.99	65.79
1973	212.97	103.85	65.76
1974	212.53	103.55	65.60
1975	212.21	103.31	65.55
1976	211.71	102.86	65.50
1977	211.38	102.59	65.42
1978	210.15	100.84	65.36
1979	209.67	100.47	65.29
1980	209.13	100.24	65.23
1981	208.91	100.13	65.16
1982	206.73	98.09	65.06

10-2 续表　Continued　　　　　　　　　　　　　　　　　　　单位：千公顷（1000 hectares）

年　份 Year	全　市 Whole Municipality	其　中　of　which 市　区 Urban Area	溧阳市 Liyang City
1983	207.14	98.61	64.99
1984	206.79	98.38	64.93
1985	206.57	98.25	64.87
1986	206.16	98.08	64.68
1987	206.05	98.04	64.65
1988	205.31	97.38	64.63
1989	204.97	97.19	64.50
1990	204.54	97.01	64.34
1991	204.27	96.86	64.26
1992	203.60	96.59	63.94
1993	203.23	96.42	63.80
1994	202.42	95.81	63.68
1995	200.88	94.80	63.44
1996	205.35	90.16	68.99
1997	204.99	80.57	68.87
1998	204.70	80.29	68.87
1999	204.81	89.31	69.19
2000	204.25	88.75	69.15
2001	202.63	87.03	69.23
2002	199.97	84.93	68.91
2003	197.67	82.78	68.64
2004	178.09	66.14	66.89
2005	176.32	64.27	66.83
2006	161.81	60.58	62.24
2007	161.09	59.89	62.34
2008	161.09	59.32	62.60
2009	148.13	60.37	55.83
2010	150.39	59.25	57.64
2011	150.00	58.60	57.59
2012	149.71	58.37	57.59
2013	149.85	58.30	57.62
2014	150.13	58.42	57.77
2015	149.94	92.01	57.93

注:1、2015年末耕地面积为初步统计数据。
　2、2015年行政区划调整，市区包含金坛区数据。
Note:1、The arable land calculated in the end of 2015 was based on the preliminary statistics.
　2、With the administrative district adjustment in 2015, the city's urban area now includes Jintan District.

10-3 历年粮食总产量
TOTAL OUTPUT OF GRAIN OVER THE YEARS

单位：万吨（10000 tons）

年 份 Year	全 市 Whole Municipality	其 中 of which 市 区 Urban Area	 溧阳市 Liyang City
1949	57.89	34.54	11.86
1950	61.23	34.57	14.86
1951	67.10	37.91	17.24
1952	78.41	42.77	19.87
1953	80.46	43.36	20.31
1954	75.69	39.74	20.15
1955	78.59	41.88	20.08
1956	80.81	42.77	20.96
1957	71.52	37.60	18.34
1958	79.50	44.68	17.92
1959	62.57	34.79	14.90
1960	59.91	35.47	12.54
1961	59.94	33.93	12.88
1962	74.80	44.49	15.45
1963	93.13	51.44	23.36
1964	103.13	58.50	24.75
1965	116.93	65.31	29.20
1966	129.16	73.06	31.62
1967	118.37	62.50	32.02
1968	109.78	60.07	29.26
1969	113.65	60.42	30.84
1970	114.48	61.81	29.11
1971	136.47	71.52	36.88
1972	130.41	67.64	37.66
1973	131.16	70.63	35.50
1974	138.11	75.45	36.74
1975	121.23	68.96	30.90
1976	140.22	74.40	38.32
1977	111.38	59.50	30.82
1978	150.25	81.96	40.03
1979	154.07	81.35	43.61
1980	139.42	75.25	37.38
1981	132.79	71.57	37.23
1982	157.60	84.85	43.84

10-3 续表 Continued

单位：万吨（10000 tons）

年 份 Year	全 市 Whole Municipality	其 中 of which 市 区 Urban Area	 溧阳市 Liyang City
1983	164.73	85.76	48.47
1984	177.75	91.79	53.12
1985	153.34	80.46	44.50
1986	162.13	85.82	45.09
1987	151.45	81.42	42.92
1988	157.63	85.37	41.56
1989	160.60	85.87	43.17
1990	164.50	89.07	41.98
1991	138.39	77.55	35.15
1992	158.62	88.06	40.53
1993	154.24	82.17	40.52
1994	144.79	77.74	37.07
1995	159.57	81.30	43.55
1996	166.37	83.73	46.03
1997	170.77	85.47	48.39
1998	153.28	72.02	47.82
1999	154.83	76.13	46.00
2000	136.22	66.11	41.87
2001	126.14	57.32	41.89
2002	122.86	53.78	42.96
2003	103.54	42.49	38.53
2004	106.08	41.43	40.96
2005	98.06	39.28	36.61
2006	95.25	36.30	36.87
2007	94.84	31.91	40.96
2008	113.35	36.84	49.41
2009	114.18	36.37	49.78
2010	115.16	34.22	52.72
2011	115.19	32.34	54.47
2012	114.80	32.02	54.52
2013	113.71	31.79	53.63
2014	112.16	30.71	53.89
2015	108.31	54.41	53.90

注:1、2006、2007年数据依据第二次农业普查数据作相应调整。
2、2015年行政区划调整，市区包含金坛区数据。

Note: 1、Data of year 2006 and 2007 are adjusted in accordance with the data of the second agricultural census.
2、With the administrative district adjustment in 2015, the city's urban area now includes Jintan District.

10-4 历年棉花总产量
TOTAL OUTPUT OF COTTON OVER THE YEARS

单位：吨（ton）

年 份 Year	全 市 Whole Municipality	其 中 of which 市 区 Urban Area	溧阳市 Liyang City
1949	261	195	
1950	269	210	
1951	367	254	
1952	390	301	
1953	403	314	
1954	124	93	
1955	215	143	
1956	42	36	
1957	50	46	
1958	11	10	
1959	10	8	
1960	102		102
1961	1		1
1962	12	10	1
1963	17	7	1
1964	33	17	2
1965	112	42	19
1966	129	17	51
1967	211	17	55
1968	219	30	88
1969	87	4	61
1970	34		27
1971	9		3
1972	221		1
1973	381		
1974	415		1
1975	503		1
1976	753		1
1977	775		
1978	2045		366
1979	3274		482
1980	5509		1831
1981	10495	104	3366
1982	11615	594	3457

10-4 续表　Continued　　单位：吨（ton）

年　份 Year	全　市 Whole Municipality	其中 of which 市　区 Urban Area	溧阳市 Liyang City
1983	11973	914	2937
1984	12860	1198	3729
1985	7240	559	2444
1986	3464	227	1591
1987	2954	252	1518
1988	3325	215	1819
1989	2259	125	1273
1990	2255	78	1193
1991	1956	86	1170
1992	2840	74	2031
1993	1828	27	1497
1994	1050		913
1995	1276		1086
1996	936		758
1997	1114		924
1998	1150		902
1999	589		388
2000	764		544
2001	708		348
2002	637		406
2003	305		182
2004	368		236
2005	298		185
2006	303		241
2007	283		204
2008	484		406
2009	454		332
2010	506		451
2011	491		457
2012	493		470
2013	462		439
2014	433		409
2015	419	12	407

注:1、2006、2007年数据依据第二次农业普查数据作相应调整。
2、2015年行政区划调整，市区包含金坛区数据。
Note: 1、Data of year 2006 and 2007 are adjusted in accordance with the data of the second agricultural ensus.
2、With the administrative district adjustment in 2015, the city's urban area now includes Jintan District.

10-5 历年油料总产量
TOTAL OUTPUT OF OIL-BEARING CROPS OVER THE YEARS

单位：吨（ton）

年份 Year	全市 Whole Municipality	其中 of which 市区 Urban Area	溧阳市 Liyang City
1949	4455	1250	1244
1950	4457	1250	1248
1951	6794	930	3844
1952	5027	936	3538
1953	3290	797	2015
1954	4501	839	3093
1955	4062	984	2560
1956	2915	435	2242
1957	4146	550	3130
1958	1816	233	1281
1959	3285	1774	1252
1960	3252	1655	1138
1961	803	353	337
1962	2154	233	1414
1963	2248	154	1479
1964	3167	199	2223
1965	2493	118	1795
1966	2606	108	1502
1967	3852	888	1490
1968	5200	2204	1674
1969	5612	2337	1564
1970	7195	2969	2209
1971	9493	3917	3158
1972	14638	6855	4258
1973	11953	5311	3825
1974	9207	3532	3619
1975	10586	4962	3385
1976	6517	2540	2593
1977	4408	1888	1645
1978	13515	4713	6046
1979	14894	5028	7040
1980	17724	5747	9473
1981	27590	9895	12578
1982	52438	13308	31780

10-5 续表　Continued　　　　单位：吨（ton）

年 份 Year	全 市 Whole Municipality	其 中　of which 市 区 Urban Area	溧阳市 Liyang City
1983	38895	10578	22205
1984	38175	10080	22780
1985	69961	13383	43870
1986	55603	12017	32795
1987	57063	11526	35544
1988	46657	10347	27518
1989	54054	10341	33295
1990	63899	11710	38899
1991	53931	10879	31126
1992	68040	10594	42774
1993	61498	10114	26942
1994	51683	10610	29530
1995	72786	12068	41895
1996	70526	12793	38632
1997	66204	11240	37689
1998	35932	5154	21286
1999	72421	9981	42509
2000	91629	17412	53102
2001	86994	15027	52238
2002	73015	10270	45111
2003	72586	8954	47360
2004	85537	8725	59109
2005	85960	8489	60469
2006	76904	7074	56485
2007	51326	4868	35198
2008	52575	4316	38703
2009	51608	4513	36561
2010	40035	3922	26411
2011	32048	3138	20710
2012	37684	3228	25847
2013	42579	2407	31582
2014	41738	2638	30801
2015	36006	9737	26269

注:1、2006、2007年数据依据第二次农业普查数据作相应调整。
2、2015年行政区划调整，市区包含金坛区数据。
Note: 1、Data of year 2006 and 2007 are adjusted in accordance with the data of the second agricultural census.
2、With the administrative district adjustment in 2015, the city's urban area now includes Jintan District.

10-6 主要年份人均占有主要农产品产量
PER CAPTIA OUTPUT OF MAJOR FARM PRODUCTS IN MAIN YEARS

单位：千克 / 人（kg/person）

年份 Year	粮食 Grain	油料 Oil-bearing Crops	蚕茧 Silkworm Cocoons	茶叶 Tea	水果 Fruit	猪肉 Pork	水产品 Aquatic Products
1952	427.68	2.74	1.30	0.01	1.30		4.06
1957	351.09	2.04	0.68	0.01	1.60		4.96
1965	485.63	1.04	0.40	0.14	0.86		4.26
1970	429.06	2.70	1.08	0.36	0.94		3.76
1975	425.84	3.72	0.87	0.47	0.85		4.48
1978	516.31	4.64	0.61	0.47	1.01		4.49
1980	471.14	5.99	0.76	0.54	1.93	23.64	4.85
1985	499.71	22.80	1.78	0.89	2.79	19.64	9.22
1986	523.43	17.95	2.04	0.96	2.96	19.17	12.01
1987	492.13	18.22	2.05	1.09	3.42	19.32	13.00
1988	497.16	14.12	2.38	1.20	3.93	19.86	15.73
1989	499.29	16.81	2.77	1.17	3.38	20.13	13.81
1990	506.40	19.67	2.69	1.15	2.98	21.55	16.36
1991	423.38	16.50	2.64	1.03	2.95	22.44	11.44
1992	482.75	20.71	2.88	1.13	3.07	23.77	15.69
1993	468.36	18.67	3.38	1.24	4.17	23.98	21.14
1994	436.85	15.59	3.54	1.20	6.08	25.31	24.27
1995	478.25	21.82	3.01	0.76	6.81	26.97	27.15
1996	492.88	20.89	1.47	0.72	6.49	25.94	29.16
1997	503.41	19.52	1.51	0.80	6.32	17.47	27.57
1998	450.83	10.60	1.43	0.79	7.10	18.32	31.11

10-6 续表 Continued

单位：千克 / 人（kg/person）

年 份 Year	粮 食 Grain	油 料 Oil-bearing Crops	蚕 茧 Silkworm Cocoons	茶 叶 Tea	水 果 Fruit	猪 肉 Pork	水产品 Aquatic Products
1999	455.78	21.32	1.28	0.81	7.92	17.56	32.16
2000	398.90	26.83	1.41	0.79	8.68	18.83	32.51
2001	369.40	25.47	1.53	0.77	10.55	19.83	33.80
2002	357.92	21.27	1.47	0.78	10.79	19.51	35.08
2003	299.06	20.97	1.30	0.78	17.30	21.30	36.02
2004	303.99	24.51	1.26	0.76	17.41	19.16	36.48
2005	278.88	24.45	0.81	0.79	19.13	18.46	37.03
2006	268.56	21.68	0.92	0.82	16.88	19.05	37.13
2007	265.37	14.36	0.68	0.93	20.69	16.52	37.83
2008	315.96	14.66	0.46	1.06	27.14	17.78	39.63
2009	317.33	14.34	0.20	1.09	23.12	17.40	39.13
2010	319.17	11.10	0.19	0.96	27.60	16.57	41.00
2011	317.45	8.83	0.14	0.95	25.61	16.74	45.31
2012	314.71	10.33	0.13	0.96	32.19	18.24	49.67
2013	310.75	11.64	0.11	0.80	30.28	20.71	50.65
2014	304.25	11.32	0.08	0.77	33.42	19.89	50.66
2015	292.06	9.71	0.05	0.76	34.78	19.57	47.97

注:1、2006、2007年数据依据第二次农业普查数据作相应调整。
2、2015年行政区划调整，市区包含金坛区数据。

Note: 1、Data of year 2006 and 2007 are adjusted in accordance with the data of the second agricultural census.
2、With the administrative district adjustment in 2015, the city’s urban area now includes Jintan District.

10-7 主要年份农村经济主要指标
MAJOR ECONOMIC INDICATORS OF AGRICULTURE IN MAIN YEARS

指标	Item	1985	1990	1995	2000	2005	2010	2015
农业机械总动力（万千瓦）	Total Power of Agricultural Machinery （10000 kw）	105.65	116.92	137.19	167.67	162.03	150.22	142.86
农林牧渔业总产值（亿元）	Total Output Value of Farming,Forestry, Animal Husbandry and Fishery （100 million yuan）	13.35	29.06	74.74	85.88	104.10	174.08	271.76
# 农业产值	Value of Farming	9.30	15.95	44.65	51.37	50.14	95.03	147.24
林业产值	Value of Forestry	0.14	0.17	0.51	0.88	1.24	1.26	1.90
牧业产值	Value of Animal Hubandry	3.10	8.28	17.52	12.97	18.74	27.41	38.75
渔业产值	Value of Fishery	0.81	2.60	12.06	20.66	29.01	42.37	68.27
粮食产量（万吨）	Total Output of Grain （10000 tons）	153.34	164.50	159.57	136.22	98.06	115.16	108.31
棉花产量（吨）	Total Output of Cotton （ton）	7240	2255	1276	764	298	506	419
油料产量（吨）	Total Output of Oil-bearing Grops （ton）	69961	63899	72786	91629	85960	40035	36006
水产品产量（吨）	Output of Aquatic Products （ton）	26848	53149	90571	111188	130198	147938	177892
蚕茧产量（吨）	Output of Silkworm Cocoons （ton）	5476	8726	10055	4815	2843	671	187
水果产量（吨）	Output of Fruits （ton）	8551	9670	22716	29639	67275	99565	128971
茶叶产量（吨）	Output of Tea （ton）	2727	3730	2550	2680	2762	3464	2819

10-8 主要年份农村经济主要指标增长速度
GROWTH RATE OF MAJOR INDICATORS OF AGRICULTURAL ECONOMY IN MAIN YEARS

单位：%

指标	Item	2015 年比下列各年增长 Growth Rate of 2015 over Following Years						
		1985	1990	1995	2000	2005	2010	2014
农业机械总动力	Total Power of Agricultural Machinery	35.2	22.2	4.1	-14.8	-11.8	-4.9	-7.7
农林牧渔业总产值	Total Output Value of Farming,Forestry, Animal Husbandry and Fishery	19.4倍	8.4倍	2.6倍	2.2倍	1.6倍	56.1	5.8
# 农业产值	Value of Farming	14.8倍	8.2倍	2.3倍	1.9倍	1.9倍	54.9	6.1
林业产值	Value of Forestry	12.6倍	10.2倍	2.7倍	1.2倍	53.0	50.6	4.8
牧业产值	Value of Animal Hubandry	11.5倍	3.7倍	1.2倍	2.0倍	106.8	41.4	3.5
渔业产值	Value of Fishery	83.3倍	25.3倍	4.7倍	2.3倍	1.4倍	61.1	5.5
粮食产量	Total Output of Grain	-29.4	-34.2	-32.1	-20.5	10.4	-6.0	-3.4
油料产量	Total Output of Oil-bearing Grops	-48.5	-43.7	-50.5	-60.7	-58.1	-10.1	-13.7
水产品产量	Output of Aquatic Products	5.6倍	2.3倍	96.4	60.0	36.6	20.2	-4.7
蚕茧产量	Output of Silkworm Cocoons	-96.6	-97.9	-98.1	-96.1	-93.4	-72.1	-42.8
水果产量	Output of Fruits	14.1倍	12.3倍	4.7倍	3.4倍	91.7	29.5	-5.6
茶叶产量	Output of Tea	3.4	-24.4	10.5	5.2	2.1	-18.6	0.0

10-9　主要年份农村基本情况
FUNDAMENTAL CONDITION OF VILLAGE IN MAIN YEARS

指　标	Item	1990	1995	2000	2005	2010	2015
农村基层组织（个）	**Village Units （unit）**						
镇政府	Town Governments	32	73	70	73	39	36
村民委员会	Number of Villagers' Committees	1933	1924	1909	1101	811	654
村民小组	Villager Group	21557	21638	21485	17999	17147	15277
乡村户数、人口数	**Households and Rural Population**						
总户数（万户）	Number of Households （10000 households）	74.68	76.80	80.41	79.98	78.72	73.69
总人口（万人）	Rural Population（10000 persons）	242.34	239.14	236.86	235.30	237.55	224.30
乡村实有从业人员（万人）	**Number of Rural Laborers （10000 persons）**	**135.80**	**136.31**	**128.67**	**126.86**	**133.95**	**129.40**
按性别分	Grouped by Sex						
男劳动力	Male	70.50	70.77	66.66	66.02	70.55	68.61
女劳动力	Female	65.30	65.54	62.01	60.84	63.40	60.79
按行业分	**Grouped by Sector**						
农林牧渔业	Farming, Forestry, Animal Husbandry and Fishery	65.45	54.65	51.03	32.21	27.39	23.56
# 种植业	Planting	59.15	47.29	43.98	26.11	21.84	18.75
工　业	Industry	37.58	42.88	36.98	48.35	58.20	59.62
建筑业	Construction	11.22	12.86	13.54	15.89	16.66	17.23
交通运输、仓储、邮电通信业	Transport, Storage, Post and Telecommunications	4.18	5.23	5.27	5.91	5.44	5.24
批发零售贸易餐饮业	Wholesale and Retail Trade, Catering Service	2.71	3.92	5.67	7.91	7.13	6.62
金融保险业	Banking and Insurance	0.10	0.11	0.17	0.49	0.76	0.77
房地产、社会服务业	Real Estate and Social Services	0.49	0.39	0.72	1.42	1.69	1.41
卫生、体育和社会福利业	Health Care, Sporting and Social Welfare	0.41	0.41	0.39	0.42	0.56	0.54
教育、文化艺术和广电业	Culture, Education and Arts, Radio, Film and Television	0.60	0.47	0.38	0.48	0.60	0.63
科研和综合技术服务业	Scientific Research and Polytechnical Services	0.08	0.07	0.14	0.16	0.24	0.22
乡经济组织管理业	Rural Economic Management	0.74	0.94	0.87	0.58	0.45	0.28
其他行业	Others	12.24	14.38	13.51	13.04	14.83	13.28

注：本表按当年口径统计，2013 年以后，交通运输、仓储、邮电通信业指交通运输、仓储和邮政业；批发零售贸易餐饮业指批发和零售业。

Notes:The table is in line with the current statistical caliber. Starting from 2013, the transportation, storage, and post and telecommunications industries refer to the transportation, storage and postal industries; and the wholesale & retail trade and catering services sectors refer to the wholesale & retail trade sector.

10-10 农林牧渔业增加值（2015 年）
VALUE ADDED OF FARMING, FORESTRY, ANIMAL HUSBANDARY AND FISHERY（2015）

指标	Item	总产值（万元）Gross Output Value（10000 yuan）	其中 of which 中间消耗 Depreciation	增加值 Value-Added	增加值率（%）Value-adding Rate（%）
总　计	**Total**	**2717635**	**1157888**	**1559747**	**57.4**
农　业	Farming	1472428	521421	951007	64.6
林　业	Forestry	18976	9350	9626	50.7
牧　业	Animal Husbandry	387493	247164	140329	36.2
渔　业	Fishery	682695	318102	364593	53.4
农林牧渔服务业	Services	156043	61851	94192	60.4

10-11 分地区农林牧渔业增加值（2015 年）
VALUE ADDED OF FARMING, FORESTRY, ANIMAL HUSBANDARY AND FISHERY BY REGION（2015）

单位：万元（10000 yuan）

地区	Region	增加值 Value-Added	其中 of which 农业 Farming	林业 Forestry	牧业 Animal Husbandry	渔业 Fishery	农林牧渔服务业 Services
全　市	**Whole Municipality**	**1559747**	**951007**	**9626**	**140329**	**364593**	**94192**
市　区	Urban Area	1075112	653202	5000	118946	225053	72911
金坛区	Jintan District	346829	175271	2663	40311	105026	23558
武进区	Wujin District	416118	290182	742	36586	60063	28545
新北区	New District	189842	122158	1116	20830	30430	15308
天宁区	Tianning District	91941	46469	479	13321	26890	4782
钟楼区	Zhonglou District	30382	19122		7898	2644	718
溧阳市	Liyang City	484635	297805	4626	21383	139540	21281

10-12 分地区农林牧渔业总产值（2015 年）
OUTPUT VALUE OF FARMING, FORESTRY, ANIMAL HUSBANDRY AND FISHERY BY REGION（2015）

指标	Item	全市 Whole Municipality	市区 Urban Area
总计	**Total**	**2717635**	**1859116**
农业产值	**Output Value of Farming**	**1472428**	**996098**
谷物及其他作物	Grain and Other Crop	378033	183996
蔬菜园艺作物	Vegetable and Horticultural Crop	747715	635809
水果、坚果、饮料和香料作物	Fruit, Nut, Beverage and Aromatic Crop	345147	175098
林业产值	**Output Value of Forestry**	**18976**	**7892**
林木培养和种植	Forest Cultivation and Planting	9938	6247
林产品	Forest Products	7524	865
竹木采运	Bamboo and Wood Cuttingand Transportation	1514	780
牧业产值	**Output Value of Animal Husbandry**	**387493**	**322821**
牲畜	Livestock	15318	11422
家禽	Poultry	236692	203059
猪的饲养	Pig Breeding	127503	102356
捕猎	Hunting	171	171
其它畜牧业	Others	7809	5813
渔业产值	**Output Value of Fishery**	**682695**	**411123**
内陆水域产品	Lnland Waters Aquatic Products	682695	411123
#养殖	Artificial Culture	656760	391965
#贝类	Shellfish	5687	4643
其他	Others	9199	8977
农林牧渔服务业	**Services**	**156043**	**121182**

单位：万元（10000 yuan）

其中 of which					溧阳市 Liyang City
金坛区 Jintan District	武进区 wujin District	新北区 Xinbei District	天宁区 Tianning District	钟楼区 Zhonglou District	
663609	**661481**	**329555**	**150526**	**53945**	**858519**
284513	**427877**	**188754**	**66407**	**28547**	**476330**
91796	34160	50897	6534	609	194037
151370	308744	128685	24244	22766	111906
40152	84973	9172	35629	5172	170049
3856	**1297**	**1984**	**755**		**11084**
2673	1230	1602	742		3691
466	67	319	13		6659
717		63			734
129847	**89232**	**56256**	**28164**	**19322**	**64672**
2862	1734	1376	847	4603	3896
88523	58110	28619	14573	13234	33633
34688	28952	24503	12728	1485	25147
171					
3603	436	1758	16		1996
204160	**98465**	**55710**	**47907**	**4881**	**271572**
204160	98465	55710	47907	4881	271572
193103	90364	55710	47907	4881	264795
1455	300	1645	1243		1044
3634	1243	2369	1731		222
41233	**44610**	**26851**	**7293**	**1195**	**34861**

10-13　分地区农业现代化情况（2015 年）
STATISTICS ON AGRICULTURAL MODERNIZATION BY REGION（2015）

指　标	Item	全　市 Whole Municipality	市 区 Urban Area
农业机械情况	**Statistics on Agricultural Machinery**		
机耕地面积（千公顷）	Area Ploughed by Tractors （1000 hectares）	156.82	85.08
#占耕地面积（%）	Percentage of Coverage Area under Cultivation （%）	104.59	92.47
机播面积（千公顷）	Seeded Area by Tractors （1000 hectares）	122.57	61.45
机械植保面积（千公顷）	Plant Protection Area by Tractors （1000 hectares）	142.62	70.87
机收面积（千公顷）	Harvest Area by Tractors （1000 hectares）	131.79	69.83
机械脱粒粮食（万吨）	Amount of Shelling by Thresher （10000 tons）	91.25	49.15
农村电气化情况	**Electrization in Rural Area**		
农村用电量（万千瓦小时）	Electricity Consumed in Rural Area （10000 kwh）	1606486	1131671
农村化学化情况	**Chemification Conditions of Village**		
化肥施用量（折纯量，吨）	Consumption of Chemical Fertilizer （ton）	67338	45203
#氮　肥	Nitrogenous Fertilizer	40077	25969
磷　肥	Phosphate Fertilizer	3009	1663
钾　肥	Potash Fertilizer	1619	1267
复合肥	Compound Fertilizer	22633	16304
农药使用量（吨）	Consumption of Agricultural Chemical Pesticide （ton）	3152	1876
农用薄膜使用量（吨）	Consumption of Agricultural Film （ton）	2975	1839
#地膜使用量（吨）	Consumption of Mulching Film （ton）	1343	804
地膜覆盖面积（公顷）	Area of Coverage of Mulching Film （hectare）	7725	2649
农用柴油（吨）	Agricultural Diesel Oil （ton）	26732	16827
自来水受益村数（个）	**Number of Villages with Access to Tap Water （unit）**	**647**	**472**

其 中 of which					溧阳市 Liyang City
金坛区 Jintan District	武进区 wujin District	新北区 Xinbei District	天宁区 Tianning District	钟楼区 Zhonglou District	
35.12	27.33	19.19	2.04	1.40	71.75
103.74	85.19	102.21	54.28	39.47	123.84
32.61	11.97	14.45	1.92	0.50	61.11
37.98	14.46	15.00	2.04	1.40	71.75
33.59	14.84	18.86	2.04	0.50	61.97
26.35	11.02	11.58	0.00	0.19	42.10
228513	704883	18254	45041	134980	474815
22302	5118	9552	5331	2900	22135
11007	2942	6852	3758	1410	14108
60	249	345	235	774	1346
126	90	412	2	637	352
11109	1837	1943	1336	79	6329
814	486	421	125	30	1276
718	462	275	272	112	1136
213	236	152	192	11	539
847	926	498	223	155	5076
5321	6920	2788	341	1457	9905
97	**197**	**60**	**60**	**58**	**175**

10-14　分地区农村基本情况（2015 年底）
FUNDAMENTAL CONDITION OF VILLAGE BY REGION（END OF 2015）

指　标	Item	全　市 Whole Municipality	市 区 Urban Area
农村基层组织情况（个）	**Village Units （unit）**		
镇政府	Town Governments	36	26
村民委员会	Number of Villagers' Committees	654	479
村民小组	Villager Group	15277	10297
乡村户数、人口	**Households and Rural Population**		
乡村总户数（万户）	Number of Households （10000 households）	73.69	53.67
乡村总人口（万人）	Rural Population （10000 persons）	224.30	163.71
乡村实有从业人员数（万人）	**Number of Rural Laborers （10000 persons）**	**129.40**	**97.64**
按性别分	**Grouped by Sex**		
男劳动力	Male	68.61	51.99
女劳动力	Female	60.79	45.65
按行业分	**Grouped by Sector**		
农林牧渔业	Farming, Forestry, Animal Husbandry and Fishery	23.56	15.6
# 种植业	Planting	18.75	12.96
工　业	Industry	59.62	50.85
建筑业	Construction	17.23	8.14
交通运输、仓储和邮政业	Transport,Storage and Post	5.24	3.45
信息传输、软件和信息技术服务业	Information Transmission, Software and IT Services Industry	0.65	0.58
批发和零售业	Wholesale and Retail Trade	6.62	4.84
住宿和餐饮业	Accommodation and Catering Services	2.47	1.73
金融保险业	Banking and Insurance	0.77	0.42
房地产、社会服务业	Real Estate and Social Services	1.41	1.17
卫生、体育和社会福利业	Health Care, Sporting and Social Welfare	0.54	0.39
教育、文化艺术和广电业	Culture, Education and Arts,Radio, Film and Television	0.63	0.5
科研和综合技术服务业	Scientific Research and Polytechnical Services	0.22	0.13
乡经济组织管理业	Rural Economic Management	0.28	0.21
其他行业	Others	10.16	9.63

其中 of which					溧阳市 Liyang City
金坛区 Jintan District	武进区 wujin District	新北区 Xinbei District	天宁区 Tianning District	钟楼区 Zhonglou District	
6	11	7	1	1	10
97	197	60	67	58	175
1505	5409	1738	683	962	4980
13.87	20.38	10.50	3.78	5.14	20.02
37.05	63.03	36.90	11.65	15.08	60.59
20.57	**37.99**	**22.08**	**8.39**	**8.61**	**31.76**
11.26	19.84	11.56	4.71	4.62	16.62
9.31	18.15	10.52	3.68	3.99	15.14
5.08	7.00	2.57	0.52	0.43	7.96
4.02	5.93	2.21	0.42	0.38	5.79
7.34	20.42	12.80	5.59	4.70	8.77
4.49	1.77	1.13	0.39	0.36	9.09
0.88	1.19	0.70	0.42	0.26	1.79
0.11	0.22	0.10	0.07	0.08	0.07
0.76	1.59	1.30	0.47	0.72	1.78
0.33	0.52	0.40	0.25	0.23	0.74
0.04	0.17	0.13	0.03	0.05	0.35
0.17	0.51	0.13	0.27	0.09	0.24
0.03	0.14	0.11	0.03	0.08	0.15
0.06	0.20	0.15	0.03	0.06	0.13
0.04	0.04	0.01	0.02	0.02	0.09
0.03	0.06	0.06	0.02	0.04	0.07
1.21	4.16	2.49	0.28	1.49	0.53

10-15　分地区农业机械拥有情况（2015 年底）
POSSESSION OF AGRICULTURAL MACHINERY BY REGION（END OF 2015）

指　标	Item	全　市 Whole Municipality	市 区 Urban Area
农业机械总动力（万千瓦）	**Total Power of Agricultural Machinery（10000 kw）**	**142.86**	**87.62**
拖拉机及配套机械	**Tractors and Subsidiary Machinery**		
大中型拖拉机（台）	Large and Medium Tractors （unit）	3796	2379
#轮式拖拉机	Roller Tractors	3796	2379
小型拖拉机（台）	Mini-tractors （unit）	15209	8339
种植业机械	**Machinery of Farm Production**		
机引犁（台）	Trailed Tractor Plow （unit）	10569	4249
农用排灌动力机械（台）	Machinery for Agricultural Drainage and Irrigation （unit）	25249	11477
机动喷雾（粉）机（台）	Motorized Duster （unit）	17478	10641
联合收割机（台）	Combined Harvesters （unit）	1940	1339
机动脱粒机（台）	Threshing and Drying Machine （unit）	16006	14106
农副产品加工机械	**Machinery of Agricultural and Sideline Products Processing**		
农副产品加工动力（台）	Machinery of Agricultural and Sideline Products Processing （unit）	13250	8910
#柴油机	Diesel Engines	2661	1920
电动机	Motor	10042	6990
农副产品加工作业机械（台）	Operation Machinery of Agricultural and Sideline Products Processing （unit）	10128	6297
畜牧养殖机械（台）	**Machinery of Livestock Husbandry（unit）**	**5684**	**5286**
饲草料加工机（台）	Fodder Grinder （unit）	2745	2360
林果机械（台）	**Forestry and Fruit Industry Machinery（unit）**	**170**	**140**
渔业机械（台）	**Machinery of Fishery （unit）**	**63117**	**33284**
农田基本建设机械（台）	**Machinery of Farmland Fundamental Construction （unit）**	**5953**	**1023**

其中 of which					溧阳市 Liyang City
金坛区 Jintan District	武进区 wujin District	新北区 Xinbei District	天宁区 Tianning District	钟楼区 Zhonglou District	
42.87	**27.65**	**11.03**	**3.96**	**2.11**	**55.24**
792	937	433	119	98	1417
792	937	433	119	98	1417
4661	2074	1050	297	257	6870
2735	693	698	123		6320
6281	3215	1052	813	116	13772
5352	3125	1600	312	252	6837
477	512	261	67	22	601
8784	701	2977	1644		1900
6191	1273	1100	333	13	4340
1140	327	350	100	3	741
5051	946	750	233	10	3052
3511	1273	1167	333	13	3831
1151	**3135**	**881**	**119**		**398**
572	849	820	119		385
73	**67**				**30**
10405	**18617**	**2420**	**737**	**1105**	**29833**
538	**280**	**168**		**37**	**4930**

10-16　分地区农作物播种面积（2015 年）
SOWN AREA OF FARM CROPS BY REGION（2015）

指　标	Item	全　市 Whole Municipality	市 区 Urban Area
农作物总播种面积	**Total Sown Area**	**214.66**	**121.86**
粮食作物	**Grain Crops**	**142.77**	**74.24**
夏收粮食	Summer Grain	58.70	33.10
谷　物	Cereal	57.19	32.45
小　麦	Wheat	56.87	32.13
大　麦	Barley	0.32	0.32
秋收粮食	Autumn Grain	84.07	41.14
谷 物	Autumn Cereal	78.08	37.55
# 稻 谷	Rice	76.26	36.98
单季晚稻	Single Harvest Late Rice	76.26	36.98
其他谷物	Other cereals	0.04	0.04
玉　米	Corn	1.78	0.53
豆　类	Beans	3.92	2.52
# 大 豆	Soybeans	3.41	2.31
薯　类	Tubers	2.07	1.07
油　料	**Oil-bearing Crops**	**14.90**	**4.30**
# 油菜籽	Rapeseeds	13.45	3.72
棉　花	**Cotton**	**0.47**	**0.01**
糖　料	**Sugar Crops**	**0.08**	**0.01**
药　材	**Crude Drugs**	**0.21**	**0.17**
蔬　菜	**Vegetable**	**29.18**	**20.06**
瓜果类	**Melon Crops**	**4.29**	**2.20**
其他农作物	**Other Farm Crops**	**22.76**	**20.87**
# 青饲料	Green Fodder	1.95	1.11
绿　肥	Green Manure	1.13	0.50

单位：千公顷（1000 hectares）

其 中 of which					溧阳市 Liyang City
金坛区 Jintan District	武进区 wujin District	新北区 Xinbei District	天宁区 Tianning District	钟楼区 Zhonglou District	
54.94	**31.50**	**27.71**	**4.83**	**2.88**	**92.80**
35.63	**14.20**	**21.78**	**2.34**	**0.29**	**68.53**
14.84	6.48	10.71	0.91	0.16	25.60
14.58	6.28	10.57	0.87	0.15	24.74
14.45	6.26	10.41	0.87	0.14	24.74
0.13	0.02	0.16		0.01	
20.79	7.72	11.07	1.43	0.13	42.93
19.12	6.93	10.17	1.23	0.10	40.53
18.76	6.86	10.10	1.19	0.07	39.28
18.76	6.86	10.10	1.19	0.07	39.28
			0.03	0.01	
0.36	0.07	0.07	0.01	0.02	1.25
1.08	0.58	0.72	0.12	0.02	1.40
0.94	0.55	0.68	0.12	0.02	1.10
0.59	0.21	0.18	0.08	0.01	1.00
2.93	**0.58**	**0.61**	**0.14**	**0.04**	**10.60**
2.54	0.51	0.51	0.13	0.03	9.73
0.01					**0.46**
		0.01			**0.07**
0.17					**0.04**
6.35	**7.24**	**3.61**	**1.78**	**1.08**	**9.12**
0.63	**1.02**	**0.21**	**0.18**	**0.16**	**2.09**
9.22	**8.46**	**1.49**	**0.39**	**1.31**	**1.89**
0.83	0.08	0.08	0.11	0.01	0.84
0.46	0.02		0.02		0.63

10-17 分地区农产品总产量（2015 年）
TOTAL YIELD OF FARM CROPS BY REGION（2015）

指 标	Item	全 市 Whole Municipality	市 区 Urban Area
粮食作物	**Grain Crops**	**1083061**	**544050**
夏收粮食	Summer Grain	309028	171528
谷 物	Cereal	305286	170038
小 麦	Wheat	304113	168865
大 麦	Barley	1173	1173
秋收粮食	Autumn Grain	774033	372522
谷 物	Cereal	748897	360054
#稻 谷	Rice	736089	356939
玉 米	Corn	12553	2860
豆 类	Beans	12318	7224
#大 豆	Soybeans	10298	6107
薯 类	Tubers	12818	5244
油 料	**Oil-bearing Crops**	**36006**	**9737**
#油菜籽	Rapeseeds	32886	8618
棉 花	**Cotton**	**419**	**12**
糖 料	**Sugar Crops**	**5866**	**700**

单位：吨（ton）

其 中 of which					溧阳市 Liyang City
金坛区 Jintan District	武进区 wujin District	新北区 Xinbei District	天宁区 Tianning District	钟楼区 Zhonglou District	
268801	**101148**	**156328**	**16048**	**1725**	**539011**
79684	31013	56091	4029	711	137500
79018	30546	55827	3949	698	135248
78475	30460	55320	3949	661	135248
543	86	507		37	
189117	70135	100237	12019	1014	401511
183420	67179	97413	11217	825	388843
181503	66751	97112	10972	601	379150
1917	428	301	64	150	9693
2688	1894	2112	394	136	5094
2331	1801	1445	394	136	4191
3009	1062	712	408	53	7574
6990	**1165**	**1215**	**297**	**70**	**26269**
6207	1055	1025	279	52	24268
12					**407**
		700			**5166**

10-18 分地区农产品单产（2015年）
YIELD OF FARM CROPS PER HECTARE BY REGION（2015）

指 标	Item	全 市 Whole Municipality	市 区 Urban Area
粮食作物	**Grain Crops**	**7586**	**7328**
夏收粮食	Summer Grain	5265	5182
谷 物	Cereal	5338	5240
小 麦	Wheat	5348	5256
大 麦	Barley	3666	3666
秋收粮食	Autumn Grain	9207	9055
谷 物	Cereal	9591	9589
#稻 谷	Rice	9652	9652
单季晚稻	Single Harvest Late Rice	9652	9652
玉 米	Corn	7052	5396
豆 类	Beans	3142	2867
#大 豆	Soybeans	3020	2644
薯 类	Tubers	6192	4901
油 料	**Oil-bearing Crops**	**2417**	**2264**
#油菜籽	Rapeseeds	2445	2317
棉 花	**Cotton**	**891**	**1200**
糖 料	**Sugar Crops**	**73325**	**70000**

单位：公斤 / 公顷（kg/hectare）

其 中 of which					
金坛区 Jintan District	武进区 wujin District	新北区 Xinbei District	天宁区 Tianning District	钟楼区 Zhonglou District	溧阳市 Liyang City
7544	**7123**	**7178**	**6858**	**5948**	**7865**
5370	4786	5237	4427	4444	5371
5420	4864	5282	4539	4653	5467
5431	4866	5314	4539	4721	5467
4177	4300	3169		3700	
9097	9085	9055	8405	7800	9353
9593	9694	9578	9120	8250	9594
9675	9730	9615	9220	8586	9652
9675	9730	9615	9220	8586	9652
5325	6114	4300	6400	7500	7754
2489	3266	2933	3283	6800	3639
2480	3275	2125	3283	6800	3810
5100	5057	3956	5100	5300	7574
2386	**2009**	**1992**	**2121**	**1750**	**2478**
2444	2069	2010	2146	1733	2494
1200					**885**
		70000			**73800**

10-19 分地区畜牧业生产情况（2015 年）
STATISTICS ON LIVESTOCK HUSBANDRY BY REGION（2015）

指 标	Item	全 市 Whole Municipality	市 区 Urban Area
当年出栏数	**Slaughtered Livestock of the Year**		
牛（头）	Cattle and Buffaloes （head）	400	400
猪（万头）	Hogs （10000 heads）	83.70	66.77
羊（万只）	Sheep and Goats（10000 heads）	10.52	6.74
家 禽（万只）	Poultry （10000 heads）	4564.45	4126.45
年末存栏数	**Livestock Being Raised at Year-end**		
牛（头）	Cattle and Buffaloes （head）	4700	4100
猪（万头）	Hogs （10000 heads）	46.87	39.56
羊（万只）	Sheep and Goats （10000 heads）	6.39	5.00
# 山 羊	Goats	6.15	5.00
家 禽（万只）	Poultry （10000 heads）	1180.70	1017.70
产 量	**Output**		
肉 类（吨）	Meat （ton）	143875	120954
#猪牛羊肉	Pork,Beef and Mutton	74381	61472
牛 肉	Beef	304	304
猪 肉	Pork	72579	60051
羊 肉	Mutton	1498	1117
禽 肉	Poultry	68903	59267
牛 奶（吨）	Cow Milk （ton）	17743	16128
蜂 蜜（吨）	Honey （ton）	161	108
禽 蛋（吨）	Poultry Eggs （ton）	33650	22026

其中 of which					溧阳市 Liyang City
金坛区 Jintan District	武进区 wujin District	新北区 Xinbei District	天宁区 Tianning District	钟楼区 Zhonglou District	
400					
22.66	20.68	14.94	7.49	1.00	16.93
3.61	0.71	1.00	1.40	0.02	3.78
1800.42	1524.27	262.00	239.76	300.00	438.00
400	1300	300		2100	600
16.87	12.35	7.80	1.86	0.68	7.31
3.44	0.51	0.80	0.20	0.05	1.39
3.44	0.51	0.80	0.20	0.05	1.15
551.06	270.64	120.00	35.00	41.00	163.00
50203	39818	17892	8479	4562	22921
24329	17425	13847	5023	848	12909
304					
23359	17315	13742	4790	845	12528
666	110	105	233	3	381
25793	22393	4045	3322	3714	9636
510	4326	1030	65	10197	1615
5	103				53
10466	5227	4360	1010	963	11624

10-20 分地区林业、蚕茧、茶叶、水果生产情况（2015年）
STATISTICS ON FORESTRY, SILKWORM COCOONS, TEA AND FRUITS BY REGION（2015）

指 标	Item	全 市 Whole Municipality	市 区 Urban Area
林 业	**Forestry**		
当年造林面积（公顷）	Forestation Area at Current Year（hectare）	1809.79	1155.59
木材产量（立方米）	Output of Timber （cu.m）	2932	2061
蚕 桑	**Silkworm Cocoons and Mulberry**		
年末桑园面积（公顷）	Mulberry Field Area at Year-en（hectare）	400.00	66.67
蚕茧产量（吨）	Output of Silkworm Cocoons （ton）	187	71
茶 叶	**Tea**		
年末茶园面积（公顷）	Tea Field Area at Year-end （hectare）	7773	2746
茶叶产量（吨）	Output of Tea （ton）	2819	1059
红 茶	Black Tea	16	6
绿 茶	Green Tea	2803	1053
水 果	**Fruits**		
年末果园面积（公顷）	Area of Orchards at Year-end （hectare）	12267	6576
# 桃 园	Peaches	2494	1919
梨 园	Pears	1210	930
葡萄园	Grapes	3306	3001
水果产量（吨）	Output of Fruits （ton）	128971	105771
# 桃	Peaches	36021	31784
梨	Pears	23993	19163
葡 萄	Grapes	52293	46863

其 中 of which					溧阳市 Liyang City
金坛区 Jintan District	武进区 wujin District	新北区 Xinbei District	天宁区 Tianning District	钟楼区 Zhonglou District	
438.33	361.86	355.40			654.20
1899	162				871
66.67					333.33
71					116
2746	227				4800
1008	51				1760
6					10
1002.1	50.9				1750
1305	3968	356	889	59	5691
217	1658	35		9	575
153	189	87	481	19	281
507	1905	154	408	27	305
18644	66031	3694	15954	1448	23200
4200	26592	797		195	4237
3150	3918	980	10323	792	4830
7400	32343	1052	5632	436	5430

10-21　分地区淡水产品生产情况（2015 年）
STATISTICS ON FRESHWATER AQUATIC PRODUCTS BY REGION（2015）

指　标	Item	全　市 Whole Municipality	市 区 Urban Area
淡水产品产量（吨）	**Output of Freshwater Aquatic Products （ton）**	**177892**	**114027**
#鱼　类	Fish	134303	85863
#青　鱼	Mackerel	7372	6058
草　鱼	Grass Carp	21599	12089
鲢　鱼	Silver Carp	20170	15189
鲫　鱼	Crucian	27350	10160
鳊　鱼	Bream	28214	22179
鳜　鱼	Mandarin Fish	912	709
甲壳类	Crustacean	40181	25892
#河　蟹	River Crabs	28279	19544
青　虾	Shrimps	11902	6348
鳖	Soft-shelled Turtle	1000	901
珍　珠	Pearl	20000	18000
淡水养殖面积（公顷）	**Freshwater Raise Areas （hectares）**	**37198**	**23708**
#特种养殖	Special Species Breeding	25295	15436
#池　塘	Pond	33033	20197
湖　泊	Lake	2191	1537
水　库	Reservoir	533	533
河　沟	Brook	1441	1441

其中 of which					溧阳市 Liyang City
金坛区 Jintan District	武进区 wujin District	新北区 Xinbei District	天宁区 Tianning District	钟楼区 Zhonglou District	
44140	**50704**	**10071**	**6737**	**2375**	**63865**
21775	45924	9862	5991	2311	48440
565	3537	963	885	108	1314
3146	4625	2928	803	587	9510
3359	8201	2586	567	476	4981
3451	2788	1495	2057	369	17190
2868	16585	842	1367	517	6035
439	218	26	26		203
21125	3950	127	626	64	14289
15411	3474	42	562	55	8735
5714	476	85	64	9	5554
580	199	72	50		99
18000					2000
15247	**5731**	**1175**	**1093**	**462**	**13490**
11918	2429	269	750	70	9859
12541	5079	1062	1093	422	12836
893	644				654
533					
1280	8	113		40	

10-22 分镇、街道基本情况（2015 年）
BASIC STATISTICS ON TOWNS AND SUBDISTRICTS（2015）

镇、街道 Towhs and Subdistricts		总户数（户）Total Households（Household）	总人口（人）Total Population（person）	从业人员（人）Employment（person）	年底耕地面积（公顷）Cultivated Area Year-end（hectare）	其中 of which #有效灌溉面积（公顷）Effective Irrigation	农业机械总动力（千瓦）Total Agricultural Machinery Power（kw）
金坛区	**Jintan District**						
西城街道	Xicheng Subdistrict	48152	120365	86754	5694	1858	66340
金城镇	Jincheng Town	19377	56674	28779	3682	2912	36760
直溪镇	zhixi Town	23221	58465	41124	4065	3840	45610
朱林镇	Zhulin Town	15253	38516	26712	3406	3077	39585
薛埠镇	Xuebu Town	25242	68122	48790	6494	4752	89870
指前镇	Zhiqian Town	19961	55891	25675	4278	3443	40453
儒林镇	Rulin Town	13522	34563	18268	1587	1541	43620
开发区	Development Zone	48973	127046	98575	5290	5180	62135
武进区	**Wujin District**						
湖塘镇	Hutang Town	112300	360922	123253	94	94	1082
牛塘镇	Niutang Town	26635	87911	40309	469	8	5616
洛阳镇	Luoyang Town	26119	84276	54413	1490	1490	20560
遥观镇	Yaoguan Town	33914	101538	56854	704	704	9100
横林镇	Henglin Town	29476	95833	49755	914	622	11075
横山桥镇	Hengshanqiao Town	28193	82066	53297	1266	1266	23869
雪堰镇	Xueyan Town	35807	101800	47182	2999	2999	35475
前黄镇	Qianhuang Town	27768	85760	39314	3388	3388	101595
礼嘉镇	Lijia Town	28387	87764	31691	2397	2063	44650
嘉泽镇	Jiaze Town	28972	86962	47275	4598	4598	38507
湟里镇	Huangli Town	28560	77296	41426	3539	3198	37069
丁堰街道	Dingya Subdistrict	5162	24591	12542	35	35	1861
潞城街道	Lucheng Subdistrict	7296	30352	19727	174	127	301
新北区	**Xinbei District**						
龙虎塘街道	Longhutang Subdistrict	10013	44962	27026	61	19	
春江镇	Chunjiang Town	52164	173438	77934	4215	3236	16952
新桥镇	Xinqiao Town	20990	64639	14526	625	625	7195
薛家镇	Xuejia Town	17046	59321	22945	450	350	7800

地区生产总值（万元） Gross Domestic Product (10000 yuan)	其中 of which 第一产业 Primary Industry	第二产业 Secondary Industry	第三产业 Tertiary Industry	工业总产值（万元） Gross Industrial Output Value	固定资产投资完成额（万元） Realized Investment in Fixed Assets	粮食总产量（吨） Total Output of Grain (ton)	乡镇财政收入（万元） Fiscal Revenue of Town and Township (10000 yuan)	其中 of which #公共财政收入（万元） Public Finance Budget Revenue	农民人均纯收入（元） Per Capita Net Income of Rural Resident (yuan)
784800	14300	220200	550300	121000	160419	11399	41148	22687	40002
535306	58306	374900	102100	1631200	596014	38641	53402	32515	25736
428900	45300	283300	100300	1118211	305050	52757	38236	16800	23886
285700	33300	184400	68000	524510	229600	33112	150618	11852	21476
384590	55581	157403	171606	563147	221137	40858	34292	16670	23726
244700	51400	123800	69500	580672	131196	48351	72276	5581	21348
272100	37500	124100	110500	601532	157305	12351	120361	8606	22181
1896100	51200	1267500	577400	5465269	1436522	31332	364421	85736	237545
1935706	1506	653100	1281100	3210697	1603089	93	275228	205990	26360
1251308	12179	738737	500392	4173031	467487	112	67780	40105	24777
1152666	20222	762066	370378	3353984	350743	5806	52223	23855	25886
1487173	4805	1014137	468231	4426405	390792	4456	120370	53560	24947
1161607	6467	624975	530165	3025477	406160	3920	63000	33642	25190
1347680	12807	714871	620002	3503122	477929	5542	81476	41846	25276
722237	36491	285729	400017	1639931	210782	17197	68405	57155	24205
706127	69915	256097	380115	1353733	375700	33595	40534	18174	24662
836423	24948	501451	310024	2167469	295650	15494	58393	18173	25024
609515	88935	100005	420575	240520	136822	61	33535	30930	25632
1306792	56720	728946	521126	3764966	341341	406	32743	20061	25220
573839	82	472512	101245	2182936	352172	9	51324	22434	23280
587899	52	431668	156179	1899747	572110	307	78295	43962	20126
1100051		674923	425128	4317395	370603		181697	84115	26456
3129112	30915	2514045	584152	11842116	2506307	48362	308280	135478	22195
378600	5600	220800	152200	1015236	600163	3778	82270	46002	24400
910000	9500	685500	215000	3661244	880000	1628	18023	101646	24117

10-22 续表 Continued

镇、街道	Towhs and Subdistricts	总户数（户） Total Households (Household)	总人口（人） Total Population (person)	从业人员（人） Employment (person)	年底耕地面积（公顷） Cultivated Area Year-end (hectare)	其中 of which #有效灌溉面积（公顷） Effective Irrigation	农业机械总动力（千瓦） Total Agricultural Machinery Power (kw)
罗溪镇	Luoxi Town	19582	60884	30530	1150	1143	92460
西夏墅镇	Xixiashu Town	17810	58100	26850	2096	1900	18140
孟河镇	Menghe Town	30782	101305	50242	3860	3647	24315
三井街道	Sanjin Town	22512	60298	44496			
奔牛镇	Benniu Town	20159	65463	33091	2574	2574	17756
天宁区	**Tianning District**						
雕庄街道	Diaozhuang Subdistrict	12098	38707	23540			
青龙街道	Qinlong Subdistrict	14879	50514	32707	90	20	102
郑陆镇	Zhenlu Town	42012	106638	50692	2819	1959	35861
钟楼区	**Zhonglou District**						
新闸镇	Xinzha Town	9670	32311	18924	1380		
五星街道	Wuxing Subdistrict	21132	69937	45621			
永红街道	Yonghong Subdistrict	13890	48322	34880			
北港街道	Beigang Subdistrict	10956	45269	25199			
西林街道	Xilin Subdistrict	8865	23351	14652			13683
邹区镇	Zhouqu Town	32750	95521	45847	2615	2615	20692
溧阳市	**Liyang City**						
溧城镇	Licheng Town	113875	335356	176533	4849	4229	26200
埭头镇	Litou Town	9160	25783	15726	2006	1725	22892
上黄镇	Shanghuang Town	8722	25905	13113	2122	2122	46867
戴埠镇	Daibu Town	19008	47826	30553	3684	3050	25000
天目湖镇	Tianmuhu Town	23213	77619	34392	5705	4369	43418
别桥镇	Bieqiao Town	23336	70922	45384	6554	5255	64230
上兴镇	Shangxing Town	27060	80155	38506	9722	3381	63440
竹箦镇	Zhuze Town	21460	66211	34576	6762	5891	45820
南渡镇	Nandu Town	25737	75488	39290	6784	6485	61846
社渚镇	Shezhu Town	23511	72916	40413	7866	7206	64499

地区生产总值（万元）Gross Domestic Product (10000 yuan)	其中 of which 第一产业 Primary Industry	第二产业 Secondary Industry	第三产业 Tertiary Industry	工业总产值（万元）Gross Industrial Output Value	固定资产投资完成额（万元）Realized Investment in Fixed Assets	粮食总产量（吨）Total Output of Grain (ton)	乡镇财政收入（万元）Fiscal Revenue of Town and Township (10000 yuan)	其中 of which #公共财政收入（万元）Public Finance Budget Revenue	农民人均纯收入（元）Per Capita Net Income of Rural Resident (yuan)
628000	22200	380800	225000	2151500	934000	17631	71900	41000	22232
402000	8000	276000	118000	1210800	322000	22937	48089	21217	18678
791171	36222	507485	247464	2257519	602890	45893	56374	26196	20629
1462000		641000	821000	3730000	546500		285913	147593	27774
631127	21602	212649	396876	1000568	212942	16017	27800	16125	23682
1639543		787932	851611	25023200	482700		102614	50002	14125
823192	395	549743	273054	3584165	132		205000	95800	29033
1249026	150526	524071	574429	2382818	562105	16585	111090	47824	25288
1041737		903675	138062	4107315	428893		62374	27614	19356
571263		267402	303861	883256	513800		35094	27835	22951
387744		174512	213232	380452	369400		46300	25546	22351
33828	1	19795	14032	3960406	510294		12569	6902	19805
307314		127597	179717	395134	320235		33802	21606	24360
950500	22700	288800	639000	1293744	407077	1573	78676	46148	26076
356939	15905	274898	66136	1180546	229925	19926	25157	12526	24876
264429	43663	100628	120138	551515	175650	15155	15077	8797	25601
458416	37700	274894	145822	1250878	259533	32047	20052	12785	22325
539025	40744	285514	212767	1340280	348400	32806	68639	39197	28297
496849	56492	296888	143469	1326753	263060	59060	20131	10176	19500
414100	56400	232500	125200	1160000	277000	105961	47600	28100	21816
342447	46653	189897	105897	875766	149100	68325	33698	11799	22245
387178	36842	189183	161153	745143	198025	67284	25746	16402	23724
686257	53002	359007	274248	1117149	284888	109746	24197	15880	21430

11

CHAPTER 11

工 业

INDUSTRY

常州统计年鉴

11 工业 INDUSTRY

2015年主要统计指标 MAJOR STATISTICAL INDICATORS OF 2015

规模以上工业总产值	Total Output Value of Industry above Designated Size	11101.64 亿元	(100 million yuan)
规模以上工业主营业务收入	Main Business Income of Industrial above Designated Size	11500.68 亿元	(100 million yuan)
规模以上工业实现利税	Profits and Taxes of Industry above Designated Size	1031.88 亿元	(100 million yuan)
规模以上工业实现利润	Profit of Industry above Designated Size	642.27 亿元	(100 million yuan)
规模以上工业总资产	Total Industrial Assets above Designated Size	8407.94 亿元	(100 million yuan)

11-1 历年工业生产发展指数
INDICES OF GROSS INDUSTRIAL OUTPUT OVER THE YEARS

按可比价计算 1949=100 　　Calculated by comparable price： 1949=100

年 份 Year	全 市 Whole Municipality	其中 of which #市 区 Urban Area
1949	100.0	100.0
1950	145.5	148.1
1951	181.0	184.8
1952	231.0	235.1
1953	281.9	288.4
1954	293.3	297.0
1955	260.0	260.4
1956	337.0	334.2
1957	325.0	315.8
1958	585.6	589.7
1959	756.8	749.3
1960	824.6	825.9
1961	496.2	497.0
1962	387.5	379.6
1963	383.8	373.3
1964	483.5	472.8
1965	614.8	603.8
1966	737.3	729.0
1967	567.9	539.7
1968	659.3	642.4
1969	872.2	872.6
1970	1161.9	1163.6
1971	1431.8	1411.5
1972	1667.0	1645.5
1973	1963.5	1923.5
1974	2047.4	2021.0
1975	2305.4	2276.4
1976	2531.8	2495.3
1977	2890.9	2836.1
1978	3208.7	3146.5
1979	3632.7	3565.9
1980	4409.7	4287.7
1981	4887.2	4765.6
1982	5206.0	5023.9
1983	5916.3	5712.2
1984	7092.8	6745.8
1985	9357.8	8807.2
1986	10410.6	9688.6
1987	12618.2	11457.3
1988	15683.8	13769.0
1989	16677.0	14582.2
1990	18500.8	16280.5
1991	21422.5	18847.3
1992	27496.4	24117.3
1993	38501.3	32980.7
1994	47311.0	39967.6
1995	53542.2	45391.8
1996	64109.9	52915.2
1997	63557.5	54208.9
1998	61998.0	52938.4
1999	69415.3	59018.4
2000	76647.0	64689.3
2001	86446.1	72835.6
2002	102096.2	86752.5
2003	130391.2	111681.7
2004	146677.1	126836.9
2005	178762.5	151521.9
2006	219517.7	191379.5
2007	266849.7	232001.2
2008	292010.9	251498.2
2009	358518.1	312735.6
2010	329998.3	287947.2
2011	305683.3	266768.9
2012	341570.1	300176.0
2013	388901.3	339555.6
2014	439939.2	379281.4
2015	472741.6	426056.2

11-2 规模以上工业企业主要经济指标（1982-2015 年）
MAJOR ECONOMIC INDICATORS OF INDUSTRIAL ENTERPRISES ABOVE DESIGNATED SIZE （1982-2015）

单位：亿元（100 million yuan）

年份 Year	主营业务收入 Main Business Income of Industrial	利税总额 Total Profits and Taxes	利润总额 Total Profits	年份 Year	主营业务收入 Main Business Income of Industrial	利税总额 Total Profits and Taxes	利润总额 Total Profits
1982	45.72	8.53	5.47	1999	718.07	46.05	16.31
1983	51.14	9.69	6.47	2000	836.10	59.64	25.44
1984	57.68	10.75	7.08	2001	944.65	68.25	31.25
1985	75.01	14.14	9.26	2002	1135.55	86.03	45.89
1986	82.63	12.93	8.10	2003	1510.77	114.41	65.62
1987	103.18	14.33	9.07	2004	2064.71	136.24	82.49
1988	136.36	17.02	10.48	2005	2459.56	161.84	96.23
1989	151.55	15.44	7.99	2006	3243.79	228.91	142.26
1990	160.85	13.21	5.26	2007	4171.08	301.73	188.78
1991	199.51	11.81	2.58	2008	5089.94	371.12	221.44
1992	264.13	17.80	6.46	2009	5868.05	450.07	276.77
1993	399.13	24.64	9.63	2010	7274.88	620.18	413.47
1994	429.87	25.63	6.22	2011	8212.53	713.30	468.43
1995	542.82	34.65	11.83	2012	9097.95	730.30	443.77
1996	562.96	32.28	8.76	2013	10223.05	844.21	512.56
1997	558.17	31.29	7.69	2014	11379.01	1006.13	618.49
1998	635.22	35.98	8.25	2015	11500.68	1031.88	642.27

注：1982-1997年规模以上工业口径为乡及乡以上全部独立核算工业企业，1998至2010年为全部国有企业及年销售收入500万元以上工业企业，2011年起为主营业务收入2000万元以上的法人工业企业。

Note:During year 1982 and 1997, the scaled industrial caliber involved industrial enterprises with wholly independent accounting;All the "state-owned companies and the industrial enterprises with annual main business income of 5 million yuan and above" cited from 1998 to 2010 has been altered to "corporate industrial enterprises with annual main business income of 20 million yuan and above".

11-3 规模以上工业企业单位数、工业总产值（1998-2015 年）
THE NUMBER AND GROSS OUTPUT VALUE OF INDUSTRIAL ENTERPRISES ABOVE DESIGNATED SIZE （1998-2015）

年 份 Year	企业单位数 （个） Number of Enterprises (unit)	工业总产值 （万元） Gross Industrial Output Value (10000 yuan)	按地区分 Grouped by Region		
			市 区 Urban Area	其中 of which 武进区 Wujin District	溧阳市 Liyang City
1998	2016	6934265	5785261	2584387	683278
1999	2054	7699337	6384288	2894976	772913
2000	2059	8746325	7307378	3238846	871781
2001	2185	10012488	8380690	3730814	990805
2002	2474	11670167	9737547	4025683	1170019
2003	2804	15272769	12705644	5560192	1504701
2004	4707	21272032	17734015	8344588	2062119
2005	3593	25041903	20323885	9350753	2790052
2006	4223	32937718	26651563	12775644	3665369
2007	4768	42539096	33985939	16307805	4950478
2008	5030	52001203	41229707	20510878	6288701
2009	6493	59829073	48011691	23980866	7283391
2010	6375	73960851	58731617	29548158	9326507
2011	3638	82707703	64466417	32237118	11372284
2012	3869	89702986	70432514	35590244	13556800
2013	3887	100678759	78735791	39465912	15589153
2014	4350	110374592	84844291	42272367	17322880
2015	4244	111016373	98889027	42731977	12127345

注：1、2010年及以前规模以上工业企业为全部国有企业及年销售收入500万元以上工业企业，2011年起规模以上工业企业调整为主营业务收入2000万元以上企业。

2、2015年行政区划调整，市区包含金坛区数据。

Note:1、Before 2010,industrial enterprises above Designated Size refers to enterprise with main business income above 10 million yuan;Form 2011,industrial enterprises above Designated Sise Refers to enterprise With main business income above 20 million yuan.

2、With the administrative district adjustment in 2015, the city's urban area now includes Jintan District.

按轻重工业分 Grouped by Light and Heavy IndustryGrouped by Light		按经济类型分 Grouped by Economic type			按企业规模分 Grouped by Size of Enterprises		
轻工业 Light Industry	重工业 Heavy Industry	#国有工业 State-owned	集体工业 Collective owned	其他工业 Other Industries	#大型企业 Large	中型企业 Medium-sized	小型企业 Small
2804344	4129922	1188513	2091252	3654500	1431178	1808339	3694748
3129671	4569666	1168296	2168551	4362490	1772567	1680778	4245992
3398700	5347625	1014739	1753500	5978086	1826100	1818832	5101393
3936827	6075661	914054	1595517	7502917	2831899	2096893	5083696
4720707	6949460	804912	992787	9872468	3331394	2436048	5902725
5564940	9707829	696256	755597	13820916	2575835	5418160	7278774
7374271	13897762	494034	894936	19883062	1512383	6976498	12783152
7441957	17599946	701147	769236	23571520	3874604	7368895	13798404
9087163	23850555	555090	1030039	31352589	4899288	10188471	17849959
10315119	32223977	712690	1206437	40619969	6157127	13680857	22701112
12069457	39931746	942058	994995	50064150	8427722	16507572	27065909
13102615	46726458	639506	267577	58921990	12657601	19059066	28112406
15965600	57995251	916713	145710	72898428	17429595	23014060	33517196
15478418	67229285	1007972	57972	81641759	29159406	22308844	30915652
19618121	70084865	1398170	56849	88247967	32166130	21069320	35847962
21149252	79529507	1350890	63819	99264049	36273837	23118847	40916135
24421624	85952968	100154	301530	109972908	37873344	24639771	47443946
27752433	83263939	101191	320971	110594211	38661916	30757348	41027913

11-4 规模以上工业企业主要经济指标（2015 年）
MAJOR ECONOMIC INDICATORS OF INDUSTRIAL ENTERPRISES ABOVE DESIGNATED SIZE （2015）

指 标	Item	企 业 单位数 （个） Number of Enterpr-ises (unit)	其中 of which # 亏损 企业 Loss-incurring Enter-prises	工 业 总产值 Gross Industrial Output Value
总 计	Total	4244	668	111016373
按地区分	Grouped by Region			
市 区	Urban Area	3852	566	98889027
金坛区	Jintan District	436	97	10255320
武进区	Wujin District	1678	205	42731977
# 经开区	Economic Development Zone	581	44	17301519
新北区	Xinbei District	991	174	26236765
天宁区	Tianning District	413	48	10355717
钟楼区	Zhonglou District	334	42	9309249
溧阳市	Liyang City	392	102	12127345
按登记注册类型分	Grouped by Registration Status			
内 资	Domestic Investment	3435	470	73866093
国 有	State-owned	4	1	101191
集 体	Collective-owned	4		320971
股份合作	Share-holding Cooperative	7	2	76597
有限责任公司	Limited Liability Corporations	250	45	8471716
股份有限公司	Share-holding Corporations Ltd.	46	3	2676525
私 营	Private	3124	419	62219094
港澳台商投资	Investment from Hong Kong, Macao and Taiwan	294	56	15845691
合资经营	Joint-Venture	140	19	8554477
合作经营	Cooperative	13	3	298078
独资经营	Sole Investment	135	34	5838993
股份有限公司	Share-holding Corporations Ltd.	6		1154142
外商投资	Foreign Investment	515	142	21304589
中外合资经营	Joint Ventures	209	44	7642730
中外合作经营	Cooperative Enterprises	10	1	293953
外商独资	Sole Foreign Investment	290	95	13029760
股份有限公司	Share-holding Corporations Ltd.	6	2	338147
按轻重工业分	Grouped by Light and Heavy Industry			
轻工业	Light Industry	1402	195	27752433
重工业	Heavy Industry	2842	473	83263939
按企业规模分	Grouped by Size of Enterprises			
大 型	Large-sized	92	5	38661916
中 型	Medium-sized	481	55	30757348
小 型	Small-sized	3588	592	41027913
微 型	Micro-sized	83	16	569195

单位：万元（10000 yuan）

工业销售产值 Value of Industrial Products Sales	流动资产合计 Current Assets	其中 of which			固定资产合计 Total Fixed Assets	固定资产原价合计 Total Original Value of Fixed Assets	累计折旧 Accumulative Depreciation	资产总计 Total Assets
		#应收帐款净额 Net Account Income	存货 Existing Stock	其中 of which #产成品 Manufac-tured Products				
110091902	**48469994**	**15905812**	**10735255**	**4208219**	**25157006**	**49785962**	**24450586**	**84079366**
98120002	43507785	14310099	9774292	3852203	22412838	44982667	22355225	74545817
10406564	4785037	1557719	812892	363692	3214574	5146544	1901188	8947010
41887254	20037103	5820757	4841309	1622681	9862869	18625175	8821984	34258294
17024804	7805215	2012257	2119570	619632	3847751	6288138	2403298	12780002
26152273	11861072	4635336	2591195	1161821	5844436	13141311	7214256	19876379
10094803	3398255	1090842	757734	356302	1803239	3032328	1215692	5534814
9579108	3426318	1205445	771163	347707	1687720	5037309	3202105	5929320
11971901	4962209	1595713	960962	356016	2744168	4803295	2095361	9533550
73210063	33904227	10527905	7499901	2800176	16620470	32931125	16197443	57910882
100671	74946	5557	19753	8111	22791	47003	24213	101881
318996	23690	5267	2573	2402	23336	79220	55884	59615
72184	33976	12927	9912	5622	20506	34751	14642	61109
8527564	4164324	1511677	1000344	360384	2409149	4843924	2409527	7425651
2688590	1874238	598855	357751	180364	2053259	3337397	1286398	4455174
61502058	27733053	8393622	6109569	2243292	12091430	24588831	12406779	45807452
15709799	5752313	1698651	1354114	622136	3854981	7734873	3845621	11192937
8511548	2650261	783665	692356	286710	1994081	4061236	2054112	5282783
298074	78248	27934	14458	7715	42269	91649	49379	123970
5804263	2553614	754067	592489	316560	1602859	2981378	1357293	5079777
1095915	470190	132985	54812	11151	215773	600610	384837	706406
21172040	8813453	3679256	1881239	785908	4681554	9119964	4407521	14975548
7559107	2729018	956307	697436	340123	1257672	2652026	1390833	4381913
294268	75280	21758	11350	4709	104038	153446	52634	195943
12980037	5710330	2614977	1143089	432129	3223955	6162589	2908040	9954972
338627	298825	86214	29365	8947	95889	151904	56015	442721
27412394	12756427	3816267	2776985	1139230	6423855	12604174	6144350	22203773
82679508	35713567	12089545	7958270	3068990	18733151	37181788	18306236	61875593
38409356	16226577	4882772	3416358	1099334	9504185	19446325	9758575	30037485
30590033	13630136	4417996	2949122	1343888	7565234	15269951	7680074	24279431
40523698	18323623	6474279	4338284	1753073	8001376	14952628	6981163	29285209
568816	289658	130764	31491	11925	86211	117059	30774	477242

11-4 续表 Continued

指标	Item	负债总计 Total Liabilities	其中 of which 流动负债合计 Total Current Liabilities	非流动负债合计 Total Non-current Liabilities	所有者权益 Owner's Equity
总 计	**Total**	**48359594**	**43581728**	**4578381**	**35620329**
按地区分	**Grouped by Region**				
市 区	Urban Area	41638093	37280329	4158317	32808286
金坛区	Jintan District	5969469	5486547	475198	2974698
武进区	Wujin District	18656105	16534166	2083602	15585351
#经开区	Economic Development Zone	7002365	6318781	652573	5762728
新北区	Xinbei District	11038923	9819515	1084092	8757702
天宁区	Tianning District	2780855	2624999	155441	2753956
钟楼区	Zhonglou District	3192741	2815103	359984	2736578
溧阳市	Liyang City	6721502	6301398	420064	2812043
按登记注册类型分	**Grouped by Registration Status**				
内 资	Domestic Investment	34125916	30902127	3092473	23713015
国 有	State-owned	77102	75102	2000	24779
集 体	Collective-owned	50341	43741	6600	9274
股份合作	Share-holding Cooperative	25546	18502	7044	35563
有限责任公司	Limited Liability Corporations	4354628	3923177	423218	3070013
股份有限公司	Share-holding Corporations Ltd.	2272680	2141125	130602	2182493
私 营	Private	27345619	24700480	2523010	18390894
港澳台商投资	Investment from Hong Kong, Macao and Taiwan	6310064	5717902	575758	4873383
合资经营	Joint-Venture	3436167	3188834	247333	1837127
合作经营	Cooperative	75045	75045		48925
独资经营	Sole Investment	2413940	2070185	327350	2665836
股份有限公司	Share-holding Corporations Ltd.	384912	383837	1075	321494
外商投资	Foreign Investment	7923614	6961699	910150	7033931
中外合资经营	Joint Ventures	2224030	2136694	87161	2157881
中外合作经营	Cooperative Enterprises	92860	88420	4439	103084
外商独资	Sole Foreign Investment	5454603	4584574	818439	4482368
股份有限公司	Share-holding Corporations Ltd.	152121	152011	111	290599
按轻重工业分	**Grouped by Light and Heavy Industry**				
轻工业	Light Industry	12174355	10850304	1290721	10008450
重工业	Heavy Industry	36185240	32731424	3287661	25611879
按企业规模分	**Grouped by Size of Enterprises**				
大 型	Large-sized	17707979	16057207	1650772	12329505
中 型	Medium-sized	13521247	11747969	1620745	10679326
小 型	Small-sized	16787485	15477459	1263074	12477141
微 型	Micro-sized	342883	299092	43791	134358

单位：万元（10000 yuan）

主营业务收入 Main Business Income	销售费用 Cost of Sales	管理费用 Cost of Management	财务费用 Finance Charge	营业利润 Business Profit	实现利税总额 Total Profits and Taxes	其中 of which 利润总额 Total Profits	 主营业务税金及附加 Main Business Tax and Surcharges	 应交增值税 Value Added Tax Payable	亏损企业亏损总额 Amount of Loss in Loss-incurring Enterprises	应付职工薪酬 Remuneration Payable to Employees
115006836	**2083808**	**4295355**	**1045999**	**7039344**	**10318801**	**6422706**	**445044**	**3451051**	**593730**	**6191981**
102776579	1882473	3951360	900422	6138529	9093591	5690288	373881	3029423	518479	5709943
10472790	205592	393200	133957	768875	1124748	785111	48139	291498	34137	532221
45671970	628760	1537345	450154	2889101	3860054	2410282	126767	1323005	179005	2797006
21072653	278492	573722	210849	1394760	1518930	940842	51878	526210	58188	982167
26297919	603211	1246097	191560	1231802	2167449	1260439	109965	797045	261599	1389838
10639558	287158	429527	58665	676453	1074133	681069	58773	334291	24329	557023
9694342	157754	345192	66087	572299	867208	553386	30237	283585	19411	433855
12230257	201336	343996	145577	900815	1225209	732418	71163	421628	75251	482038
77705281	1289868	2803622	809295	4794879	6981565	4378522	298627	2304417	235045	4092245
107722	2433	5747	401	3982	9308	4339	526	4443	1472	12586
359234	196	1685	2761	29485	41182	31181	251	9751		10479
73070	2219	4129	625	753	2643	683	226	1734	550	7211
8553547	182068	393444	89858	387547	726044	426893	27910	271241	93257	578875
2795459	106359	195789	44826	239021	360688	254924	14851	90913	15983	207384
65816250	996594	2202829	670824	4134092	5841701	3660503	254863	1926335	123783	3275710
15821546	212047	534853	88823	1149329	1518115	951226	69923	496966	120912	944380
8735076	114165	250242	47972	770004	928631	577217	48514	302900	6178	417772
309703	4814	13099	152	20627	33353	20631	1418	11304	2726	13364
5847922	84445	248823	41231	306610	484918	298294	17699	168926	112009	436814
928845	8623	22689	-531	52088	71213	55084	2293	13837		76431
21480009	581893	956881	147882	1095136	1819120	1092958	76495	649668	237773	1155355
7730771	245865	300015	56562	376716	616573	376037	32237	208299	104666	390053
309615	6651	12749	2137	34370	48278	34226	1628	12425	0	13013
13149868	327190	630870	87877	648565	1108139	646864	42475	418801	131907	730559
289755	2188	13247	1306	35485	46130	35832	155	10143	1201	21730
27815769	717608	1271382	240544	1698690	2798670	1738493	137819	922358	99460	2167502
87191067	1366201	3023973	805455	5340655	7520131	4684212	307225	2528693	494270	4024478
42585344	552930	1204596	391379	2826909	3471717	2134438	121542	1215737	92694	2345198
30954920	739172	1227523	279761	2052622	3311501	2111589	139464	1060449	234152	1741896
40906860	784401	1838867	371053	2141424	3498060	2158030	181594	1158436	255602	2089118
559712	7306	24369	3806	18389	37523	18650	2444	16429	11282	15768

11-5 规模以上工业企业分行业主要经济指标（2015 年）
MAJOR ECONOMIC INDICATORS OF INDUSTRIAL ENTERPRISES ABOVE DESIGNATED SIZE BY SECTOR（2015）

指 标	Item	企业单位数（个）Number of Enterpr-ises (unit)	其中 of which #亏损企业 Loss-incurring Enterprises	工业总产值 Gross Industrial Output Value
黑色金属矿采选业	Ferrous Metal Mining Industry	1		3591
非金属矿采选业	Nonmetal Minerals Mining and Dressing	7	1	78285
农副食品加工业	Food Processing	17	7	273170
食品制造业	Food Production	19	4	552086
酒、饮料和精制茶制造业	Beverages and Refined Tea Manufacturing	4	1	98553
纺织业	Textile Industry	357	37	6318461
纺织服装、服饰业	Textile and clothing Industry	137	24	2530079
皮革、毛皮、羽毛及其制品和制鞋业	Leather, Fur, Feathers and Their Products, and Footwear Industry	34	8	514280
木材加工及木、竹、藤、棕、草制品业	Timber Processing, Bamboo, Cane, Palm Fiber and Straw Products	60	2	731486
家具制造业	Furniture Manufacturing	9	2	32134
造纸及纸制品业	Papermaking and Paper Products	58	3	692842
印刷和记录媒介复制业	Printing and Recorded Media Duplication Industry	41	4	342409
文教、工美、体育和娱乐用品制造业	Cultural & Educational, Arts & Crafts, Sports & Entertainment Articles Manufacturing	104	18	1312374
石油加工、炼焦及核燃料加工业	Petroleum Processing, Coking and Nuclear Fuel Processing	11	3	919672
化学原料及化学制品制造业	Raw Chemical Materials and Chemica Products	391	54	18393708
医药制造业	Medical and Pharmaceutical Products	69	10	1674771
化学纤维制造业	Chemical Fiber	50	8	544445
橡胶和塑料制品业	Rubber and Plastic Products Industry	163	19	1300513
非金属矿物制品业	Nonmetal Mineral Products	199	40	3796768
黑色金属冶炼及压延加工业	Smelting and Pressing of Ferrous Metals	149	39	14698929
有色金属冶炼及压延加工业	Smelting and Pressing of Nonferrous Metals	99	11	3254366
金属制品业	Metal Products	255	37	5164940
通用设备制造业	General Equipment Manufacturing	454	85	6627522
专用设备制造业	For Special Purposes Equipment Manufacturing	348	67	6124124
汽车制造业	Automotive Industry	190	22	2622605
铁路、船舶、航空航天和其他运输设备制造	Railways, Shipping, Aerospace and other Transportation Equipment Manufacturing	94	13	4087792
电气机械及器材制造业	Electric Equipment and Machinery	512	88	18650047
计算机、通信和其他电子设备制造	Computer, Communications and other Electronic Equipment Manufacturing	267	41	6322682
仪器仪表制造业	Instrumentation Manufacturing	107	16	1757413
其他制造业	Othere Manufacturing	1		2206
废弃资源综合利用业	Comprehensive Utilization of Waste Resources Industry	5	1	331481
金属制品、机械和设备修理业	Metal Products, Machinery & Equipment Repairing Industry	2		29239
电力、热力生产和供应业	Production and Supply of Electricity & Heat Industry	17	2	815415
燃气生产和供应业	Production and Supply of Gas Industry	6		291351
水的生产和供应业	Production and Supply of water Industry	7	1	126636

单位：万元（10000 yuan）

工业销售产值 Value of Industrial Products Sales	流动资产合计 Current Assets	其中 of which		其中 of which	固定资产合计 Total Fixed Assets	固定资产原价合计 Total Original Value of Fixed Assets	累计折旧 Accumulative Depreciation	资产总计 Total Assets
		#应收帐款净额 Net Account Income	存货 Existing Stock	#产成品 Manufacured Products				
3591	3370	101	2039	1933	5106	6149	1042	8854
77859	43767	17301	2629	2529	15330	24119	8789	115379
281881	120943	26447	38011	8040	49352	87296	35015	191049
555657	170952	52230	29676	8040	123753	208720	85751	411094
100100	44317	6100	23951	2891	32677	92495	59818	88701
6269929	2676861	709013	572134	248958	1437554	2338086	898717	4905942
2534732	786766	242734	186565	83239	432783	682895	249754	1311998
527423	121545	30972	29270	8948	48889	93717	43134	182629
719730	267110	69700	111425	29316	55814	104117	48302	351407
31200	23650	8002	6654	2582	16195	20272	4121	53479
688400	350697	89443	91613	31994	110862	204047	93241	483079
340063	150284	51393	40903	16209	84607	170963	87056	254290
1291703	592135	193274	159704	62324	272084	473930	208859	1003871
901596	133465	18002	22543	10307	117588	362387	244846	263922
18375384	5965137	2067362	1203530	562000	3462868	8446004	4969010	11236871
1607959	1063254	246439	151243	75405	391397	711929	319866	1728666
540506	331740	93911	64021	39222	112956	260628	147881	491704
1274531	729729	292662	170297	79866	391784	670384	280937	1244126
3773131	2327029	716514	255573	89382	1127249	2278351	1165203	4274156
14374461	4746956	528097	1279479	447097	3323564	5863852	2541920	8784311
3268151	926433	282376	222764	70861	380463	1136617	765039	1492654
5115822	2310052	833633	604113	224091	891756	2009528	1120508	3683720
6571899	3031402	1225127	782451	318565	2475904	4073033	1584924	6166795
6070202	3667373	1254360	1124258	427620	1668046	3296935	1552908	6200853
2632087	1598661	440631	254861	106958	614783	1114382	507555	2550559
4089503	2501817	990317	637719	176177	866046	2128054	1255324	3718149
18522118	8498440	3596895	1654576	687522	3430160	7153163	3616266	13395942
6207760	3442947	1348060	637120	274032	1493044	2712422	1212678	5420716
1754300	1230738	367729	294551	105535	396947	719444	327513	1901973
2238	599	227	367	168	758	1499	741	1378
330805	14194	3939	3037	2689	25024	77239	52215	48946
28910	23788	5809	9438	3006	11051	25950	16301	38102
811913	256223	58554	32565		876191	1575869	698289	1225620
293726	111448	33177	1947	717	123640	179231	55591	290185
122632	206176	5281	34229		290780	482257	191474	558249

11-5 续表 Continued

指 标	Item	负债总计 Total Liabilities	其中 of which 流动负债合计 Total Current Liabilities	非流动负债合计 Total Non-current Liabilities	所有者权益 Owner's Equity
黑色金属矿采选业	Ferrous Metal Mining Industry	7632	7632		1221
非金属矿采选业	Nonmetal Minerals Mining and Dressing	63060	46821	16240	52318
农副食品加工业	Food Processing	133184	127513	5671	57866
食品制造业	Food Production	291702	186618	105084	119392
酒、饮料和精制茶制造业	Beverages and Refined Tea Manufacturing	55100	44134	10966	33602
纺织业	Textile Industry	3021829	2486227	535603	1884109
纺织服装、服饰业	Textile and clothing Industry	630264	618161	12103	672246
皮革、毛皮、羽毛及其制品和制鞋业	Leather, Fur, Feathers and Their Products, and Footwear Industry	129969	129767	91	52659
木材加工及木、竹、藤、棕、草制品业	Timber Processing, Bamboo, Cane, Palm Fiber and Straw Products	200088	193443	183	150309
家具制造业	Furniture Manufacturing	14387	14387		39093
造纸及纸制品业	Papermaking and Paper Products	327026	321051	4736	155718
印刷和记录媒介复制业	Printing and Recorded Media Duplication Industry	140711	140067	530	113579
文教、工美、体育和娱乐用品制造业	Cultural & Educational, Arts & Crafts, Sports & Entertainment Articles Manufacturing	602920	578834	24013	400950
石油加工、炼焦及核燃料加工业	Petroleum Processing, Coking and Nuclear Fuel Processing	139364	138242	1122	124557
化学原料及化学制品制造业	Raw Chemical Materials and Chemica Products	5911552	5421176	489374	5322218
医药制造业	Medical and Pharmaceutical Products	790247	705496	82400	938419
化学纤维制造业	Chemical Fiber	273203	261505	7515	218500
橡胶和塑料制品业	Rubber and Plastic Products Industry	568084	530721	36998	676041
非金属矿物制品业	Nonmetal Mineral Products	2970294	2817532	152558	1303859
黑色金属冶炼及压延加工业	Smelting and Pressing of Ferrous Metals	5934995	5418118	497094	2842928
有色金属冶炼及压延加工业	Smelting and Pressing of Nonferrous Metals	835883	748022	84150	654600
金属制品业	Metal Products	2187308	1921594	195740	1472223
通用设备制造业	General Equipment Manufacturing	3669774	3385594	263042	2489648
专用设备制造业	For Special Purposes Equipment Manufacturing	3430551	3142308	288223	2770298
汽车制造业	Automotive Industry	1783150	1582661	198430	766721
铁路、船舶、航空航天和其他运输设备制造	Railways, Shipping, Aerospace and other Transportation Equipment Manufacturing	1929018	1795722	132093	1789130
电气机械及器材制造业	Electric Equipment and Machinery	7346789	6454970	829850	6005142
计算机、通信和其他电子设备制造	Computer, Communications and other Electronic Equipment Manufacturing	2628115	2413835	210755	2791928
仪器仪表制造业	Instrumentation Manufacturing	1009865	920712	89153	892106
其他制造业	Other Manufacturing	980	472	507	398
废弃资源综合利用业	Comprehensive Utilization of Waste Resources Industry	45307	38944	6363	3639
金属制品、机械和设备修理业	Metal Products, Machinery & Equipment Repairing Industry	32399	19917	12482	5704
电力、热力生产和供应业	Production and Supply of Electricity & Heat Industry	679602	489160	190442	546018
燃气生产和供应业	Production and Supply of Gas Industry	166959	133775	33185	123226
水的生产和供应业	Production and Supply of water Industry	408286	346599	61687	149963

单位：万元（10000 yuan）

主营业务收入 Main Business Income	销售费用 Cost of Sales	管理费用 Cost of Management	财务费用 Finance Charge	营业利润 Business Profit	实现利税总额 Total Profits and Taxes	其中 of which 利润总额 Total Profits	主营业务税金及附加 Main Business Tax and Surcharges	应交增值税 Value Added Tax Payable	亏损企业亏损总额 Amount of Loss in Loss-incurring Enterprises	应付职工薪酬 Remuneration Payable to Employees
3468	183	504	52	32	269	44	13	212		316
78315	648	12786	2804	5774	14271	5559	6069	2643	411	3845
282619	6791	5289	2544	7975	11565	8738	305	2523	1514	8396
565924	42558	31760	11157	54807	81539	56079	7813	17647	1359	16785
100545	11390	5958	748	4992	22962	4949	9962	8051	1469	10201
6641008	77205	212931	56538	373192	645604	378816	28352	238436	9897	267769
2583281	46045	120818	-278	168827	263178	165500	14436	83243	2900	363904
528458	7495	15365	2041	35068	59844	34998	3174	21672	644	55031
723401	35161	31048	4206	45809	75673	46081	4112	25480	191	37571
33155	2042	5018	60	535	3289	1397	156	1735	350	4794
697974	13305	23108	7321	28352	49738	29107	2790	17841	87	26426
339119	9456	17348	4843	16087	28512	17022	2208	9283	602	29865
1332631	22722	60601	14708	68395	118539	69760	7423	41355	3457	103318
935880	6064	14889	3613	44018	58858	37934	2250	18674	1151	10284
18554478	261770	497121	190521	840476	1389875	854594	55554	479728	75278	653030
1564943	190426	126388	13131	153980	243277	158485	10204	74588	4397	127101
530854	15410	29031	6092	34699	54063	36869	1979	15215	906	30285
1285647	39125	80889	13926	69855	122423	73262	5905	43256	6446	96715
3806423	63654	134298	73916	322360	534156	369915	17645	146597	23292	189188
18351260	64159	190474	174572	1240378	958475	478836	34886	444753	5993	540048
3297739	23878	65988	21164	214641	307893	208474	10224	89195	11942	108533
5135336	104433	175399	59070	292459	462924	293359	18605	150960	29567	307136
6552896	137637	335265	89862	394144	633088	406989	29634	196464	39783	513093
6109383	186018	378660	63415	212067	434492	224957	39459	170076	160101	465791
2632851	60420	154421	23157	102524	188048	107346	9707	70996	26459	169861
3998705	73431	242881	29323	327310	482310	328998	19270	134043	62441	279234
18886469	370392	785291	115375	1113721	1782595	1108648	60036	613912	78573	911055
6067311	144348	343122	24119	477804	722822	493764	26065	202993	20224	632118
1743472	51389	140246	15094	146680	219218	152941	10535	55743	22322	143607
2238	98	130	-2	18	129	18	10	101		345
370069	468	1817	2782	29085	40896	30669	203	10024	144	11051
28967	1322	4712	344	1642	3474	2634	77	763		3514
816559	84	24016	17608	129496	209776	155486	4169	50121	360	37036
294425	7974	15294	2286	60078	69070	58191	1210	9669		16921
131032	6312	12490	-111	22064	25957	22290	606	3061	1472	17816

11-6 规模以上民营工业企业主要经济指标（2015 年）
MAJOR ECONOMIC INDICATORS OF PRIVATE INDUSTRIAL ENTERPRISES ABOVE DESIGNATED SIZE（2015）

指 标	Item	企业单位数（个）Number of Enterpr-ises (unit)	其中 of which #亏损企业 Loss-incurring Enterprises	工业总产值 Gross Industrial Output Value	工业销售产值 Value of Industrial Products Sales
总 计	**Total**	**3367**	**461**	**69799580**	**69128078**
按地区分	**Grouped by Region**				
市 区	Urban Area	3036	375	61808282	61230478
金坛区	Jintan District	331	69	7056755	7176380
武进区	Wujin District	1412	139	33206257	32561567
# 经开区	Economic Development Zone	516	34	13696393	13451344
新北区	Xinbei District	699	97	9841020	9774001
天宁区	Tianning District	331	39	5970013	5839165
钟楼区	Zhonglou District	263	31	5734236	5879365
溧阳市	Liyang City	331	86	7991299	7897600
按轻重工业分	**Grouped by Light and Heavy Industry**				
轻工业	Light Industry	1069	122	18922921	18704647
重工业	Heavy Industry	2298	339	50876659	50423432
按企业规模分	**Grouped by Size of Enterprises**				
大 型	Large-sized	47		24037389	23800104
中 型	Medium-sized	283	24	16053825	15965759
小 型	Small-sized	2963	426	29178264	28832366
微 型	Micro-sized	74	11	530102	529849
按工业行业分	**Grouped by Sector**				
黑色金属矿采选业	Ferrous Metal Mining Industry	1		3591	3591
非金属矿采选业	Nonmetal Minerals Mining and Dressing	6	1	73805	73379
农副食品加工业	Food Processing	15	6	203663	209474
食品制造业	Food Production	12	2	167745	159912
酒、饮料和精制茶制造业	Beverages and Refined Tea Manufacturing	2		66395	66169
纺织业	Textile Industry	296	28	4692950	4657051
纺织服装、服饰业	Textile and clothing Industry	66	10	1060254	1065972
皮革、毛皮、羽毛及其制品和制鞋业	Leather, Fur, Feathers and Their Products, and Footwear Industry	22	4	187873	190063

单位：万元（10000 yuan）

流动资产合计 Current Assets	其中 of which #应收帐款净额 Net Account Income	存货 Existing Stock	其中 of which #产成品 Manufac-tured Products	固定资产合计 Total Fixed Assets	固定资产原价合计 Total Original Value of Fixed Assets	累计折旧 Accumulative Depreciation	资产总计 Total Assets
31224435	**9492219**	**6851278**	**2567733**	**14775031**	**29414690**	**14576771**	**52751967**
27183999	8169394	6181411	2319816	13231665	26539975	13212622	45634186
3498665	1089301	564062	264927	2351699	3702420	1330499	6413884
14933790	3931659	3643079	1196125	6962670	14131732	7238576	24989699
6087538	1239164	1646981	479358	2824545	4677970	1815211	9740053
4880390	1764753	1099254	493080	1968153	4628464	2613925	7794468
2066213	739753	472473	219898	1092369	1728592	622723	3339560
1804941	643928	402543	145786	856773	2348767	1406900	3096575
4040437	1322825	669867	247918	1543367	2874715	1364149	7117781
8575991	2642377	1862860	707673	4031080	8456229	4411299	14612515
22648444	6849842	4988418	1860060	10743952	20958461	10165472	38139452
10141084	2089038	2249315	659612	6383273	13368630	6940256	19326226
7320305	2335843	1462458	680484	3476537	6873922	3347644	12459687
13515217	4939492	3110473	1215713	4880036	9115250	4267244	20631113
247830	127846	29033	11924	35186	56887	21626	334940
3370	101	2039	1933	5106	6149	1042	8854
39951	15240	2629	2529	12677	18573	5896	108050
93289	23515	30678	6531	36930	64409	26562	148638
98907	12977	14681	6020	38563	59705	21512	156909
17293	1844	8021	853	13985	40392	26407	39325
2083282	591708	401804	151536	1134346	1800293	663145	3945354
277900	96377	72872	27623	229429	348088	117464	537767
62469	20713	20384	4956	21564	37020	15668	92221

11-6 续表 1 Continued 1

指 标	Item	企 业单位数（个）Number of Enterpr-ises (unit)	其中 of which #亏损企业 Loss-incurring Enterprises	工 业总产值 Gross Industrial Output Value	工业销售产值 Value of Industrial Products Sales
木材加工及木、竹、藤、棕、草制品业	Timber Processing, Bamboo, Cane, Palm Fiber and Straw Products	57	2	565178	555598
家具制造业	Furniture Manufacturing	6	1	18306	17810
造纸及纸制品业	Papermaking and Paper Products	51	2	595385	591376
印刷和记录媒介复制业	Printing and Recorded Media Duplication Industry	34	3	271316	267759
文教、工美、体育和娱乐用品制造业	Cultural & Educational, Arts & Crafts, Sports & Entertainment Articles Manufacturing	83	15	1026102	1022816
石油加工、炼焦及核燃料加工业	Petroleum Processing, Coking and Nuclear Fuel Processing	9	3	177059	157411
化学原料及化学制品制造业	Raw Chemical Materials and Chemica Products	310	33	9667814	9704935
医药制造业	Medical and Pharmaceutical Products	50	6	1209295	1158017
化学纤维制造业	Chemical Fiber	46	8	367261	359292
橡胶和塑料制品业	Rubber and Plastic Products Industry	137	14	989240	969189
非金属矿物制品业	Nonmetal Mineral Products	176	33	3504504	3481319
黑色金属冶炼及压延加工业	Smelting and Pressing of Ferrous Metals	141	37	11592852	11309892
有色金属冶炼及压延加工业	Smelting and Pressing of Nonferrous Metals	89	7	2967237	2969599
金属制品业	Metal Products	221	30	4065469	4004893
通用设备制造业	General Equipment Manufacturing	362	58	4642306	4567836
专用设备制造业	For Special Purposes Equipment Manufacturing	260	42	3615975	3613165
汽车制造业	Automotive Industry	159	13	1869627	1843364
铁路、船舶、航空航天和其他运输设备制造	Railways, Shipping, Aerospace and other Transportation Equipment Manufacturing	67	7	2566802	2557394
电气机械及器材制造业	Electric Equipment and Machinery	397	62	9454460	9383475
计算机、通信和其他电子设备制造	Computer, Communications and other Electronic Equipment Manufacturing	188	19	2726020	2714184
仪器仪表制造业	Instrumentation Manufacturing	86	13	934487	941362
其他制造业	Other Manufacturing	1		2206	2238
废弃资源综合利用业	Comprehensive Utilization of Waste Resources Industry	5	1	331481	330805
金属制品、机械和设备修理业	Metal Products, Machinery & Equipment Repairing Industry	2		29239	28910
电力、热力生产和供应业	Production and Supply of Electricity & Heat Industry	6	1	117786	115429
燃气生产和供应业	Production and Supply of Gas Industry	2		29818	29520
水的生产和供应业	Production and Supply of water Industry	2		6079	4880

单位：万元（10000 yuan）

流动资产合计 Current Assets	其中 of which			固定资产合计 Total Fixed Assets	固定资产原价合计 Total Original Value of Fixed Assets	累计折旧 Accumulative Depreciation	资产总计 Total Assets
	#应收帐款净额 Net Account Income	存货 Existing Stock	其中 of which #产成品 Manufac-turedProducts				
228925	58584	105104	25075	43473	83734	40260	294965
17755	7193	4737	1809	5747	7731	2028	25781
330852	84398	85031	28416	100887	173699	72762	448411
114152	39408	33358	12151	52000	103735	54537	177827
419439	147860	111171	37260	224054	381464	165185	768207
35945	7364	14112	7327	35125	46393	11316	82071
3728892	1273414	750061	309469	1945122	5181348	3191459	6659874
707354	154598	93032	49503	250738	460794	209671	1138059
228085	59254	48805	30447	55496	101869	46582	325884
579755	238893	120968	54808	281423	419059	139543	966350
2063534	663090	219476	83814	948218	1971238	1036942	3793707
4451853	477237	1133295	408885	2511260	4579433	2069804	7516475
740534	225830	176658	59546	257914	966047	719619	1167154
1681359	657071	462042	137051	580350	1107140	529516	2601651
2049078	812155	509465	219413	1813591	2982143	1163860	4258656
1883937	607369	542463	188900	721187	1626128	833234	2932295
1227232	293580	180021	76297	312199	636649	322185	1725740
1214142	426075	273941	77985	378916	1153258	765713	1702929
4361444	1560188	943898	367164	1775851	3160700	1403064	7140190
1428324	629054	263175	106175	592794	1124168	539598	2256376
854401	256294	191820	77681	219721	425801	211122	1304433
599	227	367	168	758	1499	741	1378
14194	3939	3037	2689	25024	77239	52215	48946
23788	5809	9438	3006	11051	25950	16301	38102
111327	23531	21981		96409	181692	83796	226100
35923	16659	717	717	37968	50847	12880	88747
15153	674			5158	10302	5144	24547

11-6 续表 2 Continued 2

指 标	Item	负债总计 Total Liabilities	其中 of which 流动负债合计 Total Current Liabilities	非流动负债合计 Total Non-current Liabilities	所有者权益 Owner's Equity	主营业务收入 Main Business Income
总 计	**Total**	**31101553**	**28220249**	**2749988**	**21578464**	**73558246**
按地区分	**Grouped by Region**					
市 区	Urban Area	26313127	23742140	2439709	19249114	65499427
金坛区	Jintan District	4417845	4162952	247168	1993197	7258729
武进区	Wujin District	14269299	12554667	1676465	10703565	36481991
# 经开区	Economic Development Zone	5423110	4899506	492747	4302036	17452214
新北区	Xinbei District	4436827	4109925	243010	3305376	9766602
天宁区	Tianning District	1610666	1512498	97754	1728892	6082201
钟楼区	Zhonglou District	1578490	1402098	175312	1518084	5909904
溧阳市	Liyang City	4788427	4478109	310278	2329350	8058819
按轻重工业分	**Grouped by Light and Heavy Industry**					
轻工业	Light Industry	8539565	7655192	851047	6061473	19113667
重工业	Heavy Industry	22561988	20565057	1898941	15516992	54444579
按企业规模分	**Grouped by Size of Enterprises**					
大 型	Large-sized	11470422	10120666	1349756	7855804	27864683
中 型	Medium-sized	6961992	6161793	715159	5446322	16267256
小 型	Small-sized	12430877	11708541	676061	8179660	28902936
微 型	Micro-sized	238262	229250	9012	96678	523370
按工业行业分	**Grouped by Sector**					
黑色金属矿采选业	Ferrous Metal Mining Industry	7632	7632		1221	3468
非金属矿采选业	Nonmetal Minerals Mining and Dressing	62370	46131	16240	45679	73835
农副食品加工业	Food Processing	113887	112283	1604	34751	207613
食品制造业	Food Production	116897	111350	5547	40012	163036
酒、饮料和精制茶制造业	Beverages and Refined Tea Manufacturing	22313	21204	1109	17011	65564
纺织业	Textile Industry	2478861	1976085	502775	1466490	4961765
纺织服装、服饰业	Textile and clothing Industry	290318	286460	3858	247449	1079674
皮革、毛皮、羽毛及其制品和制鞋业	Leather, Fur, Feathers and Their Products, and Footwear Industry	68794	68593	91	23426	187832

单位：万元（10000 yuan）

销售费用 Cost of Sales	管理费用 Cost of Management	财务费用 Finance Charge	营业利润 Business Profit	实现利税总额 Total Profits and Taxes	其中 of which 利润总额 Total Profits	主营业务税金及附加 Main Business Tax and Surcharges	应交增值税 Value Added Tax Payable	亏损企业亏损总额 Amount of Loss in Loss-incurring Enterprises	应付职工薪酬 Remuneration Payable to Employees
1144340	**2531605**	**760593**	**4623849**	**6604141**	**4167374**	**280763**	**2156005**	**146006**	**3758104**
976265	2270955	647356	4076381	5726604	3594743	231076	1900785	116670	3403426
130667	264487	92999	505324	734968	517371	27136	190462	22824	368048
430981	1030864	388962	2180312	2742696	1670764	91904	980028	39975	1924802
206119	378967	182446	1079464	1024658	603185	37244	384229	4694	720777
248539	540656	81075	626240	1041652	647544	56964	337144	31430	596728
104090	261004	47044	403964	651807	406582	37377	207848	16139	290102
61989	173943	37276	360542	555480	352482	17695	185303	6302	223745
168074	260650	113237	547468	877537	572631	49686	255219	29337	354679
367588	806583	199633	1060496	1787454	1090427	84953	612075	28715	1235351
776752	1725022	560960	3563353	4816687	3076947	195810	1543930	117292	2522754
299848	596857	324049	1882607	2121545	1386334	68539	666671		1299843
314439	628293	161895	1231761	1946340	1251978	75163	619199	25067	937937
523455	1293124	270955	1483313	2491375	1502227	134745	854402	119782	1506247
6598	13331	3694	26169	44882	26834	2315	15733	1157	14077
183	504	52	32	269	44	13	212		316
648	10875	2804	5760	12478	5546	4935	1997	411	3475
4543	4671	2232	4895	8023	5678	304	2041	1514	6356
11105	13791	2964	8526	13534	10537	510	2486	200	8696
6174	3233	468	6259	18629	6297	6409	5923		5720
53086	160209	43942	265467	464927	269043	20600	175284	7496	185597
20669	59073	4787	47269	85266	48114	5737	31415	1107	148779
3279	8370	1592	5665	13695	5653	858	7184	525	26128

11-6 续表 3 Continued 3

指 标	Item	负债总计 Total Liabilities	其中 of which 流动负债合计 Total Current Liabilities	非流动负债合计 Total Non-current Liabilities	所有者权益 Owner's Equity
木材加工及木、竹、藤、棕、草制品业	Timber Processing, Bamboo, Cane, Palm Fiber and Straw Products	163347	156701	183	130609
家具制造业	Furniture Manufacturing	12156	12156		13626
造纸及纸制品业	Papermaking and Paper Products	309834	305632	2962	138242
印刷和记录媒介复制业	Printing and Recorded Media Duplication Industry	119212	118569	530	58614
文教、工美、体育和娱乐用品制造业	Cultural & Educational, Arts & Crafts, Sports & Entertainment Articles Manufacturing	478110	454671	23365	290097
石油加工、炼焦及核燃料加工业	Petroleum Processing, Coking and Nuclear Fuel Processing	48762	47692	1070	33309
化学原料及化学制品制造业	Raw Chemical Materials and Chemica Products	3653524	3449357	203173	3003249
医药制造业	Medical and Pharmaceutical Products	498258	431888	64019	639801
化学纤维制造业	Chemical Fiber	188763	178804	5776	137120
橡胶和塑料制品业	Rubber and Plastic Products Industry	438606	425056	13185	527743
非金属矿物制品业	Nonmetal Mineral Products	2657627	2529661	127766	1136077
黑色金属冶炼及压延加工业	Smelting and Pressing of Ferrous Metals	4715541	4229855	465903	2794546
有色金属冶炼及压延加工业	Smelting and Pressing of Nonferrous Metals	680927	632355	44861	484057
金属制品业	Metal Products	1587005	1449934	134918	1008454
通用设备制造业	General Equipment Manufacturing	2635223	2548625	65636	1616063
专用设备制造业	For Special Purposes Equipment Manufacturing	1728934	1549152	179762	1203358
汽车制造业	Automotive Industry	1305562	1207407	96096	419491
铁路、船舶、航空航天和其他运输设备制造	Railways, Shipping, Aerospace and other Transportation Equipment Manufacturing	856580	790513	65016	846348
电气机械及器材制造业	Electric Equipment and Machinery	3521920	3004129	455822	3574260
计算机、通信和其他电子设备制造	Computer, Communications and other Electronic Equipment Manufacturing	1314887	1184491	126880	940818
仪器仪表制造业	Instrumentation Manufacturing	734419	680534	53885	570013
其他制造业	Other Manufacturing	980	472	507	398
废弃资源综合利用业	Comprehensive Utilization of Waste Resources Industry	45307	38944	6363	3639
金属制品、机械和设备修理业	Metal Products, Machinery & Equipment Repairing Industry	32399	19917	12482	5704
电力、热力生产和供应业	Production and Supply of Electricity & Heat Industry	137463	103873	33591	88637
燃气生产和供应业	Production and Supply of Gas Industry	58894	25709	33185	29853
水的生产和供应业	Production and Supply of water Industry	16246	14416	1830	8300

单位：万元（10000 yuan）

主营业务收入 Main Business Income	销售费用 Cost of Sales	管理费用 Cost of Management	财务费用 Finance Charge	营业利润 Business Profit	实现利税总额 Total Profits and Taxes	其中 of which 利润总额 Total Profits	主营业务税金及附加 Main Business Tax and Surcharges	应交增值税 Value Added Tax Payable	亏损企业亏损总额 Amount of Loss in Loss-incurring Enterprises	应付职工薪酬 Remuneration Payable to Employees
557069	24913	17988	2454	34361	55741	34413	2431	18898	191	28203
18087	1149	1709	-119	1087	2027	1182	137	709	97	2270
597039	11272	20994	6571	25575	43991	26430	2133	15428	20	23131
265165	7199	11995	3753	10009	20654	10434	1837	8383	491	21460
1062917	16006	45440	11547	49405	89500	50735	5973	32793	3034	78628
150458	1574	5607	2228	-1944	7790	-444	254	7980	1151	2736
9862999	151226	331182	117100	581826	910331	589140	35983	285208	18457	475188
1121130	65488	71316	11574	96197	144918	98147	5310	41461	976	79274
347995	5396	18233	4203	21494	32536	23142	1012	8382	906	19879
975194	27390	59701	9862	50927	91477	54070	4622	32785	2523	72354
3516335	57740	117243	68290	305087	507407	352155	16455	138797	15927	160139
15120612	59717	170667	160934	909435	683916	345274	18818	319824	5154	483691
3021452	18102	45158	18377	215990	295336	209184	8298	77854	2799	94736
4025911	73971	131897	50317	242051	387109	242643	15913	128553	9791	241963
4554935	83424	212034	70109	288634	464471	298739	20108	145625	15878	318929
3689332	79543	194547	40391	236400	385415	248624	26375	110416	12918	241198
1835519	43277	85190	14711	60375	118742	64046	5184	49512	4828	98457
2483668	34766	105419	14061	263446	357766	263549	11107	83110	6728	101617
9443989	195974	368506	52559	604333	922366	607611	40920	273835	22054	506311
2665461	54211	149915	22723	152505	267925	157220	11522	99183	5341	221822
937668	29926	84664	14417	75863	120296	80117	5953	34227	5044	79101
2238	98	130	-2	18	129	18	10	101		345
370069	468	1817	2782	29085	40896	30669	203	10024	144	11051
28967	1322	4712	344	1642	3474	2634	77	763		3514
126085	64	9166	1378	20129	25442	20611	520	4311	305	5269
29526	425	5285	1238	3324	4612	3237	148	1228		1313
5641	13	364	-49	2723	3055	2884	95	75		459

11-7 规模以上外商和港澳台商投资工业企业主要经济指标（2015 年）
MAJOR ECONOMIC INDICATORS OF INDUSTRIAL ENTERPRISES ABOVE DESIGNATED SIZE WITH HONG KONG,MACAO,TAIWAN AND FOREIGN FUNDS（2015）

指 标	Item	企 业 单位数（个） Number of Enterpr-ises（unit）	其中 of which #亏损企业 Loss-incurring Enterprises	工 业 总产值 Gross Industrial Output Value	工业销售产值 Value of Industrial Products Sales
总 计	**Total**	**809**	**198**	**37150280**	**36881839**
按地区分	**Grouped by Region**				
市 区	Urban Area	759	182	33330719	33119355
金坛区	Jintan District	96	26	2677652	2709884
武进区	Wujin District	253	65	8216203	8021886
# 经开区	Economic Development Zone	56	9	2433186	2405562
新北区	Xinbei District	274	73	15695113	15660336
天宁区	Tianning District	75	8	4022637	3893410
钟楼区	Zhonglou District	61	10	2719115	2833839
溧阳市	Liyang City	50	16	3819561	3762484
按轻重工业分	**Grouped by Light and Heavy Industry**				
轻工业	Light Industry	314	71	8182864	8060504
重工业	Heavy Industry	495	127	28967416	28821336
按企业规模分	**Grouped by Size of Enterprises**				
大 型	Large-sized	36	3	13199471	13168824
中 型	Medium-sized	177	27	13219659	13142703
小 型	Small-sized	590	164	10714787	10554075
微 型	Micro-sized	6	4	16363	16237
按工业行业分	**Grouped by Sector**				
农副食品加工业	Food Processing	2	1	69508	72407
食品制造业	Food Production	6	2	267555	278966
酒、饮料和精制茶制造业	Beverages and Refined Tea Manufacturing	2	1	32158	33930
纺织业	Textile Industry	60	9	1538964	1526332
纺织服装、服饰业	Textile and clothing Industry	66	13	1439981	1435590
皮革、毛皮、羽毛及其制品和制鞋业	Leather, Fur, Feathers and Their Products, and Footwear Industry	12	4	326407	337360

单位：万元（10000 yuan）

流动资产合计 Current Assets	其中 of which # 应收帐款净额 Net Account Income	存货 Existing Stock	其中 of which # 产成品 Manufac -tured Products	固定资产合计 Total Fixed Assets	固定资产原价合计 Total Original Value of Fixed Assets	累计折旧 Accumulative Depreciation	资产总计 Total Assets
14565767	**5377907**	**3235354**	**1408043**	**8536535**	**16854837**	**8253143**	**26168485**
13864958	5160009	2991018	1328950	7490728	15201361	7641196	24192282
1154872	454270	237572	96088	676326	1145240	458354	2191273
4215246	1424928	914096	381235	2139484	3349221	1199903	7452187
901693	337541	215838	105126	301358	526086	225853	1338169
6396595	2658263	1386914	620307	3441694	7625698	4147847	10912292
1135053	289167	249203	122977	617110	1125864	509434	1884239
963192	333380	203232	108343	616114	1955337	1325658	1752290
700809	217898	244336	79093	1045808	1653476	611947	1976203
3764159	1082663	842118	394980	2167764	3690394	1501933	6858748
10801608	4295244	2393235	1013063	6368771	13164442	6751209	19309737
4814431	2164704	824253	347298	2682860	4954509	2183797	8667919
5522752	1847652	1300339	576037	3289061	7132143	3867008	10088321
4208813	1363133	1108336	484708	2563493	4763875	2199148	7391048
19771	2418	2425	1	1121	4310	3189	21196
27654	2932	7333	1509	12422	22887	8453	42411
66361	35646	13899	1773	69377	127526	58563	224366
27024	4256	15931	2038	18693	52104	33411	49377
546893	103807	150245	87512	286267	479867	194588	896960
460260	146048	112081	55617	189318	302691	115058	709509
59076	10259	8886	3992	27325	56698	27466	90408

11-7 续表 1 Continued 1

指 标	Item	企 业 单位数（个） Number of Enterpr-ises（unit）	其中 of which #亏损企业 Loss-incurring Enterprises	工 业 总产值 Gross Industrial Output Value	工业销售产值 Value of Industrial Products Sales
木材加工及木、竹、藤、棕、草制品业	Timber Processing, Bamboo, Cane, Palm Fiber and Straw Products	3		166308	164132
家具制造业	Furniture Manufacturing	3	1	13828	13390
造纸及纸制品业	Papermaking and Paper Products	7	1	97457	97025
印刷和记录媒介复制业	Printing and Recorded Media Duplication Industry	5	1	58943	60674
文教、工美、体育和娱乐用品制造业	Cultural & Educational, Arts & Crafts, Sports & Entertainment Articles Manufacturing	21	3	286272	268887
石油加工、炼焦及核燃料加工业	Petroleum Processing, Coking and Nuclear Fuel Processing	2		742614	744185
化学原料及化学制品制造业	Raw Chemical Materials and Chemica Products	75	19	8390497	8325970
医药制造业	Medical and Pharmaceutical Products	18	4	391097	379075
化学纤维制造业	Chemical Fiber	3		88008	92077
橡胶和塑料制品业	Rubber and Plastic Products Industry	25	5	264530	256191
非金属矿物制品业	Nonmetal Mineral Products	20	7	246695	249273
黑色金属冶炼及压延加工业	Smelting and Pressing of Ferrous Metals	8	2	3106077	3064569
有色金属冶炼及压延加工业	Smelting and Pressing of Nonferrous Metals	9	4	243459	250555
金属制品业	Metal Products	32	7	985782	998167
通用设备制造业	General Equipment Manufacturing	85	27	1586908	1596457
专用设备制造业	For Special Purposes Equipment Manufacturing	82	23	2189002	2138733
汽车制造业	Automotive Industry	29	8	734164	769909
铁路、船舶、航空航天和其他运输设备制造	Railways, Shipping, Aerospace and other Transportation Equipment Manufacturing	20	5	809454	819986
电气机械及器材制造业	Electric Equipment and Machinery	109	25	8591418	8543236
计算机、通信和其他电子设备制造	Computer, Communications and other Electronic Equipment Manufacturing	75	22	3266645	3162148
仪器仪表制造业	Instrumentation Manufacturing	21	3	822926	812937
电力、热力生产和供应业	Production and Supply of Electricity & Heat Industry	4	1	84581	83436
燃气生产和供应业	Production and Supply of Gas Industry	3		254580	254580
水的生产和供应业	Production and Supply of water Industry	2		54464	51659

单位：万元（10000 yuan）

流动资产合计 Current Assets	其中 of which #应收帐款净额 Net Account Income	存货 Existing Stock	其中 of which #产成品 Manufac-tured Products	固定资产合计 Total Fixed Assets	固定资产原价合计 Total Original Value of Fixed Assets	累计折旧 Accumulative Depreciation	资产总计 Total Assets
38185	11116	6321	4241	12341	20384	8043	56441
5895	809	1917	773	10448	12541	2093	27698
19845	5045	6582	3578	9975	30348	20479	34668
26101	10053	6165	3559	28985	51689	20601	60763
172696	45414	48533	25064	48030	92466	43674	235664
97520	10639	8430	2980	82464	315993	233530	181851
2120647	769158	441982	245511	1377405	3015037	1668313	4300599
300859	79591	53607	22711	124697	220101	95700	499553
40389	18872	9746	4905	28106	98108	70002	73201
142759	51227	45802	22226	68206	152057	84281	224087
152194	43213	27135	4886	112226	202933	90885	286043
295103	50860	146184	38212	812304	1284419	472116	1267837
174152	52261	43852	9795	120582	165591	42409	309867
549226	153571	105554	64980	300275	874162	573898	977969
725892	324877	201493	68333	575683	921858	338663	1460129
1458029	481812	494069	180072	826932	1485516	654345	2757555
349986	146566	74807	30662	255204	425696	180714	706852
534567	180651	134036	67018	196542	483197	288601	835126
3798342	1859317	634676	288879	1507739	3477095	1894403	5711539
1778933	639221	296091	139367	831456	1494021	646469	2831785
376337	111435	102731	27854	177226	293643	116391	597541
27301	9437	2178		89338	162871	73631	126450
68381	16518	1197		83079	123393	40314	191676
125161	3295	33893		253891	409947	156053	400560

11-7 续表 2 Continued 2

指标	Item	负债总计 Total Liabilities	其中 of which 流动负债合计 Total Current Liabilities	非流动负债合计 Total Non-current Liabilities	所有者权益 Owner's Equity	主营业务收入 Main Business Incom
总 计	**Total**	**14233678**	**12679601**	**1485908**	**11907314**	**37301555**
按地区分	**Grouped by Region**					
市 区	Urban Area	12615911	11125274	1422469	11548879	33395777
金坛区	Jintan District	1348462	1159728	188735	842810	2688899
武进区	Wujin District	3312050	3012524	299356	4140134	7890183
#经开区	Economic Development Zone	602684	550317	52211	735484	2463121
新北区	Xinbei District	5929324	5142427	735473	4955481	15772939
天宁区	Tianning District	1001057	945223	55834	883181	4193308
钟楼区	Zhonglou District	1025017	865372	143071	727272	2850449
溧阳市	Liyang City	1617767	1554327	63439	358436	3905778
按轻重工业分	**Grouped by Light and Heavy Industry**					
轻工业	Light Industry	3244857	2886303	358550	3604401	8034561
重工业	Heavy Industry	10988822	9793298	1127358	8302913	29266994
按企业规模分	**Grouped by Size of Enterprises**					
大 型	Large-sized	5150958	4891521	259438	3516961	13228044
中 型	Medium-sized	5464336	4627164	769680	4596500	13201880
小 型	Small-sized	3604171	3147703	455791	3786871	10854834
微 型	Micro-sized	14213	13213	1000	6983	16797
按工业行业分	**Grouped by Sector**					
农副食品加工业	Food Processing	19297	15230	4067	23114	75006
食品制造业	Food Production	152322	65785	86537	72045	281247
酒、饮料和精制茶制造业	Beverages and Refined Tea Manufacturing	32786	22930	9857	16590	34981
纺织业	Textile Industry	494568	461740	32827	402392	1584278
纺织服装、服饰业	Textile and clothing Industry	325058	316812	8245	374963	1470989
皮革、毛皮、羽毛及其制品和制鞋业	Leather, Fur, Feathers and Their Products, and Footwear Industry	61175	61175		29233	340626

单位：万元（10000 yuan）

销售费用 Cost of Sales	管理费用 Cost of Management	财务费用 Finance Charge	营业利润 Business Profit	实现利税总额 Total Profits and Taxes	其中 of which 利润总额 Total Profits	主营业务税金及附加 Main Business Tax and Surcharges	应交增值税 Value Added Tax Payable	亏损企业亏损总额 Amount of Loss in Loss-incurring Enterprises	应付职工薪酬 Remuneration Payable to Employees
793941	**1491734**	**236705**	**2244465**	**3337235**	**2044184**	**146417**	**1146634**	**358686**	**2099736**
766493	1427269	210181	1908627	3029304	1905632	126949	996724	312772	1995109
54733	106424	33615	233881	342706	236589	19003	87113	9840	147529
179658	416103	40613	690468	1017894	696313	30222	291359	89042	737481
56645	112419	8638	305006	409132	301064	10539	97529	3505	141203
324081	654035	100161	554043	1033966	557389	48534	428043	202867	739702
160652	145664	9509	253136	390750	253344	19751	117655	4678	234460
47368	105043	26284	177099	243988	161996	9438	72554	6344	135937
27448	64465	26523	335838	307931	138552	19469	149910	45914	104627
299835	410282	39054	589905	929464	593738	49429	286297	69274	866787
494106	1081452	197651	1654561	2407771	1450446	96989	860337	289412	1232948
189935	483167	55569	959949	1317017	758333	47366	511318	27553	870248
374941	516668	95871	745570	1185792	750906	58222	376664	201588	701158
228691	490822	85154	539111	834879	535667	40751	258461	128785	526982
374	1077	110	-164	-453	-722	78	191	760	1348
2248	618	312	3080	3542	3060		482		2039
14243	13553	8132	33449	51771	32709	7303	11759	1159	7119
5216	2726	281	-1266	4334	-1348	3553	2128	1469	4481
21558	45250	11723	105818	176818	107474	7383	61962	2401	67350
25020	55289	-5059	112583	164205	108149	8254	47802	1793	208189
4216	6995	450	29403	46149	29345	2316	14488	120	28903

11-7 续表 3 Continued 3

指 标	Item	负债总计 Total Liabilities	其中 of which 流动负债合计 Total Current Liabilities	非流动负债合计 Total Non-current Liabilities	所有者权益 Owner's Equity
木材加工及木、竹、藤、棕、草制品业	Timber Processing, Bamboo, Cane, Palm Fiber and Straw Products	36741	36741		19700
家具制造业	Furniture Manufacturing	2231	2231		25467
造纸及纸制品业	Papermaking and Paper Products	17192	15418	1774	17476
印刷和记录媒介复制业	Printing and Recorded Media Duplication Industry	18391	18391		42372
文教、工美、体育和娱乐用品制造业	Cultural & Educational, Arts & Crafts, Sports & Entertainment Articles Manufacturing	124811	124163	648	110853
石油加工、炼焦及核燃料加工业	Petroleum Processing, Coking and Nuclear Fuel Processing	90602	90550	52	91249
化学原料及化学制品制造业	Raw Chemical Materials and Chemica Products	2137266	1890862	246396	2163333
医药制造业	Medical and Pharmaceutical Products	277606	261079	16527	221947
化学纤维制造业	Chemical Fiber	37696	37696		35504
橡胶和塑料制品业	Rubber and Plastic Products Industry	104893	86528	18366	119194
非金属矿物制品业	Nonmetal Mineral Products	120492	95696	24793	165551
黑色金属冶炼及压延加工业	Smelting and Pressing of Ferrous Metals	1219454	1188263	31191	48382
有色金属冶炼及压延加工业	Smelting and Pressing of Nonferrous Metals	144354	105967	38388	165512
金属制品业	Metal Products	547520	421319	58380	412452
通用设备制造业	General Equipment Manufacturing	842253	660735	181340	617874
专用设备制造业	For Special Purposes Equipment Manufacturing	1414379	1311389	102991	1343175
汽车制造业	Automotive Industry	389818	321263	68556	317033
铁路、船舶、航空航天和其他运输设备制造	Railways, Shipping, Aerospace and other Transportation Equipment Manufacturing	370345	325427	44766	464780
电气机械及器材制造业	Electric Equipment and Machinery	3413209	3046409	366800	2298330
计算机、通信和其他电子设备制造	Computer, Communications and other Electronic Equipment Manufacturing	1139446	1059562	79876	1692337
仪器仪表制造业	Instrumentation Manufacturing	275447	240178	35268	322094
电力、热力生产和供应业	Production and Supply of Electricity & Heat Industry	35065	28764	6300	91385
燃气生产和供应业	Production and Supply of Gas Industry	106755	106755		84921
水的生产和供应业	Production and Supply of water Industry	282507	260541	21966	118053

单位：万元（10000 yuan）

主营业务收入 Main Business Income	销售费用 Cost of Sales	管理费用 Cost of Management	财务费用 Finance Charge	营业利润 Business Profit	实现利税总额 Total Profits and Taxes	其中 of which			亏损企业亏损总额 Amount of Loss in Loss-incurring Enterprises	应付职工薪酬 Remuneration Payable to Employees
						利润总额 Total Profits	主营业务税金及附加 Main Business Tax and Surcharges	应交增值税 Value Added Tax Payable		
166332	10247	13059	1752	11449	19932	11668	1682	6582		9369
15068	893	3310	178	-553	1262	215	20	1027	253	2523
100935	2033	2114	750	2777	5747	2676	657	2413	67	3295
62324	1958	3371	1106	6058	6640	6267	275	99	111	6137
269714	6716	15161	3161	18991	29038	19025	1451	8562	423	24690
785422	4490	9282	1385	45961	51068	38378	1997	10694		7548
8344266	104515	150032	66245	249887	458094	255091	18149	184854	54037	162791
376707	108237	46770	2668	48930	83923	50099	4096	29728	3421	37364
93722	4355	3946	1751	6909	10412	7129	440	2844		4931
261300	11001	19021	3888	17567	29148	17953	1225	9969	3924	21221
246538	5257	14442	2161	15021	21873	15283	1082	5508	7366	22784
3230649	4442	19807	13638	330943	274559	133562	16067	124929	838	56357
229798	4693	20265	2809	-3760	9875	-3121	1760	11236	9143	12461
997259	25594	33864	8801	49076	69796	49017	2244	18535	19776	51998
1600264	39459	94815	20850	94321	147346	95843	8437	43066	23905	150985
2095554	85797	166054	17914	-10998	49432	-11395	11210	49616	125266	193849
781135	16839	60106	8469	50830	77835	51829	4523	21484	12264	71169
811595	27850	61935	4009	89145	128885	91417	5461	32008	5725	92258
8823775	163157	391036	56540	482534	811201	472282	17688	321232	53008	372818
3024998	61013	161276	441	297295	404188	302236	12833	89119	14883	383156
805804	21463	55581	677	70818	98922	72824	4582	21516	17278	64506
82864	19	5749	1065	14262	18193	14473	513	3208	56	3456
255166	6121	9442	1190	55982	63227	54197	1012	8019		13497
53240	5293	6863	-581	17955	19820	17848	205	1767		12496

11-8 大中型工业企业主要经济指标（2015 年）
MAJOR ECONOMIC INDICATORS OF LARGE AND MEDIUM-SIZED ENTERPRISES（2015）

指 标	Item	企 业 单位数（个） Number of Enterpr-ises（unit）	其中 of which #亏损企业 Loss-incurring Enterprises	工 业 总产值 Gross Industrial Output Value	工业销售产值 Value of Industrial Products Sales
总 计	**Total**	**573**	**60**	**69419265**	**68999388**
按地区分	**Grouped by Region**				
市 区	Urban Area	513	53	60608341	60284716
金坛区	Jintan District	74	9	6057770	6159491
武进区	Wujin District	200	18	30426869	29851743
# 经开区	Economic Development Zone	65	4	12429050	12226931
新北区	Xinbei District	135	18	15787302	15828725
天宁区	Tianning District	60	6	3336388	3262617
钟楼区	Zhonglou District	44	2	5000011	5182141
溧阳市	Liyang City	60	7	8810924	8714672
按登记注册类型分	**Grouped by Registration Status**				
内 资	Domestic Investment	360	30	43000135	42687861
国 有	State-owned	2	1	72609	72609
集 体	Collective-owned	1		310006	309515
有限责任公司	Limited Liability Corporations	48	10	5689190	5790164
股份有限公司	Share-holding Corporations Ltd.	22	1	2073586	2063739
私 营	Private	287	18	34854745	34451835
港澳台商投资	Investment from Hong Kong, Macao and Taiwan	90	9	12050660	11930931
合资经营	Joint-Venture	44	4	7295756	7252381
合作经营	Cooperative	2		105211	107101
独资经营	Sole Investment	39	5	3506730	3486711
股份有限公司	Share-holding Corporations Ltd.	5		1142964	1084737
外商投资	Foreign Investment	123	21	14368470	14380597
中外合资经营	Joint Ventures	52	8	4357703	4379545
中外合作经营	Cooperative Enterprises	2		50589	53949
外商独资	Sole Foreign Investment	68	13	9704282	9689146
股份有限公司	Share-holding Corporations Ltd.	1		255896	257957
按轻重工业分	**Grouped by Light and Heavy Industry**				
轻工业	Light Industry	213	24	15545433	15341122
重工业	Heavy Industry	360	36	53873832	53658267
按企业规模分	**Grouped by Size of Enterprises**				
大 型	Large-sized	92	5	38661916	38409356
中 型	Medium-sized	481	55	30757348	30590033

单位：万元（10000 yuan）

流动资产合计 Current Assets	其中 of which #应收帐款净额 Net Account Income	存货 Existing Stock	其中 of which #产成品 Manufac-tured Products	固定资产合计 Total Fixed Assets	固定资产原价合计 Total Original Value of Fixed Assets	累计折旧 Accumulative Depreciation	资产总计 Total Assets
29856713	**9300768**	**6365479**	**2443222**	**17069420**	**34716276**	**17438649**	**54316916**
26602989	8441044	5729356	2209044	15161212	31190878	15791672	47727014
2401703	913811	431571	206541	2362420	3796842	1405306	5268694
13765559	3442995	3151503	949309	7370099	14411931	7052027	24600339
5810504	1197127	1588211	422540	3169698	5114538	1899300	9918691
6774436	2861816	1334903	646787	3308409	7867262	4481457	11441797
1666652	533718	377685	177858	1110027	1694422	568687	2928864
1994640	688703	433694	228550	1010258	3420421	2284196	3487320
3253724	859724	636124	234178	1908207	3525398	1646977	6589902
19519530	5288412	4240887	1519887	11097499	22629624	11387843	35560676
33990	3384	3005	1234	14015	28358	14344	48233
6852	176	2152	2066	21002	72385	51383	36695
2820167	1041388	715288	253701	1734505	3770399	2009691	5117005
1392321	459585	282607	137098	1736912	2639380	906736	3543206
15266200	3783880	3237836	1125788	7591065	16119101	8405690	26815537
4365637	1278843	980290	438734	3229677	6539653	3280051	8966206
2086195	592176	544723	218687	1730504	3527692	1793357	4344875
44502	19365	3026	1969	10399	15988	5590	55075
1773424	535354	378209	207323	1273132	2395624	1096398	3872655
461516	131949	54332	10756	215642	600349	384706	693601
5971545	2733513	1144302	484600	2742244	5546998	2770754	9790035
1562652	569802	426346	210573	687834	1468068	769207	2520085
27961	15062	7281	2430	16090	18781	5916	54855
4132680	2070666	699339	268562	1990783	3975097	1958114	6876624
248253	77982	11336	3036	47536	85053	37517	338471
8035282	2168287	1555338	621861	4281084	8619671	4263471	14612176
21821431	7132481	4810141	1821361	12788336	26096605	13175177	39704740
16226577	4882772	3416358	1099334	9504185	19446325	9758575	30037485
13630136	4417996	2949122	1343888	7565234	15269951	7680074	24279431

11-8 续表 Continued

指 标	Item	负债总计 Total Liabilities	其中 of which 流动负债合计 Total Current Liabilities	非流动负债合计 Total Non-current Liabilities	所有者权益 Owner's Equity
总 计	**Total**	**31229226**	**27805176**	**3271517**	**23008831**
按地区分	**Grouped by Region**				
市 区	Urban Area	26483190	23365834	2964823	21164966
金坛区	Jintan District	3508484	3271099	237385	1760210
武进区	Wujin District	13321089	11520908	1777016	11269966
# 经开区	Economic Development Zone	5467183	4873435	573076	4444141
新北区	Xinbei District	6381341	5639932	629243	4990882
天宁区	Tianning District	1389695	1317902	71793	1539169
钟楼区	Zhonglou District	1882581	1615993	249387	1604739
溧阳市	Liyang City	4746037	4439342	306694	1843865
按登记注册类型分	**Grouped by Registration Status**				
内 资	Domestic Investment	20613932	18286492	2242400	14895370
国 有	State-owned	37076	37076		11157
集 体	Collective-owned	36695	30332	6363	
有限责任公司	Limited Liability Corporations	2949326	2676252	273024	2167679
股份有限公司	Share-holding Corporations Ltd.	1826213	1752777	73436	1716993
私 营	Private	15764622	13790055	1889576	10999542
港澳台商投资	Investment from Hong Kong, Macao and Taiwan	5154994	4672934	465825	3801724
合资经营	Joint-Venture	2939726	2722761	216965	1395661
合作经营	Cooperative	39652	39652		15423
独资经营	Sole Investment	1794826	1530806	247785	2077829
股份有限公司	Share-holding Corporations Ltd.	380790	379715	1075	312811
外商投资	Foreign Investment	5460301	4845751	563292	4311737
中外合资经营	Joint Ventures	1373859	1318877	54982	1146226
中外合作经营	Cooperative Enterprises	19329	16649	2679	35527
外商独资	Sole Foreign Investment	3963556	3406668	505631	2895071
股份有限公司	Share-holding Corporations Ltd.	103557	103557		234914
按轻重工业分	**Grouped by Light and Heavy Industry**				
轻工业	Light Industry	7831471	6773375	1035073	6763850
重工业	Heavy Industry	23397756	21031801	2236444	16244981
按企业规模分	**Grouped by Size of Enterprises**				
大 型	Large-sized	17707979	16057207	1650772	12329505
中 型	Medium-sized	13521247	11747969	1620745	10679326

单位：万元（10000 yuan）

主营业务收入 Main Business Income	销售费用 Cost of Sales	管理费用 Cost of Management	财务费用 Finance Charge	营业利润 Business Profit	实现利税总额 Total Profits and Taxes	其中 of which 利润总额 Total Profits	主营业务税金及附加 Main Business Tax and Surcharges	应交增值税 Value Added Tax Payable	亏损企业亏损总额 Amount of Loss in Loss-incurring Enterprises	应付职工薪酬 Remuneration Payable to Employees
73540264	**1292102**	**2432119**	**671140**	**4879531**	**6783218**	**4246027**	**261006**	**2276185**	**326846**	**4087095**
64624983	1142844	2236416	569559	4118151	5813172	3658626	211507	1943039	290528	3774021
6210095	119990	230482	90012	518227	744061	530230	32350	181482	4167	338835
33773808	376008	948841	335775	2273105	2840950	1785795	80839	974316	109289	2022186
16274984	180683	375437	175621	1105408	1065410	649701	34072	381637	52564	710135
15952631	353852	672066	97758	720795	1333949	740790	60860	532299	166423	821891
3388962	195591	193145	10960	275090	415477	283939	22324	109214	9560	343560
5299487	97404	191882	35053	330934	478735	317872	15134	145729	1089	247549
8915281	149258	195703	101582	761380	970046	587401	49499	333146	36318	313074
47110340	727226	1432284	519700	3174012	4280409	2736788	155418	1388203	97705	2515689
79416	1899	3328	260	2590	6879	2656	383	3840	1472	9449
348991	135	1030	2710	27760	38969	29260	144	9565		9956
5819709	107081	234777	60925	267554	513280	304351	17895	191034	63682	441627
2180518	95358	159227	34741	132037	217228	145691	9589	61947	15152	175696
38681706	522754	1033923	421065	2744071	3504053	2254829	127407	1121817	17398	1878961
12004383	148558	381262	63500	987795	1247852	786232	56776	404844	96401	788402
7484975	90398	189442	37665	700777	816281	507199	42016	267066	1457	343525
113582	1644	4017	-1511	12028	15508	12103	418	2988		5899
3485951	48436	165835	27931	223919	346302	212849	12098	121355	94943	363068
919875	8080	21969	-584	51071	69760	54080	2245	13435		75910
14425541	416318	618573	87940	717724	1254957	723007	48812	483138	132741	783004
4359703	199664	193653	31834	168582	321013	171827	20540	128646	84993	262315
53948	2531	4438	1432	3467	5844	3250	369	2226		5222
9797721	214100	413067	55087	512786	886252	514914	27903	343436	47748	499473
214170	23	7416	-413	32890	41848	33017		8831		15995
15556482	448015	723963	141483	1087200	1721895	1119319	81597	520979	51882	1494118
57983782	844087	1708156	529657	3792331	5061323	3126708	179409	1755206	274963	2592977
42585344	552930	1204596	391379	2826909	3471717	2134438	121542	1215737	92694	2345198
30954920	739172	1227523	279761	2052622	3311501	2111589	139464	1060449	234152	1741896

11-9 规模以上工业企业主要经济分析指标（2015 年）
MAJOR ECONOMIC ANALYTICAL INDICATORS OF INDUSTRIAL ENTERPRISES ABOVE DESIGNATED SIZE（2015）

单位：%

指 标	Item	企业亏损面 Percentage of loss Making Enterprises	产值利税率 Percentage of Profit and Tax to Output Value	资 产 负债率 Assets Liability Ratio	工业产品 销 售 率 Sales Ratio Industrial Products	工业成本 费用利润率 Ratio of Profits to Industrial Cost
总 计	**Total**	**15.74**	**9.29**	**57.52**	**99.17**	**5.95**
按地区分	**Grouped by Region**					
市 区	Urban Area	14.69	9.20	55.86	99.22	5.89
金坛区	Jintan District	22.25	10.97	66.72	101.47	8.12
武进区	Wujin District	12.22	9.03	54.46	98.02	5.63
#经开区	Economic Development Zone	7.57	8.78	54.79	98.40	4.78
新北区	Xinbei District	17.56	8.26	55.54	99.68	5.05
天宁区	Tianning District	11.62	10.37	50.24	97.48	6.85
钟楼区	Zhonglou District	12.57	9.32	53.85	102.90	6.08
溧阳市	Liyang City	26.02	10.10	70.50	98.72	6.47
按登记注册类型分	**Grouped by Registration Status**					
内 资	Domestic Investment	13.68	9.45	58.93	99.11	6.01
#国 有	State-owned	25.00	9.20	75.68	99.49	4.20
集 体	Collective-owned		12.83	84.44	99.38	9.20
股份合作	Share-holding Cooperative	28.57	3.45	41.80	94.24	0.95
有限责任公司	Limited Liability Corporations	18.00	8.57	58.64	100.66	5.23
股份有限公司	Share-holding Corporations Ltd.	6.52	13.48	51.01	100.45	9.96
私 营	Private	13.41	9.39	59.70	98.85	5.94
港澳台商投资	Investment from Hong Kong, Macao and Taiwan	19.05	9.58	56.38	99.14	6.50
合资经营	Joint-Venture	13.57	10.86	65.04	99.50	7.26
合作经营	Cooperative	23.08	11.19	60.53	100.00	7.17
独资经营	Sole Investment	25.19	8.30	47.52	99.41	5.40
股份有限公司	Share-holding Corporations Ltd.		6.17	54.49	94.96	6.27
外商投资	Foreign Investment	27.57	8.54	52.91	99.38	5.38
中外合资经营	Joint Ventures	21.05	8.07	50.75	98.91	5.16
中外合作经营	Cooperative Enterprises	10.00	16.42	47.39	100.11	12.40
外商独资	Sole Foreign Investment	32.76	8.50	54.79	99.62	5.18
股份有限公司	Share-holding Corporations Ltd.	33.33	13.64	34.36	100.14	14.07
按轻重工业分	**Grouped by Light and Heavy Industry**					
轻工业	Light Industry	13.91	10.08	54.83	98.77	6.66
重工业	Heavy Industry	16.64	9.03	58.48	99.30	5.73
按企业规模分	**Grouped by Size of Enterprises**					
大 型	Large-sized	5.43	8.98	58.95	99.35	5.35
中 型	Medium-sized	11.43	10.77	55.69	99.46	7.33
小 型	Small-sized	16.50	8.53	57.32	98.77	5.58
微 型	Micro-sized	19.28	6.59	71.85	99.93	3.46

11-10 规模以上工业企业分行业主要经济分析指标（2015 年）
MAJOR ECONOMIC ANALYTICAL INDICATORS OF INDUSTRIAL ENTERPRISES ABOVE DESIGNATED SIZE BY SECTOR（2015）

单位：%

指 标	Item	企业亏损面 Percentage of loss Making Enterprises	产值利税率 Percentage of Profit and Tax to Output Value	资产负债率 Assets Liability Ratio	工业产品销售率 Sales Ratio Industrial Products	工业成本费用利润率 Ratio of Profits to Industrial Cost
黑色金属矿采选业	Ferrous Metal Mining Industry		7.48	86.20	100.00	1.17
非金属矿采选业	Nonmetal Minerals Mining and Dressing	14.29	18.23	54.66	99.45	8.36
农副食品加工业	Food Processing	41.18	4.23	69.71	103.19	3.18
食品制造业	Food Production	21.05	14.77	70.96	100.65	11.13
酒、饮料和精制茶制造业	Beverages and Refined Tea Manufacturing	25.00	23.30	62.12	101.57	5.74
纺织业	Textile Industry	10.36	10.22	61.60	99.23	6.02
纺织服装、服饰业	Textile and clothing Industry	17.52	10.40	48.04	100.18	6.89
皮革、毛皮、羽毛及其制品和制鞋业	Leather, Fur, Feathers and Their Products, and Footwear Industry	23.53	11.64	71.17	102.56	7.14
木材加工及木、竹、藤、棕、草制品业	Timber Processing, Bamboo, Cane, Palm Fiber and Straw Products	3.33	10.35	56.94	98.39	6.84
家具制造业	Furniture Manufacturing	22.22	10.24	26.90	97.09	4.12
造纸及纸制品业	Papermaking and Paper Products	5.17	7.18	67.70	99.36	4.36
印刷和记录媒介复制业	Printing and Recorded Media Duplication Industry	9.76	8.33	55.33	99.32	5.29
文教、工美、体育和娱乐用品制造业	Cultural & Educational, Arts & Crafts, Sports & Entertainment Articles Manufacturing	17.31	9.03	60.06	98.42	5.55
石油加工、炼焦及核燃料加工业	Petroleum Processing, Coking and Nuclear Fuel Processing	27.27	6.40	52.81	98.03	4.27
化学原料及化学制品制造业	Raw Chemical Materials and Chemica Products	13.81	7.56	52.61	99.90	4.83
医药制造业	Medical and Pharmaceutical Products	14.49	14.53	45.71	96.01	11.29
化学纤维制造业	Chemical Fiber	16.00	9.93	55.56	99.28	7.41
橡胶和塑料制品业	Rubber and Plastic Products Industry	11.66	9.41	45.66	98.00	6.01
非金属矿物制品业	Nonmetal Mineral Products	20.10	14.07	69.49	99.38	10.66
黑色金属冶炼及压延加工业	Smelting and Pressing of Ferrous Metals	26.17	6.52	67.56	97.79	2.79
有色金属冶炼及压延加工业	Smelting and Pressing of Nonferrous Metals	11.11	9.46	56.00	100.42	6.78
金属制品业	Metal Products	14.51	8.96	59.38	99.05	6.07
通用设备制造业	General Equipment Manufacturing	18.72	9.55	59.51	99.16	6.62
专用设备制造业	For Special Purposes Equipment Manufacturing	19.25	7.09	55.32	99.12	3.86
汽车制造业	Automotive Industry	11.58	7.17	69.91	100.36	4.25
铁路、船舶、航空航天和其他运输设备制造	Railways, Shipping, Aerospace and other Transportation Equipment Manufacturing	13.83	11.80	51.88	100.04	8.93
电气机械及器材制造业	Electric Equipment and Machinery	17.19	9.56	54.84	99.31	6.24
计算机、通信和其他电子设备制造	Computer, Communications and other Electronic Equipment Manufacturing	15.36	11.43	48.48	98.18	8.87
仪器仪表制造业	Instrumentation Manufacturing	14.95	12.47	53.10	99.82	9.63
其他制造业	Other Manufacturing		5.83	71.09	101.46	0.79
废弃资源综合利用业	Comprehensive Utilization of Waste Resources Industry	20.00	12.34	92.57	99.80	8.78
金属制品、机械和设备修理业	Metal Products, Machinery & Equipment Repairing Industry		11.88	85.03	98.88	9.67
电力、热力生产和供应业	Production and Supply of Electricity & Heat Industry	11.76	25.73	55.45	99.57	22.74
燃气生产和供应业	Production and Supply of Gas Industry		23.71	57.54	100.82	23.32
水的生产和供应业	Production and Supply of water Industry	14.29	20.50	73.14	96.84	17.44

11-11 规模以上民营工业企业主要经济分析指标（2015 年）
MAJOR ECONOMIC ANALYTICAL INDICATORS OF PRIVATE INDUSTRIAL ENTERPRISES ABOVE DESIGNATED SIZE（2015）

指 标	Item	企业亏损面 Percentage of loss Making Enterprises	产值利税率 Percentage of Profit and Tax to Output Value	资产负债率 Assets Liability Ratio	工业产品销售率 Sales Ratio Industrial Products	工业成本费用利润率 Ratio of Profits to Industrial Cost
总 计	**Total**	**13.69**	**9.46**	**58.96**	**99.04**	**6.05**
按地区分	**Grouped by Region**					
市 区	Urban Area	12.35	9.27	57.66	99.07	5.85
金坛区	Jintan District	20.85	10.42	68.88	101.70	7.69
武进区	Wujin District	9.84	8.26	57.10	98.06	4.86
# 经开区	Economic Development Zone	6.59	7.48	55.68	98.21	3.69
新北区	Xinbei District	13.88	10.58	56.92	99.32	7.10
天宁区	Tianning District	11.78	10.92	48.23	97.81	7.20
钟楼区	Zhonglou District	11.79	9.69	50.98	102.53	6.37
溧阳市	Liyang City	25.98	10.98	67.27	98.83	7.61
按轻重工业分	**Grouped by Light and Heavy Industry**					
轻工业	Light Industry	11.41	9.45	58.44	98.85	6.04
重工业	Heavy Industry	14.75	9.47	59.16	99.11	6.05
按企业规模分	**Grouped by Size of Enterprises**					
大 型	Large-sized		8.83	59.35	99.01	5.31
中 型	Medium-sized	8.48	12.12	55.88	99.45	8.35
小 型	Small-sized	14.38	8.54	60.25	98.81	5.50
微 型	Micro-sized	14.86	8.47	71.14	99.95	5.42
按工业行业分	**Grouped by Sector**					
黑色金属矿采选业	Ferrous Metal Mining Industry		7.48	86.20	100.00	1.17
非金属矿采选业	Nonmetal Minerals Mining and Dressing	16.67	16.91	57.72	99.42	8.78
农副食品加工业	Food Processing	40.00	3.94	76.62	102.85	2.80
食品制造业	Food Production	16.67	8.07	74.50	95.33	6.82
酒、饮料和精制茶制造业	Beverages and Refined Tea Manufacturing		28.06	56.74	99.66	11.90
纺织业	Textile Industry	9.46	9.91	62.83	99.24	5.70
纺织服装、服饰业	Textile and clothing Industry	15.15	8.04	53.99	100.54	4.68
皮革、毛皮、羽毛及其制品和制鞋业	Leather, Fur, Feathers and Their Products, and Footwear Industry	18.18	7.29	74.60	101.17	3.12

11-11 续表 Continued

单位：%

指 标	Item	企业亏损面 Percentage of loss Making Enterprises	产值利税率 Percentage of Profit and Tax to Output Value	资产负债率 Assets Liability Ratio	工业产品销售率 Sales Ratio Industrial Products	工业成本费用利润率 Ratio of Profits to Industrial Cost
木材加工及木、竹、藤、棕、草制品业	Timber Processing, Bamboo, Cane, Palm Fiber and Straw Products	3.51	9.86	55.38	98.31	6.61
家具制造业	Furniture Manufacturing	16.67	11.07	47.15	97.29	6.98
造纸及纸制品业	Papermaking and Paper Products	3.92	7.39	69.10	99.33	4.64
印刷和记录媒介复制业	Printing and Recorded Media Duplication Industry	8.82	7.61	67.04	98.69	4.11
文教、工美、体育和娱乐用品制造业	Cultural & Educational, Arts &Crafts, Sports & Entertainment Articles Manufacturing	18.07	8.72	62.24	99.68	5.03
石油加工、炼焦及核燃料加工业	Petroleum Processing, Coking and Nuclear Fuel Processing	33.33	4.40	59.41	88.90	-0.29
化学原料及化学制品制造业	Raw Chemical Materials and Chemica Products	10.65	9.42	54.86	100.38	6.34
医药制造业	Medical and Pharmaceutical Products	12.00	11.98	43.78	95.76	9.61
化学纤维制造业	Chemical Fiber	17.39	8.86	57.92	97.83	7.04
橡胶和塑料制品业	Rubber and Plastic Products Industry	10.22	9.25	45.39	97.97	5.83
非金属矿物制品业	Nonmetal Mineral Products	18.75	14.48	70.05	99.34	11.01
黑色金属冶炼及压延加工业	Smelting and Pressing of Ferrous Metals	26.24	5.90	62.74	97.56	2.42
有色金属冶炼及压延加工业	Smelting and Pressing of Nonferrous Metals	7.87	9.95	58.34	100.08	7.48
金属制品业	Metal Products	13.57	9.52	61.00	98.51	6.42
通用设备制造业	General Equipment Manufacturing	16.02	10.01	61.88	98.40	7.01
专用设备制造业	For Special Purposes Equipment Manufacturing	16.15	10.66	58.96	99.92	7.21
汽车制造业	Automotive Industry	8.18	6.35	75.65	98.60	3.62
铁路、船舶、航空航天和其他运输设备制造	Railways, Shipping, Aerospace and other Transportation Equipment Manufacturing	10.45	13.94	50.30	99.63	11.86
电气机械及器材制造业	Electric Equipment and Machinery	15.62	9.76	49.33	99.25	6.90
计算机、通信和其他电子设备制造	Computer, Communications and other Electronic Equipment Manufacturing	10.11	9.83	58.27	99.57	6.31
仪器仪表制造业	Instrumentation Manufacturing	15.12	12.87	56.30	100.74	9.33
其他制造业	Other Manufacturing		5.83	71.09	101.46	0.79
废弃资源综合利用业	Comprehensive Utilization of Waste Resources Industry	20.00	12.34	92.57	99.80	8.78
金属制品、机械和设备修理业	Metal Products, Machinery & Equipment Repairing Industry		11.88	85.03	98.88	9.67
电力、热力生产和供应业	Production and Supply of Electricity & Heat Industry	16.67	21.60	60.80	98.00	19.45
燃气生产和供应业	Production and Supply of Gas Industry		15.47	66.36	99.00	12.33
水的生产和供应业	Production and Supply of water Industry		50.25	66.19	80.28	74.59

11-12 规模以上外商和港澳台商投资工业企业主要经济分析指标（2015 年）
MAJOR ECONOMIC ANALYTICAL INDICATORS OF INDUSTRIAL ENTERPRISES ABOVE DESIGNATED SIZE WITH HONG KONG,MACAO,TAIWAN AND FOREIGN FUNDS（2015）

指 标	Item	企业亏损面 Percentage of loss Making Enterprises	产值利税率 Percentage of Profit and Tax to Output Value	资 产 负债率 Assets Liability Ratio	工业产品 销 售 率 Sales Ratio Industrial Products	工业成本费 用利润率 Ratio of Profits to Industrial Cost
总 计	**Total**	**24.47**	**8.98**	**54.39**	**99.28**	**5.85**
按地区分	**Grouped by Region**					
市 区	Urban Area	23.98	9.09	52.15	99.37	6.07
金坛区	Jintan District	27.08	12.80	61.54	101.20	9.66
武进区	Wujin District	25.69	12.39	44.44	97.63	9.69
# 经开区	Economic Development Zone	16.07	16.81	45.04	98.86	13.96
新北区	Xinbei District	26.64	6.59	54.34	99.78	3.68
天宁区	Tianning District	10.67	9.71	53.13	96.79	6.41
钟楼区	Zhonglou District	16.39	8.97	58.50	104.22	6.07
溧阳市	Liyang City	32.00	8.06	81.86	98.51	3.90
按轻重工业分	**Grouped by Light and Heavy Industry**					
轻工业	Light Industry	22.61	11.36	47.31	98.50	7.99
重工业	Heavy Industry	25.66	8.31	56.91	99.50	5.27
按企业规模分	**Grouped by Size of Enterprises**					
大 型	Large-sized	8.33	9.98	59.43	99.77	6.19
中 型	Medium-sized	15.25	8.97	54.17	99.42	6.06
小 型	Small-sized	27.80	7.79	48.76	98.50	5.20
微 型	Micro-sized	66.67	-2.77	67.05	99.23	-4.38
按工业行业分	**Grouped by Sector**					
农副食品加工业	Food Processing	50.00	5.10	45.50	104.17	4.25
食品制造业	Food Production	33.33	19.35	67.89	104.27	13.60
酒、饮料和精制茶制造业	Beverages and Refined Tea Manufacturing	50.00	13.48	66.40	105.51	-4.05
纺织业	Textile Industry	15.00	11.49	55.14	99.18	7.28
纺织服装、服饰业	Textile and clothing Industry	19.70	11.40	45.81	99.70	8.01
皮革、毛皮、羽毛及其制品和制鞋业	Leather, Fur, Feathers and Their Products, and Footwear Industry	33.33	14.14	67.67	103.36	9.50

11-12 续表 Continued

单位：%

指标	Item	企业亏损面 Percentage of loss Making Enterprises	产值利税率 Percentage of Profit and Tax to Output Value	资产负债率 Assets Liability Ratio	工业产品销售率 Sales Ratio Industrial Products	工业成本费用利润率 Ratio of Profits to Industrial Cost
木材加工及木、竹、藤、棕、草制品业	Timber Processing, Bamboo, Cane, Palm Fiber and Straw Products		11.98	65.10	98.69	7.62
家具制造业	Furniture Manufacturing	33.33	9.13	8.06	96.84	1.27
造纸及纸制品业	Papermaking and Paper Products	14.29	5.90	49.59	99.56	2.74
印刷和记录媒介复制业	Printing and Recorded Media Duplication Industry	20.00	11.27	30.27	102.94	11.18
文教、工美、体育和娱乐用品制造业	Cultural & Educational, Arts & Crafts, Sports & Entertainment Articles Manufacturing	14.29	10.14	52.96	93.93	7.63
石油加工、炼焦及核燃料加工业	Petroleum Processing, Coking and Nuclear Fuel Processing		6.88	49.82	100.21	5.20
化学原料及化学制品制造业	Raw Chemical Materials and Chemica Products	25.33	5.46	49.70	99.23	3.16
医药制造业	Medical and Pharmaceutical Products	22.22	21.46	55.57	96.93	15.37
化学纤维制造业	Chemical Fiber		11.83	51.50	104.62	8.22
橡胶和塑料制品业	Rubber and Plastic Products Industry	20.00	11.02	46.81	96.85	7.37
非金属矿物制品业	Nonmetal Mineral Products	35.00	8.87	42.12	101.05	6.64
黑色金属冶炼及压延加工业	Smelting and Pressing of Ferrous Metals	25.00	8.84	96.18	98.66	4.63
有色金属冶炼及压延加工业	Smelting and Pressing of Nonferrous Metals	44.44	4.06	46.59	102.91	-1.35
金属制品业	Metal Products	21.88	7.08	55.99	101.26	5.18
通用设备制造业	General Equipment Manufacturing	31.76	9.29	57.68	100.60	6.37
专用设备制造业	For Special Purposes Equipment Manufacturing	28.05	2.26	51.29	97.70	-0.56
汽车制造业	Automotive Industry	27.59	10.60	55.15	104.87	7.13
铁路、船舶、航空航天和其他运输设备制造	Railways, Shipping, Aerospace and other Transportation Equipment Manufacturing	25.00	15.92	44.35	101.30	12.63
电气机械及器材制造业	Electric Equipment and Machinery	22.94	9.44	59.76	99.44	5.65
计算机、通信和其他电子设备制造	Computer, Communications and other Electronic Equipment Manufacturing	29.33	12.37	40.24	96.80	11.12
仪器仪表制造业	Instrumentation Manufacturing	14.29	12.02	46.10	98.79	9.99
电力、热力生产和供应业	Production and Supply of Electricity & Heat Industry	25.00	21.51	27.73	98.65	21.19
燃气生产和供应业	Production and Supply of Gas Industry		24.84	55.70	100.00	25.28
水的生产和供应业	Production and Supply of water Industry		36.39	70.53	94.85	34.14

11-13 大中型工业企业主要经济分析指标（2015 年）
MAIN ECONOMIC ANALYTICAL INDICATORS OF LARGE AND MEDIUM-SIZED INDUSTRIAL ENTERPRISES（2015）

指 标	Item	企业亏损面 Percentage of loss Making Enterprises	产值利税率 Percentage of Profit and Tax to Output Value	资产负债率 Assets Liability Ratio	工业产品销售率 Sales Ratio Industrial Products	工业成本费用利润率 Ratio of Profits to Industrial Cost
总 计	**Total**	**10.47**	**9.77**	**57.49**	**99.40**	**6.18**
按地区分	**Grouped by Region**					
市 区	Urban Area	10.33	9.59	55.49	99.47	6.05
金坛区	Jintan District	12.16	12.28	66.59	101.68	9.36
武进区	Wujin District	9.00	9.34	54.15	98.11	5.65
#经开区	Economic Development Zone	6.15	8.57	55.12	98.37	4.28
新北区	Xinbei District	13.33	8.45	55.77	100.26	4.88
天宁区	Tianning District	10.00	12.45	47.45	97.79	9.09
钟楼区	Zhonglou District	4.55	9.57	53.98	103.64	6.40
溧阳市	Liyang City	11.67	11.01	72.02	98.91	7.19
按登记注册类型分	**Grouped by Registration Status**					
内 资	Domestic Investment	8.33	9.95	57.97	99.27	6.21
#国 有	State-owned	50.00	9.47	76.87	100.00	3.47
集 体	Collective-owned		12.57	100.00	99.84	8.88
有限责任公司	Limited Liability Corporations	20.83	9.02	57.64	101.77	5.48
股份有限公司	Share-holding Corporations Ltd.	4.55	10.48	51.54	99.53	7.07
私 营	Private	6.27	10.05	58.79	98.84	6.26
港澳台商投资	Investment from Hong Kong, Macao and Taiwan	10.00	10.36	57.49	99.01	7.15
合资经营	Joint-Venture	9.09	11.19	67.66	99.41	7.49
合作经营	Cooperative		14.74	72.00	101.80	11.96
独资经营	Sole Investment	12.82	9.88	46.35	99.43	6.55
股份有限公司	Share-holding Corporations Ltd.		6.10	54.90	94.91	6.22
外商投资	Foreign Investment	17.07	8.73	55.77	100.08	5.30
中外合资经营	Joint Ventures	15.38	7.37	54.52	100.50	4.16
中外合作经营	Cooperative Enterprises		11.55	35.24	106.64	6.43
外商独资	Sole Foreign Investment	19.12	9.13	57.64	99.84	5.55
股份有限公司	Share-holding Corporations Ltd.		16.35	30.60	100.81	18.17
按轻重工业分	**Grouped by Light and Heavy Industry**					
轻工业	Light Industry	11.27	11.08	53.60	98.69	7.73
重工业	Heavy Industry	10.00	9.39	58.93	99.60	5.77
按企业规模分	**Grouped by Size of Enterprises**					
大 型	Large-sized	5.43	8.98	58.95	99.35	5.35
中 型	Medium-sized	11.43	10.77	55.69	99.46	7.33

11-14 规模以上工业主要产品产量（2015 年）
OUTPUT OF INDUSTRIAL ENTERPRISES ABOVE DESIGNATED SIZE（2015）

产品名称	Name of Products	全 市 Whole Municipality	其 中 of which #市 区 Urban Area
原 盐（吨）	Crude Salt （ton）	4300757	4300757
大 米（吨）	Grain （ton）	9774	9774
饲 料（吨）	Feedign Stuff （ton）	497521	120890
精制食用植物油（吨）	Purified Edible Vegetable Oil （ton）	5741	5741
饮料酒（千升）	Drinks （kilolitre）	325551	128230
#啤 酒	Beer	325551	128230
纱（万吨）	Yarn （10000 tons）	26	25
#棉 纱	Cotton Yarn	21	21
布（万米）	Cloth （10000 m）	136954	136266
#棉 布	Cotton Cloth	107486	107486
#牛仔布	Jean	5650	5650
印染布（万米）	Printing and Dyeing Cloth （10000 m）	26975	26975
服 装（万件）	Garment （10000 units）	44211	41467
复合木地板（万平方米）	Laminate Flooring （10000m^2）	7903	7903
纸制品（吨）	Paper Products （ton）	60278	60278
硫 酸（折100%,吨）	Sulfuric Acid （100%, ton）	426874	426874
盐 酸（含量31%以上,吨）	Hydrochloric Acid （content above 31%, ton）	101653	101653
烧 碱（折100%,吨）	Caustic Soda （100%, ton）	266188	266188
化学农药原药（折有效成份100%，吨）	Chemical pesticide （Converted into effective components 100%,ton）	37699	37699
涂 料（吨）	Coating （ton）	361944	331828
初级形态的塑料（吨）	Primary-form Plastic （ton）	3682035	3645789

11-14 续表 1 Continued 1

产品名称	Name of Products	全 市 Whole Municipality	其中 of which #市 区 Urban Area
单晶硅（吨）	Monocrystalline silicon （ton）	45520	45520
化学药品原药（吨）	Chemical Pesticide （ton）	9039	9039
化学纤维（吨）	Chemical Fiber （ton）	41672	41672
水泥熟料（万吨）	Cement Clinker （10000 tons）	1450	112
水 泥（万吨）	Cement （10000 tons）	2364	476
钢化玻璃（平方米）	Tempered Glass （square meter）	6004845	6004845
生 铁（万吨）	Pig Iron （10000 tons）	1154	943
粗 钢（万吨）	Raw Steel （10000 tons）	1293	1078
钢 材（万吨）	Rolled-Steel （10000 tons）	1676	1274
铁合金（万吨）	Ferroalloy （10000 tons）	14	14
金属集装箱（万立方米）	Metal Container （10000 m^3）	1959	1959
金属切削机床（台）	Metal-Cutting Machine Tool （unit）	662	662
滚动轴承（万套）	Rolling Axle Bearing （10000 units）	34758	34062
电动手提式工具（台）	Portable Electric Tools （unit）	8939742	8939742
衡 器（秤,台）	Weighing Apparatus （unit）	449046	449046
减速机（台）	Reducer （unit）	1156223	1156223
挖掘机（台）	Mechanical Excavator （unit）	6849	6849
装载机（台）	Shovel Loader （unit）	1230	1230
金属冶炼设备（吨）	Melting Equipment （ton）	8412	8412
金属轧制设备（吨）	Metal Rolling Equipment （ton）	30216	30216
大中型拖拉机（台）	Large and Medium Size Tractor （unit）	69113	69113

11-14　续表 2　Continued 2

产品名称 Name of Products		全　市 Whole Municipality	其 中 of which #市　区 Urban Area
小型拖拉机（台）	Mini-tractors （unit）	47794	47794
汽　车（辆）	Motor Vehicles （City Buses,unit）	45458	45458
铁路机车（辆）	Locomotive （unit）	134	134
民用钢质船舶（载重吨）	Civil Steel Ship （deadweight tons）（DWT）	5585	5585
摩托车整车（万辆）	Finished Motorcycle （10000 units）	18	18
两轮脚踏自行车（万辆）	Bicycles （10000 units）	182	182
电动自行车（万辆）	Electric Bicycle （10000 units）	31	31
交流电动机（千瓦）	AC Machine （ kw）	254518	254518
变压器（兆伏安）	Transformer （MVA）	137088	83697
通信电缆（对千米）	Telecommunications Cable （pair,km）	134482	88159
电力电缆（千米）	Electric Cable （1000 m）	1402702	944414
光　缆（芯千米）	Fiber Optic Cable （core km）	2498585	2498585
原电池（折R20标准万只）	Primary battery （converted into R20 standard unit）	38125	24205
太阳能电池（兆瓦）	Solar Cell （megawatt）	7587	7587
房间空气调节器（台）	Air Conditioners （unit）	514690	514690
GPS接收机（台）	GPS Receiver （unit）	32805	32805
彩色电视机（台）	Color TV Sets （unit）	474566	474566
激光视盘机（台）	Video-CD Players （unit）	181690	181690
半导体分立器件（万只）	Semiconduction Separating Part （10000 units）	2238053	2238053
光学仪器（台）	Optical Instruments （unit）	307073	307073
发电量（万千瓦时）	Power Generation （10000 kwh）	1626123	1516843

12

CHAPTER 12

建 筑 业

CONSTRUCTION

常州统计年鉴

12 建 筑 业
CONSTRUCTION

2015 年主要统计指标
MAJOR STATISTICAL INDICATORS OF 2015

年底建筑业企业数（含劳务企业）	Number of Construction Enterprises (Including Labor Services Enterprises)	717个	(unit)
#施工总承包企业数	Number of Construction Contracting Enterprises	621个	(unit)
建筑业企业总产值（含劳务企业）	Construction Enterprises Output Value (Including Labor Service Enterprises)	1323.95亿元	(100 million yuan)
比上年增长	Over the Previous Year	0.7%	
房屋建筑施工面积	Floor Space of Buildings Under Construction	10050.99万平方米	(10000 sq.m)
比上年增长	Over the Previous Year	-6.4%	
房屋建筑竣工面积	Floor Space of Buildings Completed	3448.59万平方米	(10000 sq.m)
比上年增长	Over the Previous Year	-9.5%	
从事主营业务活动的从业人员平均人数（含劳务企业）	Average Number of People Engaged in Main Business (Including Labor ServiceEnterprises)	50.08万人	(10000person)
比上年增长	Over the Previous Year	3.2%	

12-1 分地区建筑业企业生产情况（2015 年）
STATISTICS ON CONSTRUCTION ENTERPRISES BY REGION（2015）

指 标	Item	全 市 Whole Municipality	市 区 Urban Area
企业个数（不含劳务企业，个）	Number of Enterprises（Excluding Labor Enterprises, unit）	621	513
签订的建筑合同金额（万元）	Value of Signed Construction Contracts （10000 yuan）	18468120	10641506
上年结转建筑合同额	Value of Construction Contracts Carried forward from Previous Year	8147491	4964444
本年新签建筑合同额	Value of Construction Contracts Signed in This Year	10320628	5677062
建筑业总产值（万元）	Gross Output Value of Construction（10000 yuan）	12885168	7229768
# 装饰装修产值	Output of Decoration and Fitment	914381	826586
在外省完成的产值	Output Achieved out of Jiangsu Province	4572949	1932482
按构成分	**Grouped by Composition**		
建筑工程	Construction Projects	11312574	7003353
安装工程	Installation Projects	1463692	203238
其它产值	Other Output Value	108902	23178
竣工产值（万元）	Output Value of Buildings Completed （10000 yuan）	11287870	5986332
房屋建筑施工面积（万平方米）	Floor Space of Buildings Under Construction （10000 sq.m）	10050.99	6185.79
房屋建筑竣工面积（万平方米）	Floor Space of Buildings Completed （10000 sq.m）	3448.59	1926.80
# 住 宅	Residential Buildings	2049.70	1137.81
平均从业人员（人）	Average Number of Staff of Calculating Labor Productivity（person）	470777	277757
从事主营业务活动的从业人员平均人数（人）	Average Number of People Engaged in Main Business （person）	462102	364548

其中 of which					溧阳市
金坛区 Jintan District	武进区 wujin District	新北区 Xinbei District	天宁区 Tianning District	钟楼区 Zhonglou District	Liyang City
74	160	121	77	81	108
3790391	3001774	1126862	773371	1949108	7826614
1703678	1407329	537108	274875	1041455	3183047
2086713	1594445	589754	498496	907653	4643567
2869546	2031451	747379	558899	1022494	5655400
107965	155306	172016	224776	166523	87795
1330522	258965	107569	94863	140563	2640467
2810530	1984226	710073	538770	959753	4309222
49981	39867	33024	18805	61561	1260455
9035	7358	4282	1324	1180	85724
2296981	1855156	609051	520806	704338	5301538
2462.45	1883.00	509.17	273.84	1057.17	3865.21
800.39	716.00	162.08	94.71	153.67	1521.79
543.04	410.00	91.81	45.09	48.26	911.89
96021	100188	27769	20100	33679	193020
35286	102683	31789	21377	173413	97554

12-2　分登记注册类型建筑业企业生产情况（2015 年）
STATISTICS ON CONSTRUCTION ENTERPRISES BY REGISTER STATUS（2015）

指　标	Item	合　计 Total	内资企业 Domestic Funded Enterprises
企业个数（不含劳务企业，个）	Number of Enterprises （Excluding Labor Enterprises, unit）	621	613
签订的建筑合同金额（万元）	Value of Signed Construction Contracts （10000 yuan）	18468120	18351966
上年结转建筑合同额	Value of Construction Contracts Carried forward from Previous Year	8147491	8113758
本年新签建筑合同额	Value of Construction Contracts Signed in This Year	10320628	10238208
建筑业总产值（万元）	Gross Output Value of Construction（10000 yuan）	12885168	12839871
# 装饰装修产值	Output of Decoration and Fitment	914381	901641
在外省完成的产值	Output Achieved out of Jiangsu Province	4572949	4564176
按构成分	**Grouped by Composition**		
建筑工程	Construction Projects	11312574	11277169
安装工程	Installation Projects	1463692	1454621
其它产值	Other Output Value	108902	108081
竣工产值（万元）	Output Value of Buildings Completed （10000 yuan）	11287870	11263138
房屋建筑施工面积（万平方米）	Floor Space of Buildings UnderConstruction （10000 sq.m）	10050.99	9998.78
房屋建筑竣工面积（万平方米）	Floor Space of Buildings Completed （10000 sq.m）	3448.59	3448.59
# 住　宅	Residential Buildings	2049.70	2049.70
平均从业人员（人）	Average Number of Staff of Calculating Labor Productivity（person）	470777	469327
直接从事生产经营活动的平均人数（人）	Average Number of Persons Directly Engaged in Production and Business Activities（person）	462102	460555

其中 of which					港澳台投资企业	外商投资企业
国有企业 State-owned Enterprises	集体企业 Collective-owned Enterprises	有限责任公司 Limited Liability Corporations	股份有限公司 Share-holding Corporations Ltd.	私营企业 Private Enterprises	Enterprises With Investment FromHongKong, Macao and Taiwan	Foreign Funded
6	1	80	8	518	4	4
361694	39919	2263506	286043	15400804	24267	91886
193888	7348	1234945	113674	6563904	683	33050
167806	32572	1028561	172369	8836900	23585	58836
127913	24561	1386559	282061	11018777	23440	21858
		168574		733067	12740	
32348		409369	168400	3954059	3758	5015
126705	24561	1270173	279868	9575862	20940	14466
1208		105697	920	1346796	2500	6571
		10689	1274	96119		820
52793	25990	1074815	238100	9871440	16061	8671
2.96		1222.66	348.31	8424.86	3.84	48.37
1.14		339.74	99.04	3008.67		
		208.28	95.01	1746.41		
4532	377	60493	18606	385319	685	765
4456	350	66932	9998	378819	724	823

12-3 分资质等级建筑业企业生产情况（2015 年）
STATISTICS ON CONSTRUCTION ENTERPRISES BY GRADE（2015）

指 标	Item	总 计 Total	施工总承包 Contracted Construction
企业个数（不含劳务企业，个）	Number of Enterprises（Excluding Labor Enterprises, unit）	621	325
签订的建筑合同金额（万元）	Value of Signed Construction Contracts（10000 yuan）	18468120	16735292
上年结转建筑合同额	Value of Construction Contracts Carried forward from Previous Year	8147491	7663805
本年新签建筑合同额	Value of Construction Contracts Signed in This Year	10320628	9071487
建筑业总产值（万元）	Gross Output Value of Construction（10000 yuan）	12885168	11327180
# 装饰装修产值	Output of Decoration and Fitment	914381	104703
在外省完成的产值	Output Achieved out of Jiangsu Province	4572949	3973633
按构成分	**Grouped by Composition**		
建筑工程	Construction Projects	11312574	10047057
安装工程	Installation Projects	1463692	1186947
其它产值	Other Output Value	108902	93176
竣工产值（万元）	Output Value of Buildings Completed（10000 yuan）	11287870	9843029
房屋建筑施工面积（万平方米）	Floor Space of Buildings Under Construction（10000 sq.m）	10050.99	9893.79
房屋建筑竣工面积（万平方米）	Floor Space of Buildings Completed（10000 sq.m）	3448.59	3383.73
# 住 宅	Residential Buildings	2049.70	2018.34
平均从业人员（人）	Average Number of Staff of Calculating Labor Productivity（person）	470777	408339
直接从事生产经营活动的平均人数（人）	Average Number of Persons Directly Engaged in Production and Business Activities（person）	462102	392400

其中 of which				专业承包 Professional Contracting	其中 of which			
一级 First Grade	二级 Second Grade	三级及以下 Under Third Grade	其他 Others		一级 First Grade	二级 Second Grade	三级及以下 Under Third Grade	不分等级 Ungraded
51	131	142	1	296	36	82	169	9
11018258	4368508	1346046	2480	1732828	789125	336573	597884	9245
5206547	1932342	522436	2480	483686	247987	59827	173321	2552
5811711	2436166	823610		1249141	541139	276746	424564	6693
7140252	2784573	1402100	256	1557988	787338	293720	462507	14424
73370	20395	10938		809677	599366	126714	78913	4685
2943617	598350	431666		599316	403514	78112	113993	3697
5941285	2760273	1345244	256	1265517	690635	217282	344691	12909
1119254	15957	51736		276745	95882	72075	107273	1515
79713	8343	5120		15726	820	4363	10543	
6119663	2409581	1313786		1444841	782370	268839	378467	15165
6170.42	2759.63	961.44	2.30	157.20	10.74	11.55	134.91	
1956.25	1035.05	392.44		64.86	10.74	10.45	43.67	
1247.51	555.46	215.38		31.36			31.36	
260329	99895	47991	124	62438	28338	15755	17717	628
237218	100222	54845	115	69702	32669	17242	18967	824

12-4　分行业建筑业企业生产情况（2015 年）
STATISTICS ON CONSTRUCTION ENTERPRISES BY SECTOR（2015）

指　标	Item	合　计 Total	房　屋 建筑业 Construction of Buildings	土木工程 建 筑 业 Civil Engineering	建　筑 安装业 Construction Installation	建筑装饰和 其它建筑业 Buildings Decoration and Other Construction
企业个数（不含劳务企业，个）	Number of Enterprises（Excluding Labor Enterprises, unit）	621	211	152	82	176
签订的建筑合同金额（万元）	Value of Signed Construction Contracts（10,000 yuan）	18468120	12272686	2182567	2902576	1110291
上年结转建筑合同额	Value of Construction Contracts Carried forward from Previous Year	8147491	5941795	1024116	889846	291735
本年新签建筑合同额	Value of Construction Contracts Signed in This Year	10320628	6330891	1158451	2012730	818557
建筑业总产值（万元）	Gross Output Value of Construction（10000 yuan）	12885168	8361191	1553362	1971823	998792
# 装饰装修产值	Output of Decoration and Fitment	914381	99241	2890	41067	771184
在外省完成的产值	Output Achieved out of Jiangsu Province	4572949	2735472	269053	1209893	358530
按构成分	**Grouped by Composition**					
建筑工程	Construction Projects	11312574	8163596	1509844	703460	935674
安装工程	Installation Projects	1463692	128624	40657	1237642	56769
其它产值	Other Output Value	108902	68970	2861	30721	6349
竣工产值（万元）	Output Value of Buildings Completed（10000 yuan）	11287870	7179794	1245305	1876594	986178
房屋建筑施工面积（万平方米）	Floor Space of Buildings Under Construction（10000 sq.m）	10050.99	9517.87	114.82	414.76	3.55
房屋建筑竣工面积（万平方米）	Floor Space of Buildings Completed（10000 sq.m）	3448.59	3280.56	26.62	141.41	
# 住　宅	Residential Buildings	2049.70	1993.17	17.00	39.53	
平均从业人员（人）	Average Number of Staff of Calculating Labor Productivity（person）	470777	316659	45400	76724	31994
直接从事生产经营活动的平均人数（人）	Average Number of People Engaged in Main Business（person）	462102	309270	48561	69996	34275

12-5 分行业建筑业企业财务状况（2015 年）
FINANCIAL CONDITIONS OF CONSTRUCTION ENTERPRISES BY SECTOR（2015）

单位：万元（10000 yuan）

指标	Item	合计 Total	房屋建筑业 Construction of Buildings	土木工程建筑业 Civil Engineering	建筑安装业 Construction Installation	建筑装饰和其它建筑业 Buildings Decoration and Other Construction
年末资产负债	**Asset and Liabilities at Year-end**					
年初存货	Opening Stock	1992393	1278512	448197	89185	176499
流动资产	Current Assets	9402618	5089759	2533560	724522	1054777
固定资产	Fixed Assets	808455	383713	249970	88204	86569
固定资产原价	Original Value of Fixed Assets	1102255	457951	416734	110384	117185
累计折旧	Accumulative Total Depreciation	489545	187310	205849	40826	55560
#本年折旧	Depreciation Within the Year	65511	30278	20987	5543	8703
在建工程	Projects Under Construction	141352	81199	22666	17937	19549
资产合计	Total Assets	11008801	5831393	3107290	868199	1201919
流动负债	Liquid Liabilities	6241307	3515324	1590092	444981	690910
长期负债	Long-term Liabilities	161456	49033	109183	498	2743
负债合计	Total Liabilities	6469583	3612493	1714953	446978	695159
所有者权益	Owners' Equity	4539218	2218900	1392337	421221	506760
损益及分配	**Expenditure,Income and Distribution**					
营业收入	Business Income	11179012	6634353	1703375	1719938	1121347
营业税金及附加	Business Tax and Surcharges	375904	227637	58867	55385	34015
其他业务利润	Other Business Profit	5428	1865	212	912	2440
销售费用	Sales Expenses	24707	3697	7438	6037	7535
管理费用	Management and Financial Expenditures	264769	104851	70399	36020	53499
财务费用	Financial Costs	98638	69658	17381	3735	7863
营业利润	Operating Surplus	458673	221969	99975	85218	51511
利润总额	Total Profits	464871	220379	102502	87540	54450
补充资料	**Supplementary Material**					
应付职工薪酬	Remuneration Payable to Employees	2189657	1417969	206366	385772	179550

注：本表统计范围不含劳务企业。
Note： The statistical rang of this table doesn't including Labour Service Enterprises.

12-6　分登记注册类型建筑业企业财务状况（2015 年）
FINANCIAL CONDITIONS OF CONSTRUCTION ENTERPRISES BY REGISTER STATUS（2015）

指　标	Item	合　计 Total	内资企业 Domestic Funded Enterprises	国有企业 State-owned Enterprises
年末资产负债	**Asset and Liabilities at Year-end**			
年初存货	Opening Stock	1992393	1979651	22788
流动资产	Current Assets	9402618	9366431	176391
固定资产	Fixed Assets	808455	801221	22192
固定资产原价	Original Value of Fixed Assets	1102255	1094609	37756
累计折旧	Accumulative Total Depreciation	489545	488346	24734
#本年折旧	Depreciation Within the Year	65511	65188	2136
在建工程	Projects Under Construction	141352	140667	7980
资产合计	Total Assets	11008801	10963367	304783
流动负债	Liquid Liabilities	6241307	6220727	121087
长期负债	Long-term Liabilities	161456	161443	
负债合计	Total Liabilities	6469583	6447174	129558
所有者权益	Owners' Equity	4539218	4516193	175225
损益及分配	**Expenditure,Income and Distribution**			
营业收入	Business Income	11179012	11134543	124752
营业税金及附加	Business Tax and Surcharges	375904	375124	4192
其他业务利润	Other Business Profit	5428	5197	
销售费用	Sales Expenses	24707	24313	339
管理费用	Management and Financial Expenditures	264769	262488	5535
财务费用	Financial Costs	98638	98362	3291
营业利润	Operating Surplus	458673	457826	13403
利润总额	Total Profits	464871	464026	13503
补充资料	**Supplementary Material**			
应付职工薪酬	Remuneration Payable to Employees	2189657	2185618	17825

单位：万元（10000 yuan）

其　中　of　which				港澳台投资企　　业 Enterprises With Investment From HongKong, Macao and Taiwan	外商投资企　　业 Foreign Funded
集体企业 Collective-owned Enterprises	有限责任公司 Limited Liability Corporations	股份有限公司 Share-holding Corporations Ltd	私营企业 Private Enterprises		
	338053	50303	1568507	3301	9441
18365	1879846	437025	6854805	21304	14883
1298	96139	67859	613734	694	6539
2990	143374	54079	856411	1493	6153
1693	63528	18619	379772	799	401
163	5813	2092	54984	94	228
	8134	30517	94036		685
20991	2023836	640207	7973550	22949	22485
16262	1196823	301652	4584903	14611	5969
	89352	10425	61667	13	
16262	1314945	312077	4674333	14623	7786
4729	708892	328130	3299217	8325	14699
25654	1314588	464012	9205537	22335	22133
643	41199	15646	313444	312	468
218	2443	199	2337	231	
	4320	4358	15296	102	292
2813	50077	18406	185658	1241	1040
	1526	6058	87588	219	57
708	52785	34911	356019	213	634
690	56269	35053	358511	213	632
7144	293124	64348	1803177	1915	2125

12-7 分资质等级建筑业企业财务状况（2015 年）
FINANCIAL CONDITIONS OF CONSTRUCTION ENTERPRISES BY GRADE（2015）

指 标	Item	总 计 Total	施工总承包 Contracted Construction	其 中 一 级 First Grade
年末资产负债	**Asset and Liabilities at Year-end**			
年初存货	Opening Stock	1992393	1662602	747110
流动资产	Current Assets	9402618	7470315	3265188
固定资产	Fixed Assets	808455	631777	269720
固定资产原价	Original Value of Fixed Assets	1102255	853788	371179
累计折旧	Accumulative Total Depreciation	489545	379603	182551
# 本年折旧	Depreciation Within the Year	65511	50109	21517
在建工程	Projects Under Construction	141352	121175	66060
资产合计	Total Assets	11008801	8665125	3703294
流动负债	Liquid Liabilities	6241307	5036642	2204583
长期负债	Long-term Liabilities	161456	63576	16077
负债合计	Total Liabilities	6469583	5151017	2221642
所有者权益	Owners' Equity	4539218	3514108	1481652
损益及分配	**Expenditure,Income and Distribution**			
营业收入	Business Income	11179012	9352856	5761946
营业税金及附加	Business Tax and Surcharges	375904	320949	192563
其他业务利润	Other Business Profit	5428	2940	784
销售费用	Sales Expenses	24707	8765	2391
管理费用	Management and Financial Expenditures	264769	172235	72911
财务费用	Financial Costs	98638	86916	48647
营业利润	Operating Surplus	458673	366839	215944
利润总额	Total Profits	464871	368465	219265
补充资料	**Supplementary Material**			
应付职工薪酬	Remuneration Payable to Employees	2189657	1865400	1201208

注：本表统计范围不含劳务企业。
Note：The statistical rang of this table doesn't including Labour Service Enterprises.

单位：万元（10000 yuan）

of which			专业承包	其中 of which			
二级 Second Grade	三级及以下 Under Third Grade	其他 Others	Professional Contracting	一级 First Grade	二级 Second Grade	三级及以下 Under Third Grade	不分等级 Ungraded
691967	223018	506	329791	145188	83621	99561	1420
2986874	1209986	8267	1932303	936695	463718	512274	19616
237450	123914	693	176678	45221	49737	78869	2850
309442	172474	693	248467	78283	75370	91044	3771
122424	74048	580	109942	45190	33898	29696	1159
15032	13508	52	15402	5859	4763	4525	256
38989	16127		20177	8279	4620	7178	100
3513379	1439492	8960	2343676	1026859	541749	749667	25401
2092038	733916	6106	1204664	572616	284453	332663	14932
43328	4171		97880	80096	1786	15998	
2148865	774404	6106	1318566	652712	287691	362962	15201
1364514	665088	2854	1025110	374147	254057	386705	10201
2500620	1088990	1301	1826156	815284	460836	519434	30602
89771	38572	43	54955	25879	13354	14841	881
900	1256		2488	465	2029	-7	
3706	2669		15942	3628	6000	6183	131
61682	37613	29	92533	29746	33542	28259	987
26889	11338	42	11722	5518	2272	3831	101
91300	59506	89	91834	47543	18635	25290	366
89605	59507	89	96406	47446	23053	25547	360
460491	202161	1540	324258	147508	92614	80976	3161

13

CHAPTER 13

交通运输　邮电通信

TRANSPORTATION,POST AND TELCOMMUNICATIONS

13 交通运输 邮电通信 TRANSPORTATION, POST AND TELECOMMUNICATIONS

2015 年主要统计指标 MAJOR STATISTICAL INDICATORS OF 2015

客运量	Passenger Traffic	7673 万人	(10000 persons)
比上年增长	Over the Previous Year	-9.3%	
货运量	Freight Traffic	12954 万吨	(10000 tons)
比上年增长	Over the Previous Year	0.9%	
邮电业务收入	Revenue from Post & Telecommunication Services	78.66 亿元	(100 million yuan)
比上年增长	Over the Previous Year	6.9%	
年底本地网电话用户数	Number of Telephone Subscribers of Local Telephone Net	132.99 万户	(10000 households)
比上年增长	Over the Previous Year	-7.9%	
年底移动电话用户	Number of Mobile Phones Subscribers at Year-End	514.35 万户	(10000 households)
比上年增长	Over the Previous Year	4.7%	
年底互联网用户	Number of Internet Subscribers	199.84 万户	(10000 households)
比上年增长	Over the Previous Year	25.3%	

13-1 主要年份客、货运量
TOTAL PASSENGER AND FREIGHT TRAFFIC IN MAIN YEARS

年份 Year	客运量（万人）Passenger Traffic（10000 ersons）	其中 of which 铁路 Railways	民航 Civil Aviation	公路 Highways	水路 Waterways	货运量（万吨）Freight Traffic（10000 tons）	其中 of which 铁路 Railways	民航 Civil Aviation	公路 Highways	水路 Waterways
1949	192	41		41	110	96	2		17	78
1952	273	68		83	122	139	7		38	95
1957	535	69		170	296	168	13		24	131
1962	867	165		295	407	289	25		68	196
1965	712	110		438	164	405	20		111	274
1970	1005	125		618	262	498	28		131	339
1975	1837	180		1194	463	1072	47		319	706
1980	3071	245		2465	361	1839	51		621	1167
1981	3701	261		2917	523	1842	54		641	1147
1982	4074	282		3396	396	1926	59		679	1188
1983	4199	353		3563	283	2299	109		938	1251
1984	4373	429		3732	212	2880	117		1510	1253
1985	4373	488		3760	125	4351	128		2330	1893
1986	4389	511	1	3773	104	4836	135	0.02	2369	2332
1987	4958	544	2	4333	79	4612	132	0.05	2627	1853
1988	5259	647	3	4534	75	4983	126	0.06	3051	1806
1989	4877	395	3	4431	48	4812	131	0.06	3061	1620
1990	5048	585	3	4428	32	4375	126	0.06	2943	1306
1991	5361	579	3	4740	39	5998	136	0.05	4246	1616
1992	5372	639	5	4706	23	6266	162	0.12	3833	2271
1993	5492	700	6	4766	19	5987	158	0.10	3707	2121
1994	5336	697	10	4620	9	6173	162	0.20	3802	2209
1995	7270	734	7	6522	6	5804	187	0.10	3551	2065

13-1 续表 Continued

年 份 Year	客运量（万人） Passenger Traffic（10000 ersons）	其中 of which 铁 路 Railways	民 航 Civil Aviation	公 路 Highways	水 路 Waterways	货运量（万吨） Freight Traffic（10000 tons）	其中 of which 铁 路 Railways	民 航 Civil Aviation	公 路 Highways	水 路 Waterways
1996	7099	570	12	6513	4	5917	127	0.15	3843	1947
1997	7687	490	27	7168	2	5246	193	0.45	3375	1677
1998	8042	492	23	7526	1	5167	193	0.50	3340	1634
1999	9216	550	22	8643	1	4909	222	0.50	3299	1388
2000	10196	557	19	9620	1	4696	223	0.60	3335	1137
2001	10507	566	13	9928		4830	240	0.30	3445	1144
2002	11216	603	15	10598		5140	246	0.30	3783	1111
2003	11413	577	16	10820		5437	254	0.30	4040	1143
2004	12679	682	24	11973		5648	361	0.40	4334	952
2005	15235	715	15	14505		6032	296	0.47	4950	786
2006	16719	741	20	15958		6855	298	0.42	5692	865
2007	19096	745	21	18330		8083	396	0.54	6710	976
2008	21018	818	34	20166		8729	258	0.54	7490	980
2009	24778	840	23	23837	78	11206	232	0.53	9839	1134
2010	29361	874	27	28380	80	13109	219	0.55	11600	1290
2011	15845	981	36	14733	95	15644	195	0.68	13936	1512
2012	17257	1100	43	16030	84	17154	190	0.91	15344	1619
2013	8401	1218	65	6657	461	11713	170	1.18	9620	1922
2014	8458	1333	79	6769	277	12836	122	1.37	10705	2008
2015	7673	1369	181	5856	267	12954	106	2	10668	2178

注：1、公路、水路客、货运量 2011 年以前年份数据为全社会口径，2011 年起为营业性口径。
2、2013 年起公路、水路客、货运量采用运输经济专项调查结果。其中：公路客运量不再核算在公路上行驶的公交车、出租车客运量；公路货运量不再核算拖拉机、农用车货运量；水路客运量增加圩塘轮渡的客运量。

Note：1、The statistical coverage of passenger and cargo by land and river throughput before 2011 refers to the whole society, which has been altered to business statistical data form 2011.
2、The result of special survey on transportation economy is adopted as passenger and frieight traffic by land and water since 2013, of which, passenger traffic by highways excludes that of bus and taxi driven on highways, freight traffic by highways excludes that of tractor and agricultural vehicle and passenger traffic of Yutang Ferry is added to that by waterways.

13-2　主要年份客、货运周转量
PASSENGER TRAFFIC AND FREIGHT TRAFFIC IN MAIN YEARS

年 份 Year	客运周转量（万人公里） Passenger-kilometers (10000 persons-km)	其中 of which 公 路 Highways	其中 of which 水 路 Waterways	货运周转量（万吨公里） Freight Ton-kilometers (10000 tons-km)	其中 of which 公 路 Highways	其中 of which 水 路 Waterways
1949	4327	610	3717	6037	40	5997
1952	5681	1235	4446	7559	84	7475
1957	10032	3153	6879	7997	68	7929
1962	20259	9859	10400	13965	1004	12961
1965	13336	9723	3613	19800	1660	18140
1970	22934	17776	5158	28970	3272	25698
1975	40465	33385	7080	73230	12065	61165
1980	68882	62748	6134	144838	27546	117292
1981	79911	70592	9319	151476	30279	121197
1982	90280	82680	7600	166308	32469	133839
1983	94294	88286	6008	209359	36518	172841
1984	107560	102404	5156	223855	47519	176336
1985	125797	121910	3887	220817	63970	156847
1986	136856	133160	3696	245502	70345	175157
1987	152028	148706	3322	262000	81134	180866
1988	164462	161268	3194	273096	99083	174013
1989	162072	159840	2232	265580	108727	156853
1990	168514	166596	1918	246937	111072	135865
1991	193806	191781	2025	287995	128732	159263
1992	223327	222135	1192	376867	133152	243715
1993	226534	225580	954	377914	154140	223774
1994	191495	190916	579	380862	154382	226480
1995	310456	309924	532	354690	139846	214844

13-2 续表 Continued

年 份 Year	客运周转量(万人公里) Passenger-kilometers(10000 persons-km)	其 中 of which		货运周转量(万吨公里) Freight Ton-kilometers(10000 tons-km)	其 中 of which	
		公 路 Highways	水 路 Waterways		公 路 Highways	水 路 Waterways
1996	316737	316392	345	344144	138748	205396
1997	324783	324585	198	319055	142140	176915
1998	321356	321172	184	307452	135819	171633
1999	395343	395174	169	327542	148289	179253
2000	440379	440154	225	273472	145475	127997
2001	454239	454239		279312	150555	128757
2002	474890	474890		274835	151418	123417
2003	479180	479180		291913	164781	127132
2004	579976	579976		299376	187981	111395
2005	640944	640944		312269	220159	92110
2006	765984	765984		379974	267524	112450
2007	888260	888260		461815	328558	133257
2008	992311	992311		505902	369226	136676
2009	1286371	1286051	320	774413	596587	177826
2010	1541228	1540900	328	898400	698600	199800
2011	897763	897373	390	1098169	858887	239282
2012	976796	976342	454	1212857	948211	264646
2013	419436	417382	2054	1358597	996836	361761
2014	420540	419383	1157	1508146	1111871	396275
2015	403404	402300	1104	1609673	1172609	437064

注 :2013 年起公路、水路客、货周转量采用运输经济专项调查结果。
Note:The result of special survey on transportation economy is adopted as passenger-kilometer and frieight ton-kilometer by land and water since 2013.

13-3 历年公路总里程
TOTAL LENGTH OF HIGHWAYS OVER THE YEARS

单位：公里（km）

年份 Year	公路总里程 Total Length of Highways	其中 of which 高速公路 Expressway	一级公路 First Class	二级公路 Second Class	三级公路 Third Class	四级公路 Fourth Class	等外公路 Substandard Highways
1949	179			45	17	116	1
1950	179			45	17	116	1
1951	220			45	17	117	41
1952	220			45	17	117	41
1953	220			45	17	117	41
1954	220			45	17	117	41
1955	220			45	17	117	41
1956	256			45	53	117	41
1957	312			60	53	138	61
1958	390			60	53	181	96
1959	393			60	53	184	96
1960	405			60	65	184	96
1961	405			60	65	184	96
1962	405			60	65	184	96
1963	405			60	65	184	96
1964	442			60	69	217	96
1965	442			60	69	217	96
1966	471			60	83	217	111
1967	480			60	83	226	111
1968	515			60	83	261	111
1969	531			60	83	262	126
1970	531			60	83	262	126
1971	572			60	98	273	141
1972	613			60	98	308	147
1973	626			60	101	318	147
1974	659			60	101	351	147
1975	659			60	101	351	147
1976	663			60	101	355	147
1977	676			60	101	368	147
1978	717			60	101	409	147
1979	737			60	102	428	147
1980	838			73	101	499	165
1981	862			73	101	523	165
1982	907			88	104	546	169

13-3 续表 Continued

单位：公里（km）

年 份 Year	公路总里程 Total Length of Highways	其 中 of which 高速公路 Expressway	一级公路 First Class	二级公路 Second Class	三级公路 Third Class	四级公路 Fourth Class	等外公路 Substandard Highways
1983	940			90	97	590	163
1984	1020			95	130	628	167
1985	1044			102	140	635	167
1986	1106			134	155	650	167
1987	1183			155	201	660	167
1988	1215			162	232	654	167
1989	1215		5	185	233	628	164
1990	1215		5	192	263	613	142
1991	1226		5	230	308	615	68
1992	1227		5	236	337	588	61
1993	1228		5	249	348	573	53
1994	1230		5	299	362	511	53
1995	1241		41	311	348	500	41
1996	1296	43	33	338	346	483	53
1997	1313	43	77	319	342	479	53
1998	1344	43	122	315	339	472	53
1999	1384	43	140	313	374	471	43
2000	1384	43	144	321	362	471	43
2001	5165	43	200	457	910	2262	1293
2002	5232	43	250	467	926	2254	1292
2003	5404	60	297	532	987	2294	1234
2004	5999	117	336	736	1033	2694	1083
2005	5444	117	406	886	1266	1816	953
2006	5546	117	459	908	1247	2278	537
2007	6732	221	558	1095	1572	2763	523
2008	7185	221	809	1130	1229	3547	249
2009	7479	221	794	1167	1227	3849	221
2010	8348	221	855	1170	1282	4768	52
2011	8446	247	882	1179	1301	4784	52
2012	8677	268	918	1215	1312	4912	52
2013	8847	268	956	1236	1321	5014	52
2014	8906	268	988	1251	1336	5013	50
2015	9010	306	1043	1250	1292	5069	50

13-4 分地区客、货运量（2015 年）
TOTAL PASSENGER AND FREIGHT TRAFFIC BY REGION （2015）

指 标	Item	全 市 Whole Municipality	市 区 Urban Area	其中 of which #金坛区 Jintan District	溧阳市 Liyang City
客运量（万人）	**Passenger Traffic （10000 Persons）**	**7673**	**6595**	**723**	**1078**
铁 路	Railway	1369	1369		
公 路	Highway	5856	4834	723	1022
水 路	Waterway	267	211		56
民 航	Civil Aviation	181	181		
旅客周转量（万人公里）	**Passenger-kilometers （10000 persons-km）**	**403404**	**330935**	**49450**	**72469**
公 路	Highway	402300	330135	49450	72165
水 路	Waterway	1104	800		304
货运量（万吨）	**Freight Traffic （10000 tons）**	**12954**	**10477**	**2066**	**2477**
铁 路	Railway	106	106		
公 路	Highway	10668	8718	1031	1950
水 路	Waterway	2178	1651	1035	527
民 航	Civil Aviation	2	2		
货运周转量（万吨公里）	**Freight Ton-kilometers （10000 tons-km）**	**1609673**	**1292512**	**319159**	**317161**
公 路	Highway	1172609	960115	114445	212494
水 路	Waterway	437064	332397	204714	104667

13-5 公路和内河航道里程数（2015 年）
TOTAL LENGTH OF HIGHWAYS AND NAVIGABLE INLAND WATERWAYS （2015）

指 标	Item	全 市 Whole Municipality	市 区 Urban Area	其中 of which #金坛区 Jintan District	溧阳市 Liyang City
公路总里程	**Total Length of Highways**	**9010**	**6453**	**2117**	**2557**
# 高速公路	Expressway	306	229	79	77
一级公路	First Class	1043	911	168	132
二级公路	Second Class	1250	952	318	298
三级公路	Third Class	1292	908	179	384
四级公路	Fourth Class	5069	3403	1324	1666
航道里程	**Length of Navigable Inland Waterways**	**1086**	**792**	**259**	**293**
# 通机动船里程	Length of Navigation of Motor Vessels	864	577	200	287

13-6 分地区全社会港口吞吐量（2015 年）
THE WHOLE-SOCIETY PORTS THROUGHPUT BY REGIONS (2015)

指 标	Item	全 市 Whole Municipality	市 区 Urban Area	其中 of which #长江港 Changzhou Yangtze River Port	溧阳市 Liyang City
码头泊位个数（个）	**Number of Berths (unit)**	**857**	**535**	**31**	**322**
货物吞吐量（万吨）	**Cargo at Ports Throughput (10 000 tons)**	**8984**	**6816**	**3620**	**2168**
#外 贸	Freight Trade	409	· 409	409	
按进出港分	Divided by Arrive at/Leave Port				
出 港	Leave Port	4364	2802	1333	1562
#外 贸	Foreign Trade	149	149	149	
进 港	Arrive at Port	4620	4014	2287	606
#外 贸	Foreign Trade	260	261	261	
集装箱吞吐量	**International Containes**				
箱 数（万标箱）	Containers (10000 TEU)	22	22	22	
重 量（万吨）	Weight (10000 tons)	309	309	309	
#货 物	Freight	265	265	265	

13-7 分地区民用船舶拥有量（2015 年）
NUMBER OF PRIVATE SHIPS BY REGION (2015)

指 标	Item	全 市 Whole Municipality	市 区 Urban Area	其中 of which # 金坛区 Jintan District	溧阳市 Liyang City
民用船舶拥有量（艘）	**Number of Private Ships (number)**	**2095**	**1399**	**849**	**696**
1、机动船合计（艘）	Total Number of Motorboats (number)	2060	1364	824	696
客 船 （艘）	Passenger Ship (number)	8	8		
（客位）	(rated seats)	1019	1019		
（千瓦）	(KW)	1407	1407		
货 船 （艘）	Cargo Ship (number)	3446	2750	823	696
（吨位）	(tonnage)	1160837	855211	524935	305626
（千瓦）	(KW)	312764	217276	125271	95488
拖 船 （艘）	Tugboat (number)	5	5	1	
（千瓦）	(KW)	6808	6808	330	
2、驳 船（艘）	Barge (number)	35	35	25	
（吨位）	(tonnage)	11450	11450	8600	

13-8　公路运输汽车拥有量（2015 年）
NUMBER OF HIGHWAY TRANSPORTATION VEHICLES （2015）

指　标	Item	合　计 Total	其 中 of which 个　体 Private
公路运输汽车拥有量	**Number of Highway Transportation Vehicles**	**60576**	**25663**
载客汽车	Passenger Service Vehicles		
辆　数	Number	2150	
客 位（客位）	Rated Seats （10000 seats）	93643	
载货汽车	Trucks		
辆　数	Number	58426	25663
# 普通载货汽车	Common Trucks	47868	23633
吨　位（吨）	Tonnage （10000 tons）	407531	136252
# 普通载货汽车	Common Trucks	260979	105817

注：表中车辆是指持有《道路运输经营许可证》的营运车辆。
Note:Vehicle indicated in the table refers to the operating vehicle with Road Transportation Operation Permit.

13-9　机动车辆数（2015 年）
NUMBER OF MOTOR VEHICLES （2015）

单位：辆（unit）

指　标	Item	合　计 Total	其 中 of which 私　人 Private
民用汽车	**Civil Vehicles**	**968334**	**821486**
客　车	Passenger Vehicles	895759	793676
# 大　型	Large-scale	6495	26
中　型	Medium-sized	4080	1297
小　型	Compact car	877539	785081
微　型	Minicar	7645	7272
# 轿　车	Sedan	648526	591507
货　车	Freight Trucks	68638	27047
# 重　型	Heavy-duty	24650	5170
中　型	Medium-sized	11357	1975
轻　型	Pick-up Truck	32429	19741
微　型	Minicar	202	161
其他汽车	Other Motorcar	3937	763
摩托车	**Motorcycle**	**134906**	**133164**
# 普通摩托车	Ordinary Motorcycle	134468	132729
轻便摩托车	Scooter	438	435
挂　车	**Trailer**	**4270**	**596**
其他机动车	**Other Motor Vehicles**	**23**	**5**
附：机动车驾驶员人数（人）	**Number of Drivers of Motor Vehicles （person）**	**1594309**	
# 汽车驾驶员人数	NumberofDriverofVehicles	1495883	

13-10 历年邮电业务主要指标
MAJOR INDICATORS OF POST AND TELECOMMUNICATIONS OVER THE YEARS

年 份 Year	邮电局所数 （个） Number of Post and Telecommun-ications Offices （unit）	邮路单程长度 （公里） Lengh of Postal Routs （one way,km）	邮电业务总量 （万元） Business Volume of Post and Telecommunications （10000 yuan）	市话交换机容量 （门） Capacity of Urban Telephones Exchanges （line）
1952	261		235	1620
1953	282		266	1640
1954	263		266	1650
1955	213		259	1670
1956	210		284	1670
1957	201		302	1670
1958	249	4190	372	1830
1959	194	3999	525	2730
1960	204	3642	619	3030
1961	203	3012	600	3030
1962	189	2740	514	3020
1963	193	3776	513	3120
1964	194	6237	537	3180
1965	171	7579	567	3280
1966	171	7953	593	3280
1967	173	8330	531	3280
1968	173	8330	503	3280
1969	170	9311	589	3180
1970	241	8937	662	3180
1971	244	8452	669	3180
1972	238	9496	747	3250
1973	203	9629	792	4100
1974	204	10043	884	4250
1975	207	10217	928	4250
1976	207	10427	964	4250
1977	208	10076	1031	5250
1978	209	10029	1127	6250
1979	210	9948	1202	6420
1980	206	10108	1368	7420
1981	212	4554	1470	7850
1982	215	2854	1561	7400
1983	212	2762	1743	7400
1984	217	2788	1920	12350
1985	218	3078	2454	17200
1986	215	2065	2780	17200

13-10 续表 Continued

年 份 Year	邮电局所数 （个） Number of Post and Telecommun-ications Offices（unit）	邮路单程长度 （公里） Lengh of Postal Routs（one way,km）	邮电业务总量 （万元） Business Volume of Post and Telecommunications（10000 yuan）	市话交换机容量 （门） Capacity of Urban Telephones Exchanges（line）
1987	211	2233	3442	17200
1988	210	1892	4776	23000
1989	204	1889	6026	32000
1990	196	1881	7477	40500
1991	193	1715	10315	44000
1992	181	1790	16184	67500
1993	167	2226	27740	121300
1994	166	2516	43122	144000
1995	220	2502	56746	160000
1996	223	2419	77169	402000
1997	233	5509	107951	539609
1998	297	5776	131919	560375
1999	255	6297	175449	539108
2000	248	9401	284105	606730
2001	263	9799	192078	675348
2002	263	9799	247394	1142675
2003	375	9947	281939	1342600
2004	250	10129	318161	1332400
2005	250	10129	348747	1311800
2006	166	9045	391996	1712600
2007	166	10161	451700	2918700
2008	160	8995	505176	2975000
2009	190	7903	538059	2884424
2010	167	3740	574083	2844144
2011	151	4269	594741	3099600
2012	150	4269	644801	3658000
2013	150	6241	735200	5818300
2014	147	6097	757006	9557200
2015	150	6946	820131	3190100

注：1、从 2006 年起邮电局所数不包括电信网点数字；1952-2000 年邮电业务总量按 1990 年价格计算，2001 年起按 2000 年价格计算。
2、年末邮路单程长度不包括速递邮路单程长度。

Note：1、The number of post stations and offices excludes the number of telecommunication network offices since the year of 2006.The total business volumes of post and telecommunication from 1952 to 2000 have been calculated by the price of 1990, The figures from the year of 2001 have been calculated according to the price in 2000.
2、The one-way postal length by the end of year does not include the one-way length of postal express.

13-11 分地区邮政电信情况（2015 年）
POSTS AND TELECOMMUNCIATIONS BY REGION（2015）

指 标	Item	全 市 Whole Municipality	市 区 Urban Area	其中 of which # 金坛区 Jintan District	溧阳市 Liyang City
年末邮政机构数（个）	**Number of Network Points of Post**	**150**	**111**	**26**	**39**
# 邮政局	Post Offices	3	2	1	1
邮政支局	Post Branches	124	106	26	18
自办所	Self-Run Post Services	20	2		18
年末邮路单程长度（公里）	**Lengh of Postal Routes （single way,km）**	**6946**	**6383**	**404**	**563**
农村投递线路（公里）	**Rural Delivery Routes （km）**	**13827**	**11076**	**2708**	**2751**
年末电话交换机总容量（万门）	**Total Capacity of Urban and Rural Telephone Exchanges （10000 lines）**	**319.01**	**309.16**	**11.11**	**9.85**
邮电业务收入（万元）	**Total Business Volume of Post & Telecommunications （10000 yuan）**	**786631**	**706180**	**67200**	**80451**
邮政行业业务收入	Total Business Volume of Post Services	259500	247074	13268	12426
# 快递业务收入	Express business income	173700			
通信业务收入	Total Business Volume of Communications Services	527131	459106	53932	68025
主要业务量	**Major Business Volume**				
函 件（万件）	Number of Letters （10000 pcs）	1211	1142	117	69
快 递（万件）	Pieces of Express Mail Services （10000 pcs）	11710			
包 件（万件）	Pieces of Courier Services （10000 pcs）	6.30	5.67	0.33	0.63
汇 票（万件）	Number of Bill of Exchange （10000 pcs）	17.00	13.40	4.90	3.60
集邮业务（万枚）	Business Volume of Philately （10000 pcs）	650.00	577.00	104.00	73.00
年末本地网电话用户数（万户）	**Number of Telephone Subscribers of Local Telephone Net （10000 households）**	**132.99**	**112.14**	**17.87**	**20.85**
城市电话用户	Urban Telephone Subscribers	68.55	59.03	8.39	9.51
# 住 宅	Residential Telephone Subscribers	40.02	33.78	6.51	6.24
农村电话用户	Rural Telephone Subscribers	50.87	39.10	8.13	11.77
# 住 宅	Residential Telephone Subscribers	37.57	22.85	8.85	14.72
无线市话用户	Wireless Urban Telephone Subscribers	0.86	0.85	0.02	0.01
年末移动电话用户数（万户）	**Number of Mobile Telephone Subscribers （10000 households）**	**514.35**	**444.06**	**58.10**	**70.29**
#3G 用户	3G users	132.15	130.56	1.43	1.59
4G 用户	4G users	260.43	253.53	5.76	6.90
年末互联网用户（万户）	**Number of Internet Subscribers（10000 households）**	**199.84**	**184.63**	**12.82**	**15.21**
# 宽带网用户	Widebband Network Subscribers	190.43	175.31	12.69	15.12

注：1、年末电话交换机总容量不包括无线市话，宽带网用户中含无线上网用户。
2、年末邮路单程长度不包括速递邮路单程长度。
3、邮政行业业务收入及快递业务量是指邮政企业和规模以上快递服务企业的业务收入和业务总量。

Note：1、Total capacity of urban and rural telephone exchanges doesn't including wireless urban telephone,internet subscribers include wireless internet subscribers.
2、The one-way postal length by the end of year does not include the one-way length of postal express.
3、Business revenues of the post service and business volumes of the express mail delivery service are the revenues and volumes of postal companies and express delivery companies above the designated size.

14

CHAPTER 14

批发零售 住宿餐饮

WHOLESALE AND RETAIL, ACCOMMODATION AND CATERING

14 批发零售　住宿餐饮
WHOLESALE AND RETAIL, ACCOMMODATION AND CATERING

2015 年主要统计指标
MAJOR STATISTICAL INDICATORS OF 2015

社会消费品零售总额	Total Retail of Consumer Goods	1990.45 亿元	(100 million yuan)
比上年增长	Over the Previous Year	10.3%	
限额以上批发零售贸易业商品销售总额	Total Sales of Wholesale and Retail Trade above Designated Size	3229.33 亿元	(100 million yuan)
超亿元商品交易市场成交额	Transaction Value of Trade Market of Goods	2001.48 亿元	(100 million yuan)
比上年增长	Over the Previous Year	0.4%	

14-1 历年分地区社会消费品零售总额
TOTAL RETAIL SALES OF CUNSUMER GOODS BY REGION OVER THE YEARS

单位：万元（10000 yuan）

年 份 Year	全 市 Whole Municipality	其 中 of which	
		市 区 Urban Area	溧阳市 Liyang City
1949	8102	5816	1389
1950	9594	7076	1576
1951	11884	8727	1869
1952	12572	8833	2215
1953	14109	9664	2685
1954	14814	10163	2813
1955	13435	9007	2773
1956	14622	9869	2927
1957	14603	10067	2725
1958	17975	12581	3279
1959	19734	14172	3220
1960	22434	16325	3589
1961	18873	13966	2794
1962	20377	14290	3541
1963	18044	12217	3569
1964	19142	12326	4055
1965	21379	13042	4857
1966	22577	13729	5002
1967	23951	14451	5329
1968	21685	12506	5356
1969	21764	11629	5945
1970	26295	14902	6897
1971	26512	14514	7461
1972	30343	17743	7551
1973	31821	17804	8376
1974	34606	20093	8639
1975	38450	23473	8692
1976	40233	24572	8951
1977	44298	27330	9594
1978	48236	28813	10881
1979	58116	34682	13371
1980	72740	42012	17880
1981	79614	48181	17532
1982	89417	53600	20312

单位：万元（10000 yuan）

年 份 Year	全 市 Whole Municipality	其中 of which 市 区 Urban Area	溧阳市 Liyang City
1983	108328	65763	22645
1984	129310	81806	25874
1985	181736	119591	35557
1986	202929	133243	39765
1987	248014	165286	46660
1988	323678	213641	61009
1989	363259	242555	63731
1990	381931	262148	66529
1991	436920	300243	76502
1992	558904	402730	97255
1993	782257	547972	132046
1994	1002394	673218	191109
1995	1317764	849886	285210
1996	1575902	1016554	330375
1997	1679581	1110655	334340
1998	1739300	1143964	341290
1999	1844235	1208355	364403
2000	2023126	1338778	391687
2001	2226101	1480205	425803
2002	2488005	1659780	469821
2003	2806470	1907533	494016
2004	3240528	2193610	581878
2005	4449415	3292101	652950
2006	5178307	3840209	753775
2007	6144075	4581050	881159
2008	7640631	5740836	1072741
2009	8915444	6745496	1218920
2010	10543943	7906496	1475388
2011	12361038	9262314	1732009
2012	14133300	10583451	1982562
2013	15970055	11923773	2274813
2014	18041930	13466600	2592161
2015	19904510	17151528	2752982

注：1、2005 年至 2008 年数据已按照第二次经济普查结果、2009 年至 2013 年数据已按照第三次经济普查结果重新进行了修订。
2、2015 年行政区划调整，市区包含金坛区数据。

Note: 1、 The statistic data from year 2005 to year 2008 was adjusted in accordance with the second economic survey and the statistic data from year 2009 to year 2013 was adjusted in accordance with the third economic survey.
2、With the administrative district adjustment in 2015, the city's urban area now includes Jintan District.

14-2　分地区社会消费品零售总额（2015 年）
TOTAL RETAIL SALES OF CONSUMER GOODS BY REGION（2015）

指　标	Item	全　市 Whole Municipality	市　区 Urban Area
总　计	**Total**	**19904510**	**17151528**
按销售地区分	**Grouped by Sales Region**		
城　镇	Urban and Town	18610576	16117348
乡　村	Countryside	1293935	1034180
按行业分	**Grouped by Sector**		
批发零售业	Wholesale,Retail Sales	18257888	15721319
住宿餐饮业	Accommodation Catering Trade	1646623	1430209

14-3　分地区限额以上批发零售贸易业商品销售总额（2015 年）
TOTAL COMMODITIES SALES VOLUME ABOVE DESIGNATED SIZE IN WHOLESALE AND RETAIL TRADE BY REGION （2015）

指　标	Item	全　市 Whole Municipality	市　区 Urban Area
限额以上企业	**Enterprises above Designated Size**	**32293341**	**30099738**
批　发	Wholesale	23942578	22342741
零　售	Retail	8350763	7756996

14-4　分地区限额以上住宿餐饮业营业额（2015 年）
SALES TURNOVER ABOVE DESIGNATED SIZE IN ACCOMMODATION & CATERING TRADE GROUPED BY REGION（2015）

指　标	Item	全　市 Whole Municipality	市　区 Urban Area
限额以上企业	**Enterprises above Designated Size**	**554271**	**482262**
住　宿	Accommodation	206075	140253
餐　饮	Catering	348196	342009

单位：万元（10000 yuan）

其　中 of which					溧阳市 Liyang City
金坛区 Jintan District	武进区 wujin District	新北区 Xinbei District	天宁区 Tianning District	钟楼区 Zhonglou District	
2226107	**4798643**	**2639478**	**4296510**	**3190790**	**2752982**
1993414	4323368	2462633	4249249	3088684	2493228
232693	475275	176845	47262	102105	259754
2039953	4313659	2492666	3945722	2929320	2536569
186154	484985	146812	350789	261470	216414

单位：万元（10000 yuan）

其　中 of which					溧阳市 Liyang City
金坛区 Jintan District	武进区 wujin District	新北区 Xinbei District	天宁区 Tianning District	钟楼区 Zhonglou District	
1751037	**7195530**	**6618024**	**7723694**	**6811453**	**2193603**
1390453	5002391	5719471	5379068	4851359	1599836
360585	2193139	898553	2344627	1960094	593767

单位：万元（10000 yuan）

其　中 of which					溧阳市 Liyang City
金坛区 Jintan District	武进区 wujin District	新北区 Xinbei District	天宁区 Tianning District	钟楼区 Zhonglou District	
20594	**84813**	**100161**	**214602**	**62093**	**72009**
9963	38788	54928	26076	10499	65822
10631	46025	45233	188526	51594	6187

14-5 限额以上批发和零售业基本情况（2015 年）
BASIC CONDITIONS ENTERPRISES ABOVE DESIGNATED SIZE IN WHOLESALE AND RETAIL TRADES（2015）

指 标	Item	法人企业数（个）Number of Corporations (unit)	零售营业面积（平方米）Floor Space Of Retail Business (sq.m)	从业人员（人）Persons Engaged (Person)
总 计	**Total**	**1895**	**2172715**	**70396**
市 区	Urban Area	1709	1945640	64465
金坛区	Jintan District	133	144142	6042
武进区	Wujin District	330	589983	18165
#经开区	Economic Development Zone	74	73031	1452
新北区	Xinbei District	406	287373	9598
天宁区	Tianning District	498	533076	18058
钟楼区	Zhonglou District	342	391066	12602
溧阳市	Liyang City	186	227075	5931
批发贸易业	**Wholesale Trade**	**1316**	**277269**	**30904**
#国有控股	State-owned and State Share Holding	16	40192	2322
按地区分	**Grouped by Region**			
市 区	Urban Area	1211	255786	29127
金坛区	Jintan District	80	39922	3643
武进区	Wujin District	234	22759	8424
#经开区	Economic Development Zone	56	1093	810
新北区	Xinbei District	344	106258	5931
天宁区	Tianning District	366	43801	6556
钟楼区	Zhonglou District	187	43046	4573
溧阳市	Liyang City	105	21483	1777
按登记注册类型分	**Group by Registration Status**			
内 资	Domestic Investment	1298	261664	29567
国 有	State-owned	5	30302	450
集 体	Collective-owned	2		28
股份合作	Share-holding Cooperative	1		142
有限责任公司	Limited Liability Corporations	124	23135	3702
股份有限公司	Share-holding Cooperative Ltd.	3	10122	2293
私 营	Private	1144	194068	21794
其 他	Others	19	4037	1158
港澳台商投资	Hong Kong,Macao and Taiwan Funded	11	6368	636
外商投资	Foreign Investment	7	9237	701
按主要行业分	**Group by Sector**			
农、林、牧产品批发	Wholesale of Products of Agriculture, Forestry and Animal Husbandry	65	14949	5110
食品、饮料及烟草制品批发	Wholesale of Food,Beverages and Tobaccos	36	46895	2576
纺织、服装及家庭用品批发	Specialized Retail of Textile, Garments and Commodity	141	15859	4059
文化、体育用品及器材批发	Specialized Retail of Stationers Goods, Sports Goods and Apparatus	16	1771	308
医药及医疗器材批发	Wholesale of Medicine and Medical Appliance	15	2476	1958
矿产品、建材及化工产品批发	Wholesale of Mineral Product, Building Material and Chemical Product	825	146862	11273
机械设备、五金产品及电子产品批发	Wholesale of Machinery, Hardware,Transport, Electric and Electronic Equipment	154	26328	4682
贸易经纪与代理	Trade Broker and Agent	23	4439	464
其他批发	Others	41	17690	474
零售贸易业	**Retail Trade**	**579**	**1895446**	**39492**
#国有控股	State-owned and State Share Holding	16	68925	1566
按地区分	**Grouped by Region**			
市 区	Urban Area	498	1689854	35338

14-5 续表 Continued

指 标	Item	法人企业数（个） Number of Corporations (unit)	零售营业面 积（平方米） Floor Space Of Retail Business (sq.m)	从业人员（人） Persons Engaged (Person)
金坛区	Jintan District	53	104220	2399
武进区	Wujin District	96	567224	9741
#经开区	Economic Development Zone	18	71938	642
新北区	Xinbei District	62	181115	3667
天宁区	Tianning District	132	489275	11502
钟楼区	Zhonglou District	155	348020	8029
溧阳市	Liyang City	81	205592	4154
按登记注册类型分	**Group by Registration Status**			
内 资	Domestic Investment	566	1736090	36393
国 有	State-owned	3	2873	161
集 体	Collective-owned	5	3952	43
股份合作	Share-holding Cooperative	1	300	12
有限责任公司	Limited Liability Corporations	77	516414	8120
股份有限公司	Share-holding Cooperative Ltd.	7	89524	1500
私 营	Private	468	1119425	26531
其 他	Others	5	3602	26
港澳台商投资	Hong Kong,Macao and Taiwan Funded	9	119420	2311
外商投资	Foreign Investment	4	39936	788
按主要行业分	**Group by Sector**			
综合零售	Comprehensive Retail	47	566512	10374
食品、饮料及烟草制品专门零售	Speicalized Retail of Food, Beverage and Tobacco	46	20043	1150
纺织、服装及日用品专门零售	Specialized Retail of Textile, Garments and Commodity	33	26997	1234
文化、体育用品及器材专门零售	Specialized Retail of Stationers Goods, Sports Goods and Apparatus	62	140384	3895
医药及医疗器材专门零售	Specialized Retail of Medicine and Medical aappliance	23	57743	4198
汽车、摩托车、燃料及零配件专门零售	Specialized Retail of Automobile, Motorcycle, Fuel and Fittings	229	751692	12525
家用电器及电子产品专门零售	Specialized Retail of Household Appliance and Electronic Products	76	214995	3324
五金、家具及室内装修材料专门零售	Specialized Retail of Hardware, Furniture and Interior Decoration Materials	44	91150	2317
货摊、无店铺及其他零售业	Stall，Retail without Shops and Other Retail	19	25930	475
按经营方式分	**Group by Means of Operation**			
独立门店	Independent Store	504	1507340	30019
连锁总店（总部）	Chain Headquarters （HQ）	11	133211	3315
连锁门店	Chain Store	21	194819	4275
其 他	Others	43	60076	1883
按零售业态分	**Group by Retail Size**			
食杂店	Traditional Grocery Stores	3	515	30
便利店	Convenience Stores	3	2460	169
超 市	Supermarket	14	46625	2923
大型超市	Large Supermarket	12	200068	3911
百货店	Composite Store	24	323618	3615
专业店	Specialized Store	360	799829	16836
专卖店	Speciality Store	135	458762	9133
家居建材店	Home Building Materials Stores	7	41930	1598
厂家直销中心	Factory Outlet Centers	12	18719	762
网上商店	Online stores	5	2200	451

14-6　限额以上个体批发零售业基本情况（2015 年）
BASIC CONDITIONS ENTERPRISES ABOVE DESIGNATED SIZE IN INDIVIDUAL WHOLESALE AND RETAIL TRADES（2015）

指　标	Item	法人企业数（个）Number of Corporations（unit）	零售营业面积（平方米）Floor Space Of Retail Business（sq.m）	从业人员（人）Persons Engaged（Person）
总　计	**Total**	**1012**	**240672**	**8537**
市　区	Urban Area	951	229006	7960
金坛区	Jintan District	67	20137	402
武进区	Wujin District	250	58886	2504
#经开区	Economic Development Zone	23	11454	223
新北区	Xinbei District	82	8075	582
天宁区	Tianning District	126	23831	1155
钟楼区	Zhonglou District	426	118077	3317
溧阳市	Liyang City	61	11666	577
批发贸易业	**Wholesale Trade**	**321**	**91416**	**3395**
按主要行业分	**Group by Sector**			
农、林、牧产品批发	Wholesale of Products of Agriculture, Forestry and Animal Husbandry	69	5352	568
食品、饮料及烟草制品批发	Wholesale of Food,Beverages and Tobaccos	90	18270	592
纺织、服装及家庭用品批发	Specialized Retail of Textile, Garments and Commodity	79	52459	1083
矿产品、建材及化工产品批发	Wholesale of Mineral Product, Building Material and Chemical Product	66	14055	1006
机械设备、五金产品及电子产品批发	Wholesale ofMachinery,Hardware, Transport, Electric and Electronic Equipment	17	1280	146
零售贸易业	**Retail Trade**	**691**	**149256**	**5142**
按主要行业分	**Group by Sector**			
综合零售	Comprehensive Retail	61	35999	828
食品、饮料及烟草制品专门零售	Speicalized Retail of Food, Beverage and Tobacco	158	21229	1118
纺织、服装及日用品专门零售	Specialized Retail of Textile, Garments and Commodity	77	21928	641
文化、体育用品及器材专门零售	Specialized Retail of Stationers Goods, Sports Goods and Apparatus	5	800	43
医药及医疗器材专门零售	Specialized Retail of Medicine and Medical Appliance	2	500	8
汽车、摩托车、燃料及零配件专门零售	Specialized Retail of Automobile, Motorcycle, Fuel and Fittings	47	7659	245
家用电器及电子产品专门零售	Specialized Retail of Household Appliance and Electronic Products	8	2360	38
五金、家具及室内装修材料专门零售	Specialized Retail of Hardware, Furniture and Interior Decoration Materials	290	51031	2007
货摊、无店铺及其他零售业	Stall，Retail without Shops and Other Retail	43	7750	214
按经营方式分	**Group by Means of Operation**			
独立门店	Independent Store	678	143008	4941
连锁总店（总部）	Chain Headquarters（HQ）	1	183	6
连锁门店	Chain Store	5	4470	103
其　他	Others	7	1595	92
按零售业态分	**Group by Retail Size**			
食杂店	Traditional Grocery Stores	59	9315	490
便利店	Convenience Stores	60	5476	265
折扣店	Discount Stores	1	180	6
超　市	Supermarket	30	24856	626
大型超市	Large Supermarket	1	6000	53
百货店	Composite Store	44	8102	320
专业店	Specialized Store	159	25143	903
专卖店	Speciality Store	18	3175	120
家居建材店	Home Building Materials Stores	316	66659	2341
厂家直销中心	Factory Outlet Centers	3	350	18

14-7 限额以上批发零售贸易业商品购进、销售、库存总额（2015 年）
TOTAL PURCHASES, SALES AND INVENTORY OF WHOLESALE AND RETAIL TRADE ABOVE DESIGNATED SIZE （2015）

单位：万元（10000 yuan）

指标	Item	购进总额 Total Purchases	销售额 Total Sales	其中 of which 批发额 Wholesale	零售额 Retail Sales	年末库存总额 Inventory (year-end)
总 计	**Total**	**28280852**	**32293341**	**23656379**	**8636962**	**1872373**
市 区	Urban Area	26296755	30099738	22116599	7983139	1781692
金坛区	Jintan District	1428276	1751037	1369041	381996	88356
武进区	Wujin District	6551913	7195530	4958031	2237499	363657
#经开区	Economic Development Zone	1550279	1631772	1541439	90333	24374
新北区	Xinbei District	6038111	6618024	5643171	974853	558356
天宁区	Tianning District	7027397	7723694	5593025	2130669	454611
钟楼区	Zhonglou District	5251059	6811453	4553331	2258122	316711
溧阳市	Liyang City	1984097	2193603	1539780	653823	90681
批发贸易业	**Wholesale Trade**	**21203478**	**23942578**	**22957185**	**985392**	**1152089**
#国有控股	State-owned and State Share Holding	887117	1966449	1516801	449648	98346
按地区分	**Grouped by Region**					
市 区	Urban Area	19737560	22342741	21439848	902894	1110001
金坛区	Jintan District	1141602	1390453	1367820	22633	59583
武进区	Wujin District	4725114	5002391	4954953	47438	157528
#经开区	Economic Development Zone	1472111	1545391	1541034	4356	17366
新北区	Xinbei District	5369932	5719471	5534542	184929	488097
天宁区	Tianning District	4964002	5379068	5358194	20874	228806
钟楼区	Zhonglou District	3536910	4851359	4224339	627020	175986
溧阳市	Liyang City	1465918	1599836	1517338	82499	42088
按登记注册类型分	**Group by Registration Status**					
内 资	Domestic Investment	20806864	23484412	22546270	938142	1143641
国 有	State-owned	532107	716517	716517		43000
集 体	Collective-owned	5206	5365	5365		181
股份合作	Share-holding Cooperative	606151	636019	636019		5013
有限责任公司	Limited Liability Corporations	4093521	4353395	4157908	195486	216134
股份有限公司	Share-holding Cooperative Ltd.	132473	964990	510976	454015	19720
私 营	Private	15308640	16658956	16374797	284158	851751
其 他	Others	128766	149170	144687	4483	7842
港澳台商投资	Hong Kong,Macao and Taiwan Funded	315077	365171	317921	47250	5941
外商投资	Foreign Investment	81537	92994	92994		2507
按主要行业分	**Group by Sector**					
农、林、牧产品批发	Wholesale of Products of Agriculture, Forestry and Animal Husbandry	795886	952080	920034	32046	85268
食品、饮料及烟草制品批发	Wholesale of Food,Beverages and Tobaccos	929349	1175709	1161130	14579	84764
纺织、服装及家庭用品批发	Specialized Retail of Textile, Garments and Commodity	1648098	1816988	1766401	50587	93171
文化、体育用品及器材批发	Specialized Retail of Stationers Goods, Sports Goods and Apparatus	128285	139508	136810	2698	266473
医药及医疗器材批发	Wholesale of Medicine and Medical Appliance	331446	367724	359554	8170	26019
矿产品、建材及化工产品批发	Wholesale of Mineral Product, Building Material and Chemical Product	14238002	15984627	15226736	757892	476693
机械设备、五金产品及电子产品批发	Wholesale ofMachineryHardware,Transport, Electric and Electronic Equipment	2350989	2641387	2526138	115250	96545
贸易经纪与代理	Trade Broker and Agent	306030	343875	343875		5518
其他批发	Others	475393	520678	516508	4170	17639
零售贸易业	**Retail Trade**	**7077374**	**8350763**	**699193**	**7651570**	**720284**
#国有控股	State-owned and State Share Holding	642475	852432	342060	510371	30925
按地区分	**Grouped by Region**					
市 区	Urban Area	6559195	7756996	676751	7080245	671691

14-7　续表　Continued

指　标	Item	购进总额 Total Purchases	销售额 Total Sales	其中 of which 批发额 Wholesale	零售额 Retail Sales	年末库存总额 Inventory (year-end)
金坛区	Jintan District	286674	360585	1222	359363	28773
武进区	Wujin District	1826799	2193139	3077	2190061	206129
#经开区	Economic Development Zone	78168	86382	405	85977	7008
新北区	Xinbei District	668179	898553	108628	789924	70259
天宁区	Tianning District	2063395	2344627	234832	2109795	225805
钟楼区	Zhonglou District	1714148	1960094	328992	1631102	140725
溧阳市	Liyang City	518179	593767	22443	571325	48593
按登记注册类型分	**Group by Registration Status**					
内资	Domestic Investment	6757885	7916132	696483	7219650	702075
国有	State-owned	16451	21298		21298	2232
集体	Collective-owned	14683	14857		14857	163
股份合作	Share-holding Cooperative	966	991	869	123	190
有限责任公司	Limited Liability Corporations	1452148	1610456	299092	1311365	147913
股份有限公司	Share-holding Cooperative Ltd.	467441	764680	106757	657923	42968
私营	Private	4780187	5477995	288214	5189781	508127
其他	Others	26009	25855	1552	24303	483
港澳台商投资	Hong Kong,Macao and Taiwan Funded	200658	303528		303528	10239
外商投资	Foreign Investment	118832	131103	2711	128393	7971
按主要行业分	**Group by Sector**					
综合零售	Comprehensive Retail	670926	1093942	6476	1087466	49090
食品、饮料及烟草制品专门零售	Speicalized Retail of Food, Beverage and Tobacco	120303	134938	20872	114066	14132
纺织、服装及日用品专门零售	Specialized Retail of Textile, Garments and Commodity	121083	142611	16477	126134	17840
文化、体育用品及器材专门零售	Specialized Retail of Stationers Goods, Sports Goods and Apparatus	688219	783822	50375	733447	75292
医药及医疗器材专门零售	Specialized Retail of Medicine and Medical Appliance	1077319	1149095	319958	829138	75632
汽车、摩托车、燃料及零配件专门零售	Specialized Retail of Automobile, Motorcycle, Fuel and Fittings	3345816	3934143	122350	3811792	334542
家用电器及电子产品专门零售	Specialized Retail of Household Appliance and Electronic Products	507256	550225	20566	529658	41360
五金、家具及室内装修材料专门零售	Specialized Retail of Hardware, Furniture and Interior Decoration Materials	508209	513673	142084	371589	107397
货摊、无店铺及其他零售业	Stall，Retail without Shops and Other Retail	38244	48315	36	48279	5001
按经营方式分	**Group by Means of Operation**					
独立门店	Independent Store	5868489	7010875	393284	6617591	596633
连锁总店（总部）	Chain Headquarters （HQ）	246621	260355		260355	37949
连锁门店	Chain Store	274436	311639	7349	304291	37444
其他	Others	687828	767894	298561	469333	48259
按零售业态分	**Group by Retail Size**					
食杂店	Traditional Grocery Stores	3294	3068	128	2940	458
便利店	Convenience Stores	3522	7729		7729	738
超市	Supermarket	144726	166597	3097	163500	13556
大型超市	Large Supermarket	306683	395853	320	395533	26271
百货店	Composite Store	246255	557383	7272	550111	11480
专业店	Specialized Store	2612388	3059280	181388	2877892	235026
专卖店	Speciality Store	2758637	3119019	66868	3052151	312985
家居建材店	Home Building Materials Stores	392029	369898	132239	237659	101558
厂家直销中心	Factory Outlet Centers	566093	618235	305007	313229	12761
网上商店	Online stores	20489	26230	14	26216	3380

14-8 限额以上个体批发零售贸易业商品购进、销售、库存总额（2015 年）
TOTAL PURCHASES, SALES AND INVENTORY OF INDIVIDUAL WHOLESALE AND RETAIL TRADE ABOVE DESIGNATED SIZE （2015）

指 标	Item	购进总额 Total Purchases	销售额 Total Sales	其中 of which 批发额 Wholesale	零售额 Retail Sales	年末库存总额 Inventory (year-end)
总 计	**Total**	**2894817**	**3433798**	**1817405**	**1616393**	**69009**
市 区	Urban Area	2770716	3290156	1792135	1498021	65938
金坛区	Jintan District	95572	136698		136698	1244
武进区	Wujin District	817816	1031810	778653	253157	37663
#经开区	Economic Development Zone	53678	56571	27891	28679	1419
新北区	Xinbei District	331435	332748	83870	248878	2272
天宁区	Tianning District	384380	385328	8675	376654	2673
钟楼区	Zhonglou District	1141514	1403572	920937	482636	22086
溧阳市	Liyang City	124100	143641	25270	118371	3071
批发贸易业	**Wholesale Trade**	**1597626**	**1980386**	**1714787**	**265599**	**43714**
按主要行业分	**Group by Sector**					
农畜产品批发	Wholesale of Agricultural and Animal Product	331059	425234	404661	20573	13113
食品、饮料及烟草制品批发	Wholesale of Food,Beverages and Tobaccos	715709	883084	783483	99601	11553
纺织、服装及日用品批发	Wholesale of Textile, Garments and Commodity	226366	294221	212627	81594	7289
矿产品、建材及化工产品批发	Wholesale of Mineral Product, Building Material and Chemical Product	249712	301174	241687	59487	10333
机械设备、五金交电及电子产品批发	Wholesale of Machinery, Hardware and Eletronic Products	74780	76673	72329	4344	1426
零售贸易业	**Retail Trade**	**1297190**	**1453412**	**102618**	**1350794**	**25295**
按主要行业分	**Group by Sector**					
综合零售	Comprehensive Retail	108876	117011	2616	114395	3611
食品、饮料及烟草制品专门零售	Speicalized Retail of Food, Beverage and Tobacco	199137	227891	9104	218787	5925
纺织、服装及日用品专门零售	Specialized Retail of Textile, Garments and Commodity	115901	140449	35029	105420	5839
文化、体育用品及器材专门零售	Specialized Retail of Stationers Goods, Sports Goods and Apparatus	8310	8730	85	8645	182
医药及医疗器材专门零售	Specialized Retail of Medicine and Medical Appliance	1863	2442		2442	322
汽车、摩托车、燃料及零配件专门零售	Specialized Retail of Automobile, Motorcycle,Fuel and Fittings	53316	64368	743	63626	1359
家用电器及电子产品专门零售	Specialized Retail of Household Appliance and Electronic Products	11612	13035	830	12205	247
五金、家具及室内装修材料专门零售	Specialized Retail of Hardware, Furniture and Interior Decoration Materials	742302	798845	54211	744634	7406
货摊、无店铺及其他零售业	Stall, Retail without Shops and Other Retail	55873	80640		80640	405
按经营方式分	**Group by Means of Operation**					
独立门店	Independent Store	1278340	1432070	102468	1329602	24320
连锁总店（总部）	Chain Headquarters （HQ）	550	724		724	34
连锁门店	Chain Store	7132	7828	149	7679	634
其 他	Others	11168	12790		12790	307
按零售业态分	**Group by Retail Size**					
食杂店	Traditional Grocery Stores	89112	101902	8270	93632	2345
便利店	Convenience Stores	60002	68986	572	68414	1125
折扣店	Discount Stores	1421	2117		2117	5
超 市	Supermarket	49523	55907	162	55744	2373
大型超市	Large Supermarket	2175	2203		2203	92
百货店	Composite Store	95307	110898	14715	96184	4401
专业店	Specialized Store	203520	229133	7798	221335	6036
专卖店	Speciality Store	31408	32556	2671	29884	426
家居建材店	Home Building Materials Stores	760572	844145	67463	776682	7976
厂家直销中心	Factory Outlet Centers	4151	5566	967	4599	515

14-9 限额以上批发零售贸易企业主要财务指标（2015 年）
MAINFINANCIAI INDICATORS OF WHOLFSALE AND RETAZLENTERISES ABOVE DESLGNATED SILE（2015）

指 标	Item	流动资产合计 Total Circulating Funds	固定资产原价 Original Value of Fixed Assets	资产总计 Total Assets	负债总计 Total Liabilities
总 计	**Total**	**10593165**	**1370214**	**14508165**	**10107822**
市 区	Urban Area	9668368	1218226	13358339	9391887
溧阳市	Liyang City	924797	151988	1149826	715935
批发贸易业	**Wholesale Trade**	**7175461**	**625790**	**8389257**	**5834015**
#国有控股	State-owned and State Share Holding	621800	133508	786157	227985
按地区分	**Grouped by Region**				
市 区	Urban Area	6394968	561228	7511531	5322703
溧阳市	Liyang City	780493	64562	877726	511312
按登记注册类型分	**Group by Registration Status**				
内 资	Domestic Investment	6970553	609679	8139975	5683150
国 有	State-owned	397146	48651	431802	90805
集 体	Collective-owned	1410	546	1633	1188
股份合作	Share-holding Cooperative	114034	5754	124308	117521
有限责任公司	Limited Liability Corporations	1202078	123995	1491567	1239826
股份有限公司	Share-holding Cooperative Ltd.	236616	63083	382725	179449
私 营	Private	4971867	367141	5659308	4010267
其 他	Others	47403	508	48632	44094
港澳台商投资	Hong Kong,Macao and Taiwan Funded	173208	10727	203781	124238
外商投资	Foreign Investment	31699	5384	45501	26627
按主要行业分	**Group by Sector**				
农、林、牧产品批发	Wholesale of Products of Agriculture, Forestry and Animal Husbandry	347765	36865	411670	304542
食品、饮料及烟草制品批发	Wholesale of Food,Beverages and Tobaccos	518811	78278	577668	169047
纺织、服装及家庭用品批发	Specialized Retail of Textile, Garments and Commodity	456531	39952	501077	391826
文化、体育用品及器材批发	Specialized Retail of Stationers Goods, Sports Goods and Apparatus	104765	2677	116668	100488
医药及医疗器材批发	Wholesale of Medicine and Medical Appliance	327926	61357	492371	407404
矿产品、建材及化工产品批发	Wholesale of Mineral Product, Building Material and Chemical Product	4429091	337641	5101878	3593939
机械设备、五金产品及电子产品批发	Wholesale of Machinery, Hardware,Transport, Electric and Electronic Equipment	731710	47673	836923	625687
贸易经纪与代理	Trade Broker and Agent	61914	15346	139645	91147
其他批发	Others	196948	6000	211359	149936
零售贸易业	**Retail Trade**	**3417704**	**744424**	**6118908**	**4273807**
#国有控股	State-owned and State Holding Majority Shares	336268	43481	408320	349450
按地区分	**Grouped by Region**				
市 区	Urban Area	3273400	656998	5846809	4069185
溧阳市	Liyang City	144305	87426	272100	204623

单位：万元（10000 yuan）

所有者权益 Creditors Equity	实收资本 Total Capital Hold	其中 of which #国家资本 State Capital	营业收入 Business Revenues	其中 of which #主营业务收入 Major Business Revenues	主营业务成本 Major Business Cost	主营业务税金及附加 Major Business Taxes and Extra Charges	营业利润 Profits from Bus iness	利润总额 Total Profits	本年应交增值税 Value Added Tax Payable	本年应交所得税 Income tax payable	应付职工薪酬 Remuneration Payable to Employees
4400343	**1852566**	**44851**	**28326011**	**28167994**	**25994597**	**132036**	**692440**	**704437**	**557485**	**125184**	**364661**
3966452	1424941	36610	26246666	26100818	24121676	125921	618009	625449	529679	107697	336659
433891	427625	8241	2079345	2067176	1872921	6115	74431	78989	27807	17486	28002
2555242	**1357687**	**27540**	**21064506**	**21012017**	**19555878**	**102208**	**555537**	**558624**	**460763**	**90118**	**183498**
558173	40754	27239	1522594	1521507	1302452	57331	111402	115649	295813	23894	22607
2188828	1010571	19302	19528094	19475804	18155457	98862	491362	491099	444252	76975	175221
366414	347116	8238	1536412	1536213	1400421	3346	64175	67526	16511	13143	8277
2456825	1280149	27540	20657712	20605224	19198385	101217	542553	545502	453756	86946	170525
340997	6070	6070	605860	605012	447817	56348	88140	89715	184761	22676	9278
445	100		4586	4586	4069	12	154	153	55	40	148
6787	362		545199	543643	536444	130	607	1114	1081	97	812
251742	220903	21169	3836863	3834451	3671305	2737	51420	47842	11180	6524	21619
203276	15626		665194	665130	627414	1022	10951	11360	112201	669	13472
1649041	1033809	300	14856898	14809288	13780595	40930	388313	392352	144412	56929	121029
4538	3279		143114	143114	130743	39	2967	2967	67	11	4166
79543	62892		316896	316895	274108	778	11142	11290	6015	2599	9284
18874	14645		89898	89898	83384	213	1842	1832	992	573	3690
107128	58368	8154	919950	916037	855636	2507	16897	19459	2912	2143	21468
408621	31379	5085	1051350	1027104	796728	56868	107508	108977	190289	23972	19248
109251	59522	800	1675346	1666481	1547467	2691	38067	39903	14714	6702	25219
16180	10906		124352	124352	113924	180	3743	3702	681	842	2014
84967	74110		327942	327470	291050	766	13480	14635	10485	1468	8726
1507939	938890	13500	13867011	13856779	13161847	12991	256871	250815	183907	41772	67124
211236	108544	1	2321584	2318362	2078814	21533	96396	98113	38811	10771	32033
48498	28364		325795	324268	293488	1631	8318	7518	2874	699	3969
61422	47603		451174	451162	416925	3041	14256	15502	16090	1749	3698
1845101	**494880**	**17311**	**7261505**	**7155977**	**6438720**	**29828**	**136903**	**145813**	**96722**	**35066**	**181163**
58870	23082	15542	723709	717562	682108	704	7037	7389	4091	1591	9784
1777624	414370	17308	6718572	6625014	5966219	27058	126647	134350	85427	30723	161438
67477	80510	3	542933	530963	472501	2769	10256	11463	11296	4343	19726

14-9 续表　Continued

指　标	Item	流动资产合　计 Total Circulating Funds	固定资产原　价 Original Value of Fixed Assets	资产总计 Total Assets	负债总计 Total Liabilities
按登记注册类型分	**Group by Registration Status**				
内　资	Domestic Investment	3364057	655361	5945536	4159353
国　有	State-owned	820	285	926	453
集　体	Collective-owned	1495	129	1903	991
股份合作	Share-holding Cooperative	306	59	320	236
有限责任公司	Limited Liability Corporations	568839	117250	716683	607909
股份有限公司	Share-holding Cooperative Ltd.	272805	74395	405311	230430
私　营	Private	2518783	463193	4819365	3318842
其　他	Others	1009	49	1028	492
港澳台商投资	Hong Kong,Macao and Taiwan Funded	40909	79954	143915	91503
外商投资	Foreign Investment	12739	9110	29457	22952
按主要行业分	**Group by Sector**				
综合零售	Comprehensive Retail	326453	248411	711597	450492
食品、饮料及烟草制品专门零售	Speicalized Retail of Food, Beverage and Tobacco	49112	9252	61902	37355
纺织、服装及日用品专门零售	Specialized Retail of Textile, Garments and Commodity	41148	35031	80272	44114
文化、体育用品及器材专门零售	Specialized Retail of Stationers Goods, Sports Goods and Apparatus	127650	33930	164939	110451
医药及医疗器材专门零售	Specialized Retail of Medicine and Medical Appliance	519134	23224	580606	456871
汽车、摩托车、燃料及零配件专门零售	Specialized Retail of Automobile, Motorcycle, Fuel and Fittings	948821	258489	1413263	1245829
家用电器及电子产品专门零售	Specialized Retail of Household Appliance and Electronic Products	176845	51549	250246	186417
五金、家具及室内装修材料专门零售	Specialized Retail of Hardware, Furniture and Interior Decoration Materials	1215145	77886	2837257	1733766
货摊、无店铺及其他零售业	Stall，Retail without Shops and Other Retail	13398	6653	18827	8513
按经营方式分	**Group by Means of Operation**				
独立门店	Independent Store	2903395	663458	5508288	3747117
连锁总店（总部）	Chain Headquarters （HQ）	88561	18184	104693	84831
连锁门店	Chain Store	73297	40320	115590	111780
其　他	Others	352452	22462	390337	330079
按零售业态分	**Group by Retail Size**				
食杂店	Traditional Grocery Stores	902	176	997	910
便利店	Convenience Stores	4007	4515	11015	11210
超　市	Supermarket	47657	31978	74198	65223
大型超市	Large Supermarket	96791	74296	166961	143400
百货店	Composite Store	185154	142076	473361	240945
专业店	Specialized Store	656325	264380	1134809	854347
专卖店	Speciality Store	936487	176715	1262772	1048570
家居建材店	Home Building Materials Stores	1166477	31233	2641657	1611900
厂家直销中心	Factory Outlet Centers	313369	15422	338779	288290
网上商店	Online stores	6993	836	8254	5087

单位：万元（10000 yuan）

所有者权益 Creditors Equity	实收资本 Total Capital Hold	其中 of which #国家资本 State Capital	营业收入 Business Revenues	其中 of which #主营业务收入 Major Business Revenues	主营业务成本 Major Business Cost	主营业务税金及附加 Major Business Taxes and Extra Charges	营业利润 Profits from Business	利润总额 Total Profits	本年应交增值税 Value Added Tax Payable	本年应交所得税 Income Tax Payable	应付职工薪酬 Remuneration Payable to Employees
1786183	425546	17311	6918523	6829949	6163779	28072	128037	134948	91368	32899	168422
472	118	58	2785	2776	2396	3	53	53	28	12	179
913	380		12699	12699	11998	15	157	159	57	9	195
84	50		1034	1034	955	1	9	9	12	1	34
108774	90065	15343	1398285	1375336	1241431	5290	29466	30836	23867	6783	37869
174881	14341	1860	662440	652049	604771	1486	26416	26486	7927	7098	11124
1500524	320513	50	4819175	4763948	4283389	21247	69598	75067	59204	18913	118885
536	80		22106	22106	18841	30	2338	2338	273	84	136
52412	58931		281290	267314	226010	1356	8082	10000	4204	2163	10686
6506	10402		61692	58714	48931	400	784	866	1151	4	2055
261105	124557	500	963761	910289	757673	7214	52873	56780	23343	14177	43431
24547	14224		103959	102259	88056	164	3434	3838	1167	471	3957
36159	23280	50	117681	117590	99796	281	3186	3180	2203	620	5085
54488	21559	1555	672693	669830	575508	8281	39129	39137	9257	3147	17331
123735	38358	15057	988793	986794	917162	1387	21453	22107	9850	3447	20238
167433	212071	149	3466219	3439958	3264492	4872	-14061	-10736	38570	5545	66125
63829	41395		451871	446087	391382	1404	2786	3257	8159	2156	14207
1103491	10423		453219	441654	312214	5969	24895	25021	3846	5298	9061
10314	9013		43309	41515	32437	256	3209	3230	327	205	1728
1761171	419786	3674	6136476	6053414	5452876	26712	116442	123217	78998	30539	143797
19862	10436		209488	205707	171131	1134	4768	5432	5582	1437	13130
3810	19820	500	257291	243007	205520	801	6574	7665	6596	1771	15663
60258	44838	13138	658251	653849	609193	1181	9119	9499	5547	1318	8573
88	232		3629	3608	3332	4	-2	1	41	3	127
-196	4656		6516	6515	5690	12	-207	-207	90	5	615
8975	7453		148853	145996	124179	802	715	1190	3415	664	11479
23561	39643	500	334449	309984	259022	1654	12282	13344	5275	3075	14647
232416	76202	50	503501	476194	394205	4806	40225	42608	14875	10547	17517
280462	145978	1904	2622556	2601576	2328213	11868	55406	57206	36515	10652	75995
214202	177535	1719	2747021	2730388	2579494	4038	5736	8068	29542	4758	49505
1029758	4760		316953	305709	204510	5503	13549	13895	3001	4635	5764
50489	34710	13138	531685	531011	505390	963	8117	8376	2709	497	3326
3167	2332		22863	21515	14256	98	270	347	614	101	1831

14-10 市区限额以上批发零售贸易企业主要财务指标（2015 年）
MAIN FINANCIAL INDICATORS OF WHOLESALE AND RETAIL ENTERPRISES ABOVE DESIGNATED SIZE IN URBAN AREA（2015）

指 标	Item	流动资产合计 Total Circulating Funds	固定资产原价 Original Value of Fixed Assets	资产总计 Total Assets	负债总计 Total Liabilities
总 计	**Total**	**9668368**	**1218226**	**13358339**	**9391887**
金坛区	Jintan District	705565	183067	1062961	758698
武进区	Wujin District	3013406	326004	3756478	2941335
#经开区	Economic Development Zone	591132	61791	702909	406981
新北区	Xinbei District	1235128	143218	1503416	1162810
天宁区	Tianning District	2659150	253965	4497144	2917896
钟楼区	Zhonglou District	2055120	311972	2538340	1611149
#国有控股	State-owned and State Share Holding	936096	167911	1157980	555550
批发贸易业	**Wholesale Trade**	**6394968**	**561228**	**7511531**	**5322703**
#国有控股	State-owned and State Share Holding	604589	125375	754599	209320
按登记注册类型分	**Group by Registration Status**				
内 资	Domestic Investment	6210709	545116	7282898	5174896
国 有	State-owned	397146	48651	431802	90805
集 体	Collective-owned	1410	546	1633	1188
股份合作	Share-holding Cooperative	114034	5754	124308	117521
有限责任公司	Limited Liability Corporations	1181984	115512	1456533	1219159
股份有限公司	Share-holding Cooperative Ltd.	236616	63083	382725	179449
私 营	Private	4232117	311062	4837265	3522679
其 他	Others	47403	508	48632	44094
港澳台商投资	Hong Kong,Macao and Taiwan Funded	152559	10727	183132	121180
外商投资	Foreign Investment	31699	5384	45501	26627
按主要行业分	**Group by Sector**				
农、林、牧产品批发	Wholesale of Products of Agriculture, Forestry and Animal Husbandry	329424	27831	378111	285806
食品、饮料及烟草制品批发	Wholesale of Food,Beverages and Tobaccos	513618	75880	570640	162165
纺织、服装及家庭用品批发	Specialized Retail of Textile, Garments and Commodity	452887	39083	496579	389336
文化、体育用品及器材批发	Specialized Retail of Stationers Goods, Sports Goods and Apparatus	103145	1426	108261	99466
医药及医疗器材批发	Wholesale of Medicine and Medical Appliance	321631	60157	484995	400124
矿产品、建材及化工产品批发	Wholesale of Mineral Product, Building Material and Chemical Product	3728054	290444	4334959	3147769
机械设备、五金产品及电子产品批发	Wholesale of Machinery, Hardware,Transport, Electric and Electronic Equipment	722557	46512	826521	618237
贸易经纪与代理	Trade Broker and Agent	61914	15346	139645	91147
其他批发	Others	161737	4549	171821	128652
零售贸易业	**Retail Trade**	**3273400**	**656998**	**5846809**	**4069185**
#国有控股	State-owned and State Holding Majority Shares	331507	42536	403382	346230
按登记注册类型分	**Group by Registration Status**				
内 资	Domestic Investment	3206149	597159	5711854	3965225

单位：万元（10000 yuan）

所有者权益 Creditors Equity	实收资本 Total Capital Hold	其中 of which #国家资本 State Capital	营业收入 Business Revenues	其中 of which #主营业务收入 Major Business Revenues	主营业务成本 Major Business Cost	主营业务税金及附加 Major Business Taxes and Extra Charges	营业利润 Profits from Business	利润总额 Total Profits	本年应交增值税 Value Added Tax Payable	本年应交所得税 Income Tax Payable	应付职工薪酬 Remuneration Payable to Employees
3966452	**1424941**	**36610**	**26246666**	**26100818**	**24121676**	**125921**	**618009**	**625449**	**529679**	**107697**	**336659**
304263	134324	185	1554015	1525984	1327290	3492	81065	81293	11249	6578	27113
815144	513596	1500	6460362	6428866	6018522	13425	111056	115430	70741	21226	89298
295928	76813	1000	1407214	1406306	1318184	1761	39719	39706	4972	8649	8145
340606	255014	5716	5765408	5755502	5472489	5557	46645	41943	42433	14557	61770
1579248	261059	5311	6683097	6640613	6060259	30189	209517	214530	62077	25118	85840
927191	260948	23898	5783785	5749853	5243115	73258	169726	172253	343178	40219	72639
602430	55895	34840	2218743	2211590	1959267	58019	119506	122477	299873	25457	31291
2188828	**1010571**	**19302**	**19528094**	**19475804**	**18155457**	**98862**	**491362**	**491099**	**444252**	**76975**	**175221**
545279	32816	19301	1501609	1500523	1282077	57331	113043	115615	295811	23874	22098
2108002	950810	19302	19159462	19107172	17836049	97879	478320	477918	437258	73803	162276
340997	6070	6070	605860	605012	447817	56348	88140	89715	184761	22676	9278
445	100		4586	4586	4069	12	154	153	55	40	148
6787	362		545199	543643	536444	130	607	1114	1081	97	812
237374	211565	13231	3801150	3798739	3638427	2702	50957	45710	11139	6495	20918
203276	15626		665194	665130	627414	1022	10951	11360	112201	669	13472
1314586	713808		13394359	13346949	12451137	37626	324543	326900	127955	43815	113483
4538	3279		143114	143114	130743	39	2967	2967	67	11	4166
61952	45116		278734	278733	236023	771	11200	11348	6002	2599	9255
18874	14645		89898	89898	83384	213	1842	1832	992	573	3690
92305	50070	216	896725	892812	833675	2423	18024	18911	2659	2035	20953
408474	31264	5085	1046478	1022232	792551	56863	107495	108967	190248	23969	19073
107243	57675	800	1643311	1634564	1519488	2542	35859	37701	14632	6647	24660
8795	5906		96019	96019	88930	180	1962	1921	681	397	1867
84871	73110		320133	319662	283715	756	14052	13940	10401	1468	8535
1187190	627045	13200	12551620	12541459	11962978	10590	198696	193339	176238	29645	61475
208284	106574	1	2289061	2285839	2051165	21419	93527	95258	38674	10612	31453
48498	28364		325795	324268	293488	1631	8318	7518	2874	699	3969
43169	30563		358951	358951	329468	2459	13429	13543	7844	1504	3238
1777624	**414370**	**17308**	**6718572**	**6625014**	**5966219**	**27058**	**126647**	**134350**	**85427**	**30723**	**161438**
57152	23079	15539	717133	711068	677190	688	6463	6862	4062	1583	9194
1746630	373560	17308	6429068	6348677	5735009	26054	120330	126036	80718	28950	151789

14-10 续表　Continued

指　标	Item	流动资产合　计 Total Circulating Funds	固定资产原　价 Original Value of Fixed Assets	资产总计 Total Assets	负债总计 Total Liabilities
国　有	State-owned	355	280	457	37
集　体	Collective-owned	1495	129	1903	991
股份合作	Share-holding Cooperative	306	59	320	236
有限责任公司	Limited Liability Corporations	527736	97634	636595	546796
股份有限公司	Share-holding Cooperative Ltd.	272805	74395	405311	230430
私　营	Private	2402443	424614	4666240	3186243
其　他	Others	1009	49	1028	492
港澳台商投资	Hong Kong,Macao and Taiwan Funded	54512	50730	105497	81008
外商投资	Foreign Investment	12739	9110	29457	22952
按主要行业分	**Group by Sector**				
综合零售	Comprehensive Retail	325933	201882	626685	409686
食品、饮料及烟草制品专门零售	Speicalized Retail of Food, Beverage and Tobacco	32873	8288	45160	22361
纺织、服装及日用品专门零售	Specialized Retail of Textile, Garments and Commodity	41148	35031	80272	44114
文化、体育用品及器材专门零售	Specialized Retail of Stationers Goods, Sports Goods and Apparatus	119189	32920	156284	104220
医药及医疗器材专门零售	Specialized Retail of Medicine and Medical Appliance	508525	22196	569016	450147
汽车、摩托车、燃料及零配件专门零售	Specialized Retail of Automobile, Motorcycle, Fuel and Fittings	867302	225936	1294277	1129712
家用电器及电子产品专门零售	Specialized Retail of Household Appliance and Electronic Products	165961	50751	238803	177311
五金、家具及室内装修材料专门零售	Specialized Retail of Hardware, Furniture and Interior Decoration Materials	1205559	77117	2827102	1726507
货摊、无店铺及其他零售业	Stall，Retail without Shops and Other Retail	6911	2878	9210	5127
按经营方式分	**Group by Means of Operation**				
独立门店	Independent Store	2781445	584689	5268146	3564630
连锁总店（总部）	Chain Headquarters （HQ）	78814	16275	93287	78102
连锁门店	Chain Store	60688	33573	95038	96373
其　他	Others	352452	22462	390337	330079
按零售业态分	**Group by Retail Size**				
食杂店	Traditional Grocery Stores	902	176	997	910
便利店	Convenience Stores	4007	4515	11015	11210
超　市	Supermarket	38572	27675	62694	57592
大型超市	Large Supermarket	86890	72675	155517	133779
百货店	Composite Store	198688	101241	406318	213997
专业店	Specialized Store	570455	239331	1019468	750855
专卖店	Speciality Store	887199	162445	1201100	994622
家居建材店	Home Building Materials Stores	1163345	31134	2638389	1609768
厂家直销中心	Factory Outlet Centers	313267	14181	337415	288186
网上商店	Online stores	6533	830	7792	4340

单位：万元（10000 yuan）

所有者权益 Creditors Equity	实收资本 Total Capital Hold	其中 of which #国家资本 State Capital	营业收入 Business Revenues	其中 of which #主营业务收入 Major Business Revenues	主营业务成本 Major Business Cost	主营业务税金及附加 Major Business Taxes and Extra Charges	营业利润 Profits from Business	利润总额 Total Profits	本年应交增值税 Value Added Tax Payable	本年应交所得税 Income Tax Payable	应付职工薪酬 Remuneration Payable to Employees
420	115	55	1874	1864	1640	2	22	22	16	4	119
913	380		12699	12699	11998	15	157	159	57	9	195
84	50		1034	1034	955	1	9	9	12	1	34
89798	69635	15343	1273394	1252048	1136951	4193	23747	25160	17779	4807	33226
174881	14341	1860	662440	652049	604771	1486	26416	26486	7927	7098	11124
1479998	288959	50	4455522	4406876	3959855	20326	67641	71863	54654	16948	106955
536	80		22106	22106	18841	30	2338	2338	273	84	136
24489	30408		227813	217623	182278	605	5534	7448	3558	1769	7594
6506	10402		61692	58714	48931	400	784	866	1151	4	2055
216999	83529	500	816935	769886	638593	5385	43052	46958	20885	11946	37440
22799	12939		96062	95515	81886	129	3779	4180	1073	456	3605
36159	23280	50	117681	117590	99796	281	3186	3180	2203	620	5085
52065	20841	1555	650298	647550	556037	8159	38261	38309	9187	3048	16387
118868	35058	15057	964067	962191	898560	1261	20240	20514	8266	2868	17678
164565	187601	146	3216855	3194274	3031656	4539	-7712	-4769	32975	5263	59168
61491	39475		425472	420163	369304	1312	2228	2219	7069	1609	13241
1100595	8527		407896	396331	271306	5954	23026	23150	3557	4830	8319
4083	3121		23307	21514	19082	40	589	609	211	83	515
1703516	347481	3670	5678798	5606730	5054087	24189	107784	113744	71919	27102	127907
15185	7331		186516	182858	153573	1011	3518	3800	4033	858	10927
-1335	14720	500	195007	181577	149366	677	6226	7307	3927	1445	14031
60258	44838	13138	658251	653849	609193	1181	9119	9499	5547	1318	8573
88	232		3629	3608	3332	4	-2	1	41	3	127
-196	4656		6516	6515	5690	12	-207	-207	90	5	615
5102	5625		107282	106559	90043	606	-966	-503	2706	228	8752
21738	38643	500	303005	280526	233653	1423	10535	11572	4740	2627	13201
192321	36502	50	412183	388332	319382	3376	33431	35850	13634	9092	15384
268613	119596	1901	2407959	2388927	2133136	11314	59801	60664	29802	10110	67457
206477	167476	1719	2622295	2608108	2470244	3772	4209	6452	27459	3782	44921
1028621	4500		282226	270981	173127	5502	11618	11964	2995	4188	5616
49228	33449	13138	527192	526518	502975	871	7096	7355	2701	459	3211
3451	2312		22808	21461	14211	98	319	396	614	101	1797

14-11 限额以上住宿餐饮企业主要情况（2015 年）
MAIN CONDITION OF ACCOMMODATION AND CATERING BUSINESS ABOVE DESIGNATED SIZE（2015）

指 标	Item	法人企业数（个）Number of Enterprises (unit)	年末餐饮营业面积（平方米）Operation Area of Catering At Year-end (sq.m)	从业人员（人）Persons Engaged (Person)
总 计	**Total**	**164**	**571918**	**33359**
市 区	Urban Area	131	486230	29798
溧阳市	Liyang City	33	85688	3561
#国有控股	State-owned and State Share Holding	6	14594	480
按登记注册类型分	**Group by Registration Status**			
内 资	Domestic Investment	152	445050	19461
国 有	State-owned	4	10274	298
集 体	Collective-owned	2	1865	155
有限责任公司	Limited Liability Corporations	15	63153	2793
股份有限公司	Share-holding Cooperative Ltd	1	6000	980
私 营	Private	129	359758	15149
其 他	Others	1	4000	86
港澳台商投资	Hong Kong,Macao and Taiwan Funded	8	42708	4706
外商投资	Foreign Investment	4	84160	9192
住宿业	**Accommodation Trade**	**76**	**210370**	**11033**
#国有控股	State-owned and State Share Holding	5	10794	321
按登记注册类型分	**Group by Registration Status**			
内 资	Domestic Investment	68	189012	9369
国 有	State-owned	4	10274	298
集 体	Collective-owned	1	1165	104
有限责任公司	Limited Liability Corporations	9	35900	1344
股份有限公司	Share-holding Cooperative Ltd	1	6000	980
私 营	Private	53	135673	6643
港澳台商投资	Hong Kong,Macao and Taiwan Funded	6	19358	1497
外商投资	Foreign Investment	2	2000	167

营业收入（万元）Operational Revenues（10000 yuan）	其中 of which				床位数（张）Number of Beds（bed）	餐位数（位）Catering Seats Available（Seat）
	客房收入 Room Rate Revenues	餐费收入 Catering Revenues	商品销售收入 Commodity Sales Revenues	其他收入 Other Revenues		
554271	**107466**	**404449**	**26576**	**15780**	**25391**	**125708**
482262	82024	363740	25876	10622	18829	109663
72009	25442	40709	700	5157	6562	16045
9089	1640	6828	266	355	873	2860
337784	87178	232530	3638	14438	21698	96394
5049	1552	2896	266	335	776	2240
3240	705	1826	123	585	518	950
56068	19100	34396	277	2296	4053	12690
28248	15280	8802	159	4006	1452	2250
243748	50541	183179	2813	7215	14899	77184
1430		1430				1080
91919	15732	74921	477	790	2934	11951
124569	4557	96999	22462	552	759	17363
206075	**82543**	**107836**	**2021**	**13675**	**20244**	**47741**
5241	1640	2980	266	355	873	2340
170717	69136	87134	1864	12584	17522	39646
5049	1552	2896	266	335	776	2240
2835	610	1675	64	486	368	650
22838	9902	10984	237	1715	2665	7389
28248	15280	8802	159	4006	1452	2250
111748	41791	62777	1138	6041	12261	27117
32519	11579	20089	61	790	2414	7540
2839	1829	614	96	301	308	555

14-11 续表　Continued

	指标 Item	法人企业数（个） Number ofEnterprises (unit)	年末餐饮营业面积（平方米） OperationArea ofCateringAt Year-end (sq.m)	从业人员（人） Persons Engaged (Person)
按星级饭店分	**Restaurants Grouped By Star Level**			
一　星	One-star	1	980	34
二　星	Two-star	1	800	54
三　星	Three-star	11	17565	685
四　星	Four-star	17	65345	3894
五　星	Five-star	9	37228	2905
其　他	Others	37	88452	3461
餐饮业	**Catering Trade**	**88**	**361548**	**22326**
#国有控股	State-owned and State Share Holding	1	3800	159
按登记注册类型分	**Group by Registration Status**			
内　资	Domestic Investment	84	256038	10092
集　体	Collective-owned	1	700	51
有限责任公司	Limited Liability Corporations	6	27253	1449
私　营	Private	76	224085	8506
其　他	Others	1	4000	86
港澳台商投资	Hong Kong,Macao and Taiwan Funded	2	23350	3209
外商投资	Foreign Investment	2	82160	9025
按主要行业分	**Group by Sector**			
正　餐	Dinner	77	256373	9055
快　餐	Fast Food	8	102625	12952
饮料及冷饮服务	Beverage and Cold Drinks		735	60
其他餐饮业	Other	3	1815	259
按经营方式分	**Group by Means of Operation**			
独立商店	Independent Store	82	260121	10424
连锁商店总店	Head Office of Chain Store	3	97035	11338
连锁商店分店	Branch Store of Chain Store	1	2502	237
其　他	Others	2	1890	327

营业收入（万元） Operational Revenues（10000 yuan）	其中 of which				床位数（张） Number of Beds（bed）	餐位数（位） Catering Seats Available（Seat）
	客房收入 Room Rate Revenues	餐费收入 Catering Revenues	商品销售收入 Commodity Sales Revenues	其他收入 Other Revenues		
454	418	34		2	171	50
457	137	296	24		145	300
10010	3978	5074	104	854	2520	4091
68792	29758	30355	481	8199	5757	13357
61151	19563	38196	677	2715	3496	16934
65212	28690	33881	736	1905	8155	13009
348196	**24923**	**296613**	**24555**	**2105**	**5147**	**77967**
3848		3848				520
167067	18042	145396	1774	1854	4176	56748
405	95	152	59	99	150	300
33231	9198	23412	40	581	1388	5301
132001	8750	120402	1675	1174	2638	50067
1430		1430				1080
59400	4153	54831	415		520	4411
121730	2728	96385	22366	251	451	16808
167696	24923	138547	2393	1833	5147	52999
172285		149851	22163	271		23835
2813		2813				438
5402		5402				695
182112	24712	152903	2393	2105	5075	56339
151917		129754	22163			19855
7657		7657				938
6510	211	6299			72	835

14-12 市区限额以上住宿餐饮企业主要情况（2015 年）
MAIN CONDITION OF ACCOMMODATION AND CATERING TRADE ABOVE DESIGNATED SIZE WITHIN CITY（2015）

指 标	Item	法人企业数（个）Number ofEnterprises（unit）	年末餐饮营业面积（平方米）OperationArea ofCateringAt Year-end（sq.m）	从业人员（人）Persons Engaged（Person）
总 计	**Total**	**131**	**486230**	**29798**
金坛区	Jintan District	18	51920	1495
武进区	Wujin District	28	126637	4385
#经开区	Economic Development Zone	6	42865	638
新北区	Xinbei District	19	65677	5172
天宁区	Tianning District	31	161270	15401
钟楼区	Zhonglou District	35	80726	3345
#国有控股	State-owned and State Share Holding	4	11574	382
按登记注册类型分	**Group by Registration Status**			
内 资	Domestic Investment	120	360752	16078
国 有	State-owned	3	7774	223
集 体	Collective-owned	2	1865	155
有限责任公司	Limited Liability Corporations	14	62633	2770
股份有限公司	Share-holding Cooperative Ltd.	0	1000	240
私 营	Private	100	283480	12604
其 他	Others	1	4000	86
港澳台商投资	Hong Kong,Macao and Taiwan Funded	8	42708	4706
外商投资	Foreign Investment	3	82770	9014
住宿业	**Accommodation Trade**	**47**	**132172**	**7771**
#国有控股	State-owned and State Share Holding	3	7774	223
按登记注册类型分	**Group by Registration Status**			
内 资	Domestic Investment	39	110814	6107
国 有	State-owned	3	7774	223
集 体	Collective-owned	1	1165	104
有限责任公司	Limited Liability Corporations	8	35380	1321
股份有限公司	Share-holding Cooperative Ltd.	0	1000	240
私 营	Private	27	65495	4219
港澳台商投资	Hong Kong,Macao and Taiwan Funded	6	19358	1497
外商投资	Foreign Investment	2	2000	167

营业收入（万元）Operational Revenues（10000 yuan）	其　中　of　which				床位数（张）Number of Beds（bed）	餐位数（位）Catering Seats Available （Seat）
	客房收入 Room Rate Revenues	餐费收入 Catering Revenues	商品销售收入 Commodity Sales Revenues	其他收入 Other Revenues		
482262	**82024**	**363740**	**25876**	**10622**	**18829**	**109663**
20594	3912	14283	554	1845	1185	10339
84813	22619	60259	734	1201	5900	24782
11100	1293	9580	227		637	4705
100161	32820	63774	527	3040	5261	21562
214602	12055	176251	23295	3001	3436	34254
62093	10617	49173	768	1535	3047	18726
8051	1131	6341	266	313	526	2260
269996	61735	196042	2938	9281	15136	80845
4202	1131	2492	266	313	526	1740
3240	705	1826	123	585	518	950
55876	19012	34311	277	2276	3956	12590
6710	4630	1921	159		570	450
198537	36258	154060	2113	6106	9566	64035
1430		1430				1080
91919	15732	74921	477	790	2934	11951
120347	4557	92777	22462	552	759	16867
140253.3	**57101**	**73236**	**1399**	**8518**	**13682**	**33038**
4202	1131	2492	266	313	526	1740
104895	43693	52533	1242	7427	10960	24943
4202	1131	2492	266	313	526	1740
2835	610	1675	64	486	368	650
22645	9814	10900	237	1695	2568	7289
6710	4630	1921	159	0	570	450
68502	27508	35545	516	4932	6928	14814
32519	11579	20089	61	790	2414	7540
2839.3	1829	613.6	95.5	301.2	308	555

14-12 续表 Continued

指 标	Item	法人企业数（个）Number of Enterprises（unit）	年末餐饮营业面积（平方米）Operation Area of Catering At Year-end（sq.m）	从业人员（人）Persons Engaged（Person）
按星级饭店分	**Restaurants Grouped By Star Level**			
一 星	One-star	1	980	34
三 星	Three-star	6	6124	382
四 星	Four-star	12	38708	2566
五 星	Five-star	6	26263	2140
其 他	Others	22	60097	2649
餐饮业	**Catering Trade**	**84**	**354058**	**22027**
#国有控股	State-owned and State Share Holding	1	3800	159
按登记注册类型分	**Group by Registration Status**			
内 资	Domestic Investment	81	249938	9971
集 体	Collective-owned	1	700	51
有限责任公司	Limited Liability Corporations	6	27253	1449
私 营	Private	73	217985	8385
其 他	Others	1	4000	86
港澳台商投资	Hong Kong,Macao and Taiwan Funded	2	23350	3209
外商投资	Foreign Investment	1	80770	8847
按主要行业分	**Group by Sector**			
正 餐	Dinner	74	250273	8934
快 餐	Fast Food	7	101235	12774
饮料及冷饮服务	Beverage and Cold Drinks		735	60
其他餐饮业	Other	3	1815	259
按经营方式分	**Group by Means of Operation**			
独立商店	Independent Store	79	254021	10303
连锁商店总店	Head Office of Chain Store	3	97035	11338
连锁商店分店	Branch Store of Chain Store		1112	59
其 他	Others	2	1890	327

营业收入（万元）Operational Revenues（10000 yuan）	其中 of which				床位数（张）Number of Beds（bed）	餐位数（位）Catering Seats Available（Seat）
	客房收入 Room Rate Revenues	餐费收入 Catering Revenues	商品销售收入 Commodity Sales Revenues	其他收入 Other Revenues		
454	418	34		2	171	50
6944	2551	3482	104	808	1290	2190
39091	15748	18761	416	4165	3897	9187
43512	14801	26430	176	2105	2410	12934
50252	23583	24528	703	1438	5914	8677
342009	**24923**	**290504**	**24477**	**2105**	**5147**	**76625**
3848		3848				520
165101	18042	143509	1696	1854	4176	55902
405	95	152	59	99	150	300
33231	9198	23412	40	581	1388	5301
130035	8750	118515	1597	1174	2638	49221
1430		1430				1080
59400	4153	54831	415		520	4411
117508	2728	92164	22366	251	451	16312
165731	24923	136659	2315	1833	5147	52153
168064		145630	22163	271		23339
2813		2813				438
5402		5402				695
180147	24712	151015	2315	2105	5075	55493
151917		129754	22163			19855
3436		3436				442
6510	211	6299			72	835

14-13 限额以上个体住宿餐饮业主要情况（2015 年）
MAIN CONDITION OF INDIVIDUAL ACCOMMODATION AND CATERING BUSINESS ABOVE DESIGNATED SIZE （2015）

指 标	Item	户 数（户）Number of Enterprises (Unit)	从业人员（人）Persons Engaged (Person)
总 计	**Total**	**243**	**7375**
市 区	Urban Area	227	7005
溧阳市	Liyang City	16	370
住宿业	**Accommodation Trade**	**24**	**500**
按主要行业分	**Group by Sector**		
旅游饭店	Tourist Hotel	2	42
一般旅馆	Regular Hotel	19	354
其他住宿服务	Other Accommodation	3	104
餐饮业	**Catering Trade**	**219**	**6875**
按主要行业分	**Group by Sector**		
正 餐	Dinner	210	6755
快 餐	Fast Food	1	9
其他餐饮业	Other	8	111
按经营方式分	**Group by Means of Operation**		
独立商店	Independent Store	212	6736
连锁商店总店	Head Office of Chain Store	1	6
连锁商店分店	Branch Store of Chain Store	6	133

营业收入（万元）Operational Revenues（10000 yuan）	其　中　of　which				床位数（张）Number of Beds（bed）	餐位数（位）Catering Seats Available（Seat）
	客房收入 Room Rate Revenues	餐费收入 Catering Revenues	商品销售收入 Commodity Sales Revenues	其他收入 Other Revenues		
222278	**20058**	**197854**	**3457**	**910**	**2984**	**66467**
206462	16196	186002	3420	844	2582	64770
15817	3862	11852	36	66	402	1697
18864	**14102**	**4356**	**131**	**274**	**1677**	**1975**
1834	799	804		232	80	184
10218	7728	2368	79	43	1215	930
6812	5576	1184	52		382	861
203414	**5956**	**193498**	**3325**	**636**	**1307**	**64492**
195584	5956	185667	3325	636	1307	63322
653		653				38
7178		7178				1132
197184	5514	187943	3091	636	1277	62796
925		925				212
5306	441	4630	234		30	1484

14-14 市区限额以上个体住宿餐饮业主要情况（2015 年）
MAIN CONDITION OF INDIVIDUAL ACCOMMODATION AND CATERING BUSINESS ABOVE DESIGNATED SIZE （2015）

指 标	Item	户 数（户）Number of Enterprises (Unit)	从业人员（人）Persons Engaged (Person)
总 计	**Total**	**227**	**7005**
金坛区	Jintan District	69	1550
武进区	Wujin District	67	2182
#经开区	Economic Development Zone	21	615
新北区	Xinbei District	23	939
天宁区	Tianning District	32	1413
钟楼区	Zhonglou District	36	921
住宿业	**Accommodation Trade**	**21**	**463**
按主要行业分	**Group by Sector**		
旅游饭店	Tourist Hotel	2	42
一般旅馆	Regular Hotel	17	345
其他住宿服务	Other Accommodation	2	76
餐饮业	**Catering Trade**	**206**	**6542**
按主要行业分	**Group by Sector**		
正 餐	Dinner	201	6479
快 餐	Fast Food	1	9
其他餐饮业	Other	4	54
按经营方式分	**Group by Means of Operation**		
独立商店	Independent Store	199	6403
连锁商店总店	Head Office of Chain Store	1	6
连锁商店分店	Branch Store of Chain Store	6	133

营业收入（万元）Operational Revenues（10000 yuan）	其中 of which				床位数（张）Number of Beds（bed）	餐位数（位）Catering Seats Available（Seat）
	客房收入 Room Rate Revenues	餐费收入 Catering Revenues	商品销售收入 Commodity Sales Revenues	其他收入 Other Revenues		
206462	**16196**	**186002**	**3420**	**844**	**2582**	**64770**
42836	4313	37629	662	232	906	20354
52192	5288	45017	1274	612	997	19118
18635	2634	15187	256	558	312	8450
20922	2525	18387	10		248	5975
52417	1236	49708	1474		181	10737
38095	2833	35262			250	8586
15797	**11069**	**4323**	**131**	**274**	**1509**	**1725**
1834	799	804	0	232	80	184
9670	7180	2368	79	43	1129	930
4294	3091	1151	52		300	611
190664	**5127**	**181679**	**3289**	**570**	**1073**	**63045**
186975	5127	177990	3289	570	1073	62307
653		653				38
3036		3036				700
184434	4685	176124	3055	570	1043	61349
925		925				212
5306	441	4630	234		30	1484

14-15 限额以上住宿餐饮企业财务指标（2015 年）
FINANCIAL INDEX OF ACCOMMODATION AND CATERING TRADE ABOVE DESIGNATED SIZE（2015）

指 标	Item	流动资产合 计 Total Circulating Funds	固定资产原 价 Original Value of Fixed Assets	资产总计 Total Assets	负债总计 Total Liabilities
总 计	**Total**	**260738**	**358064**	**615475**	**571453**
市 区	Urban Area	206726	301585	510015	499215
溧阳市	Liyang City	54013	56479	105460	72238
#国有控股	State-owned and State Holding	6128	15556	13658	3048
按登记注册类型分	**Group by Registration Status**				
内 资	Domestic Investment	183343	285320	429930	392025
国 有	State-owned	5535	14921	12504	2488
集 体	Collective-owned	1831	6589	7505	7652
有限责任公司	Limited Liability Corporations	11612	57050	59773	63618
股份有限公司	Share-holding Cooperative Ltd	14352	676	14726	376
私 营	Private	149769	205670	334948	317424
其 他	Others	245	415	474	468
港澳台商投资	Hong Kong,Macao and Taiwan Funded	45156	42663	119590	132478
外商投资	Foreign Investment	32239	30081	65954	46950
住宿业	**Accommodation Trade**	**133329**	**263695**	**382093**	**372080**
#国有控股	State-owned and State Holding	5653	14958	12626	2587
按登记注册类型分	**Group by Registration Status**				
内 资	Domestic Investment	90047	210372	260442	231719
国 有	State-owned	5535	14921	12504	2488
集 体	Collective-owned	1035	2811	2268	439
有限责任公司	Limited Liability Corporations	8123	52206	52766	50565
股份有限公司	Share-holding Cooperative Ltd	14352	676	14726	376
私 营	Private	61002	139758	178178	177852
港澳台商投资	Hong Kong,Macao and Taiwan Funded	40822	37290	109861	126952
外商投资	Foreign Investment	2460	16033	11789	13410

所有者权益 Creditors Equity	实收资本 Total Capital Hold	其中 of which #国家资本 State Capital	营业收入 Business Revenues	其中 of which #主营业务收入 Major Business Revenues	主营业务成本 Major Business Cost	主营业务税金及附加 Major Business Taxes and Extra Charges	营业利润 Profits from Business	利润总额 Total Profits	本年应交所得税 Income Tax Payable	应付职工薪酬 Remuneration Payable to Employees
44021	**200985**	**7764**	**486133**	**484052**	**195554**	**24841**	**-22663**	**-20245**	**2165**	**124460**
10800	180248	4454	415376	413630	173970	20850	-30310	-28030	1706	110412
33222	20737	3310	70757	70422	21584	3991	7648	7785	460	14048
10611	5182	4682	9089	9067	3714	455	-588	-402	25	2384
37905	145013	4683	297996	296102	124236	16681	-8616	-5978	904	70524
10016	4662	4662	5049	5027	2047	221	-652	-613		1309
-147	160		3240	3239	1243	179	-633	-667	80	488
-3845	48972	20	37164	35763	15419	1961	-1035	-876	73	9335
14350	200		21538	21538	2905	1199	7952	7954		2866
17524	91014	1	229566	229105	101870	13040	-14335	-11865	750	56175
6	5		1439	1430	752	80	88	88		351
-12887	40843		80192	80163	30191	2908	-17412	-17205	1	17556
19004	15129	3081	107946	107787	41127	5252	3365	2938	1261	36380
10012	**147678**	**7764**	**177966**	**175897**	**60001**	**9921**	**-20697**	**-17871**	**486**	**40854**
10039	4682	4682	5241	5219	2102	240	-798	-613		1498
28723	105534	4683	142977	141095	50493	7989	-3749	-1261	486	34201
10016	4662	4662	5049	5027	2047	221	-652	-613		1309
1829	140		2835	2834	973	159	274	241	80	452
2201	47754	20	14626	13225	6974	844	-2293	-2135	3	4179
14350	200		21538	21538	2905	1199	7952	7954		2866
326	52778	1	98929	98472	37593	5566	-9029	-6708	403	25395
-17091	35022		31991	31962	7365	1767	-15862	-15517		5830
-1621	7123	3081	2999	2839	2144	165	-1087	-1093		823

14-15 续表 Continued

指 标	Item	流动资产合计 Total Circulating Funds	固定资产原价 Original Value of Fixed Assets	资产总计 Total Assets	负债总计 Total Liabilities
按星级饭店分	**Restaurants Grouped By Star Level**				
一 星	One-star	2394	2162	3246	3189
二 星	Two-star	142		302	142
三 星	Three-star	14303	20034	26619	20920
四 星	Four-star	32376	89469	87202	68775
五 星	Five-star	67016	113729	198861	212902
其 他	Others	17099	38301	65863	66152
餐饮业	**Catering Trade**	**127409**	**94369**	**233382**	**199373**
#国有控股	State-owned and State Share Holding	476	598	1033	461
按登记注册类型分	**Group by Registration Status**				
内 资	Domestic Investment	93296	74948	169488	160306
集 体	Collective-owned	796	3778	5237	7213
有限责任公司	Limited Liability Corporations	3489	4843	7008	13054
私 营	Private	88766	65912	156770	139572
其 他	Others	245	415	474	468
港澳台商投资	Hong Kong,Macao and Taiwan Funded	4334	5373	9729	5526
外商投资	Foreign Investment	29779	14048	54165	33541
按主要行业分	**Group by Sector**				
正 餐	Dinner	86751	72464	158673	153224
快 餐	Fast Food	39346	20027	69838	42832
其他餐饮业	Others	1312	1878	4871	3317
按经营方式分	**Group by Means of Operation**				
独立商店	Independent Store	81348	71736	152252	145146
连锁商店总店	Head Office of Chain Store	40901	19424	71983	45968
连锁商店分店	Branch Store of Chain Store	1094	610	1702	208
其 他	Others	4066	2598	7445	8051

单位：万元（10000 yuan）

所有者权益 Creditors Equity	实收资本 Total Capital Hold	其中 of which #国家资本 State Capital	营业收入 Business Revenues	其中 of which #主营业务收入 Major Business Revenues	主营业务成本 Major Business Cost	主营业务税金及附加 Major Business Taxes and Extra Charges	营业利润 Profits from Business	利润总额 Total Profits	本年应交所得税 Income Tax Payable	应付职工薪酬 Remuneration Payable to Employees
57	1000		454	454	107	20	-204	-204		108
160	160		457	457	235	26	-107	-106		157
5699	9807	3632	9673	9617	3844	581	-943	-811	83	2738
18427	55429	3082	60563	60393	20571	3375	3611	5909	114	13661
-14042	45903		56606	54978	17754	3109	-10360	-10413	164	12227
-289	35380	1050	50214	49998	17490	2811	-12694	-12246	125	11963
34009	**53307**		**308167**	**308155**	**135553**	**14920**	**-1965**	**-2373**	**1680**	**83606**
572	500		3848	3848	1612	216	210	211	26	886
9182	39479		155019	155007	73744	8692	-4868	-4717	418	36323
-1976	20		405	405	270	20	-907	-908		36
-6046	1218		22538	22538	8445	1118	1258	1259	70	5156
17198	38236		130636	130633	64277	7475	-5306	-5157	347	30780
6	5		1439	1430	752	80	88	88		351
4203	5822		48201	48201	22826	1141	-1550	-1687	1	11727
20625	8006		104948	104948	38983	5087	4452	4032	1261	35556
5450	36948		135834	135822	63304	7615	-4328	-4565	384	32131
27006	16234		167248	167248	68938	7020	2484	2320	1284	50541
1554	125		5085	5085	3312	285	-122	-128	11	934
7106	36601		145535	145523	67879	8179	-4418	-4263	412	34460
26015	16000		151913	151913	62626	6162	2246	1688	1099	47087
1494	506		4209	4209	1155	214	669	669	167	696
-606	200		6510	6510	3894	365	-462	-467	2	1362

14-16 市区限额以上住宿餐饮企业财务指标（2015 年）
FINANCIAL INDEX OF ACCOMMODATION AND CATERING TRADE ABOVE DESIGNATED SIZE WITHIN CITY（2015）

指 标	Item	流动资产合 计 Total Circulating Funds	固定资产原 价 Original Value of Fixed Assets	资产总计 Total Assets	负债总计 Total Liabilities
总 计	**Total**	**206726**	**301585**	**510015**	**499215**
金坛区	Jintan District	22694	34408	73920	63965
武进区	Wujin District	56706	49568	135858	134597
# 经开区	Economic Development Zone	6132	12251	14730	5495
新北区	Xinbei District	42600	62872	97038	104624
天宁区	Tianning District	57809	85035	137871	129810
钟楼区	Zhonglou District	26917	69703	65328	66219
# 国有控股	State-owned and State Share Holding	5156	11093	10517	2852
按登记注册类型分	**Group by Registration Status**				
内 资	Domestic Investment	130425	229452	326173	319995
国 有	State-owned	4680	10495	9484	2392
集 体	Collective-owned	1831	6589	7505	7652
有限责任公司	Limited Liability Corporations	11495	57013	59651	63519
私 营	Private	112175	154941	249058	245964
其 他	Others	245	415	474	468
港澳台商投资	Hong Kong,Macao and Taiwan Funded	45156	42663	119590	132478
外商投资	Foreign Investment	31145	29471	64252	46742
住宿业	**Accommodation Trade**	**82046**	**208767**	**280778**	**303205**
# 国有控股	State-owned and State Share Holding	4680	10495	9484	2392
按登记注册类型分	**Group by Registration Status**				
内 资	Domestic Investment	38764	155445	159128	162843
国 有	State-owned	4680	10495	9484	2392
集 体	Collective-owned	1035	2811	2268	439
有限责任公司	Limited Liability Corporations	8006	52170	52644	50466
私 营	Private	25043	89969	94732	109547

单位：万元（10000 yuan）

所有者权益 Creditors Equity	实收资本 Total Capital Hold	其中 of which #国家资本 State Capital	营业收入 Business Revenues	其中 of which #主营业务收入 Major Business Revenues	主营业务成本 Major Business Cost	主营业务税金及附加 Major Business Taxes and Extra Charges	营业利润 Profits from Business	利润总额 Total Profits	本年应交所得税 Income Tax Payable	应付职工薪酬 Remuneration Payable to Employees
10800	**180248**	**4454**	**415376**	**413630**	**173970**	**20850**	**-30310**	**-28030**	**1706**	**110412**
9955	31163	20	21284	19884	8509	1461	-2442	-2386	118	5701
1261	33474	1030	68220	68216	28175	3571	-11848	-11547	130	13902
9235	1358	1030	10810	10809	6523	506	-182	-149	35	2289
-7586	35932	3081	62262	62102	25959	3514	-10241	-10246	138	17413
8061	34100		210876	210834	87063	9363	-2113	64	1235	61216
-891	45580	323	52734	52594	24265	2941	-3666	-3914	85	12180
7665	1873	1373	8051	8051	3492	392	-362	-323	26	1921
6177	124782	1373	231448	229889	103807	12904	-15595	-13095	611	57173
7093	1373	1373	4202	4202	1880	176	-572	-534		1036
-147	160		3240	3239	1243	179	-633	-667	80	488
-3868	48952		36972	35571	15364	1943	-889	-876	73	9146
3093	74292		185594	185447	84568	10525	-13589	-11106	457	46152
6	5		1439	1430	752	80	88	88		351
-12887	40843		80192	80163	30191	2908	-17412	-17205	1	17556
17510	14623	3081	103737	103578	39972	5038	2696	2270	1094	35683
-22426	**128113**	**4454**	**113236**	**111502**	**40555**	**6253**	**-28054**	**-25372**	**196**	**27981**
7093	1373	1373	4202	4202	1880	176	-572	-534		1036
-3715	85968	1373	78247	76701	31046	4320	-11106	-8762	196	21329
7093	1373	1373	4202	4202	1880	176	-572	-534		1036
1829	140		2835	2834	973	159	274	241	80	452
2178	47734		14434	13032	6919	826	-2147	-2136	3	3990
-14816	36721		56776	56632	21275	3160	-8661	-6333	113	15851

14-16 续表　Continued

指　标	Item	流动资产合　计 Total Circulating Funds	固定资产原　价 Original Value of Fixed Assets	资产总计 Total Assets	负债总计 Total Liabilities
港澳台商投资	Hong Kong,Macao and Taiwan Funded	40822	37290	109861	126952
外商投资	Foreign Investment	2460	16033	11789	13410
住宿业	**Accommodation Trade**	**82046**	**208767**	**280778**	**303205**
按星级饭店分	**Restaurants Grouped By Star Level**				
一　星	One-star	2394	2162	3246	3189
三　星	Three-star	3341	12676	10645	8021
四　星	Four-star	14273	82404	55579	53893
五　星	Five-star	49554	77354	153074	178565
其　他	Others	12484	34171	58235	59536
餐饮业	**Catering Trade**	**124680**	**92818**	**229236**	**196011**
#国有控股	State-owned and State Share Holding	476	598	1033	461
按登记注册类型分	**Group by Registration Status**				
内 资	Domestic Investment	91661	74007	167044	157152
有限责任公司	Limited Liability Corporations	796	3778	5237	7213
私 营	Private	3489	4843	7008	13054
其 他	Others	87132	64972	154326	136417
港澳台商投资	Hong Kong,Macao and Taiwan Funded	245	415	474	468
外商投资	Foreign Investment	4334	5373	9729	5526
按主要行业分	**Group by Sector**	28685	13438	52463	33333
正 餐	Dinner				
快 餐	Fast Food	85116	71524	156230	150070
其他餐饮业	Other	38252	19417	68136	42624
按经营方式分	**Group by Means of Operation**	1312	1878	4871	3317
独立商店	Independent Store				
连锁商店总店	Head Office of Chain Store	79713	70796	149808	141992
连锁商店分店	Branch Store of Chain Store	40901	19424	71983	45968
其　他	Others	4066	2598	7445	8051

单位：万元（10000 yuan）

所有者权益 Creditors Equity	实收资本 Total Capital Hold	其中 of which 国家资本 State Capital	营业收入 Business Revenues	其中 of which #主营业务收入 Major Business Revenues	主营业务成本 Major Business Cost	主营业务税金及附加 Major Business Taxes and Extra Charges	营业利润 Profits from Business	利润总额 Total Profits	本年应交所得税 Income tax payable	应付职工薪酬 Remuneration Payable to Employees
-17091	35022		31991	31962	7365	1767	-15862	-15517		5830
-1621	7123	3081	2999	2839	2144	165	-1087	-1093		823
-22426	**128113**	**4454**	**113236**	**111502**	**40555**	**6253**	**-28054**	**-25372**	**196**	**27981**
57	1000		454	454	107	20	-204	-204		108
2624	2733	323	6942	6912	2961	423	-61	-74	83	1676
1686	52924	3081	30870	30700	13836	1702	-4344	-2061	82	8871
-25491	38403		38935	37535	12594	2161	-10494	-10500		8468
-1302	33052	1050	36036	35901	11056	1946	-12952	-12533	32	8859
33226	**52136**		**302140**	**302128**	**133415**	**14597**	**-2256**	**-2658**	**1509**	**82431**
572	500		3848	3848	1612	216	210	211	26	886
9893	38814		153201	153188	72760	8583	-4490	-4333	415	35844
-1976	20		405	405	270	20	-907	-908		36
-6046	1218		22538	22538	8445	1118	1258	1259	70	5156
17909	37571		128818	128815	63294	7366	-4928	-4773	344	30301
6	5		1439	1430	752	80	88	88		351
4203	5822		48201	48201	22826	1141	-1550	-1687	1	11727
19130	7500		100739	100739	37828	4873	3783	3363	1094	34860
6160	36283		134016	134004	62321	7506	-3950	-4180	381	31652
25512	15728		163039	163039	67783	6806	1816	1651	1117	49845
1554	125		5085	5085	3312	285	-122	-128	11	934
7817	35936		143717	143705	66895	8070	-4040	-3879	409	33981
26015	16000		151913	151913	62626	6162	2246	1688	1099	47087
-606	200		6510	6510	3894	365	-462	-467	2	1362

14-17 亿元商品交易市场基本情况（2015 年）
MARKETS WITH TRANSACTION VOLUME OVER 100 MILLION YUAN （2015）

指　标	Item	市场个数（个）Number of Markets（unit）	市场摊位总量（个）Number of Market Booth（unit）	摊位出租率（%）Occupancy Rate（%）	市场营业面积（平方米）Operation Area（sq.m）	商品成交总额（万元）Transaction Volume（10000 yuan）
总　计	**Total**	**56**	**43798**	**85.1**	**5133921**	**20014817**
按经营环境分	**By Operation Environment**					
露天式	Outdoor	5	3010	81	718496	3132150
封闭式	Close	41	33898	83.1	3288631	14106911
其　他	Other	10	6890	96.9	1126794	2775756
按经营方式分	**By Operation Method**					
批　发	Wholesale	31	28464	86.3	4042991	17128464
零　售	Retail	25	15334	82.8	1090930	2886353
按市场类别分	**By Market Type**					
综合市场	**Comprehensive Market**	**16**	**9869**	**74.1**	**1194702**	**5094701**
工业消费品综合市场	Industrial Consumable Market	1	450	70	360000	414975
农产品综合市场	Farm and Side-line Products	13	8240	71	547402	3568753
其他综合市场	Others	2	1179	96.8	287300	1110973
专业市场	**Professional Market**	**40**	**33929**	**88.3**	**3939219**	**14920116**
生产资料市场	Markets of Means of Production	13	8718	86.7	1249922	6148971
农业生产用具市场	Agricultural Appliances Market	1	327	100	52700	50358
木材市场	Timber	2	3286	98.7	262300	549840
建材市场	Building Materials Market	4	1085	93.1	432782	796585
化工材料及制品市场	Chemical Materials and Related Prod ucts Market	2	1408	97.3	321000	1830951
金属材料市场	Metal Materials Market	3	1792	48.4	178140	2766950
机械设备市场	Mechanical Equipment Market	1	820	90.2	3000	154287
农产品市场	Agricultural Products Market	2	3389	81.6	439984	2414632
水产品市场	Aquatic Products Market	1	991	40	14000	33384

14-17 续表 Continued

指 标	Item	市场个数（个）Number of Markets (unit)	市场摊位总量（个）Number of Market Booth (unit)	摊位出租率（%）Occupancy Rate (%)	市场营业面积（平方米）Operation Area (sq.m)	商品成交总额（万元）Transaction Volume (10000 yuan)
棉麻土畜、烟叶市场	Cotton Gunny Specialty Livestock and Tobacco Market	1	2398	98.9	425984	2381248
食品、饮料及烟酒市场	Foodstuff, Beverage, Cigarette & Wine	3	1050	93.9	73555	215048
食品饮料市场	Food and Beverage Market	2	630	97.8	44960	186143
其他食品、饮料及烟酒市场	Others	1	420	88.1	28595	28905
纺织、服装、鞋帽市场	Textile, Garment, Shoes and Hat	4	5894	98.3	158360	598544
服装市场	Garment Market	1	280	99.3	45000	104105
其他纺织服装鞋帽市场	OtherTextile, Garment, Shoes and Hat Market	3	5614	98.2	113360	494439
日用品及文化用品市场	Daily Necessities and Cultural Arti cles Market	3	2507	100	27448	410196
小商品市场	Small Commodities Market	2	2063	100	19448	396844
其他日用品及文化用品市场	Other Daily Products and Stationery Market	1	444	100	8000	13352
电器、通讯器材、电子设备市场	Appliance communication Equipment and Electronic Device Market	1	426	72.8	10000	39524
计算机及辅助设备市场	Computer and Component Market	1	426	72.8	10000	39524
家具、五金及装饰材料市场	Furniture,Hardware and Decorative Material Market	10	7695	87.2	944950	1720582
家具市场	Furniture Market	3	1525	77.2	223577	213097
装饰材料市场	Decorative Materials Market	3	1228	91	225556	221460
灯具市场	Lighting Fixtures Market	1	3000	97.8	411000	925001
五金材料市场	Hardware Materials Market	3	1942	76.5	84817	361024
汽车、摩托车及零配件市场	Automobile,Motorcycle and Parts & Material Market	3	1750	75.8	575000	1728984
汽车市场	Automobile Market	2	960	95.6	515000	1691415
机动车零配件市场	Auto Parts Market	1	790	51.6	60000	37569
花、鸟、鱼、虫市场	Flowers, Birds, Fish and Insects Market	1	2500	80	460000	1643635
花卉市场	Flowers	1	2500	80	460000	1643635

15

CHAPTER 15

个体　私营经济

INDIVIDUAL AND PRIVATE ECONOMY

15 个体　　私营经济
INDIVIDUAL AND PRIVATE ECONOMY

2015 年主要统计指标
MAJOR STATISTICAL INDICATORS OF 2015

年底私营个体经济单位数	Number of Individual and Private Economy at Year-end	36.25 万户	(10000 units)
比上年增长	Over the Previous Year	14.4%	
年底私营个体企业注册资金	Registered Capital of Individual and Private Economy at Year-end	4814.71 亿元	(100 million yuan)
比上年增长	Over the Previous Year	33.5%	
年底私营个体企业从业人数	Number of Employees in Individual and Private Enterprises at Year-end	209.66万人	(10000 persons)
比上年增长	Over the Previous Year	6.8%	

15-1 个体、私营经济主要指标（2011-2015 年）
MAIN INDICATORS OF THE INDIVIDUAL AND PRIVATE ECONOMIES（2011-2015）

指 标	Item	2011	2012	2013	2014	2015
个体工商业户数（户）	**The Number of Individual Industrial and Commercial Households （Unit）**	**170755**	**182669**	**200921**	**218945**	**248196**
第一产业	Primary Industry	1091	1508	1962	2630	3406
第二产业	Secondary Industry	19315	20734	22893	25014	27899
第三产业	Tertiary Industry	150349	160420	176066	191301	216891
个体工商业从业人数（人）	**The Number of Individual Industrial and Commercial Practitioners （people）**	**331195**	**351981**	**390434**	**431671**	**496266**
第一产业	Primary Industry	2515	3599	5158	7056	9095
第二产业	Secondary Industry	62088	64805	70937	78040	88364
第三产业	Tertiary Industry	266592	283567	314339	346575	398807
私营企业户数（户）	**The Number of Private Enterprises （Unit）**	**75216**	**80216**	**88264**	**97909**	**114256**
第一产业	Primary Industry	655	768	943	1035	1207
第二产业	Secondary Industry	36638	38121	40101	42915	47256
第三产业	Tertiary Industry	37923	41327	47220	53959	65793
私营企业从业人员（人）	**The Number of Private Enterprises' Employees （ people）**	**1227556**	**1301874**	**1496597**	**1531874**	**1600356**
第一产业	Primary Industry	8667	9627	11373	11661	12838
第二产业	Secondary Industry	873611	916815	1027114	1033320	1047750
第三产业	Tertiary Industry	345278	375432	458110	486893	539768
私营企业注册资金（万元）	**Registered Capital of Private Enterprises （10000 yuan）**	**21700710**	**25040852**	**28245455**	**34717066**	**46414326**
第一产业	Primary Industry	201584	247979	423923	426660	533531
第二产业	Secondary Industry	10534812	12033309	13417488	16634609	19858776
第三产业	Tertiary Industry	10964314	12759564	14404045	17655797	26022019

15-2 分地区年底个体工商业户数（2015年）
NUMBER OF SELF-EMPLOYED BUSINESS AT YEAR-END BY REGION（2015）

单位：户（unit）

指 标	Item	全 市 Whole Municipality	市 区 Urban Area	溧阳市 Liyang City
总 计	**Total**	**248196**	**214825**	**33371**
按行业分	**Grouped By Sector**			
农林牧渔业	Farming,Forestry,Animal Husbandry and Fishery	3406	2114	1292
采矿业	Mining	5	4	1
制造业	Manufacturing	27269	24623	2646
电力、燃气及水的生产和供应业	Eletric Power, Gas and Tap Water Production and Supply	22	13	9
建筑业	Construction	603	509	94
批发零售贸易业	Wholesale and Retail Trade	148152	126439	21713
交通运输、仓储和邮政业	Transportation, Storage,Post and Telecommunications	2705	2356	349
住宿和餐饮业	Accommodation and Catering Services	26241	23468	2773
信息传输、计算机服务和软件业	Information Transmission, Computer Service and Software	872	564	308
金融业	Financial	9	4	5
房地产业	Real Estate	210	118	92
租赁和商务服务业	Lease and Commercial Service	4879	4082	797
科学研究、技术服务和地质勘查业	Scientific Research, Technology Service and Geological Prospecting	823	699	124
水利、环境和公共设施管理业	Water Conservancy, Environment and Public Facility Management	38	31	7
居民服务和其他服务业	Residents Service and Other Service	30784	27850	2934
教 育	Education	360	332	28
卫生、社会保障和社会福利业	Healthcare, Social Security and Social Welfare	166	137	29
文化、体育和娱乐业	Culture, Sport and Entertainment	1645	1475	170
其他行业	Other Sectors	7	7	
按城乡分	**Grouped By City and Village**			
城 镇	**Urban and Town**	**236932**	**208448**	**28484**
农林牧渔业	Farming,Forestry,Animal Husbandry and Fishery	2529	1731	798
采矿业	Mining	3	3	
制造业	Manufacturing	24707	22631	2076
电力、燃气及水的生产和供应业	Eletric Power,Gas and Tap Water Production and Supply	21	13	8
建筑业	Construction	575	489	86
批发零售贸易业	Wholesale and Retail Trade	141964	123325	18639
交通运输、仓储和邮政业	Transportation, Storage,Post and Telecommunications	2571	2283	288

15-2 续表 Continued 单位：户（unit）

指 标	Item	全 市 Whole Municipality	市 区 Urban Area	溧阳市 Liyang City
住宿和餐饮业	Accommodation and Catering Services	25670	23200	2470
信息传输、计算机服务和软件业	Information Transmission, Computer Service and Software	865	559	306
金融业	Financial	9	4	5
房地产业	Real Estate	209	118	91
租赁和商务服务业	Lease and Commercial Service	4819	4060	759
科学研究、技术服务和地质勘查业	Scientific Research, Technology Service and Geological Prospecting	786	680	106
水利、环境和公共设施管理业	Water Conservancy, Environment and Public Facility Management	32	29	3
居民服务和其他服务业	Residents Service and Other Service	30023	27392	2631
教 育	Education	358	331	27
卫生、社会保障和社会福利业	Healthcare, Social Security and Social Welfare	162	134	28
文化、体育和娱乐业	Culture, Sport and Entertainment	1623	1460	163
其他行业	Other Sectors	6	6	
农 村	**Countryside**	**11264**	**6377**	**4887**
农林牧渔业	Farming,Forestry,Animal Husbandry and Fishery	877	383	494
采矿业	Mining and Quarrying	2	1	1
制造业	Manufacturing	2562	1992	570
电力、燃气及水的生产和供应业	Eletric Power, Gas and Tap Water Production and Supply	1		1
建筑业	Construction	28	20	8
批发零售贸易业	Wholesale and Retail Trade	6188	3114	3074
交通运输、仓储和邮政业	Transportation, Storage,Post and Telecommunications	134	73	61
住宿和餐饮业	Accommodation and Catering Services	571	268	303
信息传输、计算机服务和软件业	Information Transmission, Computer Service and Software	7	5	2
房地产业	Real Estate	1		1
租赁和商务服务业	Lease and Commercial Service	60	22	38
科学研究、技术服务和地质勘查业	Scientific Research, Technology Service and Geological Prospecting	37	19	18
水利、环境和公共设施管理业	Water Conservancy, Environment and Public Facility Management	6	2	4
居民服务和其他服务业	Residents Service and Other Service	761	458	303
教 育	Education	2	1	1
卫生、社会保障和社会福利业	Healthcare, Social Security and Social Welfare	4	3	1
文化、体育和娱乐业	Culture, Sport and Entertainment	22	15	7
其他行业	Other Sectors	1	1	

15-3 分地区年底个体工商户从业人数（2015 年）
NUMBER OF EMPLOYEES IN SELF-EMPLOYED BUSINESS AT YEAR-END BY REGION（2015）

单位：人（person）

指标	Item	全市 Whole Municipality	市区 Urban Area	溧阳市 Liyang City
总计	**Total**	**496266**	**427458**	**68808**
按行业分	**Grouped By Sector**			
农林牧渔业	Farming,Forestry,Animal Husbandry and Fishery	9095	5602	3493
采矿业	Mining	14	9	5
制造业	Manufacturing	86227	76854	9373
电力、燃气及水的生产和供应业	Eletric Power, Gas and Tap Water Production and Supply	51	30	21
建筑业	Construction	2072	1746	326
批发零售贸易业	Wholesale and Retail Trade	239779	203579	36200
交通运输、仓储和邮政业	Transportation, Storage,Post and Telecommunications	5469	4691	778
住宿和餐饮业	Accommodation and Catering Services	73263	64486	8777
信息传输、计算机服务和软件业	Information Transmission, Computer Service and Software	1345	972	373
金融业	Financial	12	5	7
房地产业	Real Estate	435	283	152
租赁和商务服务业	Lease and Commercial Service	8245	6629	1616
科学研究、技术服务和地质勘查业	Scientific Research, Technology Service and Geological Prospecting	1933	1590	343
水利、环境和公共设施管理业	Water Conservancy, Environment and Public Facility Management	127	114	13
居民服务和其他服务业	Residents Service and Other Service	61938	55381	6557
教　育	Education	980	900	80
卫生、社会保障和社会福利业	Healthcare, Social Security and Social Welfare	556	381	175
文化、体育和娱乐业	Culture, Sport and Entertainment	4716	4197	519
其他行业	Other Sectors	9	9	
按城乡分	**Grouped By City and Village**			
城　镇	**Urban and Town**	**470944**	**412540**	**58404**
农林牧渔业	Farming,Forestry,Animal Husbandry and Fishery	6471	4518	1953
采矿业	Mining	6	6	
制造业	Manufacturing	76499	69732	6767
电力、燃气及水的生产和供应业	Eletric Power,Gas and Tap Water Production and Supply	49	30	19
建筑业	Construction	1959	1680	279
批发零售贸易业	Wholesale and Retail Trade	230422	198872	31550
交通运输、仓储和邮政业	Transportation, Storage,Post and Telecommunications	5234	4600	634

15-3 续表 Continued 单位：人（person）

指 标	Item	全 市 Whole Municipality	市 区 Urban Area	溧阳市 Liyang City
住宿和餐饮业	Accommodation and Catering Services	71732	63699	8033
信息传输、计算机服务和软件业	Information Transmission, Computer Service and Software	1334	964	370
金融业	Financial	12	5	7
房地产业	Real Estate	434	283	151
租赁和商务服务业	Lease and Commercial Service	8150	6589	1561
科学研究、技术服务和地质勘查业	Scientific Research, Technology Service and Geological Prospecting	1873	1562	311
水利、环境和公共设施管理业	Water Conservancy, Environment and Public Facility Management	108	103	5
居民服务和其他服务业	Residents Service and Other Service	60485	54473	6012
教 育	Education	974	899	75
卫生、社会保障和社会福利业	Healthcare, Social Security and Social Welfare	536	367	169
文化、体育和娱乐业	Culture, Sport and Entertainment	4658	4150	508
其他行业	Other Sectors	8	8	
农 村	**Countryside**	**25322**	**14918**	**10404**
农林牧渔业	Farming,Forestry,Animal Husbandry and Fishery	2624	1084	1540
采矿业	Mining and Quarrying	8	3	5
制造业	Manufacturing	9728	7122	2606
电力、燃气及水的生产和供应业	Eletric Power, Gas and Tap Water Production and Supply	2		2
建筑业	Construction	113	66	47
批发零售贸易业	Wholesale and Retail Trade	9357	4707	4650
交通运输、仓储和邮政业	Transportation, Storage,Post and Telecommunications	235	91	144
住宿和餐饮业	Accommodation and Catering Services	1531	787	744
信息传输、计算机服务和软件业	Information Transmission, Computer Service and Software	11	8	3
房地产业	Real Estate	1		1
租赁和商务服务业	Lease and Commercial Service	95	40	55
科学研究、技术服务和地质勘查业	Scientific Research, Technology Service and Geological Prospecting	60	28	32
水利、环境和公共设施管理业	Water Conservancy, Environment and Public Facility Management	19	11	8
居民服务和其他服务业	Residents Service and Other Service	1453	908	545
教 育	Education	6	1	5
卫生、社会保障和社会福利业	Healthcare, Social Security and Social Welfare	20	14	6
文化、体育和娱乐业	Culture, Sport and Entertainment	58	47	11
其他行业	Other Sectors	1	1	

15-4 分地区年底私营企业单位数（2015 年）
NUMBER OF PRIVATE ENTERPRISES AT YEAR-END BY REGION（2015）

单位：户（unit）

指 标	Item	全 市 Whole Municipality	市 区 Urban Area	溧阳市 Liyang City
总 计	**Total**	**114256**	**105291**	**8965**
按行业分	**Grouped By Sector**			
农林牧渔业	Farming,Forestry,Animal Husbandry and Fishery	1207	722	485
采矿业	Mining	25	9	16
制造业	Manufacturing	40882	38228	2654
电力、燃气及水的生产和供应业	Eletric Power, Gas and Tap Water Production and Supply	138	86	52
建筑业	Construction	6211	5366	845
批发零售贸易业	Wholesale and Retail Trade	35118	32417	2701
交通运输、仓储和邮政业	Transportation, Storage,Post and Telecommunications	2222	2040	182
住宿和餐饮业	Accommodation and Catering Services	820	748	72
信息传输、计算机服务和软件业	Information Transmission, Computer Service and Software	2496	2355	141
金融业	Financial	254	232	22
房地产业	Real Estate	2116	1856	260
租赁和商务服务业	Lease and Commercial Service	10087	9382	705
科学研究、技术服务和地质勘查业	Scientific Research, Technology Service and Geological Prospecting	9277	8631	646
水利、环境和公共设施管理业	Water Conservancy, Environment and Public Facility Management	283	251	32
居民服务和其他服务业	Residents Service and Other Service	2061	1988	73
教 育	Education	112	106	6
卫生、社会保障和社会福利业	Healthcare, Social Security and Social Welfare	103	95	8
文化、体育和娱乐业	Culture, Sport and Entertainment	844	779	65
按城乡分	**Grouped By City and Village**			
城 镇	**Urban and Town**	**111509**	**104012**	**7497**
农林牧渔业	Farming,Forestry,Animal Husbandry and Fishery	949	692	257
采矿业	Mining	11	6	5
制造业	Manufacturing	39376	37318	2058
电力、燃气及水的生产和供应业	Eletric Power,Gas and Tap Water Production and Supply	109	82	27
建筑业	Construction	6111	5323	788
批发零售贸易业	Wholesale and Retail Trade	34611	32276	2335
交通运输、仓储和邮政业	Transportation, Storage,Post and Telecommunications	2185	2029	156

15-4 续表 Continued　　　　单位：户（unit）

指　标	Item	全　市 Whole Municipality	市　区 Urban Area	溧阳市 Liyang City
住宿和餐饮业	Accommodation and Catering Services	811	744	67
信息传输、计算机服务和软件业	Information Transmission, Computer Service and Software	2468	2338	130
金融业	Financial	251	231	20
房地产业	Real Estate	2086	1844	242
租赁和商务服务业	Lease and Commercial Service	10023	9356	667
科学研究、技术服务和地质勘查业	Scientific Research, Technology Service and Geological Prospecting	9196	8618	578
水利、环境和公共设施管理业	Water Conservancy, Environment and Public Facility Management	267	242	25
居民服务和其他服务业	Residents Service and Other Service	2006	1938	68
教　育	Education	111	106	5
卫生、社会保障和社会福利业	Healthcare, Social Security and Social Welfare	103	95	8
文化、体育和娱乐业	Culture, Sport and Entertainment	835	774	61
农　村	**Countryside**	**2747**	**1279**	**1468**
农林牧渔业	Farming,Forestry,Animal Husbandry and Fishery	258	30	228
采矿业	Mining and Quarrying	14	3	11
制造业	Manufacturing	1506	910	596
电力、燃气及水的生产和供应业	Eletric Power, Gas and Tap Water Production and Supply	29	4	25
建筑业	Construction	100	43	57
批发零售贸易业	Wholesale and Retail Trade	507	141	366
交通运输、仓储和邮政业	Transportation, Storage,Post and Telecommunications	37	11	26
住宿和餐饮业	Accommodation and Catering Services	9	4	5
信息传输、计算机服务和软件业	Information Transmission, Computer Service and Software	28	17	11
金融业	Financial	3	1	2
房地产业	Real Estate	30	12	18
租赁和商务服务业	Lease and Commercial Service	64	26	38
科学研究、技术服务和地质勘查业	Scientific Research, Technology Service and Geological Prospecting	81	13	68
水利、环境和公共设施管理业	Water Conservancy, Environment and Public Facility Management	16	9	7
居民服务和其他服务业	Residents Service and Other Service	55	50	5
教　育	Education	1		1
文化、体育和娱乐业	Culture, Sport and Entertainment	9	5	4

15-5 分地区年底私营企业从业人数（2015 年）
NUMBER OF EMPLOYEES IN PRIVATE ENTERPRISES AT YEAR-END BY REGION（2015）

单位：人 (person)

指 标	Item	全 市 Whole Municipality	市 区 Urban Area	溧阳市 Liyang City
总 计	**Total**	**1600356**	**1389531**	**210825**
按行业分	**Grouped By Sector**			
农林牧渔业	Farming,Forestry,Animal Husbandry and Fishery	12838	7413	5425
采矿业	Mining	590	93	497
制造业	Manufacturing	822129	740914	81215
电力、燃气及水的生产和供应业	Eletric Power, Gas and Tap Water Production and Supply	1858	1051	807
建筑业	Construction	223173	151041	72132
批发零售贸易业	Wholesale and Retail Trade	225512	203526	21986
交通运输、仓储和邮政业	Transportation, Storage,Post and Telecommunications	21134	18686	2448
住宿和餐饮业	Accommodation and Catering Services	20937	16915	4022
信息传输、计算机服务和软件业	Information Transmission, Computer Service and Software	16920	15915	1005
金融业	Financial	2534	2318	216
房地产业	Real Estate	33517	29667	3850
租赁和商务服务业	Lease and Commercial Service	81971	73776	8195
科学研究、技术服务和地质勘查业	Scientific Research, Technology Service and Geological Prospecting	88728	81866	6862
水利、环境和公共设施管理业	Water Conservancy, Environment and Public Facility Management	6365	5898	467
居民服务和其他服务业	Residents Service and Other Service	34355	33375	980
教 育	Education	701	626	75
卫生、社会保障和社会福利业	Healthcare, Social Security and Social Welfare	2005	1912	93
文化、体育和娱乐业	Culture, Sport and Entertainment	5089	4539	550
按城乡分	**Grouped By City and Village**			
城 镇	**Urban and Town**	**1504264**	**1348635**	**155629**
农林牧渔业	Farming,Forestry,Animal Husbandry and Fishery	10317	7041	3276
采矿业	Mining	205	81	124
制造业	Manufacturing	776706	715863	60843
电力、燃气及水的生产和供应业	Eletric Power,Gas and Tap Water Production and Supply	1693	1001	692
建筑业	Construction	187805	143128	44677
批发零售贸易业	Wholesale and Retail Trade	220541	201039	19502
交通运输、仓储和邮政业	Transportation, Storage,Post and Telecommunications	20492	18348	2144

15-5 续表 Continued　　　　单位：人（person）

指　标	Item	全　市 Whole Municipality	市　区 Urban Area	溧阳市 Liyang City
住宿和餐饮业	Accommodation and Catering Services	20365	16514	3851
信息传输、计算机服务和软件业	Information Transmission, Computer Service and Software	16776	15810	966
金融业	Financial	2500	2306	194
房地产业	Real Estate	33153	29476	3677
租赁和商务服务业	Lease and Commercial Service	81333	73562	7771
科学研究、技术服务和地质勘查业	Scientific Research, Technology Service and Geological Prospecting	87466	81428	6038
水利、环境和公共设施管理业	Water Conservancy, Environment and Public Facility Management	5830	5566	264
居民服务和其他服务业	Residents Service and Other Service	31333	30417	916
教　育	Education	691	626	65
卫生、社会保障和社会福利业	Healthcare, Social Security and Social Welfare	2005	1912	93
文化、体育和娱乐业	Culture, Sport and Entertainment	5053	4517	536
农　村	**Countryside**	**96092**	**40896**	**55196**
农林牧渔业	Farming,Forestry,Animal Husbandry and Fishery	2521	372	2149
采矿业	Mining and Quarrying	385	12	373
制造业	Manufacturing	45423	25051	20372
电力、燃气及水的生产和供应业	Eletric Power, Gas and Tap Water Production and Supply	165	50	115
建筑业	Construction	35368	7913	27455
批发零售贸易业	Wholesale and Retail Trade	4971	2487	2484
交通运输、仓储和邮政业	Transportation, Storage,Post and Telecommunications	642	338	304
住宿和餐饮业	Accommodation and Catering Services	572	401	171
信息传输、计算机服务和软件业	Information Transmission, Computer Service and Software	144	105	39
金融业	Financial	34	12	22
房地产业	Real Estate	364	191	173
租赁和商务服务业	Lease and Commercial Service	638	214	424
科学研究、技术服务和地质勘查业	Scientific Research, Technology Service and Geological Prospecting	1262	438	824
水利、环境和公共设施管理业	Water Conservancy, Environment and Public Facility Management	535	332	203
居民服务和其他服务业	Residents Service and Other Service	3022	2958	64
教　育	Education	10		10
文化、体育和娱乐业	Culture, Sport and Entertainment	36	22	14

15-6 分地区私营企业注册资金（2015 年）
REGISTERED CAPITAL OF PRIVATE ENTERPRISES BY REGION（2015）

单位：万元（10000 yuan）

指 标	Item	全 市 Whole Municipality	市 区 Urban Area	溧阳市 Liyang City
总 计	**Total**	**46414326**	**39536947**	**6877379**
按行业分	**Grouped By Sector**			
农林牧渔业	Farming,Forestry,Animal Husbandry and Fishery	533531	318501	215030
采矿业	Mining	77788	33100	44688
制造业	Manufacturing	14938810	12501615	2437195
电力、燃气及水的生产和供应业	Eletric Power, Gas and Tap Water Production and Supply	103307	58683	44623
建筑业	Construction	4738872	3614703	1124168
批发零售贸易业	Wholesale and Retail Trade	6687951	5812220	875731
交通运输、仓储和邮政业	Transportation, Storage,Post and Telecommunications	895101	804467	90634
住宿和餐饮业	Accommodation and Catering Services	169533	132404	37129
信息传输、计算机服务和软件业	Information Transmission, Computer Service and Software	514995	500362	14632
金融业	Financial	1012378	853868	158510
房地产业	Real Estate	2675369	2296748	378620
租赁和商务服务业	Lease and Commercial Service	8482420	7853093	629326
科学研究、技术服务和地质勘查业	Scientific Research, Technology Service and Geological Prospecting	4758323	3998260	760063
水利、环境和公共设施管理业	Water Conservancy, Environment and Public Facility Management	185202	172756	12446
居民服务和其他服务业	Residents Service and Other Service	343639	329290	14349
教 育	Education	15224	8564	6660
卫生、社会保障和社会福利业	Healthcare, Social Security and Social Welfare	52884	46194	6690
文化、体育和娱乐业	Culture, Sport and Entertainment	229001	202116	26885
按城乡分	**Grouped By City and Village**			
城 镇	**Urban and Town**	**44546280**	**38951475**	**5594805**
农林牧渔业	Farming,Forestry,Animal Husbandry and Fishery	419179	312040	107139
采矿业	Mining	33948	32950	998
制造业	Manufacturing	14028516	12172379	1856137
电力、燃气及水的生产和供应业	Eletric Power,Gas and Tap Water Production and Supply	101830	57967	43863
建筑业	Construction	4424379	3489668	934711
批发零售贸易业	Wholesale and Retail Trade	6463942	5750683	713259
交通运输、仓储和邮政业	Transportation, Storage,Post and Telecommunications	882990	802457	80533

15-6 续表 Continued

单位：万元（10000 yuan）

指 标	Item	全 市 Whole Municipality	市 区 Urban Area	溧阳市 Liyang City
住宿和餐饮业	Accommodation and Catering Services	164080	130256	33824
信息传输、计算机服务和软件业	Information Transmission, Computer Service and Software	510156	498673	11482
金融业	Financial	982228	848518	133710
房地产业	Real Estate	2642028	2285538	356489
租赁和商务服务业	Lease and Commercial Service	8397462	7842605	554857
科学研究、技术服务和地质勘查业	Scientific Research, Technology Service and Geological Prospecting	4704515	3988654	715861
水利、环境和公共设施管理业	Water Conservancy, Environment and Public Facility Management	168980	161652	7328
居民服务和其他服务业	Residents Service and Other Service	334618	321129	13489
教 育	Education	9224	8564	660
卫生、社会保障和社会福利业	Healthcare, Social Security and Social Welfare	52884	46194	6690
文化、体育和娱乐业	Culture, Sport and Entertainment	225321	201546	23775
农 村	**Countryside**	**1868046**	**585472**	**1282574**
农林牧渔业	Farming,Forestry,Animal Husbandry and Fishery	114352	6461	107891
采矿业	Mining and Quarrying	43840	150	43690
制造业	Manufacturing	910293	329236	581058
电力、燃气及水的生产和供应业	Eletric Power, Gas and Tap Water Production and Supply	1477	717	760
建筑业	Construction	314493	125036	189457
批发零售贸易业	Wholesale and Retail Trade	224009	61537	162472
交通运输、仓储和邮政业	Transportation, Storage,Post and Telecommunications	12111	2010	10101
住宿和餐饮业	Accommodation and Catering Services	5453	2148	3305
信息传输、计算机服务和软件业	Information Transmission, Computer Service and Software	4839	1689	3150
金融业	Financial	30150	5350	24800
房地产业	Real Estate	33341	11210	22131
租赁和商务服务业	Lease and Commercial Service	84958	10488	74470
科学研究、技术服务和地质勘查业	Scientific Research, Technology Service and Geological Prospecting	53808	9606	44202
水利、环境和公共设施管理业	Water Conservancy, Environment and Public Facility Management	16222	11104	5118
居民服务和其他服务业	Residents Service and Other Service	9021	8161	860
教 育	Education	6000		6000
文化、体育和娱乐业	Culture, Sport and Entertainment	3680	570	3110

16
CHAPTER 16

对外经济　旅游

FOREIGN ECONOMY AND TOURISM

常州统计年鉴

16 对外经济 旅游
FOREIGN ECONOMY AND TOURISM

2015 年主要统计指标
MAJOR STATISTICAL INDICATORS OF 2015

进出口总额	Total Imports and Exports	280.46 亿美元	(USD 100 million)
比上年增长	Over the Previous Year	-2.7%	
出口总额	Total Exports	212.58 亿美元	(USD 100 million)
比上年增长	Over the Previous Year	-0.5%	
协议外资项目	Protocol foreign Investment projects	255 个	(unit)
比上年增长	Over the Previous Year	-23.2%	
协议（合同）外资金额	Amount of Foreign Capital in the Newly Signed Agreements	27.69 亿美元	(USD 100 million)
比上年增长	Over the Previous Year	-19.7%	
实际到帐注册外资	Foreign Capital Actually Utilized	24.87 亿美元	(USD 100 million)
比上年增长	Over the Previous Year	-20.3%	
国家及省级开发区	Number of State and Provincial Development Zones	10 个	(unit)
# 国家级开发区	State Development Zone	2 个	(unit)
接待国际旅游者人数	Number of International Tourists	12.70 万人次	(10000 persons-times)
比上年增长	Over the Previous Year	5.4%	

16-1 主要年份对外经济指标
MAJOR INDICATORS OF FOREIGN TRADE AND ECONOMIC COOPERATION IN MAJOR YEARS

单位：万美元（USD 10000）

年 份 Year	进出口总额 Total Import and Export	其中 of which 进口 Import	出口 Export	协议（合同）外资金额 Amount of Foreign Capital in the Signed Agreements	实际利用外资金额 Amount of Foreign Capital Actually Utilized	新签对外承包劳务合同额 Amount of Newly Signed Foreign Contracted Labor Contract	对外承包劳务营业额 Business Value of Foreign Contracted Labor
1985	128		128	3617	1455	581	567
1990	6153	1180	4973	1751	666	433	73
1991	11520	2279	9241	9002	2384	1432	599
1992	20188	2516	17672	36897	8557	3842	1619
1993	38847	6047	32800	62412	14440	3076	1408
1994	64564	8101	56463	52882	27772	2859	1843
1995	99315	22371	76944	88728	32858	4568	3817
1996	135493	35261	100232	99906	51764	7448	6623
1997	168431	45457	122974	107417	56639	7321	6849
1998	159380	28345	131035	82327	55681	8630	7544
1999	192723	65056	127667	90158	62569	9424	8309
2000	282208	96174	186034	100285	70006	12480	9409
2001	325884	109306	216577	117625	62192	10275	7644
2002	391831	126244	265587	122132	56102	13997	9837
2003	525126	172170	352956	205376	85522	16189	12371
2004	690551	218920	471631	218671	58000	20432	14594
2005	833364	220936	612428	285100	73120	26010	20561
2006	1044213	255109	789104	329575	125145	40695	26479
2007	1322596	338192	984404	440087	183481	51694	32618
2008	1762893	438540	1324353	340952	204002	52231	37175
2009	1507929	421284	1086645	422114	226129	52280	41082
2010	2227750	671944	1555806	474203	267000	57685	46913
2011	2863464	927380	1936084	463196	305238	58005	49505
2012	2904567	908397	1996170	474925	336073	59870	53985
2013	2921273	883894	2037379	438316	353000	66432	57801
2014	2881021	742593	2138428	344848	312072	69382	58917
2015	2804591	678821	2125770	276857	248700	63155	46482

注：1、从 1999 年起进出口为海关数。
2、从 2001 年起新签对外承包劳务合同额、营业额为商务部口径。
3、从 2002 年起协议合同外资金额、实际利用外资金额为新口径，即协议注册外资额、实际到帐注册外资。
4、从 2004 年起实际利用外资金额为有验资报告的实际到帐注册外资数。

Note：1.The indices of import and export are the statistical figures of the customs since 1999.
2.Since the year of 2001, the amount of newly signed foreign contracted labor contracts and the business value of foreign contracted labor belong to the statistical figures of the Ministry of Commerce.
3.The amount of foreign capital in signed agreements and contracts and foreign capital actually utilized are based on new statistical specifications since 2002,Namely the actual paid up amount of contracted foreign capital and registered foreign capital.
4.The amount of foreign capital actually utilized since 2004 has been included in capital verification report.

16-2 分地区对外经济主要指标（2015 年）
MAJOR INDICATORS OF FOREIGN TRADE AND ECONOMIC COOPERATION BY REGION（2015）

指 标	Item	全 市 Whole Municipality	市 区 Urban Area	溧阳市 Liyang City
进出口总额（万美元）	**Total Import and Export （USD 10000）**	**2804591**	**2721087**	**83504**
对外贸易公司	Foreign Trade Corporation	257476	241815	15661
自营生产企业	Self-supporting Manufacturing Enterprises	1092205	1057273	34932
三资企业	Three Types of Foreign-funded Enterprises	1454910	1421999	32911
出 口	**Export**	**2125770**	**2051167**	**74603**
对外贸易公司	Foreign Trade Corporation	237455	222523	14932
自营生产企业	Self-supporting Manufacturing Enterprises	848414	816019	32395
三资企业	Three Types of Foreign-funded Enterprises	1039901	1012625	27276
进 口	**Import**	**678821**	**669921**	**8900**
对外贸易公司	Foreign Trade Corporation	20021	19292	729
自营生产企业	Self-supporting Manufacturing Enterprises	243791	241254	2537
三资企业	Three Types of Foreign-funded Enterprises	415009	409375	5634
协议外资项目（个）	**Protocol foreign Investment projects （unit）**	**255**	**241**	**14**
# 新增协议外资项目	New Foreign Investment project agreement	146	138	8
港、澳、台商投资企业	Enterprises with Investment from Hongkong, Macao and Taiwan	48	43	5
外商投资企业	Enterprises with Foreign Investment	98	95	3
协议（合同）外资（万美元）	**Amount of Foreign Capital in the Newly Signed Agreements （USD 10000）**	**276857**	**246335**	**30522**
港、澳、台商投资企业	Enterprises with Investment from Hongkong, Macao and Taiwan	197657	173048	24609
外商投资企业	Enterprises with Foreign Investment	79200	73287	5913
实际到帐注册外资（万美元）	**Foreign Capital Actually Utilized （USD 10000）**	**248700**	**238080**	**10620**
期末实有外商投资企业数（个）	**Number of Foreign-funded Enterprises at Year-end（unit）**	**3687**	**3447**	**240**
新签对外承包工程和劳务合作	**Newly Signed Foreign Contracted Projects and Labor Cooperation**			
项目个数（个）	Number of Project （unit）	58	24	34
合同金额（万美元）	Amount of Contracts （USD 10000）	63155	47425	15730
营业额（万美元）	Business Value （USD 10000）	46482	37069	9413
派出人数（人）	Number of Persons Sent Abroad （person）	3900	3221	679
期末在外人数（人）	Number of Persons Abroad （person）	5971	4888	1083
新批海外投资企业	**Newly Approved Enterprises with Overseas Investment**			
本年新签海外投资企业（个）	Number of Newly Contracted overseas Investment Enterprises（unit）	67	62	5

16-3 按贸易方式和产品类别分的外贸进出口商品总额（2011-2015 年）
TOTAL VALUE OF IMPORTS AND EXPORTS BY TRADE AND DIFFERENT PRODUCTS（2011-2015）

单位：万美元（USD 10000）

指 标	Items	2011	2012	2013	2014	2015
进口总额	**Total Value of Imports**	**927380**	**908397**	**883894**	**742593**	**678821**
#高新技术产品	High and New Technological Products	149083	220825	98342	100882	85903
按贸易方式分	**Grouped by Trade**					
#一般贸易	Original Trade	592868	518042	565885	475730	456349
来料加工装配贸易	Processing and Assembling Trade Provided with Raw Material	10927	10157	7929	10402	13149
进料加工贸易	Raw Material Input Processing Trade	194032	170020	251432	196759	162606
外商投资企业投资设备	Goods as Invested for Import Equipments	76196	34372	23540	21146	14552
按产品类别分	**Grouped by Different Products**					
#化工产品	Chemicals and Related Products	161721	151547	133208	113956	117571
纺织服装	Textile Materials and Products	52904	52898	279	36330	31927
机电产品	Electrical and Mechanical Products	425225	389193	297475	312310	268276
出口总额	**Total Value of Exports**	**1936084**	**1996170**	**2037379**	**2138428**	**2125770**
#高新技术产品	High and New Technological Products	410518	397422	451024	318702	349464
按贸易方式分	**Grouped by Trade**					
#一般贸易	Original Trade	1376255	1389861	1462894	1585429	1577214
来料加工装配贸易	Processing and Assembling Trade Provided with Raw Material	22715	21017	16602	17828	24041
进料加工贸易	Raw Material Input Processing Trade	529221	457499	553900	528609	498429
按产品类别分	**Grouped by Different Products**					
#化工产品	Chemicals and Related Products	179065	173724	152440	156038	149790
纺织服装	Textile Materials and Products	375169	354448	164299	363183	352529
机电产品	Electrical and Mechanical Products	1033688	1054890	1009359	1121906	1149329

16-4 分国别或地区进出口总额（2015 年）
TOTAL IMPORTS AND EXPORTS BY COUNTRY OR REGION（2015）

单位：万美元（USD 10000）

国别或地区	Region	进出口总额 Total Import and Export	其中 of which 出口 Export	进口 Import
总　计	**Total**	**2804591**	**2125770**	**678821**
亚　洲	**Asia**	**1337844**	**965996**	**371847**
#日　本	Japan	310149	206743	103405
印　度	India	94614	87407	7207
中国香港	Hongkong,China	73941	72048	1893
中国台湾	Taiwan,China	118257	52107	66150
韩　国	Korea,Rep.	138132	60378	77755
越　南	Vietnam	86647	80084	6563
非　洲	**Africa**	**76345**	**73614**	**2730**
欧　洲	**Europe**	**544452**	**394601**	**149850**
#德 国	Germany	145054	71922	73132
荷 兰	Netherlands	67663	61791	5872
英 国	United Kindom	56423	50595	5829
意大利	Italy	39864	33055	6809
法 国	France	34435	28129	6306
俄罗斯	Russia	27610	26832	778
拉丁美洲	**Latin America**	**157953**	**127323**	**30630**
北美洲	**North America**	**561628**	**512429**	**49200**
#美 国	United States	518314	476419	41894
大洋洲	**Oceania**	**124947**	**50548**	**74399**
#澳大利亚	Australia	118439	44620	73819
附：东 盟	Association of Southeast Asia Nations	325784	273057	52726
欧 盟	European Union	473046	342911	130135

16-5 外商直接投资情况（2015 年）
FOREIGN INVESTMENT CONDITIONS（2015）

指 标	Item	新签项目个数（个）Number of Newly Signed Agreements (unit)	协议外资金额（万美元）Amount of Contractual Foreign Captial (USD 10000)	实际到帐注册外资（万美元）Foreign Capital Actually Utilized (USD 10000)
总 计	**Total**	**146**	**276857**	**248700**
按企业登记注册类型分	**Grouped by Type of Registration**			
合资经营企业	Joint Venture	60	39576	33762
合作经营企业	Cooperative		-19	
独资经营企业	Sole Investment	86	236623	214938
股份有限公司	Share-holding Corporations Ltd.		677	
按国民经济行业分	**Grouped by Sector**			
农、林、牧、渔业	Farming,Forestry,Animal Husbandry and Fishery	5	4282	428
制造业	Manufacturing	47	148970	129915
# 农副食品加工业	Food Processing		583	519
纺织业	Textile Industry	2	399	2257
纺织服装、鞋、帽制造业	Textile, Garments, Shoes and Hat Processing	2	3981	935
家具制造业	Furniture Manufacturing		444	326
造纸及纸制品业	Papermaking and Paper Products			328
化学原料及化学制品制造业	Raw Chemical Materials and Chemica Products	2	4016	2871
医药制造业	Medical and Pharmaceutical Products	1	804	2212
化学纤维制造业	Chemical Fiber			30
橡胶制品业	Rubber Products	1	1111	
塑料制品业	Plastic Products	1	1313	2337
非金属矿物制品业	Nonmetal Mineral Products	4	12102	1552

16-5 续表 1 Continued 1

指 标	Item	新签项目个数（个） Number of Newly Signed Agreements (unit)	协议外资金额（万美元） Amount of Contractual Foreign Captial (USD 10000)	实际到帐注册外资（万美元） Foreign Capital Actually Utilized (USD 10000)
金属制品业	Metal Products		383	2319
通用设备制造业	General Equipment Manufacturing	9	6224	8783
专用设备制造业	For Special Purposes Equipment Manufacturing	6	8536	7438
交通运输设备制造业	Transport Equipment Manufacturing	4	4405	10038
电气机械及器材制造业	Electric Equipment and Machinery	10	103042	82339
通信设备、计算机及其他电子设备制造业	Communication, Computer and Other Electronic Equipment	2	1840	2459
仪器仪表及文化、办公用机械制造业	Instruments, Meters, Cultural and Office Machinery	3	-214	2764
工艺品及其他制造业	Artcraft and Other Manufacturing		1	408
电力、燃气及水的生产和供应业	Production and Supply of Electricity, Gas and Water	5	38455	12905
建筑业	Construction	1	2	
交通运输、仓储和邮政业	Transportation , Storage and Post	3	940	4701
信息传输、计算机服务和软件业	Information Transformation, Computer Service and Software	3	548	151
批发和零售业	Wholesale and Retail Trade	40	11223	8764
住宿和餐饮业	Accommodation and Catering Services	3	41	52
金融业	Banking		4038	4201
房地产业	Real Estate Industry		-1481	8460
租赁和商务服务业	Rent and Business Services	16	46410	69891
科学研究、技术服务和地质勘查业	Scientific Research and Technology Service and Geologic Examination	19	21815	8520
水利、环境和公共设施管理业	Water Conservancy, Environment and Public Facilities Management	1	1500	480
居民服务和其他服务业	Residents Service and Other Service	1	107	106
教 育	Education	1	2	
文化、体育和娱乐业	Culture, Sports and Entertainment	1	5	126

16-5 续表 2 Continued 2

指 标	Item	新签项目个数（个） Number of Newly Signed Agreements (unit)	协议外资金额（万美元） Amount of Contractual Foreign Captial (USD 10000)	实际到帐注册外资（万美元） Foreign Capital Actually Utilized (USD 10000)
按投资国别、地区分	**Grouped by Country and Region**	**146**	**276857**	**248700**
亚 洲	**Asia**	**80**	**212638**	**212005**
#香 港	Hongkong,China	33	207606	195978
台 湾	Taiwan,China	12	1406	31
新加坡	Singapore	6	1440	6494
日 本	Japan	7	2058	5695
韩 国	Korea	14	-71	2005
非 洲	**Africa**	**3**	**339**	**294**
#塞舌尔	Seychelle		214	94
欧 洲	**Europe**	**27**	**7673**	**11075**
#英 国	United Kindom	5	522	33
德 国	Germany	7	2583	3572
法 国	France	1	10	
荷 兰	Netherlands	2	1524	3996
意大利	Italy	4	417	131
西班牙	Spain	2	27	
芬 兰	Finland		-210	305
瑞 典	Sweden	1	901	1103
瑞 士	Switzerland	3	747	330
拉丁美洲	**Latin America**		**2517**	**5784**
#开曼群岛	CaymanIslands		2158	780
英属维尔京群岛	British West Indies		-383	3620
北美洲	**North America**	**24**	**3475**	**1237**
#加拿大	Canada	5	2838	200
美 国	United States	19	638	1037
大洋洲	**Oceania**	**8**	**2266**	**3328**
#澳大利亚	Australia	6	60	63

16-6 分地区旅游人数和收入（2015 年）
NUMBER OF TOURISTS AND ERANINGS FROM TOURISM BY REGION（2015）

指 标	Item	全 市 Whole Municipality	市 区 Urban Area	溧阳市 Liyang City
旅游总人数（万人次）	**Number of Tourists （10000 persons-times）**	**5455.70**	**3993.28**	**1462.42**
国内旅游人数	Number of Dometic Tourists	5443.00	3981.03	1461.97
入境旅游人数	Number of International Tourists	12.70	12.25	0.45
旅游总收入	**Total Earnings from Tourism**	**730.96**	**571.50**	**159.46**
国内旅游收入（亿元）	Domestic Tourism （100 million yuan）	718.35	560.33	158.02
旅游创汇（亿美元）	International Tourism （USD 100 million）	1.02	0.97	0.05
出游前后花费（亿元）	Cost before and after Travel（100 million yuan）	5.16	4.04	1.12
旅游景区（点）	**Scenic Spots**			
接待游客（万人次）	Number of Tourists （10000 persons-times）	12186	9826	2360
营业收入（万元）	Operating Income （10000 yuan）	583563	400162	183401

16-7 分地区国际旅游人数和收入（2015 年）
TOTAL NUMBER OF INTERNATIONAL TOURISTS AND ERANINGS FROM INTERNATIONAL TOURISM BY REGION（2015）

指 标	Item	全 市 Whole Municipality	市 区 Urban Area	溧阳市 Liyang City
入境游客人数（人）	**Number of International Tourists（person）**	**126952**	**122456**	**4496**
外国人（人）	Foreigners（person）	108267	104674	3593
澳、台同胞（人）	Hongkong, Macao and Taiwan（person）	18685	17782	903
旅游创汇（万美元）	**Foreign Exchange Earings of Tourism （USD 10000）**	**12066**	**11577**	**489**

16-8 主要旅游区（点）情况（2015 年）
MAIN SCENIC SPOTS（2015）

名 称 Name	接待人数（万人次） Persons Reception（10000 persons-times）	营业收入（万元） Business Income（10000 yuan）	地 址 Address	联系电话 Contact Telephone Number	邮政编码 Post Code
中华恐龙园 China Dinosaur Park	783	63113	常州新区长江东路1号 No. 1 East Changjing Rd. New District, Changzhou	85106668	213022
天宁禅寺 Tianning Temple	51	3408	常州延陵东路636号 No. 636 East Yanling Rd., Changzhou	88111447	213003
红梅公园 Red Plum Park	1027	2917	常州罗汉路1号 No. 1 Luohan Rd., Changzhou	88108020	213003
东坡公园 Dongpo Park	58		常州延陵东路水门桥堍 Shuimen Bridge, East Yanling Rd., Changzhou	88815005	213003
瞿秋白纪念馆 Qu Qiubai Memorial	107		常州延陵西路102号 No.102 West Yanling Rd. ,Changzhou	86636909	213003
张太雷纪念馆 Zhang Tailei Memorial	33		常州清凉路子和里3号 No. 3 Ziheli Qingliang Rd., Changzhou	88813757	213003
青枫公园 Qingfeng Park	588	180	常州钟楼区星港大道 Xinggang Boulevard, Zhonglou District, Changzhou	88156617	213200
春秋淹城遗址旅游区 Tourist Resort of Yancheng Remains of Spring and Autumn Period	350	35865	常州市武进区武宜南路588号 No.588 South Wuyi Road, Wujin District, Changzhou	86318622	213161
太湖湾旅游度假区 Taihu Lake Bay Tourism Resort	400	52400	武进雪堰镇太湖湾 Taihu Lake Bay, Xueyan Town, Wujin	86543001	213179
环球动漫嬉戏谷 Global Animation Joyland	221	29661	常州市武进区雪堰镇太北路1号 1 North Taibei Road, Xueyan Town, Wujin District, Changzhou	88888821	213179
中华孝道园 China Filial Piety Park	60	4796	常州市武进区雪堰镇环湖路101号 101 Huanhu Road, Xueyan Town, Wujin District, Changzhou	86692018	213179

16-8 续表 Continued

名 称 Name	接待人数（万人次） Persons Reception（10000 persons-times）	营业收入（万元） Business Income（10000 yuan）	地 址 Address	联系电话 Contact Telephone Number	邮政编码 Post Code
武进横山风景旅游区 Wujin Hengshan Scenic Spot	75	86	武进区横山桥镇 Hengshanqiao Town,Wujin District	88605967	213119
武进艺林园 Wujin Horticulture Garden	36	1094	武进区夏溪镇厚余街 Huoyu St., Xiaxi Town, Wujin District	83681109	213146
常州天目湖旅游度假区 Liyang Tianmu Lake Tourism and Vacation Zone	735	108623	溧阳市天目湖镇 Tianmu Lake Town, Liyang City	87980388	213333
金鹰国际海洋世界 Golden eagle international ocean world	3441	2094	常州市钟楼区吊桥路25号 No.25 diaoqiao Rd.,Zhonglou District,Changzhou	81168280	213003
金坛茅山风景名胜区 Jintan Maoshan Scenic Spot	231	5622	金坛区茅东林场西侧 West of Maodong Forestry Center, Jintan District	82669388	213200
金坛华罗庚公园 Jintan Hua Luogeng Park	217		金坛区市府路38号 No. 38 Shifu Rd., Jintan District	82822957	213200
金坛城南风景区 Jintan Chengnan Scenic Spot	91		金坛区金城镇 Jincheng Town, Jintan District	82823427	213200
华夏宝盛园 Sino-art&craft Museum LandScape	3	140	金坛区茅东林场西侧 West of Maodong Forestry Center, Jintan District	80188888	213200
金坛长荡湖旅游度假区 Jintan Changdang Lake Tourism Resort	119	37254	金坛区蒋庄路 Jiangzhuang Rd.,Jintan District	82560086	213200
常州运河五号创意街区 Changzhou Canal 5 creativity Compus	46	5574	钟楼区三堡街141号 No.141 Sanbao Street,Zhonglou District	86884316	213016
江苏华夏工美产业博览园 Jiangsu Sino-arts Industry Expo Park	102	5394	新北区薛家镇庆阳路68号 No.68 Qingyang Rd,Xuejia Town,Xinbin District	85957750	324000

16-9 旅游涉外饭店、宾馆情况（2015 年底）
FOREIGN-CONCERNED HOTEL AND RESTAURANT CONDITIONS（END OF 2015）

名 称 Name	星级标准 Standard		地 址 Address	联系电话 Contact Telephone Number	客房数（间） Number of Guest Room（room）	客房出租率（%） Room Occupancy Rate（%）
常州大酒店	五星	Five-star	常州市延陵西路65号	88109988	216	51.17
常州富都盛贸大酒店	五星	Five-star	新区通江大道398号	85168888	378	61.76
江苏天目湖宾馆	五星	Five-star	溧阳市天目湖旅游度假区	87168888	171	53.66
溧阳宾馆	五星	Five-star	溧阳市西大街118号	87222777	281	58.41
维景国际大酒店	五星	Five-star	新北区河海东路56号	82088888	266	66.65
武进九洲喜来登	五星	Five-star	武进区延政西大道1号	69968888	317	55.29
溧阳御水温泉酒店	五星	Five-star	溧阳市戴埠镇李家园村	87938888	240	61.62
常州市和平假日大饭店	四星	Four-star	常州市和平南路151号	88163388	172	53.76
常州阳光国际大酒店有限公司	四星	Four-star	常州市怀德中路45号	86606888	333	51.37
常州市明都大饭店管理	四星	Four-star	常州市和平北路39号	88118888	236	57.49
常州中天凤凰大酒店	四星	Four-star	常州市新区通江大道555号	86187888	211	64.25
常州溧阳市假日酒店	四星	Four-star	溧阳罗湾路99号	87199999	146	52.77
常州万豪花都国际大酒店	四星	Four-star	常州晋陵北路168号	88222222	184	54.11
奥体明都国际饭店	四星	Four-star	新北区龙锦路1261号	85608888	202	76.54
涵田度假村酒店	四星	Four-star	溧阳市戴埠镇	87178888	506	75.53
常州九洲环宇大酒店	四星	Four-star	关河东路38号	85228820	185	55.99
常州香树湾花园酒店	四星	Four-star	新北区汉江路2号	85118900	121	70.58
常州海阳大酒店	四星	Four-star	通江大道371号	88516778	142	71.49
金坛颐丰大酒店有限公司	四星	Four-star	金坛市丹阳门中路188号	82796666	66	74.55
常州锦江国际大酒店有限公司	四星	Four-star	新北区通江中路769号	85198888	261	66.23
常州金色南都国际大酒店	四星	Four-star	武进区湖塘环府路58号	86319588	70	65.09
溧阳皇廷国际大酒店	四星	Four-star	天目湖中心大道20号	83106828	145	61.81
常州德泰恒大酒店	四星	Four-star	常州小河沿1号	85221688	115	60.10
常州金鼎明都国际大酒店	四星	Four-star	武进区湟里镇金鼎路8号	83349898	147	52.52
西太湖明都国际会议中心	四星	Four-star	经济开发区禾香路118号	89852888	203	58.06
溧阳市扬子国际大酒店	四星	Four-star	溧阳市溧城镇安顺路9号	87928888	118	49.75
常州市武进区新苑宾馆	三星	Three-star	武进湖塘环府路	86312888	160	59.97
新锦江商旅酒店	三星	Three-star	常州市新丰街14号	88101710	185	58.15

16-9 续表 Continued

名 称 Name	星级标准 Standard		地 址 Address	联系电话 Contact Telephone Number	客房数（间） Number of Guest Room（room）	客房出租率（%） Room Occupancy Rate（%）
国瑞宾馆	三星	Three-star	武进横山桥镇	88603888	167	55.00
溧阳市天目水庐宾馆	三星	Three-star	溧阳市天目湖旅游度假区	87981798	67	45.29
武进城区金龙酒店	三星	Three-star	武进湖塘人民路1号	86550978	86	67.67
溧阳虹枫美食休闲度假村	三星	Three-star	溧阳天目湖旅游度假区内	87167718	243	47.82
宫苑宾馆	三星	Three-star	常州市延陵西路85号	86602606	106	44.01
常州馨雅楼宾馆	三星	Three-star	戚机厂工房1区1号	85052122	116	70.32
武进漕桥石头大酒店	三星	Three-star	雪堰镇漕桥金三角东路61号	81182000	36	73.99
常瑞宾馆	三星	Three-star	常州市浦南路8号	86183888	131	63.90
常州椿庭大酒店有限公司	三星	Three-star	常州市局前街27号	88152222	111	50.01
常州锦海城市大酒店	三星	Three-star	常州市会馆浜路11号	86856577	80	60.78
金坛市九龙宾馆	三星	Three-star	金坛市东环二路39号	82399000	68	72.77
武进区郑陆舜杰名都大酒店	三星	Three-star	武进区郑陆镇焦溪路2号	81231777	54	64.78
溧阳市翠谷庄园	三星	Three-star	溧阳市戴埠镇南山竹海大道旁	87933888	60	55.73
溧阳市李家园大酒店	三星	Three-star	溧阳市戴埠镇	87938777	53	58.31
星港中信国际商务酒店	三星	Three-star	钟楼区星港路88号	88891888	77	77.70
景尚大成假日酒店	三星	Three-star	天宁区关河东路44号	85220000	167	48.70
竺山湖小镇酒店	三星	Three-star	太湖湾旅游度假区竺山路	83591000	137	78.38
溧阳天目湖煜景大酒店	三星	Three-star	溧阳市天目湖镇牌楼东侧	87033666	86	48.90
湖塘逸都宾馆	三星	Three-star	武进区武宜中路165号	81198119	55	42.50
溧阳天目湖大酒店	二星	Two-star	溧阳天目湖镇	87980396	51	57.00
溧阳市翠竹园宾馆	二星	Two-star	溧阳市天目湖旅游度假区	87980358	125	49.03
溧阳交通大酒店	二星	Two-star	西大街142号	87225188	79	63.94
武进假日酒店	准评星	Units Qualified for Star Levels	武进区延政中路33号	86313888	280	57.36
凯纳豪生大酒店	准评星	Units Qualified for Star Levels	钟楼区通江南路8号	88808888	343	60.74
福记逸高酒店	准评星	Units Qualified for Star Levels	新北区汉江东路99号	83098888	303	60.65
万达喜来登	准评星	Units Qualified for Star Levels	新北区通江中路88-1号	81588888	247	72.39
华美达国际大酒店	准评星	Units Qualified for Star Levels	新北区晋陵北路85号	68000888	159	67.68
常州金陵江南大饭店	准评星	Units Qualified for Star Levels	新北区通江路466号	85119988	205	77.43

16-10 开发区建设情况（2015 年）
CONSTRUCTION OF THE DEVELOPMENT ZONES（2015）

指　标	Item	合　计 Total	常州高新技术产业开发区 Changzhou High and New Technology Industries Development Zone	武进国家高新技术产业开发区 Wujin National Hi-tech Industrial Zone
本年全社会固定资产投资（亿元）	Total Investment in Fixed Assets at This Year（100 million yuan）	2215.70	759.90	243.00
本年批准外商投资企业（个）	Approved Foreign-funded Enterprises in Year（unit）	101	31	20
本年新签协议注册外资（万美元）	Accumulated Contractual Foreign Capital of Approved Enterprises at This Year（USD 10000）	236326	27482	83303
本年实际到帐注册外资（万美元）	Accumulated Actual Foreign Investment at This Year（USD 10000）	225453	37073	51692
本年外贸进出口额（万美元）	Accumulated Export-import Volume at This Year（USD 10000）	1974418	1064061	320374
工业产品销售收入	Sales Revenue from Industrial Products	10410.71	3209.85	1430.00
公共财政预算收入（亿元）	Public Finance Budget Revenue（100 million Yuan）	299.70	98.20	58.00

注：各开发区包括进区企业。
Note:All development zones include the enterprises settled down in the zone.

江苏省武进经济开发区 Wujin Economic Development Zone, Jiangsu	江苏省金坛经济开发区 Jintan Economic Development Zone, Jiangsu	江苏省溧阳经济开发区 Liyang Economic Development Zone, Jiangsu	江苏省常州天宁经济开发区 Tianning Economic Development Zone, Changzhou, Jiangsu	江苏省常州钟楼经济开发区 Zhonglou Economic Development Zone, Changzhou, Jiangsu	江苏省常州经济开发区 Changzhou Economic Development Zone , Jiangsu	天目湖旅游度假区 Tianmu Lake Tourist Resort
110.60	273.40	207.50	189.30	176.80	220.40	34.80
19	13	1	3	9	5	
9247	5656	17550	6513	14125	9158	3144
2616	4827	2738	2315	7230	1363	6169
35930	90605	39164	90532	89899	231331	12522
397.13	863.48	1341.72	893.36	846.46	1301.00	127.71
9.40	17.60	39.40	36.00	13.90	23.30	3.90

17

CHAPTER 17

能源消费

CONSUMPTION OF ENERGY

常州统计年鉴

17 能源消费
CONSUMPTION OF ENERGY

2015 年主要统计指标
MAJOR STATISTICAL INDICATORS OF 2015

全社会用电量	Total Electriccity Consumed	408.04亿千瓦时	(100 million kw.h)
比上年增长	Over the Previous Year	3.3%	
工业用电量	Industrial Electricity Consumption	325.49亿千瓦时	(100 million kw.h)
比上年增长	Over the Previous Year	3.0%	
城乡居民生活用电量	Electricity Consumption by Urban and Rural Residents	34.39亿千瓦时	(100 million kw.h)
比上年增长	Over the Previous Year	6.0%	
规模以上工业企业生产综合能源消费量	Production of the Comprehensive energy Consumption of Industrial Enterprises above Designated Size	1709.43万吨	(10000 tons)
同比增长	Over the Previous Year	2.3%	

17-1 全社会用电量（1980-2015 年）
TOTAL ELECTRICITY CONSUMPTION（1980-2015）

单位：万千瓦时（10000 kw.h）

年 份 Year	全社会用电量 Total Electricity Consumption	其中 of which # 农林牧渔水利业 Farming, Forestry, Animal Husbandry, Fishery and Water Conservancy	工 业 Industry	交通运输、邮电通信业 Transportation, Post and Telecommuni-cations Services	城乡居民生活 Electricity Consumption by of Urban and Rural Residents
1980	134387	27134	102715	459	4079
1981	144076	33226	105738	375	4737
1982	155004	35467	113498	293	5746
1983	166728	41084	119095	321	6228
1984	180092	45608	126691	291	7502
1985	195387	54628	131151	287	9321
1986	226192	27971	183961	778	7059
1987	253060	28737	207018	340	9549
1988	268665	31616	214548	921	12346
1989	270752	32965	213121	1322	14256
1990	293370	38930	223449	1709	17283
1991	330885	42703	250208	3915	18973
1992	378832	47382	286052	2024	25103
1993	424120	51949	310357	2627	33968
1994	483755	57671	342772	3287	46000
1995	522521	60136	362325	3726	57620
1996	557030	63478	381807	4248	62910
1997	586748	71269	391600	5735	68439
1998	601148	72676	391733	6975	77286
1999	641191	79090	421049	7435	78497
2000	743453	87042	492989	7924	97199
2001	813527	96264	542864	8812	108352
2002	988809	112040	686011	10134	110380
2003	1269745	142175	915670	12391	118145
2004	1522392	164706	1107854	15586	128541
2005	1826605	34748	1452046	36287	149200
2006	2126844	23952	1749992	16396	172817
2007	2306172	17285	1908046	12272	186762
2008	2373291	17634	1920858	15038	213800
2009	2554100	18246	2054113	15913	229934
2010	2911875	21420	2318221	23790	275163
2011	3316562	22438	2672080	32690	280418
2012	3515102	23255	2778770	35876	321920
2013	3909821	26777	3080572	40964	373899
2014	3950643	25900	3160866	46026	324278
2015	4080444	29662	3254879	49140	343885

注:本表按当年口径统计, 1986年行业用电分类按调整口径统计, 1991年以前交通运输、邮电通信业仅指交通运输业。2006年以后交通运输、邮电通信业也指交通运输、仓储和邮政业。

Notes: This form is in compliance with the specification of this year. The statistic data of the electricity consumption by sectors in 1986 was based upon the regulatory specification. The transportation, post and telecommunications had only indicated the transportation before 1991.After 2006, transportation, post and telecommunications refers to transportation, storage and postal industry.

17-2 全社会分月用电量（2015 年）
TOTAL ELECTRICITY CONSUMPTION BY MONTH（2015）

单位：万千瓦时 （10000 kw.h）

月 份 Month		全社会用电量 Total Electricity Consumption	其 中 of witch #工 业 Industry	城乡居民生活用电 Electricity Consumption by of Urban and Rural Residents
总 计	**Total**	**4080444**	**3254879**	**343885**
第一季度	First Quarter	966902	764497	90247
1		360208	285724	29154
2		267135	201698	34134
3		339559	277075	26959
第二季度	Second Quarter	979121	793852	78276
4		318075	251140	30083
5		336922	271559	26350
6		324124	271153	21843
第三季度	Third Quarter	1067654	828355	95104
7		348147	279575	23425
8		376646	300822	30218
9		342861	247958	41461
第四季度	Fourth Quarter	1066767	868175	80258
10		332458	258150	33087
11		344451	285428	23403
12		389858	324597	23768

17-3 分地区全社会用电量（2015 年）
TOTAL ELECTRICITY CONSUMPTION BY REGION（2015）

单位：万千瓦时（10000 kw.h）

指 标	Item	全 市 Whole Municipality	市 区 Urban Area	溧阳市 Liyang City
总 计	**Total**	**4080444**	**3399272**	**681172**
农林牧渔业	Farming,Forestry,Animal Husbandry and Fishery	29662	22853	6809
农 业	Agriculture	3709	3134	575
林 业	Forestry	974	801	173
畜牧业	Animal Husbandry	4404	4072	332
渔 业	Fishery	10998	7356	3642
农、林、牧、渔服务业	Farming,Forestry, Animal Husbandry and Fishery	9577	7490	2087
#排 灌	Irrigation and Drainage	6182	4484	1698
工 业	Industry	3254879	2680826	574053
采矿业	Mining	487	487	
制造业	Manufacturing	3049933	2522649	527284
食品、饮料和烟草制造业	Production of Food ,Beverages and Tobacco	18983	14538	4445
纺织业	Textiles	273957	260464	13493
服装鞋帽、皮革羽绒及其制品业	Garments, leather Down and Related Products	30014	27822	2192
木材加工及制品和家具制品业	Timber Processing and products, and Furniture Manufacturing	34968	32446	2522
造纸及纸制品业	Papermaking and Paper Production	16243	15348	895
印刷业和记录媒介的复制	Printing and Record Duplicating	5973	5686	287
文体用品制造业	Culture and Sports Goods	3126	3111	15
石油加工、炼焦及核燃料加工业	Petroleum Processing, Coking and Nuclear Fuel Processing	1520	1500	20
化学原料及化学制品制造业	Raw Chemical Materials and Chemica Production	212580	202397	10183
医药制造业	Medical and Pharmaceutical Production	28074	25554	2520
化学纤维制造业	Chemical Fiber	27293	27136	157
橡胶和塑料制品业	Rubber and Plastic Production	167918	159660	8258
非金属矿物制品业	Nonmetal Mineral Production	328840	148340	180500
黑色金属冶炼及压延加工业	Smelting and Pressing of Ferrous Metals	657844	547828	110016
有色金属冶炼及压延加工业	Smelting and Pressing of Nonferrous Metals	48840	47338	1502

17-3 续表 continued　　单位：万千瓦时（10000 kwh）

指 标	Item	全 市 Whole Municipality	市 区 Urban Area	溧阳市 Liyang City
金属制品业	Metal Products	315904	214387	101517
通用及专用设备制造业	Universal & Special Equipments Manufacturing	421722	364426	57296
交通运输、电气、电子设备制造业	Electronic and Transportation Equipment	391794	361451	30343
工艺品及其他制造业	Other Industry	57123	56339	784
废弃资源和废旧材料回收加工业	Waste Resources and Materials Recycling and Processing	7217	6878	339
电力、燃气及水的生产和供应业	Production and Supply of Electric Power, Gas and Water	204459	157690	46769
电力、热力的生产和供应业	Production and Supply of Electric Power and Thermal Power	164743	120852	43891
燃气生产和供应业	Production and Supply of Gas	8355	8282	73
自来水生产和供应业	Production and Supply of Running Water	31361	28556	2805
建筑业	Construction	28266	23141	5125
交通运输、仓储和邮政业	Communication and Transportation, Storage and Post Industry	49140	40437	8703
商业、住宿和餐饮业	Commerce, Accommodation and Catering Industry	141145	121277	19868
信息传输、计算机服务和软件业	Information transmission, computer service and software	19394	16230	3164
金融、房地产、租赁和商务、居民服务和其他服务业	Finance, Real Estate, Renting and Business, Residents Services and Other Services	96048	89537	6511
卫生、社会保障和社会福利事业	Health Care,Social Security and Social Welfare	21089	19229	1860
教育、文化体育和娱乐业	Education,Culture,Sports and recreation	41935	39163	2772
科学研究、技术服务和地质堪查业	Scientific Research,Polytechnical Services and Geological Exploration	3327	3188	139
公共管理和社会组织、国际组织	Public Administration and Social or International Organizations	20854	18646	2208
水利、环境和公共设施管理业	Water, Environment and Public Facilities	30820	28154	2666
城乡居民生活用电	Electricity Consumption by Urban and Rural Residents	343885	296591	47294
农 村	Villiage	192623	162904	29719
城 市	City	151262	133687	17575

17-4 规模以上工业企业分行业生产综合能源消费量（2015 年）
COMPREHENSIVE ENERGY CONSUMPTION IN PRODUCTION OF ABOVE-SCALE INDUSTRIAL ENTERPRISES BY SECTOR（2015）

指 标	Item	企业单位数（个）Number of Enterpr-ises（unit）	综合能源消费量（吨标准煤）Comprehensive Energy Consumption（tce）
总 计	**Total**	**4016**	**17094314**
按地区分	**Grouped by Region**		
市 区	Urban Area	3676	12310104
金坛区	Jintan District	404	980376
武进区	Wujin District	1591	7803802
#经开区	Economic Development Zone	560	6127000
新北区	Xinbei District	957	2576614
天宁区	Tianning District	400	620396
钟楼区	Zhonglou District	324	328916
溧阳市	Liyang City	340	4784210
按轻重工业分	**Grouped by Light and Heavy Industry**		
轻工业	Light Industry	1244	1548426
重工业	Heavy Industry	2772	15545889
按行业分	**Grouped by Sector**		
黑色金属矿采选业	Ferrous Metal Mining Industry	1	588
非金属矿采选业	Nonmetal Minerals Mining and Dressing	7	8891
农副食品加工业	Food Processing	16	11286
食品制造业	Food Production	17	218051
酒、饮料和精制茶制造业	Beverages and Refined Tea Manufacturing	4	14889
纺织业	Textile Industry	343	638831
纺织服装、服饰业	Textile and clothing Industry	136	86305
皮革、毛皮、羽毛及其制品和制鞋业	Leather, Fur, Feathers and Their Products, and Footwear Industry	38	15683
木材加工及木、竹、藤、棕、草制品业	Timber Processing, Bamboo, Cane, Palm Fiber and Straw Products	56	16105
家具制造业	Furniture Manufacturing	7	335
造纸及纸制品业	Papermaking and Paper Products	57	56393
印刷和记录媒介复制业	Printing and Recorded Media Duplication Industry	39	13112

17-4 续表 continued

指 标	Item	企业单位数（个）Number of Enterpr-ises（unit）	综合能源消费量（吨标准煤）Comprehensive Energy Consumption（tce）
文教、工美、体育和娱乐用品制造业	Cultural & Educational, Arts & Crafts, Sports & Entertainment Articles Manufacturing	97	70586
石油加工、炼焦及核燃料加工业	Petroleum Processing, Coking and Nuclear Fuel Processing	11	9145
化学原料及化学制品制造业	Raw Chemical Materials and Chemical Products	376	1222986
医药制造业	Medical and Pharmaceutical Products	65	94369
化学纤维制造业	Chemical Fiber	48	36840
橡胶和塑料制品业	Rubber and Plastic Products Industry	151	71291
非金属矿物制品业	Nonmetal Mineral Products	184	2518568
黑色金属冶炼及压延加工业	Smelting and Pressing of Ferrous Metals	142	8313386
有色金属冶炼及压延加工业	Smelting and Pressing of Nonferrous Metals	93	95277
金属制品业	Metal Products	241	236337
通用设备制造业	General Equipment Manufacturing	424	223255
专用设备制造业	For Special Purposes Equipment Manufacturing	325	183897
汽车制造业	Automotive Industry	168	52424
铁路、船舶、航空航天和其他运输设备制造	Railways, Shipping, Aerospace and other Transportation Equipment Manufacturing	92	72328
电气机械及器材制造业	Electric Equipment and Machinery	477	449413
计算机、通信和其他电子设备制造	Computer, Communications and other Electronic Equipment Manufacturing	260	172884
仪器仪表制造业	Instrumentation Manufacturing	105	44094
其他制造业	Other Manufacturing	1	131
废弃资源综合利用业	Comprehensive Utilization of Waste Resources Industry	4	1338
金属制品、机械和设备修理业	Metal Products, Machinery & Equipment Repairing Industry	2	713
电力、热力生产和供应业	Production and Supply of Electricity & Heat Industry	17	2121301
燃气生产和供应业	Production and Supply of Gas Industry	5	1694
水的生产和供应业	Production and Supply of water Industry	7	21588

17-5　年耗能 5000 吨标煤及以上工业企业生产综合能源消费量（2015 年）
COMPREHENSIVE ENERGY CONSUMPTION IN PRODUTTION OF INDUSTRIAL ENTERPRISES WITH ANNUAL CONSUMPTION OF 5000 TCE AND ABOVE（2015）

指　标	Item	企业单位数（个）Number of Enterpr-ises（unit）	综合能源消费量（吨标准煤）Comprehensive Energy Consumption（tce）
总　计	**Total**	**195**	**15137763**
按地区分	**Grouped by Region**		
市　区	Urban Area	160	10594520
金坛区	Jintan District	28	782307
武进区	Wujin District	50	7094788
#经开区	Economic Development Zone	15	5887300
新北区	Xinbei District	33	2138359
天宁区	Tianning District	33	417548
钟楼区	Zhonglou District	16	161517
溧阳市	Liyang City	35	4543243
按轻重工业分	**Grouped by Light and Heavy Industry**		
轻工业	Light Industry	63	845921
重工业	Heavy Industry	132	14291842
按行业分	**Grouped by Sector**		
食品制造业	Food Production	2	199965
酒、饮料和精制茶制造业	Beverages and Refined Tea Manufacturing	1	10435
纺织业	Textile Industry	36	359395
纺织服装、服饰业	Textile and clothing Industry	4	34085
皮革、毛皮、羽毛及其制品和制鞋业	Leather, Fur, Feathers and Their Products, and Footwear ndustry	1	6353

17-5 续表 continued

指 标	Item	企业单位数（个）Number of Enterpr-ises（unit）	综合能源消费量（吨标准煤）Comprehensive Energy Consumption（tce）
造纸及纸制品业	Papermaking and Paper Products	2	36362
文教、工美、体育和娱乐用品制造业	Cultural & Educational, Arts & Crafts, Sports & Entertainment Articles Manufacturing	2	13328
石油加工、炼焦和核燃料加工业	Petroleum Processing, Coking and Nuclear Fuel Processing	1	6899
化学原料及化学制品制造业	Raw Chemical Materials and Chemical Products	33	977244
医药制造业	Medical and Pharmaceutical Products	3	42974
橡胶和塑料制品业	Rubber and Plastic Products Industry	2	12315
非金属矿物制品业	Nonmetal Mineral Products	15	2413128
黑色金属冶炼及压延加工业	Smelting and Pressing of Ferrous Metals	23	8202938
有色金属冶炼及压延加工业	Smelting and Pressing of Nonferrous Metals	2	30848
金属制品业	Metal Products	7	92597
通用设备制造业	General Equipment Manufacturing	6	59088
专用设备制造业	For Special Purposes Equipment Manufacturing	6	73323
汽车制造业	Automotive Industry	1	7543
铁路、船舶、航空航天和其他运输设备制造	Railways, Shipping, Aerospace and other Transportation Equipment Manufacturing	1	24437
电气机械及器材制造业	Electric Equipment and Machinery	22	285959
计算机、通信和其他电子设备制造	Computer, Communications and other Electronic Equipment Manufacturing	6	86361
仪器仪表制造业	Instrumentation Manufacturing	2	25571
电力、热力生产和供应业	Production and Supply of Electricity & Heat Industry	15	2121147
水的生产和供应业	Production and Supply of water Industry	2	15468

17-6 规模以上工业企业分行业主要能源品种消费量（2015 年）
ENERGY CONSUMPTION OF MAIN VARIETIES OF ABOVE-SCALE INDUSTRIAL ENTERPRISES BY SECTOR（2015）

指 标	Item	原 煤（吨）Raw Coal（ton）
总 计	**Total**	**10614579**
按地区分	**Grouped by Region**	
市 区	Urban Area	7495497
金坛区	Jintan District	614477
武进区	Wujin District	2201230
#经开区	Economic Development Zone	1576593
新北区	Xinbei District	4146194
天宁区	Tianning District	494777
钟楼区	Zhonglou District	38819
溧阳市	Liyang City	3119082
按轻重工业分	**Grouped by Light and Heavy Industry**	
轻工业	Light Industry	193897
重工业	Heavy Industry	10420682
按行业分	**Grouped by Sector**	
非金属矿采选业	Nonmetal Minerals Mining and Dressing	
农副食品加工业	Food Processing	2597
食品制造业	Food Production	
酒、饮料和精制茶制造业	Beverages and Refined Tea Manufacturing	12174
纺织业	Textile Industry	56944
纺织服装、服饰业	Textile and clothing Industry	16476
皮革、毛皮、羽毛及其制品和制鞋业	Leather, Fur, Feathers and Their Products,and Footwear Industry	2693
木材加工及木、竹、藤、棕、草制品业	Timber Processing, Bamboo, Cane, Palm Fiber and Straw Products	1559
造纸及纸制品业	Papermaking and Paper Products	10297
印刷和记录媒介复制业	Printing and Recorded Media Duplication Industry	4691

洗精煤（吨）Fien Coal（ton）	焦 炭（吨）Coke（ton）	天然气（万立方米）Natural Gas（10000 cubicmeters）	汽 油（吨）Gasoline（ton）	煤 油（吨）Kerosene（ton）	柴 油（吨）Diesel Oil（ton）	燃料油（吨）Fuel Oil（ton）	液化石油气（吨）LPG（ton）	热 力（百万千焦）Heat（1million kilojoule）
2505594	**4465916**	**153522**	**42087**	**727**	**61478**	**1183**	**5712**	**33874816**
1671493	3392519	149246	40816	604	56645	1183	4281	33372742
	451	3882	2885	61	5895		89	6722787
1671478	3385283	121876	6772	285	19964	35	1816	6800685
1671391	2688497	112316	2208	28	12715	9	1297	4031117
15	831	11514	7584	225	14424	1028	1729	12336926
	53	4774	1867	7	3421	121	34	7489970
	5901	7199	21709	26	12941		613	22375
834101	1073397	4276	1271	123	4833		1431	502074
		10790	11928	28	6211	19	2506	18620386
	4465916	142732	30159	699	55268	1165	3206	15254430
					2319			
		84	140					7801
		180	584		146			5146358
			118		117			91721
		3890	1626	1	816	4	251	9516835
		1521	929	7	690		2	585639
		38	704		353		5	180617
		103	18		57			
		183	170		1006	9		812935
		43	298		114			

17-6　续表　continued

指　标	Item	原　煤（吨）Raw Coal（ton）
文教、工美、体育和娱乐用品制造业	Cultural & Educational, Arts & Crafts, Sports & Entertainment Articles Manufacturing	13903
石油加工、炼焦及核燃料加工业	Petroleum Processing, Coking and Nuclear Fuel Processing	
化学原料及化学制品制造业	Raw Chemical Materials and Chemical Products	424537
医药制造业	Medical and Pharmaceutical Products	35333
化学纤维制造业	Chemical Fiber	6034
橡胶和塑料制品业	Rubber and Plastic Products Industry	11359
非金属矿物制品业	Nonmetal Mineral Products	2948786
黑色金属冶炼及压延加工业	Smelting and Pressing of Ferrous Metals	1346178
有色金属冶炼及压延加工业	Smelting and Pressing of Nonferrous Metals	11335
金属制品业	Metal Products	19606
通用设备制造业	General Equipment Manufacturing	6474
专用设备制造业	For Special Purposes Equipment Manufacturing	39190
汽车制造业	Automotive Industry	307
铁路、船舶、航空航天和其他运输设备制造	Railways, Shipping, Aerospace and other Transportation Equipment Manufacturing"	967
电气机械及器材制造业	Electric Equipment and Machinery	25539
计算机、通信和其他电子设备制造	Computer, Communications and other Electronic Equipment Manufacturing	7600
仪器仪表制造业	Instrumentation Manufacturing	14943
其他制造业	Other Manufacturing	
废弃资源综合利用业	Comprehensive Utilization of Waste Resources Industry	
金属制品、机械和设备修理业	Metal Products, Machinery & Equipment Repairing Industry	
电力、热力生产和供应业	Production and Supply of Electricity & Heat Industry	5595057
燃气生产和供应业	Production and Supply of Gas Industry	
水的生产和供应业	Production and Supply of water Industry	

洗精煤 (吨) Fien Coal (ton)	焦 炭 (吨) Coke (ton)	天然气 (万立方米) Natural Gas (10000 cubicmeters)	汽 油 (吨) Gasoline (ton)	煤 油 (吨) Kerosene (ton)	柴 油 (吨) Diesel Oil (ton)	燃料油 (吨) Fuel Oil (ton)	液化石油气 (吨) LPG (ton)	热 力 (百万千焦) Heat (1million kilojoule)
		629	486		210		348	388163
		134	24		60			165276
		5857	5171	181	3025	240	11	11902081
		518	1245		213			792338
		211	44		102		25	15152
		611	914		376		1	173784
	8182	7598	2035		23872	782	2	212239
2504514	4439694	6204	288		5260	101	113	3187487
	11	2487	1732		387			17451
	1440	5428	3184	36	2640	6	1509	25716
867	11163	2426	5344	177	3929	42	3	28668
102		2775	3289	10	2356		28	9955
	88	547	1299	2	370		21	37575
	68	560	1604	201	7826		3060	193651
	5211	8466	7969	100	4061		220	379548
		824	1645		526		84	3826
111	48	101	782	13	277		28	3
			8					
		85	15		20			
	10		12					
		102017	29		329			
		1	255					
			126		22			

17-7 年耗能 5000 吨标煤及以上工业企业主要能源品种消费量（2015 年）
ENERGY CONSUMPTION OF MAIN VARIETIES OF INDUSTRIAL ENTERPRISES WITH ANNUAL CONSUMPTION OF 5000 TCE AND ABOVE（2015）

指 标	Item	原 煤（吨）Raw Coal（ton）
总 计	**Total**	**10311808**
按地区分	**Grouped by Region**	
市 区	Urban Area	7270972
金坛区	Jintan District	564728
武进区	Wujin District	2092349
#经开区	Economic Development Zone	1517463
新北区	Xinbei District	4117777
天宁区	Tianning District	472360
钟楼区	Zhonglou District	23758
溧阳市	Liyang City	3040836
按轻重工业分	**Grouped by Light and Heavy Industry**	
轻工业	Light Industry	89449
重工业	Heavy Industry	10222359
按行业分	**Grouped by Sector**	
食品制造业	Food Production	
酒、饮料和精制茶制造业	Beverages and Refined Tea Manufacturing	12174
纺织业	Textile Industry	24928
纺织服装、服饰业	Textile and clothing Industry	9408
皮革、毛皮、羽毛及其制品和制鞋业	Leather, Fur, Feathers and Their Products,and Footwear Industry	
造纸及纸制品业	Papermaking and Paper Products	

洗精煤（吨）Fien Coal（ton）	焦炭（吨）Coke（ton）	天然气（万立方米）Natural Gas（10000 cubicmeters）	汽油（吨）Gasoline（ton）	煤油（吨）Kerosene（ton）	柴油（吨）Diesel Oil（ton）	液化石油气（吨）LPG（ton）	热力（百万千焦）Heat（1million kilojoule）
2504514	**4451816**	**134645**	**5801**	**139**	**18708**	**1533**	**28349166**
1671280	3382161	132490	5480	39	18061	1533	28191368
		1778	516		420		6243445
1671280	3376305	114316	603	13	11472	1533	5103666
1671280	2686794	109908	183	12	9966	1297	3619713
		7367	147		915		10529181
		3744	440		1060		6292700
	5856	5286	3775	26	4194		22375
833234	1069656	2155	321	100	648		157798
		4420	862	1	1540	123	14780800
2504514	4451816	130226	4939	138	17169	1410	13568366
							4978387
			31		35		
		1585	341	1	240	123	7014144
		913	249		202		273474
			24				135766
					622		783801

17-7　续表　continued

指　标	Item	原　煤 （吨） Raw Coal （ton）
文教、工美、体育和娱乐用品制造业	Cultural & Educational, Arts & Crafts, Sports & Entertainment Articles Manufacturing	
石油加工、炼焦及核燃料加工业	Petroleum Processing, Coking and Nuclear Fuel Processing	
化学原料及化学制品制造业	Raw Chemical Materials and Chemical Products	333050
医药制造业	Medical and Pharmaceutical Products	21872
橡胶和塑料制品业	Rubber and Plastic Products Industry	4119
非金属矿物制品业	Nonmetal Mineral Products	2925127
黑色金属冶炼及压延加工业	Smelting and Pressing of Ferrous Metals	1303640
有色金属冶炼及压延加工业	Smelting and Pressing of Nonferrous Metals	
金属制品业	Metal Products	5077
通用设备制造业	General Equipment Manufacturing	
专用设备制造业	For Special Purposes Equipment Manufacturing	35688
汽车制造业	Automotive Industry	
铁路、船舶、航空航天和其他运输设备制造	Railways, Shipping, Aerospace and other Transportation Equipment Manufacturing	30
电气机械及器材制造业	Electric Equipment and Machinery	22990
计算机、通信和其他电子设备制造	Computer, Communications and other Electronic Equipment Manufacturing	3733
仪器仪表制造业	Instrumentation Manufacturing	14915
电力、热力生产和供应业	Production and Supply of Electricity & Heat Industry	5595057
水的生产和供应业	Production and Supply of water Industry	

洗精煤（吨）Fien Coal (ton)	焦炭（吨）Coke (ton)	天然气（万立方米）Natural Gas (10000 cubicmeters)	汽油（吨）Gasoline (ton)	煤油（吨）Kerosene (ton)	柴油（吨）Diesel Oil (ton)	液化石油气（吨）LPG (ton)	热力（百万千焦）Heat (1million kilojoule)
		203					149410
			9		3		165276
		3320	104		861		10559214
		112	101		171		439136
		92					112369
	6678	6752	15		2416		143334
2504514	4435513	4897	91		4809	113	3187480
		1235			78		
		2786	1364		116		
	5856	890	190	24	1341		22835
		1560	32	2	702		
		449					
	23		117	12	6141	1297	175375
	3746	7332	2924	100	714		209165
		487	72				
		16					
		102017	29		239		
			110		18		

18

CHAPTER 18

财政 金融 保险

PUBLIC FINANCE, BANKING AND INSURANCE

18 财政 金融 保险
PUBLIC FINANCE, BANKING AND INSURANCE

2015 年主要统计指标
MAJOR STATISTICAL INDICATORS OF 2015

一般公共预算收入	General Public Budgetary Revenue	466.28亿元	（100 million yuan）
比上年增长	Over the Previous Year	7.5%	
一般公共预算支出	General Public Budgetary Expenditure	485.33亿元	（100 million yuan）
比上年增长	Over the Previous Year	11.6%	
年底金融机构本外币存款余额	Balance of Domestic and Foreign Currency Deposits in Financial Institutions at Year-end	7664.98亿元	（100 million yuan）
比上年增长	Over the Previous Year	7.2%	
年底金融机构人民币存款余额	RMB Deposits Balance of Banking Institutions at Year-end	7438.68亿元	（100 million yuan）
比上年增长	Over the Previous Year	7.4%	
年底金融机构本外币贷款余额	Balance of Domestic and Foreign Currency Loans in Financial Institutions at Year-end	5418.85亿元	（100 million yuan）
比上年增长	Over the Previous Year	10.7%	
年底金融机构人民币贷款余额	RMB Loans Balance of Banking Institutions at Year-end	5354.58亿元	（100 million yuan）
比上年增长	Over the Previous Year	11.8%	

18-1 历年财政收入、财政支出
FINANCIAL REVENUE AND FINANCIAL EXPENDITURE OVER THE YEARS

单位：万元（10000 yuan）

年 份	财政收入	其中 of which	财政支出	其中 of which
		#市 区		#市 区
Year	Financial Revenue	Urban Area	Financial Expenditure	Urban Area
1949	1209	861	17	17
1950	2664	1974	207	93
1951	3885	3074	357	254
1952	5155	4129	741	538
1953	6258	4886	854	591
1954	6956	5500	1033	750
1955	6338	5084	957	678
1956	7146	5900	1431	993
1957	7813	6602	2025	1557
1958	18880	17106	7633	6408
1959	18662	17008	3048	2065
1960	18853	17106	2766	1563
1961	11878	10729	2041	1279
1962	8694	7503	1915	1341
1963	9551	8280	1977	1441
1964	13225	11873	2306	1634
1965	16044	14639	2533	1832
1966	20250	18886	2674	1880
1967	12603	11205	2574	1793
1968	13793	12354	2411	1641
1969	21562	20027	4376	3419
1970	31837	29958	3917	2706
1971	33681	31894	6148	4888
1972	37363	35414	6843	5382
1973	43564	40973	6180	4860
1974	44651	42029	6162	4394
1975	49437	46665	5470	3992
1976	52558	49769	6359	4561
1977	57904	54827	6843	4970
1978	62128	58560	9259	6583
1979	62364	58983	13585	8481
1980	66960	63122	11603	8293
1981	72163	67767	10615	7837
1982	70139	65046	13109	9805
1983	73628	67892	16885	12799
1984	80543	77320	21601	16794
1985	100364	92691	25231	19660
1986	103337	94451	31333	24513
1987	109850	99516	32565	25238
1988	115680	103528	38331	29560
1989	126680	113446	47647	36535
1990	130953	116644	51082	38698
1991	117190	103734	55849	41716
1992	136516	119384	59228	43719
1993	198857	171003	99387	74698
1994	246778	210378	114387	86228
1995	285043	239948	133252	101585
1996	343032	289773	153820	116570
1997	401779	337700	193880	150801
1998	450937	376665	224114	176498
1999	492092	415554	257172	202273
2000	602271	507742	325043	259763
2001	753317	633537	414753	331521
2002	1029032	866120	610099	495583
2003	1361047	1136921	847597	690368
2004	1447666	1181910	1048820	1181910
2005	2204491	1821223	1402776	1126903
2006	2772705	2269853	1710373	1341912
2007	4143811	3399957	2743954	2192203
2008	5426800	4536087	3844112	3178717
2009	6817200	5737600	5208061	4297952
2010	8416700	7101100	6382050	5291309
2011	9777913	8102756	7430767	6050417
2012	11170283	9305089	8849217	7263458
2013	11693220	9337031	9277601	7177898
2014	12837620	10679467	10069635	8211588
2015	13675433	11589292	11060907	9161638

注：1、2002年7月起财政收入包括行政性收费收入、基金收入。2014年起财政收入、财政支出均未含社保基金、国有资本经营预算。
2、2015年行政区划调整，市区包含金坛区数据。

Note: 1、The financial revenue includes the incomes from administrative charge and funds since July 2002.Starting from 2014, social security funds and government-owned capital management budgets are not included in government revenues and spending.
2、With the administrative district adjustment in 2015, the city's urban area now includes Jintan District.

18-2 分地区一般公共预算收入、支出（1997-2015）
PUBLIC FINANCE BUDGETARY REVENUE AND EXPENDITURE BY REGION （1997-2015）

单位：万元（10000 yuan）

年份 Year	一般公共预算收入 General Public Budgetary Revenue	其中 of which 市区 Urban Area	其中 of which 溧阳市 Liyang City	年份 Year	一般公共预算支出 General Public Budgetary Expenditure	其中 of which 市区 Urban Area	其中 of which 溧阳市 Liyang City
1997	189210	157949	17173	1997	186742	144839	23756
1998	222536	185568	19889	1998	219440	172644	26428
1999	251712	210724	21946	1999	254124	199993	30822
2000	322524	270430	28035	2000	318283	254115	36046
2001	420961	351387	36968	2001	411581	329178	45098
2002	461972	386364	40399	2002	518223	418456	53993
2003	566729	473538	52977	2003	630490	514181	67521
2004	673407	556044	68201	2004	756627	611906	87767
2005	949905	791432	91088	2005	978458	797957	109280
2006	1188818	984472	118008	2006	1176965	945667	135700
2007	1580688	1305365	162588	2007	1546367	1250226	175098
2008	1851888	1527880	196188	2008	1866796	1510855	218523
2009	2158888	1786378	231688	2009	2187465	1715610	284866
2010	2861788	2391480	290028	2010	2814401	2258104	334681
2011	3508800	2906762	371280	2011	3618123	2877736	443228
2012	3789900	3153808	404988	2012	3912183	3136649	458353
2013	4088800	3373890	456018	2013	4179007	3325841	520117
2014	4338800	3531440	506188	2014	4349289	3404648	570050
2015	4662800	4100932	561868	2015	4853330	4239511	613819

注：2015年行政区划调整，市区包含金坛区数据。
Note: With the administrative district adjustment in 2015, the city's urban area now includes Jintan District.

18-3　分地区财政收入（2015 年）
FINANCIAL REVENUE BY REGION（2015）

单位：万元（10000 yuan）

指　标	Item	全　市 Whole Municipality	其　中 of which 市　区 Urban Area	溧阳市 Liyang City
总　计	**Total**	**13675433**	**11589292**	**2086141**
中央收入	Revenue of Central Government	2881698	2628153	253545
增值税（75%）	Value-added Tax （75%）	1835416	1681127	154289
消费税	Consumption Tax	59773	56256	3517
企业所得税（60%）	Corporate Income Tax （60%）	638607	582121	56486
个人所得税（60%）	Individual Income Tax （60%）	347902	308649	39253
一般公共预算收入	General Public Budgetary Revenue	4662800	4100932	561868
税收收入	Tax Revenue	3737009	3276183	460826
#增值税25%及营改增增值税	VAT 25% and VAT Transformed from Business Tax	708039	642525	65514
营业税	Operation Tax	1138408	973227	165181
企业所得税（40%）	Enterprise's Income Tax （40%）	425738	388081	37657
个人所得税（40%）	Individual Income Tax （40%）	231935	205766	26169
资源税	Resources Tax	6655	4016	2639
城市维护建设税	Tax on Urban Construction and Maintenance	260829	234177	26652
房产税	Tax on Real Estates	178874	161647	17227
印花税	Stamp Tax	59507	52191	7316
城镇土地使用税	Tax on Use of Urban Land	161044	144259	16785
土地增值税	Land Value Added Tax	152660	133546	19114
车船税	Vehicle and Vessel Usage Tax	33035	29773	3262
耕地占用税	Tax on the Occupancy of Cultivated Land	23788	18488	5300
契　税	Contract Tax	356497	288487	68010
非税收入	Non-tax Revenue	925791	824749	101042
#专项收入	pecial Revenue	274021	241922	32099
行政性收费收入	Income From Administrative Fees	223267	193380	29887
罚没收入	Fine and Confiscatory Revenue	100810	83168	17642
政府性基金收入	Government Fund Revenue	6130935	4860207	1270728

注：2015年财政收入仅指中央收入、一般公共预算收入和政府性基金收入三项合计。
Note: Government revenue of 2015 comprises revenue contributions to the central government, general public budget revenues and governmentmanaged funds.

18-4 分地区财政支出（2015年）
FINANCIAL EXPENDITURE BY REGION （2015）

单位：万元（10000 yuan）

指 标	Item	全 市 Whole Municipality	其中 of which 市 区 Urban Area	溧阳市 Liyang City
总 计	**Total**	**11060907**	**9161638**	**1899269**
一般公共预算支出	General Public Budgetary Expenditure	4853330	4239511	613819
#一般公共服务	General Public Services	418493	363492	55001
国 防	National Defense	26595	25267	1328
公共安全	Public Security	282481	244744	37737
教 育	Education	792137	679714	112423
科学技术	Science and Technology	227499	197312	30187
文化体育与传媒	Culture, Sports and Media	68467	62196	6271
社会保障和就业	Social Security and Employment	552599	484461	68138
医疗卫生与计划生育	Expenditure on healthcare and family planning	385091	309566	75525
节能环保	Energy saving and Environmental Protection	146771	124147	22624
城乡社区	Urban and Rural Community Affairs	877686	832202	45484
农林水	Agriculture, Forestry and Water Affairs	411555	337056	74499
交通运输	Traffic and Transportation	125479	115517	9962
资源勘探电力信息等	Resource Exploration and Power Information	68906	62743	6163
商业服务业等	Business and Services	52254	45471	6783
金 融	Financial expenditure	5232	5098	134
援助其他地区	Expenditure on aid to other regions	20688	18694	1994
国土海洋气象等	Expenditure on land resources, maritime affairs and meteorology	24702	20092	4610
住房保障	Housing Security Expenditure	159704	119000	40704
粮油物资储备	Expenditure on food, oil and material reserves	8354	7159	1195
债务付息	Expenditure on debt interest	7905	6607	1298
债务发行费用支出	Spending on bond issuance	937	855	82
其 他	Others	189795	178118	11677
政府性基金支出	Government Fund Expenditure	6207577	4922127	1285450

注：2015年财政支出仅指一般公共预算支出和政府性基金支出两项合计。
Note: Government spending of 2015 only consists of general public budget spending and spending of government-managed funds.

18-5 五区财政收支（2015 年）
FINANCIAL REVENUE AND EXPENDITURE OF FIVE DISTRICTS（2015）

单位：万元（10000 yuan）

指 标	Item	金坛区 Jintan District	武进区 wujin District	新北区 Xinbei District	天宁区 Tianning District	钟楼区 Zhonglou District
财政收入	**Financial Revenue**	**1231280**	**3780049**	**2053220**	**775705**	**618341**
中央收入	Revenue of Central Government	207251	1028664	711027	314805	228586
一般公共预算收入	General Public Budgetary Revenue	361508	1403798	975917	447861	359657
税收收入	Tax Revenue	311871	1154167	784978	380352	300566
#增值税25%及营改增增值税	VAT 25% and VAT Transformed from Business Tax	54695	258050	171790	74843	56967
营业税	Operation Tax	81675	337760	223061	138360	101635
企业所得税	Enterprise's Income Tax	27725	152780	115285	49974	35633
个人所得税	Individual Income Tax	13693	64525	45953	29986	22758
城市维护建设税	Tax on Urban Construction and Maintenance	21203	79451	61816	28928	20866
房产税	Tax on Real Estates	12914	58260	40234	17283	20048
印花税	Stamp Tax	6437	18662	13952	5313	4261
契 税	Contract Tax	50992	71152	44380		
非税收入	Non-tax Revenue	49637	249631	190939	67509	59091
政府性基金收入	Government und Revenue	662521	1347587	366276	13039	30098
财政支出	**Financial Expenditure**	**1129917**	**2795135**	**1016579**	**262702**	**268721**
一般公共预算支出	General Public Budgetary Expenditure	465893	1417241	630174	246005	238406
# 一般公共服务	General Public Services	41042	108248	45126	34497	28662
国 防	National Defense	3402	7460	2706	1047	358
公共安全	Public Security	24998	53591	20774	11988	8033
教 育	Education	85305	195730	102407	60768	44270
科学技术	Science and Technology	13308	92733	63381	9909	6462
文化体育与传媒	Culture, Sports and Media	6040	11174	6457	7467	801
社会保障和就业	Social Security and Employment	51776	103340	115691	41772	39296
医疗卫生与计划生育	Expenditure on healthcare and family planning	45408	73135	33680	14194	17844
节能环保	Energy saving and Environmental Protection	17641	28946	26045	2392	4590
城乡社区	Urban and Rural Community Affairs	17731	463897	140173	29768	61514
农林水	Agriculture, Forestry and Water Affairs	72463	156419	32476	14199	12095
交通运输	Traffic and Transportation	11685	36068	369	85	
资源勘探电力信息等	Resource Exploration and Power Information	8140	15336	10888	6992	5068
商业服务业等	Business and Services	6824	20618	7323	3104	1658
金 融	Financial expenditure	20	1264	195	111	159
住房保障	Housing Security Expenditure	45729	21716	3541	6314	6589
其 他	Others	14381	27566	18942	1398	1007
政府性基金支出	Government Fund Expenditure	664024	1377894	386405	16697	30315

18-6 分地区金融机构存、贷款余额（1990-2015 年）
DEPOSIT AND LOAN BALANCE OF FINANCIAL INSTITUTIONS BY REGION（1990-2015）

单位:亿元（100 million yuan）

年份 Year	存款余额 Deposits Balance	其中 of which 市区 Urban Area	溧阳市 Liyang City	年份 Year	贷款余额 Loans Balance	其中 of which 市区 Urban Area	溧阳市 Liyang City
1990	59.37	46.24	7.50	1990	74.24	58.52	8.98
1991	81.35	64.79	9.64	1991	93.10	73.94	10.95
1992	104.84	83.34	12.83	1992	112.46	89.96	13.27
1993	127.73	101.60	17.06	1993	132.16	105.84	15.81
1994	192.71	158.68	21.74	1994	180.48	148.54	19.31
1995	257.61	205.93	32.12	1995	211.88	170.12	25.43
1996	308.89	251.34	35.73	1996	237.04	192.43	26.71
1997	403.16	329.26	44.15	1997	304.83	242.25	36.05
1998	479.80	387.49	56.17	1998	342.13	272.79	39.93
1999	560.03	454.81	62.86	1999	369.06	298.86	40.39
2000	629.36	511.00	69.00	2000	389.26	324.19	39.52
2001	735.25	596.55	79.78	2001	444.54	376.32	40.08
2002	904.71	738.30	95.75	2002	559.85	476.15	46.97
2003	1170.56	964.37	117.88	2003	799.14	683.11	66.72
2004	1362.22	1129.93	134.10	2004	956.38	835.85	70.05
2005	1649.61	1375.25	159.62	2005	1113.25	966.84	87.90
2006	1974.05	1644.73	190.81	2006	1348.60	1164.62	108.67
2007	2263.84	1893.65	216.59	2007	1590.11	1349.12	140.68
2008	2819.42	2348.91	281.79	2008	1851.69	1550.76	181.86
2009	3765.91	3141.89	382.84	2009	2513.97	2100.23	256.02
2010	4550.47	3800.47	454.64	2010	3011.67	2518.92	299.11
2011	4902.15	4024.70	541.80	2011	3406.35	2817.27	361.26
2012	5604.90	4558.74	645.20	2012	3832.80	3109.26	436.64
2013	6348.10	5080.49	795.50	2013	4318.32	3443.36	536.21
2014	6758.57	5365.33	848.45	2014	4789.74	3766.69	604.06
2015	7438.68	6572.31	866.37	2015	5354.58	4655.86	698.72

注：2015年行政区划调整，市区包含金坛区数据。
Note: With the administrative district adjustment in 2015, the city's urban area now includes Jintan District.

18-7 历年分地区城乡居民储蓄存款余额
URBAN AND RURAL SAVINGS DEPOSITS BALANCE OVER THE YEARS BY REGION

单位：万元（10000 yuan）

年份 Year	全市 Whole Municipality	其中 of which 市区 Urban Area	溧阳市 Liyang City	年份 Year	全市 Whole Municipality	其中 of which 市区 Urban Area	溧阳市 Liyang City
1949	8	8		1983	36154	26686	5139
1950	59	57	2	1984	48512	34826	7328
1951	280	239	28	1985	67304	48969	10596
1952	598	544	37	1986	92511	67526	13841
1953	734	664	43	1987	134174	96557	21849
1954	913	782	69	1988	157915	117394	22716
1955	970	833	73	1989	230962	170915	34123
1956	1256	1070	124	1990	342914	254479	52128
1957	1666	1329	250	1991	462939	348651	67370
1958	1580	1400	119	1992	568704	429591	83516
1959	2267	1945	137	1993	673404	496160	115022
1960	2333	2013	165	1994	909347	675495	153622
1961	2281	1951	148	1995	1286526	969196	207815
1962	1594	1410	99	1996	1726519	1321397	259967
1963	1968	1719	151	1997	2246590	1733748	302559
1964	2662	2311	204	1998	2841400	2324026	414700
1965	2829	2453	232	1999	3326100	2522385	479400
1966	3144	2737	283	2000	3555700	2681100	511000
1967	2974	2658	189	2001	4126500	3099500	596000
1968	2981	2477	302	2002	4999400	3798700	697100
1969	2503	2059	263	2003	6229200	4783000	832900
1970	2566	2197	208	2004	7243600	5609100	946100
1971	3236	2621	388	2005	8653900	6718200	1137300
1972	3577	2975	336	2006	10140100	7903800	1310600
1973	4313	3520	478	2007	10921400	8514000	1397400
1974	4530	3803	412	2008	14312100	11181700	1855300
1975	4960	4148	464	2009	17562400	13727400	2303800
1976	5137	4317	455	2010	20092400	15672600	2629800
1977	5928	4942	551	2011	21573900	16740000	2865800
1978	7182	6008	652	2012	24732700	19111400	3325400
1979	12032	9256	1403	2013	27533110	21012491	3873755
1980	16337	12704	1960	2014	29341866	22211493	4140285
1981	20123	15454	2623	2015	31937707	27311225	4626482
1982	26767	20211	3767				

注：2015年起表中数据为住户存款余额。
Note: Starting from 2015, the figure in the table refers to the balance of individual deposits.

18-8 分地区金融机构信贷收支情况（2015 年）
CREDIT FUNDS BALANCE OF FINANCIAL INSTITUTIONS GROUPED BY REGION（2015）

单位：亿元（100 million yuan）

指 标	Item	全 市 Whole Municipality	市 区 Urban Ared	溧阳市 Liyang City
金融机构存贷款余额（本外币）	**Balance of Deposits and Loans in Financial Institutions（Domestic and Foreign Currency）**			
各项存款余额	Balance of Deposits	7664.98	6791.07	873.91
#住户存款	Individual Deposits	3223.43	2759.01	464.42
各项贷款余额	Balance of Loans	5418.85	4718.49	700.36
金融机构存贷款余额（人民币）	**Balance of Deposits and Loans in Financial Institutions（RMB）**			
各项存款余额	Balance of Deposits	7438.68	6572.31	866.37
境内存款	Domestic Deposits	7431.12	6565.22	865.90
住户存款	Individual Deposits	3193.77	2731.12	462.65
非金融企业存款	Deposits of Non-financial Businesses	2641.37	2409.96	231.41
广义政府存款	General Government Deposits	1126.24	962.21	164.03
非银行金融机构存款	Deposits of Non-bank Financial Institutions	469.74	461.93	7.81
境外存款	Overseas Deposits	7.55	7.08	0.47
各项贷款余额	Balance of Loans	5354.58	4655.86	698.72
境内贷款	Domestic Loans	5354.03	4655.31	698.72
住户贷款	Individual Loans	1233.82	1071.79	162.03
短期贷款	Short-term Loans	326.72	250.38	76.34
消费贷款	Consumption Loans	72.50	67.61	4.89
经营贷款	Operating Loans	254.22	182.77	71.45
中长期贷款	Medium-term and Long-term Loans	907.10	821.41	85.69
消费贷款	Consumption Loans	814.40	738.32	76.08
经营贷款	Operating Loans	92.70	83.09	9.61
非金融企业及机关团体贷款	Loans of Non-financial Businesses, Government Agencies and Non-profit Institutions	4120.21	3583.52	536.69
短期贷款	Short-term Loans	2303.35	1977.29	326.06
中长期贷款	Medium-term and Long-term Loans	1478.84	1282.40	196.44
票据融资	Bill Financing	287.12	273.28	13.84
融资租赁	Financial Leasing	44.62	44.62	
各项垫款	Various types of Advance Money	6.28	5.93	0.35
境外贷款	Overseas Loans	0.55	0.55	

18-9　分地区金融机构外汇信贷收支情况（2015 年）
CREDIT FUNDS BALANCE IN FOREIGN CURRENCIES OF FINANCIAL INSTITUTIONS GROUPED BY REGION（2015）

单位：万美元（USD 10000）

项　目	Item	全　市 Whole Municipality	市　区 Urban Area	溧阳市 Liyang City
金融机构外币存款余额	**Deposits Balance in Foreign Currencies of Banking Institutions**	**348510**	**336890**	**11620**
#非金融企业存款	Deposits of Enterprises	277514	268641	8873
住户存款	personal deposits	45682	42956	2726
金融机构外币贷款余额	**Loans Balance in Foreign Currencies of Banking Institutions**	**98980**	**96453**	**2527**
短期贷款	Short-term Loans	78952	77723	1229
中长期贷款	Medium-term and Long-term Loans	1864	1073	791
贸易融资	Export and Import Trade Financing	72026	70812	1214

18-10　证券交易情况（2015 年）
TRADING SUMMARY FOR SECURITIES（2015）

单位：亿元（100 million yuan）

指　标	Item	全　市 Whole Municipality
证券交易总额（亿元）	Total Transaction Volume of Securities （100 million yuan）	32172.29
A　股	A Shares	28946.82
B　股	B Shares	34.98
基　金	Funds	749.36
债　券	Bonds	2441.13
资金帐户总数（万户）	Total Capital Accounts （10000 households）	95.95

18-11 保险业务情况（2014—2015 年）
BASIC STATISTICS ON INSURANCE （2014-2015）

单位：万元（10000 yuan）

指标	Item	2014	2015
财产险	**Property Insurance**		
承保金额	**Insurance Value**	**288909595**	**290760081**
企业财产险	Enterprise Property Insurance	40165030	45186830
机动车辆险	Motor Vehicle Insurance	54908747	69008608
货物运输险	Freight Transport Insurance	11987565	11183945
工程险	Project Liability Insurance	1746543	2409586
家庭财产险	Family Property Insurance	11876093	12996024
责任险	Liability Insurance	83160892	69850091
其它险	Other Insurance	85064725	80124997
保费收入	**Premium Income**	**456607**	**517037**
企业财产险	Enterprise Property Insurance	31252	32428
机动车辆险	Motor Vehicle Insurance	368835	417591
货物运输险	Freight Transport Insurance	5760	5557
工程险	Project Liability Insurance	2130	4907
家庭财产险	Family Property Insurance	1705	2007
责任险	Liability Insurance	18762	22553
其它险	Other Insurance	28162	31995
赔付支出	**Indemnity Experditur**	**258125**	**334289**
企业财产险	Enterprise Property Insurance	9626	30779
机动车辆险	Motor Vehicle Insurance	224328	265499
货物运输险	Freight Transport Insurance	2557	2647
工程险	Project Liability Insurance	721	360
家庭财产险	Family Property Insurance	408	2716
责任险	Liability Insurance	10249	15581
其它险	Other Insurance	10237	16707

18-11 续表 Continued

单位：万元（10000 yuan）

指 标	Item	2014	2015
人寿险	**Life Insurance**		
保费收入	**Premium Income**	**897205**	**1048570**
意外伤害险	Personal and Accident Insurance	18005	20840
健康险	Health Insurance	21165	26110
一般寿险	General Life Insurance	420683	541060
分红险	Participating Insurance	428282	440421
万能险	Universal Life Insurance	5901	15256
投连险	Investment-linked Insurance	250	225
其他险	Other Insurance	2920	4658
赔付支出	**Indemnity Experditur**	**35639**	**45197**
意外伤害险	Personal and Accident Insurance	4620	5124
健康险	Health Insurance	15077	21958
一般寿险	General Life Insurance	12397	14515
分红险	Participating Insurance	3194	3123
万能险	Universal Life Insurance	328	374
投连险	Investment-linked Insurance	17	92
其他险	Other Insurance	7	11
其它各类给付支出	**Other Payments or Expenditure**	**196197**	**171564**
一般寿险	General Life Insurance	46278	47138
分红险	Participating Insurance	149317	123520
万能险	Universal Life Insurance	530	863
投连险	Investment-linked Insurance	13	13
其他险	Other Insurance	59	30

18-12 分地区保险业务情况（2015 年）
BASIC STATISTICS ON INSURANCE BY REGION （2015）

单位：万元 (10000 yuan)

指 标	Item	全 市 Whole Municipality	市 区 Urban Area	溧阳市 Liyang City
财产险	**Property Insurance**			
保费收入	Premium Income	517037	460099	56938
#企业财产险	Enterprise Property Insurance	32428	29975	2453
机动车辆险	Motor Vehicle Insurance	417591	374620	42971
货物运输险	Freight Transport Insurance	5557	4272	1285
工程险	Project Liability Insurance	4907	4784	123
家庭财产险	Family Property Insurance	2007	1708	299
责任险	Liability Insurance	22553	20651	1901
其它险	Other Insurance	31995	24089	7906
赔付支出	Indemnity Experditur	334289	303021	31268
人寿险	**Life Insurance**			
保费收入	Premium Income	1048570	984978	63592
#意外伤害险	Personal and Accident Insurance	20840	19005	1835
健康险	Health Insurance	26110	25431	679
赔付支出	Indemnity Experditur	45197	42728	2469
其它各类给付支出	Other Payments or Expenditure	171564	155140	16424

18-13 分地区企业职工基本养老保险情况（2015 年）
BASIC CONDITIONS OF PENSION INSURANCE OF ENTERPRISES' STAFF AND WORKERS GROUPED BY REGION（2015）

指 标	Item	全 市 Whole Municipality	市 区 Urban Area	其中 of which 金坛区 Jintan District	武进区 wujin District	溧阳市 Liyang City
参保单位数（个）	Number of Units Covered by Insurance （unit）	52047	47568	3113	16636	4479
参保职工人数（人）	Number of Employees Covered by Insurance （person）	1337735	1176202	131570	374933	161533
领取养老保险金人数（人）	Number of People Receiving Pension Insurance （person）	474644	407060	41639	115037	67584
基金总收入（万元）	General Fund Revenue （10000 yuan）	1364713	1211661	157897	387403	153052
#基本养老保险费	Basic Pension Insurance Premiums	1267563	1125081	142456	346180	142482
基金总支出（万元）	General Fund Expenditure （10000 yuan）	1220083	1086725	90717	246761	133358
#基本养老金	Basic Pension	1156999	1029303	85788	229121	127696

18-14 分地区城乡居民社会养老保险情况（2015 年）
BASIC CONDITIONS OF THE URBAN AND RURAL SOCIAL PENSION INSURANCE GROUPED BY REGION（2015）

指 标	Item	全 市 Whole Municipality	市 区 Urban Area	其中 of which 金坛区 Jintan District	武进区 wujin District	溧阳市 Liyang City
参保人数（人）	Number of People Covered by Insurance （person）	322633	224638	76532	100103	97995
领取养老金人数（人）	Number of Pensioners （person）	476113	353218	96904	179853	122895
基金总收入（万元）	General Fund Revenue （10000 yuan）	151922	122368	32496	65282	29554
基金总支出（万元）	General Fund Expenditure （10000 yuan）	126785	99953	22260	54806	26832

18-15 分地区基本医疗保险情况（2015 年）
BASIC CONDITIONS OF MEDICAL INSURANCE GROUPED BY REGION（2015）

指 标	Item	全 市 Whole Municipality	市 区 Urban Area	其中 of which 金坛区 Jintan District	武进区 wujin District	溧阳市 Liyang City
参保人数（人）	Number of People Covered by Insurance （person）	1882401	1684473	167853	521416	197928
在职职工	Employed Staff and Workers	1403695	1259733	129738	413810	143962
退休人员	Retirees	478706	424740	38115	107606	53966
基金总收入（万元）	General Fund Revenue （10000 yuan）	571312	526215	52170	162684	45097
#统筹账户	Pool Account	336956	313249	37485	103218	23707
基金总支出（万元）	General Fund Expenditure （10000 yuan）	474581	428524	32340	114562	46057
#统筹账户	Pool Account	273852	246498	19761	62710	27354

18-16 分地区失业保险情况（2015年）
BASIC CONDITIONS OF UNEMPLOYMENT INSURANCE GROUPED BY REGION（2015）

指 标	Item	全 市 Whole Municipality	市 区 Urban Area	其中 of which 金坛区 Jintan District	其中 of which 武进区 wujin District	溧阳市 Liyang City
参保人数（人）	Number of People Covered by Insurance （person）	1086719	963069	97973	324160	123650
领取失业保险金人数（人）	Number of People Receiving Unemployment Insurance （person）	50833	46826	4750	14379	4007
基金总收入（万元）	General Fund Revenue （10000 yuan）	96609	87577	7081	25216	9033
基金总支出（万元）	General Fund Expenditure （10000 yuan）	63610	60058	3962	21622	3552

18-17 分地区工伤保险情况（2015年）
BASIC CONDITIONS OF WORK-RELATED INJURY INSURANCE GROUPED BY REGION（2015）

指 标	Item	全 市 Whole Municipality	市 区 Urban Area	其中 of which 金坛区 Jintan District	其中 of which 武进区 wujin District	溧阳市 Liyang City
参保人数（人）	Number of People Covered by Insurance （person）	1136295	1019980	132015	318287	116315
基金总收入（万元）	General Fund Revenue （10000 yuan）	59581	51464	7893	14892	8117
基金总支出（万元）	General Fund Expenditure （10000 yuan）	48298	41125	7313	14281	7173
当年享受工伤保险待遇人次（人次）	Number of People Receiving Work-Related Injury Insurance （person-time）	10730	9586	2191	3012	1144

18-18 分地区生育保险情况（2015年）
BASIC CONDITIONS OF MATERNITY INSURANCE GROUPED BY REGION（2015）

指 标	Item	全 市 Whole Municipality	市 区 Urban Area	其中 of which 金坛区 Jintan District	其中 of which 武进区 wujin District	溧阳市 Liyang City
参保人数（人）	Number of People Covered by Insurance （person）	1109761	1016319	98675	329252	93442
基金总收入（万元）	General Fund Revenue （10000 yuan）	23081	21439	1890	6102	1642
基金总支出（万元）	General Fund Expenditure （10000 yuan）	33966	31260	1771	9593	2706
当年享受生育保险待遇人次（人次）	Number of People Receiving Maternity Insurance （person-time）	54859	50441	3031	16008	4418

19

CHAPTER 19

城市建设 环境保护

URBAN CONSTRUCTION AND ENVIRONMENTAL PROTECTION

常州统计年鉴

19 城市建设　环境保护
URBAN CONSTRUCTION AND ENVIRONMENTAL PROTECTION

2015 年主要统计指标
MAJOR STATISTICAL INDICATORS OF 2015

城区人口密度	Urban Population Density	2399 人 / 平方公里	(person/sq.km)
城区实有道路面积	Area of Existing Road in Urban District	4431.85 万平方米	(10000 sq.m)
城区人均公园绿地面积	Per Capita Green Area of Parks in Urban District	13.85 平方米	(sq.m)
城区出租车营运数量	Number of Taxi in Operation in Urban Area	3321 辆	(coach)
城区燃气普及率	Gas Penetration Rate in Urban District	100.0%	

19-1　市区城市公用事业基本情况（1978-2015 年）
BASIC STATISTICS ON URBAN PUBLIC UTILITIES（1978-2015）

年　份 Year	建成区面积（平方公里） Developed Area（sq.km）	年末实有铺装道路长度（公里） Length of Roads at Year-end（km）	年末实有铺装道路面积（万平方米） Area of Paved Roads at Year-end（10000 sq.m）	城市下水道总长度（公里） Total Length of Urban Sewerage Drain（km）	园林绿地面积（公顷） Parkes,Gardens and Green Areas（hectare）
1978	24.44	98	83	140	145
1979	26.80	102	86	145	150
1980	27.85	105	89	150	161
1981	28.98	109	90	155	171
1982	29.58	119	93	161	174
1983	31.00	124	103	190	177
1984	32.52	127	108	195	272
1985	34.30	121	104	225	275
1986	35.10	198	154	231	283
1987	35.90	320	263	284	294
1988	37.20	326	273	289	310
1989	37.80	332	279	229	322
1990	39.00	336	296	231	343
1991	39.60	354	312	238	364
1992	41.10	355	314	260	389
1993	54.80	415	359	271	920
1994	57.40	449	432	312	947
1995	60.60	483	450	698	1067
1996	65.00	559	606	714	1105
1997	67.00	593	662	736	1188
1998	68.14	648	713	818	1300
1999	68.14	671	777	894	1378
2000	68.95	697	868	929	1441
2001	70.95	821	1024	1040	1509
2002	90.50	2497	2907	1544	4779
2003	92.28	3828	3563	2414	4813
2004	98.50	3548	3772	2775	5213
2005	104.31	3584	3954	2918	5529
2006	107.58	1349	2158	2366	4037
2007	112.50	1551	2247	2918	6057
2008	120.51	1565	2606	3223	6468
2009	133.90	1656	2809	3458	6773
2010	153.05	1753	3023	3627	7222
2011	173.15	1811	3230	3807	7535
2012	183.24	1892	3451	4214	7914
2013	185.67	1956	3719	5003	8088
2014	203.80	2111	3934	4876	8813
2015	250.31	2444	4432	5503	10768

注：1、本表数据按当年行政区划统计；从1995年起，供水总量中不包括单位自备水量。
2、由于建设局统计口径发生变化，2006年起均为城区口径，同时公共绿地面积调整为公园绿地面积。
3、自2010年起年末实有公共汽车营运车辆统计口径调整为市区口径。

Note：1、The data in the tabal were calculated according to the administrative division of that year;Since 1995,the total volume of water supply excludes the volume oh self-prepared water supply by units.
2、Due to the change of statistic coverage of municipal construction authorities, the data were calculated as per statistic coverage of urban area since the year of 2006, meanwhile, public green area was adjusted as green area of park.
3、Since 2010, the actual number of buses in operation by the end of year has been calculated as per statistical coverage of urban areas.

其 中 of which #公园绿地面积（公顷）Green Space of Park（hectare）	供水总量（万立方米）Total Annual Volume of Water Supply（10000 m3）	年末实有公共汽车营运车辆（辆）Number of Operating Public Transport Vehicles at Year-end（coach）	全年公共汽车客运总数（万人次）Total Number of Annual Passengers Despatched by Public Transport Vehicles（10000 persons/time）	年末实有出租汽车营运车辆（辆）Number of Operating Taxies at Year-end（coach）	管道燃气供气总量（万立方米）Total Pipe Natural Gas Supply（10000 m3）	液化气供气总量（吨）Total Liquefied of Gas Supply（ton）
54	20578	117	7184			
55	20876	133	9706			
56	21219	147	10862		109	
59	21385	157	11023		143	
61	21881	167	10907		115	
64	22911	182	10171		224	
68	24332	205	10119		333	
71	25759	227	11271		515	
76	26611	217	11082	92	996	2386
80	26878	209	10762	116	1058	2798
99	27050	211	10519	131	1157	4161
107	24871	208	10290	136	1415	3757
121	25994	232	9482	137	1601	5469
137	26066	244	9632	146	1655	10556
147	28353	254	10201	290	1654	22877
223	26240	283	9129	356	1667	20802
233	25789	297	8354	419	1729	22940
283	11257	307	8704	592	1783	24662
301	11491	348	8768	1029	2624	28995
357	14870	371	9199	1209	3224	28923
412	15310	1415	11490	1173	3533	33405
440	15291	1423	12624	1564	3846	35443
458	16631	1572	14616	1443	4256	38827
500	20123	1703	14865	1442	4502	43835
1101	31431	1651	14195	1442	5058	92852
1193	30517	1804	15523	1442	5898	87464
1433	30965	2065	18089	1642	5694	77510
1568	32384	2105	21829	1842	8030	80800
1333	20940	1608	18940	1842	14892	42115
1389	23636	1779	25973	2142	26943	37025
1450	23220	1788	33150	2142	31298	26656
1561	23633	1934	35583	2142	33444	23532
1632	21981	2518	38948	2542	48099	11037
1704	21664	2600	40717	2542	52355	8182
1759	21801	2590	41190	2542	55209	7043
1873	21759	2705	41890	3042	58829	6123
2036	21278	2657	35675	3042	63432	5689
2479	25048	2858	34054	3321	77578	11069

19-2 主要年份市区城市设施水平
URBAN CIVIL FACILITIES IN MAIN YEARS

指 标	Item	2000	2005	2010	2015
人均日生活用水量（升）	Per Capita Daily Consumption of Tap Water for Rrsidential Use （liter）	224.2	181.6	238.7	229.8
自来水普及率（%）	Percentage of Population with Access to Tap Water （%）	100.0	92.7	100.0	100.0
每万人拥有公交车辆（标台）	Average Public Service Vehicles per 10000 Persons （coach）	15.6	9.0	13.1	20.5
燃气普及率（%）	Percentage of Population with Access to Fuel Gas （%）	99.8	92.0	99.0	100.0
人均拥有道路面积（平方米）	Per Capita Area of Roads （sq.m）	10.7	17.9	22.9	24.8
污水处理率（%）	Rate of Sewerage Disposal（%）	69.0	86.8	89.8	95.4
人均公园绿地面积（平方米）	Per Capita Green Area of Parks （sq.m）	5.6	7.1	12.4	13.9
建成区绿化覆盖率（%）	Rate of the Green Space in Constructed Areas （%）	31.7	38.8	42.2	43.1
生活垃圾无害化处理率（%）	Rate of No Harm Disposal of Living Garbage （%）	50.5	92.1	100.0	100.0

注：每万人拥有公交车辆数从2013年起按交通部规定采用建成区人口计算。
Note：Since 2013, the number of buses per 10000 people has been calculated according to the population of built-up area as required by the Ministry of Transport of the People's Republic of China.

19-3 分地区城市建设用地情况（2015 年）
LAND USE OF URBAN CONSTRUCTION BY REGION（2015）

单位：平方公里（sq.km）

指 标	Item	市 区 Urban Area	其中 of which #金坛区 Jintan District	溧阳市 Liyang City
建成区面积	Area of Constructed Regions	250.31	22.2	28.48
城市建设用地面积	Floor space of Urban Constructed Area	250.22	22.13	27.36
居住用地	Residential Area	64.38	7.26	8.63
公共管理与公共服务用地	Public Management & Public Service Sites	15.50	2.48	2.65
商业服务业设施用地	Business Services Facilities	15.66	5.27	2.21
工业用地	Industrial Area	70.28	0.27	7.03
物流仓储用地	Logistics & Warehousing Space	6.37	1.45	0.65
道路与交通设施用地	Road and Transportation Facilities	34.80	2.36	2.91
公用设施用地	Communal Facilities	7.59	0.96	1.09
绿地与广场用地	Green Area and squares	35.64	2.08	2.19

19-4 分地区城市市政设施情况（2015 年） URBAN CIVIL FACILITIES BY REGION（2015）

指标	Item	市区 Urban Area	其中 of which #金坛区 Jintan District	溧阳市 Liyang City
实有道路长度（公里）	Length of Roads （km）	2444	247	240
实有道路面积（万平方米）	Area of Roads （10000 sq.m）	4431.85	351.72	429.65
桥梁数（座）	Number of Bridges （unit）	1222	59	56
排水管道长度（公里）	Length of Sewage Pipelines （km）	5503	474	306
污水日处理能力（万立方米）	Capacity of Sewage Disposal （10000 m^3）	108	7	5
路灯盏数（千盏）	Street Lamps （1000 sets）	239.08	29.18	11.01

19-5 分地区城市园林绿化情况（2015 年） URBAN PARKS, GARDENS AND GREEN AREAS BY REGION（2015）

指标	Item	市区 Urban Area	其中 of which #金坛区 Jintan District	溧阳市 Liyang City
园林绿地面积（公顷）	Parkes,Gardens and Green Areas （hectare）	10768	999	1337
公园绿地面积（公顷）	Green Space of Park （hectare）	2479	281	273
建成区绿化覆盖面积（公顷）	Green Space in Constucted Areas （hectare）	10783	929	1215
人均公园绿地面积（平方米）	Per Capita Green Area of Park （sq.m）	13.85	13.18	12.73
建成区绿地率（%）	Rate of the Green Space in Constructed Areas （%）	39.1	37.9	38.4
建成区绿化覆盖率（%）	Rate of the Green Space in Constructed Areas （%）	43.1	41.9	42.7
城市公园个数（个）	Urban Parks （unit）	38	6	8
公园面积（公顷）	Park Area （hectare）	1063	199	154

19-6　分地区城市公共汽车、出租汽车情况（2015 年）
URBAN PUBLIC SERVICE VEHICLES AND TAXIES BY REGION（2015）

指　标	Item	市　区 Urban Area	其中 of which # 金坛区 Jintan District	溧阳市 Liyang City
公共汽车	Public Service Vehicles			
年底营运车辆数（辆）	Number in Operation at Year-end （coach）	2858	150	197
年底营运线路条数（条）	Number of Operating Routes at Year-end （line）	278	15	28
年底营运线路网长度（公里）	Length of Operating Route Net at Year-end （km）	4171	207	262
客运总量（万人次）	Total volume of travellers （10000 Persons/times）	34054	1335	2912
每万人拥有公交车辆（标台）	Average Public Service Vehicles per 10000 Persons （coach）	20.5	8.1	9.3
出租汽车	Taxies			
营运车辆（辆）	Operation Vehicles （coach）	3321	279	359

19-7　分地区城市自来水情况（2015 年）
URBAN TAP WATER CONDITION BY REGION（2015）

指　标	Item	市　区 Urban Area	其中 of which # 金坛区 Jintan District	溧阳市 Liyang City
自来水综合生产能力（万立方米 / 日）	General Production Capacity of Water Treatment Plant （10000 m^3 /day）	172.0	5.0	25.0
供水管道长度（公里）	Length of Water Supply Piplines （km）	13066	1191	731
供水总量（万立方米）	Total Water Supply （10000 m^3）	25048	2577	2856
# 生产用水量	Water for Production	6845	728	974
生活用水量	Water for Livelihood	15009	1360	1515
用水人口（万人）	Population with Access to Tap Water （10000 persons）	178.97	21.30	21.46
人均日生活用水量（升）	Per Capita Daily Comsumption of Tap Water for Livelihood （litre）	229.77	174.92	193.44
自来水普及率（%）	Percentage of Population with Access to Tap Water （%）	100.0	100.0	100.0

19-8 分地区城市燃气情况（2015 年）
URBAN GAS SUPPLY BY REGION（2015）

指 标	Item	市 区 Urban Area	其中 of which #金坛区 Jintan District	溧阳市 Liyang City
天然气	**Natural Gas**			
燃气管道长度（公里）	Length of natural gas pipelines （km）	6171	584	453
供气总量（万立方米）	Total Gas Supply （10000 m^3）	77578	7668	8615
#家庭用量	Consumption for Residential Use	10447	1015	2572
用气户数（户）	Total Number of Residents with Access to Gas （household）	623853	65383	62994
#家庭用户	Households Consumers	613106	63733	61944
用气人口（万人）	Total Population with Access to Gas （10000 persons）	174.31	19.20	18.57
天然气汽车加气站（座）	Natural Gas Filling Stations for Automobiles （unit）	18	3	4
液化石油气	**Liquefied Petroleum Gas**			
供气总量（吨）	Total Gas Supply （ton）	11069	5800	1419
#家庭用量	Consumption for Residential Use	3460	2100	1419
用气户数（户）	Total Number of Residents with Access to Gas （household）	28016	17900	8091
#家庭用户	Households Consumers	18967	9900	8091
用气人口（万人）	Total Population with Access to Gas （10000 persons）	4.66	2.10	2.79
燃气普及率（%）	**Percentage of Population with Access to Fuel Gas （%）**	**100.0**	**100.0**	**99.5**

19-9 分地区城市环境卫生情况（2015 年）
URBAN ENVIRONMENT SANITATION BY REGION（2015）

指 标	Item	市 区 Urban Area	其中 of which #金坛区 Jintan District	溧阳市 Liyang City
实际清扫面积（万平方米）	Actually Cleaned Area （10000 sq.m）	3278	528	360
生活垃圾清运量（万吨）	Volume of Residential Garbage Disposal （10000 tons）	76.48	8.49	7.18
粪便清运量（万吨）	Clearing of Excrement and Urine （10000 tons）	1.77	1.07	0.15
公共厕所（座）	Public Lavatories （unit）	929	71	86
环卫机械数（台）	Environmental Sanitation Equipment （unit）	520	144	88

19-10　市区城市生态自然环境情况（2011-2015 年）
URBAN ECOLOGICAL NATURAL ENVIRONMENT（2011-2015）

指　标	Item	2011	2012	2013	2014	2015
园林绿化	**Parks,Gardens and Green Areas**					
园林绿地面积（公顷）	Parkes,Gardens and Green Areas （hectare）	7535	7914	8088	8813	10768
公园绿地面积（公顷）	Green Space of Park （hectare）	1704	1759	1873	2036	2479
建成区绿化覆盖面积（公顷）	Green Space in Constucted Areas （hectare）	7302	7735	7960	8756	10783
建成区绿化覆盖率（%）	Rate of Green Space in Constructed Areas （%）	42.2	42.2	42.9	43.0	43.1
人均公园绿地面积 （平方米）	Per Capita Green Area of Park （sq.m）	12.41	12.49	12.83	13.21	13.85
城市公园个数（个）	Urban Parks （unit）	25	26	27	29	38
公园面积（公顷）	Park Area （hectare）	520	553	666	716	1063
水、空气和噪声情况	**Water, Air and Noise**					
城市集中式饮用水源地水质达标率（%）	Rate up to the Standards of Water Quality for Urban Potable Water Sources （%）	100.0	100.0	100.0	100.0	100.0
空气污染指数小于100天数占全年天数的比例（%）	Proportion of Days with Air Pollution Index less than 100 to Whole Year （%）	92.1	92.1	58.6	63.8	67.3
区域环境噪声平均值（分贝）	Average Value of Noise in Whole Area （dB）	54.7	53.9	53.9	52.6	52.4
交通干线噪声平均值（分贝）	Average Value of Noise Along Main Traffic Artery （dB）	67.3	67.5	67.7	67.8	68.2
生活垃圾无害化处理	**Harmless Disposal of Household Garbage**					
垃圾清运量（万吨）	Wastes Transported （10000 Tons）	54.95	58.08	59.24	61.83	76.48
垃圾无害化处理量（万吨）	Volume of Garbage Disposal （10000 ton）	54.95	58.08	59.24	61.83	76.48
生活垃圾无害化处理率（%）	Rate of Harmless Disposal of Household Garbage （%）	100.0	100.0	100.0	100.0	100.0

注：2013年起执行新的环境空气质量标准，“空气污染指数小于100天数占全年天数的比例”按AQI指数评价。
Note：The new ambient air quality standards were implemented in 2013, and the "percent of days with air quality index （AQI） lower than 100" is calculated in accordance with the AQI thereinafter.

19-11 环境保护情况（1986-2015 年）
ENVIRONMENTAL PROTECTION（1986-2015）

年 份 Year	工业废水排放总量（万吨） Total Volume of Industrial Wastewater Discharged（10000 tons）	工业废水中 COD 排放总量（吨） Total Volume of COD in Industrial Wastewater Discharged（ton）	工业废气中二氧化硫排放总量（吨） Total Volume of Sulphur Dioxide Emission in Industrial Waste Gas（ton）	工业废气中烟尘排放总量（吨） Total Volume of Soot Emission in Industrial Waste Gas（ton）	工业废气中粉尘排放总量（吨） Total Volume of Dust Emission in Industrial Waste Gas（ton）
1986	20681	64856	42527	49395	32500
1987	22647	51396	41072	38406	27800
1988	22386	43617	46968	37395	33700
1989	20546	35879	56252	56307	32700
1990	20439	30508	56099	55662	43400
1991	21455	28797	73472	62014	25700
1992	18697	31121	75671	57791	19200
1993	12070	27998	45906	26704	19000
1994	10931	22308	55355	28196	31300
1995	11489	22865	55971	25282	34300
1996	10523	15979	57236	28991	65900
1997	11193	26763	74320	35814	104600
1998	10183	17436	51476	26563	30300
1999	16455	19873	47409	33895	48700
2000	14728	16436	39042	30798	41200
2001	27086	29903	48242	17590	46400
2002	23912	29289	45133	19329	41447
2003	24071	30015	45722	15375	43986
2004	23082	43018	62958	28086	54602
2005	32519	51579	86215	35804	61091
2006	27300	36215	82930	31465	59396
2007	31875	30944	72243	29496	52085
2008	32601	28273	66656	25392	14904
2009	35942	26354	62255	24917	11299
2010	37715	24827	48000	19582	10784
2011	17371	9416	43734	38563	
2012	14630	8158	35984	27589	
2013	12017	6948	35830	35161	
2014	11909	7046	35308	115086	
2015	12977	7446	34420	97999	

注：从2011年起工业废气中烟尘、粉尘排放总量合并成烟（粉）尘排放量。2014年起增加无组织烟粉尘排放量统计。
Note: The Total Dust and Powder Emissions in Industrial Emissions was combined as Smoke（Powder）Dust Emissions starting from 2011.
Staatistics of fugitive dust emissions was added from 2014.

19-12　分地区环境保护情况（2015 年）
ENVIRONMENTAL PROTECTION BY REGION（2015）

指标	Item	全市 Whole Municipality	其中 of which 市区 Urban Area	溧阳市 Liyang City
废水排放	**Wastewater Discharged**			
工业废水排放总量（万吨）	Total Volume of Industrial Wastewater Discharged（10000 tons）	12977	10519	2458
废水中化学需氧量排放量（吨）	Volume of Chemical Oxygen Demand in Wastwater Discharged（ton）	7446	5967	1480
废水中氨氮排放量（吨）	Ammonia Emissions from Wastewater（ton）	422	327	95
废气排放	**Waste Gas**			
工业废气排放总量（万标立方米）	Total Volume of Industrial Waste Gas Emission（10000 Nm^3）	35061894	29150435	5911458
二氧化硫排放量（吨）	Volume of Sulphur Dioxide Emission（ton）	34420	25139	9281
氮氧化物排放量（吨）	Nitrogen Oxides（ton）	58492	32938	25554
烟（粉）排放量（吨）	Smoke（Powder）Dust Emissions（ton）	97999	72477	25522
工业固体废物	**Industrail Solid Wastes**			
工业固体废物产生量（万吨）	Volume of Industrial Solid Wastes Produced（10000 tons）	680.47	593.29	87.18
工业固体废物综合利用量（万吨）	Volume of Industrial Solid Wastes Utilized（10000 tons）	668.06	580.88	87.18
工业固体废物处置量（万吨）	Volume of Industrial Solid Wastes Treated（10000 tons）	12.41	12.41	0.00
工业固体废物综合利用率（%）	Percentage of Industrial Solid Wastes Utilized（%）	98.2	97.9	100.0
环境建设	**Environmental Construction**			
自然保护区覆盖率（‰）	Coverage Rate of Nature Reserves（‰）	1.56		4.45

20

CHAPTER 20

科技 教育 文化

SCIENCE,TECHNOLOGY,
EDUCATION AND CULTURE

常州统计年鉴

20 科技 教育 文化
SCINECE & TECHNOLOGY EDUCATION AND CULTURE

2015 年主要统计指标
MAJOR STATISTICAL INDICATORS OF 2015

普通高等学校数	Number of Institutions of Higher Education	10 所	(unit)
普通高等学校在校学生数	Students Enrollment of Institutions of Higher Education	12.44 万人	(10000 persons)
普通中学数	Regular Secondary Schools	160 所	(unit)
普通中学在校学生数	Student Enrollment of Regular Secondary Schools	16.25 万人	(10000 persons)
小学学校数	Primary Schools	201 所	(unit)
小学学校在校学生数	Student Enrollment of Primary Schools	27.37 万人	(10000 persons)
年底公共图书馆	Number of Public Libraries	4 个	(unit)
电视台数	Number of Television Stations	4 座	(unit)
广播电台数	Number of Broadcasting Stations	4 座	(unit)

20-1　分地区规模以上工业企业研发活动情况（2015）
R&D ACTIVITIES OF INDUSTRIAL ENTERPRISES ABOVE THE DESIGNATED SIZE BY REGION（2015）

指　标	Item	全　市 Whole Municipality	市　区 Urban Area
企业基本情况	**Statistics on Industrial Enterprises**		
有 R&D 活动企业数（个）	Number of Enterprises Having R&D Activities （unit）	1296	1140
有科技机构企业数（个）	The Number of Companies with Scientific Institutions（unit）	1507	1332
有 R&D 活动企业所占比重（%）	Percentage of Enterprises Having R&D Activities to Total Number of Enterprises （%）	30.5	29.6
企业办科机构覆盖率（%）	The Coverage of Scientific Institutions Established by Companies （%）	35.5	34.6
R&D 活动情况	**Statistics on R&D Activities**		
R&D 人员（人）	Total Number of R&D Personnel （person）	57431	50296
R&D 经费内部支出（万元）	Intramural Expenditure on R&D （10000 yuan）	1361163	1193919
R&D 项目数（项）	Total Number of R&D Projects（unit）	4936	4305
企业办科技机构情况	**Scientific and Technological Institutions Run by Enterprises**		
企业办科技机构数（个）	Number of Scientific and Technological Institutions Run by Enterprises（unit）	1730	1529
机构科技活动人员（人）	Number of Scientific and Technological Personnel in Technological Institutions （person）	51946	46128
# 博士生	Ph.D. Owners	625	509
硕士生	Master's Degree Owners	3793	3415
新产品开发及生产情况	**Statitstics on New Product Development and Production**		
新产品开发项目数（个）	Number of New Products （unit）	5655	4996
新产品开发经费支出（万元）	Expenditure on New Product Development （10000 yuan）	1648960	1479751
新产品产值（万元）	Output Value of New Products （10000 yuan）	22887034	20850990
新产品销售收入（万元）	Sales Income of New Products （10000 yuan）	23147640	21055413
# 新产品出口	Export	4548510	4432460
专利情况	**Statistics on Patent**		
当年专利申请受理数（件）	Patent Applications （piece）	10530	9949
# 发明专利	Inventions	3262	3036
期末有效发明专利数（件）	Number of Effective Patents by End of Year （piece）	7831	7413
技术改造和技术获取情况	**Technical Innovation and Technology Acquisition**		
引进境外技术经费支出（万元）	Spending on Imported Techonologies （10000 yuan）	36744	36369
引进境外技术的消化吸收经费支出（万元）	Spending on Conversion of Imported Technologies （10000 yuan）	16845	13801
购买境内技术经费支出（万元）	Expenditure on Purchasing Domestic Technology （10000 yuan）	14288	10757
技术改造经费支出（万元）	Appropriation Expenditure on Technical Inovation （10000 yuan）	1014781	902650

	其 中 of which					
金坛区 Jintan District	武进区 wujin District	其 中 of which #经开区 Economic Development Zone	新北区 Xinbei District	天宁区 Tianning District	钟楼区 Zhonglou District	溧阳市 Liyang City
129	508	157	236	134	133	156
150	560	181	343	135	144	175
29.9	30.3	27.1	23.8	32.4	39.6	39.8
34.7	33.4	31.1	34.6	32.6	42.9	44.6
4080	24253	7442	9679	5863	6421	7135
144114	494870	170802	280968	146023	127944	167244
463	1913	525	925	462	542	631
177	613	204	416	160	163	201
3555	20571	6968	13052	3491	5459	5818
83	201	69	126	52	47	116
268	1659	753	802	297	389	378
490	2148	628	1388	422	548	659
140248	578687	208783	498337	131103	131375	169209
1610212	10057324	2790534	5994731	1159976	2028747	2036044
1901368	9938571	2795963	5992230	1198428	2024817	2092227
293337	2311111	941113	1536995	99498	191519	116050
559	4532	1312	3120	551	1187	581
268	1229	441	1075	190	274	226
347	3046	1057	2602	466	952	418
570	12171	1127	14253	6546	2828	375
2098	4868	4134	5673	1162		3043
558	6212	5518	640	2739	608	3531
92964	579299	277601	113907	70736	45745	112130

20-2　分地区大中型工业企业研发活动情况（2015 年）
R&D ACTIVITIES OF LARGE-AND-MEDIUM SIZED INDUSTRIAL ENTERPRISES BY REGION （2015）

指　标	Item	全　市 Whole Municipality	市　区 Urban Area
企业基本情况	**Statistics on Industrial Enterprises**		
有 R&D 活动企业数（个）	Number of Enterprises Having R&D Activities （unit）	411	367
有科技机构企业数（个）	The Number of Companies with Scientific Institutions（unit）	475	425
有 R&D 活动企业所占比重（%）	Percentage of Enterprises Having R&D Activities to Total Number of Enterprises （%）	72.1	71.4
企业办科机构覆盖率（%）	The Coverage of Scientific Institutions Established by Companies （%）	83.3	82.7
R&D 活动情况	**Statistics on R&D Activities**		
R&D 人员（人）	Total Number of R&D Personnel （person）	37000	32402
R&D 经费内部支出（万元）	Intramural Expenditure on R&D （10000 yuan）	966144	853360
R&D 项目数（项）	Total Number of R&D Projects（unit）	2427	2077
企业办科技机构情况	**Scientific and Technological Institutions Run by Enterprises**		
企业办科技机构数（个）	Number of Scientific and Technological Institutions Run by Enterprises（unit）	619	552
机构科技活动人员（人）	Number of Scientific and Technological Personnel in Technological Institutions （person）	31185	27872
#博士生	Ph.D. Owners	361	287
硕士生	Master's Degree Owners	2470	2279
新产品开发及生产情况	**Statitstics on New Product Development and Production**		
新产品开发项目数（个）	Number of New Products （unit）	2733	2395
新产品开发经费支出（万元）	Expenditure on New Product Development （10000 yuan）	1196389	1090797
新产品产值（万元）	Output Value of New Products （10000 yuan）	18515848	16896363
新产品销售收入（万元）	Sales Income of New Products （10000 yuan）	18700618	17036199
#新产品出口	Export	3806721	3708427
专利情况	**Statistics on Patent**		
当年专利申请数（件）	Patent Applications （piece）	4985	4670
#发明专利	Inventions	1749	1604
期末有效发明专利数（件）	Number of Effective Patents by End of Year （piece）	3703	3474
技术改造和技术获取情况	**Technical Innovation and Technology Acquisition**		
引进境外技术经费支出（万元）	Spending on Imported Techonologies （10000 yuan）	32827	32827
引进境外技术的消化吸收经费支出（万元）	Spending on Conversion of Imported Technologies （10000 yuan）	14696	12752
购买境内技术经费支出（万元）	Expenditure on Purchasing Domestic Technology （10000 yuan）	10582	8748
技术改造经费支出（万元）	Appropriation Expenditure on Technical Inovation （10000 yuan）	710264	622989

其中 of which						
金坛区 Jintan District	武进区 wujin District	其中 of which #经开区 Economic Development Zone	新北区 Xinbei District	天宁区 Tianning District	钟楼区 Zhonglou District	溧阳市 Liyang City
55	168	57	69	40	35	44
65	174	58	108	42	36	50
78.6	83.6	84.1	49.6	67.8	77.8	78.6
92.9	86.6	85.5	77.7	71.2	80.0	89.3
2594	16658	5220	6031	3193	3926	4598
109564	374350	131614	213716	70405	85324	112784
217	1011	314	379	202	268	350
80	217	79	148	54	53	67
2029	13403	4808	7496	1816	3128	3313
41	115	49	87	31	13	74
151	1217	571	518	186	207	191
224	1110	374	589	194	278	338
106439	439155	163974	390003	63893	91306	105593
1421251	8467082	2083036	4903357	767116	1337558	1619486
1637722	8404054	2107377	4833297	795547	1365580	1664419
249961	1833476	582355	1389252	96291	139448	98294
285	2315	800	1460	227	383	315
160	717	334	534	95	98	145
218	1623	777	1079	187	367	229
420	12137	1127	14064	3378	2828	
2033	4740	4128	5163	817		1944
283	5093	5091	446	2326	600	1834
77902	378599	162934	98369	37311	30808	87275

20-3　科研开发基本情况（2011-2015 年）
BASIC STATISTICS OF SCIENCE RESEARCH DEVELOPMENT（2011-2015）

指　标	Item	2011	2012	2013	2014	2015
机构数（个）	**Number of Institutes（unit）**	**17**	**17**	**16**	**14**	**16**
从业人数（人）	**Number of Employed Persons（person）**	**3741**	**3170**	**3163**	**2945**	**2711**
# 从事科技活动人数	Number of Personnel Engaged in Science and Technology	1496	1208	1606	1562	1254
从事 R&D 人员数	Number of Personnel Engaged in R&D	964	1002	1006	990	1083
课题活动人数	Number of Persons Engaged in Subject Activity	893	887	895	815	987
经费收入总额（万元）	**Total Funds Income（10000 yuan）**	**301408**	**291966**	**308773**	**318595**	**336591**
# 政府资金	Government Funds	3316	8432	6582	6332	4819
技术性收入	Technological Income	11809	8912	7198	8295	9475
经营收入	Operating Income	279966	272142	291734	300977	319299
经费支出总额（万元）	**Total Expenditure（10000 yuan）**	**237057**	**191865**	**207697**	**273518**	**267170**
#R&D 经费支出	Expenditure on Research and Development	24310	19197	18301	12008	22312
# 购置科研仪器设备	Purchasing Scientific Research Instruments and Equipments	4715	3605	2281	2335	1726
发表科技论文（篇）	**Number of Published Scientific and Technological Thesis（piece）**	**197**	**226**	**195**	**203**	**206**

注：机构数是指由江苏科技中心确认的研发机构数。
Note: The number of institutions listed in this table is the number of R&D institutions confirmed by the Jiangsu Provincial Science and Technology Center.

20-4 国家级、省级科技计划数（2015 年）
NUMBER OF SCIENTIFIC AND TECHNOLOGICAL PLANS AT STATE LEVEL OR PROVINCE LEVEL（2015）

计划名称 Name of Plan		合计（项） Total (Unit)	其中 of which 国家级 State Level	省级 Province Level	上级拨款（万元） Higher Organizations Appropriations (10000 yuan)	其中 of which 国家 State	省 Province
科技型中小企业技术创新基金	Technology Innovation Funds for Scientific and Technical Type Small and Medium Enterprises	2	2		11000	11000	
国家重大科技专项	Major National Science and Technology Projects	1	1		329	329	
国家自然科学基金	National Natural Science Foundation of China	64	64		2735	2735	
国家国际科技合作	National and International Scientific and Technological Cooperation	2	2		136	136	
国家专利行政执法	National patent administrative law enforcement	1	1		22	22	
省科技支撑计划（工业）	Provincial Scientific and Technological Support Plan （Industry）	42		42	5360		5360
省科技支撑计划（社会发展）	Provincial Scientific and Technological Support Plan （Social Development）	9		9	950		950
省工程技术研究中心	Provincial Engineering and Technology Reaearch Center	35		35			
省国际科技合作计划	International Scientific and Technologic Cooperation Plan	7		7	490		490
省科技成果转化专项资金	Special Fund for Scientific and Technological Achievements Transfer	23		23	12400		12400
省知识产权战略推进计划	Provincial Promotion Plan of Intellectual Property Rights Strategy	11		11	180		180
省软科学研究	Provincial Soft Science Research	4		4	20		20
省科技创新资金	Provincial Science & Technology Innovation Capital	27		27	878		878
省企业院士工作站	Provincial Enterprise Academician Workstations	3		3			
省级专利行政执法	Provincial patent administrative law enforcement	3		3	83		83

注：本表项目数和上级拨款为当年新上项目数及新上项目的上级拨款总额。

Note：The number of projects and appropriation from higher authorities in this table shall be the number of new projects and total appropriations of the current year.

20-5　市级科技计划项目情况（2015 年）
SCIENTIFIC AND TECHNOLOGICAL PLAN AT CITY LEVEL（2015）

单位：万元（10000 yuan）

项目名称	Name of Project	项数（项）Number of Project（unit）	科技拨款 Scientific and Technological appropriations
农业科技	Agricultural Science and Technology	29	515
工业科技	Industrial Science and Technology	91	1920
社会发展科技	Social Development Science and Technology	65	895
软课题	Research Task	63	127

注：本表未包括指导性计划。
Note：This table doesn't include guidance plans.

20-6　科技进步获奖情况（2015 年）
STATISTICS ON PRIZE OF ADVANCE OF SCIENCE AND TECHNOLOGY（2015）

单位：项（unit）

奖励级别	Prize Grade	合计 Total	其中 of which 一等奖 First Prize	二等奖 Second Prize	三等奖 Third Prize	省创新奖 Innovation Award	省国合奖 The prize
省　级	Provincial Level	18	2	6	7	1	2
市　级	City Level	78	8	24	46		

20-7　分地区专利申请及授权情况（2015 年）
STATISTICS ON PATENT APPLICATIONS EXAMINED AND GRANTED BY REGION（2015）

单位：项（unit）

指　标	Item	合　计 Total	其中 of which 市　区 Urban Area	溧阳市 Liyang City
专利申请量	**Number of Patent Applications Examined**	**38559**	**37460**	**1099**
发明专利	Patent for Invention	13211	12691	520
实用新型专利	Practical New-type Patent	17481	16965	516
外观专利	Appearance Patent	7867	7804	63
专利授权量	**Number of Patent Authorizations Granted**	**21585**	**20643**	**942**
发明专利	Patent for Invention	2664	2306	358
实用新型专利	Practical New-type Patent	13121	12606	515
外观专利	Appearance Patent	5800	5731	69

20-8 分地区政府科技拨款数（2015 年）
GOVERNMENT APPROPRIATION OF SCIENCE AND TECHNOLOGY BY REGION（2015）

单位：万元（10000 yuan）

指 标	Item	全 市 Whole Municipality	其 中 of which	
			市 区 Urban Area	溧阳市 Liyang City
总 计	**Total**	**295479**	**265292**	**30187**
科学技术管理事务	Scientific & Technical Management Affairs	4384	3205	1179
基础研究	Basic Research	200	200	
应用研究	Applied Research	1192	1192	
技术研究与开发	Technology Research and Development	91584	73548	18036
科技条件与服务	Scientific & Technical Conditions and Service	4016	3385	631
科学技术普及	Science & Technology Popularization	1704	1449	255
科技交流与合作	Science and Technology Exchange and Cooperation	1946	1946	
科技重大专项	Special science and Technology Major	43000	43000	
其他科学技术支出	Other Expenditure For Science & Technology	147453	137367	10086

20-9 分地区高新技术企业情况（2015 年）
STATISTICS ON HIGH AND NEW TECHNOLOGY ENTERPRISES BY REGION（2015）

指 标	Item	全 市 Whole Municipality	其 中 of which	
			市 区 Urban Area	溧阳市 Liyang City
年末高新技术企业数（家）	Number of High and New Technology Enterprises at Year-end （unit）	1050	985	65
# 当年确认数	Confirmed Number at Current Year	139	125	14
企业总产值（亿元）	Gross Output Value of Enterprises （100 million yuan）	2593.91	2352.75	241.16
新技术产品产值（亿元）	Output Value of New Technological Products （100 million yuan）	1392.74	1295.49	97.25
出口创汇总额（亿美元）	Total Exports （USD 100 million）	84.88	82.23	2.65
利税总额（亿元）	Total Amount of Pre-tax （100 million yuan）	314.37	295.71	18.66
研究与开发经费（亿元）	Research and Development Funds （100 million yuan）	118.11	109.57	8.54
职工总数（万人）	Number of staff and workers （10000 persons）	25.3	23.62	1.68

20-10 分地区高新技术产品情况（2015 年）
STATISTICS ON HIGH AND NEW TECHNOLOGICAL PRODUCTS BY REGION（2015）

指标	Item	全市 Whole Municipality	其中 of which 市区 Urban Area	其中 of which 溧阳市 Liyang City
省级高新技术产品累计数（只）	Accumulated Number of High and New Technological Products at Provincial Level（unit）	5971	5424	547
当年经省确认的高新技术产品数（只）	Number of High and New Technological Products Confirmed by the Province at This Year（unit）	816	738	78

20-11 技术（市场）贸易情况（2015 年）
STATISTICS ON TECHNOLOGY （MARKET） TRADE（2015）

指标	Item	全市 Whole Municipality
网上登记技术合同（项）	Number of Online Registered Technology Contracts（unit）	1762
网上登记技术合同成交金额（万元）	Business Volume of Online Registered Technology Contracts（10000 yuan）	440473

20-12 科技企业孵化器、加速器情况（2015 年）
STATISTICS ON SCIENTIFIC AND TECHNOLOGICAL ENTERPRISE INCUBATORS AND ACCELERATORS（2015）

指标	Item	全市 Whole Municipality	其中 of which 市区 Urban Area	其中 of which 溧阳市 Liyang City
孵化器个数（个）	Number of Incubators and Accelerators（unit）	108	96	12
#省级以上	Provincial Level and Above	41	38	3
场地面积（万平方米）	Site Area（10000 square meters）	789	708	81
#省级以上	Provincial Level and Above	573	535	38
本年在孵企业数（家）	Number of Entered Enterprises（unit）	5444	5036	408
#省级以上	Provincial Level and Above	4235	3934	301
在孵企业总收入（万元）	Gross Income of Entered Enterprises（10000 yuan）	1387872	1321013	66859
#省级以上	Provincial Level and Above	989317	941521	47796
在孵企业从业人员数（人）	Persons Employed in Entered Enterprises（person）	54099	48630	5469
累计毕业企业数（家）	Accumulated Number of Incubated Enterprises（unit）	1440	1368	72
#当年毕业企业数	Number of Incubated Enterprises at Current Year	150	145	5

20-13 历年各类学校数
NUMBER OF SCHOOLS BY TYPE OVER THE YEARS

单位：所（unit）

年份 Year	合计 Total	其中 of which			
		#普通高等院校 Institutions of Higher Education	普通中等专业学校 Specialized Secondary Schools	普通中学 Regular Secondary Schools	小学 Primary Schools
1949	1666		3	54	1607
1950	1865		4	52	1807
1951	1983		5	54	1923
1952	2076		5	55	2015
1953	2033		3	55	1974
1954	2017		2	58	1956
1955	2003		2	59	1941
1956	2281		3	66	2211
1957	2138		2	68	2067
1958	2862	4	9	110	2465
1959	2921	3	9	116	2634
1960	2651	3	10	123	2367
1961	2436	2	6	116	2217
1962	2391		2	117	2245
1963	2348		2	116	2199
1964	3181		2	115	2974
1965	3726		2	103	3322
1966	3252		5	117	2855
1967	3038		5	120	2636
1968	2907		5	129	2467
1969	2615		4	183	2380
1970	2649		4	192	2445
1971	2712		5	308	2390
1972	2736		6	333	2390
1973	2769		6	300	2457
1974	2638		7	345	2281
1975	2641		8	427	2201
1976	2691		7	635	2043
1977	2612		7	632	1967
1978	2477		8	509	1952
1979	2466		10	478	1968
1980	2490		13	360	2104
1981	2386	2	12	266	2093
1982	2400	2	11	282	2092

20-13　续表　Continued　　　　单位：所（unit）

年　份 Year	合　计 Total	其　中　of　which			
		# 普通高等院校 Institutions of Higher Education	普通中等专业学校 Specialized Secondary Schools	普通中学 Regular Secondary Schools	小　学 Primary Schools
1983	2369	2	11	278	2061
1984	2294	2	14	282	1974
1985	2253	3	14	275	1933
1986	2212	3	15	270	1895
1987	2176	3	16	266	1862
1988	2136	3	16	260	1830
1989	2072	3	16	248	1776
1990	2021	3	16	235	1736
1991	1955	3	17	219	1678
1992	1822	3	16	212	1550
1993	1758	3	16	205	1497
1994	1633	3	16	199	1374
1995	1597	3	17	201	1332
1996	1448	3	17	193	1189
1997	1228	3	17	184	978
1998	1018	3	17	178	771
1999	927	3	17	176	683
2000	816	3	14	174	581
2001	736	5	12	177	498
2002	681	8	8	177	450
2003	550	8	8	174	327
2004	528	9	8	173	307
2005	499	9	7	172	284
2006	468	9	8	172	252
2007	446	9	8	169	234
2008	430	9	8	168	221
2009	408	9	8	166	206
2010	388	9	12	163	190
2011	384	9	13	162	186
2012	382	9	12	162	187
2013	379	9	12	163	182
2014	379	9	12	158	187
2015	395	10	11	160	201

20-14 历年在校学生数
NUMBER OF STUDENTS OVER THE YEARS

单位：人（person）

年 份 Year	合 计 Total	其中 of which			
		# 普通高等院校 Institutions of Higher Education	普通中等专业学校 Specialized Secondary Schools	普通中学 Regular Secondary Schools	小 学 Primary Schools
1949	154997		586	13223	140949
1950	158060		855	12568	144402
1951	186276		1404	16334	168353
1952	260160		1919	25587	221884
1953	270719		923	28973	230248
1954	264525		740	31813	231904
1955	284551		726	34113	249646
1956	311969		1243	30826	279829
1957	321017		1010	44123	275815
1958	416767	1069	2099	53013	338334
1959	436537	855	2991	59030	351695
1960	475975	1004	4614	65497	380691
1961	424200	1037	3487	61509	347389
1962	361579		1406	50482	306269
1963	353245		571	47779	301894
1964	412149		213	50043	355244
1965	447588		468	5225	372321
1966	464351		1027	74009	382302
1967	441394		1113	69817	364815
1968	450651		890	60215	360821
1969	500982		479	95506	403911
1970	446826			90659	352914
1971	497600			102324	391535
1972	558081		625	134911	419129
1973	549911		1220	124534	422645
1974	574459		1785	128937	442630
1975	601646		1725	159492	439205
1976	614776		464	193235	419580
1977	645041		1203	261068	381334
1978	598917	434	1980	215461	379391
1979	561234	542	2962	185704	369719
1980	539645	481	3064	173164	360399
1981	513322	1312	3686	161621	343001
1982	492065	1036	3878	158452	324956

20-14　续表　Continued　　　　单位：人（person）

年 份 Year	合 计 Total	其中 of which #普通高等院校 Institutions of Higher Education	普通中等专业学校 Specialized Secondary Schools	普通中学 Regular Secondary Schools	小 学 Primary Schools
1983	486181	1240	5100	161380	312593
1984	487492	2059	6655	155577	314954
1985	491522	3161	9717	148865	319954
1986	493492	4044	12462	150555	313588
1987	483933	4578	13657	150979	301508
1988	476768	4839	14024	147573	296839
1989	468608	5079	14777	146394	289683
1990	461007	5085	15715	149037	277043
1991	453827	5190	15616	153409	262497
1992	452175	5469	16799	157068	253370
1993	460296	8897	20868	153547	255823
1994	478422	10908	26562	155908	261261
1995	501879	11644	33885	158586	271583
1996	526262	12182	42918	157074	289272
1997	542890	13156	49260	149390	305431
1998	550361	14251	52981	146903	312446
1999	561141	15120	53704	159995	309019
2000	571011	20013	49925	182332	300091
2001	584831	26668	49267	203570	287717
2002	603213	35159	52535	221258	273755
2003	622271	53059	50887	229845	263522
2004	642190	73862	51821	228206	255632
2005	648778	95396	48848	220718	244589
2006	648373	107742	46247	215938	234874
2007	643540	119131	39477	211346	229781
2008	630821	123174	36448	205966	224181
2009	614813	125468	34523	199351	216791
2010	603938	122802	36029	188436	221533
2011	600423	123947	38231	177639	229035
2012	596907	124637	40527	169063	234305
2013	600365	126254	38462	164809	243614
2014	604560	126137	36896	162484	253265
2015	624613	124405	36013	162527	273682

20-15 教育事业基本情况（2015 年）
BASIC STATISTICS ON EDUCATION（2015）

单位：人（person）

指标	Item	学校数（所）Number of Schools (Unit)	毕业生数 Number of Graduates	招生数 Number of New Students Enrollment	在校学生数 Number of Students Enrollment	毕业班学生数 Number of Students in Graduate Class	教职工数 Number of Staff and Teachers	其中 of which #专任教师 Number of Full-time Teachers
总计	**Total**	**395**	**147786**	**164654**	**624613**	**147001**	**44248**	**37870**
按地区分	**Grouped by Region**							
市区	Urban Area	318	129323	146907	552109	128958	37634	32191
溧阳市	Liyang City	77	18463	17747	72504	18043	6614	5679
按学校类型分	**Grouped by Type of School**							
普通高等学校	Institutions of Higher Education	10	39478	39116	124405	39315	8098	5685
普通中等专业学校	Specilized Secondary Schools	11	12144	11924	36013	12009	2909	2480
技工学校	Technical Schools	8	6279	11011	27115		2082	1915
普通中学	Regular Secondary Schools	160	52669	54901	162527	53894	17057	13970
高中	Senior Secondary Schools	34	18450	16832	51624	17911		4814
初中	Junior Secondary Schools	126	34219	38069	110903	35983		9156
小学	Primary Schools	201	37064	47596	273682	41783	13955	13701
特殊教育学校	Special Education Schools	5	152	106	871		147	119

20-16 市区教育事业基本情况（2015 年）
BASIC STATISTICS ON EDUCATION OF URBAN AREA（2015）

单位：人（person）

指标	Item	学校数（所）Number of Schools (Unit)	毕业生数 Number of Graduates	招生数 Number of New Students Enrollment	在校学生数 Number of Students Enrollment	毕业班学生数 Number of Students in Graduate Class	教职工数 Number of Staff and Teachers	其中 of which #专任教师 Number of Full-time Teachers
总计	**Total**	**318**	**129323**	**146907**	**552109**	**128958**	**37634**	**32191**
按地区分	**Grouped by Region**							
金坛区	Jintan District	57	11538	11750	47323	11465	4912	4300
武进区	Wujin District	107	32223	38752	162749	34968	10235	9261
#经开区	Economic Develpment Zone	27	6752	7803	34770	7288	1998	1816
新北区	Xinbei District	47	11758	15957	64967	12987	4026	3661
天宁区	Tianning District	29	7277	8285	40393	7315	2418	2340
钟楼区	Zhonglou District	30	6026	7353	38783	6651	2058	1916
按学校类型分	**Grouped by Type of School**							
普通高等学校	Institutions of Higher Education	10	39224	38878	123944	39092	8098	5685
普通中等专业学校	Specilized Secondary Schools	9	9684	9827	29682	9830	2333	1980
技工学校	Technical Schools	8	6279	11011	27115		2082	1915
普通中学	Regular Secondary Schools	124	42879	46083	135817	44643	13542	11164
高中	Senior Secondary Schools	27	14437	13905	42023	14373		3752
初中	Junior Secondary Schools	97	28442	32178	93794	30270		7412
小学	Primary Schools	163	31121	41019	234784	35393	11444	11335
特殊教育学校	Special Education Schools	4	136	89	767		135	112

20-17　成人教育基本情况（2015 年）
BASIC STATISTICS ON ADULT EDUCATION（2015）

单位：人（person）

指　标	Item	学校数（所）Number of Schools（Unit）	毕业生数 Number of Graduates	招生数 Number of New Students Enrollment	在校学生数 Number of Students Enrollment	毕业班学生数 Number of Students in Graduate Class	教职工数 Number of Staff and Teachers	其中 of which #专任教师 Number of Full-time Teachers
总　计	**Total**	**246**	**1344680**	**18215**	**1254354**	**18185**	**7553**	**6070**
按地区分	**Grouped by Region**							
市　区	Urban Area	201	1215880	18086	1238291	18051	7003	5640
溧阳市	Liyang City	45	128800	129	16063	134	550	430
按学校类型分	**Grouped by Type of School**							
成人高等学校	Institutions of Higher Education for Adults		14060	18215	43302	18185	408	342
职业技术培训学校	Technical Training School for Adults	246	1330620		1211052		7145	5728

20-18　市区成人教育基本情况（2015 年）
BASIC STATISTICS ON URBAN ADULT EDUCATION（2015）

单位：人（person）

指　标	Item	学校数（所）Number of Schools（Unit）	毕业生数 Number of Graduates	招生数 Number of New Students Enrollment	在校学生数 Number of Students Enrollment	毕业班学生数 Number of Students in Graduate Class	教职工数 Number of Staff and Teachers	其中 of which #专任教师 Number of Full-time Teachers
总　计	**Total**	**201**	**1215880**	**18086**	**1238291**	**18051**	**7003**	**5640**
成人高等学校	Institutions of Higher Education of Adults		14060	18086	43039	18051	408	342
职业技术培训学校	Technical Training School for Adults	201	1201820		1195252		6595	5298

20-19 分地区中小学专任教师学历和职称情况（2015 年）
EDUCATIONAL BACKGROUNDS AND PROFESSIONAL TITLES OF FULL-TIME TEACHERS IN MIDDLE SCHOOL AND PRIMARY SCHOOLS BY REGION（2015）

单位：人（person）

指 标	Item	全 市 Whole Munici pality	其 中 of which 市 区 Urban Area	其 中 of which 溧阳市 Liyang City
总 计	**Total**	**27671**	**22499**	**5172**
高 中	**Senior Secondary School**	**4814**	**3752**	**1062**
按学历分	Grouped by Educational Background			
研究生毕业	Postgraduate	709	528	181
本科毕业	Graduate	4085	3206	879
专科毕业	Junior College	19	17	2
高中阶段毕业	Senior Secondary School	1	1	
按职称分	Grouped by Professional Titles			
中学高级	Senior Teacher	1812	1494	318
中学一级	Teacher 1st Grade	2022	1579	443
中学二级	Teacher 2nd Grade	881	591	290
未定职级	Unspecified Position Level	99	88	11
初 中	**Junior Secondary School**	**9156**	**7412**	**1744**
按学历分	Grouped by Educational Background			
研究生毕业	Postgraduate	414	361	53
本科毕业	Graduate	8337	6711	1626
专科毕业	Junior College	394	329	65
高中阶段毕业	Senior Secondary School	11	11	
按职称分	Grouped by Professional Titles			
中学高级	Senior Teacher	3071	2510	561
中学一级	Teacher 1st Grade	4117	3288	829
中学二级	Teacher 2nd Grade	1752	1415	337
中学三级	Teacher 3rd Grade	3	3	
未定职级	Unspecified Position Level	213	196	17
小 学	**Primary School**	**13701**	**11335**	**2366**
按学历分	Grouped by Educational Background			
研究生毕业	Postgraduate	256	236	20
本科毕业	Graduate	11575	9510	2065
专科毕业	Junior College	1582	1360	222
高中阶段毕业	Senior Secondary School	286	227	59
高中阶段毕业以下	High school education or below	2	2	
按职称分	Grouped by Professional Titles			
中学高级	Senior Teacher of Secondary School	2912	2342	570
小学高级	Senior Teacher of Primary School	6700	5340	1360
小学一级	Teacher 1st Grade	3019	2657	362
小学二级	Teacher 2nd Grade	246	221	25
未定职级	Unspecified Position Level	824	775	49

20-20　普通高校基本情况（2015 年）
BASIC CONDITIONS OF INSTITUTIONS OF HIGHER EDUCATION（2015）

单位：人（person）

学校名称	Name of Institutions	招生数 Number of New Students Enrollment	在校学生数 Number of Students Enrollment	毕业班学生数 Number of Students in Graduate Class	教职工数 Number of Staff and Teachers	其中 of which #专任教师 Number of Full-time Teachers
总　计	**Total**	**39116**	**124405**	**39315**	**8098**	**5685**
常州大学	Changzhou University	4122	14739	3718	1432	955
江苏理工学院	Jiangsu University of Technology	4530	16098	3759	1116	858
常州工学院	Changzhou Institute of Technology	3687	12677	2456	1082	748
常州信息职业技术学院	Changzhou Vocational Technological College of Information	3917	11554	3755	687	476
常州纺织服装职业技术学院	Changzhou Technical College of Textile and Garment	3015	9586	3210	619	456
常州轻工职业技术学院	Changzhou Vocational Technological College of Light Industry	3490	10205	3310	589	443
常州工程职业技术学院	Changzhou Vocational Technological College of Engineering	3550	10241	3274	643	435
常州机电职业技术学院	Changzhou Vocational Technological College of Electromechanical	3593	10078	3235	696	481
江苏城乡建设职业学院	Jiangsu Urban and Rural Construction College	189	189		404	343
建东职业技术学院（民办）	Jiandong College （Private）	1451	4821	1470	239	148
河海大学常州校区	Hohai University Changzhou Branch	1597	6024	1557	591	342
常州大学怀德学院	Changzhou University Huaide College		2589	1343		
常州工学院延陵学院	Yanlin Campus of Changzhou Instutute of Technology		1572	1081		
江苏技术师范学院东方学院	Dongfang Campus of Jiangsu Teachers University of Technology		1234	850		
江苏城市职业学院常州办学点	Changzhou Campus of The City Vocational College Of Jiangsu	310	980	536		
江苏城市职业学院武进办学点	Wujin Cámpus of The City Vocational College Of Jiangsu	675	1879	812		
江苏城市职业学院金坛办学点	Jintan Campus of The City Vocational College Of Jiangsu	123	251	128		
江苏城市职业学院溧阳办学点	Liyang Campus of The City Vocational College Of Jiangsu	238	461	223		
江苏联合职业技术学院常州分院	Changzhou Campuses of Jiangsu Union Technical Institute	4164	8416	4252		
江苏教育学院常州学前教育分院	Changzhou Pre-school Campus of Jiangsu Institute of Education	465	811	346		

20-21 中等专业学校基本情况（2015 年）
BASIC CONDITIONS OF SPECIALIZED SECONDARY SCHOOLS（2015）

单位：人（person）

学校名称	Name of Institutions	招生数 Number of New Students Enrollment	在校学生数 Number of Students Enrollment	毕业班学生数 Number of Students in Graduate Class	教职工数 Number of Staff and Teachers	其中 of which #专任教师 Number of Full-time Teachers
总　计	**Total**	**11924**	**36013**	**12009**	**2909**	**2480**
常州铁道高等职业技术学校	Changzhou Railway Vocational Technical School	961	2546	706	174	130
常州卫生高等职业技术学校	Changzhou Senior Vocational School of Health	808	2531	843	188	144
常州艺术高等职业学校	Changzhou Art Vocational College of Jiangsu Province	301	926	332	136	106
常州刘国钧高等职业技术学校	Changzhou Liu Guojun Higher Vocational School	1177	3603	1205	347	287
常州旅游商贸高等职业技术学校	Changzhou Tourism and Commerce Vocational Technology Academy	1486	3669	934	341	306
常州市体育运动学校	Changzhou Sports School	74	307	131	40	34
常州幼儿师范学校	Kindergarten Normal School	694	2279	876	213	191
江苏省武进中等专业学校	Jiangsu Wujin Vocational Secondary School	1780	5586	1846	593	520
江苏省溧阳中等专业学校	Jiangsu Liyang Vocational Secondary School	1295	3768	1296	376	322
江苏省溧阳市天目湖中等专业学校	Tianmuhu Specialized Secondary School, Liyang, Jiangsu	568	1903	660	200	178
江苏省金坛中等专业学校	Jiangsu Jintan Vocational Secondary School	529	1547	555	301	262
江苏城乡建设职业学院	Jiangsu Urban and Rural Construction College	893	3798	1526		
江苏省常州技师学院	Changzhou Technician College of Jiangsu Province	280	893	305		
江苏城市职业学院常州办学点	Changzhou Campus, The City Vocational College of Jiangsu	186	405	121		
江苏省城市职业学院武进办学点	Jiangsu City Vocational Institute Wujin Campus	487	1144	318		
江苏省城市职业学院溧阳办学点	Jiangsu City Vocational Institute Liyang Campus	234	660	223		
江苏省城市职业学院金坛办学点	Jiangsu City Vocational Institute Jintan Campus	171	448	132		

20-22　技工学校基本情况（2015 年）
BASIC CONDITIONS OF TECHNICAL SCHOOLS（2015）

单位：人（person）

学校名称 Name of School		招生数 Number of New Students Enrollment	在校学生数 Number of Students Enrollment	其中 of which #高级班 Senior Classes	毕业生数 Number of Students in Graduate Class	教职工数 Staff and Teachers
总　计	**Total**	**11011**	**27115**	**7817**	**6279**	**2082**
江苏省常州技师学院	Changzhou Technician College Jiangsu Province（Main Campus）	3532	9875	3347	2644	720
常州交通技师学院	Changzhou Communication College of Technician	1320	3319	1125	1017	202
常州冶金技师学院	Changzhou Metallurgy College of Technician	1182	2577	663	453	98
武进技师学院	Wujin Technician College	1398	3367	2032	1002	695
常州航空技工学校	Changzhou Aviation Technical School	798	2156	204	524	78
常州市工贸技工学校	Changzhou Industry and Trade Technical School	1209	2925	168	473	142
常州科技经贸技工学校	Changzhou Vocational School of Tech & Trade	1416	2494			93
金坛市技工学校	Jintan Technical School	156	402	278	166	54

20-23　中小学师资配备情况（2015 年）
TEACHERS IN MIDDLE SCHOOLS AND PRIMARY SCHOOLS（2015）

指　标 Item		班级数（个） Number of Classes（unit）	学生数（人） Number of Students（person）	教师数（人） Number of Teachers（person）	每班教师数（人/班） Number of Teachers Per Class（persons/class）	每一教师负担学生数（人） Student-Teacher Ratio（person）
小　学	Primary Schools	6058	273682	13701	2.26	19.98
#市　区	Urban Area	5140	234784	11335	2.21	20.71
初　中	Junior Secondary Schools	2493	110903	9156	3.67	12.11
#市　区	Urban Area	2053	93794	7412	3.61	12.65
高　中	Senior Secondary Schools	1129	51624	4814	4.26	10.72
#市　区	Urban Area	903	42023	3752	4.16	11.20

20-24 分地区幼儿教育基本情况（2015 年）
BASIC STATISTICS ON INFANT EDUCATION BY REGION（2015）

单位：人（person）

指 标	Item	全 市 Whole Municipality	其 中 of which 市 区 Urban Area	溧阳市 Liyang City
学校数（所）	Number of Schools （unit）	296	234	62
毕业生数	Number of Graduates of Kindergartens	40804	34118	6686
招生数	Number of New Students Enrollment	48502	41550	6952
在校学生数	Number of Students Enrollment	125271	105416	19855
教职工数	Number of Staff & Teachers	12400	10397	2003
# 专任教师	Full-time Teachers	7475	6269	1206

20-25 分地区升学率、入学率（2015 年）
PERCENTAGE OF GRADUATES AND ENROLLMENT RATE BY REGION（2015）

单位：%

指 标	Item	全 市 Whole Municipality	其 中 of which 市 区 Urban Area	溧阳市 Liyang City
小学入学率	Enrollemnt Rate in Primary Schools	100.0	100.0	100.0
小学升学率	Percentage of Graduates in Primary Schools	102.7	103.4	99.1
初中入学率	Enrollemnt Rate in Junior Secondary Schools	100.0	100.0	100.0
初中升学率	Percentage of Graduates in Junior Secondary Schools	99.9	99.9	99.9

20-26　分地区每一专任教师负担学生数（2015 年）
STUDENT-TEACHER OF FULL-TIME RATIO BY REGION（2015）

单位：人（person）

指 标	Item	全 市 Whole Municipality	其中 of which 市 区 Urban Area	其中 of which 溧阳市 Liyang City
总　计	**Total**	**16.52**	**17.19**	**12.76**
普通高等学校	Institutions of Higher Education	21.88	21.80	
普通中等职技校	Regular Secondary Vocation & Technical School	14.36	14.58	12.66
普通中学	Regular Secondary Schools	11.63	12.17	9.52
小　学	Primary Schools	19.98	20.71	16.44

20-27　分地区每万人拥有在校学生数（2015 年）
NUMBER OF STUDENTS ENROLLMENT PER 10000 PERSONS BY REGION（2015）

单位：人（person）

指 标	Item	全 市 Whole Municipality	其中 of which 市 区 Urban Area	其中 of which 溧阳市 Liyang City
总　计	**Total**	**1692.01**	**1906.11**	**911.95**
普通高等学校	Institutions of Higher Education	337.47	428.50	5.81
普通中等职技校	Regular Secondary Vocation & Technical School	171.25	196.36	79.75
普通中学	Regular Secondary Schools	440.88	469.55	336.44
小　学	Primary Schools	742.41	811.70	489.96

20-28 分地区文化事业机构数（2015 年底）
NUMBER OF INSTITUTIONS OF CULTURE BY REGION（END OF 2015）

单位：个（unit）

指标	Item	全市 Whole Municipality	其中 of which 市区 Urban Area	溧阳市 Liyang City
艺术事业	**Art**			
艺术表演团体	Art Performance Troupes	11	10	1
艺术表演场所	Art Performance Places	7	6	1
图书馆	**Libraries**	**4**	**3**	**1**
群众文化事业	**Mass Cultural**			
博物馆	Museums	26	24	2
群众艺术馆、文化馆	Mass Art Centers and Cultural Centers	8	7	1
文化站（文化部门）	Cultural Stations （Cultural Department）	59	49	10
教育事业	**Education**	**1**	**1**	
其他文化事业	**Others**	**5**	**4**	**1**

20-29 分地区文化事业人员数（2015 年底）
NUMBER OF PERSONS ENGAGED IN CULTURE BY REGION（END OF 2015）

单位：人（person）

指标	Item	全市 Whole Municipality	其中 of which 市区 Urban Area	溧阳市 Liyang City
艺术事业	**Art**			
艺术表演团体	Art Performance Troupes	293	245	48
艺术表演场所	Art Performance Places	356	356	
图书馆	**Libraries**	**118**	**102**	**16**
群众文化事业	**Mass Cultural**			
博物馆	Museums	390	363	27
群众艺术馆、文化馆	Mass Art Centers and Cultural Centers	109	95	14
文化站（文化部门）	Cultural Stations （Cultural Department）	270	229	41
教育事业	**Education**	**140**	**140**	
其他文化事业	**Others**	**55**	**45**	**10**

20-30　分地区博物馆、图书馆基本情况（2015 年）
BASIC STATISTICS ON MUSEUMS AND LIBRARIES BY REGION（2015）

指　标	Item	全　市 Whole Municipality	其　中 of which 市　区 Urban Area	溧阳市 Liyang City
博物馆	**Museums**			
文物藏品（件）	Number of Collections （piece）	236638	220790	15848
#一级品	Grade One	72	69	3
参观人次（千人次）	Number of Visitors （1000 person-times）	3298	2613	685
图书馆	**Libraries**			
总藏量（千册、千件）	Total Collections （1000 volumes）	3140	2762	378
#图　书	Books Published	2430	2062	368
#古　籍	Ancient Books	118	118	
报　刊	Newspapers and Magazines	549	539	10
图书流通人次（千人次）	Number of Books Circulation（1000 persons-times）	2172	1922	250

注：图书总藏量中不包括电子图书。
Note：The total number of collection of books excludes e-books.

20-31　分地区艺术事业基本情况（2015 年）
BASIC STATISTICS ON ART BY REGION（2015）

指　标	Item	全　市 Whole Municipality	其　中 of which 市　区 Urban Area	溧阳市 Liyang City
艺术表演场所	**Art Performance Places**			
座席数（个）	Number of Seats （unit）	7214	7214	
演（映）出场次（场）	Number of Performance （time）	41318	41318	
#电影放映场次	Number of Films Projection	41127	41127	
观众人次（千人次）	Number of Spectators （1000 persons-times）	1692	1692	
#电影放映	Films Projection	1560	1560	
艺术表演团体	**Art Performance Troupes**			
新排上演节目（个）	Newly Staged Shows （unit）	5	5	
#本团创作首演剧目	First Performance Drama created by the Troupe	5	5	
国内演出场次（场）	Number of Domestic Performance （time）	3310	3170	140
国内观众人次（千人次）	Number of Domestic Spectators （1000 persons-times）	2038	1868	170

20-32 广播电视事业基本情况（2015 年）
BASIC STATISTICS ON BROADCASTING AND TELEVISION（2015）

指 标	Item	全 市 Whole Municipality	其中 of which #市 区 Urban Area
广 播	**Broadcasting**		
广播电台数（座）	Number of Broadcasting Stations （unit）	4	3
对内广播节目套数（套）	Number of Home Broadcasting Programs （set）	7	6
广播全年自办播出时间（小时）	Broadcasting Hours of the Whole Year （hour）	48805	42600
广播全年自制节目时间（小时）	Broadcasting Self-made Program Hours of the Whole Year （hour）	33182	28941
中、短波发射台（座）	Number of Broadcasting Transmitting Stations with Medium and Short Wave（unit）	1	1
广播人口综合覆盖率（%）	Listener Rating （%）	100	100
电 视	**Television**		
电视台数（座）	Number of Television Station （unit）	4	3
自办电视节目套数（套）	Number of Television Programs （set）	7	6
电视节目全年自办播出时间（小时）	Broadcasting Hours of Television Program of the Whole Year （hour）	48404	43322
电视全年自制节目时间（小时）	Time of Self-made Television Program of the Whole Year （hour）	9864	7928
电视发射台数（座）	Number of Television Transmitting Stations （unit）	4	3
电视综合覆盖率（%）	Televiewer Rating （%）	100	100
有线广播电视	**Wire Broadcasting and Television**		
模拟有线广播电视传输节目（套）	Number of Modeling Cable Radio & TV Programs （set）	7	7
数字有线广播电视传输节目套数（套）	Number of Digital Cable TV Programmes（set）	225	225
#标清广播电视传输节目套数	Number of SDTV Programmes	174	174
高清广播电视传输节目套数	Number of HDTV Programmes	51	51
有线电视用户数（万户）	Number of Subscribers of Wire Television （10000 households）	117.90	98.30

20-33 分地区广播电视从业人员数（2015 年底）
NUMBER OF PERSONNEL ENGAGED IN BROADCASTING AND TELEVISION（END OF 2015）

单位：人（person）

指 标	Item	全 市 Whole Municipality	其 中 of which 市 区 Urban Area	溧阳市 Liyang City
总 计	**Total**	**3083**	**2583**	**500**
行政管理人员	Administration Staff	389	327	62
专业人员	Professional Technical Personnel	1638	1415	223
#编辑、记者	Editor and Reporter	424	391	33
播音员、主持人	Announcer and host	92	82	10
工程技术人员	Engineering and Technical Personnel	464	349	115
艺术人员	Artistic Personnel	135	130	5
经营人员	Operating Personnel	285	225	60
其他人员	Others	1065	850	215

21

CHAPTER 21

常州统计年鉴

卫生 体育

HEALTH AND SPORTS

21 卫生　体育
HEALTH AND SPORTS

2015年主要统计指标
MAJOR STATISTICAL INDICATORS OF 2015

年底全社会卫生事业机构数	Health Care Institutions （Year-end）	1196个	（unit）
年底卫生机构床位数	Beds of health Care Institutions （Year-end）	24263张	（bed）
年底医院（含妇保院）数	Number of Hospitals （Including Those of Women's and Children's Hospitals） By The End of The Year	51个	（unit）
年底医院（含妇保院）床位数	Number of Hospital Beds （Including Those of Women's and Children's Hospitals） By The End of The Year	19088张	（bed）
年底全社会卫生技术人员数	Medical Technial Personnel （Year-end）	35819人	（person）
执业（助理）医师数	Practicing （Assistant） Doctors	12009人	（person）
等级裁判员发展人数	Number of Certified Referees	391人	（person）
等级运动员发展人数	Number of Certified Athletes	455人	（person）

21-1　历年卫生事业基本情况
BASIC STATISTICS ON PUBLIC HEALTH OVER THE YEARS

年　份 Year	机构数（个） Institutions（unit）	其中 of which #医院（含妇保院）、卫生院 Hospitals（include Women-Children Health Care Hospitals）and Health Care Centers	床位数（张） Beds（bed）	其中 of which #医院（含妇保院）、卫生院 Hospitals（include Women-Children Health Care Hospitals）and Health Care Centers	卫生技术人员（人） Medical Technical Personnel（person）	其中 of which #医　生（含见习医生） Doctors（Includes Trainee Doctors）
1949	13	6	325	291	1450	1270
1950	19	6	376	371	1559	1315
1951	92	5	649	447	1752	1431
1952	249	5	970	675	2072	1625
1953	272	7	1296	1078	2378	1622
1954	296	7	1392	1049	2594	1641
1955	321	7	1930	1138	2877	1714
1956	359	8	2147	1222	2834	1963
1957	374	8	2171	1229	3020	2007
1958	440	105	3273	2449	3138	2036
1959	693	107	3824	2633	3884	2127
1960	926	133	4254	3350	4141	2118
1961	665	147	3929	3096	4381	2445
1962	531	94	3047	2277	4179	2577
1963	633	95	3489	2696	4362	2821
1964	509	89	3586	2828	4190	2653
1965	540	89	3975	3168	4245	2677
1966	444	146	4125	3199	3950	2467
1967	403	146	3024	2877	3944	2360
1968	337	152	3860	3164	3893	2265
1969	294	151	4166	3299	3656	2027
1970	426	147	5378	3767	3570	2083
1971	475	150	5893	4379	3868	2290
1972	466	150	6276	4631	4517	2332
1973	552	152	7063	5497	4916	2278
1974	527	154	8045	6021	5272	2389
1975	566	155	7802	5743	6027	2368
1976	621	156	8477	6368	6454	2668
1977	663	156	7401	5896	6973	2633
1978	684	158	8222	6982	7499	3021
1979	772	159	8371	7313	8194	3110
1980	803	159	8422	7337	8615	3238
1981	814	161	9553	7864	9178	3749
1982	823	162	9474	7775	9711	4039

21-1 续表 Continued

年 份 Year	机构数（个） Institutions（unit）	其中 of which #医院（含妇保院）、卫生院 Hospitals（include Women-Children Health Care Hospitals）and Health Care Centers	床位数（张） Beds（bed）	其中 of which #医院（含妇保院）、卫生院 Hospitals（include Women-Children Health Care Hospitals）and Health Care Centers	卫生技术人员（人） Medical Technical Personnel（person）	其中 of which #医 生（含见习医师） Doctors（Includes Trainee Doctors）
1983	802	160	9773	7937	9759	4198
1984	827	161	9282	7839	10061	4384
1985	831	162	9405	7993	10458	4437
1986	841	162	9883	8505	10957	4586
1987	859	163	10054	8734	11397	4570
1988	913	163	9996	8979	12098	5268
1989	881	163	10253	9313	12539	5923
1990	890	163	10460	9495	12942	6144
1991	880	163	10454	9538	13470	6345
1992	873	159	10607	9693	13695	6511
1993	855	160	11190	9992	13971	6411
1994	855	161	11138	10000	14580	6973
1995	855	161	11566	10339	14963	7073
1996	855	162	11268	10893	15538	7520
1997	833	161	11273	10843	16031	7567
1998	833	161	11223	10813	16405	7685
1999	824	161	11213	10803	16495	7680
2000	782	117	11143	10730	16731	7779
2001	769	114	11393	11030	16743	7737
2002	620	111	11842	11613	15242	6424
2003	625	111	12135	11687	15597	6592
2004	611	109	12352	11932	15707	6586
2005	1269	113	12474	11734	17859	8356
2006	1180	116	13247	12207	18414	8570
2007	1173	111	14696	14100	18091	8323
2008	1261	99	15113	14242	19795	8725
2009	1089	100	16170	15278	20244	9512
2010	1103	93	16701	15263	21921	9962
2011	1101	94	16936	15589	22877	10376
2012	1128	109	20497	19140	25274	10943
2013	1123	103	21286	19745	26733	11583
2014	1182	109	23634	22166	28090	12030
2015	1196	109	24263	22741	29616	12637

注：1、2002年起卫生技术人员包含领取医师执业证书和注册护士证书的人数以及药师（士）、技师（士）、其他卫技人员；
2、2005年起机构数的统计口径调整为含村级卫生室；
3、2008年起，规范城市社区和乡村卫生机构统计口径后，卫生院机构数有所减少。

Note：1. Since year 2002, the medical technical personnel has been including Physician Practice Certificate holders, Registered Nurse Certificate holders, pharmacists, technicians and other medical technical personnel.
2. Since year 2005, the statistics of institution numbers has been including village health stations.
3. Since year 2008, the scope of statistics of health service institutions in urban communities and villages has been regulated, which caused the reduction of health service institutions.

21-2 分地区卫生事业机构数（2015 年底）
NUMBER OF HEALTH SERVICE INSTITUTIONS BY REGION（END OF 2015）

单位：个（unit）

指 标	Item	全 市 Whole Municipality	其 中 of which 市 区 Urban Area	其 中 of which 溧阳市 Liyang City
总 计	**Total**	**1196**	**957**	**239**
医 院	Hospitals	49	37	12
# 综合医院	Polyclinics	26	17	9
中医医院	Hospitals for Maternity and Child Care	5	4	1
儿童医院	Children's Hospitals	1	1	
卫生院、社区卫生服务中心（站）	Health Center and Community Health Service Center （Station）	206	189	17
门诊部	Outpatient Department	63	63	
疗养院	Sanatoriums	1	1	
急救中心（站）	First-aid Center （station）	2	2	
采供血机构	Flood Extraction and Supply Organizations	3	2	1
妇幼保健院（所、站）	Maternity and Child Care Centers （Office, Station）	7	6	1
专科疾病防治院（所、站）	Specialized Disease Prevention and Cure Hospitals （Office,Station）	2	1	1
疾病预防控制中心（防疫站）	Disease Prevention and Control Centers （Epidemic Prevention Station）	7	6	1
卫生监督所	Sanitation Supervise Offices	7	6	1
医学科学研究机构	Institutions of Medical Sciences Research	2	2	
医学在职培训机构	On-the-job Training Institute of The Hospital	4	3	1
其他卫生机构	Other Health Institutions	40	40	
诊所、卫生保健所、医务室机构	Clinics, Health Care Centers and Medical Institutions	342	342	
村卫生室	Village Health Station	461	461	

21-3 分地区卫生机构床位和人员数（2015 年底）
HEALTH INSTITUTIONS, BEDS AND PERSONS ENGAGED BY REGION（END OF 2015）

指标	Item	全市 Whole Municipality	其中 of which 市区 Urban Area	其中 of which 溧阳市 Liyang City
床位数（张）	**Number of Beds（bed）**	**24263**	**21446**	**2817**
#医院（含妇保院）床位	Number of Hospital Beds（Including Those of Women's and Children's Hospitals）	19088	17186	1902
卫生院床位	Number of Rural Township Hospital Beds	3653	2789	864
人员数（人）	**Personnel（person）**	**35819**	**30519**	**5300**
卫生技术人员	Medical Technical Personnel	29616	25564	4052
#执业（助理）医师	Practicing（Assistant）Doctors	12009	10229	1780
注册护士	Certified Junior Nurses	12531	10957	1574
药 师（士）	Pharmacists	1501	1315	186
技 师（士）	Technicians	1464	1248	216
其他卫生技术人员	Other Medical Technical Personnel	2111	1815	296
其他技术人员	Other Technical Personnel	1511	1339	172
管理人员	Managerial Personnel	1467	1294	173
工勤技能人员	Personnel with Professional Qualification Serving at Government and State-owned Enterprises	2418	1823	595

注：本表人员合计中包括乡村医生和卫生员807人。
Note：The total number of staff in this table includes 807 rural doctors and health workers.

21-4 分地区乡卫生院运营情况（2015 年）
STATISTICS ON HOSPITALS AT AND ABOVE COUNTY LEVEL BY REGION（2015）

指 标	Item	全 市 Whole Municipality	其 中 of which 市 区 Urban Area	溧阳市 Liyang City
机构数（个）	Number of Medical Institution （unit）	58	43	15
总诊疗人次（万人次）	Number of Persons Diagnosed and Treated （10000 persons-times）	2960.02	2659.28	300.74
#门诊人次	Number of Outpatients	2484.46	2214.37	270.09
急诊人次	Number of Persons Received Emergency Treatment	319.05	296.07	22.98
健康检查（万人）	Health Examination （10000 persons）	154.75	125.79	28.96
出院人数（万人）	Number of Patients Left Hospitals （10000 persons）	65.19	55.38	9.81
年末实有床位数（张）	Number of Beds of Hospitals by the End of Year （Bed）	3653	2789	864

21-5 分地区医院（含妇保院）运营情况（2015 年）
STATISTICS ON HOSPITALS INCLUDE WOMEN-CHILDREN HEALTH CARE HOSPIRALS OPERATION BY REGION（2015）

指 标	Item	全 市 Whole Municipality	其 中 of which 市 区 Urban Area	溧阳市 Liyang City
医院（含妇保院）（个）	Hospitals （Include Women-Children Health Care Hospitals）（unit）	51	39	12
总诊疗人次（万人次）	Number of Persons Diagnosed and Treated （10000 persons-times）	1324.12	1186.32	137.80
#门诊人次	Number of Outpatients	1029.61	915.55	114.06
急诊人次	Number of Persons Received Emergency Treatment	199.41	181.35	18.06
健康检查（万人）	Health Examination （10000 persons）	73.85	64.79	9.06
出院人数（万人）	Number of Patients Left Hospitals （10000 persons）	51.73	45.24	6.49
年末实有医院（含妇保院）床位数（张）	Number of Beds of Hospitals （Include Women-Children Health Care Hospitals） by the End of Year （Bed）	19088	17186	1902

21-6 分地区体育事业情况（2015 年）
STATISTICS ON SPORTS CAUSE BY REGION（2015）

指 标	Item	全 市 Whole Municipality	其 中 of which 市 区 Urban Area	溧阳市 Liyang City
运动会	**Sports Meets**			
举办县级以上运动会次数（含单项）（次）	Number of Sports Meets Held at and above County Level（Including Individual Events）（time）	173	157	16
参加县级以上运动会人数（含单项）（人）	Number of Athletes Participating Sports Meets at and above County Level（Including Individual Events）（person）	93626	44940	48686
等级运动员发展人数（人）	**Number of Athletes Developed in Grades（person）**	**455**	**405**	**50**
#女 性	Female	184	165	19
等级裁判员发展人数（人）	**Number of Referees Developed in Grades（person）**	**391**	**369**	**22**
#女 性	Female	101	91	10
公共体育运动场地	**Public Stadiums and Gymnasiums**			
体育场地个数（个）	Number of Stadiums and Gymnasiums（unit）	204	164	40
体育场	Stadiums	26	20	6
体育馆	Gymnasiums	35	26	9
室内外游泳池	Indoor and Outdoor Swimming Pools	143	118	25

注：等级运动员发展人数中不含三级运动员。
Note: The number of sportspersons with grade under development excludes those third grades.

21-7 参加体育竞赛获奖数（2015 年）
NUMBER OF PRIZES WON IN SPORTS GAMES（2015）

单位：枚（unit）

指 标	Item	金 牌 Gold Medals	银 牌 Silver Medals
总 计	**Total**	**104.5**	**97.5**
参加国际比赛获奖数	Number of Prizes Won in International Sports Games	3	4
参加全国比赛获奖数	Number of Prizes Won in National Sports Games	45	31
参加全省比赛获奖数	Number of Prizes Won in Provinical Sports Games	56.5	62.5

22

CHAPTER 22

民政 司法 其他

CIVIL ADMINISTRATION
JUDICATURE AND OTHERS

常州统计年鉴

22 民政　司法　其他
CIVIL ADMINISTRATION JUDICATURE AND OTHERS

2015 年主要统计指标
MAJOR STATISTICAL INDICATORS OF 2015

社会福利院数	Socail Welfare Institutions	3个	(unit)
精神病福利院数	Psychotics Welfare Institutions	1个	(unit)
老年福利机构数	Aged People's Homes	108个	(unit)
社会福利院床位数	Beds of Socail Welfare Institutions	1216张	(bed)
精神病福利院床位数	Beds of Psychotics Welfare Institutions	1166张	(bed)
老年福利机构床位数	Beds of Aged People's Homes	40880张	(bed)
律师事务所	Lawyer Offices	112家	(unit)
专职律师数	Full-time Lawyers	1292人	(person)
公证处数	Notary Public Offices	5个	(unit)
办理公证件数	Notarized Documents	49411件	(case)
人民调解委员会数	People's Mediation Committees	1240个	(unit)
调解民间纠纷数	Civil Disputes Mediated	17247件	(case)

22-1　分地区社会福利事业情况（2015 年底）
BASIC STATISTICS ON SOCIAL WELFARE BY REGION（END OF 2015）

指　标	Item	全　市 Whole Municipality	市　区 Urban Area	溧阳市 Liyang City
社会福利院	**Social Welfare Homes**			
院　数（个）	Number of Homes（unit）	3	3	
年底职工人数（人）	Number of Staff and Workers at Year-end（person）	158	158	
年底床位数（张）	Number of Beds at Year-end（bed）	1216	1216	
年底在院人数（人）	Number of Persons Housed at Year-end（person）	590	590	
#老　人	Elders	378	378	
精神病福利院	**Mental Homes**			
院　数（个）	Number of Homes（unit）	1	1	
年底职工人数（人）	Number of Staff and Workers at Year-end（person）	228	228	
年底床位数（张）	Number of Beds at Year-end（bed）	1166	1166	
年底在院人数（人）	Number of Persons Housed at Year-end（person）	1028	1028	
老年福利机构	**Elderly Welfare Unit**			
单位数（个）	Number of Unit（unit）	108	88	20
年底职工人数（人）	Number of Staff and Workers at Year-end（person）	1465	1186	279
年底床位数（张）	Number of Beds at Year-end（bed）	40880	36470	4410
年底在院人数（人）	Number of Persons Housed at Year-end（person）	15504	12117	3387
#老　人	Elders	12064	8694	3370

注：老年福利机构床位数包括城镇各类养老机构（含公办和民办）、农村五保供养服务机构、以老年人为主的综合性社会福利机构、老年人社区日间照料机构、光荣院、农村老年人互助幸福院中的养老床位数之和。

Note:Note: The number of beds of social welfare institutions for the aged is the total number of beds of all kinds of institutions for the aged（including public and private ones）in cities and towns, institutions of the Five-guarantees System in rural areas, elderly-based comprehensive social welfare agencies, community day-care institutions for the aged, Guangrong Homes, and mutual-aid Xingfu Homes for the aged.

22-2　分地区集体社会福利企业情况（2015 年）
STATISTICS ON COLLECTIVE SOCIAL WELFARE ENTERPRISES BY REGION（2015）

指　标	Item	全　市 Whole Municipality	市　区 Urban Area	溧阳市 Liyang City
单位数（个）	Number of Units（unit）	218	187	31
职工人数（人）	Number of Staff & Workers（person）	22097	18838	3259
销售收入（亿元）	Sales Income（100 million yuan）	114.56	110.13	4.43
利润总额（亿元）	Total Profits（100 million yuan）	4.25	0.15	4.10

22-3 分地区居民最低生活保障情况（2015 年底）
STATISTICS ON LOWEST COST-OF-LIVING WELFARE FOR RESIDENTS BY REGION（END OF 2015）

指 标	Item	全 市 Whole Municipality	市 区 Urban Area	溧阳市 Liyang City
城镇居民最低生活保障人数（人）	Number of Urban Residents Receiving Lowest Cost-of-living Welfare （person）	13123	12151	972
#在职人员	Persons Employed	385	384	1
老年人	Elderly	2747	2571	176
城镇居民最低生活保障家庭数（户）	Number of Urban Households Receiving Lowest Cost-of-living Welfare （Household）	7906	7368	538
农村居民最低生活保障人数（人）	Number of Rural Residents Receiving Lowest Cost-of-living Welfare （person）	26611	16638	9973
农村居民最低生活保障家庭数（户）	Number of Rural Households Receiving Lowest Cost-of-living Welfare （Household）	15445	10172	5273

22-4 分地区优抚对象享受优待抚恤情况（2015 年底）
STATISTICS ON PERSONS RECEIVING PERIODICAL COMPENSATION AND SUBSIDIES BY REGION（END OF 2015 ）

单位：人（person）

指 标	Item	全 市 Whole Municipality	市 区 Urban Area	溧阳市 Liyang City
抚恤、补助优抚对象人数	Number of People Subject to Pension, Subsidy and Special Care	21931	14626	7305
优抚对象定期抚恤人数	Number of Persons Receiving Periodical Compen-sation	541	417	124
烈士家属	Family Members of Martyrs	265	225	40
牺牲军人家属	Family Members of Sacrificed Servicemen	126	99	27
病故军人家属	Family Members of Deceased Servicemen	150	93	57
优抚对象定期补助人数	Number of Persons Receiving Periodical Subsidies	19112	12548	6564
#在乡复员军人	Servicemen Demobilized before Nov. 1,1954 in Rural Area	1710	1364	346

22-5 分地区社区服务情况（2015 年底）
COMMUNITY SERVICES BY REGION（END OF 2015）

	指 标 Item	全 市 Whole Municipality	市 区 Urban Area	溧阳市 Liyang City
社区服务设施数（个）	Number of Urban Community Service Facilities（unit）	1574	1271	303
从业人员数（人）	Number of Persons Engaged（person）	8365	7825	540
社区指导中心（个）	Number of Community Instruction Centers（unit）	5	4	1
社区服务中心（个）	Number of Community Service Centers（unit）	74	58	16
社区服务站（个）	Number of Community Service Stations（unit）	1011	834	177

22-6 分地区婚姻登记情况（2015 年）
BASIC STATISTICS ON MARRIAGE REGISTRATION BY REGION（2015）

	指 标 Item	全 市 Whole Municipality	市 区 Urban Area	溧阳市 Liyang City
结婚登记数（对）	Marriage Legally Registered（couple）	34105	25271	8834
初 婚（人）	First Marriages（person）	56836	42538	14298
再 婚（人）	Remarriages（person）	11374	8004	3370
离婚登记数（对）	Legally Registered Divorces（couple）	10324	8059	2265

22-7 律师、公证、调解工作情况（2015 年）
STATISTICS ON LAWYERS, NOTARIZATION AND MEDIATION（2015）

指标	Item	全市 Whole Municipality	其中 of which #市区 Urban Area
律师工作	**Lawyers**		
律师事务所（个）	Number of Law Offices （unit）	112	95
取得律师资格（人）	Persons with Lawyer's Qualification （person）	1319	1109
专职律师	Full-time Lawyers	1292	1082
兼职律师	Part-time Lawyers	27	27
聘请担任常年法律顾问单位（个）	Number of Units with Permanent Legal advisors （unit）	5424	4334
民事诉讼代理（件）	Agent of Civil Cases （case）	25798	19502
刑事诉讼辩护及代理（件）	Defender and Agent of Criminal Cases （case）	2346	1840
行政诉讼代理（件）	Agent of Administrative Action （case）	457	326
非诉讼法律事务（件）	Agent of Non-litigious Legal Affairs （case）	3874	3634
法律咨询（件）	Agent of Legal Advisory services （case）	18627	10498
代写法律事务文书（件）	Agent of Legal Documents Written on Behalf of Clients （case）	2574	2242
公证工作	**Notarization**		
公证处（个）	Number of Notary Offices （unit）	5	4
公证人员（人）	Notarial Personnel （person）	34	31
#公证员（一、二、三、四级）	Notaries （Grade1, 2,3,4）	24	22
公证员助理	Assistant Notaries	23	21
办理公证件数（件）	Number of Notarial Documents Issued （case）	49411	45978
国内业务	Domestic Business	32606	30898
涉外及港澳台公证	Foreign-related and Hongkong,Macao and Taiwan Notarization	16805	15080
人民调解工作	**People's Mediation**		
专职司法助理员（名）	Number of Full-time Judical assistants （person）	303	259
人民调解委员会（个）	Number of People's Mediation Committees （unit）	1240	969
调解人员数（人）	Number of Mediators （person）	4286	2893
调解民间纠纷数（件）	Number of Civil Disputes Mediated （case）	17247	15205

22-8　国内公证文书分类情况（2011-2015 年）
DOMESTIC NOTARIAL DOCUMENT BY TYPE（2011-2015）

单位：件（unit）

指　标	Item	2011	2012	2013	2014	2015
总　计	**Total**	**22346**	**26160**	**28596**	**34438**	**32606**
# 购　销	Purchases and Sales of products	12	20	220	198	57
拍　卖	Auctions			42	36	25
贷　款	Loans	49	1194	415	174	310
招标、投标	Bidding	507	908	90	84	90
劳务合同	Labor Contracts		5		29	32
建筑工程承包	Construction Project Contracts			16	22	14
其他经济合同	Other Business Contracts	347	304		91	255
法人（代表人）资格	Legal Person（agent）Identification	48	23		48	35
委托书	Letter of Authorization	1807	10236	11325	14501	12925
继承权	Rights of Inheritance	2990	3544	3931	4111	4111
遗　嘱	Testaments	260	151	129	144	198
产　权	Property Rights		20			
亲属关系	Kinship Confirmation	221	210	280	151	86
房屋买卖	Purchases and Sales of House	318	153		52	
房屋租赁	House Leases	23				8
遗赠抚养协议	Donations and Family Fostering	3	2			9
赠与书	Presentaton Documents	6924	460	67	53	44
声明书	Declarations	942	3475	3366	5435	4585
现场监督	Field Supervision	606	66	236	208	214

22-9 涉外及涉港澳台公证文书分类情况（2011-2015 年）
FOREIGN AND HONG KONG, MACAO AND TAIWAN NOTARIAL DOCUMENT BY TYPE（2011-2015）

单位：件（unit）

指标	Item	2011	2012	2013	2014	2015
总　计	**Total**	**11686**	**11680**	**14474**	**14597**	**16805**
出　生	Births	1481	1469	1784	1727	2226
学　历	Schooling	903	297	182	222	159
经　历	Personal Histories	125	67	46	31	12
生存、居住	Survial and Residence	391	8	16	10	6
死　亡	Deaths	112	22	16	21	12
亲属关系	Family Relationship	964	1161	1428	1399	1361
婚姻状况	Marriages	689	261	212	213	169
委托书	Trust Deeds	331	184	192	145	119
声明书	Declarations	193	378	388	304	232
受、未受刑事处分	Criminal Records and Uncriminal Records	1263	1907	1882	1917	1845
文本相符	Confirmation of Copies & Photo-Offest Copies to Originals	2217	4257	3589	2820	2096
其　他	Others	3017	1674	4739	5788	8568

22-10 调解民事纠纷分类情况（2011-2015 年）
STATISTICS ON CIVIL DISPUTES MEDIATED BY TYPE（2011-2015）

单位：件（unit）

指标	Item	2011	2012	2013	2014	2015
总　计	**Total**	**16230**	**15001**	**17477**	**19346**	**17247**
婚　姻	Marriages	3465	3347	2328	2283	1854
房屋宅基地	Housing And Housing Sites	621	470	211	236	278
生产经营	Business	225	140	33	41	61
邻　里	Neighbor Disputes	4114	4236	3715	4364	4777
损害赔偿	Compensation for Damages	4084	3723	2479	2765	2557
其　他	Others	3721	3085	8711	9657	7720

22-11 主要年份住房公积金情况
STATEMENT OF PUBLIC ACCUMULATION FUND FOR HOUSING CONSTRUCTION IN MAIN YEARS

年 份 Year	缴存人数（人）Number of Paypable Persons (person)	缴存比例（%）Payment proportion (%)	人均月缴存额（元）Per capita monthly payment amount (yuan)	缴存金额（万元）Payment Amount (10000 yuan)	提取金额（万元）Withdrawed Amount (10000 yuan)	缴存余额（万元）Payment Balance (10000 yuan)
1992	278000	10	14	2929	103	2825
1995	323230	10	37	8775	854	23229
2000	334997	12-14	121	39759	11750	134776
2001	316781	14-16	142	49727	18076	168577
2002	321151	14-16	192	59676	28973	210625
2003	311722	16-24	264	80298	34153	259442
2004	303994	20-24	330	106998	45344	325051
2005	313772	20-24	384	132568	46627	410992
2006	322824	20-24	437	163392	83478	500853
2007	344071	20-24	510	196771	113598	584026
2008	373059	20-24	587	250796	125442	709381
2009	370396	20-24	616	275505	189093	795793
2010	430171	20-24	627	323831	204934	914690
2011	485392	20-24	732	405620	216913	1103397
2012	530158	20-24	831	528639	293277	1338758
2013	569251	20-24	908	620347	377223	1581882
2014	609936	20-24	964	705467	425304	1862045
2015	651096	20-24	999	780456	425304	2132646

22-11 续表 Continued

年 份 Year	个人贷款发放户数（户）Number of Household with loan (houshold)	个人贷款发放金额（万元）Amount of Loans (10000 yuan)	个人贷款回收金额（万元）Individual Loan Repayment Amount (10000 yuan)	个人贷款逾期率（%）Overdue Rate of Loans (%)	提取廉租房补充资金总额（万元）Accumulated Amount of Withdrawn Supplementory Financing to Low Rent Houses (10000 yuan)
1992					
1995	5	15			
2000	4241	26742	6940	0.050	
2001	4242	32886	11603	0.050	5003
2002	6510	65839	20259	0.050	6669
2003	6869	85740	32594	0.030	8505
2004	7213	111401	57474	0.020	9503
2005	8472	150552	64320	0.010	10694
2006	12071	212077	84107	0.004	12410
2007	12647	225062	101970	0.0004	14349
2008	10132	184035	100529	0.0007	18510
2009	12350	264884	140548	0	23000
2010	10185	239414	143443	0	27541
2011	11272	286306	144702	0	35856
2012	15051	409421	174069	0.0001	55385
2013	17561	502232	208954	0	78208
2014	16301	489099	230925	0.00032	108737
2015	17666	572700	272524	0	162059

22-12 分地区住房公积金情况（2015 年）
CONDITION OF PUBLIC ACCUMULATION FUND FOR HOUSING CONSTRUCTION （HOUSING FUND） BY REGION（2015）

指　标	Item	全 市 Whole Municipality	市 区 Urban Area	溧阳市 Liyang City
住房公积金缴存	**Payment of Housing Fund**			
应缴单位（个）	Work Unit Payable （Unit）	21797	20211	1586
当年新开户单位（个）	New Account-opening Unit （Unit）	2961	2654	307
缴存人数（人）	Number of Paypable Persons （person）	651096	597529	53567
当年新开户人数（人）	Number of New Account-opening Persons （person）	111445	102926	8519
缴存金额（万元）	Payment Amount （10000 yuan）	780456	712093	68363
缴存余额（万元）	Payment Balance （10000 yuan）	2132646	1930663	201983
累计缴存金额（万元）	Accumulated Payment Amount （10000 yuan）	4876498	4466526	409972
住房公积金提取	**Withdrawal of Housing Fund**			
提取人数（人）	Number of Person Withdrawed Fund （person）	218174	203128	15046
#转帐还贷提取	Withdrawal for Transfer Account and Repay Loan	145903	135199	10704
提取金额（万元）	Withdrawed Amount （10000 yuan）	509855	467582	42273
#转帐还贷提取	Withdrawal for Transfer Account and Repay Loan	267479	245527	21952
累计提取金额（万元）	Accumulated Withdrawed Amount （10000 yuan）	2743852	2535863	207989
住房公积金个人贷款	**Housing fund for Individual Loan**			
贷款户数（户）	Number of Household with loan （household）	17666	16102	1564
贷款金额（万元）	Amount of Loans （10000 yuan）	572700	519973	52727
平均贷款年数（年）	Average Loan Term （year）	16.38	16.40	15.24
平均贷款金额（万元）	Average Loan Amount （10000 yuan）	32.42	32.29	33.71
贷款余额（万元）	Balance of Loans （10000 yuan）	2090899	1914111	176788
贷款逾期率（%）	Overdue Rate of Loans （%）	0.00	0.00	0.00
累计贷款金额（万元）	Accumulated Amount of Loans （10000 yuan）	3878180	3551622	326558
住房公积金运用	**Application of Housing Fund**			
廉租房补充资金（万元）	Supplementary Fund of Bargain Tenement （10000 yuan）	53321	47800	5521
资金使用率（%）	Fund Utility Rate （%）	98.69	99.86	87.53
个人贷款比率（%）	Individual Loan Ratio （%）	98.04	99.14	87.53

附　录

APPENDIX

常州统计年鉴

附录 1　全国经济社会发展主要指标（2015 年）
MAJOR INDEX IN THE DEVELOPING OF SOCIETY AND ECONOMY IN CHINA（2015）

指标	Item	2015	比上年增减（%）Increase/Decrease over the previous year（%）
年末总人口（万人）	Total Population By the End of the Year（10000 persons）	137462	0.5
就业人员（万人）	Employed Persons	77451	0.3
#城　镇	Urban	40410	2.8
农民工总量（万人）	Total Number of Peasant Workers（10000 persons）	27747	1.3
#外出农民工	Migrant Workers from Rural Areas	16884	0.4
年末城镇登记失业率（%）	Registred Unemployment rate by the end of the Year（%）	4.05	-0.04个百分点 percentage points
国内生产总值（亿元）	GDP（100 million yuan）	676708	6.9
第一产业	Primary Industry	60863	3.9
第二产业	Secondary Industry	274278	6.0
第三产业	Tertiary Industry	341567	8.3
全社会固定资产投资总额（亿元）	Total Investment in Fixed Assets（100 million yuan）	562000	9.8
#固定资产投资总额	Investment in Fixed Assets	551590	10.0
第一产业	Primary Industry	15561	31.8
第二产业	Secondary Industry	224090	8.0
第三产业	Tertiary Industry	311939	10.6
#房地产开发	Real Estate Development	95979	1.0
货物运输总量（亿吨）	Total Freight Traffic（100 million tons）	417	0.2
货物周转量（亿吨公里）	Total Volume of Cargo Transported（100 million tons kilometers）	177401	-1.9
旅客运输总量（亿人）	Total Passenger Traffic（100 million persons）	194	-4.4
旅客周转量（亿人公里）	Total Volume of Passenger Transported（100 million persons kilometers）	30047	4.9
邮电业务总量（亿元）	Business Volume of Post and Telecommunications（100 million yuan）	28220	29.2
移动电话普及率（部/百人）	Popularized Rate of Telephone（set/100 persons）	95.5	1.5部（sets）

附录1 续表 Appendix 1 Continued

指 标	Item	2015	比上年增减（%） Increase/Decrease over the previous year（%）
互联网普及率（%）	Internet Penetration Rate （%）	50.3	2.4个百分点 percentage points
社会消费品零售总额（亿元）	Total Volume of Social Consumption Retail Sale （100 million yuan）	300931	10.7
按消费形态分	Group by Consumption Patterns		
商品零售额	Retail Sales	268621	10.6
餐饮收入额	Revenue of Restaurant and Catering	32310	11.7
居民消费价格指数（上年=100）	Consumption Price Index of Residents （preceding year=100）	101.4	1.4个百分点 percentage points
进出口总额（亿美元）	Gross Value of Export and Import （USD 100 million）	245741	-7.0
出 口	Export	141255	-1.8
进 口	Import	104485	-13.2
实际外商直接投资（亿美元）	Actual Foreign Direct Investment （USD 100 million）	7813.5	6.4
金融机构本外币存款余额（亿元）	Total Deposit of Financiai Departments （100 million yuan）	1397752	12.4
#住户存款	Household Deposit	551929	8.9
#人民币余额	Balance of RMB	546078	8.7
金融机构本外币贷款余额（亿元）	Total Loans of Financial Departments （100 million yuan）	993460	13.4
一般公共预算收入（亿元）	General Public Budgetary Revenue （100 million yuan）	152217	5.8
一般公共预算支出（亿元）	General Public Budgetary Expenditure （100 million yuan）	175768	13.2
全体居民人均可支配收入（元）	Per Capita Disposable Income of All Residents（yuan）	21966	8.9
城镇常住居民人均可支配收入（元）	Per Capita Disposable Income of Permanent Urban Residents（yuan）	31195	8.2
农村常住居民人均可支配收入（元）	Per Capita Disposable Income of Permanent Rural Residents（yuan）	11422	8.9
普通高等学校本专科在校学生（万人）	Students in Regular Institutions of Higher Education（10000 persons）	2625.3	3.0
科学研究与试验发展（R&D）经费支出（亿元）	Appropriation Expenditure on Science Research and Development （100 million yuan）	14220	9.2
专利申请量（万件）	Number of Patent Applications Examined（10000 units）	279.9	18.5
专利授权量（万件）	Number of Patent Authoriations Granted（10000 units）	171.8	31.9

附录 2　全国主要工农业产品产量（2015 年）
OUTPUT OF MAJOR INDUSTRIAL AND AGRICULTURAL PRODUCTS（2015）

产品名称	Name of Products	2015	比上年增减（%）Increase/Decrease over the previous year（%）
农产品产量（万吨）	**Output of Agricultural Products （10000 tons）**		
粮　食	Grain	62144	2.4
夏　粮	Summer Grain	14112	3.3
早　稻	Early Season Rice	3369	-0.9
秋　粮	Autumn Grain	44662	2.3
油　料	Oil-bearing Crops	3547	1.1
棉　花	Cotton	561	-9.3
糖　料	Sugar Crops	12529	-6.2
茶　叶	Tea	224	6.9
肉类总产量	Total Output of Meat	8625	-1.0
水产品产量	Total Output of Aquatic Products	6690	3.5
工业产品产量	**Output Of Industrial Products**		
纱（万吨）	Yarn （10000 tons）	3538	4.7
布（亿米）	Cloth （100 million meters）	892.6	-0.1
化　纤（万吨）	Chemical Fibre （10000 tons）	4831.7	10.1
成品糖（万吨）	Finished Sugar （10000 tons）	1474.1	-10.3
卷　烟（亿支）	Cigarette （100 million pieces）	25890.7	-0.8
彩色电视机（万台）	Colour TV （10000 units）	14475.7	2.5
家用电冰箱（万台）	Household Refrigerator （10000 units）	7992.8	-9.1
房间空调器（万台）	Household Air-conditioner （10000 units）	14200.4	-1.8
一次能源生产总量（亿吨标准煤）	Total Output of Primary Energy （100 million tons of SCE）	36.2	0.0
原　煤（亿吨）	Coal （100 million tons）	37.5	-3.3
原　油（亿吨）	Crude Oil （100 million tons）	2.15	1.5
天然气（亿立方米）	Natural Gas （100 million cu.m）	1346.1	3.4
发电量（亿千瓦时）	Electricity （100 million kw.h）	58105.8	0.3
粗　钢（万吨）	Steel （10000 tons）	80382.5	-2.2
钢　材（万吨）	Steel Products （10000 tons）	112349.6	-0.1
十种有色金属（万吨）	10 Kinds of Nonferrous Metals （10000 tons）	5155.8	6.8
#电解铜（铜）	Refined Copper （copper）	796.2	4.2
电解铝	Electrolytic Aluminum	3141.0	8.8
水　泥（亿吨）	Cement （100 million tons）	23.6	-5.3
硫　酸（万吨）	Sulfuric Acid （10000 tons）	8975.7	0.8
纯　碱（万吨）	Soda Ash （10000 tons）	3020.7	-1.4
乙　烯（万吨）	Ethene （10000 tons）	1714.6	1.1
化　肥（折100%,万吨）	Chemical Fertilizer （10000 tons）	7432	8.1
发电设备（万千瓦）	Electricity Generation Equiments （10000 kw）	12431.4	-17.4
汽　车（万辆）	Motor Vehicles （10000 coaches）	2450.4	3.3
#轿　车	Cars	1163.0	-6.8
大中型拖拉机（万台）	Tractors （10000 units）	68.8	6.9
集成电路（亿块）	Integrated Citcuit （100 million pcs）	1087.2	7.1
程控交换机（万线）	Distance Exchange and Transmitting Machine （10000 lines）	1880.3	-12.5
移动通信手持机（万部）	Mobile Telephone （10000 units）	181261.4	7.8
微型电子计算机（万部）	Micro-computers （10000 units）	31418.7	-10.4

附录 3　江苏省经济社会发展主要指标（2015 年）
MAJOR INDEX IN THE DEVELOPING OF SOCIETY AND ECONOMY IN JIANGSU PROVINCE（2015）

指 标	Item	2015	比上年增减（%）Increase/Decrease over the previous year （%）
常住人口（万人）	permanent population（10000 persons）	7976.30	0.2
就业人口（万人）	Employed Persons（10000 persons）	4758.50	-0.05
年末城镇登记失业率（%）	Registred Unemployment rate by the end of the Year （%）	3.0	0.0个百分点 percentage points
地区生产总值（亿元）	GDP （100 million yuan）	70116.38	8.5
第一产业	Primary Industry	3987.94	3.2
第二产业	Secondary Industry	32043.63	8.4
第三产业	Tertiary Industry	34084.81	9.3
规模以上工业增加值（亿元）	Added Value of Industry （100million yuan）	33422.50	8.3
#国有企业	State-owned Enterprises	875.35	1.6
集体企业	Collective Enterprises	178.44	10.4
股份制企业	Joint-share Enterprises	19764.40	10.0
外商及港澳台投资企业	Enterprises with Investment from Foreign, Hong Kong, Macao and Taiwan.	11950.27	6.0
工业企业实现利税总额（亿元）	Pre-tax Profit realized By Industrial Enterprises （100 million yuan）	15907.07	9.3
工业企业实现利润总额（亿元）	Gross Profit realized By Industrial Enterprises （100 million yuan）	9617.10	9.1
工业产品销售率（%）	Sales Rate of Industrial Products （%）	98.06	-0.3个百分点 percentage points
建筑业总产值（亿元）	Gross Output Value of Construction	24785.81	0.8
固定资产投资总额（亿元）	Investment in Fixed Assets （100 million yuan）	45905.17	10.5
第一产业	Primary Industry	232.24	12.2
第二产业	Secondary Industry	22890.96	12.8
第三产业	Tertiary Industry	22781.97	8.3
#房地产开发	Real Estate Development	8153.68	-1.1
货物周转量（亿吨公里）	Total Volume of Cargo Transported （100 million tons kilometers）	7374.00	5.0
旅客周转量（亿人公里）	Total Volume of Passenger Transported （100 million persons kilometers）	1566.40	1.0

附录 3 续表 Appendix 3 Continued

指 标	Item	2015	比上年增减（%）Increase/Decrease over the previous year（%）
电话普及率（部/百人）	Popularized Rate of Telephone （set/100 persons）	128.1	0.0部（sets）
社会消费品零售总额（亿元）	Total Volume of Social Consumption Retail Sale （100 million yuan）	25876.77	10.3
居民消费价格指数（上年=100）	Consumption Price Index of Residents （preceding year=100）	101.7	1.7个百分点 percentage points
商品零售价格指数（上年=100）	Retail Price Index （preceding year=100）	100.6	0.6个百分点 percentage points
进出口总额（亿美元）	Gross Value of Export and Import （USD 100 million）	5456.14	-3.2
出 口	Export	3386.68	-0.9
进 口	Import	2069.45	-6.7
协议（合同）外资金额（亿美元）	Amount of Foreign Capital in the Newly Signed Agreements （USD 100 million）	393.61	-8.9
实际到帐注册外资（亿美元）	Foreign Capital Actually Utilized （USD 100 million）	242.75	-13.8
金融机构人民币存款余额（亿元）	RMB Deposits Balance of Financial Departments（100 million yuan）	107873.03	11.7
金融机构人民币贷款余额（亿元）	RMB Loans Balance of Financial Departments （100 million yuan）	78866.34	13.4
一般公共预算收入（亿元）	General Public Budgetary Revenue（100 million yuan）	8028.59	11.0
一般公共预算支出（亿元）	General Public Budgetary Expenditure（100 million yuan）	9681.47	14.3
居民人均可支配收入（元）	Per Capita Disposable Income of All Residents （yuan）	29539	8.7
城镇常住居民人均可支配收入（元）	Per Capita Disposable Income of Permanent Urban Residents （yuan）	37173	8.2
农村常住居民人均可支配收入（元）	Per Capita Disposable Income of Permanent Rural Residents （yuan）	16257	8.7
普通高校在校学生（万人）	Students in Ordinary High Schools （10000 persons）	171.57	1.0
科学研究与试验发展（R&D）经费支出（亿元）	Appropriation Expenditure on Science Research and Development （100 million yuan）	1788	9.7
专利申请量	Number of Patent Applications Examined	428337	1.5
专利授权量	Number of Patent Authorizations Granted	250290	25.1
报纸出版量（亿份）	Total Volume of Newspaper Issued （100 million copies）	26.83	-4.2

附录 4 江苏省主要工农业产品产量（2015 年）

OUTPUT OF MAJOR INDUSTRIAL AND AGRICULTURAL PRODUCTS IN JIANGSU PROVINCE（2015）

产品名称	Name of Products	2015	比上年增减（%）Increase/Decrease over the previous year（%）
农产品产量（万吨）	**Output of Agricultural Products （10000 tons）**		
粮 食	Grain	3561.34	2.0
棉 花	Cotton	11.69	-26.7
油 料	Oil-bearing Crops	143.11	-2.4
#油菜籽	Rapeseeds	106.3	-3.4
花 生	Peanut	35.1	0.7
蚕 茧	Silkworm Cocoons	4.97	-12.7
茶 叶	Tea	1.45	-0.7
水 果	Fruits	937.27	8.8
肉 类	Meat	369.35	-2.7
禽 蛋	Poultry Eggs	198.80	0.9
牛 奶	Cow Milk	59.60	-1.8
水产品	Aquatic Products	522.10	0.6
工业产品产量	**Output Of Industrial Products**		
纱（万吨）	Yarn （10000 tons）	568.76	3.0
布（亿米）	Cloth （100 million meters）	95.68	5.2
化 纤（万吨）	Chemical Fibre （10000 tons）	1430.62	7.9
卷 烟（亿支）	Cigarette （100 million piece）	1046.09	0.7
彩色电视机（万部）	Colour TV （10000 sets）	1626.20	33.1
家用电冰箱（万台）	Household Refrigerator （10000 units）	907.65	-9.2
房间空调器（万台）	Household Air-conditioner （10000 units）	404.29	-21.4
发电量（亿千瓦·时）	Electricity （100 Million kw·h）	4351.78	0.2
粗 钢（万吨）	Crude Steel （10000 tons）	10995.17	10.4
钢 材（万吨）	Steel Products （10000 tons）	13560.81	6.5
十种有色金属（万吨）	10 Kinds of Nonferrous Metals （10000 tons）	39.76	30.1
水 泥（万吨）	Cement （10000 tons）	18013.66	-7.3
硫 酸（万吨）	Sulfuric Acid （10000 tons）	371.77	4.2
纯 碱（万吨）	Soda Ash （10000 tons）	279.86	-12.2
乙 烯（万吨）	Ethene （10000 tons）	154.34	-0.7
化 肥（折100%,万吨）	Chemical Fertilizer （10000 tons）	203.76	-3.8
汽 车（万辆）	Motor Vehicles （10000 coach）	121.75	-3.9
#轿 车	Cars	67.56	-9.3
发电设备（万千瓦）	Electricity Generation Equiments （10000 kw）	651.58	-5.9
集成电路（亿块）	Integrated Citcuit （100 million pcs）	369.52	12.1
程控交换机（万线）	Distance Exchange and Transmitting Machine （10000 lines）	0.80	-58.9
微型电子计算机（万部）	Micro-computers （10000 units）	5911.59	-15.3
移动通讯基站设备（信道）	Mobile Communication Devices （Channels）	3497206	-34.7

附录 5　江苏省市、县主要经济指标（2015 年）
MAJOR ECONOMY INDICATORS OF CITIES AND COUNTIES OF JIANGSU PROVINCE（2015）

指　标	Item	南京市 Nanjing City	无锡市 Wuxi City	江阴市 Jiangyin City
年末总人口（万人）	Year-end Population （10000 persons）	653.40	480.90	124.10
年末常住人口（万人）	Year-end permanent population（10000 persons）	823.59	651.10	163.68
土地面积（平方公里）	Area of Land （sq.km）	6587	4627	987
地区生产总值（亿元）	Gross Domestic Products （100 million yuan）	9720.77	8518.26	2880.86
#工　业	Industry	3395.26	3837.28	1515.18
按产业分	Grouped by Industries			
第一产业	Primary Industry	232.39	137.72	46.28
第二产业	Secondary Industry	3916.77	4197.43	1584.42
第三产业	Tertiary Industry	5571.61	4183.11	1250.16
人均地区生产总值（元）	Per Capita GDP （yuan）	118171	130938	176119
固定资产投资完成额（亿元）	Investment in Fixed Assets（100 million yuan）	5425.98	4888.55	1128.59
一般公共预算收入（亿元）	Public Finance Budget Revenue（100 million yuan）	1020.03	830.00	218.92
#税收收入	Tax Revenue	838.67	668.18	180.31
一般公共预算支出（亿元）	Public Finance Budget Expenditure（100 million yuan）	1045.57	821.86	205.35
年底金融机构存款余额（亿元）	Balance of Deposits of Financial Institutions at Year-end（100 million yuan）	25887.77	12710.45	2954.56
#住户存款	Individual Deposits	5535.53	4639.66	1027.51
年底金融机构贷款余额（亿元）	Balance of Loans of Financial Institutions at Year-end（100 million yuan）	18217.80	9332.27	2396.17
规模以上工业企业主要指标	**Major Economic Indicators of Industrial Enterprises Above Designated Size**			
工业总产值（亿元）	Gross Industrial Output Value （100 million yuan）	12905.13	14549.87	5744.96
主营业务收入（亿元）	Main Business Income （100 million yuan）	12180.70	14083.94	5502.22
利润总额（亿元）	Total Profits （100 million yuan）	837.39	895.09	351.63
工业用电量（亿千瓦时）	Industrial Electricity Consumption （100 million kw.h）	300.54	472.24	208.47
社会消费品零售总额（亿元）	Total Retail Sales of Consumer Goods （100 million yuan）	4590.17	2847.61	705.16
进出口总额（亿美元）	Total Imports （USD 100 million）	532.40	684.67	203.11
#出　口	Exports	315.03	422.32	124.12
实际到账注册外资（亿美元）	Foreign Capital Actually Utilized （USD 100 million）	33.35	32.02	10.11
全体居民人均可支配收入（元）	Per Capita Disposable Income of All Residents（yuan）	40455	39461	42756
全体居民人均消费性支出（元）	Per Capita Consuming Expenditures of All Residents（yuan）	24876	25954	23670
城镇常住居民人均可支配收入（元）	Per Capita Disposable Income of Permanent Urban Residents（yuan）	46104	45129	50701
城镇常住居民人均消费支出（元）	Per Capita Consuming Expenditures of Permanent Urban Residents（yuan）	27794	29466	26970
农村常住居民人均可支配收入（元）	Per Capita Disposable Income of Permanent Rural Residents（yuan）	19483	24155	26012
农村常住居民人均消费支出（元）	Per Capita Consuming Expenditures of Permanent Rural Residents （yuan）	14041	16469	16716

附录 5 续表 1

指 标	Item	宜兴市 Yixing City	徐州市 Xuzhou City
年末总人口（万人）	Year-end Population （10000 persons）	108.29	1028.70
年末常住人口（万人）	Year-end permanent population（10000 persons）	125.33	866.90
土地面积（平方公里）	Area of Land （sq.km）	1997	11765
地区生产总值（亿元）	Gross Domestic Products （100 million yuan）	1285.66	5319.88
#工 业	Industry	559.96	1976.57
按产业分	Grouped by Industries		
第一产业	Primary Industry	50.34	504.76
第二产业	Secondary Industry	659.05	2355.06
第三产业	Tertiary Industry	576.27	2460.07
人均地区生产总值（元）	Per Capita GDP （yuan）	102652	61511
固定资产投资完成额（亿元）	Investment in Fixed Assets（100 million yuan）	663.55	4266.12
一般公共预算收入（亿元）	General Public Budgetary Revenue （100 million yuan）	102.50	530.68
#税收收入	Tax Revenue	86.87	429.13
一般公共预算支出（亿元）	General Public Budgetary Expenditure （100 million yuan）	109.11	752.46
年底金融机构存款余额（亿元）	Balance of Deposits of Financial Institutions at Year-end （100 million yuan）	1821.70	4747.01
#住户存款	Individual Deposits	909.83	2780.60
年底金融机构贷款余额（亿元）	Balance of Loans of Financial Institutions at Year-end （100 million yuan）	1373.06	3069.90
规模以上工业企业主要指标	**Major Economic Indicators of Industrial Enterprises Above Designated Size**		
工业总产值（亿元）	Gross Industrial Output Value （100 million yuan）	2779.18	12215.91
主营业务收入（亿元）	Main Business Income （100 million yuan）	2673.64	12034.33
利润总额（亿元）	Total Profits （100 million yuan）	119.31	978.53
工业用电量（亿千瓦时）	Industrial Electricity Consumption （100 million kw.h）	65.58	254.36
社会消费品零售总额（亿元）	Total Retail Sales of Consumer Goods （100 million yuan）	506.96	2358.45
进出口总额（亿美元）	Total Imports （USD 100 million）	38.20	54.13
#出 口	Exports	29.18	43.89
实际到账注册外资（亿美元）	Foreign Capital Actually Utilized （USD 100 million）	1.85	14.28
全体居民人均可支配收入（元）	Per Capita Disposable Income of All Residents（yuan）	34413	20425
全体居民人均消费性支出（元）	Per Capita Consuming Expenditures of All Residents（yuan）	22116	13174
城镇常住居民人均可支配收入（元）	Per Capita Disposable Income of Permanent Urban Residents（yuan）	42750	26219
城镇常住居民人均消费支出（元）	Per Capita Consuming Expenditures of Permanent Urban Residents（yuan）	26862	16143
农村常住居民人均可支配收入（元）	Per Capita Disposable Income of Permanent Rural Residents（yuan）	21910	13982
农村常住居民人均消费支出（元）	Per Capita Consuming Expenditures of Permanent Rural Residents（yuan）	14999	9873

Appendix 5 Continued 1

丰县 Feng County	沛县 Pei County	睢宁县 Shuining County	新沂市 Xiyi City	邳州市 Pizhou City	常州市 Changzhou City	溧阳市 Liyang City	苏州市 Suzhou City
120.67	130.92	144.28	112.66	187.49	370.85	79.60	667.01
94.72	111.47	102.28	90.91	143.54	470.14	76.09	1061.60
1450	1806	1769	1592	2085	4372	1535	8657
370.33	605.84	451.89	507.63	731.71	5273.15	738.15	14504.07
122.89	217.06	151.79	180.99	271.77	2269.99	311.86	6490.44
69.53	85.59	77.51	61.93	104.59	146.55	46.32	215.71
160.32	277.91	192.72	212.36	313.59	2516.04	367.07	7045.12
140.48	242.34	181.66	233.34	313.53	2610.56	324.76	7243.24
39124	54394	44210	55891	51015	112221	97055	136702
215.83	487.09	269.77	473.69	652.69	3398.97	442.40	5965.44
43.09	59.30	43.68	51.33	62.38	466.28	56.19	1560.76
37.32	49.68	38.37	43.56	53.29	373.70	46.08	1338.61
74.72	92.35	78.89	82.50	103.43	485.33	61.38	1527.17
297.36	378.88	329.98	265.82	411.79	7438.68	866.37	23659.10
225.12	289.38	251.69	192.61	302.15	3193.77	462.65	7358.04
147.50	187.39	192.61	221.85	319.57	5354.58	698.72	19200.10
616.91	1521.09	922.79	1599.25	2225.10	11101.64	1212.73	30249.25
602.43	1485.31	887.82	1581.70	2171.54	11500.68	1223.03	29768.65
49.76	95.36	97.56	113.04	183.26	642.27	73.24	1529.04
11.14	24.04	14.07	33.38	16.32	325.49	57.41	1074.20
133.36	217.22	158.55	153.71	223.55	1990.45	275.30	4461.62
1.00	3.18	5.56	4.05	9.47	280.41	8.35	3053.50
0.99	3.12	4.09	2.08	8.20	212.56	7.46	1814.59
0.51	0.83	1.06	0.07	1.88	17.21	1.06	60.00
16481	19372	16515	17100	18842	35379	28737	42987
11548	12452	9863	11521	11051	22234	17527	26847
21094	25163	21478	22901	26334	42710	38445	50390
15678	15951	12188	15312	14749	25358	20294	31136
12850	14441	12656	13281	14028	21912	19880	25580
8296	9473	8054	9025	8674	14764	15003	16761

附录 5 续表 2

指 标	Item	常熟市 Changshu City	张家港市 Zhangjiagang City
年末总人口（万人）	Year-end Population （10000 persons）	106.82	92.28
年末常住人口（万人）	Year-end permanent population（10000 persons）	151.01	125.31
土地面积（平方公里）	Area of Land （sq.km）	1276	987
地区生产总值（亿元）	Gross Domestic Products （100 million yuan）	2044.88	2229.82
#工 业	Industry	1011.88	1132.68
按产业分	Grouped by Industries		
第一产业	Primary Industry	40.76	30.34
第二产业	Secondary Industry	1064.27	1190.76
第三产业	Tertiary Industry	939.85	1008.72
人均地区生产总值（元）	Per Capita GDP （yuan）	135431	177987
固定资产投资完成额（亿元）	Investment in Fixed Assets（100 million yuan）	622.47	733.79
一般公共预算收入（亿元）	General Public Budgetary Revenue （100 million yuan）	157.70	174.22
#税收收入	Tax Revenue	128.40	143.64
一般公共预算支出（亿元）	General Public Budgetary Expenditure （100 million yuan）	155.26	171.34
年底金融机构存款余额（亿元）	Balance of Deposits of Financial Institutions at Year-end （100 million yuan）	2418.40	2372.21
#住户存款	Individual Deposits	1104.60	958.77
年底金融机构贷款余额（亿元）	Balance of Loans of Financial Institutions at Year-end （100 million yuan）	1930.91	1824.69
规模以上工业企业主要指标	**Major Economic Indicators of Industrial Enterprises Above Designated Size**		
工业总产值（亿元）	Gross Industrial Output Value （100 million yuan）	3612.54	4485.74
主营业务收入（亿元）	Main Business Income （100 million yuan）	3547.87	4577.74
利润总额（亿元）	Total Profits （100 million yuan）	168.60	142.81
工业用电量（亿千瓦时）	Industrial Electricity Consumption （100 million kw.h）	136.76	268.16
社会消费品零售总额（亿元）	Total Retail Sales of Consumer Goods （100 million yuan）	675.64	494.87
进出口总额（亿美元）	Total Imports （USD 100 million）	221.57	292.69
#出 口	Exports	146.10	148.29
实际到账注册外资（亿美元）	Foreign Capital Actually Utilized （USD 100 million）	8.05	6.50
全体居民人均可支配收入（元）	Per Capita Disposable Income of All Residents（yuan）	41506	41445
全体居民人均消费性支出（元）	Per Capita Consuming Expenditures of All Residents（yuan）	25472	24860
城镇常住居民人均可支配收入（元）	Per Capita Disposable Income of Permanent Urban Residents（yuan）	50413	50618
城镇常住居民人均消费支出（元）	Per Capita Consuming Expenditures of Permanent Urban Residents（yuan）	29323	29664
农村常住居民人均可支配收入（元）	Per Capita Disposable Income of Permanent Rural Residents（yuan）	25811	25715
农村常住居民人均消费支出（元）	Per Capita Consuming Expenditures of Permanent Rural Residents （yuan）	18686	16623

Appendix 5 Continued 2

昆山市 Kunshan City	太仓市 Taicang City	南通市 Nantong City	海安县 Haian County	如东县 Rudong County	启东市 Qidong City	如皋市 Rugao City	海门市 Haimen City	连云港市 Lianyungang City
78.70	47.96	766.77	94.01	103.96	112.06	143.63	100.04	530.56
165.12	70.95	730.00	86.63	98.20	95.40	125.30	90.43	447.37
932	810	10549	1184	2791	1715	1576	1144	7615
3080.01	1100.08	6148.40	680.44	672.69	803.14	812.46	915.02	2160.64
1597.62	529.25	2453.38	261.35	262.62	306.70	333.43	390.45	767.27
28.88	37.21	354.90	53.77	64.97	65.45	60.47	51.80	282.69
1695.68	564.53	2977.53	323.18	314.83	389.13	401.57	471.59	959.00
1355.45	498.34	2815.97	303.49	292.90	348.56	350.41	391.63	918.95
186582	155159	84236	78551	68506	84099	64761	101298	48416
799.15	483.48	4376.03	510.00	486.98	539.06	503.15	565.32	2077.35
284.76	114.54	625.64	62.06	58.54	76.86	77.10	78.40	291.77
251.85	97.78	521.08	53.51	49.34	63.44	63.63	65.04	237.55
255.36	109.07	748.97	84.40	93.82	86.24	101.02	85.55	425.92
3062.60	1269.17	9659.15	1104.37	843.70	1073.30	980.91	1169.05	2128.22
1046.03	486.49	5115.51	634.40	543.95	715.85	649.64	699.66	1048.27
2174.54	1139.46	5997.24	752.65	419.66	644.85	602.88	688.40	1781.05
8270.97	1993.08	13515.33	1992.15	1860.27	1631.36	1759.43	1871.30	5433.14
8225.99	1918.99	13322.91	1956.87	1847.23	1584.10	1752.44	1876.72	5356.08
401.42	126.23	1015.25	141.97	146.21	121.24	80.09	206.81	434.64
159.37	77.05	253.05	33.91	33.88	18.10	32.84	25.02	116.57
714.68	264.70	2379.46	247.39	287.43	293.06	308.99	311.15	830.71
834.53	127.27	315.79	16.16	24.46	30.67	30.53	22.54	80.45
537.96	63.09	228.26	13.64	14.41	24.81	26.10	14.19	40.60
11.01	5.01	23.16	3.01	3.17	1.37	2.41	2.20	8.01
42755	40428	27584	24916	24463	26071	24416	27554	19418
25992	25878	18358	17323	15840	20244	15744	18441	13260
50749	50134	36291	34445	34338	34566	33792	37404	25728
30363	31488	23680	21611	20275	28060	20558	24555	17259
25978	25643	17267	16549	15827	18287	15532	18986	12778
16819	17333	12052	13559	11960	13083	11182	13124	9052

附录 5　续表 3

指　标	Item	东海县 Donghai County	灌云县 Guanyun County
年末总人口（万人）	Year-end Population （10000 persons）	122.84	104.82
年末常住人口（万人）	Year-end permanent population（10000 persons）	96.35	80.10
土地面积（平方公里）	Area of Land （sq.km）	2037	1538
地区生产总值（亿元）	Gross Domestic Products （100 million yuan）	393.54	300.13
#工　业	Industry	150.82	101.23
按产业分	Grouped by Industries		
第一产业	Primary Industry	61.89	59.81
第二产业	Secondary Industry	173.71	133.52
第三产业	Tertiary Industry	157.94	106.80
人均地区生产总值（元）	Per Capita GDP （yuan）	40947	37542
固定资产投资完成额（亿元）	Investment in Fixed Assets（100 million yuan）	251.09	205.10
一般公共预算收入（亿元）	General Public Budgetary Revenue （100 million yuan）	41.02	39.32
#税收收入	Tax Revenue	35.52	34.67
一般公共预算支出（亿元）	General Public Budgetary Expenditure （100 million yuan）	68.72	61.80
年底金融机构存款余额（亿元）	Balance of Deposits of Financial Institutions at Year-end （100 million yuan）	269.90	216.82
#住户存款	Individual Deposits	186.69	132.21
年底金融机构贷款余额（亿元）	Balance of Loans of Financial Institutions at Year-end （100 million yuan）	210.18	165.91
规模以上工业企业主要指标	**Major Economic Indicators of Industrial Enterprises Above Designated Size**		
工业总产值（亿元）	Gross Industrial Output Value （100 million yuan）	929.82	636.22
主营业务收入（亿元）	Main Business Income （100 million yuan）	917.62	600.27
利润总额（亿元）	Total Profits （100 million yuan）	64.30	39.97
工业用电量（亿千瓦时）	Industrial Electricity Consumption （100 million kw.h）	12.64	5.25
社会消费品零售总额（亿元）	Total Retail Sales of Consumer Goods （100 million yuan）	156.21	106.57
进出口总额（亿美元）	Total Imports （USD 100 million）	3.69	1.98
#出　口	Exports	2.90	1.79
实际到账注册外资（亿美元）	Foreign Capital Actually Utilized （USD 100 million）	0.55	0.33
全体居民人均可支配收入（元）	Per Capita Disposable Income of All Residents（yuan）	18381	16059
全体居民人均消费性支出（元）	Per Capita Consuming Expenditures of All Residents（yuan）	12769	10341
城镇常住居民人均可支配收入（元）	Per Capita Disposable Income of Permanent Urban Residents（yuan）	25281	21240
城镇常住居民人均消费支出（元）	Per Capita Consuming Expenditures of Permanent Urban Residents（yuan）	17748	13019
农村常住居民人均可支配收入（元）	Per Capita Disposable Income of Permanent Rural Residents（yuan）	13286	11881
农村常住居民人均消费支出（元）	Per Capita Consuming Expenditures of Permanent Rural Residents（yuan）	9092	8181

Appendix 5 Continued 3

灌南县 Guannan County	淮安市 Huaian City	涟水县 Lianshui County	洪泽县 Hongze County	盱眙县 Xuyu County	金湖县 Jinhu County	盐城市 Yancheng City	响水县 Xiangshui County	滨海县 Binhai County
82.17	564.45	114.97	39.65	80.25	35.96	828.03	62.37	122.35
63.19	487.20	84.68	33.76	65.25	33.10	722.85	50.19	94.10
1028	10030	1678	1273	2497	1378	16931	1474	1950
281.63	2745.09	340.87	230.81	320.13	216.53	4212.50	244.30	361.30
118.56	985.66	107.49	81.49	102.39	73.23	1653.90	99.46	128.24
48.23	307.67	53.14	31.58	51.98	30.94	516.53	40.35	55.97
136.86	1176.66	132.51	95.46	128.57	83.31	1923.47	113.68	148.98
96.54	1260.76	155.22	103.77	139.58	102.28	1772.50	90.27	156.35
44682	56460	40290	68459	49145	65476	58299	48646	38359
175.69	2203.24	276.32	170.03	328.00	164.37	3372.89	250.02	321.08
38.85	350.31	33.32	25.21	34.98	23.91	477.50	32.54	38.65
34.11	284.05	28.45	21.31	29.19	21.00	384.31	26.83	31.64
60.91	512.47	62.85	47.78	57.52	41.14	746.31	50.82	69.45
146.83	2328.63	275.77	179.32	218.90	186.24	4363.99	134.23	233.83
94.02	1183.92	160.93	78.94	139.65	114.86	2397.52	76.75	153.17
116.82	1864.76	182.69	132.34	206.20	148.60	3045.50	121.35	184.67
619.80	6560.50	729.48	645.47	912.50	476.94	8253.62	718.52	657.39
613.33	6542.23	699.73	635.23	943.05	472.94	8038.97	710.29	640.92
43.08	374.36	36.87	43.00	38.93	21.62	564.34	81.15	32.16
27.06	108.89	8.88	14.50	9.80	7.33	206.28	43.24	17.06
83.51	970.74	117.20	84.75	111.07	81.02	1468.60	59.90	99.46
2.51	41.30	3.71	2.10	2.74	3.45	81.19	4.37	3.84
2.08	30.09	3.18	1.98	2.13	3.40	51.24	3.88	3.04
0.37	12.14	1.21	1.24	1.17	1.27	7.95	0.56	0.64
15941	20840	16698	21043	20007	20565	22419	17949	18485
10625	12349	10426	11563	10651	14845	14348	9628	12230
22657	28105	23325	28120	28359	28454	28200	23642	24451
14557	15867	14877	13128	15104	18537	16539	10659	14831
11408	13128	12259	14385	13295	14352	15748	13088	13683
7972	8615	7444	10091	7073	11938	11819	8748	10137

附录 5 续表 4

指 标	Item	阜宁县 Huning County	射阳县 Sheyang County
年末总人口（万人）	Year-end Population （10000 persons）	112.28	96.32
年末常住人口（万人）	Year-end permanent population（10000 persons）	83.82	89.10
土地面积（平方公里）	Area of Land （sq.km）	1439	2606
地区生产总值（亿元）	Gross Domestic Products （100 million yuan）	363.20	407.61
#工 业	Industry	118.42	139.38
按产业分	Grouped by Industries		
第一产业	Primary Industry	52.97	78.41
第二产业	Secondary Industry	159.27	147.61
第三产业	Tertiary Industry	150.95	181.59
人均地区生产总值（元）	Per Capita GDP （yuan）	43315	45737
固定资产投资完成额（亿元）	Investment in Fixed Assets（100 million yuan）	279.69	241.99
一般公共预算收入（亿元）	General Public Budgetary Revenue （100 million yuan）	39.17	20.56
#税收收入	Tax Revenue	32.55	17.48
一般公共预算支出（亿元）	General Public Budgetary Expenditure （100 million yuan）	71.51	59.38
年底金融机构存款余额（亿元）	Balance of Deposits of Financial Institutions at Year-end （100 million yuan）	318.38	334.53
#住户存款	Individual Deposits	228.03	239.44
年底金融机构贷款余额（亿元）	Balance of Loans of Financial Institutions at Year-end （100 million yuan）	213.57	217.36
规模以上工业企业主要指标	**Major Economic Indicators of Industrial Enterprises Above Designated Size**		
工业总产值（亿元）	Gross Industrial Output Value （100 million yuan）	682.56	630.61
主营业务收入（亿元）	Main Business Income （100 million yuan）	674.67	620.99
利润总额（亿元）	Total Profits （100 million yuan）	31.30	30.13
工业用电量（亿千瓦时）	Industrial Electricity Consumption （100 million kw.h）	24.21	12.21
社会消费品零售总额（亿元）	Total Retail Sales of Consumer Goods （100 million yuan）	117.01	151.19
进出口总额（亿美元）	Total Imports （USD 100 million）	2.14	3.07
#出 口	Exports	1.66	1.67
实际到账注册外资（亿美元）	Foreign Capital Actually Utilized （USD 100 million）	0.40	0.26
全体居民人均可支配收入（元）	Per Capita Disposable Income of All Residents（yuan）	18502	19864
全体居民人均消费性支出（元）	Per Capita Consuming Expenditures of All Residents（yuan）	12793	14182
城镇常住居民人均可支配收入（元）	Per Capita Disposable Income of Permanent Urban Residents（yuan）	23528	24460
城镇常住居民人均消费支出（元）	Per Capita Consuming Expenditures of Permanent Urban Residents（yuan）	19019	20842
农村常住居民人均可支配收入（元）	Per Capita Disposable Income of Permanent Rural Residents（yuan）	14138	15136
农村常住居民人均消费支出（元）	Per Capita Consuming Expenditures of Permanent Rural Residents （yuan）	7386	7330

Appendix 5 Continued 4

建湖县 Jianhu County	东台市 Dongtai City	扬州市 Yangzhou City	宝应县 Baoying County	仪征市 Yizheng City	高邮市 Gaoyou City	镇江市 Zhenjiang City	丹阳市 Danyang City
80.01	112.65	461.12	91.16	56.46	81.58	271.67	81.21
73.71	98.71	448.36	75.54	56.47	74.01	317.65	98.02
1157	3176	6591	1462	902	1922	3840	1047
431.05	670.23	4016.84	458.02	408.19	483.86	3502.48	1070.25
161.61	243.49	1749.58	165.96	157.12	177.86	1588.95	518.22
45.19	87.92	241.86	65.63	21.69	66.34	132.89	50.94
189.25	279.21	2012.10	204.00	186.44	215.53	1726.96	540.95
196.61	303.10	1762.88	188.39	200.06	201.98	1642.63	478.36
58483	67916	89647	60669	76792	65420	110351	109276
311.36	510.54	2856.82	287.57	383.11	360.50	2541.07	457.74
50.61	71.55	336.75	30.49	39.44	33.24	302.85	67.06
42.33	60.85	274.67	25.31	33.95	27.36	245.40	57.58
83.64	101.72	442.78	53.02	46.83	53.62	348.73	80.07
365.00	631.03	4719.40	406.05	501.92	453.80	3969.11	885.13
258.21	480.02	2376.68	262.60	273.21	309.85	1741.48	508.40
265.99	347.76	3095.77	259.49	306.22	278.44	2982.60	858.08
895.06	1060.47	9194.19	990.88	1462.10	1157.32	8403.82	2512.23
852.53	1057.30	8973.50	914.62	1453.77	1101.43	8211.10	2453.93
59.50	57.64	605.64	54.92	101.50	78.61	556.73	151.22
13.91	27.17	152.49	11.26	35.39	22.90	165.33	52.22
155.43	228.30	1236.96	135.63	100.19	153.06	1113.71	283.94
3.16	7.12	103.38	8.90	3.72	4.40	100.64	28.03
3.02	6.81	77.11	6.75	2.86	4.07	68.73	23.50
0.63	0.70	8.48	0.09	0.27	0.60	13.05	3.31
20997	24372	26253	19613	24739	21874	31263	30366
12128	14257	16720	12719	17021	15464	19570	19059
27393	30330	32946	24746	33808	29007	38666	38574
14867	16803	19780	15102	19540	19427	22859	20907
15687	18097	16619	15507	16138	15608	19214	19892
9854	11576	12316	10813	14632	11984	14217	16701

附录 5　续表 5

指　标	Item	扬中市 Yangzhong City	句容市 Jurong City
年末总人口（万人）	Year-end Population （10000 persons）	28.16	59.13
年末常住人口（万人）	Year-end permanent population（10000 persons）	34.21	62.50
土地面积（平方公里）	Area of Land （sq.km）	327	1378
地区生产总值（亿元）	Gross Domestic Products （100 million yuan）	475.80	468.50
#工　业	Industry	240.57	200.51
按产业分	Grouped by Industries		
第一产业	Primary Industry	11.87	41.32
第二产业	Secondary Industry	249.82	223.85
第三产业	Tertiary Industry	214.11	203.33
人均地区生产总值（元）	Per Capita GDP （yuan）	139184	75020
固定资产投资完成额（亿元）	Investment in Fixed Assets（100 million yuan）	256.19	306.44
一般公共预算收入（亿元）	General Public Budgetary Revenue （100 million yuan）	34.03	40.01
#税收收入	Tax Revenue	29.22	33.62
一般公共预算支出（亿元）	General Public Budgetary Expenditure （100 million yuan）	38.53	49.49
年底金融机构存款余额（亿元）	Balance of Deposits of Financial Institutions at Year-end （100 million yuan）	471.92	473.28
#住户存款	Individual Deposits	260.03	265.69
年底金融机构贷款余额（亿元）	Balance of Loans of Financial Institutions at Year-end （100 million yuan）	384.11	371.86
规模以上工业企业主要指标	**Major Economic Indicators of Industrial Enterprises Above Designated Size**		
工业总产值（亿元）	Gross Industrial Output Value （100 million yuan）	1255.91	1361.19
主营业务收入（亿元）	Main Business Income （100 million yuan）	1206.65	1322.13
利润总额（亿元）	Total Profits （100 million yuan）	82.80	74.50
工业用电量（亿千瓦时）	Industrial Electricity Consumption （100 million kw.h）	12.18	14.76
社会消费品零售总额（亿元）	Total Retail Sales of Consumer Goods （100 million yuan）	126.77	129.16
进出口总额（亿美元）	Total Imports （USD 100 million）	5.62	5.28
#出　口	Exports	4.80	4.54
实际到账注册外资（亿美元）	Foreign Capital Actually Utilized （USD 100 million）	1.31	2.80
全体居民人均可支配收入（元）	Per Capita Disposable Income of All Residents（yuan）	32728	26527
全体居民人均消费性支出（元）	Per Capita Consuming Expenditures of All Residents（yuan）	18904	17061
城镇常住居民人均可支配收入（元）	Per Capita Disposable Income of Permanent Urban Residents（yuan）	42407	37548
城镇常住居民人均消费支出（元）	Per Capita Consuming Expenditures of Permanent Urban Residents（yuan）	22486	21497
农村常住居民人均可支配收入（元）	Per Capita Disposable Income of Permanent Rural Residents（yuan）	21886	17355
农村常住居民人均消费支出（元）	Per Capita Consuming Expenditures of Permanent Rural Residents（yuan）	14890	13369

Appendix 5 Continued 5

泰州市 Taizhou City	兴化市 Xinghua City	靖江市 Jingjiang City	泰兴市 Taixing City	宿迁市 Suqian City	沭阳县 Suyang County	泗阳县 Siyang County	泗洪县 Sihong County
507.85	158.16	66.61	119.53	586.28	195.37	106.76	110.10
464.16	125.50	68.69	107.72	485.38	154.30	83.70	88.90
5787	2395	656	1170	8524	2299	1378	2694
3687.90	667.40	748.32	740.77	2126.19	630.13	362.24	361.32
1565.28	230.97	344.89	311.06	873.04	260.29	154.09	129.25
218.93	93.62	20.55	49.10	258.11	81.68	52.74	55.38
1811.04	268.49	384.08	357.97	1031.33	293.28	185.31	154.91
1657.93	305.29	343.69	333.70	836.75	255.17	124.19	151.03
79479	53186	108973	68768	43853	40719	43072	40394
2693.75	349.63	495.86	560.62	1838.97	455.59	336.10	336.04
316.56	40.85	61.61	52.79	235.67	71.75	33.68	31.59
256.89	33.52	50.83	43.81	196.95	58.85	28.27	26.72
429.90	82.50	69.95	67.45	405.78	112.69	69.46	66.96
4441.70	580.79	823.68	754.29	1819.81	394.83	263.26	250.02
2242.46	430.57	433.87	428.60	949.51	281.04	174.11	168.40
3228.08	392.98	615.11	502.24	1696.70	338.74	269.13	265.86
11063.14	1558.69	2002.83	2589.50	3863.32	1319.01	584.28	720.78
10792.62	1535.05	1946.08	2564.30	3714.77	1295.56	579.16	668.79
840.00	89.27	148.99	235.97	374.85	116.37	43.51	66.57
172.53	47.56	26.79	41.18	106.04	28.85	13.15	8.17
1001.64	154.61	159.41	191.52	626.64	175.49	88.88	93.41
102.29	5.40	29.89	24.34	25.99	5.80	3.27	1.42
63.77	4.92	18.07	12.54	18.50	4.63	3.19	1.17
10.66	0.49	2.56	3.24	2.98	0.73	0.35	0.07
25927	22558	27097	25508	17342	17521	16943	16191
16777	13760	19817	16122	11328	11721	11679	10619
34092	31170	36790	33800	22233	22098	21720	21191
21008	17798	24843	21117	14494	14770	14021	14117
16410	15527	18045	16392	12772	12940	12800	12477
11844	10464	15124	10630	8444	9031	9512	7005

附录 6 长江三角洲地区各城市主要经济指标（2015 年）
MAIN ECONOMIC INDICATORS BY CITY IN THE YANGSE RIVER DELTA（2015）

指 标	Item	上海市 Shanghai City	南京市 Nanjing City	无锡市 Wuxi City
土地面积（平方公里）	Area of Land （sq.km）	6341	6587	4627
年末户籍人口（万人）	Year-end Population （10000 persons）	1442.97	653.40	480.90
年末常住人口（万人）	Year-end permanent population （10000 persons）	2415.27	823.59	651.10
地区生产总值（亿元）	Gross Domestic Products （100 million yuan）	24964.99	9720.77	8518.26
#工 业	Industy	7109.94	3395.26	3837.28
按产业分	Grouped by Industries			
第一产业	Primary Industry	109.78	232.39	137.72
第二产业	Secondary Industry	7940.69	3916.77	4197.43
第三产业	Tertiary Industry	16914.52	5571.61	4183.11
人均地区生产总值（元）	Per Capita GDP （yuan）	103141	118171	130938
规模以上工业总产值（亿元）	Total Output Value of Industry above Designated Size （100 million yuan）	31322.62	12905.13	14549.87
社会消费品零售总额（亿元）	Total Retail of Consumer Goods （100 million yuan）	10131.50	4590.17	2847.61
固定资产投资完成额（亿元）	Investment in Fixed Assets （100 million yuan）	6352.70	5425.98	4888.55
#房地产投资	Real Estate Investment	3468.94	1429.02	991.66
进出口总额（亿美元）	Total Imports and Exports（USD 100 million）	4517.33	532.40	684.67
#出 口	Exports	1969.69	315.03	422.32
实际到帐注册外资（亿美元）	Foreign Capital Actually Used （USD 100 million）	184.59	33.35	32.02
一般公共预算收入（亿元）	General Public Budgetary Revenue （100 million yuan）	5519.50	1020.03	830.00
一般公共预算支出（亿元）	General Public Budgetary Expenditure （100 million yuan）	6191.56	1045.57	821.86
年底金融机构存款余额（亿元）	Balance of Deposits of Financial Institutions at Year-end （100 million yuan）	98266.49	25887.77	12710.45
年底金融机构贷款余额（亿元）	Balance of Loans of Financial Institutions at Year-end （100 million yuan）	48090.75	18217.80	9332.27
全体居民人均可支配收入（元）	Per Capita Disposable Income of All Residents（yuan）	49867	40455	39461
全体居民人均消费性支出（元）	Per Capita Consuming Expenditures of All Residents（yuan）	34784	24876	25954
城镇常住居民人均可支配收入（元）	Per Capita Disposable Income of Permanent Urban Residents（yuan）	52962	46104	45129
城镇常住居民人均消费支出（元）	Per Capita Consuming Expenditures of Permanent Urban Residents（yuan）	36946	27794	29466
农村常住居民人均可支配收入（元）	Per Capita Disposable Income of Permanent Rural Residents（yuan）	23205	19483	24155
农村常住居民人均消费支出（元）	Per Capita Consuming Expenditures of Permanent Rural Residents （yuan）	16152	14041	16469
全社会用电量（亿千瓦时）	Total Electriccity Consumed （100 million kw.h）	1405.56	495.18	600.50
#工 业	Industrial	787.03	300.54	472.24

常州市 Changzhou City	苏州市 Shanghai City	南通市 Nantong City	扬州市 Yangzhou City	镇江市 zhenjiang City	泰州市 Taizhou City	杭州市 Hangzhou City	宁波市 Ningbo City	嘉兴市 Jiaxing City	湖州市 Huzhou City
4372	8657	10549	6591	3840	5787	16596	9816	3915	5820
370.85	667.01	766.77	461.12	271.67	507.85	723.55	586.57	349.48	263.71
470.14	1061.60	730.00	448.36	317.65	464.16	901.80	782.50	458.50	295.00
5273.15	14504.07	6148.40	4016.84	3502.48	3687.90	10050.21	8003.61	3517.81	2084.26
2269.99	6490.44	2453.38	1749.58	1588.95	1565.28	3497.83	3632.86	1668.57	920.47
146.55	215.71	354.90	241.86	132.89	218.93	287.95	284.68	139.09	122.60
2516.04	7045.12	2977.53	2012.10	1726.96	1811.04	3909.01	4098.22	1850.68	1021.05
2610.56	7243.24	2815.97	1762.88	1642.63	1657.93	5853.25	3620.71	1528.04	940.60
112221	136702	84236	89647	110351	79479	112230	102374	76850	70893
11101.64	30249.25	13515.33	9194.19	8403.82	11063.14	12415.68	13869.46	7569.31	4413.10
1990.45	4461.62	2379.46	1236.96	1113.71	1001.64	4697.23	3349.63	1494.57	963.92
3398.97	5965.44	4376.03	2856.82	2541.07	2693.75	5556.32	4506.58	2513.82	1402.64
508.04	1864.95	690.94	378.18	355.78	245.57	2472.07	1228.84	458.41	323.39
280.41	3053.50	315.79	103.38	100.64	102.29	665.66	1003.72	310.85	102.07
212.56	1814.59	228.26	77.11	68.73	63.77	500.67	713.73	229.27	88.55
17.21	60.00	23.16	8.48	13.05	10.66	71.13	42.34	26.84	9.42
466.28	1560.76	625.64	336.75	302.85	316.56	1233.88	1006.41	350.35	191.31
485.33	1527.17	748.97	442.78	348.73	429.90	1205.48	1252.64	424.13	273.74
7438.68	23659.10	9659.15	4719.40	3969.11	4441.70	29003.07	15400.24	5775.41	3034.64
5354.58	19200.10	5997.24	3095.77	2982.60	3228.08	22395.29	14966.92	4718.35	2509.83
35379	42987	27584	26253	31263	25927	42642	41373	37139	34251
22234	26847	18358	16720	19570	16777	30181	26056	22336	22020
42710	50390	36291	32946	38666	34092	48316	47852	45499	42238
25358	31136	23680	19780	22859	21008	33818	29645	25544	26815
21912	25580	17267	16619	19214	16410	25719	26469	26838	24410
14764	16761	12052	12316	14217	11844	19334	17800	17522	16112
408.04	1311.72	349.19	211.50	216.27	227.46	646.38	585.07	413.35	198.91
325.49	1074.20	253.05	152.49	165.33	172.53	407.02	434.90	339.92	151.16

附录 6 续表 Appendix 6 continued

指 标	Item	绍兴市 Shaoxing City	舟山市 Zhoushan City	台州市 Taizhou City
土地面积（平方公里）	Area of Land （sq.km）	8279	1455	9411
年末户籍人口（万人）	Year-end Population （10000 persons）	443.11	97.36	597.49
年末常住人口（万人）	Year-end permanent population （10000 persons）	496.80	115.20	604.90
地区生产总值（亿元）	Gross Domestic Products （100 million yuan）	4465.97	1092.85	3553.85
#工 业	Industy	1957.29	356.17	1339.56
按产业分	Grouped by Industries			
第一产业	Primary Industry	198.94	111.01	229.75
第二产业	Secondary Industry	2252.87	449.63	1567.65
第三产业	Tertiary Industry	2014.15	532.21	1756.45
人均地区生产总值（元）	Per Capita GDP （yuan）	90003	95113	58917
规模以上工业总产值（亿元）	Total Output Value of Industry above Designated Size （100 million yuan）	9746.38	1633.37	3852.24
社会消费品零售总额（亿元）	Total Retail of Consumer Goods （100 million yuan）	1621.06	415.52	1826.68
固定资产投资完成额（亿元）	Investment in Fixed Assets （100 million yuan）	2582.84	1134.76	1996.03
#房地产投资	Real Estate Investment	622.65	193.59	438.69
进出口总额（亿美元）	Total Imports and Exports（USD 100 million）	299.02	117.01	211.66
#出 口	Exports	271.42	61.85	188.29
实际到帐注册外资（亿美元）	Foreign Capital Actually Used （USD 100 million）	9.42	0.78	1.16
一般公共预算收入（亿元）	General Public Budgetary Revenue （100 million yuan）	362.89	112.72	298.02
一般公共预算支出（亿元）	General Public Budgetary Expenditure （100 million yuan）	421.41	239.65	457.21
年底金融机构存款余额（亿元）	Balance of Deposits of Financial Institutions at Year-end （100 million yuan）	6820.96	1694.26	6188.65
年底金融机构贷款余额（亿元）	Balance of Loans of Financial Institutions at Year-end （100 million yuan）	5947.21	1458.38	5429.60
全体居民人均可支配收入（元）	Per Capita Disposable Income of All Residents（yuan）	38389	38254	33788
全体居民人均消费性支出（元）	Per Capita Consuming Expenditures of All Residents(yuan）	23906	25774	23822
城镇常住居民人均可支配收入（元）	Per Capita Disposable Income of Permanent Urban Residents（yuan）	46747	44845	43266
城镇常住居民人均消费支出（元）	Per Capita Consuming Expenditures of Permanent Urban Residents（yuan）	28156	30128	28892
农村常住居民人均可支配收入（元）	Per Capita Disposable Income of Permanent Rural Residents（yuan）	25648	25903	21225
农村常住居民人均消费支出（元）	Per Capita Consuming Expenditures of Permanent Rural Residents （yuan）	17123	17615	17102
全社会用电量（亿千瓦时）	Total Electriccity Consumed （100 million kw.h）	366.25	46.03	252.75
#工 业	Industrial	293.97	23.45	167.79

附录 7　主要统计指标解释

1. **地区生产总值**　指一个国家（地区）所有常住单位在一定时期内生产活动的最终成果。国内生产总值有三种表现形态，即价值形态、收入形态和产品形态。从价值形态看，它是所有常住单位在一定时期内所生产的全部货物和服务价值超过同期投入的全部非固定资产货物和服务价值的差额，即所有常住单位的增加值之和；从收入形态看，它是所有常住单位在一定时期内所创造并分配给常住单位和非常住单位的初次分配收入之和；从产品形态看，它是最终使用的货物和服务减去进口货物和服务。在实际核算中，国内生产总值的三种表现形态表现为三种计算方法，即生产法、收入法和支出法。三种方法分别从不同的方面反映地区生产总值及其构成。

2. **可比价格**　指对不同时期的价值进行对比时，扣除了价格变动的因素，以确切反映物量的变化情况。按可比价格计算的方法有两种：一是直接按产品产量乘不变价格计算；二是用物价指数换算。

3. **不变价格**　指以同类产品某年的平均价格作为固定价格，用于计算各年的产品价值。按不变价格计算的产品价值消除了价格变动因素，不同时期对比可以反映生产的发展速度。新中国成立后，随着工农业产品价格水平的变化，国家统计局先后五次制定了全国统一的工业产品不变价格和农业产品不变价格。从1952年到1957年使用1952年工（农）业产品不变价格，从1957年到1970年使用1957年不变价格，从1971年到1980年使用1970年不变价格，从1981年到1990年使用1980年不变价格，从1991年开始使用1990年不变价格。

4. **各个计划时期**　各个计划“时期”代表的年份如下：恢复时期为1950-1952年；第一个五年计划时期（简称“一五”时期）为1953-1957年；第二个五年计划时期（简称“二五”时期）为1958-1962年；调整时期为1963-1965年；第三个五年计划时期（简称“三五”时期）为1966-1970年；第四个五年计划时期（简称“四五”时期）为1971-1975年；第五个五年计划时期（简称“五五”时期）为1976-1980年；第六个五年计划时期（简称“六五”时期）为1981-1985年；第七个五年计划时期（简称“七五”时期）为1986-1990年；第八个五年计划时期（简称“八五”时期）为1991-1995年；第九个五年计划时期（简称“九五”时期）为1996-2000年；第十个五年计划时期（简称“十五”时期）从2001-2005年；第十一个五年计划时期（简称“十一五”时期）为2006-2010年；第十二个五年计划时期（简称“十二五”时期）为2011-2015年。

5. **平均增长速度**　指某种现象在一个较长时期中逐年增长的平均速度。其计算方法有两种：一是习惯上经常使用的“水平法”，又称几何水平法，是以间隔期最后一年的水平同基期水平对比来计算平均每年增长（或下降）速度；二是“累计法”，又称代数平均法或方程法，是以间隔期内各年水平的总和同基期水平对比来计算平均每年增长（或下降）速度。在一般正常情况下，两种方法计算的数值比较接近，但在经济发展不平衡，出现大起大落时，该两个数值差别较大。

本《年鉴》内所列的平均每年的增长速度，均用“水平法”计算。从某年到某年平均每年增长速度的年份，均不包括基期年在内。如改革开放35年以来的平均每年增长速度是以1978年为基期计算的，则写为1979-2013年平均每年增长速度，其余类推。

6. **企业（单位）登记注册类型**　是以在工商行政管理机关登记注册的各类企业为划分对象，以工商行政管理部门对企业登记注册的类型为依据，将企业登记注册类型分为内资企业、港澳台商投资企业和外商投资企业三大类。内资企业包括国有企业、集体企业、股份合作企业、联营企业、有限责任公司、股份有限公司、私营公司和其他企业;港澳台商投资企业和外商投资企业分别包括合资经营企业、合作经营企业、独资经营企业和股份有限公司。对不在工商行政管理部门进行登记注册的行政机关、事业单位和社会团体，主要按其经费来源和管理方式进行划分。

7. **国有企业**　指企业全部资产归国家所有，并按《中华人民共和国企业法人登记管理条例》规定登记注册的非公司制经济组织。不包括有限责任公司中的国有独资公司。

8. **集体企业**　指企业资产归集体所有，并按《中华人民共和国企业法人登记管理条例》规定登记注册的经济组织。

9. **股份合作企业**　指以合作制为基础，由企业职工共同出资入股，吸收一定比例的社会资产投资组建，实行自主经营，自负盈亏，共同劳动，民主管理，按劳分配与按股分红相结合的一种集体经济组织。

10. **联营企业**　指两个及两个以上相同或不同所有制性质的企业法人或事业单位法人，按自愿、平等、互利的原则，共同投资组成的经济组织。联营企业包括国有联营企业、集体联营企业、国有与集体联营企业和其他联营企业。

11. **有限责任公司**　指根据《中华人民共和国公司登记管理条例》规定登记注册，由两个以上、五十个以下的股东共同出资，每个股东以其所认缴的出资额对公司承担有限责任，公司以其全部资产对其债务承担责任的经济组织。有限责任公司包括国有独资公司以及其他有限责任公司。

12. **股份有限公司**　指根据《中华人民共和国公司登记管理条例》规定登记注册，其全部注册资本由等额股份构成并通过发行股票筹集资本，股东以其认购的股份对公司承担有限责任，公司以其全部资产对其债务承担责任的经济组织。

13. **私营企业**　指由自然人投资设立或由自然人控股，以雇佣劳动为基础的营利性经济组织。包括按照《公司法》、《合伙企业法》、《私营企业暂行条例》规定登记注册的私营有限责任公司、私营股份有限公司、私营合伙企业和私营独资企业。

14. **其他企业**　指上述企业之外的其他内资经济组织。

15. **港、澳、台投资企业**　指港、澳、台地区投资者参照中华人民共和国有关涉外经济的法律、法规，以合资、合作或独资的形式在祖国大陆举办的企业。包括合资经营企业、合作经营企业和独资企业。

16. 外商投资企业 指外国投资者根据中华人民共和国有关涉外经济的法律、法规，以合资、合作或独资的形式在中国大陆境内开办的企业。包括中外合资经营企业、中外合作经营企业和外资企业。

17. 三次产业 根据社会生产活动历史发展的顺序对产业结构的划分，产品直接取自自然界的部门称为第一产业，对初级产品进行再加工的部门称为第二产业，为生产和消费提供各种服务的部门称为第三产业。它是世界上通用的产业结构分类，但各国的划分不尽一致。我国的三次产业划分是：

第一产业是指农、林、牧、渔业（不含农、林、牧、渔服务业）。

第二产业是指采矿业（不含开采辅助活动），制造业（不含金属制品、机械和设备修理业），电力、热力、燃气及水生产和供应业，建筑业。

第三产业即服务业，是指除第一产业、第二产业以外的其他行业。第三产业包括：批发和零售业，交通运输、仓储和邮政业，住宿和餐饮业，信息传输、软件和信息技术服务业，金融业，房地产业，租赁和商务服务业，科学研究和技术服务业，水利、环境和公共设施管理业，居民服务、修理和其他服务业，教育，卫生和社会工作，文化、体育和娱乐业，公共管理、社会保障和社会组织，国际组织，以及农、林、牧、渔业中的农、林、牧、渔服务业，采矿业中的开采辅助活动，制造业中的金属制品、机械和设备修理业。

18. 人口数 指一定时点、一定地区范围内的有生命的个人的总和。年度统计的年末人口数是指每年12月31日24时的常住人口数。不包括户籍不在本市的外来人数。

19. 出生率（又称粗出生率） 指在一定时期内（通常为一年）出生的人数与同期平均人数（或期中人数）比率，一般用千分率表示。计算公式：

出生率=年出生人数/年平均人数×1000‰

出生人数是指活产婴儿，即胎儿脱离母体时（不管怀孕月数），有过呼吸或其他生命现象。

目前出生率的计算，在市级有公安的户籍口径、计生委的常住人口统计口径；国家、省级还有年度人口抽样调查公布口径等。本年鉴用的为公安口径出生数，包括补报往年出生数在内。

年平均人数是年初、年底人口数的平均数，也可用年中人口数代替。

20. 死亡率（又称粗死亡率） 指在一定时期内（通常为一年）一定地区的死亡人数与同期平均人数（或期中人数）之比，一般用千分率表示。计算公式：

死亡率=年死亡人数/年平均人数×1000‰

21. 人口自然增长率 指在一定时期内（通常为一年）人口自然增加数（出生人数减死亡人数）与该时期内平均人数（或期中人数）之比，一般用行千分率表示。计算公式：

人口自然增长率＝（本年出生人数—本年死亡人数）/年平均人数×1000‰

人口自然增长率＝人口出生率—人口死亡率

22. 人口预期寿命 指在一定年龄组死亡率水平下，对某一确定的年龄日后平均还能继续生存的年数（或该年龄组未来的平均预期寿命）。

23. 从业人员 指从事一定社会劳动并取得劳动报酬或经营收入的人员，包括在岗职工、再就业的离退休人员、私营业主、个体户主、私营和个体就业人员、乡镇企业就业人员、农村就业人员、其他就业人员（包括民办教师、宗教职业者、现役军人等）。这一指标反映了一定时期内全部劳动力资源的实际利用情况，是研究我国基本国情国力的重要指标。

24.单位从业人员 指在各级国家机关、政党机关、社会团体及企业、事业单位中工作，取得工资或其他形式的劳动报酬的全部人员。包括在岗职工、再就业的离退休人员、民办教师以及在各单位中工作的外方人员和港澳台方人员、兼职人员、借用的外单位人员和第二职业者。不包括离开本单位仍保留劳动关系的职工。各单位的就业人员反映了各单位实际参加生产或工作的全部劳动力。

25. 职 工 指在内资（国有、集体、股份合作、联营、有限责任公司、股份有限公司）单位、港澳台投资单位和外商投资单位及其附属机构工作，并由其支付工资的在岗人员以及不在岗但劳动关系在本单位的离岗人员。

26. 在岗职工 指在本单位工作并由单位支付工资的人员，以及有工作岗位，但由于学习、病伤产假等原因暂未工作，仍由单位支付工资的人员。

27. 离岗职工 指由于各种原因，已经离开本人的生产或工作岗位，并已不在本单位从事其他工作，但仍与用人单位保留劳动关系的职工。

28. 从业人员工资总额 指各单位在一定时期内直接支付给本单位全部从业人员的劳动报酬总额。包括在岗职工工资总额、劳务派遣人员工资总额和其他从业人员工资总额三部分。

29. 在岗职工工资总额 指各单位在一定时期内直接支付给本单位全部在岗职工的劳动报酬总额。

工资总额的计算原则应以直接支付给职工的全部劳动报酬为根据。各单位支付给职工的劳动报酬以及其他根据有关规定支付的工资，不论是计入成本的还是不计入成本的，不论是按国家规定列入计征奖金税项目的，还是未列入计征奖金税项目的，不论是以货币形式支付的还是以实物形式支付的，均包括在工资总额内。

30. 在岗职工平均工资 指各单位的在岗职工在一定时期内平均每人所得的货币工资额。它表明一定时期内职工工资收入高低程度，是反映职工工资水平的主要指标。计算公式为：

在岗职工平均工资=报告期实际支付的全部在岗职工工资总额/报告期全部在岗职工平均人数

31. 城镇登记失业人员 指在劳动年龄（16周岁至退休年龄）内，有劳动能力，有就业要求，处于无业状态，并在公共就业人才服务机构进行失业登记的城镇人员。

32.居民消费价格指数 居民消费价格，指城乡居民支付生活消费品和服务项目消费的价格，是社会产品和服务项目的最终价格，同人民生活密切相关，在整个国民经济价格体系中具有极为重要的地位。居民消费价格指数，就是指反映一定时期内居民消费价格变动趋势和变动程度的相对数。

33.商品零售价格指数 是反映一定时期内城乡商品零售价格变动趋势和程度的相对数。商品零售价格的变动直接影响到城乡居民的生活支出和国家的财政、影响居民购买力和市场供需平衡，影响消费与积累的比例。因此，计算零售价格指数，可以从一个侧面对上述经济活动进行观察和分析。

34.服务项目价格指数 指居民非商品服务性支出的相对数。服务项目包括：电信费、邮费、交通费、洗理美容费、文娱费、学杂保育费、修理及其他服务费、医疗保险服务费8个大类。

35.可支配收入 指调查户在调查期内获得的、可用于最终消费支出和储蓄的总和，即调查户可以用来自由支配的收入。可支配收入既包括现金，也包括实物收入。按照收入的来源，可支配收入包含四项，分别为：工资性收入、经营净收入、财产净收入和转移净收入。

36.工资性收入 指就业人员通过各种途径得到的全部劳动报酬和各种福利，包括受雇于单位或个人、从事各种自由职业、兼职和零星劳动得到的全部劳动报酬和福利。

37.经营净收入 指住户或住户成员从事生产经营活动所获得的净收入，是全部经营收入中扣除经营费用、生产性固定资产折旧和生产税之后得到的净收入。

38.财产净收入 指住户或住户成员将其所拥有的金融资产、住房等非金融资产和自然资源交由其他机构单位、住户或个人支配而获得的回报并扣除相关的费用之后得到的净收入。财产净收入包括利息净收入、红利收入、储蓄性保险净收益、转让承包土地经营权租金净收入、出租房屋净收入、出租其他资产净收入和自有住房折算净租金等。

39.转移净收入 指转移性收入减去转移性支出得到的净收入。

40.转移性收入 指国家、单位、社会团体对住户的各种经常性转移支付和住户之间的经常性收入转移。包括政府、非行政事业单位、社会团体对居民转移的养老金或退休金、社会救济和补助、惠农补贴、政策性生活补贴、救灾款、经常性捐赠和赔偿以及报销医疗费等；住户之间的赡养收入、经常性捐赠和赔偿以及农村地区（村委会）在外（含国外）工作的本住户非常住成员寄回带回的收入等。

41.转移性支出 指调查户对国家、单位、住户或个人的经常性或义务性转移支付。包括缴纳的税款、各项社会保障支出、赡养支出、经常性捐赠和赔偿支出以及其他经常转移支出等。

42.消费支出 指住户用于满足家庭日常生活消费需要的全部支出，包括用于消费品的支出和用于服务性消费的支出。根据用途不同，消费支出可划分为食品烟酒、衣着、居住、生活用品及服务、交通通信、教育文化娱乐、医疗保健、其他用品及服务八大类。根据来源不同，消费支出可划分为现金消费支出、实物消费支出（含自产自用、来自单位、来自政府和其他社会组织）。

43. 固定资产投资 固定资产投资是社会固定资产再生产的主要手段。固定资产投资额是以货币表现的建造和购置固定资产活动的工作量，它是反映固定资产投资规模、结构和发展速度的综合性指标，又是观察工程进度和考核投资效果的重要依据。

44. 房地产开发投资 指各种登记注册类型的房地产开发公司、商品房建设公司及其他房地产开发单位统一开发的包括统代建、拆迁还建的住宅、厂房、仓库、饭店、宾馆、度假村、写字楼、办公楼等房屋建筑物和配套的服务设施、土地开发工程（如道路、给水、排水、供电、供热、通讯、平整场地等基础设施工程）的投资。还包括非房地产企业实际从事房地产开发或经营活动，不包括单纯的土地交易活动。

45. 固定资产投资的资金来源 根据固定资产投资的资金来源不同，分为上年末结余资金、本年实际到位资金小计。其中本年实际到位资金小计又分为国家预算资金、国内贷款、债券、利用外资、自筹资金和其他资金来源6种。

46. 固定资产投资按构成分 固定资产投资活动按其工程内容和实现方式分为建筑工程、安装工程、设备工器具购置、其他费用4个部分。

47. 新增固定资产 指通过投资活动所形成的新的固定资产价值。包括已经建成投入生产或交付使用的工程投资和达到固定资产标准的设备、工具、器具的投资及有关应摊入的费用。它是以价值形式表示的固定资产投资成果的综合性指标。

48. 固定资产交付使用率 指在一定时期所增固定资产与同期完成投资额的比率。它是反映各个时期固定资产动用速度，衡量建设过程中投资改革的一个综合性指标。

49. 施工项目 指报告期内正式进行过建筑或安装施工活动的建设项目。包括报告期内新开工项目、报告期以前开工跨入报告期继续施工的项目，报告期施过工并在报告期内全部建成投产的项目，报告期之前全部停缓建在报告期恢复施工的项目，报告期进行过施工又在报告期内全部停缓建的项目。

50. 全部建成投产项目 工业项目是指设计文件规定形成生产能力的主体工程及其相应配套的辅助设施全部建成，经负荷试运转，证明具备生产设计规定合格产品的条件，并经过验收鉴定合格或达到竣工验收标准，与生产性工程配套的生产福利设施可以满足近期正常生产的需要，正式移交生产的建设项目。非工业项目是指设计文件规定的主体工程和相应的配套工程全部建成，能够发挥设计规定的全部效益，经验收鉴定合格或达到竣工验收标准，正式移交使用的建设项目。

51. 房屋施工面积 指在报告期内施工的全部房屋（包括地下室、半地下室以及配套房屋）建筑面积。包括本期新开工的面积和上年开工跨入本期继续施工的房屋面积，以及上期已停建在本期恢复施工的房屋面积。本期竣工和本期施工后又停建缓建的房屋面积仍包括在施工面积中，多层建筑应填各层建筑面积之和。

52. 房屋竣工面积 指在报告期内房屋建筑按照设计要求已全部完工，达到住人和使用条件，经验收鉴定合格或达到竣工验收标准，可正式移交使用的各栋房屋建筑面积的总和。

53. 住宅面积 指施工和竣工房屋建筑面积中供居住用的施工房屋建筑面积。

54. 商品房销售面积 指报告期内出售商品房屋的合同总面积（即双方签署的正式买卖合同中所确定的建筑面积）。本月销售面积指从本月1日起至本月最后一天止出售商品房屋的合同总面积。商品房销售面积由现房销售面积和期房销售面积两部分组成。

55. 待售面积 指报告期末已竣工的可供销售或出租的商品房屋建筑面积中，尚未销售或出租的商品房屋建筑面积，包括以前年度竣工和本期竣工的房屋面积，但不包括报告期已竣工的拆迁还建、统建代建、公共配套建筑、房地产公司自用及周转房等不可销售或出租的房屋面积。

56. 农林牧渔业总产值 是以货币表现的农、林、牧、渔业全部产品的总量和对农林牧渔业生产活动进行的各种支持性服务活动的价值。它反映一定时期内农林牧渔业生产的总规模和总成果。农、林、牧、渔业的统计范围是：

（1）农业 包括农作物种植业和其他农业。

农作物种植业包括谷物、豆类、薯类、棉花、油料、糖料、麻类、烟叶、蔬菜、药材、瓜类和其他农作物的种植以及茶园、桑园、果园的生产经营。

其他农业包括采集野生植物的果实、纤维、树胶、树脂、油料以及柴草、野生药材、菌类等及农民家庭兼营的商品性工业。

（2）林业 包括林木的栽培（不包括茶园、桑园和果园的栽培、管理和收获等活动）、林产品的采集和村及村以下合作经济组织和农户的竹木采伐。

（3）牧业 包括除渔业养殖以外的一切动物饲养和放牧以及野生动物的捕猎和饲养。

（4）渔业 包括水生动物和海藻类植物的养殖和捕捞。

（5）农林牧渔服务业 包括灌溉服务、农产品初级加工服务、其他农业服务、林业服务、兽医服务、其他畜牧服务、渔业服务业等。

57. 粮食产量 指全社会的粮食产量。包括国有经济经营的、集体统一经营的和农民家庭经营的粮食产量，还包括工矿企业家属办的农场和其他生产单位的产量。（粮食除包括稻谷、小麦、玉米、高粱、谷子及其他杂粮外，还包括薯类和豆类）。1989年以前全国粮食产量数据主要靠全面报表取得，1989年开始使用抽样调查数据。

58. 油料产量 指全部油料作物的生产量。包括花生、油菜籽、芝麻、向日葵籽、胡麻籽（亚麻籽）和其他油料。不包括大豆，也不包括木本油料和野生油料。花生以带壳干花生计算。

59. 水产品产量 指人工养殖的水产品和天然生长的水产品捕捞量，包括海水的鱼类、虾蟹类、贝类和藻类以及内陆水域的鱼类、虾蟹类和贝类，不包括淡水生植物。

60. 猪、牛、羊肉产量 指当年出栏并已屠宰后除去头蹄下水后带骨肉的重量（即胴体重）。

61. 耕地面积 指可以用来种植农作物、经常进行耕锄的田地，除包括熟地、当年新开荒地、连续撂荒未满三年的耕地和当年的休闲地（轮歇地）外，还包括以种植农作物为主并附带种植桑树、茶树、果树和其他林木的土地，以及沿海、沿湖地区已围垦利用的“海涂”、“湖田”等面积。但不包括属于专业性的桑园、茶园、果园、果木苗圃、林地、芦苇地、天然或人工草地面积。

62 农作物播种面积 指实际播种或移植有农作物的面积。凡是实际种植有农作物的面积，不论种植在耕地上还是种植在非耕地上，均包括在农作物播种面积中，同时还包括因遭灾而重新改种和补种的农作物面积。目前，农作物播种面积主要包括粮食、油料、棉花、麻类、糖料、烟叶、药材、蔬菜、瓜类和其他农作物等十大类。

63. 有效灌溉面积 指具有一定的水源，地块比较平稳，灌溉工程或设备已经配套，在一般年景下当年能够进行正常灌溉耕地面积。在一般情况下，该面积应等于灌溉工程或设备已经配套，能够进行正常灌溉的水田和水源地面积之和。

64. 农用化肥使用量 指本年内实际用于农业生产的化肥数量，包括氮肥、磷肥、钾肥和复合肥。并要求按折纯量计算数量。折纯量指氮肥、磷肥、钾肥分别按氮、五氧化二磷、钾的100%成分进行折纯后的数量，复合肥按其所含主要成分折算的。

65. 农业机械总动力 指主要用于农、林、牧、渔业的各种动力机械的动力总和。包括耕作机械、排灌机械、收获机械、农产品加工机械、运输机械、植物保护机械、牧业机械、林业机械、渔业机械和其他农业机械[内燃机按引擎马力折成瓦（特）计算，电动机按功率折成瓦（特）计算]。不包括专门用于乡、镇、村、组办工业、基本建设、非农业运输、科学试验和教学等非农业生产方面用的动力机械与作业机械。但从事农副产品初级加工的村户工业的机械动力统计在内。

66. 期初（末）畜禽存栏数 指本期期初（末）农村各种合作经济组织和国营农场、农民个人、机关、团体、学校、工矿企业、部队等单位以及城镇居民饲养的大牲畜、猪、羊、家禽等畜禽的存栏数。从1997年起，猪及家禽调查方法，由全面调查改为抽样调查。

67. 工 业 指从事自然资源的开采，对采掘品和农产品进行加工和再加工的物质生产部门。具体包括：（1）对自然资源的开采，如采矿、晒盐、森林采伐等（但不包括禽兽捕猎和水产捕捞）；（2）对农副产品的加工、再加工，如粮油加工、食品加工、轧花、缫丝、纺织、制革等；（3）对采掘品的加工、再加工，如炼铁、炼钢、化工生产、石油加工、机器制造、木材加工等，以及电力、自来水、煤气的生产和供应等；（4）对工业品的修理、翻新，如机器设备的修理、交通运输工具（包括小卧车）的修理等。

68. **轻工业** 指主要提供生活消费品和制作手工工具的工业。另一定义为：指生产消费资料的工业。包括：（1）以农产品为原料的。如棉、毛、麻、丝的纺织及缝纫，皮革及其制品，纸浆及造纸，食品制造等工业；（2）以非农产品为原料的。如日用金属、日用化工、日用玻璃、日用陶瓷、化学纤维及其织品、火柴、生活用木制品等工业。轻工业产品大部分是生产消费品，一部分作为原料和半成品用于生产，如化学纤维、工业用布、纸张、盐等。

69. **重工业** 指为国民经济各部门提供物质技术基础的主要生产资料的工业。按其生产性质和产品用途，可以分为下列三类：（1）采掘（伐）工业，是指对自然资源的开采，包括石油开采、煤炭开采、金属矿开采、非金属矿开采和木材采伐等工业；（2）原材料工业，是指向国民经济各部门提供基本材料、动力和燃料的工业。包括金属冶炼及加工、炼焦及焦炭化学、化工原料、水泥、人造板以及电力、石油和煤炭加工等工业；（3）加工工业，是指对工业原材料进行再加工制造的工业。包括装备国民经济各部门的机械设备制造工业、金属结构、水泥制品等工业，以及为农业提供的生产资料如化肥、农药等工业。

根据上述划分原则，修理业中以重工业产品为修理作业对象的划为重工业，反之划为轻工业。

70. **工业总产值** 指工业企业在报告期内生产的以货币形式表现的工业最终产品和提供工业劳务活动的总价值量。包括：生产的成品价值、对外加工费收入、自制半成品在制品期末期初差额价值。

71. **工业销售产值** 指以货币表现的工业企业在一定时期内销售的本企业生产的工业产品总量。包括已销售的成品、半成品价值，对外提供的工业性作业价值和对本单位基本建设部门、生活福利部门等提供的产品和工业性作业及自制设备的价值。已销售的成品、半成品不论是本期生产的、还是上期生产的，只要是本期销售出去的均包括在内。对外提供的工业性作业是指企业按合同对外提供的工业性劳务。企业为本单位基本建设部门、生活福利部门等提供的产品和工业性作业及自制设备也应视同销售，这部分也作为销售统计。

工业销售产值的计算范围、计算价格和计算方法与工业总产值一致，但两者计算的基础不同；工业销售产值计算的基础是产品销售总量，工业总产值计算的基础是工业产品生产总量。

72. **应收账款** 指企业因销售商品、提供劳务等经营活动，应向购货单位或接受劳务单位收取的款项，主要包括企业销售商品或提供劳务等应向有关债务人收取的价款及代购货单位垫付的包装费、运杂费等。

73. **实收资本** 指企业各投资者实际投入的资本（或股本）总额，包括货币、实物、无形资产等各种形式的投入。按投资主体可分为国家资本、集体资本、法人资本、个人资本、港澳台资本和外商资本。

74. **资产总计** 指企业过去的交易或者事项形成的、由企业拥有或者控制的、预期会给企业带来经济利益的资源。

75. **流动资产合计** 资产满足以下条件之一应归为流动资产：（1）预计在一个正常营业周期中变现、出售或耗用，主要包括存货、应收账款等；（2）主要为交易目的而持有；（3）预计在资产负债表日起一年内（含一年）变现；（4）自资产负债日起一年内，交换其他资产或清偿负债的能力不受限制的现金或现金等价物。

76. **固定资产合计** 指企业为生产商品、提供劳务、出租或经营管理而持有的，使用寿命超过一个会计年度的有形资产。

77. **固定资产原价** 指固定资产的成本，包括企业在购置、自行建造、安装、改建、扩建、技术改造某项固定资产时所发生的全部支出总额。

78. **累计折旧** 指企业在报告期末提取的历年固定资产折旧累计数。

79. **本年折旧** 指企业在报告期内提取的固定资产折旧合计数。根据会计“财务状况变动表”中“固定资产折旧”项的数值填报。

80. **负债合计** 指企业过去的交易或者事项形成的，预期会导致经济利益流出企业的现时义务。负债一般按偿还期长短分为流动负债和非流动负债。

81. **流动负债合计** 负债满足下列条件之一的应归为流动负债：（1）预计在一个正常营业周期中清偿；（2）主要为交易目的而持有；（3）自资产负债表日起一年内到期应予清偿；（4）企业无权自主地将清偿推迟至资产负债表日后一年以上。包括短期借款、应付票据、应付账款、应付职工薪酬、应交税费等项目。

82. **非流动负债** 指流动负债之外的负债。包括长期借款、应付债券等。根据会计“资产负债表”中“非流动负债合计”项目的期末余额数填报。

83. **所有者权益合计** 指企业资产扣除负债后由所有者享有的剩余权益。公司的所有者权益又称股东权益。包括实收资本、资本公积、盈余公积、未分配利润等。

84. **主营业务收入** 指企业确认的销售商品、提供劳务等主营业务的收入。

85. **主营业务税金及附加** 指企业经营主要业务应负担的营业税、消费税、城市维护建设税、教育费附加等。

86. **利税总额** 指企业产品销售税金及附加、应交增值税和利润总额之和。

87. **工业成本费用利润率** 该指标反映工业投入的生产成本及费用的经济效益，同时也反映企业降低成本所取得的经济效益。计算公式为：

工业成本费用利润率=利润总额/成本费用总额

88. 工业产品销售率 该指标反映工业产品已实现销售的程度，是分析工业产销衔接情况、研究工业产品满足社会需求的指标。计算公式为：

工业产品销售率 =（现价工业销售产值/现价工业总产值）×100%

89. 建筑业总产值 是以货币表现的建筑业企业在一定时期内生产的建筑业产品和服务的总和。建筑业总产值包括三部份内容：

①建筑工程产值：指列入建筑工程预算内的各种工程价值。

②设备安装工程产值：指设备安装工程价值。

③其他产值：指房屋构筑物修理产值、非标准设备制造产值、总包企业向分包企业收取的管理费以及不能明确划分的施工活动所完成的产值。

90.竣工产值 一般是以单位工程为对象,当该工程按照设计所规定的工程内容全部完成,达到了设计规定的交工条件,经有关部门检查验收鉴定合格的单位工程价值工程,即为竣工产值。竣工产值包括范围应是报告期内竣工单位工程从开工到竣工的全部自行完成的价值，如果一个单位工程跨两个年度施工,其竣工价值应当包括上年度完成的价值。有些大型单位工程，如大型厂房、高级宾馆、各种管道、公路、铁路等，能够分跨、分层、分段施工并按合同规定，能够分开交付使用的，可以分开计算竣工产值。竣工产值不包括附属辅助企业或内部核算的其他单位为外单位生产和服务的价值。

91.房屋建筑施工面积 指报告期内施过工的全部房屋建筑面积，它包括本期新开工的面积、上期跨入本期继续施工的房屋面积、上期停缓建在本期恢复工的房屋面积、本期竣工的房屋面积以及本期施工后又停缓建的房屋面积。

92.房屋建筑竣工面积 指在报告期内房屋建筑按照设计要求已全部完工，达到了使用条件，经检查验收鉴定合格的房屋建筑面积。计算房屋竣工面积，必须严格执行房屋竣工验收标准。对民用建筑来讲，一般应按设计要求在土建工程和房屋本身附属的水、卫、气、暖等工程已经完工，通风、电梯等设备已安装完毕，做到水通、灯亮、经验收鉴定合格，并正式交付使用单位后，才能计算竣工面积。对于工业及科研单位等生产性房屋建筑：一般应按设计要求在土建工程（包括水、暖、电、卫、通风）及属于房屋组成部分的生活间、操作间等已经完成，经验收合格后才计算竣工面积。只差安装工艺设备、管线工程的亦可以计算竣工面积。

93. 自有机械设备年底总台数 指归本企业（或单位）所有，属于本企业固定资产的生产性机械设备年末总台数。包括施工机械、生产设备、运输设备以及其他设备。

94. 自有施工机械设备年底总功率 指本企业（或单位）自有施工机械、生产设备、运输设备以及其他设备等列为在册固定资产的生产性机械设备年末总功率，按设定能力或查定能力计算。包括机械本身的动力和为该机械服务的单独动力设备，如电动机等。计量单位用千瓦，动力换算可按1马力 = 0.735千瓦折合成千瓦数。电焊机、变压器、锅炉不计算动力。

95. 公路里程 指在一定时期内实际达到《公路工程技术标准JTJ0l—88》规定的等级公路，并经公路主管部门正式验收交付使用的公路里程数。其计算单位为：KM。它包括大中城市的郊区公路以及通过小城镇街道部分的公路里程，也包括桥梁、渡口的长度，但不包括大中城市的街道、厂矿、林区生产用道和农业生产用道的里程。两条或多条公路共同经由同一路段，只计算一次，不得重复计算里程长度。公路里程是反映公路建设发展规模的重要指标，也是计算运输网密度等指标的基础资料。

96. 内河航道里程 也称“内河通航里程”，是反映内河水运网规模、水平和发展情况的主要指标，是指在一定时期内，能通航运输船舶及排筏的天然河流、湖泊水库、运河及通航渠道的长度。包括全年季节性通航累计三个月以上的航道，但不包括仅供零散流放竹、木排的河道。

97. 货（客）运量 指在一定时期内，各运输部门实际运送的货物（旅客）数量。是反映运输业为国民经济和人民生活服务的数量指标，也是制定和检查运输生产计划，研究运输发展规模和速度的重要指标。货运按吨计算，客运按人计算。货物不论运输距离长短，货物类别，均按实际重量统计；旅客不论行程远近或票价多少，均按一人一次作为客运量统计。半价票、小孩票也按一人统计。

98. 货物（旅客）周转量 指在一定时期内，由各种运输工具运送的货物（旅客）数量与其相应运输距离的乘积之总和，是反映运输业生产总成果的重要指标，也是编制和检查运输生产计划，计算运输效率、劳动生产率以及核算运输单位成本的主要基础资料。通常以吨公里和人公里为计算单位。计算货物周转量通常按发出站与到达站之间的最短距离，也就是计费距离计算。

99. 邮电业务总量 指以价值量形式表现的邮电通信企业为社会提供各类邮电通信服务的总数量。邮电业务量按专业分类包括函件、包件、汇票、报刊发行、邮政快件、特快专递、集邮、固定电话、出租电路、移动电话、分组交换数据通信、出租代维等。计算方法为各类产品乘以相应的平均单价（不变价）之和，再加上出租电路和设备、代用户维护电话交换机和线路等的服务收入。

100. 移动电话用户 是指通过移动电话交换机进入移动电话网、占用移动电话号码的电话用户。用户数量以报告期末在移动电话营业部门实际办理登记手续进入移动电话网的户数进行计算，一部移动电话统计为一户。

101. 英特网用户数 指办理登记手续且已接入国际互联网的用户数，包括局域网、城域网和广域网，包括拨号上网用户和专线上网用户。

102. 社会消费品零售总额 指企业（单位、个体户）通过交易直接售给个人、社会集团非生产、非经营用的实物商品金额，以及提供餐饮服务所取得的收入金额。个人包括城乡居民和入境人员，社会集团包括机关、社会团体、部队、学校、企事业单位、居委会或村委会等。

103. 批发零售贸易业 指不直接从事商品的生产，而是从工农业生产者或从商品流通企业购进商品，不做任何加工，或只做简单的加工（如清洗、整理、分类、包装等），通过转卖以获取经济利益的单位。

104.住宿业 指有偿为顾客提供临时住宿的服务活动。

105. 餐饮业 指在一定的场所内，以烹饪、调制等手段，向购买者提供各种主要供现场消费的食品、饮料，并且所提供的这种服务要大于所提供的其他服务（如娱乐）的单位。

106. 限额以上批发企业 指年主营业务收入在2000万元及以上的批发贸易企业。

107. 限额以上零售企业 指年主营业务收入在500万元及以上的零售企业。

108. 限额以上餐饮企业 指年主营业务收入在200万元及以上的餐饮企业。

109. 商品销售总额 指对本企业以外的单位和个人出售的商品（包括售给本单位消费用的商品）金额。这个指标反映批发零售贸易企业在国内市场上销售商品以及出口商品的总量。包括：（1）售给城乡居民和社会集团消费的商品；（2）售给工业、农业等各行业作为生产、经营使用的商品；（3）售给批发零售贸易业作为转卖或加工后转卖的商品；（4）对国（境）外直接出口的商品。

110. 商品交易市场成交额 指商品交易市场内所有经营者所实现的商品销售金额。商品交易市场包括消费品市场和生产资料市场。

111. 私营企业注册资本 指私营企业办理开业登记，或变更登记时核准的资金数，不包括银行贷款。

112. 个体工商业户数 指已经领取《营业执照》或《临时营业执照》的个体工商户的数量。

113. 个体工商业从业人员 指经过工商行政管理部门核准的、参加经营活动并领取报酬的所有人员，包括个体经营者本人、帮手、学徒等。

114. 个体工商业注册资金 指申请登记或变更登记时核准的资金。

115. 利用外资 指我国各级政府、部门、企业和其他经济组织通过对外借款、吸收外商直接投资以及用其他方式筹措的境外现汇、设备、技术等。

116. 外商直接投资 是指外国企业和经济组织或个人（包括华侨、港澳台胞以及我国在境外注册的企业）按我国有关政策、法规，用现汇、实物、技术等在中国大陆开办外商独资企业、与中国大陆的企业或经济组织共同举办中外合资经营企业、合作经营企业或者合作开发资源的投资（包括外商投资收益的再投资）以及经政府有关部门批准的项目投资总额内，企业从境外借入的资金。

117. 对外承包工程 包括各对外承包公司以招标议标承包方式承揽的下列业务（1）承包国外工程建设项目。（2）承包我国对外经援项目。（3）承包我国驻外机构的工程建设项目。（4）与外国承包公司合营或联合承包工程项目时我国公司分包部分。（5）以服务成果向业主收费的技术服务项目（包括承担地形地貌测绘；地质资源勘探与普查；建设区域规划；提供设计文件、图纸、生产工艺技术资料和工程技术经济咨询；工程项目的可行性考察、研究和评估；进行技术指导和培训人员等）。（6）对外承包兼营的房屋开发业务。对外承包工程的营业额是以货币表现的本期内完成的对外承包工程的工作量，包括以前年度签订的合同和本年度新签订的合同在报告期完成的工作量。

118. 对外劳务合作 指以收取工资的形式向业主或承包商提供技术和劳动服务的活动。我国对外承包公司在境外开办的合营企业，中国公司同时又提供劳务的，其劳务部分也纳入劳务合作统计。劳务合作营业额按报告期内向雇主提交的结算数（包括工资、加班费和奖金等）统计。

119. 国际旅游人数 指来中国大陆参观、访问、旅行、探亲、访友、休养、考察、参加会议和从事经济、科技、文化、教育、体育、宗教等活动的外国人、华侨、港澳和台湾同胞的人数。不包括外国在我国的常驻机构，如使领馆、通讯社、企业办事处的工作人员；来我国常住的外国专家、留学生以及在岸逗留不过夜人员。

120. 全社会用电量 指全年用电的总量，按用户的用电性质分为："农村用电"、工业用电"、"交通运输用电"和"城乡居民生活用电"等，各类用电中均包括电力企业售给本市用户的电量、自备电厂自发自用电量（包括余热发电量）和自备电厂售给附近用户的电量以及趸售电量。

121. 工业企业能源消费量 指工业企业在生产过程中作为燃料、原材料、动力、辅助材料使用的能源、工艺用能及非生产用能。

122. 财政总收入 指国家财政参与社会产品分配所取得的收入，是实现国家职能的财力保证。按我省口径，财政总收入为公共财政预算收入、基金收入和上划中央四税之和。

123. 财政支出 指国家财政将筹集起来的资金进行分配使用的数额。以满足经济建设和各项事业的需要。

124. 存　款 指企业、机关、团体或居民根据可以收回的原则，把货币资金存入银行或其他信用机构保管并取得一定利息的一种信用活动形式。根据存款对象的不同可划分为企业存款、财政存款、机关团体存款、基本建设存款、城镇储蓄存款、农村存款等项目。它是银行信贷资金的主要来源。

125. 城乡储蓄存款余额 城乡储蓄存款，包括城镇居民储蓄存款和农民个人储蓄存款两部分，不包括居民的手存现金和工矿企业、部队、机关团体等集团存款。城乡居民储蓄存款余额指城乡居民存入银行及农村信用社储蓄的时点数（存入数扣除取出数的余额），如月末、季末或年末数额。

126. 贷　款 指银行或其他信用机构根据必须归还的原则，按一定利率，为企业、个人等提供资金的一种信用活动形式。我国银行贷款，分流动资金贷款、固定资产贷款、城乡个体工商户贷款以及农户贷款等科目。

127. 承保额（保险金额） 指保险人对被保险人负担损失补偿或约定给付的金额。它是保险合同上的最高责任额，也是计算保费的依据。

128. 保费（保险费） 指保险人根据保险合同的有关规定，为被保险人取得因约定危险事故发生所造成的经济损失补偿（或给付）权利，付给保险人的代价。

129. 保险赔款 指保险事故发生后，经查证确属保险责任范围以内的保险标的损失，保险人根据保险合同的规定履行赔偿义务，给予被保险人的款项。

130. 年底实有铺装道路长度 指除土路外，路面经过铺装宽度在3.5米以上的道路，包括高级、次高级道路和普通道路。

131. 城市桥梁 指城市范围内，修建在河道上的桥梁和道路与道路立交、道路跨越铁路的立交桥，以及人行天桥。包括永久性桥和半永久性桥，不包括临时性桥、铁路桥、涵洞。

132. 城市下水道总长度 指所有排水总管、干管、支管及暗渠、检查井、连接井进出水口等长度之和。

133. 城市污水日处理能力 指污水处理厂每昼夜处理污水量的设计能力。

134. 城市园林绿地面积 指城市公共绿地、专用绿地、生产绿地、防护绿地、郊区风景名胜区的全部面积。

135. 公园绿地 指城市中向公众开放的、以游憩为主要功能，有一定的游憩设施和服务设施，同时兼有健全生态、美化景观、防灾减灾等综合作用的绿化用地。

136. 年底自来水生产能力 指年底城建部门管理的自来水厂和自备水源的社会单位取水、净化、送水、出厂输水干管等环节的实际生产能力。

137. 年底实有公共汽车 指年底可参加营运的全部车辆数，包括年底营运车辆和库存查封未参加营运的车辆，不包括非营运车辆，如架线车、油罐车、工程车、货车及其他专用车辆和借入的客运车辆。

138. 营运线路长度 指设置的固定营运的线路长度，包括郊区营运线路长度。不包括临时行驶的线路长度。

139. 年底供水管道长度 指从送水泵到用户水表之间所有管道的长度。

140. 全年供水总量 指公用自来水厂和自备水源的社会单位全年的供水总量，包括有效供水量及损失水量。

141. 生活用水量 指居民日常生活与公共福利设施的用水量。包括居民、饮食店、旅馆、医院、理发店、浴池、洗衣店、游泳池、商店、学校、机关、部队等单位的用水量。

142. 城市人口用水普及率 指城市用水的非农业人口数（不包括临时人口和流动人口）与城市非农业人口总数之比，计算公式：

用水普及率＝城市用水的非农业人口数/城市非农业人口数×100%

143. 输气管道长度 指由压缩机、鼓风机、储气罐的出口到用户立管之间的全部管道长度。

144. 全年供气总量 指全年售给各类用户的全部煤气量。包括工业用量、家庭用量和其他用量。

145. 城市用气普及率 指使用煤气（包括人工煤气、液化石油气、天然气）的城市非农业人口数（不包括临时人口和流动人口）与城市非农业人口总数之比。计算公式：

城市用气普及率＝城市用气的非农业人口数/城市非农业人口数×100%

146. 废水排放总量 指生产废水和生活污水的排放总量。生产废水指企、事业单位在生产、科研过程中向外排放的所有排放口的废水量总和。生活污水指城镇居民区和企、事业单位职工集中居住区排放的污水量。

147. 工业废水排放量 指经过企业厂区所有排放口排到企业外部的工业废水量。包括生产废水、外排的直接冷却水、废气治理设施废水、超标排放的矿井地下水和与工业废水混排的厂区生活污水，不包括独立外排的间接冷却水（清浊不分流的间接冷却水应计算在内）。

148. 工业废气排放总量 指企业厂区内燃料燃烧和生产工艺过程中产生的各种排入空气中含有污染物的气体的总量，以标准状态（273K，101325Pa）计。

149. 一般工业固体废物综合利用量 指通过回收、加工、循环、交换等方式，从固体废物中提取或者使其转化为可以利用的资源、能源和其他原材料的固体废物量（包括当年利用的往年工业固体废物累计贮存量）。如用作农业肥料、生产建筑材料、筑路等。

150. 一般工业固体废物处置量 指调查年度企业将工业固体废物焚烧和用其他改变工业固体废物的物理、化学、生物特性的方法，达到减少或者消除其危险成分的活动，或者将工业固体废物最终置于符合环境保护规定要求的填埋场的活动中，所消纳固体废物的量。处置方式如：填埋、焚烧、专业贮存场（库）封场处理、深层灌注、回填矿井及海洋处置（经海洋管理部门同意投海处置）等。

151. 工业烟（粉）尘排放量 指企业在燃料燃烧和生产工艺过程中排入大气的烟尘及工业粉尘的总质量之和。

152. R & D 是"研究与发展"（Research and development）的英文缩写。其含义是指在科学技术领域（包括自然科学、农业科学、医药科学、工程与技术科学、人文与社会科学领域），为了增加知识的总量，以及运用这些知识而进行的系统的、创造性的活动。R&D包括基础研究、应用研究、试验发展三类活动。

153. 独立研究与开发机构 指有明确的任务和研究方向，有一定学术水平的业务骨干和一定数量的研究人员，具有研究、开发、开展学术工作的基本条件，主要进行科学研究与技术开发活动，并且在行政上有独立的组织形式，财务上独立核算盈亏，有权与其他单位签订合同，在银行有单独户头的单位。

154. 科学家和工程师 指具有大学本科以上学历的人员和不具备上述学历但已评定为高、中级职称的人员。

155. 独立研究与开发机构职工　指在科学研究与技术开发机构工作，并由其支付工资的各种人员。包括长期职工和临时职工，不包括编制以外的离休、退休人员和停薪留职人员，但包括招聘人员。

156. 研究与发展经费支出　指报告期内用于研究与实验发展课题活动（基础研究、应用研究、实验发展）的全部实际支出。包括用于研究与发展课题活动的直接支出，还包括间接用于研究与发展活动的一切支出。

157. 发　明　专利法及其实施细则所称的发明是指对有关产品、方法或其改进所提出的新的技术方案。

158. 实用新型　专利法及其实施细则所称的实用新型是指对产品的形状、构造或者其结合所提出的适于实用的新的技术方案。

159. 外观设计　专利法及其实施细则所称的外观设计是指对产品形状、图案、色彩或者其结合所作出的富有美感并适于工业上应用的新设计。

160. 网上登记技术合同数　指本地区在全国技术合同网上登记系统中登记的技术合同数。

161. 网上登记技术合同成交金额　指本地区在全国技术合同网上登记系统中登记的技术合同成交金额。

162. 科技企业孵化器　是指以促进科技成果转化、培养高新技术企业和企业家为宗旨的科技创业服务机构。包括科技创业服务中心、大学科技园、归国留学人员创业园、软件园等综合型、专业技术型科技企业孵化器。

163. 在孵企业总收入　指在统计年度内由孵化器孵化的企业所实现的技、工、贸等各种收入之和。

164. 在孵企业从业人员　指本报告期末在孵化器孵化的企业的人员总数。

165. 毕业企业　指经孵化器扶持，发展到一定规模后脱离孵化器实现独立发展的企业。（毕业企业的数据仅按毕业时的数据累计，不进行跟踪）。

166. 普通高等学校　是指按国家规定的设置标准和审批程序批准举办的，通过全国普通高等教育统一招生考试，招收高中毕业生为主要培养对象，实施高等学历教育的全日制大学、独立设置的学院和高等专科学校、高等职业学校及其他机构（独立学院和分校、大专班）。

167. 成人高等学校　是指按国家规定的设置标准和审批程序批准举办的，通过全国成人高等教育统一招生考试,招收具有高中毕业或同等学历的人员为主要培养对象，利用函授、业余、脱产的多种形式对其实施高等学历教育的学校。包括：职工高等学校、农民高等学校、管理干部学院、教育学院、独立函授学院、广播电视大学、其他机构。

168. 专任教师数　教师是指专职从事教学工作的人员，包括临时调去帮助做其他工作的人员，不包括调离教学岗位担负行政领导工作的原教学人员。

169. 文化事业机构　指从事专业文化工作和为专业文化工作服务的独立建制的单独核算的单位。不包括这些单位另外举办独立核算的其他机构和各部门的业余文化组织。

170. 艺术表演团体　指从事戏曲、音乐、舞蹈、杂技等专业艺术表演，有独立账户，实行单独核算的团体。不包括半工半艺、半农半艺的业余剧团。

171. 艺术表演观众人数（人次）　指售票、包场演出或民族地区免费演出的艺术表演观众人次数。不包括彩排审查和内部观摩演出的观看人次数。

172. 医　院　指名称为医院，设有固定床位能收容病人住院并能为病人提供医疗、护理服务的医疗机构。包括县及以上医院、其他医院两部分。按所属性质分为卫生部门、工业及其他部门、集体所有制单位3类。其中县及以上医院按业务性质分为综合医院和专科医院。

173. 卫生技术人员　指卫生事业机构支付工资的全部固定职工和合同制职工中现任职务为卫生技术工作的专业人员。包括中医师、西医师、中西医结合高级医师、护师、中药师、西药师、检验师、其他技师、中医士、西医士、护士、助产士、中药剂士、西药剂士、检验士、其他技士、其他中医、护理员、中药剂员、西药剂员、检验员、其他初级卫生技术人员。

174. 医　生　指经卫生部门审查合格，从事医疗工作的专业人员。分为中医医生和西医医生。包括卫生技术人员中的中医师、西医师、中西结合高级医师、中医士、西医士和其他中医。

175. 等级运动员人数　指经考核正式批准授予等级运动员称号的人数。运动员等级分为国际级运动健将、运动健将、一级运动员、二级运动员。

176. 等级裁判员人数　指经考核正式批准授予等级裁判员称号的人数。裁判员等级分为国际裁判、国家级裁判、一级裁判、二级裁判、三级裁判。

177. 社会福利事业单位　指集中收养社会孤老、残、幼的机构。包括由民政部门管理的社会福利院、儿童福利院、精神病人福利院和城镇集体办的福利院，以及农村集体办的敬老院。

178. 社会福利事业单位收养人数　指由民政部门管理的和城镇及农村集体举办的社会福利事业单位中收养的老人、少年儿童、缺乏生活自理能力的残疾人员和精神病人。

179. 社会福利企业单位　指以安置城镇有一定劳动能力的盲、聋、哑和肢体残疾人员就业为目的，享受国家减免税待遇的国有或集体经济性质的企业。包括福利工厂、福利商品服务业、假肢厂和安置农场等单位。

180. 律　师　指受聘参加法律顾问处工作，担任法律顾问、刑（民）事代理人、刑事辩护人，办理非诉讼事件、解答法律询问，代写法律事务文书等主要从事律师业务的专职法律工作者和兼职律师。

181. **公证人员**　指在国家公证机关依法办理公证事务的司法人员。包括公证员、助理公证员和在公证处工作的其他人员，

182. **办理公证文书**　指公证处在一定时期内办结的公证文书件数。公证文书应按司法部规定或批准的格式制作。包括国内公证和涉外公证两部分。其中国内公证分为经济合同公证和民事法律关系公证两大类。

183. **调解人员**　指在人民调解委员会担负调解民间一般民事纠纷和轻微违法行为所引起的纠纷的工作人员。包括调解委员会的委员和调解小组的调解员。

184. **调解民间纠纷**　指调解委员会依照法律规定，根据自愿原则，用说服教育的方法调解民间发生的有关民事权利和义务的争执，促成当事双方达到协议和谅解，解决纠纷．包括婚姻家庭纠纷，财产权益纠纷等。不包括法院受理的纠纷案。

APPENDIX7 EXPLANATORY NOTES ON MAIN STATISTICAL INDICATORS

1 Gross Domestic Product （GDP） refers to the final products of all resident units in a country （or a region） during a certain period of time. Gross domestic product is expressed in three different forms, i.e. value, income, and products respectively. The form of value refers to the total value of all products and services produced by all resident units during a certain period of time minus total value of intimidate input of materials and services of the nature of non-fixed assets or the summation of the value-added of all resident units; the form of income includes all the income created by all resident units and distributed primarily to all resident and non-resident units; the form of products refers to the value of all final goods and services for final use by all resident units plus the value of net exports of goods and services during a given period of time. In the practice of national accounting, gross domestic product is calculated with three approaches, i.e. production approach, income approach, and expenditure approach, which reflect gross domestic product and its composition from different aspects.

2 Comparable Prices refers to prices that removed the factors of price change so as to exactly reflect the change of aggregate when comparing the value of different periods. Two methods are used for calculating comparable prices: 1. Multiplying the output of products by their fixed prices of certain year; 2. Converting prices by relevant price index.

3 Constant Price refers to the average price of a given product in certain year, which is used for comparison of output value over time. As the output value at constant prices removes the factor of price changes, it reflects the trend of production development over time. Since 1949, with the changes in general price level, National Bureau of Statistics has issued nationally unified constant prices five times: the 1952 constant prices for 1949-1957; the 1957 constant prices for 1957-1971; the 1970 constant prices for 1971-1981; the 1980 constant prices for 1981-1990; and the 1990 constant prices have been used since 1991.

4 Various Planning periods The conventional division of time period in this statistical yearbook is as follows: Economic Rehabilitation Period, 1950-1952; the First Five-Year Plan period, 1953-1957; The Second Five-Year Plan period, 1958-1962; The Third Five-Year Plan period, 1966-1970; The Fourth Five-Year Plan period, 1971-1975; The Fifth Five-Year Plan period, 1976-1980;The Sixth Five-Year Plan period, 1981-1985; The Seventh Five-Year Plan period, 1986-1990;The Eighth Five-Year Plan period, 1991-1995;The Ninth Five-Year Plan period, 1996-2000;The TenthFive-Year Plan period,2001-2005;The Eleventh Five-Year Plan period,2006-2010;The Twelfth Five-year plan period ,2011-2015.

5 Average Annual Growth Rate refers to the average growth rate year after year in a long period of time. There are two methods for calculating: one is "level approach", or the method of geometric level calculation, is the annual average growth （decrease） rate, which derived by comparing the level of the last year of the interval with that of the beginning year; the other is called "accumulative approach", or algebraic average or equation method, is the annual average growth （decrease） rate, which is derived by summation of the actual figure of each year in the interval divided by the figure in the base year. Usually, the results calculated by the two methods are fairly close, but they differed sharply when uneven economic development occurred with striking fluctuations in growth.

The average annual growth rates listed in this statistical yearbook are all calculated by "level approach". The base years are not listed when the years are listed for average annual growth rates. For example, the average annual growth rate of the 35 years since reform & opening-up implemented is listed as 1979-2013 without listing the base year 1978, the rest of the years are analogized as the same.

6 Registration Status of Enterprises Enterprises are classified into 3 categories, namely domestic-funded enterprises, enterprises with investment from Hong Kong, Macao and Taiwan, and enterprises with foreign investment, in the light of the registration status of an enterprise in industrial and commercial administration agencies. Domestic-funded enterprises include state-owned enterprises, collective-owned enterprises, cooperative enterprises, joint ownership enterprises, limited liability corporations, share-holding corporations Ltd., private enterprises and other enterprises. Included in the enterprises with investment from Hong Kong, Macao and Taiwan and enterprises with foreign investment are joint-venture enterprises, cooperative enterprises, sole investment enterprises and share-holding corporations Ltd. For government agencies, institutions and social organizations, which are not requested to be registered in industrial and commercial administration agencies, they are classified mainly by their sources of funds and way of management.

7 State-owned Enterprises refer to non-corporation economic units where the entire assets are owned by the state and which have registered in accordance with the Regulation of the People's Republic of China on the Management of Registration of Corporate Enterprises. Excluded from this category are sole state-funded corporations in the limited liability corporations.

8 Collective-owned Enterprises refer to economic units where the assets are owned collectively and which have registered in accordance with the Regulation of the People' s Republic of China on the Management of Registration of Corporate Enterprises.

9 Cooperative Enterprises refer to a form of collective economic units (enterprises) where capitals come mainly from employees as their shares, with certain proportion of capital from the outside, where production is organized on the basis of independent operation, independent accounting for profits and losses, joint work, democratic management, and a distribution system that integrates remuneration according to work with dividend according to capital share.

10 Joint Ownership Enterprises refer to economic units established by two or more corporate enterprises or corporate institutions of the same or different ownership, through joint investment on the basis of equality, voluntary participation and mutual benefits. They include state joint ownership enterprises, collective joint ownership enterprises, joint state-collective enterprises, and other joint ownership enterprises.

11 Limited Liability Corporations refer to economic units established with investment from 2-50 investors and registered in accordance with the Regulation of the People' s Republic of China on the Management of Registration of Corporations, each investor bearing limited liability to the corporation depending on its share of investment, and the corporation bearing liability to its debt to the maximum of its total assets. Limited liability corporations include exclusive state-funded limited liability corporations and other limited liability corporations.

12 Share-holding Corporations Ltd. refer to economic units registered in accordance with the Regulation of the People' s Republic of China on the Management of Registration of Corporations, with total registered capitals divided into equal shares and raised through issuing stocks. Each investor bears limited liability to the corporation depending on the holding of shares, and the corporation bears liability to its debt to the maximum of its total assets.

13 Private Enterprises refer to profit-making economic units invested and established by natural persons, or controlled by natural persons using employed labour. Included in this category are private limited liability corporations, private share-holding corporations Ltd., private partnership enterprises and private-funded enterprises registered in accordance with the Corporation Law, Partnership Enterprises Law and Interim Regulations on Private Enterprises .

14 Other Domestic-funded Enterprises refer to domestic-funded economic units other than those mentioned above.

15 Enterprises with Investment from HongKong, Macao and Taiwan refers to enterprises set up in mainland China in the forms of joint investment,cooperation or solely-owned investment by investors from HongKong, Macao and Taiwan in accordance with foreign-related economic laws & regulations of China. They include joint-venture enterprises, cooperative enterprises & solely-owned enterprises.

16 Enterprises with Foreign Investment refers to enterprises set up in mainland China in the forms of joint investment, cooperation or solely-owned investment by foreign investors in accordance with foreign-related economic laws & regulations of China. They include joint-venture enterprises with foreign investment, cooperation enterprises with foreign investment and enterprises with sole (exclusive) foreign investment.

17 Three industries Industry structure has been classified according to the historical sequence of development. Primary industry refers to extraction of natural resources; secondary industry involves processing of primary products; and tertiary industry provides services of various kinds for production and consumption. The above classification is universal although it varies to some extent from country to country. The three industries in China are classified as follows:

Primary industry refers to farming, forestry, animal husbandry and fishery (excluding services related to farming, forestry, animal husbandry and fishery) .

Secondary industry refers to mining and quarrying (excluding auxiliary activities related to mining and quarrying) , manufacturing (excluding repair services to metalware, machinery and equipment) , production and supply of electricity, water and gas, and construction.

Tertiary industry, namely service industry, refers to all other sectors not included in primary and secondary industry. It includes wholesale and retail trade, transportation, storage, post and telecommunications, catering and accommodation, information transmission, software and information technology, financing, real estate, lease and commercial service, scientific research and technology service, management of water conservancy, environment and public facilities, residents service, repair and other service, education, healthcare and social work, public management, social security and social organization, international organization as well as services related to farming, forestry, animal husbandry and fishery, auxiliary activities related to mining and quarrying and repair services to metalware, machinery and equipment.

18 Total Population refers to the total number of people alive at a certain point of time within a given area.The annual statistics on total population is taken at midnight, the 3lst of December, excluding migrant population without household register in Changzhou city.

19 Birth Rate (or Crude Birth Rate) refers to the ratio of the number of births to the average population (or mid-period population) during a certain period of time (usually a year) which is often expressed in ‰. Birth rate in the chapter refers to annual birth rate. The following formula is used:

Birth Rate = Number of Births/Average Number of Population × 1000‰

Number of births refers to live births i.e. the births when babies had showed any vital phenomena regardless of the length of pregnancy.

The current calculation of birth rate is based on data residency by the public security data of permanent residency by the family planning commission at city levels, and can also be based on annual population sampling at country and provincial levels, including the late registration for births of previous year.

Annual average number of population is the average of the number of population at the beginning of the year and that at the end of the year, and can be substituted with the mid-year population.

20 Death Rate (or Crude Death Rate) refers to the ratio of the number of deaths to the average population (or mid-period population) during a certain period of time (usually a year) which is often expressed in ‰. Death rate in the chapter refers to annual death rate. The following formula is used:

Death Rate= Number of Deaths/Annual Average Number of Population × 1000‰

21 Natural Growth Rate of Population refers to the ratio of natural increase in population (number of births minus number of deaths) in a certain period of time (usually a year) to the average population (or mid-period population) of the same period which is often expressed in ‰. The following formulas are applied:

Natural Growth Rate of Population = (Number of Births-Number of Deaths) /Average Number of Population × 1000‰

Natural Growth Rate of Population = Birth Rate-Death Rate

22 Life Expectancy refers to the average number of years a person of a certain age will live (or the average life-span of an age group if the pattern of morality for this age group remains as it is.)

23 Employed persons refer to individuals engaged in social labor and receive remuneration payment or earn business income, including fully employed staff and workers, re-employed retirees, private business owners, individual business owners, persons employed in private and individual businesses, township enterprises and agricultural sector, and other employed persons (including community-sponsored teachers, religion workers, active servicemen, etc.) This indicator reflects the actual utilization of overall labor resource within a given period and serves as an important indicator used for research of the basic national conditions and strength of our country.

24 Employed persons in units refer to individuals working in government agencies at various levels, political and party organizations, social organizations, enterprises and institutions, and receiving wages or other forms of payment. They include fully-employed staff and workers, re-employed retirees, community-sponsored teachers, foreigners and Chinese compatriots from Hong Kong, Macao, and Taiwan working in various units, part-time employees, employees of other units working temporarily at current posts, and employees holding a second job, but exclude staff and workers who have left their working units while keeping their labour contracts/employment relations unchanged. This indicator reflects the total number of laborers actually engaged in production or other operations in various units.

25 Staff and Workers refer to the persons who work in (and receive payment therefrom) enterprises and institutions of state ownership, collective ownership, joint ownership, share holding, foreign ownership, and ownership by entrepreneurs from Hong Kong, Macao, and Taiwan, and other types of ownership and their affiliated units and get paid also include the staff and workers who have left their working units while keeping their labour contract/employment relation unchanged.

26 Fully Employed Staff and Workers refer to persons who work in, and receive wages from their working units, as well as persons who have their work posts, but are temporarily absent from work for reasons of study or on sick, injury or maternal leave and still receive wages from their working units.

27 Staff and Workers Who Have Left Working Units but Still Remaining the Relationship with the Units refer to those who have left the production or working posts due to various reasons and are not taking other positions in the same units, but whose labor relationship still remained in the units.

28 Total Wages of Persons Employed refer to the total remuneration payment to the whole staff and workers in various units during a certain period of time, including the total wages of fully employed staff and workers, the total salaries of assigned personnel and the total earnings of other employed persons.

29 Total Wages of Fully Employed Staff and Workers refers to the total remuneration payment to fully employed staff and workers in various units during a certain period of time. The calculation of total wages is based on the total remuneration payment to the staff and workers. Therefore, all the wages and salaries and other payments to staff and workers are included in the total wages regardless of their sources, category, and forms（in kind or cash）.

30 Average Wage of Fully Employed Staff and Workers refers to the average wage in monetary terms per person during a certain period of time for fully employed staff and workers in various units, which is one of the main indicators reflecting the general level of wage and is calculated as follows:

Average Wage of Fully Employed Staff and Workers = Total Wages of Fully Employed Staff and Workers in Given Period / Average Number of Fully Employed Staff and Workers in Given Period.

31 Registered urban unemployed people refer to unemployed people at working age （from 16 years old to retirement age） in urban areas that have the ability to work and the need for jobs and have registered at public employment service agencies.

32 Consumer Price Index Consumer price, refers to the price that consumer goods and services purchased by urban and rural residents, is the final price of social products and services, which influences the people' s livehood and lay a prominent role in the whole national economic price system. Consumer price index reflects the trend and degree of changes in prices of consumer goods purchased by residents.

33 Retail Price Index The the general change in retail prices of commodities . The change and adjustment in retail prices directly affect the living expenditure of urban and rural residents ,government revenue, purchasing power of residents and the equilibrium of market supply and demand ,and the ratio of consumption to accumulation.Therefore,the calculation of retail price index is useful to analyze the changes of the above economic activities.

34 Service Price Index refer to the comparative number of the expenditure of non-commercial and service consumption. The items involve: telecommunication expense, postal expense, transportation expense, hairdressing & beautification expense, culture and entertainment expense, school and baby-sitting expense, mending and other expense, medical insurance service expense, total classifications.

35 Disposable Income refers to the sum of income of the surveyed households obtained during the survey period that can be used for final consumption or expenditure and savings, that is, the income that can be freely disposed by the surveyed households. Disposable income includes both money and in-kind income. According to the source of income, disposable income consists of four categories, namely, wage income, net operating income, net property income and net transfer income.

36 Wage Income refers to the total remuneration and various benefits of employed people obtained through various channels, including the total remuneration and benefits acquired by those employed by units or individuals, or engaged in various freelance, part-time or sporadic jobs.

37 Net Operating Income refers to the net income obtained by households or household members engaged in production and business activities, which is the net income acquired after deducting operating expenses, depreciation of fixed assets for production and production tax from the overall operating income .

38 Net property Income refers to the net income obtained by households or household members by means of entrusting other institutional units, households or individuals to manage their own financial assets, non-financial assets like housing, and other natural resources after deducting related expenses. Net property income includes net interest income, dividend income, net income derived from depositing insurance, net rents by transfer of contracted land use rights, net rents of housing, net rents of other assets, and commuted net rents of owner-occupied housing.

39 Net transfer Income refers to the net resulted from transfer income minusing transfer expenses.

40 Transfer Income refers to a variety of regular transfer payments to households made by state, units and social groups, and regular income transfers among households. Regular transfer payments include pension or retirement welfare, social relief and subsidies, agricultural subsidies, policy-guaranteed living allowance, disaster relief, regular donations and compensation, and reimbursement of medical expenses transferred to residents by government, non-administrative institutions and social groups. Regular income transfers among households include alimony, regular donations and compensation, and the income sent or brought back to a household in rural areas （village committees） by a non-permanent member of the household working outside （including overseas）, and so on.

41 Transfer Expenditure refers to regular or obligatory transfer payments made by the surveyed households to state, units, households or individuals, including the payment of taxes, social security expenses, alimony expenses, regular donations and compensations, and other regular transfer payments.

42 Consumption Expenditure refers to all the expenses for household consumption meeting daily needs, including the expenditure on consumer goods and services. According to different purposes of use, consumption expenditure can be divided into eight categories of food, alcohol and tobacco, clothing, housing, supplies and services, transportation and communications, education, culture and entertainment, health care, and other supplies and services. According to different sources, consumption expenditure can be divided into cash expenditure and in-kind expenditure (self-produced and consumed or by units, governments and other social organizations).

43 Investment in Fixed Assets Investment in fixed assets is the essential means for social reproduction of fixed assets. Amount of investment in fixed assets refers to the volume of activities in construction and purchases of fixed assets in monetary terms. It is a comprehensive indicator which shows the size, pace, proportional relations and use orientation of the investment in fixed assets. It is also an important basis to observe the progress of the project and the effect of investment.

44 Investment in Real Estate Development refers to the investment by the real estate development companies, commercial buildings construction companies and other real estate development units of various types of ownership in the construction of house buildings, such as residential buildings, factory buildings, warehouses, hotels, guesthouses, holiday villages, office buildings, and the complementary service facilities and land development projects, such as roads, water supply, water drainage, power supply, heating, telecommunications, land leveling and other projects of infrastructure. It excludes the activities in simple land transactions.

45 Capital Source of Fixed Asset Investments There are two categories of capital for fixed asset investments, balance from the previous year and the actual amount of capital the local government receives in the current year. The actual funding is subdivided into 6 types, i.e. budgetary funding from the central government, domestic bank loans, bonds, foreign capital and funding collected by the local government itself.

46 Fixed Asset Investments by Category In terms of contents and forms, there are four categories of fixed asset investments, i.e. investments on construction projects, investments on installation projects, equipment purchases, and other expenses.

47 Newly-increased Fixed Assets The term refers to the value of newly-created fixed assets through investment. It includes investments on projects that are already operational or delivered for use, investments on equipment and facilities, and other expenses that should be accounted for. The term is a value-based comprehensive indicator of fixed asset investments.

48 Rate of Projects of Fixed Assets Completed and Put into Operation refers to the ratio of the newly increased fixed assets to the total investment made in the same period. This is a comprehensive indicator, reflecting the speed of the employment of fixed assets and the investment efficiency.

49 Construction Projects Construction projects are those that are constructed in the time span covered by the report. They include newly-started projects, projects that were started before the time span but are still under construction during the time span, projects that are started and finished in the time span, projects were completely suspended before the time span and are resumed during the time span and projects that are constructed but later completely suspended in the time span.

50 Projects Completed and Put into Use Industrial projects refer to the major projects and accessory facilities completed which result in forming production capacity and have been checked and accepted while the living and welfare facilities have been completed and can ensure normal production and formally put into production. Non-industrial projects refer to the major projects and accessory facilities completed which possess the designed capacity and have been checked, accepted and formally put into production.

51 Floor space under construction refers to the floor space of all buildings (including basement, semibasement and supporting buildings) is being constructed within the period of the report. It consists of the floor space newly constructed in current phase and the floor space constructed from last year to current phase, and the floor space which stopped constructing in the previous phase but restarted to construct in current phase. The floor space completed in the current phase and the floor space stopped constructing or delayed construction of the current phase shall be included in the floor space under construction. As to multi storey building, floor space completed shall be filled in the total floor space of each storey.

52 Floor space completed refers to the total of building area of all buildings which are completed as per design requirement, meet the requirements for residence and use, and are inspected and accepted as qualified or meeting the completion acceptance criteria and can be transferred to normal use.

53 Floor Space of Residential Buildings refers to the floor space of the residential buildings under construction and completed among the total space of buildings under construction and completed.

54 Sold Floor Space of Commercial Residential Housing This term refers to the total floor space sold (gross floor space identified in formal sales contracts) in the time span covered by the report. The term "Sold Floor Space of the Month" refers to the total sold floor space identified in formal sales contracts from the first day of the month till the last day of the month. Sold floor space includes floor space of completed housing units and that of forward delivery housing units.

55 Floor Space to be Sold This term refers to the unsold or unrent floor space of commercial residential housing among all salable or rentable floor space that is completed. It includes floor space that is completed before and during the time span covered by the report. However, it does not include unsalable or rentable floor space that is completed for relocation, for real estate developers' own use, for temporary use or as part of public supporting facilities.

56 Gross Output Value of Farming,Forestry,Animal Husbandry and Fishery refers to the total volume of products of farming, forestry, animal husbandry and fishery in value terms and the value of all kinds of supporting serving activities to farming, forestry, animal husbandry and fishery producing activities, which reflects the total scale and total result of agricultural production during a given period of time.The statistical scopes for Farming, Forestry, Animal Husbandry and Fishery are:

(1) Farming include crop cultivation and other farming crop cultivation, include planting of grain, beans, tubers, cotton, oil bearing crops,sugar crops,fiber crops,tobacco,vegetables,medicinal materials, melons and others, as well as tea,mulberry and fruit plantation.

Other farming include gathering of wild plant fruits, fiber,gum, oil, firewood, wild medicinal materials, fungi and commodity industry run by rural household.

(2) Forestry include planting of trees (not including planting,management & harvest of tea, mulberry and fruit plantation), collection of forest products,cutting and felling of bamboo and trees by villages and other cooperative organizations under villages.

(3) Animal Husbandry include raising and grazing of any kind of animal and hunting and raising of wild animal, excluding fish breeding.

(4) Fishery include cultivation and catches of acquatic animals and seaweed.

(5) The trade of farming, forestry, animal husbandry and fishery, including irrigation service, elementary processing service of farming products, other agricultural service, forestry service, veterinarian service, other animal husbandry service, fishery service, and so on.

57 Grain Yield refers to the yield in the whole country including grains produced by state farms, collective units, industrial enterprises and mines. (Grain includes rice, wheat, corn, sorghum, millet and other miscellaneous grains as well as tubers and beans) .Data on grain production before 1989 were obtained through the Comprehensive Statistical Reporting System.Since 1989,data from sample sunveys are used.

58 Yield of Oil-bearing Crops refers to the total yield of oil bearing crops of various kinds, including peanuts, (dry, in shell) rapeseeds, sesame, sunflower seeds, flax seeds, and other oil bearing crops. Soybeans, oil-bearing woody plants, and wild oil-bearing crops are not included.

59 Output of Aquatic Products refers to catches of both artificially cultured and naturally grown aquatic products, including fish, shrimps, crabs and shellfish in sea and inland water as well as seaweed. Freshwater plants are not included.

60 Output of Pork, Beef, and Mutton refers to the meat of slaughtered hogs, cattle, sheep and goats with head, feet, and offal taken away.

61 Cultivated Area (Area under cultivation) refers to farmland which is plowed constantly for growing crops, including cultivated land, newly cultivated land in the current year, farmland left without cultivation for less than three years and fallow land in the current year, rotation land, rotation land of grass and crops, farmland with some fruit trees, mulberry trees and other trees and cultivated seashore land, lake land, and etc. The land of mulberry fields, tea plantations, orchards, nurseries of young plants, forestland, reed land, natural and man-made grassland and other land are not included in cultivated land.

62 Sown Area of Crops refers to area of land sown or transplanted with crops regardless of being in cultivated area or non cultivated area. Area of land re-sown due to natural disasters is also included.At present ,the sown area of crops:grain,oil-bearing crops ,lotton,hamp,sugar crops,tobacco,medicinal materials,vegetables,melons and other farm crops.

63 Irrigated Area refers to areas that are effectively irrigated, i.e. level land which has water source and complete sets of irrigation facilities to lift and move adequate water for irrigation purpose under normal conditions. Under normal conditions, irrigated area is the sum of watered fields and irrigated fields where irrigation systems or equipment have been installed for regular irrigation purpose.

64 Consumption of Chemical Fertilizers in Agriculture refers to the quantity of chemical fertilizers applied in agriculture in the year, including nitrogenous fertilizer, phosphate fertilizer, potash fertilizer, and compound fertilizer. The consumption of chemical fertilizers is required in calculation to convert the gross weight into weight containing 100% effective component (e.g. 100% nitrogen content in nitrogenous fertilizer, 100% phosphorous pentoxide contents in phosphate fertilizer, 100% potassium oxide contents in potash fertilizer) . Compound fertilizer is converted with its major component.

65 Total Power of Farm Machinery refers to total mechanical power of machinery used in farming, forestry, animal husbandry, and fishery, including ploughing, irrigation and drainage, harvesting, transport, plant protection, stock breeding, forestry and fishery. The power of internal combustion engines is required to convert horsepower into watts and the power of electric motors is required to be converted into watts. Machinery employed for non-agricultural purposes, such as the machines used in township run and village-run industry, construction, non-agricultural transport, scientific experiments and teaching, is excluded.But mechanical power that engage in agriculture and sideline products for primary processing of villiage industrial mechanical power are included.

66 Number of Livestock or Poultry in Stock at Beginning (or End) refers to the total number of large animals, pigs, sheep, fowls, etc. raised by rural cooperative organizations, state farms, rural individuals, government agencies, schools, industrial and mining enterprises, army, and urban residents at the beginning (or end) of the reference period. The investigated method of the pigs and poultry has changed from overall investigation to sampling investigation since 1997.

67 Industry refers to the material production sector which is engaged in extraction of natural resources and processing and reprocessing of minerals and agricultural products, including (1) extraction of natural resources, such as mining, salt production, logging (but not including hunting and fishing) ; (2) processing and reprocessing of farm and sideline produces, such as rice husking, flour milling, wine making, oil pressing, cotton ginning, silk reeling, spinning and weaving, and leather making; (3) manufacture of industrial products, such as steel making, iron smelting, chemicals manufacturing, petroleum processing, machine building, timber processing; water and gas production and electricity generation and supply; (4) repairing of industrial products such as the repairing of machinery and means of transport (including cars) .

68. Light Industry refers to the industry that produces consumer goods and hand tools. It also refers to the industry that produces consumer goods. The light industry consists of the following two branches: (1) the industrial sectors using agricultural products as raw materials, such as textile and sewing of cotton, wool, hemp and silk, leather and relative products, pulp and paper production, food production, etc.; (2) the industrial sectors using non-agricultural products as raw materials, such as metal, chemicals, glass, porcelain and ceramics, chemical fiber and relative fabric, matches, wood products and so on for daily use. Most of the light industrial products are production consumer goods, while some of them are used in the production of raw materials and semi-finished products, such as chemical fibers, industrial fabrics, paper products, salt, etc.

69 Heavy Industry refers to the industry, which produces capital goods, and provides various sectors of the national economy with necessary material and technical basis. It consists of the following three branches according to the purpose of production or the use of products: (1) Mining, quarrying and logging industry refers to the industry that extracts natural resources, including extraction of petroleum, coal, metal and non-metal ores and logging. (2) Raw materials industry refers to the industry that provides various sectors of the national economy with raw materials, fuels and power. It includes smelting and processing of metals, coking and coke chemistry, chemical materials and building materials such as cement, plywood, and power, petroleum refining and coal dressing. (3) Manufacturing industry refers to the industry that processes raw materials. It includes machine-building industry, which equips sectors of the national economy, industries of metal structure and cement products, industries producing means of agricultural production, such as chemical fertilizers and pesticides.

According to the above principle of classification, the repairing trades, which are engaged primarily in repairing products of heavy industry, are classified into heavy industry while these engaged in repairing products of light industry are classified into light industry.

70 Gross Industrial Output Value refers to the total volume of final industrial products produced and industrial services provided during a given period in monetary terms, including the value of finished products, the income of processing rendered to other units and the changes in the value of home-made semi-finished products between the beginning and closing of the period.

71 Industrial Sales Output Value refers to the total volume of industrial products sold by an industrial enterprise during a given period and in the form of currency. It includes the value of finished products, semi-finished products, and industrial operations rendered to other units, products, industrial operations and self-made equipment provided to the basic construction department, welfare department, etc. of the enterprise. As to those finished products and semi-finished products, no matter whether products are manufactured in this calculation period or the previous one, so long as they are sold out in this calculation period, they should be included. The industrial operations are industrial services rendered to other units according to contracts. The products, industrial operations and self-made equipment provided to basic construction department, welfare department, and etc. of the enterprise should be regarded as act of sale, and included in sales statistics.

The scope, price and method of calculation of industrial sales output value are the same as those for gross industrial output value. However, the calculation base are different: the base for sales output value is the total volume of products sold; the base for gross industrial output value is total volume of production of industrial products.

72 Accounts Receivable refer to money owed to a business on the sale of products, services and other business activities by its customers that have purchased goods or received services, mainly including money owed by concerning debtor（s）to a business on the sale of products or services, as well as the packaging costs, transport charges and so on paid in advance by a purchasing agent.

73 Paid-in Capital refers to the total capital （or equity） actually contributed to a corporation by investors in monetary terms, in kind, with intangible assets, etc. The investment entities can be divided into state capital, collective capital, corporate capital, personal capital, Hong Kong, Macao and Taiwan capital, and foreign capital.

74 Total Assets refer to all resources collected via past transactions or events of a business, owned or controlled by the business and expected to bring economic benefits to the business.

75 Total Circulating Assets refer to assets that meet one of the following conditions: （1） assets expected to be liquidated, sold or consumed within a normal business cycle, including inventory, accounts receivable, etc.; （2） assets held for trading purposes; （3） assets expected to be liquidated within one year （including one year） after the balance sheet date; and （4） cash or cash equivalents that have unrestricted ability for exchange of other assets or to pay off the liabilities within one year after the balance sheet date.

76 Total Fixed Assets refer to tangible assets, with service life over one fiscal year, held by a business for production, services, rental or operation and management.

77 Original Value of Fixed Assets refers to the cost of fixed assets, including the total amount of all expenses incurred at the time of purchase, construction, installation, reconstruction, expansion and technical improvement of a particular fixed assets.

78 Accumulated Depreciation refers to the accumulated amount of depreciation on fixed assets of a business during the past years drawn in the end of given period.

79 Depreciation Drawn in Current Year refers to the total amount of depreciation on fixed assets of a business drawn within given period, the data of which is collected according to the “Depreciation of Fixed Assets” of “Statement of Changes in Financial Position” in accounting.

80 Total Liabilities refer to the current obligations that are expected to result in outflow of economic benefits of a business incurred from past transactions or events of the said business. Liabilities are generally divided into liquid liabilities and non-liquid liabilities based on the length of the repayment period.

81 Total Liquid Liabilities refer to liabilities that meet one of the following conditions: （1） liabilities expected to be settled within a normal business cycle; （2） liabilities held for trading purposes; （3） liabilities that shall be settled within one year after the balance sheet date; and （4） liabilities that a business has no right to defer the settlement to more than one year after the balance sheet date by their own. Such liabilities include short-term borrowings, bills payable, accounts payable, remuneration payable to employees, taxes payable and other items.

82 Non-liquid Liabilities refer to liabilities other than in current liabilities, including long-term loans, bonds payable and so on, the data of which is collected according to the ending balance of “Total Non-liquid Liabilities” of “Balance Sheet” in accounting.

83 Total Creditors’ Equity refers to residual interest owned by creditors in corporate assets after deducting liabilities. Company creditors’ equity is also known as shareholders’ equity, including paid-up capital, capital surplus, earned surplus, undistributed profits, etc.

84 Main Business Income refers to income of sales of goods and services and other main business recognized by a business.

85 Main Business Tax and Surcharges refer to the business tax, consumption tax, urban maintenance and construction tax, education surtax, etc. that should be borne by a company from main business.

86 Total Value of Profit and Tax （pre-tax Profits） refers to the total sum of profits, products sales tax and surcharges and the value added tax payable of industrial enterprises. It is also called pre-tax profits.

87 Ratio of Profits to Total Industrial Costs refers to the ratio of profits realized in a given period to the total costs in the same period, which reflects the economic efficiency of input cost and is calculated as follows:

Ratio of Profits to Total Industrial Cost（%）=（Total Profits/ Total Costs）× 100%

88 Sales Ratio of Industrial Products refers to the sales of industrial products to the gross industrial output value in given period, which is important in reflecting the linkage between production and sales and the extent of the needs of the society that has been met by the supply of industrial products. It is calculated as follows:

Sales Ratio of Industrial Products = [Industrial Sales / Gross Industrial Output Value (at current prices)] × 100%

89 Gross Output Value of Construction refers to total output value as expressed in monetary terms of the production and service of construction enterprises within certain period of time. The total value consists of three parts:

(1) Output value of construction projects, that is the value of projects covered by the project budgets;

(2) Output value of installation projects, that is the value of the installation of equipment, (excluding the value of the equipment to be installed) ;

(3) Other output value: refers to the value of production including repairing of auxiliary parts of housing, non-standard equipment manufacturing, administration cost of contractor on sub-contractor and other construction output which cannot be clearly categorized.

90 Output Value of Completed Projects usually refers to output value of single construction project concerned within reference period, calculated when the projected is completed as required by the plan of the project, meeting the requirements of turning over to the user and pass the examination of authorized department. The scope of output includes: the value created from start to completion of the projects. If the construction of the projects took more than one year, the output value should include the value completed in previous year. The output can be calculated on section by section bases on large projects if they can be divided by sections, levels of construction. Large plants, deluxe hotels, pipe work, highway, railway etc are examples of these large projects.

91 Floor Space of Buildings Under Construction refers to all the floor space of buildings in construction reported in reference period, including those starting construction, construction relayed from previous period, construction resumed after the delay of the previous period, completed construction and construction started in present period and stopped at present.

92 Floor Space of Buildings Completed refers to floor space of construction project concerned within reference period, calculated when the projected is completed as required by the plan of the project, meeting the requirements of turning over to the user and pass the examination of authorized department. The calculation of the floor space should strictly adhere to the standard requirements for check up the completion of the construction projects. For civil construction projects, generally speaking, the floor space should be calculated when the building itself and its water, sewage, gas, heating, ventilation, elevator etc have been completed according to the construction plan, passed the examination for completion and turned over to the user. For the industrial construction as well as the construction of R&D buildings, the floor space should be calculated, generally speaking, when the building was completed with water, heating, sewage and ventilation as well as auxiliary parts in living quarter and operational quarter, even without the installation of manufacturing equipment as well as pipelines.

93 Total Number of Machinery and Equipment Owned by the End of Year refers to the number of machines and equipment owned by the enterprises, and listed as the fixed assets of the enterprises by the end of the year, including machinery and equipment for construction, production and transportation.

94 Total Power of Machinery and Equipment Owned by the End of Year refers to the total power of machinery and equipment owned by the enterprises, and listed as the fixed assets of the enterprises by the end of the year, including machinery and equipment for construction, production and transportation. The power of the machinery is calculated on basis of the designed or verified capacity, covering the power of the machinery/equipment and the separate power equipment serving the machinery/ equipment (such as electric motors) , but excluding welders, transformers and boilers. The unit used for the calculation of power is kilowatt, with horsepower converted to kilowatt by 1 horsepower=0.735 kilowatt.

95 Length of Highways refers to the length of highways which are builted in conformity with the grades specified by the Highway Engineering Standard JTJ01-88 formulated by the Ministry of Communications,and have been formally checked and accepted by the departments of highways and put into use. The length of highways includes that of the suburb highways at large and medium-sized cities, highways passing through streets at small cities and towns, and also the length of bridges and ferries. It does not include the length of streets in big and medium-sized cities and highways built for the production purpose at factories, mines, forest areas and agricultural areas. If two or more highways go the same section of the way, the length of the section is only calculated for once and no duplication is allowed. The length of highways is an important indicator to show the development of the highway construction and to provide essential information to calculate the transport network density.

96 Length of Navigable Inland Waterways an indicator reflecting the size and development of inland water network, it refers to the length of the natural rivers, lakes, reservoirs, canals, and ditches open to navigation during a given period, which enables the transport by ships and rafts. It includes the channels open to navigation for over an accumulative 3 months in a year, yet this does not include the river courses which are only used to float odd logs and bamboo rafts.

97 Freight (Passenger) Traffic refers to the volume of freight (passenger) transported with various means. Freight transport is calculated in tons and passenger traffic is calculated in the number of persons. Despite the type of freight and travelling distance, the freight transport is calculated in the actual weight of the goods: and despite the travelling distance and ticket price, the passenger traffic is calculated by the principle that one person can be counted only once in one travel. The passenger who travels with a half price ticket or a child ticket is also calculated as one person. The freight (passenger) traffic provides a quantitative measure to show how the transport industry serves the national economy and people, and is also an important indicator for planning the transport industry and for studying the development scale and speed of the transport industry.

98 Freight Ton-kilometers (Passenger-kilometers) refer to the sum of the products of the volume of transported cargo (passengers) multiplying by the transport distance, usually using ton-kilometer and passenger-kilometer as units for measurement. Normally, the shortest distance between the departure station and the destination station (i.e., the payable distance) is the basis to calculate the freight ton-kilometers. This is an important indicator to show the total results of the transport industry, to prepare and examine the transport plan and to measure the efficiency, the labor productivity and the unit cost of transport.

99 Business Volume of Post and Telecommunications Services refer to the total amount of services provided to society by post and telecommunications enterprises with the form of value. Post and telecommunications services can be divided by category as letter, parcel, bill of draft, newspaper and magazine distribution, EMS, philately, fixed telephone, lending circuit, mobile phone, packet switched data traffic and lending telephone switchboard maintenance. The calculation method shall be the sum of various kinds of product time average unit price (fixed price) then plus the service incomes from lending circuit, telephone switchboard and circuit maintenance on behalf of customers.

100 Mobile Telephone Subscribers refer to subscribers of the telephone using mobile telephone network, and occupying mobile telephone number. The number of subscribers shall be calculated as per the number dealt with the formalities of mobile telephone network at cell-phone business office as of the report date, each cell-phone shall be recorded as one subscriber.

101 Number of Internet Subscribers refers to the number of subscribers who have registered and accessed into the international network, including local network area, metropolitan area network, wide area network, and dial-up network subscribers and private wire network subscribers.

102 Total Retail Sales of Consumer Goods refers to the activities of selling wholesale commodities for daily use and capital goods to enterprises of wholesale and retail trades (including self-employed individuals) and other enterprises, institutions and government organs and organizations, and the activities of engaging in import and export and acting as a trade agent.The wholesaler may have the ownership of the commodities for wholesale and trade in the name of its own (a company), and the wholesaler can act as commission agent or commodity broker without the ownership of commodities Also included are the wholesale activities at the fixed stalls in wholesale market and the acquisition for sales purpose.

103 Wholesale and Retail Sales Trade refers to units not directly involved in the manufacturing of commodities, rather purchasing the commodity from manufacturers or circulating units without processing, or with simple processing (cleaning, tidying, categorizing, packaging, etc) and achieving benefits by reselling the commodities.

104 Accommodation refers to service provided to clients with payment.

105 Catering trade refer to the units offer various food and drinks consumed at once in certain places and this kind of service is more important than other services (entertainment, e.g.) offered.

106 Wholesale enterprises above designated size refer to wholesale companies with the main business income of more than RMB 20 million yuan.

107 Retail enterprises above designated size refer to retail companies with the main business income of more than RMB 5 million yuan.

108 Catering enterprises above designated size refer to catering companies with the main business income of more than RMB 2 million yuan.

109 Total Sales of Commodities refer to value of commodities sold by the establishments to other establishments and individuals (including direct export). This indicator reflects the total value of sales of commodities at domestic markets and export, including: (1) commodities sold to urban and rural residents and social groups for their consumption; (2) commodities sold to establishment in all industries for their production and opration; (3) commodities sold to wholesale and retail establishments for re-selling with or without further processing; (4) commodities for direct exprt to abroad.

110 Value of Business Transaction in Trading Markets refers to the total sales valus of commodities realized by the operators in the transaction market.Commodity transaction markets include consumer good markets and means of production markets .

111 Registered Capital of Private Enterprises refer to the checked registered capital when the private enterprises do the start or change registered, exclude the bank loans.

112 The Units of the Private owned industrial and Commercial Enterprises refers to the amount of the private owned industrial and commercial enterprises, which have got the business licence or the temporary business licences.

113 Staff and Workers in the Private Owned Industrial and Commercial Enterprises refer to the whole people take part in the business and get paid, which are checked by the industrial and commercial department, involved the manager of the private industrial and commercial enterprises, helper and the apprentices.

114 Registered Capital of the Private owned Industrial and commercial enterprises refer to the checked registered capital when apply for or change the registration.

115 Utilization of Foreign Capital refers to remittance, equipment and technology financed from abroad, by loans, foreign direct investment and other forms undertaken by the Chinese governments at all levels, by various departments, enterprises and other economic units.

116 Direct Investment by Foreign Entrepreneurs refers to the investments inside China by foreign enterprises and economic organizations or individuals （including overseas Chinese, compatriots from Hong Kong and Macao, and Chinese enterprises registered abroad ）, following the relevant policies and laws of China, for the establishment of ventures exclusively with foreign own investment, Sino-foreign joint ventures and cooperative enterprises or for cooperative exploration of resources with enterprises or economic organizations in China. It includes the re-investment of the foreign entrepreneurs with the profits gained from the investment and the funds that enterprises borrow from abroad in the total investment of projects which are approved by the relevant department of the government.

117 Contracted Projects with Foreign Countries refers to projects undertaken by Chinese contractors （project contracting companies） through bidding process. They include: （1） overseas civil engineering construction projects financed by foreign investors. （2） overseas projects financed by the Chinese government through its foreign aid programs. （3） construction projects of Chinese diplomatic missions, trade offices and other institutions stationed abroad. （4） construction, projects in China Financed by foreign investment. （5） sub-contracted projects to be taken by Chinese contractors through a joint umbrella project with foreign contractor （Including bear terrain mapping; geological resource exploration and census ;construction regional planning; provide the design documents, drawings, production technology and engineering technical economic advice; feasibility investigation, research and evaluation of project;carry out technical guidance and training personnel）; （6） housing development projects. The business income from international contracted projects is the work volume of contracted projects completed during the reference period, expressed in monetary terms, including completed work on projects singed in previous years.

118 Service Cooperation with Foreign Countries refers to the activities of providing technology and labor services to employers or contractors in the forms of receiving salaries and wages. Labor services providing by contractual joint ventures of Chinese international contracting corporations should be included in the statistics of service cooperation with foreign countries. The business income of labor service cooperation is the income in the form of wages and salaries, overtime pay, bonuses and other remuneration received from the employers during the reference period.

119 International Tourists refers to foreigners, overseas Chinese, Chinese compatriots from Hong Kong, Macao and Taiwan coming to China for sightseeing, visits, tours, family reunions, vacations, study tours, conferences and other activities of a business, scientific and technological, cultural, educational and religious nature. It does not include representatives and employees of resident institutions of foreign countries in China such as embassies, consulates, news agencies and offices of foreign companies and organizations, nor does it include long term foreign experts or students residing in China, or persons in transition without spending a night in China.

120 Total Electricity Consumption refer to the total amount of electricity consumed, it can be divided into countryside used electricity,industry used electricity, transportation used electricity , urban and rural residents used electricity and so on, all kinds of the electricity consumption all involved the electricity sold to the city' s consumer by power stations, the electricity produced for self use （involved the electricity made by the waste heat）.

121 Energy Consumption of Industry Enterprises refer to the energy, artificial used energy and energy used in other fields as fuel, material and supplementary material.

122 Total Fiscal Revenue refers to income for the government finance through participating in the distribution of social products.It is the financial guarantee to ensure government functioning. In our province, total financial revenue is the sum of public finance budgetary revenue， funds budgetary revenue and four taxes turned over to central government

123 Government Expenditure refers to the distribution and use of the funds the government finance has raised, so as to meet the needs of economic construction and various causes.

124 Deposit is a form of credit by which enterprises, institutions, organizations or households can put money into banks and other credit institutions for safekeeping and interest earning under the principle of free withdrawal. According to different depositors, deposits are divided into enterprise deposits, treasury deposits, deposits of government agencies and organizations, capital construction deposits, urban savings deposits, rural deposits and other deposits. Deposits are major sources of the credit funds of banks.

125 Saving Deposits Balance of Urban and Rural residents Saving deposits include the bank savings deposits of organizations such as industrial and mining enterprises, army units, institutions, ect. The outstanding amount of savings deposits refers to the money put into banks and rural credit unions at certain time points （balance between deposit and withdrawal）, such as the end of the month, quarter or year.

126 Loan is a form of credit by which banks and other credit institutions provide funds at certain interest rate to enterprises and individuals in the light of the principle of unconditional repayment. Loans from Chinese banks include circulating capital loans, fixed assets loans, loans to urban and rural individuals engaged in industrial and commercial business and agricultural loans.

127 Amount Insured refers to the maximum that the insurant will get for the claim of the case insured.

128 Premium is the fee paid by the insurant to the insurer to obtain the obligation of compensation from the insurance within the agreed terms.

129 Insurance Indemnity refers to the compensation paid by the insurer to the insurant in accordance with the stipulations of the insurance contract after confirmed the insured event within the scope of insurance coverage by means of verification.

130 Length of Paved Roads at the Year-end refers to the length of roads with a paved surface, and with a width of more than 3.5 meters, including high quality, medium quality and ordinary roads.

131 Urban Bridges refer to bridges over river courses, great separated junctions and overpasses in urban areas. Permanent bridges and semi-permanent bridges are included. Temporary bridges, railway bridges and culverts are excluded.

132 Length of Urban Sewage Pipes refers to the total length of general drainage, trunks,branch and blind drainage, inspection wells, connection wells, inlets and outlets, etc.

133 Daily Disposal Capacity of Urban Sewage refers to the designed 24-hour capacity of sewage disposal at the sewage treatment works.

134 Floor Space of the Park, Gardens and Green Area Of Urban refers to the total area of urban public green land, special green land, production green land, protection green land and suburban scenic spots.

135 Green Space in Park refers to the green area with main function of opening for the public, and recreation, which possesses certain recreation facilities and service facilities, integrated the effects of ecology perfection, scenery beautification, prevention and mitigation of the effects of disasters.

136 Production Capacity of Tap Water at the Year-end refers to the actual comprehensive production capacity of the waterworks administered by the urban construction department and those owned by enterprises or institutions, taking the capacity of the main links, such as water inflow, purification, conveyance and outflow of the trunk pipelines into account.

137 Number of Public Vehicles （Buses and Trolley buses） at the Year-end refers to the total number of operational buses available at the year-end, including the year-end operational vehicles and vehicles in stock. Non-operational vehicles such as stringing cars, tank cars, machine shop cars, trucks and other special vehicles and the borrowed passenger vehicles are excluded.

138 Length of Roads in Operation refers to the length of designated regular routes in operation, including the length of suburban routes in operation. The length of temporary operational lines is not included.

139 Length of Water Supply Pipelines at the Year-end refers to the total length of all the pipelines between the water pumps and the users water meters.

140 Annual Volume of Water Supply refers to the total volume of water supplied by the public water-works and those owned by individual enterprises and institutions during the whole year, including both the effective water supply and loss during the water supply.

141 Consumption of Water for Residential Use refers to the water consumption of households for daily life and the water consumption of public welfare facilities, including the consumption of restaurants, hotels, hospitals, barber shops, public bathhouses, laundries, swimming pools, shops, schools, institutions, army units and other units.

142 Percentage of Urban Population with Access to Tap Water refers to the ratio of the urban non-agricultural population (excluding temporary and mobile population) with access to tap water to the total urban non-agricultural population. The formula is:

Percentage of Population with Access to Tap Water= (Urban Non-agricultural Population with Access to Tap Water) / (Urban Non-agricultural Population) × 100%

143 Length of Gas Pipelines refers to the total length of pipelines between the outlet of the compressor, blower or gas tank and the gas meters of users.

144 Volume of Gas Supply refers to the total volume of gas sold to users in a year, including the volume for industrial use, residential use and other uses.

145 Percentage of Urban Population with Access to Gas refers to the ratio of the urban non-agricultural population with access to gas (including gas, liquefied petroleum gas and natural gas) to the urban non-agricultural population (excluding temporary and mobile population). The formula is:

Percentage of Population with Access to Gas = (Urban Non-agricultural Population with Access to Gas) / (Urban Non-agricultural Population) × 100%

146 Total Amount of Waste Water refers to the total amount of industrial waste water and resident waste water. The industrial refers to the total of the waste water produced in the producing, studying period of the enterprises and institutions. The resident waste water refers to the waste water produced in the residences.

147 Volume of Industrial Waste Water Discharged refers to the volume of industrial waste water discharged, through all outlets, to the outside of industrial enterprises, including waste water produced, direct-cooling water, underground water from mines that does not meet the standard of discharge, and the domestic sewage mixed up with industrial waste water when discharged, but excluding discharged indirect-cooling water.

148 Total Amount of Industrial Waste Gas Discharged refers to the total volume of all kinds of gas containing pollutants discharged to the air by factories in the process of fuel combustion and production, which is measured by standard conditions (273K, 101325Pa).

149 Volume of General Industrial Solid Wastes Utilized in a Comprehensive Way refers to the volume of solid wastes from which useful materials can be extracted or which can be transformed to utilizable resources, energy or other raw materials through recycling, processing, circulation, exchange, and so on, including the volume of industrial solid wastes stored up in the previous years and utilized in the current year, such as the solid wastes utilized as fertilizers, building materials, road construction materials, etc.

150 Volume of General Industrial Solid Wastes Treated refers to the amount of solid wastes eliminated by enterprises in the survey year through incineration of industrial solid wastes and other methods of changing the physical, chemical and biological properties of the industrial solid wastes, to reduce or eliminate their risk components, or by means of burying the industrial solid wastes in the landfill meeting the requirements for environmental protection. Such treatments include: burying, burning, piling in designated sites (warehouses), pouring water into the deep strata, filling of old mines, ocean disposal (as approved by Ocean Management Authorities), and so on.

151 Total Amount of Industrial Smoke, (Powder) and Dust Discharged refers to the total amount of smoke and industrial dust discharged to the air by enterprises in the process of fuel combustion and production.

152 R & D is the abbreviation of research and development, and refers to the systemic and creative activities for the purpose of increasing knowledge and applying the knowledge within the field of science and technology (including the fields of natural science, agricultural science, medical science, engineering and technological science and humanities and social science). R & D consists of three kinds of activities, including fundamental research, application research and experimental development.

153 Independent Research and Development Institutions refer to the state- owned institutions which have direct mission and research purpose, a certain number of core members with higher research level and certain number of research personal, favourable conditions for R&D and engaging in scientific research and technological development. The institutions also have their own independent organization and finance, authority to sign contracts with other units, their bank accounts. Independent research and development institutions include the institutions attached to central government agencies, Chinese Academy of Sciences, Chinese Academy of Social Sciences and the institutions attached to the local government.

154 Scientists and Engineers refer to persons who have completed university or higher education or obtained titles of senior and middle level professional positions.

155 Personnel of Independent Research and Development Institutions refers to the persons working in and receiving payment from research and development institutions. It includes regular full-time and temporary staff and workers and employees working on contracts, but excludes retirees and persons leaving their work without payment but still retaining their posts, who are not on the employee list.

156 Total Expenditure on Research and Development refers to all actual expenditure made for R&D （basic research, applied research and experimental development） in reference period. It includes direct expenditure on R&D and indirect expenditure on R&D （including management and necessary administrative expenses of research institutes, investment in capital construction relating to R&D）.

157 Inventions refer to the inventions as specified by the patent law and its detailed rules and regulations for implementation. They refer to the new technical proposals to the products or methods or their modifications.

158 Utility Models The utility models specified by the patent law and its detailed rules for implementation refer to the new technical proposals on the shape, structure or combination of shape and structure of product, which is suitable for practical use.

159 Designs refer to the designs as specified by the patent law and its detailed rules and regulation for implementation. They refer to the aesthetics and industry applicable new designs for the shape, pattern and color of the product, or their combinations.

160 Number of online registered technology contracts refers to the number of local technology contracts registered via the national technology contracts on-line registration system （http://www.ctmht.net.cn/）.

161 Business volume of online registered technology contracts refers to the business volume of local technology contracts registered via the national technology contracts on-line registration system （http://www.ctmht.net.cn/）.

162 Science and Technology Enterprises Incubator refers to the scientific and technological innovation service organization aiming to promote the transfer of scientific and technological achievements, and to nurture high-tech enterprises and entrepreneurs. It includes technological innovation service center, university technology parks, innovation （venture） park for returned overseas students, software parks and professional technological enterprises incubators.

163 Total income of enterprises under incubation refers to the sum of various incomes achieved from technology, industry and trade by the enterprises under incubation within the statistical year.

164 Persons employed by enterprises under incubation refer to the total number of persons employed by the enterprises under incubation at the end date of this report.

165 Incubated Enterprises refer to the enterprises realize independent development after developed to a certain scale so that divorce from the incubator. （The data of incubated enterprises is only accumulated based on the data of graduation time, without tracking）.

166 Regular Institutions of Higher Learning refer to educational establishments set up according to the government evaluation and approval procedures, enrolling graduates from senior secondary schools via national entrance examination and providing higher diploma education. They include full time universities, independent colleges and senior professional schools, senior vocational universities and other institutions （such as independent institutes, branch schools and junior colleges）.

167 Institutions of Higher Learning for Adults refer to educational establishments set up according to the government evaluation and approval procedures, enrolling personnel with senior secondary school or equivalent education via national entrance examination and providing higher diploma education by means of correspondence, part time or full time. They include workers' colleges, peasants' colleges, institutes for administration, educational colleges, independent correspondence colleges and etc.

168 The number of Full-time Teachers refers to the number of personnel engaged in education as full-time teachers, including those who are temporarily designated （within one year） to assist in other fields. The former teachers transferred from teaching to undertake administrative management are excluded.

169 Cultural Institutions refer to units which have their own organizational system and independent accounting system and specialize in or serve cultural development. They exclude other establishments run by these cultural institutions and amateur cultural groups established by various departments.

170 Art Troupe refers to the troupe which is engaged in drama, opera, music, dance, acrobatics or other art performance, opens independent accounts with banks and has self-supporting accounting system; excluding the troupes which are engaged partly in industrial or agricultural activities, partly in art performance and the professional troupes organized by the people.

171 Number of Spectators at Art Performance refers to the number of attendants at commercial shows, completely booked shows or free shows given in minority national areas, and does not include the number of spectators at rehearsals for examination and internal shows for study.

172 Hospitals refer to medical institutions with permanent hospital beds, which are able to take in patients and provide them with medical and nursing services. Hospitals are classified into three categories: hospitals at or above the county level, hospitals of rural townships, and other hospitals. According to their ownership, hospitals can be classified into three categories: hospitals under the public health departments, hospitals under industrial and other departments and collective-owned hospitals. Hospitals at or above county level are divided into comprehensive and specialized hospitals.

173 Medical Technical Personnel refers to all medical staff and workers employed by medical institutions, including doctors of Chinese and Western medicine, senior doctors who integrate traditional Chinese therapeutics with Western therapeutics in practice, senior nurses, pharmacists of Chinese and Western medicine, laboratory specialists, other specialists, paramedics of Chinese and Western medicine, nurses, midwives, druggists in Chinese and Western medicine, laboratory technicians, other technicians, other practitioners of Chinese medicine, nursing attendants, pharmacological workers of Chinese and Western medicine, laboratory workers, and other primary medical personnel.

174 Doctors refer to qualified professional medical workers approved to practice by public health departments. They are classified into doctors of Chinese medicine, doctors of Western medicine, senior doctors who integrate traditional Chinese therapeutics with Western therapeutics in practice, paramedics of Chinese medicine and Western medicine, and other specialists of Chinese medicine.

175 Number of Athletes in Grades refers to the number of athletes who have been given titles through examination. The titles of athletes include international masters of sports, masters of sports, first-grade and second-grade.

176 Number of Referees in Grades refers to the number of referees who have been given titles after examination. They are classified as international referees, national referees and referees of the first, second and third grades.

177 Social Welfare Institutions refer to institutions taking care of old people without children,handicapped people and orphans. They include social welfare institutions run by civil affairs departments, children welfare institutions, social welfare institutions for mental patients, and collective-owned old peoples homes in rural areas.

178 Number of People Taken in by Social Welfare Institutions refers to the number of old people, children, totally dependent handicapped people and mental patients taken in by social welfare institutions run by civil affairs departments and those run by collective units in urban and rural areas.

179 Social Welfare Enterprises are collective owned enterprises which employ the blind, deafmute, and other handicapped people who are able to work in cities and towns and enjoy exemption from state taxes, including welfare plants, welfare commercial services, artificial limb plants and farms, etc.

180 Lawyers are legal workers who are employed full time by legal counseling firms to act as legal advisers, agents in criminal or civil lawsuits, or defenders in criminal lawsuits, or to handle non-litigious legal affairs, to advise on matters of law or to write legal papers for others. Both full-time and part time lawyers are included.

181 Notary Personnel refers to judicial workers of the state notary offices handling notarization work according to law. They include notaries, assistant notaries, and other people working for notary offices.

182 Notarized Documents refer to the documents settled by notary offices in a year. The notary documents are drawn up in accordance with the regulations of the Ministry of Justice, including domestic documents and foreign-related documents. Domestic documents are divided into two major categories, documents on economic contracts and documents on civil legal relations.

183 Mediators refer to workers on peoples mediation committees responsible for mediating in civil disputes and cases of slight infraction of the law. They include members of the mediation committees and mediators of mediation groups.

184 Mediation of Civil Disputes refers to mediation committees work in mediating in civil disputes concerning civil rights and duties through persuasion and education in accordance with the provisions of law on a voluntary basis, so as to solve disputes by helping the parties involved come to an agreement and understanding. These disputes include divorce cases and disputes over property ownership, but exclude the civil cases to be handled by the court.

中国统计出版社最新图书简目

（仅供参考，以实际出书为准）

图书在版编目（CIP）数据

常州统计年鉴 . 2016 / 常州市统计局 , 国家统计局常州调查队编 .
-- 北京 : 中国统计出版社 , 2016.8
ISBN 978-7-5037-7853-7

Ⅰ . ①常…
Ⅱ . ①常… ②国…
Ⅲ . ①统计资料 – 常州市 – 2016 – 年鉴
Ⅳ . ① C832.533-54

中国版本图书馆 CIP 数据核字（2016）第 161744 号

常州统计年鉴 -2016

作　者 / 常州市统计局 国家统计局常州调查队

责任编辑 / 陈越月

装帧设计 / 常州青云阁艺术有限公司

出版发行 / 中国统计出版社

地　址 / 北京市丰台区西三环南路甲 6 号 邮政编码 /100073

电　话 / 邮购（010）63376909 书店（010）68783171

网　址 / http://csp.stats.gov.cn

印　刷 / 常州市武进第三印刷有限公司

经　销 / 新华书店

开　本 / 890mm × 1240mm 1/16

字　数 / 1150 千字

印　张 / 34

版　别 / 2016 年 8 月第 1 版

版　次 / 2016 年 8 月第 1 次印刷

定　价 / 300 元

如有印装差错，由本社发行部调换。